ROLL OF THE
INDIAN MEDICAL SERVICE
1615–1930

ROLL OF THE INDIAN MEDICAL SERVICE 1615–1930

Compiled by
LIEUT.-COLONEL D. G. CRAWFORD
BENGAL MEDICAL SERVICE, RETIRED

ICHABOD
1 Samuel, iv. 21

LONDON
W. THACKER & CO. 2 CREED LANE, E.C.
CALCUTTA & SIMLA: THACKER, SPINK & CO.
1930
All rights reserved

TO THE MEMORY
OF THE THOUSANDS FORGOTTEN
OF THE FEW FAINTLY REMEMBERED

WHO, DURING THE PAST THREE CENTURIES, HAVE

SERVED THEIR KING AND COUNTRY IN THE

INDIAN MEDICAL SERVICE, THESE BRIEF

RECORDS OF THEIR CAREERS

ARE DEDICATED

"On the bones of the English, the English flag is stayed."
KIPLING, *The Flag of England.*

PREFACE

THE Roll of the I.M.S. is, to a certain extent, compiled on the model of Colonel Johnston's *Roll of the Army Medical Service;* but with one important difference. Colonel Johnston's Roll gives the names of commissioned officers only. This excludes the great majority of the Surgeons' Mates (Assistant Surgeons), who served during the eighteenth century. Most of these officers were not commissioned officers, serving with commissions conferred by the King, but warrant officers, serving with warrants given by the Colonel commanding their regiment. It has been my endeavour to give the name of every man who served, even for the shortest period, in the Company's land medical services; and to include those who were posted or gazetted to the service, but never joined. Indeed, in Appendix I to each of the three chief services, Bengal, Madras, and Bombay, are included the names of many men who not only never served in the I.M.S., but who never existed. This sounds absurd, but is easily explained. The clerks in the East India House who kept up the Service Army Lists, Medical, in the first half of the nineteenth century, used to begin a new sheet of paper for the entries about each new name which came in from India. Among these are a number of names, at least fifty, with only one entry under each, with nothing to show how or when they entered or left the service. These are simply misreadings or misspellings of the names of men previously in the service; *e.g.* John Mowland for John Rowland, Charles Tyffe for Charles Fyffe. The most curious of these names is William Jandisith, which is a misreading of the name of William Sandwith, a prominent Surgeon in Bombay from 1783 to 1808 (Bo. No. 208).

As far as possible, I have tried to give the following information about each man: (1) date of birth; (2) medical school; (3) degrees and diplomas; (4) dates of successive commissions; (5) date of retirement; (6) date of death; (7) service relationships; (8) any service or event of special interest; (9) honours and decorations; (10) war services; (11) authorship, works. This makes a very large order, and if all this information were available for every individual, would have filled not one large volume, but several. But, up to the organisation of the Service in 1763, it is as much as one can hope for if one can give the name, with dates of appointment, and of retirement or death. Prior to 1763, degrees can be given for only two men, and

PREFACE

medical school for one other. It is not necessary to give the medical school of men holding British University degrees, other than London, for all such men must necessarily have derived part at least of their medical education from the University which gave their degrees, except in a few cases of degrees given at Aberdeen and St. Andrews. There are few entries of services of interest, other than war services. A great many more such entries might have been made, but to have done so would have taken up too much room. The only entries of any length are those under the names of Sir Joseph Fayrer and Sir Ronald Ross. Few comparatively have any orders or honours; up to 1850 practically none. Few have any service relationships. Before the war of 1914–18, less than half had any war service. And the great majority have not been guilty of writing a book.

As regards birth, the great majority, of course, were born either in the British Isles, or in India. I have given the birthplace, where ascertained, only in other cases, of men born in the colonies or in foreign countries. Degrees and diplomas taken after entering the service are entered, in order of date, among successive commissions. The cause of death has been given only in cases of violent death. In no case has suicide been mentioned. I have given relationships in cases in which an officer was the father, brother, or son, of another officer in the public medical services; and in a very few cases of near relationship to some more or less famous man. The number of service relationships is, I am sure, much larger than those ascertained with certainty; and entered. But one cannot enter as a fact what is merely guess-work.

War services are first entered in the Madras Army List in 1853, in Bengal in 1863, in Bombay between the other two. For long officers were allowed to enter pretty much what they liked. Many never sent in their war services at all. One officer, whom I knew, who had seen more active service than most, entered his war service in three words, " Sutlej, Panjab, Mutiny." A curious contrast to the great length at which services in the South African war are entered in the Army List. For the war of 1914–18 the pendulum has swung back again the other way, and very little official information is available. War services previous to those shown in the first official records have been gathered from various sources, such as gazettes, histories, and accounts of campaigns, and especially from the Service Army Lists, Medical. When the reference P.R. (Prize Rolls) is given for an officer's war service, it is taken from these lists. I have not myself seen the Prize Rolls.

Up to the year 1751 the official year began on 25 March, the period from 1 January to 24 March being reckoned in the previous year; *e.g.* the date we should call 1 February 1748 was then called 1 February 1747. To avoid confusion, in all dates in the first quarter of the year, up to 1751, both years have been given, thus, 1 February 1747/48.

PREFACE

I have used, as far as possible, the Hunterian system of spelling for place-names in Northern India. A few of the most famous names, such as Lucknow and Cawnpore, are spelt in the usual way; if one were to write Lakhnau and Khanpur, one might as well go to the limit, and write Kalikata and Mambai for Calcutta and Bombay. I do not know how far the Hunterian system should apply to names in Southern India. It does not seem to suit them. And of course it has no application to place-names in Burma and the Far East.

Letters from the Court of Directors to India are usually referred to as despatches (Desp. from C.), letters from India to the Court as letters. The names Bengal, Calcutta, and Fort William are used almost indiscriminately for Bengal; similarly Madras and Fort St. George for Madras. Men who officiated for some time before being confirmed in the service, are entered from the date of their first officiating service, not from that of confirmation.

All names beginning with Mac are spelt with the prefix in full, followed by a capital letter, *e.g.* MacDonald. In early times the spelling of these, like other proper names, was quite indiscriminate. Even in our own time, I have seen the application for examination from an officer not much senior to myself, whom I knew personally, on which there are three signatures, one of which is spelt differently from the other two, and this officer and his brother always spelt their names differently.

The most senior officer whom I have personally met, and served under, was Surgeon-General A. J. Payne (B. 1544), born 1826, entered 1848, retired 1885, died 1915. The most senior officer I have met was Deputy Surgeon-General C. B. Chalmers (B. 1359), born 1818, entered 1840, retired 1871, died 1889. After his retirement he settled in Australia. I remember his coming to stay with my father, when on a visit to Europe, shortly before I entered the service, and at the time it struck me what a young-looking and well-preserved man he was, though he had entered the service forty years before, had served thirty years in India, including the Mutiny, and had recovered from the severest injuries, a shikar accident, which I have ever heard of a man surviving; (*v. Hist. of I.M.S.*, Vol. II, p. 252).

Numerous sins of omission there must be, in a list of this kind. I hope that there are few sins of commission, in the way of incorrect statements.

I have to thank many friends for help given in the compilation of the Roll, especially Sir William Foster, C.I.E., late Historiographer in the India Office, Major V. Hodson, and the late Mr. S. C. Hill, formerly of the Indian Educational Service, and officer in charge of the Imperial Records Department, Calcutta.

ADDENDA ET CORRIGENDA

I. BENGAL

94. Patton, Robert. A.S. 2 Feb. 1764; (B. Cons.). No further information. Major Hodson suggests that he is identical with Robert Patton, D. and M.'s Infy list; Ensign, 22 July 1766; Lieut. 18 June 1767; Capt. 4 July 1771. Resigned, 2 Mar. 1775; (should be 2 Mar. 1776), gazetted Col. 2 Mar. 1776. In 1770 was Mily. Secy. to Govr. of Bengal; in 1771 O.C. Body Guard. Appointed Govr. of St. Helena, Mar. 1802, retired July 1807. *d.* at Wallington, Hants., 14 July 1812.

140. Haydon, Thomas. *d.* at Bankipur, 20 July 1770; (D. and M.). Haydon, Thomas, Bengal Surgeon, buried at Madras, 9 Dec. 1769; (Malden).

148. Matheson, William. *d.* June 1773; (D. and M.). *d.* 6 June 1773, at Kushalganj, Lucknow; (MacPherson, Soldiering in India, 1764–1787, p. 132, where name is spelt Matthewson).

191. Wedderburn, Charles. *b.* 1 Aug. 1748. St. A. Univ. *d.* 5 Feb. 1829.

279. Grant James. Allowed three years' furlough on full pay, 6 Feb. 1786, to accompany expedition to N.-W. Coast of America; did not rejoin; no further information. Captain John Meares commanded two expeditions to Nootka Sound, Vancouver Island, in 1786–87 and 1788–89, to open up a trade in furs. He mentions an epidemic of scurvy at Nootka Island in Jan. 1787, in which many of the officers and crew died, among them the Surgeon; (Meares' Voyages, pp. xviii, xx). The Surgeon's name is not mentioned, but apparently he was James Grant.

*790. Cussones, Roderick. A combatant officer, appointed Cornet, Baddeley's Horse, G.O. 20 June 1817, when described as "late of Skinner's Horse." No further information. (Hodson.)

*791. Frobisher, Thomas. A combatant officer. *b.* 5 Feb. 1789. Cadet, 1801; Ensign, 23 Apr. 1806; Lieut. 14 Mar. 1808; Capt. 11 July 1823; R. 6 May 1833; Hony. Major, 28 Nov. 1854. *d.* at Cheltenham, 8 Jan. 1863. Capture of Cape of Good Hope, 1806; capture of Java, 1811, medal; Nipal War, 1814–15, medal; Third Maratha war, 1817–18. (Hodson.)

*793. Morland, Richard Scrope Bernard. Combatant officer. *b.* 13 Aug 1793. Cadet, Bengal Artillery, 1810; Lt. Fireworker, 20 Nov. 1811; Lt. 25 Sept. 1817; Capt. 28 Sept. 1827. *d.* at Dumdum, 15 Oct. 1833. Nipal war, 1814–15, Kalanga; Third Maratha war, 1817–18, siege and capture of Hathras; siege and capture of Bhartpur, 1826. (Hodson.)

* Whether Cussones, Frobisher, Herbert, Morland, and Picard ever did any medical work appears very doubtful. More probably their names were entered in S.A.L.M.B. by mistake.

ADDENDA ET CORRIGENDA

*794. Picard, Edward. A combatant officer. Second Lieut., Third (Baddeley's) Horse, 1 Oct. 1817; Lieut. G.O. 6 Feb. 1819; (Hodson). No further information.

836. MacKinnon, Charles. Resigned, 1 May 1829. Became an indigo-planter in Tirhut. Left India, 1849. *d.* in Edinburgh about 1865. His younger daughter, Susan Margaret, married the 15th Duke of Somerset. Brother of K. MacKinnon, B. 1085, infra.

891. Paterson, George Murray. *d.* at Southampton, 9 Apr. 1829; (E.I. Regr. 1830). An account of this unfortunate officer's death is contained in the Western Gazette of 26 Apr. 1829. His body was found in a remote part of the New Forest, on Thursday (18 Apr. ?), very emaciated, and naked except for a uniform jacket and flannel waistcoat, the rest of his clothes being found about 100 yards away. At the inquest it was stated that he had been seen wandering in the New Forest, and was supposed to be insane. The coroner's jury returned a verdict of death from starvation and exposure.

1424. Roper, George Trevor. *b.* 14 May 1820. His father took name Trevor-Roper in 1809. *d.* 14 Nov. 1870.

2124. Gimlette, G. H. D. *d.* at Southsea, 7 Mar. 1930. Brother of Surg. Rear-Admiral Sir T. D. Gimlette, K.C.B., R.N. War of 1914–18. Hosp. ship 'Sicilia,' France, Gallipoli, Egypt; Iraq, 1917.

2139. Waddell, L. A. Hony. F.R.C.P.S. Glas. 1930. Add to works, The Makers of Civilisation in Race and History, 1929; The British Edda, 1929.

2293. Bedford, C. H. Kt. Grand Cross, Order of Civil Merit, Spain, 1929.

2319. Seton, B. G. Claim to Barony of Gordon disallowed by House of Lords; (Times, 2 May 1929).

2384. Stephenson, J. F.R.S. 1930. Author of Zoological Section of Mustaufi's Nuzhatu-L-Kulab, trans. from Arabic, 1928.

II. MADRAS

8. Jardin, —. At Court of Committees, 24 Oct. 1670, passage to India granted to Clement du Jordan, whose father is a Chirurgeon at Madras; (Sainsbury, Court Minutes, Vol. 1668–70, p. 374).

—. Brooke, Peter. Entertained as Surg. for Masulipatam, 25 Nov. 1669; (Sainsbury, Court Minutes, Vol. 1668–70, p. 276).

* *Vide* note, p. xi.

ADDENDA ET CORRIGENDA

401. Gordon, John. *b.* 5 June 1775. King's Coll. Ab. 1787–89; Marischal Coll. Ab. 1789–91.

745. Blood, Michael. In practice at St. Heliers over fifty years. *d.* at St. Heliers, 10 Sept. 1877.

1252. Gamack, Alex. *d.* at Hampstead, 8 Mar. 1930. The last survivor of the E.I. Co.'s medical officers.

1326. Summerhayes, Henry. Afterwards in practice in England. Name omitted from Med. Dir. 1891.

1348. Lupton, A. W. Afterwards Surgeon, Trans.-Atlantic Mail Service. *d.* in 1876.

1538. Sharman, E. H. D.T.M. Liv. 1904. *d.* at Bournemouth, 5 Mar. 1930.

1560. Rost, E. R. *d.* at Putney, 23 June 1930. Son of Dr. Reinhold Rost, Librarian, India Office. War of 1914–18, add East Africa.

III. BOMBAY

160. Durham, Andrew. *d.* Dec. 1811. Brother of John Durham, No. 251, infra.

233. Lockhart, Alex. Took name of MacKonochie in 1794; (L.G. 23 Aug. 1794).

344. Gordon, Alex. *b.* Apr. 1786. Mar. Coll. Ab. Brother of George Gordon, No. 357, infra.

357. Gordon, George. *d.* at Aberdeen, 4 May 1832. Brother of Alex Gordon, No. 344, supra.

477. MacTavish, Colin. Footnote. A book by J. G. Lockhart on the loss of the 'Blenden Hall' is announced, in July 1930, by Messrs. P. Allan and Co., as nearly ready for publication.

1126. Hooton, Alfred. R. 16 Feb. 1930.

ADDENDA ET CORRIGENDA

IV. GENERAL LIST

97. Megaw, J. W. D. Director Genl. 24 Mar. 1930. K.H.S. 16 Feb. 1930.

122. Cazaly, W. H. *d.* at Earl Soham, Suffolk, 10 Apr. 1930.

166. Kerans, G. C. L. Col. 1 Apr. 1930. Also third name should be Lovell, not Scott.

456. Watson, W. L. Promotion ante-dated, to Major, to 1 Aug. 1919; to Lieut.-Col. to 1 Aug. 1927.

628. Chand, Hari. Promotion to Major ante-dated to 31 July 1925.

642. Baker, C. H. N. Promotion to Major ante-dated to 31 July 1925.

666. Harty, A. H. Promotion to Major ante-dated to 7 Feb. 1926.

697. Prasad, B. Promotion to Major ante-dated to 2 June 1926.

1049. Wace, M. H. Ranked as Capt. from 27 Jan. 1927.

VII. ST. HELENA

34. Statham, T. *d.* at Ross, Hereford, Nov. 1797; (Monthly Mag. iv (1797), p. 410).

CONTENTS

	PAGE
Preface	vii
Addenda et corrigenda	xi
List of Abbreviations	xvii
Introduction	xxiii

ROLL
I.	Bengal, 1645–1896	1
	Appendix I, Bengal, extra names	235
II.	Madras, 1630–1896	244
	Appendix I, Madras, extra names	383
III.	Bombay, 1615–1896	391
	Appendix I, Bombay, extra names	493
IV.	General List, 1897–1930	497
V.	Eastern Factories, 1605–1775	602
VI.	Sumatra or West Coast, 1696–1825	605
VII.	St. Helena, 1684–1831	618
VIII.	China, 1763–1834	623
IX.	Prince of Wales Island	625

APPENDICES—
II.	List of Officers Killed in Action	629
III.	List of Officers who also Served as Combatants	631
IV.	List of Officers who also Served in Colonial Services	633
V.	List of Examining Physicians, and Presidents Medical Board	633
VI.	List of Officers, Successively Senior on Retired List	634
VII.	Strength of Service, 1915–1930	635
VIII.	Table of Honours and Rewards	636
IX.	Analysis of Degrees and Diplomas: Bengal, Madras, Bombay, General List	638

CONTENTS

APPENDICES

X. Analysis of Medical Schools: Bengal, Madras, Bombay, General List 643

XI. Analysis of Birthplaces, Bengal, Madras, Bombay . . 648

XII. Analysis of Parentage, Bengal, Madras, Bombay . . 650

XIII. Analysis of Final Results, Bengal, Madras, Bombay . 652

Index 657

LIST OF ABBREVIATIONS

(The common abbreviations for degrees and diplomas, M.D., M.R.C.S., etc.; and the common abbreviations for orders, C.B., D.S.O., etc., are not included, being universally known.)

(a)	Name not in Dodwell and Miles List.
A.A. Regr.	Asiatic Annual Register.
A.J.	Asiatic Journal.
A.L.	Army List.
A.M.D.	Army Medical Department.
App.	Appendix.
A.S.	Assistant Surgeon.
A.S. Certs.	Assistant Surgeons' Certificates.
(b)	Had served in Marine Service.
b.	Born.
B.A.O.	Bachelor Artis Obstetricæ.
Bart's.	St. Bartholomew's Hospital.
B. Cons.	Bengal Consultations.
B.C.S.	Bengal Civil Service.
B.G.O.	Bengal Government Order.
B. Genl. L.	Bengal General Letter.
B.I.	Bengal Infantry.
B.I.S.S.	British India Steam Ship.
B. Mily. Cons.	Bengal Military Consultations.
B.M.J.	British Medical Journal.
Bo.	Bombay.
Bo. Cons.	Bombay Consultations.
Bo. Genl. L.	Bombay General Letter.
Bo. I.	Bombay Infantry.
Bo. Mily. Cons.	Bombay Military Consultations.
Bo. P.L.	Bombay Press Lists.
Bo. Pub. Cons.	Bombay Public Consultations.
B.P. and P.	Bengal Past and Present.
Broome	Broome's History of Bengal Army.
Brux.	Brussels.
B.S.	Brigade Surgeon.
B.S. Lieut.-Col.	Brigade Surgeon Lieutenant-Colonel.
Bt.	Brevet.
(c)	Locally appointed.
Cal.	Calcutta.
Cal. Chron.	Calcutta Chronicle.

LIST OF ABBREVIATIONS

Cal. Cons.	Calcutta Consultations.
Cal. Pub. L.	Calcutta Public Letter.
Cantab.	Cantabrigiensis, Cambridge.
C.C.S.	Certificate of Corporation of Surgeons.
C.G.	Calcutta Gazette.
C.M.B.	Calcutta Medical Board.
Co.	East India Company.
Co.	County.
Cons.	Consultations.
Corp. Surgeons	Corporation, now Royal College, of Surgeons.
Cotton	Cotton's Monumental Inscriptions in Madras.
C.P.	Central Provinces.
C.P.L.	Calcutta Press Lists.
C. Pub. Cons.	Calcutta Public Consultations.
d.	Died.
(d)	Never joined.
D. and M.	Dodwell and Miles East India Medical List.
Desp.	Despatches.
Desp. from C.	Despatch from Court.
Desp. to M.	Despatch to Madras.
D.G.	Director General.
D.I.G.	Deputy Inspector General.
dist.	Distinction.
D.M.R.E.	Diploma, Medical Radiology and Electricity.
D.M.S.	Director Medical Services.
D.N.B.	Dictionary of National Biography.
D.O.M.S.	Diploma, Ophthalmic Medicine and Surgery.
D.P.M.	Diploma, Psychological Medicine.
D.S.G.	Deputy Surgeon General.
D.T.M.	Diploma, Tropical Medicine.
D.T.M. and H.	Diploma, Tropical Medicine and Hygiene.
Dunelm	Durham (University).
Dy.	Deputy.
(e)	Name in Dictionary of National Biography.
Ed.	Edinburgh.
E.F. in I.	Foster's English Factories in India.
E.I. Co.	East India Company.
F.A.	Field Ambulance.
F.C.P.	Fellow, College of Physicians (Philadelphia).
F.C.P.S. Bo.	Fellow, College of Physicians and Surgeons, Bombay.
F.F.P.S.G.	Fellow, Faculty of Physicians and Surgeons, Glasgow.
F.I.	Friend of India.
F.K.Q.C.P.	Fellow, King's and Queen's College of Physicians (Ireland).
Fort St. D. Cons.	Fort St. David Consultations.
Fort St. G. Cons.	Fort St. George Consultations.

LIST OF ABBREVIATIONS

Fort St. G. Genl. L.	Fort St. George General Letter.
Fort Wm. Genl. L.	Fort William General Letter.
F.P.	Full Pay.
F.R.	Factory Records.
F.R.S.	Fellow Royal Society.
Genl. L. from B.	General Letter from Bengal.
Genl. L. from C.	General Letter from Court.
Genl. L. from Fort Wm.	Genl. Letter from Fort William.
Genl. L. from M.	Genl. Letter from Madras.
G.G.O.	Government General Order.
Glas.	Glasgow.
G.M.	Gentleman's Magazine.
G.O.	General Order.
G. of I.	Gazette of India.
G.S.P.	Good Service Pension.
Hardy	Hardy's Shipping Register.
Hickey	Hickey's Memoirs.
H.M.'s	His Majesty's.
H.M.S.	His Majesty's Ship.
Hodson	Hodson's List of Officers of Bengal Army, 1758–1834.
Hosp. App.	Hospital Apprentice.
I.A.C.	Indian Army Circulars.
I.G.	Inspector General.
I.G. Hosps.	Inspector General of Hospitals.
I.M.D.	Indian Medical Department.
I.M.G.	Indian Medical Gazette.
I.M.S.	Indian Medical Service.
Ind. Gaz.	India Gazette.
Inf.	Infantry.
K.C.Ab.	King's College Aberdeen.
K.O.S.B.	King's Own Scottish Borderers (25th Foot).
K.T.S.	Knight of the Tower and Sword (Portugal).
L.	Letter.
L. from B.	Letter from Bengal.
L. from C.	Letter from Court.
L. from Fort St. D.	Letter from Fort St. David.
L. from Fort St. G.	Letter from Fort St. George.
L.A.H.	Licentiate Apothecary's Hall (Dublin).
Lancs.	Lancaster.
L.Ch.	Licentiate in Surgery (Trinity College Dublin).
L.D.S.	Licentiate in Dental Surgery.
L.G.	London Gazette.
L.K.Q.C.P.	Licentiate King's and Queen's College of Physicians (Ireland).
L.M.	Licentiate in Medicine (Trinity College, Dublin).

LIST OF ABBREVIATIONS

L.M.S.	Licentiate in Medicine and Surgery (India).
Love	Love's Vestiges of Old Madras.
L.S.Sc.	Licentiate in Sanitary Science (Durham).
M.	Madras.
Malden.	Malden's List of Burials at Madras.
M.A.O.	Magister Artis Obstetricæ.
Mar. Coll. Ab.	Marischal College, Aberdeen.
Mas. or Masul. Cons.	Masulipatam Consultations.
Mat. Med.	Materia Medica.
M. Ch.	Magister Chirurgeriæ, Master of Surgery.
M. Cons.	Madras Consultations.
Med. Dir.	Medical Directory.
Med. Exp. Force	Mediterranean Expeditionary Force.
M.F.P.S.G.	Member Faculty of Physicians and Surgeons, Glasgow.
M.I.	Madras Infantry.
Mills	Mills' List of Officers in Calcutta, 1756–57.
Mily. Chron.	Military Chronicle.
Mily. Desp. from C.	Military Despatch from Court.
Mily. L. from B.	Military Letter from Bengal.
Mily. L. from Bo. or M.	Military Letter from Bombay or Madras.
M.K.Q.C.P.	Member King's and Queen's College of Physicians (Ireland).
M.M.B.	Member Medical Board.
M. Mily. Cons.	Madras Military Consultations.
M.O.H.	Medical Officer of Health.
M.P.	Member of Parliament.
M.P.L.	Madras Press Lists.
M. Pub. Cons.	Madras Public Consultations.
M.R.C.V.S.	Member, Royal College of Veterinary Surgeons.
Nomd.	Nominated.
N. Park St.	North Park St. Cemetery, Calcutta.
N.W.P.	North West Provinces.
O.C.	Officer Commanding.
P.A.	Private affairs.
P. and O.	Peninsular and Oriental Steam Navigation Company.
Ph.D.	Doctor of Philosophy; Doctor of Physics.
Phil. Doc.	Doctor of Philosophy (Padua).
Phys. Genl.	Physician General.
P.M.O.	Principal Medical Officer.
P.R.	Prize Rolls.
Pres.	President.
Presy. Surg.	Presidency Surgeon.
Proc. C.M.B.	Proceedings, Calcutta Medical Board.
Prof.	Professor.
Pub. L. from B.	Public Letter from Bengal.

LIST OF ABBREVIATIONS

Pub. L. from Bo. or M.	Public Letter from Bombay or Madras.
P.W.I.	Prince of Wales Island.
Q.C.	Queen's College (Belfast, Cork, Galway).
Q.H.P.	Queen's Honorary Physician.
Q.H.S.	Queen's Honorary Surgeon.
Q.U.I.	Queen's University, Ireland.
R.	Retired.
R.A.M.C.	Royal Army Medical Corps.
R.C.P.S.	Royal Colleges of Physicians and Surgeons.
R.C.P.S.Ed.	Royal Colleges of Physicians and Surgeons, Edinburgh.
R.C.P.S.I.	Royal Colleges of Physicians and Surgeons, Ireland.
R.C.S.	Royal College of Surgeons.
Regr.	Register.
R.N.	Royal Navy.
R.U.I.	Royal University, Ireland.
S.	Sumatra.
Sainsbury	Calendar of State Papers, edited by W. Noel Sainsbury.
Sainsbury, Court Minutes	Calendar of Court Minutes of E.I. Co., Series 3, edited by Miss Ethel Sainsbury.
St. H. Cons.	St. Helena Consultations.
S.A.L.M.B.	Service Army Lists, Medical, Bengal.
S.A.L.M.Bo.	Service Army Lists, Medical, Bombay.
S.A.L.M.M.	Service Army Lists, Medical, Madras.
S.A.S.	Sub-Assistant Surgeon.
S.C.	Sick certificate.
S. Capt.	Surgeon Captain.
S. Cons.	Sumatra Consultations.
Sel. Com. L.	Select Committee Letter.
S.G.	Surgeon General.
S. List	Selected List for Promotion.
S. Lieut.	Surgeon Lieutenant.
S. Lieut.-Col.	Surgeon Lieutenant-Colonel.
S.M.	Surgeon Major.
S.M.D.	Sub-Medical Department.
S.M.O.	Senior Medical Officer.
Spring	Spring's Roll of Bombay Artillery.
S.R.	Special Reserve (R.A.M.C.; S.R.).
S.S.	Steam Ship.
S.S. or Supg. Surg.	Superintending Surgeon.
S.S.C.	Sanitary Science Certificate (Cambridge).
Stubbs.	List of Officers, Bengal Artillery.
Supy. Surg.	Supernumerary Surgeon.
T.C.	Temporary Commission.
T.C.D.	Trinity College, Dublin.

LIST OF ABBREVIATIONS

T.D.	Territorial Decoration.
T.F.	Territorial Force (R.A.M.C.; T.F.).
T.H.P.	Temporary Half Pay.
U.P.	United Provinces, Agra and Oudh.
U.S.A.	United States of America.
V.C.	Victoria Cross.
V.D.	Volunteer Decoration.
Wilson	Wilson's History of Madras Army.
Wilson	Wilson's Monumental Inscriptions in Bengal.

INTRODUCTION

The introduction is a continuation of the History of the I.M.S., and consists partly of notes on the events and changes of the past fifteen years, partly of supplementary information about former times, which has come to hand since the History was published. The Chapter headings and pages refer to those of that History.

CHAPTER II.—*European Surgeons in the Service of Oriental Potentates.*
Page 10.—Dr. Lloyd. After his escape from Haidar Ali in 1780, Dr. Lloyd settled in practice at Madras. He died there on 1 April 1815, aged ninety. The *Madras Courier* of 11 April 1815 gives him an obituary notice, as follows :—

"1st April. Suddenly, at his House, in Black Town, Charles Loyd, Esq., M.D., in the 91st year of his age. In compliance with his last request, that he shall be buried as a Mason, all the Lodges in the neighbourhood were convened, and met at his house in the evening—and under their immediate direction, in Masonic procession, decorated with their badges, etc., the funeral rites were conducted, with great decorum and solemnity, from Black Town to the burial ground, attended by a numerous concourse of other respectable friends, to many of whom the deceased had endeared himself by innumerable acts of benevolent attention, professional, as well as otherwise.

"Dr. Loyd was a Hanoverian by birth (his Father having been sent over as Commissary-General by George the 2nd), descended from an ancient Welsh family, and until a few hours before his death had never been seriously indisposed, and was always found ready to administer relief to the needy and helpless. He arrived in Madras in 1772, and whilst on his intended journey overland in 1777, he was stopt at Calicut by order from Hyder Ally, and being conveyed to Seringapatam, was forced into his service, and for several years filled the situation of Physician General and Secretary to that Prince ; in which capacities he had many opportunities of affording relief to the unfortunate prisoners taken by Hyder, particularly after the defeat of Colonel Baillie. In 1781, he contrived to effect his escape from Hyder's camp, and joined Sir Eyre Coote, at Cuddalore, to whom he rendered every (*sic*—very ?) important services, and continued to enjoy the particular confidence of that renowned General, until his death. Dr. Loyd's memoirs of his own life, containing some very interesting accounts of Hyder's policy and character, are now in the Press in London, and may be expected out by the first arrivals."

Dr. Lloyd's experiences would certainly have furnished material for an interesting book, but no such work appears ever to have been published. Nothing is known of it at the British Museum Library.

Page 15.—Besides Honigberger, Ranjit Sinh had two other

INTRODUCTION

European surgeons in his pay. Colonel Alexander Gardner, in his *Memoirs* (p. 296), gives their names, Dr. Harvey, an Englishman, and Dr. Benet, a Frenchman, who in 1838 was in receipt of Rs. 500 a month.

Kaye, in his *History of the Afghan War* (Vol. I, p. 221), mentions a Monsieur Euler as Surgeon to Shah Kamran, Shah of Persia, at the siege of Herat in 1837–38.

CHAPTER III.—*Surgeon-General John Woodall.*

Page 17.—The exact date of Woodall's appointment as Surgeon-General to the E.I. Co. was 13 December 1613, as ordered in Court Minutes of that date, quoted in Foster's *John Company*, p. 72. A portrait of Woodall, engraved by G. Glover, is given in the 1659 edition of his works, and is reproduced in *John Company*, opposite p. 74.

Page 26.—Henry Boone, Woodall's nephew, who succeeded him in the post and duties of Surgeon-General, though he was never given that title, died in July 1666, possibly of plague, that being the year of the great plague of London, *annus mirabilis*.

CHAPTER IV.—*Early History; the Islands; Amboyna.*

Page 30.—" No reparation was ever made " (for the massacre at Amboyna in 1623). This is not quite correct. In 1654 Cromwell exacted from the Dutch, under the treaty of April 1654, a payment of £35,000, in satisfaction of various claims, plus a special payment of £3,615, for the representatives of those who had suffered at Amboyna (Foster, E.F. in I, 1651–54, p. xx). Few of their immediate heirs can have been living in 1654, a generation after the massacre.

CHAPTER V.—*The Legend of Gabriel Boughton.*

Pages 37 *and* 57.—A copy of the farman granted to Boughton by Shah Shuja has since been found in the British Museum Library, in a volume of documents on the E.I. Co.'s trade with India between 1663 and 1712, which was formerly the property of H. H. Wilson. See Foster's *English Factories in India*, 1655–60, pp. 413, 414. The farman was not in favour of the English nation, or of the E.I. Co., but of Boughton personally. And, though the Company's trade with Bengal, one ship a year, could be, and doubtless was, imported duty free under Boughton's name, its validity ceased with his death. It appears to have been granted about 1650, and Boughton was dead before August 1653.

Page 44.—Grose's note refers, not to Boughton, but to William Hamilton.

Page 46.—The " Hopewell " in which Bouton served in 1663, cannot have been the same ship as Boughton's, which was past repair

INTRODUCTION

in 1645. The name was kept up in the Company's fleet. In the Sumatra Consultations of 12 August 1706 is mentioned the departure of the 'Hopewell,' Captain Hope (or Hone), from Bencoolen for Bengal. The same Consultations of 20 March 1732/33 record that Dr. James Ouchterlony was sent in the 'Hopewell' to Moko Moko, to take the place of Dr. Gerrard White, deceased.

Page 55.—Gabriel Boughton left a son, named after himself, by the 'Mogullana.' The Court of Committees of 25 October 1670 record the grant of a passage from England to Bengal to Gabriel Bowden. What he was doing in England, or what subsequently became of him, does not seem to have been recorded.

CHAPTER VI.—*Early History, Bombay and the West.*

Page 62.—President Freeman. The name should be Fremlen.

Page 67.—W. W. Crooke should be Mr. W. Crooke.

Dr. N. G. is Dr. Nehemiah Grew, Secretary to the Royal Society in 1677–79.

Page 68.—Dr. Bird. When Captain Kirgwin seized Bombay, and governed the settlement for a year, 1683–84, only four of the European inhabitants of Bombay refused to take an oath of fidelity to him. Of these four Dr. Bird was one. Kirgwin offered a free passage to Surat to any one who chose to leave Bombay, but only one man, a Mr. Church, availed himself of the offer.

CHAPTER X.—*The First Half of the Eighteenth Century.*

Page 109.—Robert Turing, junior, joined in 1766, not in 1765. The date of letter appointing Belsches Surgeon was 21 March 1738/39.

Pages 139 *and* 140.—Richard Harvey twice officiated as Lector, reading prayers in church. The Bengal Consultations of 1 February 1719/20 report his being paid Rs. 400, the usual gratuity, for having officiated in church service for over twelve months, since the death of the Revd. Mr. Briercliffe, and state that the Revd. Joshua Tomlinson has now arrived, and taken over the duties of Chaplain. Tomlinson died just four months later, on 30 May 1720, and Harvey again acted as Lector, and received Rs. 400 again, in the Consultations of 27 November 1721.

The Bengal Consultations of 1721 note two cases of deceased officers leaving legacies to the medical officers. On 5 January 1720/21 it is noted that James Williamson, Member of Council, who died on 3 January, leaves Rs. 2,000 to Dr. Harvey, and Rs. 500 to Dr. Robert Broadfoot. And on 31 July, Thomas White, junior merchant, who died on 21 July, leaves Rs. 300 to Dr. Harvey and Rs. 200 to Dr. Broadfoot.

INTRODUCTION

Richard Harvey survived his retirement for five years, and died in London on 16 May 1734.

CHAPTER XI.—*John Holwell.*

Page 170.—Hancock resigned the second Surgeoncy of Calcutta on 23 March 1761, having held the post for less than six months. His wife, Philadelphia, was an aunt of Jane Austen, the novelist.

Page 171.—William Alves had served at Basra for two years, 1755–56 (Bo. Cons. 31 Dec. 1756).

CHAPTER XII.—*William Fullerton.*

A good deal of information about Fullerton is given in the *History of the Counties of Ayr and Wigton*, by the Revd. James Paterson. Dr. William Fullerton was the elder son of Patrick Fullerton or Fullartoun of Rosemount, in the parish of Symington, in Ayrshire, and of his wife Margaret Harper. The estate of Rosemount had formerly been called Goldring. After his return from India William Fullerton added considerably to the estate he had inherited from his father. He married Annabella, third daughter of Ronald Craufurd, W.S., of Restalrig, but had no children. The *Gentleman's Magazine* of 1805, Vol. II, records his death at Rosemount on 22 October 1805. So he had nearly forty years of retirement. His widow survived until 11 November 1826. His younger brother, John Fullarton (his name is spelt Fullarton by Dodwell and Miles, Fullartoun by Paterson), served in the Company's Bengal Infantry, to which he was appointed as a Cadet in 1762, and rose to the rank of Major-General on 20 December 1793. He married an Indian lady, and died childless at Patna on 29 June 1804, sixteen months before his brother William.

CHAPTER XIV.—*Strength from Time to Time.*

Page 207.—The orders of Court of 5 July 1797, giving final orders as to the rank of the officers appointed from 1781 to 1784, contain 51 names. In the Bengal Roll, 123 names are entered as appointed in these years. The other 72 are thus accounted for—dead, 46; unknown, 8 (probably dead, but one or two may never have joined); resigned, 8; cashiered, 3; ranked earlier, above Dick, 2; given up promotion, 2; transferred to China, 1; serving as P.M.O. in Sumatra, 1; reverted to combatant, 1 (Staunton).

A table of the strength of the service for each year, from 1914 to 1930, including the war years, is given in Appendix VII.

CHAPTER XV.—*The Double Commissions.*

Page 224.—Francis Balfour died at Fernie, Fife, on 7 May 1818 (*Scot's Magazine*, 1818, i, 598).

INTRODUCTION

Page 233.—Another officer, who held a combatant commission before joining the I.M.S., and who rose to the top of the Medical Service, was Andrew Williams, who received a commission as Ensign in the 84th Foot on 4 September 1761 (Army List, 1763); was appointed Surgeon, Bengal, on 27 November 1762, and on the foundation of the Medical Board, on 29 May 1786, was appointed second member of that Board.

Page 234.—Besides Heydon, Strachan, and Stevenson, a few other instances occurred in the minor medical services of officers holding double commissions, military and medical. David Kay, appointed Assistant Surgeon at St. Helena in 1775, was appointed Lieutenant of Artillery, in addition to his medical duties on 23 December 1776, but only held his commission as Lieutenant for a year and a half, up to July 1778, after which he served as a medical officer only.

Page 234.—Appointments from the ranks. George Mead, a Sergeant in the St. Helena garrison, who had served as assistant to the Surgeons for fifteen years, though unqualified, was appointed junior Assistant Surgeon on the St. Helena Establishment from 17 September 1804. He resigned in 1808, went to England, qualified as M.R.C.S. in 1808, and was reappointed Assistant Surgeon in 1811. In ten years more, he rose to be Superintending Surgeon and head of the service. A Sergeant named Savage was appointed Surgeon on the West Coast Establishment in 1721. In 1769 John Russell, a private, who had been assistant to a Surgeon in Bristol before enlisting, was appointed Surgeon in the West Coast Service. His history is given in a petition for appointment as Surgeon, recorded in Sumatra Consultations of 20 December 1769 (*v. Sumatra Service*, p. 606).

Pages 240 *and* 241.—Archibald Swinton served in the Circars in 1758–59, at the battle of Biderra, on 25 November 1759, at the battle of Gaya, on 15 January 1761, after which he was deputed to receive Shah Alam; at Undwa Nala, on 4 September 1863, at the capture of Monghyr, where he was wounded in the left hand, and at the capture of Patna, on 4 September 1763, when he was wounded in the right hand, and had his right arm amputated above the elbow. He resigned the service on 23 January 1766.

After his retirement, Swinton bought the estate of Kimmerghame, in Berwickshire, in 1771. On 17 October 1776 he married, at Edinburgh, Henrietta, daughter of James Campbell of Blythswood. He died at Bath, on 7 March 1804, and was buried in the Abbey Church, Bath. (*Memoirs of Swinton Family, Records and Portraits at Kimmerghame*, by A. C. and J. L. C. Swinton).

The firm of Burn and Co., Engineers, in Calcutta, was founded by Col. Swinton and Mr. Burn in 1790. The date shows that this was a different Swinton.

In the India Office there is a large picture entitled " Shah Alam

INTRODUCTION

(the Great Mogul) conveying the grant of the Diwani to Lord Clive, August 1765;" presented to the E.I. Co. by the Right Honourable Earl Powis, 1820. Painted by B. West, R.A. (afterwards Sir Benjamin West, P.R.A.). A key to the figures in the picture shows that No. 4 is Captain Archibald Swinton. Shah Alam is shown handing the grant to Clive, behind Clive stands General Carnac, and behind Carnac is Swinton. The picture shows Swinton as clean shaven, with a large nose; his right arm appears in the picture, his left arm is covered by the next figure.

In the library of the India Office hangs, framed, the original treaty between the E.I. Co. and Shuja-al-Daulat, Nawab of Oudh. The treaty is signed on behalf of the E.I. Co. by Clive and Carnac, while Swinton's signature appears below as one of the witnesses. The treaty is dated 17 August 1765.

In the British Museum Library there is a "Catalogue of a valuable collection of Persian and a few Arabic MSS., selected many years ago in the East by Archibald Swinton, Esq." To be sold by auction; London, 1813.

CHAPTER XVI.—*Military and Civil.*

Page 271.—The correspondence between the Madras Council and the Madras Medical Board, on the proposed division of the Service into two separate branches, military and civil, is contained in the Madras Military Consultations of 26 July 1796. The Medical Board objected to the proposed scheme, and the Council suspended action, pending reference to the Court in England. The same question is discussed at length in the Bombay Consultations of 29 July and 24 August 1796.

Disputes arose from time to time as to the respective control over hospitals by the officer commanding the local garrison and the Chief Civil officer. The Bombay Military Consultations of 20 August 1790 report one such dispute. Lt.-Colonel J. Peché, commanding the 1st European Infantry at Salsette, had ordered the Assistant Surgeon of that regiment, John Twiss, to inspect the General Hospital at Thana. Thomas Drummond, Surgeon in charge of Thana Hospital, objected to being inspected by a junior officer. The Chief of Thana forwarded Drummond's protest to the Bombay Council, who ordered that if the officer commanding a regiment wished one of his medical officers to visit a General Hospital, he should apply to the Chief of the station, who would then direct the Surgeon of the General Hospital to allow the regimental medical officer to visit the hospital, on the same footing as the officer of the day. The Bombay Military Consultations of 12 May 1795 contain a report on a similar dispute between the Chief and Council at Surat, and the officer commanding that station, on which the Bombay Council passed orders that the General Hospital and its medical staff are under the orders of the Chief only.

INTRODUCTION

Page 286.—Indian Navy. In 1800 the Bombay Medical Board recommended that the 'Mornington,' and similar ships in the Indian Marine, should carry both a Surgeon and an Assistant Surgeon, as in the Royal Navy. (Bombay Mily. Cons. 7 Feb. 1800.)

In the Sumatra Consultations of 13–17 July 1778, it is stated that the officers of the West Coast Medical Service are civil, not military officers. When medical officers from Bengal, who of course were military officers, began to be deputed for service in Sumatra, the officers of the local service were distinguished from them by the title of Civil Surgeons.

To come to the present time, it is obvious that increasing decentralization, with greater independence of the provincial governments, and the growth of the provincial medical services, must reduce the number of civil appointments, especially of district civil surgeoncies, held by officers of the I.M.S. The civil appointments reserved for the I.M.S. now seem to be chiefly scientific, sanitary, and jail appointments, with those in the political department. For many years to come a number of the more important civil surgeoncies, and of teaching appointments in the medical schools, will probably continue to be held by the I.M.S., but the number of these seems certain to diminish, and perhaps will do so more rapidly than now seems probable.

CHAPTER XVII.—*Rank.*

The Bombay Consultations of 2 July 1790 contain a letter from the Council at Fort William, fixing the relative rank of officers of the A.M.D. and I.M.S. It is laid down that the Company's Surgeons only are eligible for the charge of General Hospitals, except in the field, where officers of both services are equally eligible. The King's and the Company's Assistant Surgeons are to take rank according to the dates of their respective warrants. All King's Surgeons, in virtue of their Royal Commissions, rank above all Company's surgeons, except that a Company's Surgeon in charge of a General Hospital must not be superseded by a regimental Surgeon of the A.M.D.

The Royal Warrant of 30 November 1796 gave the title of Assistant Surgeon, with commissions as such, to all regimental surgeon's mates in the British Army. The surgeon's mates of the Indian Army had already received Company's commissions as such by Lord Cornwallis' order of 1788.

Page 312.—In addition to the twenty-one instances given in which Bengal Assistant Surgeons gave up promotion to Surgeon in order to retain their civil stations, three more may be added : J. Reid, Delhi; A. Murray, Shahabad; and A. Fraser, Gorakhpur.

Page 314.—Bombay Consultations of 17 August 1798 contain a list of appointments "made in accordance with the new regulations."

INTRODUCTION

The four senior Surgeons are posted as follows:

Thomas Cruso, Superintending Surgeon at Cannanore and North Malabar.
Helenus Scott, Medical Storekeeper.
William Sandwith, Presidency General Hospital, Bombay.
Joseph James, Superintending Surgeon at Calicut and South Malabar.

In 1912 the rank of Surgeon-General, instead of Colonel, was conferred on the I.G.C.H., Bengal, and an extra I.G.C.H. sanctioned for the new province of Bihar and Orissa.

In 1917 Lieutenants of the I.M.S. were promoted to Captain on completion of one year's service, such promotion taking effect for the first cases from 1 September 1915, but not carrying pay and allowances from an earlier date than 1 September 1916. This promotion, at one year's service, only continued during the war; after the end of the war promotion of Lieutenant to Captain again took place after three years' service.

The title of Surgeon General, in the Army Medical Service, was changed to Major-General in the *London Gazette* of 27 February 1918. The same change was made for the I.M.S. in the *Gazette* of 11 June 1918.

Officers of the I.M.S. had always, since 1881, been eligible for the appointment of D.M.S. in India, but no I.M.S. officer had ever been appointed until, in 1923, it was ruled that this post should be held by officers of the British and Indian armies alternately. The first I.M.S. officer appointed under this ruling was Major-General C. H. Bowle-Evans, from 6 September 1923, but owing to ill-health he was only able to hold the post for a few months, retiring on 19 December 1923. His successor, of course, was an officer of the British service, who in turn was succeeded by Major-General Sir W. H. Ogilvie, K.B.E. on 3 January 1927.

The Director General of the Army Medical Services has for many years past held the rank of Lieutenant-General. The same rank may be conferred on the D.G. of the I.M.S., should the Government think fit. The only D.G. of the I.M.S. on whom this rank has been conferred was Surgeon-General Sir Charles Pardey Lukis, to whom it was granted on 22 September 1916.

CHAPTER XVIII.—*Pay*.

The rates of pay of all ranks were somewhat increased in 1917, and to a further extent in 1920, when they were raised to the rates still in force, roughly about fifty per cent. higher than the pre-war rate. The present rates are given as follows in the memo issued to intending candidates by the India Office in 1928 (paras. 23 to 27). Officers of Asiatic domicile do not receive overseas pay.

INTRODUCTION

"24. The following are the monthly rates of Indian pay payable from the date of arrival in India :—

Rank.	Service in Rank.	Basic Pay.	Overseas Pay.	Year of Total Service.
1.	2.	3.	4.	5.
		Rs.	Rs.	
Lieut.	. . . .	500	150	1st
			150	2nd
			150	3rd
Capt.	(i) During first 3 years' service as Captain	650	150	4th
			15	5th
			15	6th
	(ii) With more than 3 and less than 6 years' service as Captain .	750	25	7th
			25	8th
			25	9th
	(iii) With more than 6 years' service as Captain	850	25	10th
			25	11th
			30	12th
Major	(i) During first 3 years' service as Major	950		
	(ii) With more than 3 and less than 6 years' service as Major .	1,100		
	(iii) With more than 6 years' service as Major	1,250		
Lieut.-Col.	(i) Until completion of 23 years' total service . . .	1,500	30	13th and over
	(ii) During 24th and 25th years' service	1,600		
	(iii) After completion of 25 years' total service . . .	1,700		
	(iv) When selected for increased pay	1,850		

Note.—(1) Until the completion of 23 years' total service, basic pay is regulated according to rank and service in rank (columns 1 and 2), which, owing to the system of accelerated promotion, may be in advance of the time scale of promotion.

(2) Overseas pay is admissible only in the case of officers who, at the date of their appointment to the Indian Medical Service, had their domicile elsewhere than in Asia, and is regulated solely with reference to length of total service (column 6).

"25. *Allowances.*—In addition to the above rates of pay, various allowances are admissible to officers holding special appointments, such as :—

(a) Command pay drawn in addition to pay of rank by Indian Medical Service officers for the command and second in command of Indian Military Hospitals :—

	Command.	Second in Command.
	Rs.	Rs.
1st class Station Hospital . .	240	120
2nd class ,, . . .	180	90
3rd class ,, . . .	120	Nil

(b) Allowances for charge of Cantonment Hospitals and Cantonment Dispensaries at rates approved by the Cantonment authority concerned and sanctioned by the General Officer Commanding-in-Chief, the Command.

INTRODUCTION

(c) Charge pay varying from Rs. 30 to Rs. 240 per mensem for the medical charge of staffs of certain stations, depôts, factories, etc.

(d) Specialist pay attaching to specialists' appointments in certain subjects including :—

> Advanced Operative Surgery
> Medicine
> Ophthalmology
> Gynæcology and Midwifery
> Dermatology, including Venereal Diseases
> Prevention of Disease
> Charge of Brigade Laboratory

} Rs. 100 per mensem.

There are 50 such specialists' appointments, for which officers of the Indian Medical Service in military employment below the rank of Lieutenant-Colonel are eligible together with officers of the Royal Army Medical Corps. A candidate for one of these appointments must give proof to the satisfaction of the Director-General, Indian Medical Service, of special knowledge in the subject selected.

(e) Allowances for officers holding certain civil posts, as for instance :—

	Rs. per mensem.
Professorial or Bacteriological appointments	250
Principalships of Medical Colleges	150

Appointments as Superintendents of Central Jails—

(a) 1st class Jails	150
(b) 2nd class Jails	50

" 26. The following are the principal administrative appointments and the salaries attaching to them when they are held by officers of the Indian Medical Service :—

The Director-General, I.M.S.	Rs. 3,500 per mensem.
Director, Medical Services (Lieutenant-General or Major-General)*	Rs. 3,200 per mensem.
†Deputy Director, Medical Services, Command, Major-General	Rs. 2,750 per mensem.
†Deputy Director, Medical Services and Director, Hospital Organisation, Army Headquarters*	Rs. 2,500 per mensem.
†Assistant Director, Medical Services District †Director, Medical Organisation for War †Director, Hygiene and Pathology, Army Headquarters	Rs. 2,400 per mensem.
†Assistant Director, Medical Services, Army Headquarters	Rs. 2,150 per mensem.
Deputy Assistant Director (Medical Services or Hygiene and Pathology), Army Headquarters, Commands Districts Assistant Director of Hygiene and Pathology, Commands	Indian Medical Service pay of rank and service *plus* an additional pay of Rs. 250 per mensem.

* Normally one or the other of these posts is held by an officer of the British Service.
† I.M.S. officers holding these posts may, if they fulfil the conditions laid down in Army Instruction (India), 401 of 1925, draw in addition sterling overseas pay at £13 6s. 8d. per month.

INTRODUCTION

" 27. Unemployed pay is granted to Administrative Officers at the following rates :—

(a) *Out of India*.—A Colonel will receive the half-pay of rank of a Royal Army Medical Corps officer of corresponding rank, as laid down in the Royal Warrant,* *i.e.* £1 9s. 6d. a day = £538 7s. 6d. a year, with an Indian allowance, at present £200 a year.

A General Officer will receive the half-pay of rank of a British Service officer of corresponding rank, as laid down in the Royal Warrant,* *i.e.* £2 5s. a day = £821 5s. a year.

(b) *In India*.—The rates of unemployed pay for officers remaining in India during such unemployment will be the same as those issuable in this country, converted into rupees at the current rate of exchange as defined in Indian Army Regulations.

Unemployed pay cannot be drawn for any period exceeding three years and in no case will time on the unemployed list count as service for pension."

A subject somewhat akin to pay is that of practice. Para. 29 of the memo. given to candidates states :—

" With the exception of Administrative officers, military or civil, and officers holding certain special appointments, officers of the Indian Medical Service are not debarred from taking private practice, so long as it does not interfere with their proper duties."

CHAPTER XIX.—*Furlough and Leave.*

The leave rules have been considerably changed since the war, and in two respects have been altered greatly for the better ; leave pay has been increased, and concession passages granted, for an officer and also for his wife, up to a maximum of four passages in his total service.

The rules for leave, are set forth in paras. 30 to 40 of the memorandum of 1928, are as follows :—

Para. 30.—" Leave cannot be claimed as a right, but is granted on the discretion of the competent authority in India under whom an officer may be serving.

Para. 31.—" Officers of the I.M.S. in military employ, below the rank of Colonels, may be granted :—

(1) Privilege leave on full Indian pay under such regulations as may from time to time be in force.

(2) Furlough out of India on private affairs or on medical certificates for a period not exceeding one year in the first instance, on the rates of pay shown below.

* The Royal Warrant rates of half-pay are subject to alteration on account of a rise or fall in the cost of living as compared with the year 1919. With effect from the 1st July 1927 a reduction of 6 per cent. on this account has been made from the amounts shown above. A further revision will take place on 1st July 1930 and every three years thereafter to an extent not exceeding 20 per cent. in all.

INTRODUCTION

	Per diem.			Per annum.		
	£	s.	d.	£	s.	d.
Lieutenant	1	2	0	401	10	0
Captain	1	7	0	492	15	0
Captain after eight years' commissd. service	1	10	0	547	10	0
Captain after ten years' commissd. service	1	12	6	593	2	6
Captain holding higher brevet rank, in addition		2	0	36	10	0
Major	1	17	6	684	7	6
Major after 15 years' commissd. service	2	2	6	775	12	6
Major after 18 years' commissd. service	2	5	0	821	5	0
Major after 20 years' commissd. service	2	10	0	912	10	0
Lieutenant-Colonel	2	17	6	1048	7	6
Lieutenant-Colonel after three years as such	3	2	6	1140	12	6

Plus ration allowance at the rate laid down from time to time in Army Council Instructions.

These rates are subject to alteration on account of a rise or fall in the cost of living as compared with the year 1919. With effect from 1 July 1927 a reduction of six per cent. on this account has been made from the accounts shown above. A further revision may take place on the 1 July 1930, and every three years thereafter, to an extent not exceeding twenty per cent. in all.

Para. 32.—" No extension of leave involving absence from duty for more than two years, whether taken in or out of India, can be granted except on specially urgent grounds and without pay."

Para. 33.—(States that an officer, unable to rejoin at the end of two years' leave, will be placed on the temporary non-effective list, or on the retired list.)

Para. 34.—" An officer on leave, whether in India or out of India, is required to rejoin at once on being recalled to duty, unless certified by a Medical Board to be unfit to do so."

Para. 35.—(Leave of officers of administrative grades; entitled to privilege leave, and to six months' furlough, in one or two instalments.)

Para. 36.—(An officer in civil employment becomes subject to civil leave rules from the date of his first substantive civil appointment, or from completion of three years' officiating duty, whichever is earlier. Then follows a summary of the civil leave rules.)

Para. 37.—(Rules for study leave.)

Para. 38.—(Passages. Free passage to India given on first appointment, also for wife and family, if married.)

Para. 39.—(Rules for concession passages, going on furlough. Such passages given to self and wife, up to a maximum of four in total service; also one single adult passage for each child.)

Para. 40.—(Passages on retirement.)

CHAPTER XX.—*Pensions.*

The rates of pensions were considerably increased after the war, in 1920. The present rates, as shown in the memo. for candidates of April 1928, are as follows :—

Para. 41.—" Officers of the I.M.S. are allowed, subject to the right of

INTRODUCTION

Government to suspend retirements in times of emergency, to retire on the following scale of pension, on completion of the required periods of service.

After 17 years' service for pension £400 per annum.
,, 18 ,, ,, ,, £430 ,,
,, 19 ,, ,, ,, £460 ,,
,, 20 ,, ,, ,, £500 ,,
,, 21 ,, ,, ,, £540 ,,
,, 22 ,, ,, ,, £580 ,,
,, 23 ,, ,, ,, £620 ,,
,, 24 ,, ,, ,, £660 ,,
,, 25 ,, ,, ,, £700 ,,
,, 26 ,, ,, ,, £750 ,,
,, 27 ,, ,, ,, £800 ,,

(These rates are subject to revision, as in the footnote to para. 31.)

Para. 42.—(Reckoning of service for pension.)

Para. 43.—(Pensions to Major-Generals, additional, £350, £315, £285, for three, two, and one year respectively in that rank.)

Para. 44.—(Pensions to Colonels, additional, £250, £185, £125, £65, for four, three, two, and one year respectively in that rank.)

Para. 45.—(Retirement with gratuity, after six years £1,000, after twelve years £2,500.)

Para. 46.—(Ages of retirement. General officers at 60, Colonels at 57, Lieut.-Colonels and Majors at 55. Previously, the age for retirement was 60 for administrative, 55 for executive ranks.)

Para. 47.—(Retired officers liable to recall up to age of 55.)

Para. 48.—(Invalid pensions for officers under 17 years' of service, and special disability pensions.)

Para. 49.—(Rates of pay on temporary non-effective list.)

The benefits of the increased rates of pay in para. 41 was, after the war, given to officers on the retired list who had served for at least six months during the war.

Page 451.—Extra compensation pensions. These were first allotted, not in 1887/88, but in 1886/87. The first two officers to receive them were Brigade Surgeons J. Fairweather, retired 19 October 1886, and C. J. J. Jackson, retired, 31 March 1887. As only officers who entered the service before the end of 1889 were eligible for these pensions, the grant of these pensions ceased over ten years ago. Most of the recipients, indeed, are now dead.

CHAPTER XXI.—*The Funds.*

Two paragraphs in the memo. of April 1928 refer to family pensions.

Para. 50.—" The claims to pensions of widows and families of officers are treated under the provisions of such Royal Warrant regulating the grant of pensions to the widows and families of British officers as may be in force at the time being."

Para. 51.—" The widows and families of officers are also entitled to pensions under the Regulations of the Indian Military Widows and Orphans Fund. Subscription under these regulations is a condition of appointment, except in the case of Indians, for whom it is optional."

INTRODUCTION

CHAPTER XXII.—*Appointment to the Service; Examinations.*

Page 494.—Other instances of appointments from the ranks are given above, under CHAPTER XV, The Double Commissions.

Pages 494 *and* 504.—Previous to 1855, British nationality was not considered essential to appointment in the I.M.S. Many foreigners have been appointed from time to time, two of whom achieved considerable reputation. Nathaniel Wallich, the celebrated botanist, was a Danish Jew; Aloys Spenger, a world-famed Oriental scholar, was a Swiss. In addition to those enumerated in the text, several others may be mentioned. Theodore Duka (B. 1623) was a Hungarian; Thomas Moore (B. 1513), an American; Benjamin Heyne (M. 377), " a gentleman from Tranquebar," a Dane; George Lubbren (M. 858), a Hanoverian; J. F. Lyke or Luecke (B. 270), a Prussian. Hanover was never a British possession, but at the time of Lubbren's appointment, 1828, the King of Hanover was also King of England.

Page 504.—Chuckerbutty took the second, not the first place, in the first competitive examination in January 1855. The first man, George Marr, went to Madras.

Page 511.—In addition to the eleven names given in the text, of men who gained commissions as prizes at their medical schools, the following twelve more may be added. The names of the medical schools recommending them and of their nominators, are also given.

B. 1594.	G. R. Skinner.	R.C.S. Lond.	Sir J. M. Hogg.
B. 1620.	J. Ewart.	Guy's.	J. H. Astell.
B. 1655.	W. J. Palmer.	King's Coll. Lond.	W. B. Bayley.
M. 1154.	J. Wilson.	Guy's.	J. Masterman.
M. 1178.	W. H. Harris.	London Hosp.	J. Cotton.
M. 1180.	W. H. Rean.	Middlesex Hosp.	W. H. C. Plowden.
M. 1189.	W. R. Cornish.	St. George's.	W. H. C. Plowden.
M. 1202.	W. Pearl.	King's Coll. Lond.	Major Moore.
M. 1254.	S. G. Johnson.	Guy's.	W. B. Bayley.
M. 1274.	W. Fry.	King's Coll. Hosp.	Major Moore.
Bo. 845.	J. P. Stratton.	Mar. Coll. Ab.	J. Shepherd.
Bo. 847.	G. Nayler.	St. George's.	Lieut.-Genl. Campbell.

Competitive examination for the I.M.S. practically ceased with the outbreak of war. One examination was held in 1915, for seven appointments, the successful competitors were commissioned from 16 July 1915.

Since that date all appointments to the I.M.S. have been made by nomination. One temporary officer was nominated to a permanent commission in December 1914; the next nomination being dated October 1915. At first all the men nominated were actually serving in the war, either in the R.A.M.C. or I.M.S. After the war ended, for a while all, or nearly all, the men nominated were men who had served as medical officers during the war. Later, when this source of supply ceased, partly owing to the men who had served as doctors during the

INTRODUCTION

war becoming too old to enter on a new career, a large number of those nominated were men who had served in the war as combatants, either as subalterns or in the ranks, and had taken up the study of medicine after leaving the army.

Over a thousand temporary commissions were given in the I.M.S. during the war.

The last survivor of the medical officers appointed by the E.I. Co., Alexander Gamack (M. 1252), died at Hampstead on 8 March 1930, aged ninety-six. He was born on 13 February 1834, graduated at Marischal College, Aberdeen, as M.A. in 1853 and as M.D. in 1856, joined as Assistant Surgeon on 4 August 1856, retired on 1 August 1879, and drew his pension for just half a century.

For twenty years past, there has been a demand in India for the holding of competitive examinations for the I.M.S. in that country. This demand has been strongly pressed of late, and should the I.M.S. continue to exist, and should competitive examination for the I.M.S. be reintroduced, it seems probable that examinations will be held simultaneously in England and in India.

CHAPTER XXIII.—*Administration. The Medical Boards.*

Pages 14, 21, and 22.—It is stated on pp. 21 and 22 that the William Horsman who served on the Madras Hospital Board in 1786, and the William Horsman who entered the Madras Medical Service in 1798, were different men. Incredible as it may seem, the two were actually the same man, as shown in his record of service in the Roll (M. No. 419, p. 285.).

Page 15.—James Anderson was born on 17 January, 1738, at Long Hermiston, near Edinburgh, where his father, Dr. Andrew Anderson, was in practice, and was educated at Edinburgh University (A.A. Register, 1809, p. 458). He left England in 1758 as Surgeon's Mate of the 'Drake' Indiaman, which sailed from the Downs on 10 May 1758. The Surgeon, James Yuile, died at Canton on 3 October 1759, and Anderson succeeded to his place. The 'Drake' reached Gravesend on 25 September 1760. Anderson's further career is given in the Roll (M. No. 125, p. 257).

Pages 17 and 18.—William Duffin was Churchwarden of St. Mary's Church, Madras. (Penny, *The Church in Madras,* i. 373, 559.)

Page 17.—William Gordon went on furlough to England in 1792, and qualified the same year, taking the Certificate of the Corporation of Surgeons, London. Up to that time, during his service of thirty years, he had no qualifications at all, and had been passed over for promotion to administrative rank on that account. On his return to India, he was duly promoted to Head Surgeon from 4 June 1793, and posted to Masulipatam; two months later he got sick leave to

INTRODUCTION

Madras, and died there on 4 September 1793. A sick certificate, signed by Assistant Surgeons W. Norman and D. Mudie at Masulipatam on 18 August, states that he had an attack of a " severe nervous affection " on 12 August, from the symptoms described evidently cerebral hæmorrhage.

The term Medical Board for Hospital Board is used in the Madras Military Consultations of 26 July 1796, when the number of the Board was reduced from three to two members. Anderson was, in the same order, allowed to retain the title of Physician General.

Page 25.—The Bombay Hospital Board. On Dr. Clugstone's return from furlough, he protested, in a letter dated 21 June 1790, against being posted as a supernumerary, when he was senior to all three members of the Hospital Board (Bo. Mily. Cons. 22 June 1790). A copy of this letter was forwarded to Court. In a letter dated 24 September (Bo. Mily. Cons. same date), Clugstone claims to be appointed to the medical charge of the troops in the field (for the Third Maisur War). This was approved, and he was informed that he would be appointed Physician General on a vacancy occurring. He seems to have been so appointed in the same year, 1790, displacing the actual holder, Toomey. He died at Bombay on 14 July 1792 (Bo. No. 158, p. 405).

The Bombay Military Consultations of 5 November 1793 contain a letter from the Hospital Board, requesting that they may be granted the same pay as the members of the Bengal and Madras Boards; the Bombay Council recorded their agreement, and forwarded the representation to Court. There it was turned down. Four years later, another representation, in the Bombay Military Consultations of 24 February 1797, give a table of the pay granted in Bengal and Bombay respectively; First member, £2,500 and £2,000; Second Member, £2,000 and £1,500; Third Member, and Head Surgeon, Presidency Hospital, £1,500 and £1,000; other Head Surgeons, £1,000 and £800.

In the Bombay Military Consultations of 21 March and 23 May 1794, Toomey, the Physician General and President of the Hospital Board, signs his name with the title " Director Medical Department "; an anticipation of the modern title of Director General.

When the title of Director General was revived for the head of the Service, and his authority was extended over all three Presidencies, forty years ago, a Bengal officer was appointed Director General, and his successors were all Bengal officers, until the appointment of Sir Thomas Symons, a Madras officer, in 1926; the last officer of the old Establishments to hold the post. His successor is an officer of the General List, the first man of that Service to reach the post.

INTRODUCTION

Chapter XXIV.—*The Sea Service.*

Pages 47–49.—The ' Mocha ' frigate, on which John Leckie served as Surgeon, was not an Indiaman, but a vessel of the Bombay Marine.

Pages 57–58.—Mungo Park, the most famous man who served as Surgeon of an Indiaman. A doctor, named Mungo Park, took the M.R.C.S. in 1837, and in 1846–1851 was in practice in Old Street, London. Whether he was any, and if so what, relation to the great African explorer, cannot be stated.

Pages 60 and 61.—Charles MacLean, said to have served in the A.M.D. in 1804. He was never a regular commissioned officer of the A.M.D., though he may have temporarily served therein. His name is not in Johnston's *Roll of the Army Medical Service*. The Charles MacLean, No. 2981 in that roll, is obviously a different man.

Page 63.—Blackbeard and Teach were the same man, Blackbeard being Teach's nickname.

Surgeon General W. C. MacLean, in his *Memories of a Long Life* (p. 58), states that William Jardine and James Matheson, the founders of the great business firm of Jardine and Matheson, China Merchants, were both originally Surgeons of Indiamen. Matheson I have not been able to identify as such. William Jardine was Surgeon's Mate of the ' Brunswick ' in 1802–03, Surgeon of that ship in 1804–05, of the ' Glatton ' in 1806–1813, three voyages, and of the ' Wyndham ' in 1816–17.

Another Surgeon of an Indiaman who attained notable success in life and a considerable reputation was Robert Wigram, who was Surgeon of the ' Admiral Watson ' in 1765–66, of the ' Duke of Dorset ' in 1768–69, of the ' Duke of Richmond ' in 1768, and of the ' British King ' in 1770–72. He was born on 30 January 1743. In later life he was M.P. for Fowey in 1802–06, and for Wexford in 1806–07. He was created a Baronet on 30 October 1805, and died aged eighty-seven, on 6 November 1830. He was twice married, and had seventeen children. His son, Sir Robert Wigram, second Baronet, changed his name in 1832 to FitzWigram.

The firm of Thacker and Spink in Calcutta was founded in 1819 by William Thacker, who was Surgeon of the ' Earl St. Vincent ' in 1810–11.

The most singular career of any medical officer in the Sea Service, however, was that of Sir Robert MacAra, K.C.B., who served the E.I. Co. as Surgeon of various Indiamen for nearly twenty years, all the time holding a combatant commission in the British Army, in which he rose from Ensign to Captain during these years. He was the only child of the Revd. Duncan MacAra, Minister of Fortingall, Glenlyon, Perthshire, and of his wife Susanna Robertson, a native of Kirkmichael, in the same county. Robert was baptised at Fortingall on 6 May 1759, so was probably born early in that year. Of his life

INTRODUCTION

as a boy, the only fact known is that he matriculated at the United Colleges of St. Leonard and St. Salvator, at St. Andrews, at the age of fourteen, in the session of 1773-74, and went through the four-year course in the Faculty of Arts, but left without taking a degree. On 17 August 1782 he was gazetted Ensign in the 95th Foot. In the following year that battalion was disbanded, and its officers were placed on half-pay. An Ensign's half-pay is not a living wage, MacAra had to find some other means of livelihood, and chose medicine. Where he studied is not known, probably he entered the profession by way of apprenticeship. He was twenty-three when gazetted Ensign, so may have studied and qualified before joining the army. What qualification he had, if any, is not known. His name does not appear in any of the lists of graduates published by the Scottish Universities.

On 25 March 1785 he sailed from Portsmouth as Surgeon of the Indiaman 'Rodney.' In all he made six voyages to the East, as Surgeon, on the 'Rodney,' 13 December 1784 to 20 May 1786; the 'Thetis,' 22 October 1786 to 25 June 1788; the 'Ceres,' 1 January 1790 to 1 September 1791; the 'Valentine,' 22 January 1792 to 21 August 1793; the 'King George,' 31 January 1794 to 23 July 1795, and, after an interval of six years, the 'Marquess Wellesley,' 7 December 1801 to 31 July 1803. The logs of these voyages are all extant in the India Office. Nothing of much interest happened on any of them; there was no fighting, though there were several false alarms.

As stated above, MacAra's regiment, the 95th Foot, was disbanded in 1783, when almost all the regiments numbered above seventy were reduced. On 16 December 1795 he was promoted to Captain on full pay in the 94th Foot, and in the Army Lists of 1796-97-98 his name is included as Captain 94th Foot on full pay, but doing no duty, as the regiment was not embodied in these years. The Army Lists of 1799-1803 show him as Captain 95th Foot, on half-pay since 1795. On 9 July 1803, three weeks before the 'Marquess Wellesley' reached England, MacAra was gazetted Captain in the 42nd Foot, the Royal Highlanders, or Black Watch, and joined his regiment as soon as his ship arrived. His real military career then began, at the age of forty-four, after over twenty-one years nominal service in the army. His army rank as Captain dated from 16 Dec. 1795. The Army List of 1804 shows him as fifteenth out of eighteen Captains in his regiment, that of 1805 as seventh. On 14 November 1805 he was promoted to Major. There were four Majors in the regiment. In 1809 he had risen to third, in 1810 to second, and in 1811 became senior major. He was promoted to Lieut.-Colonel in the army on 1 January 1812, and got that rank in his regiment on 14 April 1812. There were then two Lieut.-Colonels. In 1813 he became the senior, and attained the command of his regiment.

The order of the Bath was reorganized by the Statute of 2 January

INTRODUCTION

1815. Previously there had only been one grade in the order, Knight of the Bath, K.B. In 1815 three grades were instituted; all the previous Knights became Grand Crosses, G.C.B., and a large number of Knight Commanders, K.C.B., and Companions, C.B., were gazetted from 2nd January 1815, among whom MacAra got the K.C.B.

Much of MacAra's service in the Black Watch was spent in hard campaigning in the Peninsula. The first battalion went out to Gibraltar in September 1805, and on 14 August 1808 embarked at Gibraltar for Portugal. It served under Sir John Moore in the retreat to Corunna and in the battle there on 16 January 1809. In February 1809 it returned to England, and in August to September 1809 served at Walcheren. The second battalion landed at Lisbon on 4 July 1809, and took part in the battle of Busaco on 27 September 1810, the defence of the lines of Torres Vedras in the winter of 1810–11, the battle of Fuentes d'Onoro on 3 May 1811, and in the siege of Ciudad Rodrigo and the storm of that fortress on 19 January 1812. The first battalion returned from England to the Peninsula in 1812, landing at Lisbon on 20 April. The two battalions were then combined, and served at Salamanca on 23 July 1812, Burgos 19 September 1812, Vittoria 21 June 1813, battle of the Pyrenees 25 July 1813, capture of San Sebastian September 1813, passage of the Bidassoa 7 October 1813, capture of Pampeluna 31 October 1813, battles of Nivelle 10 November 1813, Nives 9 December 1813, Orthez 27 February 1814, and Toulouse 10 April 1814. In how many of these actions MacAra took part cannot be stated with certainty. He received a medal for the battle of the Pyrenees, and clasps for Nivelle, Nives, Orthez, and Toulouse; also the Peninsular Gold Cross, having commanded the regiment in the last four. Shortly before the battle of Nivelle, Colonel Stirling, his predecessor in the command, went home, and was promoted to Major-General.

On 21 June 1814 the Black Watch embarked for Ireland, but were at home less than a year. In March 1815 Napoleon returned from Elba, and re-established himself in Paris. Among the troops sent over to the Netherlands to oppose him was the 42nd, which landed at Ostend in the middle of May 1815. The first general engagement took place at Quatre Bras on 16 June 1815, and there Sir Robert MacAra fell, commanding one of the finest regiments in the British Army, in the greatest campaign in which that army had ever been engaged previous to 1914.

While forming his regiment into square to repel a charge of French cavalry, MacAra was wounded by a musket ball, and fell from his horse, and while lying on the ground was pierced by a lance driven home under his chin. The command of the regiment passed through four hands in a few minutes, Lieut.-Col. MacAra killed, Lieut.-Col. Dick severely wounded, Brevet-Major Davidson mortally wounded, and Brevet-Major Campbell.

INTRODUCTION

In the Waterloo campaign the 42nd lost 4 officers, 2 sergeants, and 45 rank and file killed; 19 officers, 12 sergeants, and 216 men wounded. Nearly all these casualties occurred at Quatre Bras. At Waterloo itself they lost only 6 men killed, 4 officers, and 33 rank and file wounded.

MacAra was an only child, he had no near relatives, and never married. No portrait of him appears to be in existence. A joint monument to him, and to Lieut.-Colonel Cameron, of the Gordons, who also fell at Quatre Bras, stands on the hill of Tor-Alvie, north of Kingussie, in Inverness-shire.

CHAPTER XXV.—*Contracts and Trade.*

Page 77.—Alexander Gray's fortune was used to build and endow Gray's Hospital, Elgin.

Hickey mentions in his *Memoirs* (Vol. III, p. 315), that Assistant Surgeon Humphrey Howarth (B. No. 217, 1778–1785), went home at the end of 1785, with a fortune of at least £40,000, made by getting a share of the opium contract.

CHAPTER XXVI. —*The Minor Medical Services.*

Page 85.—St. Helena. The Dutch annexed the island in 1633, but never actually occupied it. It was occupied by John Dutton, for the E.I. Co., in January 1659.

Page 86.—As shown in the E.I. Regrs., the staff at St. Helena in 1798 consisted of fourteen civilians, four companies of infantry, two companies of artillery, and two medical officers. In 1820 there were twenty civilians, one regiment of infantry, one brigade of artillery, and seven medical officers; one superintending surgeon, three surgeons, and three assistant surgeons.

Page 90.—The medical officers of the P.W.I. Service were all transferred to the Bengal list in 1830, but continued to serve in the Straits till they retired.

The East India Company for a few years kept up another, even smaller, medical service, the Sagar Island Establishment, which consisted of one man, for a period of seven years. A project for the reclamation of Sagar Island excited much interest in Calcutta in the beginning of the nineteenth century. The island has an extent of 143,268 acres. A certain amount of reclamation was done in 1801, and fifteen to twenty years later the project was more seriously attacked, a company for the purpose was formed, and part of the island was cleared and cultivated. The portion cleared was named Trowerland, after Mr. Charles Trower, Collector of Calcutta, who was one of the chief supporters of the scheme.

Thomas Hodges (B. 892), was appointed Surgeon at Sagar Island

INTRODUCTION

on 13 October 1820. After the ruin of the settlement, he was transferred to the Bengal Service from 4 December 1828, being ranked in that service, not from the date of his original appointment in 1820, but from December 1828. He died in Calcutta on 16 December 1831, so the loss of rank made not much difference to him.

The settlement was destroyed by a storm wave in 1826, and the greater part of the island lapsed again into jungle. The island now has a lighthouse, built in 1808, a conspicuous object to all vessels leaving or entering the Hughli, a telegraph station, and a meteorological observatory. A large mela or religious fair is held yearly for three days in January, at the south or seaward end of the island, which is largely attended by pilgrims from Calcutta and other parts of Bengal.

CHAPTER XXVII.—*The Uncovenanted and Subordinate Medical Services.*

Page 102.—Peachey's petition, dated 5 August 1737. The date is misprinted 1837.

Page 105.—Gabriel Alvares. The Bombay Consultations of 9 March 1786 contain a petition from Alvares, recounting his services, and asking to be placed on the list of Assistant Surgeons. Orders were given that he could not be placed on the list of Assistant Surgeons, but would be ranked as senior native assistant, and would receive the allowances of an Assistant Surgeon.

Thirteen years later, the Bombay Consultations of 24 September 1799 contain another long petition from Assistant Surgeon G. Alvares, so he had succeeded in getting recognised as a Commissioned Officer. He states that, after apprenticeship in the General Hospital, he was appointed an Assistant Surgeon, and sent on active service at Caranja in 1775, was then Surgeon to Onore factory for nearly four years, and along with the Resident, Mr. Charles Stewart, was taken prisoner by Haidar Ali, was released four months later, but lost all his property. On his arrival at Bombay, he was appointed Surgeon of the snow ' Morning Star,' served on her three years, and was present at the raising of the siege of Tellicherry. He then served as Surgeon of the grab ' Bombay ' on the coast during the war, often serving with troops ashore. He then served as Surgeon to the garrison of Onore, in charge of a large hospital; was then Surgeon of the ' Sir Edward Hughes,' and was afterwards posted to the General Hospital, but served temporarily several times as Surgeon on various cruisers. He asks for promotion and increase of pay. The Medical Board state that his statement of his services is correct, that he served as Surgeon to the General Hospital at Onore in 1783, that he has always served with credit, that he is now an unranked Assistant Surgeon, serving as Mate in the General Hospital, and draws pay of Rs. 100 a month, plus Ensign's batta, Rs. 45 a month. The Bombay Council order the

INTRODUCTION

application to be referred to the Commander-in-Chief, with what result is not recorded. But he never was promoted to a higher rank than Assistant Surgeon.

From 2 October 1918 the title of the Military Indian Subordinate Medical Department was changed to Indian Medical Department, dropping out the word subordinate, in recognition of the services of the department during the war, so it is now known as the I.M.D.

Fifty years ago, the initials I.M.D. were often used instead of I.M.S., for the Indian Medical Service, on the analogy of A.M.D. This phraseology was quite incorrect, the I.M.S. always having been a Service, not a Department. The title has long since been discontinued, and few can now remember that it was ever in use.

The Uncovenanted Medical Service has long ago died out. Practically, its place has been taken by the Provincial Medical Services, recruited in India for local, *i.e.* provincial service; services which must expand as the I.M.S. diminishes in numbers, and the autonomy of the Provinces increases.

CHAPTER XXIX.—*Other Extra-Professional Work.*

Page 157.—John Leyden. Scott mentions him in Canto IV, Stanza XI, of *The Lord of the Isles*—" A distant and a deadly shore, holds Leyden's cold remains."

Page 158.— Horace Hayman Wilson took great interest in the drama. His wife was a grand-daughter of Mrs. Siddons. For many years he managed the Calcutta theatre as an amusement. Of course all dramatic performances in India were then amateur.

Page 160.— Oliver Goldsmith. An article in the *Nineteenth Century* of April 1913, states that Goldsmith took the B.A. degree at Trinity College, Dublin, on 27 July 1749, and the M.B. about 1751, and was admitted to the M.D. degree, *ad eundem*, at Oxford on 17 February 1769.

CHAPTER XXX.—*Medical Officers Employed in England.*

Page 163.—John Lorimer had served in the A.M.D. from 1761 to 1784 (Johnston's Roll, No. 614).

Page 164.—John Robert Hume also had a distinguished career in the A.M.D., from 1800 to 1821, and had served in the Peninsula and at Waterloo (Johnston's Roll, No. 1988).

Page 164.—William Dick, after retiring from the Bengal Service, was appointed Head Surgeon of the P.W.I. Service, but served there for only one year, 1805–06.

Page 167.—The President of the Medical Board, India Office, was, by an order dated 30 June 1916, appointed Medical Adviser to the

INTRODUCTION

Secretary of State for India, in addition to his other duties. One of the special duties attached to the office was supervision of recruitment for the I.M.S.

Chapter XXXI.—*After Retirement.*

Page 176.—James Laurie's successor in the chair of Surgery at Glasgow was Mr. afterwards Lord Lister.

Page 177.—Since the *History of the I.M.S.* was published, three other retired officers of the I.M.S. have been appointed Inspectors under the Department formally called Local Government Board, now the Health Ministry; Lieut.-Colonels E. Wilkinson and S. P. James, and Major F. N. White. The two former are still serving (1930); the third soon gave up his post for that of Chief Commissioner of the Epidemic Commission, League of Nations.

Pages 181-183.—Parliament. Lieut.-Colonel T. E. B. Williams (G. 178), entered the House of Commons at the Election of 1923, as a Labour M.P., winning the Seat at Kennington, but lost it in the election of 1924.

Page 183.—The Church. Another man who entered the Church, after retiring from the I.M.S., was John Coleridge (M. 1005).

Under this chapter may be mentioned that a large number of retired officers of the I.M.S. rejoined for duty in the war of 1914-18. Many of them only served at home, in the British Isles, but some served in France and Flanders, and in Iraq.

Chapter XXXII.—*War Services.*

The quotation from *Othello* which heads this chapter may have been applicable to warfare from ancient times up to the end of last century, say up to the South African War. Nothing could be more unsuitable to the era of mechanical mass destruction ushered in by the war of 1914-18. A better heading would be another sentence from the same play: " Othello's occupation's gone."

Page 187.—James Wilson, senior (M. 85), served at Trichinopoly, Wilson, Junior (M. 99), at Arcot.

Page 188.—Captain Archibald Swinton (M. 100), was also present at Undwa Nala.

Page 190.—Surgeon T. Gahagan (M. 159), was also present in Colonel Baillie's defeat at Perambakam. Colonel Braithwaite, who commanded the force defeated and cut up at Anagudi on 18 February 1782, had been in command of the troops in Sumatra in 1769-70.

Page 191.—Robert Briscoe, Surgeon of the 100th Foot, served in the A.M.D. for a few years from 1783 (Johnston's Roll, No. 1047). Gabriel Alvares (Bo. 188), was taken prisoner at Onore, in the second Maisur War, in 1783.

INTRODUCTION

Page 195.—Surgeon Alexander Home, of the 36th Foot, served in the A.M.D. for nearly twenty years, 1773 to 1792. He was taken prisoner near Bangalore in September 1791, and put to death at Naurindrug on 15 or 16 January 1792 (Johnston's Roll, No. 817). When Home was taken prisoner, Lord Cornwallis, the Commander-in-Chief, appointed Assistant Surgeon Francis Duncan (M. 293), as Surgeon of the 36th Foot, in his place. Duncan's appointment gave rise, four years later, to an interesting and somewhat amusing dispute as to his position, whether he was an officer of the A.M.D. or of the I.M.S. The Madras Military Consultations of 2 August 1796 contain an application from Duncan for sick leave to Europe, in which he states that Cornwallis had appointed him to act as Surgeon to the 36th Foot after Home's being taken prisoner, and that it is not certain that Home is dead. There is also a petition from thirteen Madras Assistant Surgeons, junior to Duncan, protesting against his being allowed to retain a place on the list of Madras Assistant Surgeons, while for six years past he has been Surgeon to the 36th Foot. The Council ordered that Duncan should have the furlough requested, and state that he was only lent to the 36th Foot, with a stipulation that he should retain his rank in the Company's service, and that of course, without question, he does so.

Page 196.—Besides the four mentioned, Cheek, MacKenzie, Twining, and Fasken, a fifth I.M.S. officer, James Lawder (M. 768), had also served in the Peninsula, as Assistant Surgeon of the 29th Foot; he also served in the War in America, in 1814 (Johnston's Roll, No. 3516). Cheek served in the Waterloo campaign, but was not present at the actual battle of Waterloo.

Page 197.—The names of twenty-five officers of the I.M.S. are given as having served in the Crimean war. One of them, F. H. Brett, a retired Bengal officer, though deputed to serve in the Crimea as Field Surgeon, does not appear to have actually gone there. At least six other officers, however, did serve in the Crimean War: J. MacAlister (Bo. 790), W. B. MacEgan (B. 1517), E. L. M. Larking (Bo. 901), B. Williamson (M. 1233), G. A. Watson (B. 1687), and H. J. Blanc (Bo. 932). Larkin served in the Turkish contingent, Blanc in the French army. The last I.M.S. survivors of the Crimea were R. Boustead (Bo. 927), who died on 8 October 1916, and B. Williamson, who died on 21 February 1917.

The last I.M.S. survivor of the Indian Mutiny was D.S.G. Philip Warren Sutherland (B. 1639), who died on 6 May 1925. A medical officer, however, not in the I.M.S., lived nearly five years longer; Major Thomas Henry Hill, C.I.E., I.M.D., who died in London on 19 February 1930, aged eighty-six. He was born on 14 February 1844, and entered the Laurence Military Asylum School for sons of soldiers, at Sanawar, in 1849. When the mutiny broke out, he joined the

INTRODUCTION

I.S.M.D. as a hospital apprentice, at the age of thirteen; he retired in 1903.

Page 198.—The following names may be added to the short list of I.M.S. officers who served in British wars in which the Indian army took no part; G. Babington (B. 639), in Flanders, in 1799, in the 3rd Foot Guards; J. W. Martin (B. 867), at Walcheren, in 1809; J. T. C. Ross (B. 1482), in the Zulu war of 1879, as Commissioner for the Stafford House Committee.

Page 198.—Four more names are to be added to those who served in foreign wars: Franco-German War, C. J. F. MacDowall (Bo. 902); Russo-Turkish War, 1877–78, C. Monks (Bo. 1045); Balkan Wars, 1912, A. N. Dickson (G. 437), and F. R. Thornton (G. 668).

Page 198.—In addition to the six names given, three more served in the South African War, J. S. Wilkins (Bo. 1006), A. F. W. King (Bo. 1127), and J. C. Robertson (B. 2395).

Page 201.—It was on her second, not on her first, voyage that the Indiaman 'Warren Hastings' was taken by the French frigate 'Piémontaise.'

Page 204.—An even earlier instance of mention in despatches, than that of Harris and Davies in 1810, is contained in Bengal G.O. of 21 May 1806, where Henry Wise (M. 368), is mentioned for services in the second Maratha War.

Page 208.—Zoar, where Assistant Surgeon John Gordon was reported killed in action, in 1819, is not on the Red Sea, but on the Mekran coast. The name should be spelt Sohar.

Pages 208 *and* 209.—A list of thirty-four I.M.S. officers killed in action, up to 1903, is given on these pages. One more name may be added, making thirty-five. The *India Gazette and Calcutta Public Advertiser* of 9 June 1781, in a list of killed in Genl. Goddard's action of 24 April 1781, the capture of Laher, gives the name of Surgeon Rennie, Madras detachment. But no further mention of this officer's name or existence has been found.

In the Great War of 1914–18, including the fighting on the Indian frontier up to 1921, seventeen more officers of the I.M.S. were killed; five in France and Flanders, one in Gallipoli, seven in Iraq, and three on the Indian Frontier. All these were officers of the General List, five of them being temporary officers. One retired officer of the Bengal list was lost in a torpedoed ship. And since the war Lieut.-Colonel P. Murphy, a retired Bombay officer, was killed in the sack of Smyrna by the Turks, on 13 September 1922. A complete list of officers killed in action is given in Appendix II.

Even before the war of 1914–21, officers of the I.M.S. had served in most parts of the world. During these years of war the I.M.S. were represented in Flanders, France, and Belgium, in Italy, the

INTRODUCTION

Balkans, Gallipoli, Egypt, Palestine, Asia Minor, Transcaucasia, Persia, China, and East and West Africa. Certainly no I.M.S. officer took part in the Australian campaign which captured the German islands in the Pacific in the beginning of the war, or in Botha's campaign in South West Africa. Whether any took part in the campaigns in Northern Russia and Siberia I cannot say.

CHAPTER XXXIII.—*Honours and Rewards.*

Page 211.—Assistant Surgeon James Penrose (Bo. 291) is stated, in the C.G. of 2 January 1900, to have been Surgeon Extraordinary to the King. This is a mistake. The officer who held that post was his father. The roll of the Corporation of Surgeons, London, shows for many years, from 1794 on, the name of James Penrose, Surgeon Extraordinary to the King, as in practice at Hatfield, Herts. In the roll for 1799, in addition to his name, appears that of James Penrose, junior, Surgeon, East Indies.

Page 212.—The Baronetcy conferred on Sir William Russell is now extinct. Since the *History of the I.M.S.* was published, a third Baronetcy has been conferred on an I.M.S. officer, Sir Richard Havelock Charles, on 2nd January 1928. Two other I.M.S. officers have inherited Baronetcies, Sir Bruce Seton succeeded his cousin as 9th Baronet on 6 March 1915, and Sir Dodington G. R. S. Baker succeeded his father as fifth Baronet on 15 March 1923. Sir Bruce Seton put forward a claim to the dormant Barony of Gordon in 1928, but failed to prove his claim.

Page 219.—A table on this page gives a list of honours and decorations bestowed on officers of the I.M.S. up to the end of 1913. A similar table is given in Appendix VIII, showing the numbers conferred up to January 1930. The war of 1914-18, with the institution of new orders, the British Empire and the Military Cross, led to a great increase. The total is now 691, almost three times the number in 1913, which was 239. Incidentally, it will be seen that the General List, a little over a thousand strong, in a little more than thirty years, have earned 313 honours, a much larger number than the Bengal Service, 2,400 strong, have gained in almost three centuries.

The table in Appendix VIII extends up to January 1930. Since then, on 3 June 1930, a K.C.B. has, for the first time, been conferred upon an ex-member of the General List, Sir David Munro; though this honour, doubtless, was given for his services as head of the Medical Department of the Royal Air Force, not for his former service in the I.M.S.

Two Victoria Crosses were gained by I.M.S. officers during the war, one by Capt. J. A. Sinton, I.M.S., in Iraq, on 21 June 1916; the other by Temporary Capt. H. J. Andrews, in Waziristan, on 22 October

INTRODUCTION

1919, conferred posthumously in the *London Gazette* of 10 September 1920. The *Gazette* notifications are quoted below.

London Gazette, 21 June 1916.—" John Alexander Sinton, M.B., Captain, Indian Medical Service. For most conspicuous bravery and devotion to duty. Although shot through both arms and through the side, he refused to go to the hospital, and remained as long as daylight lasted attending to his duties under very heavy fire. In three previous actions Captain Sinton displayed the utmost bravery."

London Gazette, 10 September 1920.—" The late Temporary Captain, Henry John Andrews, M.B.E., Indian Medical Service. For most conspicuous bravery and devotion to duty on 22 October 1919, when as Senior Medical Officer in charge of Khajuri post (Waziristan), he heard that a convoy had been attacked in the vicinity of the post, and that men had been wounded. He at once took out an Aid Post to the scene of action, and approaching under heavy fire, established an Aid Post under conditions which afforded some protection to the wounded, but not to himself. Subsequently he was compelled to remove his Aid Post to another position, and continued most devotedly to attend to the wounded. Finally, when a Ford van was available to remove the wounded, he showed the utmost disregard of danger in collecting the wounded under fire, and in placing them in the van, and was eventually killed whilst himself stepping into the van on the completion of his task."

CHAPTER XXXIV.—*Courts Martial.*

Page 234.—Duelling. It is rather a curious fact that no officer of the I.M.S. appears ever to have been killed in a duel; while, on the other hand, no less than six cases are recorded, in which I.M.S. officers killed other men. Four of these cases, Betty, Ford, Key, and Malcolmson, are recorded in the *History of the I.M.S.*, in Vol. II, pp. 234, 239, and 241, in which the survivor was tried and acquitted. Two more may now be added; in neither of them did any legal action follow.

In Seton Karr's *Selections from the Calcutta Gazettes*, Vol. II, pp. 213–215, it is recorded that Surgeon R—, of the Madras Service, in a duel at Pondicherry in 1789, shot dead Mr. J. W— of the Civil Service. Surgeon R—'s leg was fractured by his adversary's bullet. No prosecution followed, the duel having been fought on foreign territory. Mr. J. W. was Mr. James Woolley. One would have thought it would not be difficult to identify Surgeon R—. But at the time there were no less than six officers of the Madras Medical Service, of the rank of Surgeon, whose surnames began with R: William Raine, William Ruddiman, William Roxburgh, James Richardson, John Ruding, and Robert Rollo, and it has not been found possible to identify the duellist.

Surgeon Kenneth Murcheson, of the Bengal Service, in a duel at Lucknow in 1780, shot dead a Captain Croftes, of the King of Oudh's Service. In this case also the duel took place on foreign territory, Captain Crofts, moreover, was not in the Company's service, and no official notice of the duel appears to have been taken.

INTRODUCTION

Page 242.—Crime in Madras. It is noted as curious that almost all the cases of crime in the I.M.S. seem to have occurred in Madras. The S.A.L.M.M. record two other cases in which Madras Medical Officers were tried for murder; Assistant Surgeon S. Stokes (M. 725), in 1835, tried by court martial for murder of Bellary, a camp follower (G.O.C.C. 25 February 1835); and Assistant Surgeon G. Daubeny (M. 1105), indicted in 1848 for the murder of the infant child of the late Mr. Frere, a brother officer (*Indian Mail*, 5 January 1849). Both were acquitted. No details are given of either case. One might surmise that the first was a case of assault, and rupture of the spleen; the second a case of alleged careless prescribing or dispensing.

CHAPTER XXXVIII.—1865–1896.

In the period of thirty-two years, just a generation, covered by this chapter, nearly a thousand men, 997 to be exact, entered the I.M.S. All have now retired, the last two quite recently; and now, in July 1930, some 725, or nearly three-fourths, are dead. The figures for the three services are: Bengal, entered 540, living 162; Madras, 267 and 68; Bombay, 190 and 42. The senior officer now (July 1930) living, on the retired list, is Surgeon Major H. D. S. Compigné (B. 1910), who was born on 11 January 1844, entered on 1 October 1866, and retired on 13 November 1884.

CHAPTER XLIII.—*Medical Education in India.*

Since the *History of the I.M.S.* was published, about a dozen more medical schools have been opened in India. A list is given below. Three of these are female schools, two are private schools. The Agra Medical School was raised to teach up to the L.M.S. standard in 1916; the Patna school was started, as a College of Patna University, in 1925, the Patna vernacular school being then transferred to Darbangha. The Lady Hardinge Medical College for Women at Delhi also teaches up to University standard, and is affiliated to the Panjab University at Lahore. The Nagpur Medical School might be considered a resuscitation of an older school, opened in 1867, which only lasted some fifteen years.

The School of Tropical Medicine in Calcutta, opened in 1914, stands on a somewhat different footing, as a post graduate and special school.

The following new medical schools have been opened since 1914. Probably the list is incomplete.
    Nagpur, reopened, 1914.
    Lady Hardinge Medical College for Women, Delhi, February 1916.
    Calicut, 1 July 1916.
    Belgachia Medical College, Calcutta, private, 6 July 1916.

INTRODUCTION

Vellore, female, July 1918.
Coimbatore, September 1919.
Bardwan, 16 January 1922.
National Medical College, Calcutta, private, August 1922.
Egmore, Madras, female, August 1923.
Darbangha, transferred from Patna, 1925.

Medical schools have also been projected at several other places, and some of them may have been opened by now: (1) Bhowanipur, Calcutta, in connection with the Sambhu Nath Pandit Hospital; (2) Howrah; (3) Lytton Medical School, Maimansinh; (4) Chittagong; (5) Barhampur; (6) Sylhet.

Page 442.—Dr. Bhola Nath Bose died in November 1884, not, as stated, in 1885.

CHAPTER XLIV.—*Medical Societies and Medical Journalism in India.*

A medical journal called *The Antiseptic* was started at Madras in 1904, by the late Dr. T. M. Nair, and edited by him up to his death in 1919. The *Madras Medical Journal* first appeared in 1914, the *Burma Medical Times* in July 1921.

A number of new medical societies have been started in India during the past twenty years; some have survived, others have come to a premature end. They include:—

Kathiawar Medical Society, April 1913.
Sind Medical Union, 1916.
Puna Medical Society, 1916.
Bombay War Hospitals Medical Society, February 1918.
Bagdad Medical Society, 1920.

From time to time branches of the British Medical Association have been founded in India. Some have died out from time to time, but several have been founded during the past twenty-five years. There appear to be some ten now in existence.

South India Branch, Madras, founded 1884.
Bombay, 1889.
Panjab, 1889.
Burma, 1891.
Assam, 1908.
Baluchistan, 1910.
Mesopotamia, 1921.
Northern Bengal, 1922.
Haidarabad, Dekkan, started 1894, died out, reorganised 1924.
Calcutta, 1928. A former branch was started in Calcutta in 1863, by Norman Chevers, under the name of Bengal Branch, but only lasted for a few years.

ROLL OF THE INDIAN MEDICAL SERVICE

(a) *Signifies name not in Dodwell and Miles' list, 1763–1838;* (b) *had served in an Indiaman, in E.I. Co.'s Sea Service;* (c) *locally appointed in India;* (d) *never joined;* (e) *name included in Dictionary of National Biography.*

I. BENGAL

1645

1. **Whiting, Edward.** Surgeon at Jambi, 1645, transferred Madras Sept. 1649; (L. from Fort St. George, 16 Jan. 1650/51). Resigned, Jan. 1656/57; (L. from Fort St. George, 28 Jan. 1656/57). Returned to Madras 1662, transferred to Bengal as Surgeon to the Bay Factories, Feb. 1662/63; (L. from Fort St. George, 26 Feb. 1662/63). M. No. 2.

1652

2. **Archer, Samuel.** Surgeon in Pegu in 1652. (List of Co.'s servants, 10 Jan. 1651/52). Pegu was under Fort St. George at this time.

1669

3. **Harwar, Ralph** (b, c). Surgeon of 'Dilligence,' 1668–69. Resigned and set up as a trader in Bengal. Surg. Hugli 1672; (Letter from Hugli, 11 Dec. 1672). Exchanged with Douglas, and went home, Dec. 1676; (Balasore Cons. Dec. 1676). Reappointed Hugli, on dismissal of Douglas, July 1682. Served in Charnock's war against the Nawab of Bengal, 1686–87. *d.* at Hijli, during siege of the Fort, 1687. v. Hist. of the I.M.S. i. 102.

1676

4. **Douglas, Robert** (b, c). Surgeon of 'Eagle,' 1675–76, exchanged with Harwar, Dec. 1676, and appointed Surgeon to Bay Factories. Dismissed, July 1682; (Hugli Cons. 28 July 1682). Remained at Hugli till 1684, when he went to England via Persian Gulf. Living in England in 1701. v. Hist. of I.M.S. i. 102, 103.

1684

5. **Watson, Henry.** Appointed Surgeon's Mate, Bengal, 1684; (L. from C. 26 Nov. 1684). Went as Surg. of 'Hopewell' to Siam, taken prisoner by pirates, reached Madras end of 1688; (Fort St. G. Cons. 7 Jan. 1688/89). One Henry Watson, who may have been the same man, went home from Madras in 1705; (L. from Fort St. G. 14 Sept. 1706, para. 73). M. No. 18.

6. **Plomer,** or **Plummer, John** (b, c). Surgeon's Mate of 'Royal James,' Appointed Mate, Madras, (M. Cons. 28 July 1684). Surgeon, Madras, May 1685. Went home as Surgeon of 'Royal James,' May 1688, (M. Cons. 7 May 1688). Surgeon at Calcutta, 1695, possibly from 1693 or 1694; (B. Cons. 7 Mar. 1694/95). Resigned, 7 Sept. 1695, (B. Cons.).* Reappointed, 1696. Resigned, 26 July 1697; (B. Cons.). v. Hist. of I.M.S. i. 105.

* When no date is given with a reference, its date is the same as that of the event referred to.

7. **Warren, William.** Surgeon at Madras 1684; (M.P.L. No. 2618 of 26 Sept. 1684). Transferred Bengal, Aug. 1698; (Fort St. G. Cons. 30 June 1698). Resigned, 11 Nov. 1706; (B. Cons.). Settled at Madras. d. on a voyage to Tonquin, 1716; (Fort St. G. Cons. 4 Dec. 1716). v. Hist. of I.M.S. i. 106–108. M. No. 20.

1686

8. **Hart, Samuel.** Appointed Surgeon in the Bay, 17 Aug. 1686; (F.R. Cal. vol. i. List of servants, 1690). Transferred Madras, going there with Charnock, Feb. 1688/89, when he was appointed Surg. at Madras. Discharged 29 Dec. 1692; (Fort St. G. Cons.). Living at Madras up to 1707. v. Hist. of I.M.S. i. 104. Charnock's war against Nawab of Bengal, 1686–87, at Hugli, Hijli, and Ulubaria. M. No. 24.

1688

9. **Bird, —.** A Surgeon, at Chutanuti (Calcutta) in June 1688; (M.P.L. No. 1633 of 1688).

1690

10. **A Dutchman,** name not recorded. The first Surgeon of Calcutta. Resigned on account of ill-health 24 Sept. 1691; (B. Cons.).

1695

11. **Simson, Francis** (b, c). Surgeon of 'Martha.' Appointed Surg. Calcutta, v. Plomer, 7 Sept. 1695; (B. Cons. 23 Nov. 1695). No further information. In bad health when appointed, probably died before Plomer's reappointment in 1696.

1696

12. **Cholmeley, John** (b, c). Surgeon of 'Ffleete' frigate, acted as Surgeon of Calcutta during Plomer's illness in 1696; (B. Cons. 30 Jan. 1696/97). Appointed Surg. of 'Mocha' frigate at Bombay, 22 Aug. 1707; (Bo. Cons.); of ship 'Bombay,' 27 Sept. 1707. Bo. No. 48.

1698

13. **Richardson, Philip** (b, c). Surgeon of 'Tavistock,' acted as Surg. of Calcutta, Feb. to Aug. 1698, till relieved by Warren; (B. Cons. 7 Nov. 1698). Surgeon of 'Loyall Hester,' appointed Surgeon of Calcutta, 13 Dec. 1706; (B. Cons.). Resigned, 11 Jan. 1710/11; (B. Cons.).

1699

14. **Pendleton, Thomas.** Surgeon to New Company, 1699. d. Dec. 1699.

15. **Bigland, Henry.** Surgeon's Mate to New Company, 1699. d. 30 Aug. 1699.

1701

16. **Gray, Michael.** Surgeon to New Company at Masutipetam, 1701, transferred to Fort. St. David, 1702; (L. from C. 31 July 1702). Second Surgeon, Calcutta, 20 Aug. 1705; (B. Cons. 20 Aug. 1705). Resigned on account of ill-health, 4 Nov. 1706; (B. Cons. 4 Nov. 1706). Living in Calcutta as a free inhabitant, up to 1726; (B. Cons. 17 Oct. 1726). v. Hist. of I.M.S. i. 109. M. No. 36.

1703

17. Peterson, Julian. "A Dutch Musteese, lately Chirurgeon's Mate." Resigned and died in Calcutta between Feb. and July 1704; (B. Cons. 6 July 1704).

1707

18. Orme, Alexander. Went out to India as an adventurer about 1686. Appointed Surgeon at Anjengo, in 1707 or earlier. In 1712 shown in a list of seafaring men, not constant residents, at Madras. Appointed Senior Merchant and second in Council at Anjengo in 1721; (Bo. Genl. L. 28 Dec. 1721, para. 89). Soon after promoted to Chief at Anjengo. Removed by order of Court in 1728; (Bo. Genl. L. 30 Sept. 1728, para. 110). At Calcutta 1731, appointed to succeed to next vacancy as Surgeon, but superseded by R. Coult; (B. Genl. L. 25 Feb. 1731/32, and 28 Dec. 1735). *d.* in Calcutta, 19 April 1736; (St. Anne's Regr.). Father of Robert Orme, the historian. v. Hist. of I.M.S. i. 141, 142. Bo. No. 61.

1710

19. Parney, John. Surgeon's Mate at Calcutta 1710, resigned 11 Jan. 1710/11 (B. Cons. 17 Jan. 1710-11). At Bombay as Surgeon of a Bengal ship, and appointed Surgeon, Bombay, 29 June 1711; (Bo. Cons.). Resigned 1715. Practised at Bassein two years, then appointed Surgeon, Karwar factory; (Bo. Cons. 11 Feb. 1716/17). No further information. Bo. No. 66.

1711

20. James, William. Surgeon of 'Bouverie.' Appointed Surgeon of Calcutta, Jan. 1710/11, and nominated to accompany Surman's Embassy to Delhi; (B. Cons. 30 Nov. 1711). Did not go. Resigned, 4 Dec. 1712; (B. Cons.).

21. Hamilton, William (b, c). Went to India as Surgeon of 'Sherborne.' Deserted at Madras, 3 May 1711; (M. Cons. 7 May 1711). Second Surgeon, Calcutta, 27 Dec. 1711; (B. Cons. 27 Dec. 1711). Accompanied Surman's Embassy to Delhi, 1714-17. *d.* in Calcutta, 4 Dec. 1717; (tombstone). v. Hist. of I.M.S. i. chap. ix.

1712

22. Greene, Benjamin. Surgeon's Mate, Calcutta. *d.* in Calcutta, 30 May 1712.

23. Stacey, Thomas. Surgeon's Mate, Calcutta, in 1713; (B. Cons. 7 Aug. 1713).

24. Broadfoot, Robert. Surgeon's Mate, Calcutta, 1712; (Fort Wm. Genl. L. 18 Jan. 1722/23). Surgeon, 5 Feb. 1728/29; (B. Cons. 31 Mar. 1729). Resigned, Jan. 1737/38; (B. Cons. 17 Nov. 1737).

1713

25. Harvey, Richard (b, c). Surgeon of 'Recovery,' appointed Surgeon, Calcutta, 1 Jan. 1712/13; (B. Cons. 26 Mar. 1713). Resigned, 2 Feb. 1728-29; (Fort Wm. Genl. L. 2 Feb. 1728/29). *d.* London, 16 May 1734; (G.M. 1734, p. 275).

26. Colt or **Coult, Oliver** (b, c). Surgeon of 'Hallifax,' appointed Surgeon, Calcutta, 7 Sept. 1713; (B. Cons. 20 Nov. 1713). Resigned, 2 Feb. 1728/29; (Fort Wm. Genl. L. 2 Feb. 1728/29).

1723

27. Hunter, John. Surgeon at Anjengo in 1723; (Bo. Cons. 6 May 1723). Surgeon, Kasimbazar, Oct. 1723; (B. Cons. 18 Nov. 1723). d. in Calcutta, 31 Aug. 1742; (St. Anne's Regr.). Bo. No. 84.

28. Corbett, Benjamin. Surgeon at Kasimbazar. d. there 13 Nov. 1724; (St. Anne's Regr.). Signature on will Corbett; in Regr. name given as Corbet.

1725

29. Goodwin, —. Surgeon's Mate, Calcutta, 1725; (Fort. Wm. Genl. L. 28 Jan. 1727/28).

30. Knox, John, Senior. Surgeon's Mate, Calcutta, 1725; (served thirty years, L. from B, 8 Dec. 1755, para. 113). Appointed Second Surgeon, Calcutta, v. Holwell, 16 Aug. 1750; (L. from B. 23 Aug. 1750, paras. 80, 81). Removed to make room for W. Fullerton, by orders of Court, Aug. 1751; (L. from B. 20 Aug. 1751, para. 115). d. in Calcutta, 5 Feb. 1758. Siege and surrender of Calcutta, June 1856. v. Hist. of I.M.S. i. 144-149.

1728

31. Barlow, Nathaniel. Surgeon's Mate, Calcutta, 1728; (Fort Wm. Genl. L. 11 Feb. 1729/30). Appointed Second Surgeon, Madras, 25 Nov. 1729; (M. Cons. Dec. 1729, List of Salaries). Served there up to 1749. His name is in the list of 1749 as Senior Surgeon, Madras; not in list of 1754. v. Hist. of I.M.S. i. 135. M. No. 68.

1729

32. Littlejohn, Alexander. Surgeon, Calcutta, 19 Sept. 1728; (B. Cons. 14 Oct. 1728). Went home early in 1738; (B. Cons. 17 Nov. 1737, name not in salary list, April 1738).

1730

33. Coult, Robert. Surgeon's Mate, Calcutta, 1730; (B. Genl. L. 25 Feb. 1731/32). Surgeon 9 Jan. 1737/38; (B. Cons. 3 Apr. 1738, salary list). Resigned, 8 Jan. 1741/42; (B. Cons. 31 Mar. 1742, salary list). Resigned, 8 Jan. 1741/42; (B. Cons. 31 Mar. 1742, salary list). Went home Jan. 1742/43; (B. Cons. 3 Jan. 1742/43).

1732

34. Holwell, John Zephaniah (b, c, e). b. Sept. 1711. Guy's. Surgeon's Mate, 'Duke of Cumberland,' 1732. Remained in India, in E.I.Co.'s Service, 1732. Surgeon of 'Prince of Wales,' 1733-34. At Patna, 1734. Surgeon of 'Prince of Orange,' 1735-36. Surgeon, Dakka, 1736. Surgeon's Mate, Calcutta, 1736. To succeed to next vacancy as Surgeon, 1742. Alderman, and twice Mayor of Calcutta. Second Surgeon, Calcutta, 1 Aug. 1749; (B. Cons. 2 Oct. 1749). Resigned 30 Apr. 1750; (B. Cons. 30 Apr. 1750), returned to England. Rejoined, as twelfth member of Council, 6 July 1752; (B. Cons. 6 July 1752). Went home, Feb. 1757; (B. Cons. 31 Jan. 1757). Rejoined, 1758. Governor of Bengal, 24 Jan. to 27 July 1760. Resigned, 29 Sept. 1760. Left for England, 10 March 1761. d. at Pinner, 5 Nov. 1798. F.R.S. 1767. Siege and surrender of Calcutta, June 1756, conducted the defence after the flight of Drake, the Governor, taken prisoner, was one of the twenty-three survivors of the Black Hole. v. Hist. of I.M.S. i. chap. xi. Author of Narrative of the Black Hole, 1758; India Tracts, 1758; Interesting Historical Events in Bengal and Hindostan, three vols. 1765–1771; The East India Observer Extraordinary, 1766; Inoculation for Smallpox in the East Indies, 1767; Address to Luke Scrafton, 1767; A New Species of Oak, 1772; Dissertation an Origin of Intelligent Beings, 1786; An Experiment for the Prevention of Crimes, 1786.

35. **Gray, George** (c). Surgeon, Fort. St. David, 10 Apr. 1732; (M. Cons. 12 Dec. 1732). Resigned, 14 Sept. 1733, appointed Surgeon Kasimbazar. Second Surgeon, Calcutta, 13 Jan. 1737/38; (B. Cons. 3 Apr. 1738, salary list). First Surgeon, 17 Dec. 1741; (B. Cons. 31 Mar. 1742, salary list). Resigned, 3 Mar. 1760: (B. Cons. 3 Mar. 1760). d. at Huntington, East Lothian, 26 Mar. 1781; (G.M. Apr. 1781). v. Hist. of I.M.S. i. 142, 143. Siege and Surrender of Calcutta, June 1756, taken prisoner. M. No. 70.

1738

36. **Coleman, John.** Surgeon at Dakka, d. there 1738; ("Lately," B. Cons. 15 May 1738).

37. **Lindesay, William** (b, c). Surgeon of 'Marlborough,' 1729, of 'Wager,' 1735–38. Surgeon's Mate, Calcutta, 1738; (Genl. L. from B. 10 Dec. 1738). Surgeon, 17 Dec. 1741; (B. Cons. 31 Mar. 1742, salary list). d. in Calcutta, 27 July 1749; (B. Cons. 30 July 1749).

1740

38. **Mahony, Daniel.** Surgeon at Kasimbazar, 1740; (B. Cons. 13 Aug. 1740). No further information.

39. **Belsches, William** (b, c). Surgeon of 'Winchester.' Lost a leg at Canton; (L. from C. 21 Mar. 1738/39). Surgeon's Mate, Calcutta, 11 Sept. 1740; (Fort St. G. Genl. L. 12 Oct. 1740). Surgeon, Fort St. David, 4 Feb. 1741/42; (Fort St. G. Genl. L. 4 Feb. 1741/42). Resigned, 12 Feb. 1749/50; (L. from Fort St. David, 12 Feb. 1749/50, para. 49). Living at Madras, as a free merchant, up to 1756; (Lists of Inhabitants). v. Hist. of I.M.S. i. 139. M. No. 76.

1744

*40. **Fullerton, William.** Appointed by Court, 1744; (L. from B. 13 Jan. 1749/50, paras. 80, 81). Second Surgeon, Calcutta, 3 July 1751; (Salary List, B. Cons. 30 Sept. 1751). Mayor of Calcutta, 8 Dec. 1757. Transferred to Bihar, 1760. Resigned and returned to Europe, 2 Mar. 1761; (B. Cons. 9 Mar. 1761). Returned 1763, posted as Surgeon, Patna Agency. Offered post of Head Surgeon at Calcutta, after Crooke's death, but declined; (B. Cons. 9 Nov. and 25 Nov. 1763). Resigned 31 Mar. 1766. d. 22 Oct. 1805, at Rosemount, Ayr; (G.M. Nov. 1805). Siege and capture of Calcutta, June 1756. War with Shah Alam in 1760, battle of Mohsinpur, was only surviving European officer; defence of Patna. War with Mir-Kasim, 1763, attack on Patna, 25 June 1763, action at Manjhi, 1 July. Only survivor of the Patna massacre. v. Hist. of I.M.S. i. chap. xii.

41. **Lewis, Thomas.** In Calcutta, 1745; (L. from B. 9 Feb. 1744/45). Possibly same as — Lewis, No. 62, infra, 1756.

* See Diaries of three Surgeons of Patna; (William Fullerton, William Anderson, and Peter Campbell). Edited by W. K. Firminger, for Calcutta Historical Society, 1909.

1745

42. Lightfoot, Stephen (b, c). Surgeon's Mate of 'Benjamin'; (M. Cons. 4 Feb. 1744/45). Appointed Surgeon's Mate, Madras 12 Oct. 1745; (M. Cons.). *d.* at Dakka, Sept. 1749.

1746

43. Irwin, Christopher. In Calcutta, Dec. 1746; (B. Cons. 4 Dec. 1746). Name in list of 1749. *d.* in Calcutta, 13 Feb. 1751–52.

1748

44. Knox, John, junior. Name in list of 1749. Still living in Calcutta in 1762; (B. Cons. 17 Oct. 1762). His widow died in Calcutta on 10 Oct. 1815; (C.G. 19 Oct. 1815). Siege and surrender of Calcutta, June 1756. v. Hist. of I.M.S. i. 145, 146.

45. Jones, Owen. Name in list of 1749. Resigned, 8 Oct. 1853.

*****46. Hancock, Tyso Saul** (a). Surgeon's Mate, Fort St. David, 1748. Surgeon, Fort St. George, 23 June 1758. Transferred Bengal, 28 June 1759, posted Kasimbazar. Second Surgeon, Calcutta, Sept. 1760. Resigned 23 Mar. 1761; (B. Cons. 23 Mar. 1761). Lived in Calcutta as a merchant for next ten years. Reappointed Supy. Surgeon at Presidency, " not to rise," 25 Jan. 1770; (Genl. L. from Fort William, 25 Jan. 1770, para. 56). *d.* in Calcutta, 5 Nov. 1775, aged 64. War with French in Karnatak, 1752, treated Clive for wounds at Samiavaram, Apr. 1752. v. Hist. of I.M.S. i. 169–171. M. No. 87.

1749

47. Alexander, George (b, c). Surgeon in Marine for eleven years. Surgeon, Dakka, v. Lightfoot, Sept. 1749; (B. Cons. 25 Aug. 1751). Resigned, 11 Oct. 1753. Surg. of 'Colchester,' 1755; (St. H. Cons. 26 May 1755).

48. Taylor, John. Surgeon's Mate, Madras, 1749 or earlier. Name in list of 1749. Transferred Bengal, 4 Jan. 1754; (L. from B. 4 Jan. 1754, para. 135). Second Surg., Calcutta, 3 Mar. 1760. Head Surgeon, 1768. Resigned, 12 Feb. 1771; (B. Cons. 12 Feb. 1771). Siege and surrender of Calcutta, June 1756. War with Sirajaldaulat, 1757. Plassey ? M. No. 88.

1750

49. Putham, John (b). Surg. of 'Edgbaston,' 1750; (St. H. Cons. 25 June 1750). Married in Calcutta, 18 July 1751; (St. Anne's Regr.). In Calcutta in 1756, where first name is given as William; (Genl. Journal, Sept. 1756). Compensated for losses in siege; (B. Cons. 13 Oct. 1757). Siege and surrender of Calcutta, June 1756.

1751

50. Bristow, John (b, c). Surgeon's Mate of 'Princess Amelia,' 1748, when she was taken by French in Madras Roads, was prisoner of war 23 months. Steward, Calcutta hospital, Feb. 1750/51. Surgeon's Mate, 15 July 1751; (B. Cons. 15 July 1751). Resigned, 9 Dec. 1751. Surg. Mate, 'London,' 1752; (St. H. Cons. 13 Apr. 1752). Reappointed . . . Resident at Balasore, 1755, at Cuttack, 28 Apr. 1757. Removed from appointment, 3 July 1758. Employed at Balasore, Feb. 1761. *d.* in Calcutta, 2 Nov. 1761. War in Northern Circars, 1758, battle of Condore, 8 Dec. 1758. v. Hist. of I.M.S. i. 165–167.

* Hancock married at Kadalur, in 1753, Philadelphia Austen, aunt of the novelist, Jane Austen.

1752

51. Wilson, Nathaniel (b). Surg. Mate of 'Duke of Newcastle,' 1750; (St. H. Cons. 28 May 1750). Surg. Mate 2 Jan. 1752. *d.* at Fulta or Calcutta, Jan. 1757. v. Hist. of I.M.S. i. 164.

52. Fletcher, Henry. Surg. Mate at Fort St. David, 1752; (Fort St. D. Cons. Dec. 1752 and Dec. 1753, and list of 1754). Transferred Calcutta 1755 ? Siege and capture of Calcutta, June 1756.

53. Huet, Robert. Surg. Mate, Bombay Marine, ship 'Guardian,' 1752–53, discharged 15 Nov. 1757. Came to Calcutta with troops from Bombay; (B. Cons. 7 Nov. 1757). Bo. No. 121.

1753

54. Hunter, Robert. Surg. Mate, Fort Marlbro, 1753; (Pay list, S. Cons. 26 June 1753). Surg. Croee, in list of Dec. 1753. In charge of Croee factory, 1755–56. Surg. Natal, 17 Mar. 1758; (S. Cons.). Factor, 28 Feb. 1759; (S. Cons.). Taken prisoner at Natal when Sumatra was taken by French, April 1760. In S. list of 30 Dec. 1762 is shown as " Surgeon, Fort Marlbro, a hostage at Mauritius." Rejoined, 26 June 1764; (S. Cons.). Sent to Bengal as Surg. of 'Bute'; (S. Cons. 26 June 1764). Serving at Kadalur, 23 Feb. 1764; (M. Mily. Cons.). Appointed Surg. to Army, Bengal, 25 Nov. 1763; (B. Cons.). Surg. Calcutta, 12 Aug. 1765. Dismissed, 28 Nov. 1766; (L. from B. 28 Nov. 1766, para. 125). Reinstated, 9 Feb. 1767; (B. Cons.). Surg. Patna, 1768; (B. Cons. 9 Feb. 1768). Shown among "Subordinate Surgeons" in list of 1774. At Dakka, 1776. Shown as dead in Warren Hastings' list of 6 Oct. 1777. M. No. 121. S. No. 55.

*55. Anderson, William (b, c). Surg. Mate of 'Edgbaston.' Appointed Surg. Negrais Island, 29 Oct. 1753; (M. Mily. Cons.). Sick leave 1756. Serving in Bengal, and killed in Patna Massacre, 11 Oct. 1763. v. Hist. of I.M.S. i. 187.

56. Inglis, William. Surg. Mate, 12 Nov. 1753. Went to England as Surg. of 'Falmouth,' 20 Feb. 1754. Rejoined, 29 Sept. 1755. *d.* at Fulta in 1756. Siege and capture of Calcutta, June 1756.

57. Wasmus, Charles. Surg. Mate, 1753; (had served 36 years, Proc. C.M.B. 30 Dec. 1789). A German, Educated at Univ. of Helmstadt. Served at Kasimbazar and Patna 1764; (B. Cons. 8 Aug. 1769). Surg. of 'Mercury,' 1775–76; (Hardy). Appointed by Court, Surg. Fort Marlbro, 1 Dec. 1777; joined, 1 Jan. 1779; (S. Cons. 20 Mar. 1779). Head Surg. 1791. Sick leave to Bengal in latter part of 1792; (S. Cons. 30 June 1792). Pensioned and allowed to return to Europe, 31 Dec. 1796; (Mily. L. from B. 31 Dec. 1796, paras. 11–13). *d.* in 1800, apparently in Calcutta; (Mily. L. from B. 31 July 1800, para. 142). War with Mir-Kasim, 1763; battles of Katwa and Undhwa Nala, capture of Monghir and Patna. Author of Memoirs of a Gentleman who resided several years in the East Indies during the late Revolutions, by C. W. London, 1774. S. No. 78. v. Hist. of I.M.S. ii. 188, 189.

1754

58. Chandler, Samuel (a, d). Appointed in Letter from Court 23 Jan. 1754, para. 78. Apparently never joined.

* v. Note on William Fullerton, No. 40, supra.

59. **Andrews, Henry** (b, c). Surg. of 'Egmont,' Appointed Surg. Negrais Island, 1754–55. Surg. 'Egmont,' 1755; (St. H. Cons. 28 July 1755).

60. **Menzie, —.** Surg. Mate 1754 (?). At Calcutta in list of 1754.

61. **Forth, William.** Surg. of 'Winchelsea,' 1743. In Calcutta, 1747; (B. Cons. 19 Jan. 1746/47). Surg. Mate, 1754 (?). At Kasimbazar in War of 1756. Resigned, 29 Dec. 1759; (L. from B. 29 Dec. 1759, para. 104). d. 1774; (Court Minutes, 9 Mar. 1774). v. Hist. of I.M.S. i. 164 165.

62. **Lewis, —.** Surgeon, Siege and Capture of Calcutta, June 1756; (Mills' list). Possibly same as Thomas Lewis, No. 41, supra, 1744.

1755

63. **Alves, William.** Surg. at Basra, 1755–56; at Bombay, Dec. 1756; (Bo. Cons. 31 Dec. 1756). Surg. Calcutta, 7 Nov. 1757, came with troops from Bombay; (B. Cons. 7 Nov. 1757). At Kasimbazar, Aug. 1759. d. at Madras, 17 June 1762; (Malden). Bo. No. 123.

1758

64. **Dubois, James.** Surg. Mate, St. Helena, 1741; (pay list, 19 Jan. 1741/42). Resigned, 13 May 1746; (St. H. Cons.). Surg., Sumatra, Croee, 15 Mar. 1758; (S. Cons.). Second Surg., Fort Marlbro, 22 Mar. 1759; (S. Cons.). Served up to capture of Sumatra by French, in April 1760. Did not rejoin in 1762. Surg. Mate, Bengal, 2 Feb. 1764; (B. Cons.). S. No. 57. St. H. No. 22.

65. **Lauray, Jean.** Surg. served five years, goes home 1763; (B. Cons. 1 Apr. 1763).

1759

66. **Plenderleath, William** (b, c). Surg. 'Prince Edward,' 1753–55; of 'Royal Duke,' 1758–59; (St. H. Cons. 10 Mar. 1755 and 3 July 1758). Surg. Mate 23 Mar. 1759. Surg. Calcutta, 23 Mar. 1761. Drowned at Calcutta, Mar. 1762.

67. **Ellis, James** (b, c). Surg. Mate, 'Streatham,' 1758–59, lost. A. S. . . . 1759. Ensign, 1760. Resigned combatant commission on promotion to Surgeon, 1 Oct. 1761. Second Surgeon, Calcutta, 25 Nov. 1763. Head Surgeon, 12 Feb. 1771. Resigned and went to England, Apr. 1774. Returned to India, May 1783, and succeeded Campbell as Surg. Genl. First President of Medical Board at its foundation, 29 May 1786. Phys. Genl. 28 Aug. 1786. Resigned, 24 Dec. 1789. d. on 'Burbidge' on passage to England. War with Mir-Kasim, 1763, Senior Surgeon of army under Major Adams, battles of Katwa, Gharia, and Undhwa Nala, capture of Monghir and Patna. v. Hist. of I.M.S. i. 231; ii. 183.

68. **Howison, Archibald.** Surg. 1759? Resigned, 3 Apr. 1762.

1760

69. **Edwards, Patrick** (b, d). Appointed by Letter from Court, 1 Apr. 1760, para. 115. Name also in S.A.L.M. and Bo. Never joined in India. Surg. 'Earl Temple,' appointed Surg. Fort Marlbro, 5 Mar. 1762; (S. Cons.). d. at Fort Marlbro, 6 Sept. 1773; (S. Cons.). S. No. 60.

70. **Stewart,** or **Stuart, William.** Appointed by L. from C. 1 Apr. 1760, para. 115. *d.* at Kasimbazar, May 1763. Name also in S.A.L.M. Bo. Possibly same as William Stewart, M. No. 107.

71. **Crooke, Clement.** M.D. Ed. 1753. *b.* in St. Kitts, West Indies. Appointed by L. from C. 1 Apr. 1760, para. 204. Surg. Calcutta, 8 Apr. 1762. Killed in Patna Massacre, 6 Oct. 1763. v. Hist. of I.M.S. i. 186.

72. **Winsley,** or **Wensley, James** (a, b). Surg. ' Wager,' 1751, ' Stormont,' 1756–60. Surg. Bombay, 19 Aug. 1760; (Bo. Cons.). Surg. Bengal, 12 Nov. 1764; (B. Cons.). Retransferred Bombay, 1767; (Bo. Cons. 8 July 1767). R. 11 Apr. 1768; (Bo. Cons.), and went to England on ' Greenwich,' which sailed 21 Apr. Bo. No. 130.

73. **Davidson, John** (a). A.S. 1760 (?). Surg. Chittagong, Mar. 1762. Calcutta, 6 May 1766. R. 11 Jan. 1768; (B. Cons.). Living in 1792. v. Hist. of I.M.S. i. 190, 191.

74. **Ham, John** (a). A.S. 1760 (?). Surg. Kasimbazar, 23 May 1763. One of the prisoners in war of 1763. *d.* at Monghir, as a prisoner, Sept. 1763.

75. **Smith, Peter** (a). A.S. 1760 (?). Surg. 15 Nov. 1762. In list of 1777, he and G. M. Kenderdine are shown at the bottom of the list of Surgeons, " to remain youngest Surgeons." *d.* at Dakka, Jan. 1779; (B. Cons. 1 Feb. 1779).

76. **Carnac, William** (a). A.S. 1760 (?). Lent from Calcutta hospital as Surgeon to ' Godolphin,' to return to India; (Genl. L. from C. 12 Feb. 1764, para. 123). Went out as Surg. of ' Fort William,' 17 May 1764. Surgeon of the ' Cuddalore,' 24 Feb. 1767; (B. Cons.), sent to search for survivors of the ' Earl Temple,' lost in China Seas. No further information.

1761

77. **Lepage, —** (a). A.S. 1761, had served four years; (B. Cons. 25 Feb. 1765).

78. **Russell, Francis** (a). A.S. 1761 (?). *b.* 1723. Surg. at Dakka 1763; (B. Cons. 9 Nov. 1763). Resigned, 24 Feb. 1775; (Genl. L. from B. 24 Feb. 1775, para. 38). *d.* at Bath, 5 Aug. 1791.

1762

79. **Campbell, Daniel** (b). Surg. ' Norfolk,' 1760–62. A.S. 22 Mar. 1762. Surg. 13 Apr. 1762. Surg. Calcutta, 25 Nov. 1768. Head Surg. 22 Feb. 1768. Surg. Genl. 1 Mar. 1773, superseding T. Anderson. Resigned, 29 Nov. 1783. Permitted to return; (L. from C. 27 Jan. 1785, para. 2). *d.* on voyage to India at Johanna, Madagascar; (C.G. 9 Sept. 1785).

80. **Bagnall, Thomas** (a, b). Surg. Mate, ' Osterley,' appointed acting A.S. Sumatra, Mar. 1762; (S. Cons. 14 May 1762). Surg. 1762. Transferred to Bengal, 1765; (Desp. from C. 15 Feb. 1765; para. 77, S. Cons. 5 July 1765). A.S. Bengal, 30 Apr. 1765. Surg. Chittagong, 5 May 1766; (B. Cons.); Calcutta, 7 Nov. 1768. Resigned, 8 Dec. 1769. S. No. 61.

81. **Williams, Andrew.** Ensign, 84 Foot, 4 Sept. 1761; (A.L. 1763); Lt. 8 Aug. 1763; H.P. 25 Dec. 1764. Surg. Bengal, 27 Nov. 1762. Surg. Major, 1st Brigade, 1772; (Muster Roll of 1772). Granted pay and rank of Lt.-Col. 6 Jan. 1784; (B. Mily. Cons.). Second Member of Medical Board, on its foundation, 29 May 1786. Chief Surgeon, 28 Aug. 1786. Permitted to resign, 15 Dec. 1787; (Genl. L. from B. 15 Dec. 1787, para. 37). D. and M. give date of resignation as 15 Jan. 1787. Permitted to return, to be appointed President Medical Board; (Mily. Desp. from C. 6 May 1791, para. 61), but did not rejoin.

82. **Harlan,** or **Harling, Henry** (b, c). Surg. 'Norfolk,' 1754-55, 'Delaware,' 1756. Dismissed. Lt. King's Train (Royal Arty.), Bombay, 1759-60; (Bo. Cons. 12 Jan. 1759, and 26 Aug. 1760). Ordered to be dismissed and sent to England, deserted to the "Morattoes"; (Bo. Cons. 25 Nov. 1760). Employed as Surg. Bengal, 1762? Killed in Patna Massacre, 6 Oct. 1763. v. Hist. of I.M.S. i. 188-189.

83. **Smith,** or **Schmidt.** A.S. 1762 (?). A Swiss. Killed in Patna massacre, 6 Oct. 1763.

*84. **Campbell, Peter** (b, c). A.S. 1762 (?). Late Surg. of an Indiaman. Killed in Patna massacre, 11 Oct. 1763.

1763

85. **Lowle, Robert Wilkes** (a). Sent out as Surg. to Bombay; (Desp. from C. 9 Mar. 1763, para. 20). Supy. Surg. Bengal, 9 Feb. 1764, came as Surg. with detachment from Bombay; (B. Cons.). d. in Calcutta, 8 Feb. 1765. Bo. No. 136.

86. **Fisher, Robert** (a, b, c). Surg. 'Winchelsea,' 1761-63; lost on Gasper Sands, 20 Mar. 1764. Supy. Surg. 12 Apr. 1763; (B. Cons.). d. at Kasimbazar, 1765; ("some time ago," B. Cons. 12 Aug. 1765).

87. **Ecroyd, Richard** (a, b, c). Surg. 'Royal George,' appointed Supy. Surg. 12 Apr. 1763; (B. Cons.). d. in Calcutta, 1765; ("lately," B. Cons. 12 Aug. 1765).

88. **Anderson, Thomas** (b, c). Surg. Mate 'Onslow,' 1761; (St. H. Cons. 22 June 1761). Appointed Surg. to Army, 25 Nov. 1763; (B. Cons.). Surg. Genl. 18 Nov. 1769; (Genl. L. from B. 25 Jan. 1770, para. 403, where first name is erroneously given as James). Superseded by Daniel Campbell, 1 Mar. 1773. d. at Bombay, 1 Mar. 1777.

89. **MacDonald, William** (or J.) (a, c). Appointed Surg. to Army, 25 Nov. 1763; (B. Cons.). d. before 1787; (C. G. 24 May 1787). Rohilla War, 1774.

90. **Laird, John** (b). Surgeon, Canton, 1763-69; had previously served six years at Canton, so was appointed full Surgeon on joining; (Genl. L. from B. 4 Jan. 1775, para. 26; and Desp. from C. 15 Dec. 1775, para. 23). Surg. Mate, 'York,' 1769. Surg. 'Prince,' 1770. Surg. Bengal, 23 Feb. 1771. Surg. 'Earl of Lincoln,' 1772-73, 'Seahorse,' 1774-75. Surg. Major of Bengal Forces in Karnatak, 25 Mar. 1782; (B. Mily. Cons.). Surg. Major to 1st Brigade " in consideration of his meritorious services in late war in Carnatic "; (B. Mily. Cons. 28 Jan. 1785). Head Surg. 30 June 1786. Resigned to go on furlough, 15 Dec. 1788; (M.S. Army List, Nov. 1788). Returned, 1791, appointed

* v. Note on William Fullerton, No. 40, supra.

M.M.B. and President, v. Hunter removed, 15 June 1791. Furlough to Europe, 8 Dec. 1800; (C.G. 1 Jan. 1801). R. 2 June 1802. Elder brother of No. 226 Charles Laird, 1779, and of James Laird, No. 241, 1780; (Hickey's Memoirs, ii. 130). Benares war, 1781, capture of Patita, Sept. 1781. Second Maisur war, 1782–83. Third Maisur war, 1791–92, capture of Seringapatam, 6 Feb. 1792, as Head Surgeon of Grand Army. C. No. 1.

1764

91. **Knight, Robert** (b, c). Surg. of 'Walpole,' captured by French off Ceylon, Sept. 1762; taken prisoner and released on parole. Supy. Surg. 1 Feb. 1764; (B. Mily. Cons. 2 Feb. 1764). Surg. Major and Senior Surgeon; (D. and M.). Resigned, 10 Oct. 1780.

92. **Campbell, James** (c). Supy. Surg. 1 Feb. 1764; (B. Mily. Cons. 2 Feb. 1764). Surgeon Major; shown as Surg. Major, Barhampur, in B. Mily. Cons. of 24 Dec. 1777. d. 6 Dec. 1781; (G. of I. 19 Jan. 1782). S.A.L.M.B. and D. and M. say d. 7 July 1782. Rohilla war, 1774.

*93. **Hunter, Andrew** (b, c). Surg. Mate, 'Princess Augusta,' 1762; (St. H. Cons. 28 Apr. 1762). A.S. 2 Feb. 1764. Surg. 30 Mar. 1767. Surg. Major, v. Campbell deceased; (G. of I. 19 Jan. 1782). Head Surgeon, 30 June 1786. M.M.B. 24 Dec. 1789. President, v. Ellis R. 31 Dec. 1789. Removed from Board, 15 June 1791. Retired, Oct. 1797. v. Hist. of I.M.S. ii. 12, 13.

94. **Patton, Robert** (a, c). A.S. 2 Feb. 1764; (B. Cons.). No further information.

95. **Nicholson, Robert** (a, d). Appointed Surg. 22 Feb. 1764; (Desp. from C. 22 Feb. 1764, para. 65). No further information. Apparently never joined.

96. **Gordon, John** (a, c). A.S. 1 Mar. 1764; (B. Cons. 9 Apr. 1764). d. in Calcutta, 4 Nov. 1768.

97. **Stormonth, John** (b, c). Surg. Mate of 'Winchelsea,' 1761–64, lost on Gasper Sands, 20 Mar. 1764. A.S. 2 Apr. 1764; (B. Cons.). Resigned on account of ill-health, 2 Jan. 1766. Surg. 'Kent,' 1766–69. Reappointed A.S. 25 Nov. 1768. Surg. ... 1777. Resigned, with leave to return, 29 Dec. 1788; (M.S. Army List, Nov. 1788). Went home as Surg. of 'Glatton.' Did not rejoin. Struck off 1793. D. and M. call him P. Stormonth, and give date of first commission as 25 Nov. 1768. S.A.L.M.B. gives date of first commission as 24 Nov. 1769. First name sometimes given as James in records.

98. **Lowe, Joseph** (a, c). Late A.S. to Monson's regiment. Appointed A.S. Bengal, 21 May 1764; (B. Cons.). Resigned, 11 Nov. 1765. Name not in Johnston's Roll of R.A.M.C.

99. **Logan, James.** Surg. 23 Sept. 1744. Granted leave to travel in Nipal and Tibet, 1769; (B. Cons. 31 Oct. 1769). d. at Bardwan, Dec. 1770.

100. **Kenderdine, George Mainwaring** (a). St. Thomas. L.S.A. 1850. C.C.S. 1761. Had served in A.M.D. in Germany for three years; (B. Cons. 23 Nov. 1767), but name not in Johnston's Roll of R.A.M.C. Surg. Bengal, 24 Sept. 1764; (B. Cons.). Dismissed for neglect of duty, 1 Oct. 1767; (B. Cons.). Reappointed "youngest Surgeon, not to rise"; (L. from B. 17 Oct. 1774, para. 58). d. in Calcutta, 19 May 1787

* Andrew Hunter, presumably a different man, was serving as Surgeon of the 'Pigot' in 1767.

101. Gardiner, George (c). A.S. 24 Sept. 1764; (B. Cons.). Surg. 30 Mar. 1767. *d.* at Serampur, 1 Jan. 1795.

102. Walker, John (a, c). A.S. 24 Sept. 1764; (B. Cons.). Surg. 29 Apr. 1767. No further information.

103. Bagot, William (a, c). A.S. 24 Sept. 1764; (B. Cons.). Surg. to 1st Brigade at Monghir in 1766; (Broome, p. 608). No further information.

104. Ferguson, John (a, b, c). Surg. Mate ' Vansittart,' appointed A.S. 19 Nov. 1764; (B. Cons.). No further information, unless he is the same as the John Ferguson shown by D. and M. as appointed on 20 July 1772, No. 186, infra.

105. Crawford, Moses (a, c). A.S. . . . 1764 (?). *b.* 1745. Had served as Surg. Mate for some time prior to 1766; (Broome, p. lxxiii.). Ensign, May 1766; Lieut. 30 Aug. 1767; Capt. 28 Nov. 1772; Major, 27 Jan. 1781. Resigned, 14 Oct. 1782. *d.* at Newfield, Scotland, 3 Mar. 1794; (Scots Mag. 1794, p. 178). Father of P. Crawford, M. No. 606, 1811. Benares war, 1781, capture of Bijaigarh, 10 Nov. 1781. v. Hist. of I.M.S. i. 242.

1765

106. Allen, Matthew (c). Surg. 96 Foot, 4 Mar. 1761; Resigned 21 Apr. 1764; (Johnston's Roll of R.A.M.C. No. 617). Supy. Surg. Bengal, 19 Feb. 1765; (B. Cons.). Resigned, 28 Jan. 1772.

107. Walker, William (b, c). Surg. Mate of ' Clinton,' 1757; (St. H. Cons. 14 June 1757); of ' Fort William,' appointed A.S. Bengal, 19 Feb. 1765; (B. Cons.). Surg. 1777. Furlough to Europe three years, 2 Feb. 1786. Did not rejoin. Struck off, 1793. S.A.L.M.B. and D. and M. give date of first appointment as 12 June 1769. Capture of Cannanore, 16 Dec. 1783, wounded; (C.G. 4 Mar. 1784).

108. Carnegie, Thomas (a, b, c). Surg. of ' Chesterfield,' 1756–57; of ' Tilbury,' 1760–61. A.S. 30 Apr. 1765. Surg. Patna, 5 May 1766; (B. Cons.). *d.* in Calcutta, 31 Oct. 1768; (Burial Regr.).

109. Arnoth, Robert (a, d).
110. Cummins, Michael (a, d).
111. Gairdner, Archibald (a, d).
112. Mansell, Thomas (a, d).
113. St. Aubyn, James (a, d).

These five names are all entered in Service Army Lists, Medl. both Bengal and Madras, as " Nomd. by Court, List of Packet, 30 Apr. 1765." Apparently none of these ever joined. Gairdner was Surg. Mate of ' Ilchester ' in 1755, Surg. of ' Ilchester,' 1759; of ' Plassey,' 1761–66, of ' Fox,' 1767; of ' Plassey,' 1769–70. Cummins name is spelt Commins in S.A.L.M.B.

114. Ingham, Samuel (a). Surg. Apr. 1765. Went out as Surg. to Lord Clive when appointed Governor of Bengal for the second time. Arrived, April 1765. Returned to England, Jan. 1767. *d.* 18 May 1770; (London Mag. 1770, p. 386); ("lately" G.M. June 1770).

115. Connellan, John Peter (c). A.S. 25 July 1765; (B. Cons.). Surg. 24 Aug. 1767. Resigned, 4 Feb. 1778. Name given twice in S.A.L.M.B. as Peter and as Patrick Connellan. His signature is J. P. Connellan, in his letter of resignation, dated 10 Jan. 1778, in B. Cons. of that date. First Maisur war, 1767–68; (B. Cons. 24 Aug. 1767).

1766

116. Ford, James. A.S. 12 Jan. 1766. Surg. 11 Oct. 1769. Surg. Major 6 Mar. 1781; (B. Mily. Cons.). Tried in Calcutta Supreme Court in Dec. 1777, for killing Lt. Sydney Smith in a duel, acquitted. *d.* at Barhampur, 6 Apr. 1783. Rohilla war, 1774. First Maratha war, 1781, as Senior Surgeon to Col. Carnac's force. v. Hist. of I.M.S. ii. 239.

117. Lethan, or Lithan, Thomas. A.S. 20 Feb. 1766. Nominated by Court to Madras; (List of Packet, 20 Feb. 1766); then to Bombay; (List of Packet, 12 Mar. 1766). A.S. Bo. 20 Feb. 1766. Permitted to proceed to Bengal, 26 Aug. 1766; (Bo. Pub. Cons.). Resigned Bombay Service, having been appointed Surg. in Bengal, 23 Dec. 1767; (Bo. Pub. Cons.). Surg. 7 June 1769. Resigned, 1782; (Ind. Gaz. 2 Nov. 1782). Name spelt Lithan in S.A.L.M.B., Lethan in D. and M. Bo. No. 145.

118. Grant, Daniel (a, c). Surg. 105 Foot, 17 Oct. 1761; H.P. regiment disbanded, 1764; name shown on H.P. List up till 1771; (Johnston's Roll of R.A.M.C. No. 648). A.S. Bengal, 20 Feb. 1766. No further information, unless he is the same as Dr. Daniel Grove, buried in Calcutta, 6 Sept. 1767; (Burial Regr.). A Daniel Grant was serving as Surg. of 'Norfolk' in 1767–68.

119. Forbes, Walter (a, d).
120. Gibson, John (a, d).
121. Hayward, William (a, d).
122. Rickman, William (a, d).
123. Skirvin, David (a, d).

These five names are all entered in Service Army Lists, Medl. both Bengal and Madras, as "Nominated by Court, List of Packet, 20 Feb. 1766." Apparently none of them ever joined, except possibly Hayward. The Calcutta Burial Regr. records the death of William Hayward, inhabitant, on 14 June 1770, but he is not stated to be a Surgeon.

124. MacKellar, Charles. Nominated by Court, List of packet, 20 Feb. 1766; (with the five preceding). *d.* in Calcutta, 27 May 1767; (Burial Regr.).

125. Simmons, James (b, c). *b.* 1732. Surg. of 'Falmouth,' wrecked with great loss of life on Sagar Sands, 13 June 1766. A.S. 26 July 1766; (B. Cons.). Surg. 11 Oct. 1769. Surg. Major 24 July 1782, and resigned from that date; (B. Cons.). Name given twice in S.A.L.M.B. as James Simmons and as Mr. Symmonds.

126. Flor, Peter John (a, b, c). *b.* at Bergen, Norway, 14 May 1738. Surg. Mate of 'Falmouth,' 1766. A.S. 28 July 1766; (B. Cons.). *d.* 28 Aug. 1778; (tombstone at Malda, Wilson). Name given as Four in S.A.L.M.B. also occurs in Records as Flors and Dufour. His will, dated at Puruea on 15 May 1772, is signed Peter John Flor. It was proved on 28 Dec. 1772, so probably the date of 1778 on tombstone has been misread.

127. Hunter, Robert (a, b, c). Surg. of 'Hector' applied for appointment in Oct. 1760; (B. Cons.). Nominated by Court, List of Packet, 5 Mar. 1767; (but this may apply to Robert Hunter, No. 54, supra). Taking contracts in Calcutta, 1767 and 1768; (B. Cons. 15 Nov. 1767 and 18 Feb. 1768). *d.* in Calcutta, 23 Sept. 1769; (Burial Regr.). Doubtful if ever appointed.

128. Routledge, John (a, b, c). Surg. 'Godolphin,' 1753; (St. H. Cons. 31 Dec. 1753). M.D., K.C. Ab. 1763. Supy. Surg. 28 Nov. 1766; (L. from B. 28 Nov. 1766, paras. 82–84). Resigned, 4 Jan. 1775. In S.A.L.M.B. name is given as Routledge or Routlige.

129. Clugh, Patrick. A.S. 8 Dec. 1766; (B. Cons. 14 Nov. 1770). d. in Calcutta, 4 Nov. 1774; (Burial Regr.). S.A.L.M.B. and D. and M. give date of appointment as 27 Nov. 1767, and both say " died at Madras," without date.

1767

130. Thomas, Francis Ballenden, or Balladon. A.S. 12 Jan. 1767. Surg. 11 Oct. 1769. Surg. Major, 3rd Brigade, 12 Oct. 1780; (B. Mily. Cons.). Discharged by Court Martial, 26 Jan. 1785; (Hough's Court Martials, p. 784). Afterwards recovered damages, Rs. 5000, in Calcutta Supreme Court, from his accuser, Mr. Bristow, Resident at Lucknow; (C.G. 15 Oct. 1787). S.A.L.M.B. gives his second name as Ballentine or Balladon. D. and M. call him Surg. Genl. apparently erroneously. First Maisur war, 1767–68. Rohilla war, 1774. v. Hist. of I.M.S. ii. 228–230.

131. Milne, William (a, d).
132. Newton, Samuel (a, d).

These two names are entered in Service Army Lists, Medl. both Bengal and Madras, as " Nominated by Court, List of Packet, 5 Mar. 1767," but apparently never joined, though in S.A.L.M.B. Milne is said to have sailed in the ' Egmont,' and Newton in the ' Northington.'

133. Chandler, Henry John (a). Nominated by Court, List of Packet, 5 Mar. 1767. A.S. 3 Aug. 1767; (B. Cons.). Surg. 1769. Surg. Calcutta, 8 Dec. 1769; (B. Cons. 13 Feb. 1770). Resigned, 2 Nov. 1779; (B. Cons. 17 January 1780). Name also in S.A.L.M.M.

134. Urquhart, David. b. 1745. A.S. 30 Mar. 1767; (B. Cons.). Surg. 11 Oct. 1769. Surg. Major, 1 Aug. 1781; (B. Mily. Cons. 13 June, 1781). Resigned, 21 Dec. 1784; (B. Mily. Cons.). S.A.L.M.B. and D. and M. say " struck off 1793."

135. Armstrong, John (b). b. 1741. Surg. ' Earl of Middlesex,' 1766–67. A.S. 3 Aug. 1767; (B. Cons.). Surg. 11 June 1771. Resigned, 21 Dec. 1784; (B. Mily. Cons.). Benares war, 1781, capture of Bijaigarh, 10 Nov. 1781.

136. Nelson, James. A.S. 14 Sept. 1767. Not to be traced; (D. and M.). No further information. Possibly the same as James Nelson, M. No. 111, 1757. In S.A.L.M.B. first name is given as James or John.

137. Luckett, Michael. A.S. 27 Nov. 1767. Surg. 17 June 1777. d. at Budge Budge, 25 Apr. 1790. In the Field Officers' List of 20 Oct. 1777, Luckett and Kenderdine are shown as " Fixed Youngest Surgeons." Rohilla war, 1774.

1768

138. Oliphant, John (a, b, d). Surg. Mate, ' Neptune,' 1763–64; Surg. ' Hardwicke,' 1765–66. A.S. 11 Jan. 1768; (B. Cons.). Nominated by Court, List of Packet, 5 Mar. 1767. No further information. Name also in S.A.L.M.M. In S.A.L.M.B. stated to have sailed in the ' Pocock.'

139. **Buchanan, Francis,** M.D. . . . A.S. 1 July 1768. Resigned, 17 July 1769.

140. **Haydon, Thomas.** A.S. 2 July 1768. *d.* at Bankipur, 20 July 1770.

*141. **Fleming, John** (e). C.C.S.; (B. Cons. 20 Dec. 1770). A.S. 17 Aug. 1768. Surg. 11 Dec. 1771. Head Surg. Calcutta, and third Member of Medl. Board, on foundation of Board, 29 May 1786. M.D. Ed. 1804. F.R.S. 25 Feb. 1813. R. 10 Nov. 1813. M.P. for Gatton, 1818–20. *d.* in London, 17 May 1829; (G.M. May 1829). First Maratha war, 1780–81, as Senior Surg. to Bengal troops under Genl. Goddard, wounded in action of 24 Apr. 1781 (Ind. Gaz. 9 June 1781). Author of A Catalogue of Indian Medicinal Plants and Drugs, 1810.

142. **Young, Maurice.** C.C.S. A.S. 19 Aug. 1768. Surg. 20 Dec. 1771. Not to be traced (D. and M.). Signs a cert. on 25 Sept. 1775; (B. Cons.). No further information. First name given as Mark in list of 1774.

143. **Harington, Thomas.** A.S. 1 Nov. 1768. Surg. 18 Dec. 1772. Invalided, 20 Nov. 1775; ("having lost his eyesight, proceeds on the 'Salisbury';" Genl. L. from B. 20 Nov. 1775, para. 105). *d.* before 1787; (C.G. 24 May 1787). D. and M. say "not to be traced." Rohilla war, 1774.

144. **Hamilton, Thomas** (b). *b.* 1738. Surg. of 'Prince George,' 1761–62. Surg. Mate, 'Egmont,' 1764–65. A.S. 20 Nov. 1768. Surg. Dec. 1771. *d.* at Fatehgarh, 12 Aug. 1788.

145. **Yule,** or **Yuill, John** (b). Surg. 'Dutton,' 1768. A.S. 20 Dec. 1768. *d.* . . . 1772.

1769

146. **Mitchell, William.** *b.* 1745. M.D. Ed. 1766. A.S. 17 Mar. 1769. Surg. 20 July 1772. Not to be traced; (S.A.L.M.B. and D. and M.). *d.* in Calcutta, 14 Apr. 1780; (St. John's Burial Regr.; B.P. and P. vol. xxxi, part ii, p. 153).

147. **Balfour, Francis** (e). M.D. Ed. 1767. A.S. 3 July 1769. Ensign 11 July 1769. Lieut. 26 June 1771. Resigned combatant commission on promotion to Surgeon, 10 Aug. 1777. Head Surg. 20 Oct. 1786. M.M.B. 15 Jan. 1788. Furlough, with leave to return, 6 Dec. 1788; (M.S. Army List, Dec. 1788). Returned and reappointed to Medl. Board, . . . 1792. Lost his seat when Board reduced to two members, 30 Apr. 1796. M.M.B. again, 18 Dec. 1800. R. 16 Sept. 1807. *d* at Fernie, Fife, 7 May 1818; (Scots Mag. 1818, i. 598). Author of Dissertatio de Gonorrhea virulenta, 1767; The Forms of Herkern 1781; Treatise on Sol-Lunar Influence in Fevers, 1784; Treatise on Putrid Intestinal Remitting Fever, 1790; translation of Seir-i-Mutakherin (lost).

148. **Matheson, William.** A.S. 11 Aug. 1769. *d.* 6 June 1773, at Kushalgauj, Lucknow; (Soldiering in India, 1764–1787, p. 132, where name is spelt Matthewson.

149. **Campbell, William.** A.S. 18 Aug. 1769. Surg. 11 Aug. 1777. Resigned, 20 Nov. 1782; (B. Cons. 9 Dec. 1782). D. and M. say " resigned, date not known."

---

* The D.N.B. gives the date of Fleming's death, erroneously, as 10 May 1815. This was another Dr. John Fleming, whose death is also noted in G.M. of June 1815. The E.I. Regr. gives 25 Dec. 1827 as the date of death. The C.G. of 14 Sept. 1829 and A.J. June 1829, p. 803, also give 17 May 1829 as the date of death.

150. Aspinal, James. A.S. 26 Sept. 1769. *d.* at Sultanpur, Aug. 1782.

151. Smith, John (b). *b.* 1744. Surg. 'Warren,' 1761–62; 'Earl of Ashburnham,' 1769. A.S. 14 Oct. 1769. Surg. 12 Aug. 1777. Invalided 4 Feb. 1778; (Genl. L. from B. 4 Feb. 1778, para. 14; and S.A.L.M.B.). Resigned, 1782; (D. and M. and S.A.L.M.B.). *d.* in Edinburgh, 12. June 1827.

152. Cranston, Andrew (b). *b.* 1746. Surg. 'Northumberland,' 1765–68. A.S. Oct. 1769. Cadet, 1769. Ensign, 5 Oct. 1769. Lieut. 22 Mar. 1773. *d.* at Barhampur, 5 Sept. 1776.

153. Redman, David. *b.* 1742. A.S. 6 Nov. 1769 *d.* . . . 1775; (D. and M.). Application from his widow for pension in B. Cons. 20 Dec. 1775.

154. Ashe Samuel. A.S. . . . 1769 (?) Buried in Calcutta, 18 Oct. 1769; (Burial Regr.).

1770

— . Hancock, Tyso Saul. Reappointed Supy. Surg. "not to rise," 25 Jan. 1770. v. No. 46, supra.

155. Gillies, Thomas. *b.* 1750. A.S. 21 Feb. 1770. Surg. 14 Aug. 1777. First Secy. to Medl. Board, 2 June 1786. Furlough, 22 Dec. 1786; (Genl. L. from B. 22 Dec. 1786, paras. 82–84). M.D. Mar. Coll. Ab. 1788. F.R.C.P. Ed. 1789. Did not rejoin. Struck off, 1793. *d.* in Kincardineshire, — July 1808. Second Maisur war, 1781.

156. Forbes, John, or **Nicholas** (b, c). Surg. of 'Earl of Ashburnham,' 1762–64; of 'Speke,' 1766–67. Mily. A.S. 24 Apr. 1770; (B. Cons.). *d.* in Calcutta, 6 Nov. 1770; (Burial Regr.). S.A.L.M.B. and D. and M. give first name as Nicholas, and date of appointment as 26 Aug. 1770.

157. Munro, Walter Ross. *b.* 1747. A.S. Apr. 1770; (Muster Roll of 1st Brigade for 1772). Originally posted to Madras, serving there in 1771; (M. Mily. Cons. 15 Apr. 1771). A.S. Bengal 27 July 1771. Surg. 1 Sept. 1778. Head Surg. 1 Feb. 1787. M.M.B. 31 Dec. 1789 to 1 Jan. 1794; and again 24 Dec. 1802 to 4 Jan. 1815. Furlough, 4 Jan. 1815. R. 30 June 1815. M.D. K.C. Ab. 1806. *d.* 9 Aug. 1818. D. and M. give name in Bengal, but not in Madras List. First Maratha war, 1780–81, with Bengal detachment to Bombay. M. No. 180.

158. Douglas, James. C.C.S. A.S. 16 May 1770. *d.* at Chittagong, Sept. 1775; (death reported 24 Sept., B. Cons. 5 Oct. 1775). S.A.L.M.B. and D. and M. give date of death as Nov. 1775.

159. Wilson, Robert (b). *b.* 1740. Surg. Mate, 'Triton,' 1769–70. A.S. 16 May 1770. Surg. 24 Apr. 1778. Gave up promotion. *d.* at Gurhatty, (Ghireti near Serampur), 8 May 1813. S.A.L.M.B. and D. and M. give date of death as 17 June 1813. B. Cons. of 18 June 1778, noting his promotion to Surg., gives his name as William Wilson.

160. Kerr, James (b). *b.* 1738. M.D. . . . Surg. 'Cruttenden,' 1763–68; 'Asia,' 1771–72. A.S. 16 May 1770. Surg. 25 Apr. 1778. *d.* in Calcutta, 17 Sept. 1782.

161. Elliot, Thomas. A.S. 16 May 1770. Surg. 26 Apr. 1778. *d.* at Cawnpur, 30 July 1783.

162. **Scarlin, Samuel.** M.D. . . . A.S. 16 May 1770. Surg. 27 Apr. 1778. Resigned, 8 Feb. 1780; (Muster Roll of 1st Brigade for 1780). S.A.L.M.B. and D. and M. give date of retirement as 30 Dec. 1779.

163. **Blane, William.** A.S. 22 Sept. 1770. Surg. 22 Aug. 1778. Resigned, 4 Feb. 1793. F.R.S. 4 April 1795. d. . . . 1836. Brother of I. G. Gilbert Blane, R.N.

*164. **Bruce, Robert** (a, b). b. 1746. Surg. ' Ponsborne,' 1765–66 and 1768–69. A.S. 1 Nov. 1770; (Muster roll of 1st Brigade for 1772). Resigned on account of ill-health, 16 Feb. 1784; (B. Cons. 20 Feb. 1784). Surg. to Sir Eyre Coote in Karnatak in 1778. Bo. App. i. 23.

165. **Inglis, Charles** (b, c). Surg. ' Clinton,' 1763–64; ' Lord Camden,' 1766–67. A.S. 5 Dec. 1770. Resigned, 5 Mar. 1771.

166. **Johnson, Wellwood.** A.S. 5 Dec. 1770. Resigned, 19 Jan. 1773.

167. **Parratt,** or **Perrott, Ebenezer.** A.S. 5 Dec. 1770. d. in Calcutta, 23 Nov. 1771; (Burial Regr. where name is spelt Perrot). D. and M. say " not to be traced." In S.A.L.M.B. name is spelt Parratt, also in D. and M.

168. **Watson, John.** b. 1749. A.S. 5 Dec. 1770. Surg. 23 Aug. 1778. d. at Patna, June 1786 (C.G. 6 July 1786). D. and M. say " not to be traced." Cal. Chron. of 17 Jan. 1788 gives date of death as 20 May 1786.

169. **Duckworth, James.** b. 1740. A.S. 31 Dec. 1770. Surg. 24 Aug. 1778. d. " on the river," June 1781; (D. and M.), d. in Calcutta, 4 May 1781; (St. John's Burial Regr.; B.P. and P. xxxi, Part ii, p. 154).

1771

170. **Dunn, Thomas.** A.S. 31 Jan. 1771. Surg. 25 Aug. 1778. d. at Buxar, 25 Sept. 1782. First name given as James in Field Officers' List, 1777.

——. **Laird, John.** Surg. 23 Feb. 1771. v. No. 90, supra.

171. **Walters, Hopkins.** A.S. 17 Apr. 1771. C.C.S. 1777. Resigned, . . . 1782.

172. **Mills, James** (a). A.S. 26 Apr. 1771. d. at Dakka, 16 Oct. 1773; (tombstone).

173. **Birch, Thomas.** b. 1748. A.S. 7 May 1771. d. at Chinsura, Aug. 1775.

†174. **Lynd,** or **Lind, James.** L.R.C.P. Ed. 1770. A.S. 7 May 1771. Surg. 26 Aug. 1778. Head Surg. 10 Mar. 1789. M.M.B. 10 Mar. 1789 to 31 Dec. 1789, and again 6 June 1794. Furlough, 16 Jan. 1795. R. 11 Jan. 1797. d. 13 Sept. 1816. Rohilla war, 1774.

* Genl. Stibbert's list, dated 12 Nov. 1783, shows two full Surgeons named Robert Bruce, the first between C. Francis and T. Calcraft, the second between John Henderson and William Ronald. No dates of appointment are given in this list.
† At least three Surgeons, named James Lynd or Lind, were in India, as members of public medical services, in the latter half of the eighteenth century; No. 174, supra, in the Bengal Medl. Service; Surgeon James Lynd, R.N. author of the well-known work on Tropical Diseases, and James Lind, Surgeon of the Indiaman ' Drake' in 1762–63, afterwards Physician to the Royal Household at Windsor. v. Hist. of I.M.S. ii. 58, 59.

175. **Walker, Alexander.** A.S. 30 July 1771. Surg. 2 Sept. 1778. Resigned and went on furlough, 22 Jan. 1785; (B. Mily. Cons.). Did not rejoin. Struck off, 1793.

176. **Mair, Hugh.** *b.* 1750. A.S. 30 July 1771. Surg. 3 Sept. 1778. Head Surg. 28 Dec. 1788. R. 25 Oct. 1797.

177. **MacDonald, Roderick** (a, b). Surg. Mate, 'Devonshire,' 1769–70. A.S. 21 Sept. 1771. Surg. 4 Sept. 1778. *d.* at Goalpara, 14 June 1794. First name given as Robert in Field Officer's List, 1772.

178. **Francis, Clement** (b). Surg. 'Thames,' 1768–69. C.C.S. 1776 or earlier. A.S. 9 Dec. 1771. Surg. 6 Sept. 1778. Resigned, 17 Jan .1785. *d.* in England, Oct. 1792. Surg. to Warren Hastings.

179. **Calcraft,** or **Chalcraft, Thomas.** A.S. 15 Dec. 1771. Surg. 24 Feb. 1780. *d.* at Patna, 1 May 1790; (C.G. 20 May 1790). S.A.L.M.B. and D. and M. say "resigned, 1791." Name spelt Calcraft in D. and M.; Chalcraft in Field Officer's List, in Muster Rolls, and in S.A.L.M.B.

180. **Manton,** or **Martin, Thomas.** A.S. 19 Dec. 1771. *d.* at Fort William, 22 July 1772; (Burial Regr. where name is given as Thomas Martin). S.A.L.M.B. and D. and M. both give the same date of death, but spell his name Manton.

1772

181. **Fergusson, Archibald R.** A.S. 19 Feb. 1772. *d.* Aug. 1776. Rohilla war, 1774.

182. **Cunningham, William** (b). Surg. Mate, 'Cruttenden,' 1766–67; Surg. 'Verelst,' 1767–69; 'Egmont,' 1770–71. A.S. 28 Apr. 1772. Surg. 25 Feb. 1780. Resigned, 17 Apr. 1782; (B. Cons. 22 Apr. 1782). S.A.L.M.B. and D. and M. say "not to be traced."

183. **Craigie, John.** A.S. 28 Apr. 1772. Surg. 26 Feb. 1780. L.R.C.P. Ed. 1789. F.R.C.P. Ed. 1789. R. 10 Jan. 1795. *d.* on board the 'Haughton,' on passage to Europe, 10 Feb. 1795. Name also in S.A.L.M.M. as "Nominated by Court, List of Packet, 22 Mar. 1769." Claim to rank from 1769 rejected; (B. Mily. Cons. 24 Aug. 1786).

184. **Hunter, James.** A.S. 28 Apr. 1772. Surg. 27 Feb. 1780. *d.* at Dakka, 16 Mar. 1785; (tombstone). D. and M. say "not to be traced."

185. **Blohme,** or **Bluhme, Lewis.** A.S. 6 July 1772. Resigned, 19 Dec. 1776 ("on account of age and long illness," Genl. L. from B. 19 Dec. 1776, para. 12; S.A.L.M.B.). D. and M. say "not to be traced."

186. **Fergusson, John.** A.S. 20 July 1772. Surg. 26 Feb. 1780. *d.* 4 Nov. 1785; (C.G. 10 Nov. 1785). S.A.L.M.B. and D. and M. say "died at Chunar, 4 Nov. 1784"). Rohilla war, 1774.

187. **Johnson, Robert.** A.S. 1 Oct. 1782. Surg. 29 Feb. 1780. Resigned 15 Dec. 1784. First Maratha war, 1778–82, with Bengal detachment to Bombay under Col. Leslie.

188. **Knilans,** or **Neelans, Abraham.** A.S. 14 Nov. 1772; (Warren Hastings' List, dated 6 Oct. 1777, where his name is entered between Robert Johnson and John Reid, and he is noted as dead). No further information.

189. **Reid, John.** A.S. 18 Dec. 1772. Surg. 1 Mar. 1780. Gave up promotion to remain at Delhi. *d.* at Mirat, 10 Mar. 1810; (tombstone). S.A.L.M.B. and D. and M. say "died at Delhi, Apr. 1810."

190. **Carnegie, Alexander** (b, c). *b.* 1743. Surg. Mate, 'Devonshire,' 1766–67; Surg. 'Nottingham,' 1769–70. A.S. 22 Dec. 1772. Resigned, 27 Mar. 1775; (Genl. L. from B. 27 Mar. 1775, para. 50, where he is called Charles Carnegie). Readmitted; (Genl. L. from B. 4 Feb. 1778, paras. 16, 17). Surg. 2 Mar. 1780. Head Surg. 31 Dec. 1789. *d.* in Calcutta, 23 May 1806.

191. **Wedderburn, Charles** (a). A.S. . . . 1772; (Muster Roll, Artillery, 1772). Removed to Infantry, 24 Dec. 1772. Cadet, 1770. Ensign, 29 Nov. 1771. Lieut. 9 Aug. 1776. Capt. 1 Mar. 1781. Resigned, 8 Jan. 1785. Was serving in the Light Infantry at Chuckye, (Chakai, Monghir district), on 30 Sept. 1777, and signed a medl. cert. there; (B. Mily. Cons. 16 Oct. 1777), so was still doing some medical work. D. and M. give his name in their Bengal Infantry List, where it is spelt Wedderburne, but not in their Medical List. Name not in S.A.L.M.B.

192. **Dohardy, Andrew.** A.S. 6 Mar. 1773. *d.* 4 Apr. 1773.

193. **Boyd, George.** *b.* 1748. A.S. 6 Mar. 1773. Surg. 3 Mar. 1780. Head Surg. 31 Dec. 1789. M.M.B. 1 Jan. 1794 to — 1794. *d.* in Calcutta, 17 July 1808. First Maratha war, 1778–82, with Bengal detachment to Bombay under Col. Leslie.

194. **Inglis, William** (b). Surg. Mate, 'Lord Camden,' 1770–71. A.S. 1 June 1773. Surg. 21 Oct. 1780. Head Surg. 29 Apr. 1796. R. 2 Jan. 1802. *d.* 27 July 1806; (S.A.L.M.B.). D. and M. spell name Inglish, say R. in 1801.

195. **Starke, James.** A.S. 8 Sept. 1773. Surg. 5 Sept. 1778. Resigned, with leave to return, 22 Dec. 1788; (M.S. Army List, Nov. 1788). Did not rejoin. Struck off, 1793.

196. **Hamilton, Alexander** (a, b, c). Surg. 'Lord North,' 1771–72; 'Bridgwater,' 1773. A.S. 6 Dec. 1773; (Genl. L. from B. 15 Mar. 1774, para. 56; Name and date of appointment given in Warren Hastings' list of 6 Oct. 1777). Accompanied Bogle's mission to Tibet, 1773, and sent on missions to Bhutan, 1775, and 1777. S.A.L.M.B. gives date of appointment as 1774. *d.* at Baksa, Duars, Oct. 1777. (Will dated Buxadwar, 2 Aug. 1777; proved 15 Nov. 1777.)

1774

197. **Allen, Charles** (c). A.S. 15 Feb. 1774. M.A., M.D. Glas. 1778. Surg. 22 Oct. 1780. *d.* at Barhampur, 12 July 1791. Rohilla war, 1774, battle of St. George, 23 Apr. 1774; (Genl. L. from B. 6 Mar. 1788, para. 56).

198. **Harwood, Bussick** (b, c). *b.* 1745. Surg. 'Harcourt,' 1773–74. A.S. 19 Feb. 1774. Resigned, 4 May 1778. F.R.S. 27 May 1784. M.B. 1785, M.D. 1790, Cantab. Prof. of Anatomy, Cambridge, 1785–1814, also Downing Professor of Medicine, 1800–1814. Knighted, 1806. *d.* at Downing College, Cambridge, 10 Nov. 1814. Author of Lectures on Anatomy, 1787; System of Comparative Anatomy and Physiology, 1796).

199. **Phillips, Thomas** (c). *b.* 1750. A.S. 19 Feb. 1774. Surg. 23 Oct. 1780. Head Surg. 7 Dec. 1797. R. 9 Sept. 1807. Name spelt Philipps in S.A.L.M.B. First Maratha war, 1781–82, with Bengal detachment to Bombay.

200. **Armstrong, John** (a). A.S. . . . July 1774 (?). No further information. Name not given in either S.A.L.M.B. or D. and M. In both the list of 1774, and Warren Hastings' list of 6 Oct. 1777, two officers named John Armstrong are given, the senior a full surgeon (No. 135, supra), the junior an Asst. Surgeon, between W. Inglis and John Stark.

201. **Stack**, or **Stark, John** (b). Surg. Mate, 'Morse,' 1771–72; Surg. 'Mercury,' 1773–74. A.S. 1 July (?) 1774. Cadet, Artillery, 7 July 1778. Lieut. Fireworker, 18 Sept. 1778. First Lieut. 16 Sept. 1779. Struck off list of Asst. Surgeons, 3 Nov. 1780; (B. Mily. Cons. 2 Nov. 1780). *d.* in Calcutta, date unknown; (Stubbs). S.A.L.M.B. and D. and M. spell name Stack, in the M.S. Medl. Lists it is spelt Stark. D. and M. say "not to be traced" in their Artillery lists. First Maratha war, 1778–81, under Genl. Goddard.

202. **Witherstone, Robert.** A.S. 1 July 1774. Cadet, Infantry, 27 Feb. 1778. Ensign, 1778. Struck off list of Asst. Surgeons, 3 Nov. 1780; (B. Mily. Cons. 2 Nov. 1780). Lieut. 14 Feb. 1789. Capt. 1 June 1796. Major, 8 Jan. 1801. Lt.-Col. 30 Sept. 1803. *d.* at Cawnpur 7 May 1806. First Maratha war, 1778–81, under Genl. Goddard.

203. **Bannatyne, Richard** (b). Surg. 'Haughton,' 1773–74. A.S. 7 Oct. 1774. *d.* . . . 1778; (Muster Roll of Artillery, 1778). S.A.L.M.B. and D. and M. say "died, date not known."

1775

204. **Robertson, James** (b). Surg. Mate, 'Earl of Ashburnham,' 1772–73, A.S. 30 Mar. 1775. Surg. 24 Oct. 1780. Resigned, with leave to return, 10 Dec. 1788; (M.S. Army List, Nov. 1788). Did not rejoin. Struck off, 1793.

205. **MacDonald, Roderick.** A.S. 21 Sept. 1775. Surg. . . . 1778. *d.* at Patna, 26 June 1779; (S.A.L.M.B. and D. and M.); 26 May 1779; (Muster Roll of 1st Brigade for 1779).

1776

206. **Murchison, Kenneth** (b). *b.* 1751. Ed. and Glas. Univs. C.C.S. Surg. 'Fox,' 1772–73. A.S. 30 Oct. 1776. Surg. 25 Oct. 1780. Furlough, 27 Jan. 1784. Resigned from that date; (G.O. 5 Feb. 1784). *d.* at Bathampton, . . . 1796. S.A.L.M.B. spells name Murcheson. Attended Nanda Kumar in prison. Father of Sir Roderick Murchison. Killed Capt. Crofts in a duel at Lucknow in 1780.

1777

207. **Cheere, James,** or **John.** C.C.S. 1776. A.S. 3 Feb. 1777. Surg. 26 Oct. 1780. *d.* at Fort William, 3 Oct. 1782. Name spelt Chear on tombstone in S. Park St. In Muster Roll of 1st Brigade for 1778 his name is entered as " John Cheers, Asst. Surgeon and Chaplain." In Roll of Corp. Surg. name is given as " John Cheere, India, Surgeon." Second Maisur war, 1781–82.

208. **Gowdie, Walter** (b). Surg. ' Worcester,' 1761–65 ; ' Plassey,' 1765–70 ; ' Horsenden,' 1771–72. A.S. 26 Feb. 1777. Surg. 27 Oct. 1780. *d*. in Calcutta, 20 Jan. 1793. Benares war, 1781.

209. **Inglis, Charles** (b). Surg. ' Lord Mansfield,' 1770–71 ;. ' Duke of Grafton,' 1772–73. A.S. 5 Mar. 1777. Surg. 28 Oct. 1780. *d*. at Bidgee Ghur (Bijaigarh in Mirzapur), 25 Oct. 1781. Benares war, 1781.

210. **Baillie, James** (b). Surg. ' Triton,' 1772–73. A.S. 5 May 1777. Surg. 29 Oct. 1780. Resigned, 6 Feb. 1791. Second Maisur war, 1781–82.

211. **MacFie, James.** *b*. 1753. M.D. Ed. 1774. A.S. Madras, 5 May 1777 ; (M. Mily. Cons.). A.S. Bengal, 26 Jan. 1778. Surg. 25 Oct. 1781. *d*. at Commercolly (Kumarkhali, Nadiya district), 11 Apr. 1790. D. and M. give name in Bengal but not in Madras List. M. No. 210.

212. **Burnett, William.** A.S. 14 Aug. 1777. Resigned, 7 Jan. 1779 ; (S.A.L.M.B. and D. and M.). *d*. . . . 1784 ; (Advt. of Estate in C.G. 13 Jan. 1785).

213. **Totty, John** (b). Surg. ' Godfrey,' 1775–76. C.C.S. 1776. A.S. 16 Nov. 1777 ; (B. Mily. Cons. 4 Nov. 1780). Surg. 24 Feb. 1780. *d*. at Cossomah, Oct. 1781. Benares war, 1781.

214. **Gardiner, William Fullerton.** A.S. 30 Nov. 1777. Surg. 30 Oct. 1780. R. 1 Dec. 1798. *d*. . . . 1827.

215. **Ward, Joseph** (b). Surg. ' London,' 1776–77. C.C.S. 1777. A.S. 1 Dec. 1777 ; (B. Mily. Cons. 2 Feb. 1778). Surg. 19 Nov. 1781. Invalided, 25 July 1789. Resigned, 19 Feb. 1794. *d*. in London, Feb. 1798 ; (G. M. Mar. 1798).

1778

216. **Clevelands, John.** C.C.S. 1776. A.S. 8 Jan. 1778. *d*. in Calcutta, 28 Sept. 1781. Name also spelt Claveland (S.A.L.M.B.), Cleveland, (Hickey's Memoirs), and Clavelands. S.A.L.M.B. gives name twice, as Claveland and Clevelands. In Roll of Corp. Surg. is given as " John Cleveland, Bengall " ; in St. John's Burial Regr. Cleveland.

217. **Howarth, Humphrey.** C.C.S. 1776. A.S. 15 Jan. 1778. Surg. 20 Nov. 1781. Retired on full pay for three years, 31 Oct. 1785 ; (Genl. L. from B. 31 Oct. 1785, para. 45). Did not rejoin. Struck off 1793.

218. **Robinson, James** (a). A.S. 9 Mar. 1778 ; (B. Cons. 13 Mar. 1778). A.S. Infantry, appointed Lieut. Fireworker ; (Muster Roll of 1st Brigade for 1778). Cadet, Artillery, 9 Sept. 1778. Lieut. Fireworker, 6 Oct. 1778. First Lieut. 23 June 1782. Capt. 23 Jan. 1794. Major, 28 May 1804. *d*. at Cawnpur, 27 Feb. 1806 (D. and M.'s List of Bengal Artillery, where name is given as James Robertson). His signature is James Robinson ; (Stubbs, List of Bengal Artillery).

219. **Steele, James** (b). Surg. ' Duke of Kingston,' 1766–67 ; ' Salisbury,' 1768–69 ; ' Europa,' 1777–78. A.S. 24 Mar. 1778. Surg. 22 Nov. 1781. *d*. at Purnea, June 1791. S.A.L.M.B. and D. and M. spell name Steel. Second Maisur war, 1781–82.

220. **Harrison, George** (b, c). Surg. Mate, ' Ankerwyke,' 1775–76 ; Surg. ' Royal Charlotte,' 17 Aug. 1778, and to rank as A.S. from that date ; (B. Mily. Cons. 2 Aug. 1779). Surg. 4 Mar. 1782, special promotion ; (B. Mily. Cons.). *d*. 22 Dec. 1784. Second Maisur war, 1781–82.

221. Carstairs, John, or **James** (b, c). Surg. 'Eagle,' 1777–78. A.S. 11 Aug. 1778; (B. Mily. Cons.). Resigned, 9 Mar. 1787; (B. Cons. 16 Mar. 1787). In both these references his first name is given as John. Both S.A.L.M.B. and D. and M. give it as James, the date of his appointment as 1783, and say resigned, without date. He appears to have been first appointed locally from 11 Aug. 1778, afterwards nominated by Court from 10 Apr. 1783.

222. Hotchkes, Adam. C.C.S. 1778. A.S. 29 Sept. 1778. Murdered by dakaits at Simaria, en route from Chitra to Gaya, 10 Sept. 1781; (Ind. Gaz. 27 Oct. 1781). Both S.A.L.M.B. and D. and M. say "died in Bihar, 31 Oct. 1781."

223. Stewart, John (c). A.S. 10 Dec. 1778. Surg. 24 Oct. 1782. Head Surg. 1790. *d.* at Trichinopoly, while serving as Head Surg. Bengal troops; (C.G. 20 Jan. 1791, where name is spelt Stuart). S.A.L.M.B. and D. and M. give date of appointment as 1779, and say "died in Carnatic, 1790."

224. Ross, Andrew, or **Alexander** (a, c). A.S. 26 Dec. 1778; (B. Mily. Cons. 28 Dec. 1778). Three years furlough to Europe, 24 Jan. 1786; (B. Mily. Cons. where first name is given as Alexander). Did not rejoin. No further information.

1779

225. Breton, Frederick (a). Cadet, Infantry, 1770. Ensign, 22 Dec. 1772. Lieut. 25 Mar. 1777. Appointed to act as Surgeon to Major Carnac's detachment, 1 Jan. 1779; (B. Mily. Cons. where name is spelt Britton). Reverted to combatant branch. Capt. 23 Mar. 1781. Resigned, Dec. 1790. *d.* at Bourn, Cambridgeshire, 22 Nov. 1791; (G.M. 1791, ii. 1160).

226. Laird, Charles (b, c). Surg. 'Stafford,' 1774–77; 'Gatton,' 1778–79. A.S. 21 Jan. 1779; (B. Mily. Cons.). Cadet, Infantry, 2 June 1781. Ensign, 24 June 1781. Lieut. 21 July 1781. Brevet-Surgeon, for bravery at capture of Gwalior, 16 June 1781. Surg. 21 Oct. 1783. Resigned, with leave to return, 22 Dec. 1788; (G.O. 12 Mar. 1789). Did not rejoin. Struck off. 1793. *d.* at Florence, ... 1795. Brother of No. 90, supra, John Laird, and of No. 241, infra, James Laird. S.A.L.M.B. and D. and M. give date of appointment as 10 Apr. 1780. First Maratha war, 1780–81, capture of Gwalior, 3 Aug. 1780, promoted. Benares war, 1781, action at Patita, Sept. 1781.

227. Henderson, John (b, c). M.D. Ed. 1774. Surg. 'Duke of Portland,' 1773–74; 'Rochford,' 1775–76. A.S. 21 Jan. 1779; (B. Mily. Cons.). Had been in King's service; (Proc. C.M.B. 2 July 1789). Name not in Johnston's Roll of R.A.M.C. Surg. 22 Oct. 1783. *d.* at Bankipur, 9 April 1783.

228. Williams, John Lloyd (b). Surg. 'Seahorse,' 1771–72. A.S. 17 Mar. 1779. Surg. 23 Oct. 1783. Gave up promotion to remain at Benares. R. 28 Oct. 1801. Second Maisur war, 1781–82, with Col. Pearse's detachment.

229. Henderson, John Grey. *b.* 1759. A.S. 28 June 1779. Surg. 24 Oct. 1783. Head Surg. 2 Jan. 1802. M.M.B. 18 June 1807. *d.* in Calcutta, 28 Sept. 1814.

230. Bruce, Robert (b). Surg. 'Duke of Albany,' 1769–72, lost on Long Sand, 25 July 1772. A.S. 12 Aug. 1779. Surg. 25 Oct. 1783. *d.* at Serampur, 31 May 1800.

231. **Ronald, William.** A.S. 13 Aug. 1779; (B. Mily. Cons. 2 Oct. 1779). Surg. 27 Oct. 1783. *d.* in Calcutta, 2 Aug. 1784. Name given as Rolland in S.A.L.M.B.

232. **Robinson, Thomas** (a). A.S. ... 1779 (?). Name in Muster Roll of 1st Brigade for 1779, as " Asst. Surgeon promoted and struck off." Not the same as No. 218, supra, James Robinson, whose name is also given in Muster Roll for 1779. No further information.

1780

*233. **Collins, Robert** (b). Surg. ' Godfrey,' 1778–79. A.S. 6 Jan. 1780. Taken prisoner in the ' Mount Sturt,' in Aug. 1780, by French fleet, on voyage to India. Surg. 30 Oct. 1783. Resigned, 24 Feb. 1794. M.R.C.S. 1812. *d.* at Leyton, Essex, 15 Feb. 1856. Father of Alfred Collins, No. 1561, infra. First Maratha war, 1780–81, with Bengal detachment to Bombay.

*234. **Murray, Archibald.** C.C.S. 1776. A.S. 6 Jan. 1780. Sailed for India, 27 July 1780, in ship which was taken by French on 9 Aug. 1780; (the ' Mount Sturt ' (?)). Nominated by Court in Desp. of 12 May 1780, para. 15. Joined and appointed 29 Jan. 1781; (B. Mily. Cons.). Surg. 28 Oct. 1783. Gave up promotion to remain at Shahabad. Resigned, 1 Mar. 1796; (Mily. L. from B. 1 Mar. 1796, para. 18). S.A.L.M.B. gives his name as Archibald or Alexander, appointment, 1779, furlough, 1796, gave up promotion. D. and M. give date of appointment as 1779, and say gave up promotion.

*235. **Mathews, Stephen** (b). Surg. Mate, ' Prince of Wales,' 1770–71; Surg. ' Prince of Wales,' 1772–73; ' York,' 1773–75; ' Prince of Wales,' 1776–77; ' Duke of Portland,' 1780–82. A.S. 6 Jan. 1780. Surg. 30 Oct. 1783. R. 30 July 1800. *d.* Mar. 1813. S.A.L.M.B. gives name as Mathews or Matthews, and date of appointment as 1779. D. and M. also give 1779 as date of appointment. Author of Treatise on Hepatic Diseases of India, 1783.

236. **Penny, Staunton.** A.S. 24 Feb. 1780. Surg. 31 Oct. 1783. Head Surg. 9 June 1803. *d.* at Dinapur, 1 July 1810.

†237. **Bengough, Edmund** (b, c). *b.* 1731. Surg. ' Lord Holland,' 1766–68. C.C.S. 1776, Surg. ' Stafford,' 1778–79, lost in Bengal River, 29 Aug. 1779. A.S. 3 Apr. 1780. Surg. 1 Nov. 1783. *d.* in Calcutta, 10 Jan. 1787; (C.G. 18 Jan. 1787). D. and M. give first name as Henry, and say " not to be traced." In S.A.L.M.B. first name is corrected from Henry to Edmund, and death in 1787 is reported. First Maratha war, 1780–81.

†238. **Campbell, Alexander** (c). A.S. 4 Apr. 1780. Surg. 3 Nov. 1783. R. 2 July 1806; (D. and M.); R. 11 Mar. 1806 in E.I. Regr.

†239. **Collie, James** (b). Surg. Mate, ' Tilbury,' 1768–69. Surg. ' Earl of Elgin,' 1770–72; ' Duke of Kingston,' 1773–74; ' Talbot,' 1775–76. A.S. 5 Apr. 1780. Surg. 30 Dec. 1789. *d.* at Allahabad, 30 Dec. 1802.

---

* B. Mily. Cons. of 18 Mar. 1781, note the appointment in Desp. from C. 12 May 1780, para 15, of the following Asst. Surgeons, for service where required ; Archibald Murray, Henry Miller, Charles Ogilvie, Edward Smart (Stuart), Bartholomew Hartley ; Robert Collins, Stephen Matthews. Miller, Ogilvie, and Stuart were posted to Madras.

† B. Mily. Cons. of 11 Apr. 1780, note the appointment of the following Asst. Surgeons ; Bengough, 3 Apr. ; Campbell, 4 Apr. ; Collie, 5 Apr. ; Cockraine (Cochrane), 6 Apr. ; Laird, 7 Apr. ; Baillie, 8 Apr. ; Kinloch, 9 Apr. ; MacGrath, 10 Apr.

1781]   INDIAN MEDICAL SERVICE

*240. Cochrane, Peter (b). Surg. ' York,' 1777–78. A.S. 6 Apr. 1780. Surg. 5 Feb. 1790. Head Surg. 11 Apr. 1805. M.M.B. 17 Dec. 1811. R. 5 June 1821. *d.* at Beauvais, France, 18 June 1831; (A.I. July 1831, p. 239). In S.A.L.M.B. first name is given as Peter or Patrick.

*241. Laird, James (b). Surg. ' Seahorse,' 1777–78 ; ' Earl Talbot,' 1779–80. A.S. 7 Apr. 1780. Cadet, Infantry, 1781. Ensign, 13 Aug. 1781. Lieut. 1 June 1783. Resigned combatant commission, 23 July 1789 ; (G.O. 23 July 1789). Surg. 2 May 1790. R. 27 May 1801. M.D. Ed. 1803. *d.* in London, 6 Jan. 1816. Brother of No. 90, John Laird, and of No. 226, Charles Laird, supra. Benares war, 1781.

*242. Baillie, William. A.S. Apr. 1780. Surg. 7 Feb. 1791. *d.* at Barhampur, 24 Aug. 1795.

*243. Kinloch, Frederick P. (a, c). A.S. 9 Apr. 1780. Resigned, date unknown. *d.* in Calcutta, 4 May 1806 ; (C.G. 7 Aug. 1806, where he is stated to be " formerly of Bengal Establishment "). Second Maisur war, 1782–83.

*244. MacGrath, Michael (c). A.S. 10 Apr. 1780. Surg. 16 July 1791. R. 21 Sept. 1803. In S.A.L.M.B. name is given twice, as Michael MacGrath and Magrath. Second Maisur war, 1781–82.

245. Taylor, or Tailour, John (c). A.S. 22 May 1780 ; (B. Mily. Cons. 12 June 1780). Ensign, Infantry, 25 Feb. 1781. Lieut. 29 Oct. 1781. *d.* in Calcutta, 1 Dec. 1791. D. and M. give his name in Medl. List as John Taylor, in Infantry List as John Tailour. S.A.L.M.B. gives name twice, as John Tailour, Cadet, 1781, served as Surgeon in Maratha war ; and as John Taylor, A.S. 10 Apr. 1780, appointed Lieut. of Infantry. First Maratha war, 1780–81, with Major Carnac's detachment ; (B. Mily. Cons. 12 June 1780 ; Secret L. from B. 11 Nov. 1786, paras. 127, 128 ; this letter also shows that he had served both in Infantry and in Medl. Dept.).

246. Mahon, Hugh (c). Asst. Surg. R.N. in H.M.S. ' Exeter ' ; (Proc. C.M.B. 4 Nov. 1794). A.S. Bengal, 1 Dec. 1780, appointed by Sir Eyre Coote in Karnatak ; (B. Mily. Cons. 2 Mar. 1782). Name shown among invalids in Muster Roll of 1783. *d.* at Lucknow, 23 Aug. 1786 ; (D. and M.) Cal. Chron. of 17 Jan. 1788 gives date of death as 11 Sept. 1787. Second Maisur war, 1781–82.

1781

†247. Williamson, Alexander (a, b, c). Formerly Surgeon's Mate of ' Besborough.' Asst. Surg. 29 Jan. 1781 ; (B. Mily. Cons. 29 Jan. 1781). *d.* at Bangalore, 9 July 1791 ; (M.S. Army List of 1792, casualties of 1791). Third Maisur war, 1790–91.

* *Vide* note to Bengough, No. 237, on p. 23.
† During the years 1781 to 1783 a considerable number of Asst. Surgeons were appointed locally in Bengal, in addition to those sent out from home, to meet the demand for medical officers caused by the second Maisur and first Maratha wars. For the next fifteen years, constant disputes went on between these officers, as to their relative rank and seniority. Numerous memorials on the subject were submitted to the Council at Calcutta and to the Court of Directors in London. Finally, in a letter dated 5 July 1797, paras. 37 to 47, contained in Bengal Minutes of Council of 20 Feb. 1798, and published in the Calcutta Gazette of 1 Mar. 1798, the Court directed that these officers should be ranked in the order there given, and that these orders should be final. The list, which includes only those still serving in 1797, contains 52 names. Of the

248. Bainbridge, Thomas. C.C.S. 1780. Asst. Surg. Madras, 2 Feb. 1781. Left England, 10 Mar. 1781, landed at Cape of Good Hope, and took part in capture of that port; landed at Bombay Mar. 1782. Went to Madras, and thence transferred to Bengal; (Proc. C.M.B. 2 Oct. 1792). Asst. Surg. Bengal, 10 Sept. 1782; (B. Mily. Cons. 9 Sept. 1782). Surg. 21 Oct. 1794. S.S. 18 June 1807; (first use of term Superintending Surgeon, in G.O. of 28 May 1807, C.G. of 18 June 1807, v. Hist. of I.M.S. i. 315). Lost on passage home, on or about 28 Oct. 1808, in 'Experiment,' which parted company from the rest of the fleet on that day, in the South of the Indian Ocean, and was not heard of again. v. also John Bainbridge, No. 33, App. I.

249. Morton, Joseph (a, d). C.C.S. 1780. Asst. Surg. 21 Mar. 1781 (date of covenant). Arriving at Fort Marlborough, was detained for duty there till 1784; (B. Mily. Cons. 12 Apr. 1784, Mad. Cons. 31 May 1782, and 25 July 1784). Ranked as Asst. Surg. Bengal from 13 Jan. 1784; (B. Mily. Cons.). Joined at Madras July 1784; (Mad. Cons. 25 July 1784). Retransferred to West Coast (Sumatra), as acting Surgeon, 3 Aug. 1785; (Mad. Cons.). Apparently never joined Bengal. d. at Fort Marlborough, 10 Jan. 1787; (S. Cons.). M. No. 238; S. No. 79.

250. Glas, John (b, c). b. 1750. Surg. Mate, 'Speaker,' 1769–70. Surgeon of 'Prime,' 1773–4 and 1777–78. Asst. Surg. 15 Apr. 1781; (B. Mily. Cons.). Gave up promotion to remain at Bhagalpur. d. at Bhagalpur, 3 Aug. 1822. D. and M. give name as Glass, but it is always spelt Glas in records.

251. Fraser, Crichton. Asst. Surg. 17 Apr. 1781. Ranked from 20 May 1782; (B. Mily. Cons. 14 Jan. 1783). Gave up promotion to remain at Tirhut, and omitted in list of 1807; (C.G. 30 Oct. 1794). d. in Edinburgh, 6 Oct. 1810 (Royal Mily. Chron. i. Nov. 1810).

252. Ogilvy, or Ogilvie, Walter. Asst. Surg. 15 Apr. 1781. Ranked from 23 May 1782; (B. Mily. Cons. 12 June 1783). Surg. 21 Oct. 1794. S.S. 28 Sept. 1808. M.M.B. 20 Dec. 1814. Resigned 21 Jan. 1819. d. on board 'Eliza,' on passage home, 2 May 1826. Second Maisur war, 1781–82. Third Maisur war, 1791–92, Capture of Seringapatam.

253. Coote, Chidley. b. 1759. C.C.S. 1781. Asst. Surg. 19 Apr. 1781. Ranked from 26 May 1782; (B. Mily. Cons. 12 June 1783). Surg. 21 Oct. 1794. d. in Calcutta, 5 Dec. 1807. Nephew of Sir Eyre Coote.

---

officers originally appointed, 43 had died, 17 resigned, three had been dismissed or cashiered, and two had given up promotion. The order fixed in 1797 runs as follows.

1. W. Dick.
2. A. Burt.
3. T. Bainbridge.
4. W. Ogilvie.
5. C. Coote.
6. T. Phillips.
7. J. Hutton.
8. W. Spottiswood.
9. R. Anderson.
10. J. B. Gilchrist.
11. J. P. Wade.
12. J. Lamb.
13. W. Hunter.
14. J. Shaw.
15. P. Ivory.
16. J. Gillman.
17. John Williams.
18. John Macrae.
19. Walter Williams.
20. T. Stokes.
21. J. Burgh.
22. J. Meek.
23. G. Rankin.
24. J. Corse.
25. John Smith.
26. James Smith.
27. G. Macleod.
28. T. Casement.
29. E. Turner.
30. C. Fyffe.
31. G. Toshach.
32. J. Nasmyth.
33. C. Todd.
34. John Henderson.
35. George Davidson.
36. J. Campbell.
37. A. Russell.
38. William Davidson.
39. W. Cooke.
40. A. Gray.
41. W. Boyd.
42. P. Ewart.
43. W. Anderson.
44. R. Wilson.
45. A. Gibb.
46. J. Ross.
47. G. Fraser.
48. N. Fontana.
49. W. Moore.
50. J. Howison.
51. John Henderson.
52. C. Kegan.

In the Nominal Roll following the names have been entered in the actual order of the dates of appointment, as far as it could be ascertained.

254. **Phillips, Thomas** (e). *b.* 6 July 1760. M.R.C.S. Surg. Mate, R.N. 1780–81. C.C.S. 1782. Asst. Surg. 20 Apr. 1781. Ranked from 27 May 1782; (B. Mily. Cons. 12 June 1783). Surg. 21 Oct. 1794. S.S. 2 July 1810. M.M.B. 4 Jan. 1815. Retired, 6 Aug. 1817. *d.* in London, 13 June 1851, leaving by will large sums for Education in Wales, St. David's College, Lampeter, and Llandovery schools; (v. Hist. of I.M.S. ii. 77). Inspector of Hosps. Botany Bay, New South Wales, 1796. War with France, taken prisoner on voyage home in 1798. Java war, 1811, capture of Java, as S.S.

255. **Williamson, Christopher** (a). Asst. Surg. 21 April 1781. Appointed by Court, next above James Hutton, No. 256; (B. Mily. Cons. 28 Aug. 1783). Serving in 1785. Noted as "not to be found" in M.S. Army List of 1788. Serving as Surgeon of 'Marquis of Lansdowne,' 1787–88. No further information. S.A.L.M.B. gives his name as Christian Williamson.

256. **Hutton, James** (b). Surg. Mate, 'Lord North,' 1774–76. Surgeon of 'Earl of Mansfield,' 1778–81. Asst. Surg. 21 Apr. 1781. Ranked from 29 Oct. 1733; (B. Mily. Cons. 15 Dec. 1783). Retired, 27 Dec. 1805. *d.* 2 Aug. 1838. S.A.L.M.B. says *d.* 2 Oct. 1838.

257. **Minchin, Thomas** (b). Surgeon of 'York,' 1780–81. Asst. Surg. 22 Apr. 1781 (?). Name between No. 256, J. Hutton and No. 258, W. Spottiswood, in B. Mily. Cons. 28 Aug. 1783. Killed by a fall from his house (sic, horse?) at Cawnpur, Jan. 1785; (C.G. 27 Jan. 1785). D. and M. give his name as Thomas Munchin, entered, 1782, died, date not known. S.A.L.M.B. spells name Minchin, and says A.S. 1782, died, date not known.

258. **Spottiswood, William.** *b.* 1755. Asst. Surg. 23 Apr. 1781. C.C.S. 1782. Ranked from 1 Nov. 1783; (B. Mily. Cons. 15 Dec. 1783). Surg. 21 Oct. 1794. S.A.L.M.B. and D. and M. spell name Spottiswoode; also Roll of Corp. Surg. Killed in action, on passage home, 14 Aug. 1803, on the 'Lord Nelson,' taken by a French privateer off Ferrol; (G.M. Sept. 1803).

259. **Henderson, John** (b). Surgeon of 'Besborough,' 1777–81. Asst. Surg. 24 Apr. 1781. Surg. 1 June 1796. Retired, 20 May 1806; (D. and M.). The E.I. Regr. gives date as 14 Jan. 1806. *d.* in Scotland, 9 Dec. 1822.

260. **Hartley, Bartholomew.** C.C.S. 1779. Asst. Surg. 20 May 1781; (B. Mily. Cons. 21 May 1781). Surg. 29 Oct. 1783. Senior Surgeon at Bencoolen, Dec. 1792; (Proc. C.M.B. 25 Jan. 1793); to end of 1802. *d.* at Serampur, 13 Mar. 1803. D. and M. give date of appointment as 1779.

261. **Syme,** or **Sime, Edward** (a, c). Asst. Surg. 21 May 1781; (B. Mily. Cons. 21 May 1781). Name in Genl. Stibbert's List of 12 Nov. 1783. No further information. Second Maisur war, 1781–82.

262. **Henderson, Alexander** (b, c). C.C.S. 1776. Surgeon of 'Prime,' 1779–81. Asst. Surg. 25 June 1781; (B. Mily. Cons. 16 July 1781). Resigned, 3 Mar. 1789; (G.O. 9 Mar. 1789). Permitted to return, 18 Nov. 1793. Apparently did not rejoin. D. and M. say Resigned, 22 Dec. 1788.

263. **Freer, Adam** (c). M.D. Ed. 1767. Served for some years as Surgeon to factory at Aleppo; (Proc. C.M.B. 29 Dec. 1786). Asst. Surg. 6 July 1781. Surg. 6 Mar. 1793. Head Surg. 27 May 1806. *d.* at Barhampur, 18 Jan. 1811. First Maratha war, 1781–82, with Bengal detachment to Bombay.

264. **Milne, George** (c). *b.* 1759. Asst. Surg. 15 July 1781; (B. Mily. Cons.). *d.* at Chunar, 18 Nov. 1791. In S.A.L.M.B. name is given as Milne or Mylne.

265. **Nanyn, Alexander** (or **Andrew**) (c). Asst. Surg. 16 July 1781; (B. Mily. Cons.). *d.* at Barrackpur, March 1784. First name given as Andrew in Cal. Cons. of 16 July 1781, in Calcutta Record Office; as Alexander, in B. Mily. Cons. of same date in India Office. S.A.L.M.B. and D. and M. give date of appointment as 1782.

266. **Oldmeadow, John** (or (**James**). C.C.S. 1778. Asst. Surg. 27 Sept. 1781; (B. Mily. Cons.). *d.* in Fort William, 24 June 1782. D. and M. give Christian name as James, and date of appointment as 1780.

267. **Skelton, William.** C.C.S. 1780. Asst. Surg. 21 Oct. 1781; (B. M. Cons.) *d.* at Barhampur, 11 Apr. 1786. D. and M. give date of appointment as 1782.

268. **Staunton, Thomas** (a, c). Cadet and Asst. Surg. Oct. 1781. Ensign, 11 July 1782. Resigned medical service in 1783. Lieut. 8 Jan. 1785. Applied to return to Medical Dept. in 1787; (Proc. C.M.B. 24 May 1787); without success. Capt. 17 July 1801. *d.* at Fatehgarh, 21 Nov. 1805. D. and M. give name in Infantry list, but not in Medl. list.

269. **Wilson, James** (c). Asst. Surg. 5 Nov. 1781; (B. Mily. Cons. 7 Nov. 1781). Surg. 10 Apr. 1793. Permitted to retire and proceed to Europe in G.O. of 28 Nov. 1801. Did not go, (Hickey, iv. 271, 272). *d.* at Murshidabad, 26 Aug. 1803.

*270. **Lyke, John Frederick**, or **Lycke**, or **Luecke** (c). *b.* at Egeln, Magdeburg, Prussia. Asst. Surg. Nov. 6 1781; (B. Mily. Cons. 7 Nov. 1781) *d.* at Kalkapur (Murshidabad), 11 Dec. 1789.

271. **Brown, Charles** (c). Asst. Surg. 7 Nov. 1781; (B. Mily. Cons.). *d.* at Cawnpur, 29 Aug. 1784. D. and M. give date of appointment as 1782.

272. **Dick, William** (b). Surg. Mate, 'Queen,' 1778–79. C.C.S. 1780. Surgeon of 'Queen,' 1781. Asst. Surg. 8 Nov. 1781. Surg. 20 Oct. 1794. Supt. and owner of first Lunatic Asylum in Calcutta, 1787–1802. Retired, 17 Dec. 1802. Head Surgeon, Prince of Wales Island, 20 Sept. 1805; (P.W.I. Cons.); to 25 Mar. 1807; (P.W.I. Cons. 2 June 1807). Consulting Surgeon to E.I. Co. in London, 1808–18. *d.* in Scotland, 16 Jan. 1821. Father of Genl. Sir Robert Dick. P.W.I. No. 1.

1782

273. **Anderson, Robert** (b, c). C.C.S. 1776. Surgeon of 'Grosvenor,' 1778–79; of 'Rochford,' 1781. Cadet, 1781. Ensign, 29 Sept. 1781. Asst. Surg. 2 Jan. 1782, and resigned combatant commission from same date; (B. Mily. Cons. 10 Apr. 1783). Gave up promotion to remain at Jessore; (C.G. 25 Feb. 1796). *d.* at Jessore, 11 Apr. 1810. D. and M. give name in both Infantry and Medical lists, with date of appointment, 2 Apr. 1783. v. Hist. of I.M.S. i. 236, 237.

274. **Grant, Robert** (a, c). Asst. Surg. 30 Jan. 1782; (B. Mily. Cons. 4 Mar. 1782). Sent to Coromandel Coast. No further information. Not the same man as James Grant, No. 279, for both names are mentioned together in Ind. Gaz. 16 Mar. 1782. Second Maisur war, 1782.

* In Lyke's will, dated at Kalkapur, 6 Dec. 1789, he states that his name was erroneously entered as Lycke, but that his father's name was Luecke, and that he was born at Egeln, near Magdeburg.

275. Gilchrist, John Borthwick (c, e). *b.* 1759. Went to India as Asst. Surg. R.N.; (Proc. C.M.B. 21 Nov. 1795). Asst. Surg. Feb. 1782; (B. Mily. Cons, 3 Apr. 1783, when ranked next above No. 276, J. P. Wade). Surg. 21 Oct. 1794. Head of College of Fort William on its foundation in 1800–1804. Granted furlough to Europe, Feb. 1804; (Cal. Pub. L. of 29 Feb. 1804). Did not rejoin. Retired, 6 Jan. 1809. LL.D. Ed. 1804. Professor of Hindustani to E.I. Co. in London, 1818–26. *d.* in Paris, 9 Jan. 1841. S.A.L.M.B. and D. and M. give date of appointment as 3 Apr. 1783. Second Maisur war, 1782. Employed on Philological work for almost the whole of his service. Author of English and Hindustani Dictionary, 1787–90, Appendix, 1800, reprinted 1825; British Indian Monitor, or Antijargonist, 1800; Oriental Linguist, 1802; Stranger's East India Guide, 1802; Hindustani Philology, 1810; Hindi Roman Orthoepigraphical Ultimatum, 1820; Hindi Moral Preceptor, 1821; Persian Grammar, 1821; General East India Guide, 1825; also of many translations and minor works. Many of the above works went through two or more editions.

276. Wade, John Peter (c). *b.* 1762. M.D. Educated Ed. Univ. held licence to practise from King of Portugal, came to India as Surgeon of Portuguese ship 'Arabida'; (Proc. C.M.B. 21 Nov. 1795). Asst. Surg. 25 Feb. 1782; (B. Mily. Cons. 4 Nov. 1782). Surg. 21 Oct. 1794. *d.* in Calcutta, 14 Oct. 1802. D. and M. give date of appointment as 4 Apr. 1783, and add M.D. to name. First Maratha war, 1782, under Genl. Goddard. Author of Evidences of a successful method of treating Fever and Dysentery in Bengal, 1791; Nature and Effects of emetics, purgatives, mercurials, and low diet in Disorders of Bengal and similar latitudes, 1792; Prevention and Treatment of Disorders of Seamen and Soldiers in Bengal, 1793.

277. Lamb, John (c). Previously served in Navy, went to India as Surgeon of H.M.S. 'Active'; (Proc. C.M.B. 21 Nov. 1795). Asst. Surg. 1 Mar. 1782; (B. Mily. Cons.). Surg. 29 Oct. 1794. *d.* at Kanchan Ghat, (Allahabad), 29 May 1804. First Maratha war, 1782. S.A.L.M.B. and D. and M. give date of appointment as 5 Apr. 1783.

278. Morris, Thomas (c). Asst. Surg. 2 Mar. 1782; (B. Mily. Cons. 4 Mar. 1782). Returned name as Surgeon of 'Warren'; (B. Mily. Cons. 26 Sept. 1782). Resigned in England; (Genl. L. from Court, 8 July 1795, paras. 12–14). S.A.L.M.B. and D. and M. say struck off 15 Nov. 1784. Second Maisur war, 1782.

279. Grant, James (b, c). Surgeon of 'Earl of Dartmouth,' 1780–82. Asst. Surg. 3 Mar. 1782; (B. Mily. Cons. 4 Mar. 1782). Permitted to accompany expedition to N.W. Coast of America, Jan. 1786; (B. Mily. Cons. 24 Jan. 1786). Granted three years' furlough on full pay for this purpose; (Fort Wm. Genl. L. of 6 Feb. 1786, paras. 27, 28). Did not rejoin. D. and M. give date of appointment as 15 Nov. 1784, and say struck off 1786. No further information. Second Maisur war, 1782.

280. Hunter, William (c, e). *b.* 1755. M.A. 1777; M.D. 1805, Mar. Coll. Ab. Came out as Surgeon's Mate of 'Neptune,' 1780, left sick at Madras; (Proc. C.M.B. 21 Nov. 1795). Asst. Surg. 4 Mar. 1782; (B. Mily. Cons). C.C.S. 1788. Surg. 21 Oct. 1794. S.S. 19 Jan. 1811. *d.* in Java, 15 Dec. 1812. S.A.L.M.B. and D. and M. give date of appointment as 6 Apr. 1783. Second Maisur war, 1782. Java war, 1811–12, capture of Java, 1811, and of Palembang, 1812; (P. R.). Author of Concise Account of Kingdom of Pegu, 1785; Diseases of Indian Seamen, 1804; Hindustani and English Dictionary, 1808. v. Hist. of I.M.S. i. 207.

281. Saunders, Robert (c). C.C.S. 1780. Asst. Surg. 13 Mar. 1782; (B. Mily. Cons. 3 July 1782). Accompanied Capt. Turner's mission to Tibet, 1783–84; (B. Mily. Cons. 13 Mar. 1783). Resigned, 16 July 1790; (M.S. Casualty List for 1790). S.A.L.M.B. and D. and M. give date of appointment as 12 May 1782, and resignation, 6 Feb. 1791. Name is also in S.A.L.M.M. where it is spelt Sanders. First Maratha war, 1782, under Genl. Goddard. Contributed Observations Botanical Mineralogical and Medical, to Capt. Turner's Account of an Embassy to the Teshoo Lama in Tibet, 1800.

282. Shaw, John (e). Surgeon's Mate of 'Earl of Dartmouth,' 1780–82, lost on Car Nicobar, 24 June 1782, and of 'Resolution.' Asst. Surg. 18 Mar. 1782; (B. Mily. Cons. 1 Apr. 1782). C.C.S. 1785. Surg. 21 Oct. 1794. Invalided, 1 Nov. 1815. d. 21 Mar. 1816. S.A.L.M.B. and D. and M. give date of appointment as 7 Apr. 1783.

*****283. Ivory, Patrick** (b, c). M.A. 1770; M.D. 1773, Paris. C.C.S.; (Proc. C.M.B. 21 Nov. 1795). Surgeon of 'Valentine,' 1781–82. Asst. Surg. 1 Apr. 1782; (B. Mily. Cons.). Surg. 21 Oct. 1794. Retired, 17 Mar. 1802; (S.A.L.M.B.). d. in London, 28 May 1810. S.A.L.M.B. and D. and M. give date of appointment as 8 Apr. 1783, no date of retirement in D. and M.

284. Gillman, John (c). b. 1760. Had been a medl. student at Barts., but had no medical qualifications. Cadet Bo. Infy. Apr. 1781. Asst. Surg. 6 Apr. 1782, appointed by Sir Eyre Coote in Karnatak; (Proc. C.M.B. 21 Apr. 1795). Ranked from 22 May 1782; (B. Mily. Cons. 27 Feb. 1783). Surg. 21 Sept. 1795. S.S. 17 Dec. 1811. M.M.B. 30 Jan. 1817. Retired, 24 Mar. 1824. d. at Cheltenham, 8 Jan. 1830. Second Maisur war, 1781–82. Nipal war, 1815–16, as S.S.

285. Burt, Adam. C.C.S. 1779. Asst. Surg. 13 May 1782. Surg. 21 Oct. 1794. Head Surg. 17 July 1806. M.D.St.A. 1808. L.R.C.P. and F.R.C.P. Ed. 1809. M.M.B. 29 Sept. 1814. d. in Calcutta, 20 Dec. 1814. Author of Biliary complaints of Europeans in Bengal, 1785.

286. Watts, Thomas. Said to have been originally appointed to Madras; (Proc. C.M.B. 24 July 1789). C.C.S. 1780. Asst. Surg. 14 May 1782. d. at Bangalore, 8 Jan. 1792. Second Maisur war, 1782. Third Maisur war, 1791–92.

†**287. Kelly, Michael** (a). C.C.S. 1781. Asst. Surg. 15 May 1782; (B. Mily. Cons. 14 Jan. 1783). Noted as dead in Proc. C.M.B. 8 July 1788.

288. Hitchin, Edward (a, b). C.C.S. 1781. Surgeon of 'Nottingham,' 1782. Asst. Surg. 16 May 1782; (B. Mily. Cons. 14 Jan. 1783). Noted as dead in Proc. C.M.B. 8 July 1788.

289. Gaulland (or **Galland**), **George Bretland** (a). C.C.S. 1781. Asst. Surg. 17 May 1782; (B. Mily. Cons. 14 Jan. 1783). Noted as dead in Proc. C.M.B. 8 July 1788. Name spelt Galland in Roll of Corp. Surg.

---

* Though holding a commission as Asst. Surg. Patrick Ivory was still serving as Surg. of 'Valentine' in 1784–85, of 'Berrington' in 1786–87.

† Bengal Mily. Cons. 14 Jan. 1783; Adam Burt, 13 May 1782; T. Watts, 14 May; M. Kelly, 15 May; E. Hitchin, 16 May; G. B. Galland, 17 May; F. Rendall, 18 May; A. Duncan, 19 May; C. Frazer, 20 May; A. Dalziel, 21 May.

INDIAN MEDICAL SERVICE [1782

*290. Rundell (or **Rendall**), **Francis.** *b.* 1749. C.C.S. 1782. Asst. Surg. 18 May 1782; (B. Mily. Cons. 14 Jan. 1783, where name is spelt Rendall). *d.* in Calcutta, on board ' Queen,' 2 Sept. 1791; (Hickey, iv. p. 493), also tombstone in S. Park St. D. and M. say, *d.* at sea, Sept. 1791. S.A.L.M.B. Hickey, B. and M. and Roll Coll. Surg. spell name Rundell.

291. Duncan, Alexander (b). C.C.S. 1781. Surg. Mate, ' London,' 1780–81. Asst. Surg. 19 May 1782; (B. Mily. Cons. 14 Jan. 1783). Sick leave to Canton, to visit his brother, Surgeon to Canton factory; (Proc. C.M.B. 29 Dec. 1786). Officiating Surg. at Canton, 14 Jan. 1788; (Proc. C.M.B. 25 Mar. 1788). Struck off 2 Dec. 1790, having been appointed Surg. at Canton; (C.G. 2 Dec. 1790). Name out of China list, 1800. D. and M., and S.A.L.M.B. say resigned, 1793. China No. 9.

292. Dalzell, Alexander. C.C.S. 1781. Asst. Surg. 21 May 1782; (B. Mily. Cons. 14 Jan. 1783). *d.* at Prince of Wales Island, 9 Aug. 1788; (M.S. Army List, 1 Nov. 1788). S.A.L.M.B. and D. and M. give date of death as 9 Aug. 1787.

†293. MacCulloch, William (a, c). Asst. Surg. 22 May 1782; (B. Mily. Cons. 12 June 1783). Out of list in 1800. Name not in list of final settlement of rank in 1797. No further information. Name not in Genl. Stibbert's list of 12 Nov. 1783. Perhaps same as No. 342, Frederick MacCulloch. S.A.L.M.B. gives 1784 as date of commission.

294. Bever, Robert (a). C.C.S. (Calendar, 1777). Asst. Surg. 24 May 1782; (B. Mily. Cons. 12 June 1783). Noted as dead in Proc. C.M.B. 8 July 1788. No further information.

295. Borradaile, Joseph (a). Asst. Surg. 25 May 1782; (B. Mily. Cons. 12 June 1783). Noted as dead in Proc. C.M.B. 8 July 1788. Second Maisur war, 1782. No further information.

296. Hudson, John (a). Asst. Surg. 28 May 1782; (B. Mily. Cons. 12 June 1783). Name not in Genl. Stibbert's list of 12 Nov. 1783. Apparently still living in 1788, as name occurs in Proc. C.M.B. 8 July 1788, with no note against name. No further information.

297. Davis, John (a). Asst. Surg. 23 June 1782; (B. Mily. Cons. 4 and 14 Nov. 1782). Name in list of 1786. *d.* Dec. 1786; ("lately," C.G. 28 Dec. 1786). Name spelt Darris in S.A.L.M.B. Second Maisur war, 1782.

298. Williams, John (b, c). C.C.S. 1776, or earlier. Surgeon of ' Seahorse,' 1771–72; of ' Queen,' 1774–76; of ' Hawke,' 1777–78; • of ' Colebrooke,' 1778; of ' Hawke,' 1779; left sick in China. Asst. Surg. 9 Sept. 1782; (B. Mily. Cons.). Surg. 22 Sept. 1795. *d.* at Cawnpur, 20 July 1808.

299. Paton (or **Patton**), **George.** Asst. Surg. 4 Nov. 1782. C.C.S. 1783. *d.* at Chittagong, 4 June 1788; (C.G. 12 June 1788). S.A.L.M.B. and D. and M. call him George Patton, and say *d.* 1789.

* Francis Rundell managed the Calcutta theatre with great success in 1784, a very good actor; (Hickey's Memoirs, vol. iii. pp. 206–208).
† Bengal Mily. Cons. 12 June 1783; Wm. MacCulloch, 22 May 1782; W. Ogilvy, 23 May; Robt. Bever, 24 May; Joseph Borradaile, 25 May; C. Coote, 26 May; T. Phillips, 27 May; John Hudson, 28 May.

INDIAN MEDICAL SERVICE [1783

300. Rowland, (or Rolland), John (b). Surgeon of 'Norfolk,' 1771–73; of 'Ankerwyke,' 1775–76; of 'Stormont,' 1777–78, and 1780–81. Asst. Surg. 4 Nov. 1782. *d.* at Jaunpur, 5 May 1789; (M.S. Casualty list of 1789, where name is spelt Rolland). In all other cases in records is spelt Rowland. D. and M. spell name Rolland, and give date of death as 5 July 1789. In Service Army Lists Medl. Bengal, the name John Mowland, No. 38, App, 1784, is probably the same man. S.A.L.M.B. gives name thrice, as John Rolland, A.S. 4 Nov. 1782, *d.* at Jaunpur, 5 July 1789; and as John Rowland, A.S. 6 Jan. 1783, nothing more; as well as John Mowland.

301. Young, Alexander (b, c). Surgeon's Mate of 'Earl of Dartmouth,' 1781–82, lost on Car Nicobar, 24 June 1782. Asst. Surg. 4 Nov. 1782; (B. Mily. Cons.). *d.* at Burragon, (Baragaon in Ballia), 9 Dec. 1789.

302. MacRae, or MacRa, John (c). *b.* 3 Nov. 1760. Went out to Madras in 1782 as Hosp. Mate in Genl. Hosp., with troops under Genl. Medows; (Proc. C.M.B. 21 Nov. 1795). Name not in Johnston's Roll of R.A.M.C. Asst. Surg. 16 Dec. 1782; (B. Mily. Cons.). C.C.S. 1787. Gave up promotion to remain at Barisal. Also Sub. Asst. Commy. Genl. 1812–23. *d.* at Barisal, 8 Oct. 1823. Father of John MacRae, No. 1030, infra. D. and M. spell name Macra, and give date of appointment as 13 Apr. 1783. S.A.L.M.B. and Roll Coll. Surg. spell name Macrae, S.A.L.M.B. gives date of appointment as 13 Apr. 1784. Second Maisur war, 1782.

*****303. Williams, Walter** (b, c). Surg. Mate, 'Shrewsbury,' 1775–77. Surgeon of 'Norfolk,' 1779–82. Asst. Surg. 18 Dec. 1782; (B. Mily. Cons. 14 Jan. 1783). Surg. 23 Sept. 1795. Retired, 12 June 1811. *d.* in London, 31 May 1820. D. and M. give date of appointment as 14 Apr. 1783.

*****304. Stokes, Thomas Luke** (b, c). Surgeon of 'Trial,' 1781–82. Asst. Surg. 19 Dec. 1782; (B. Mily. Cons. 14 Jan. 1783). Surg. 24 Sept. 1795. Retired, 19 Aug. 1807; (C.G. 16 Nov. 1809). S.A.L.M.B and D. and M. give date of appointment as 15 Apr. 1783, and of retirement as 9 Sept. 1807.

*****305. Burgh, or Brugh, John** (c). Went to India in 1782, in 'Worcester,' as a Volunteer for Army; (Proc. C.M.B. 21 Nov. 1795). Asst. Surg. 20 Dec. 1782; (B. Mily. Cons. 14 Jan. 1783). Entered under name of Burgh, resumed spelling Brugh by G.O. of 2 Apr. 1793. Surg. 19 May 1796. Third Maisur war, 1790–92. Second Maratha war, 1803–04. Killed near Fatehpur Sikri in Menson's retreat, 29 Aug. 1804; (C.G. 11 Oct. 1804). D. and M. spell name Bragh, give date of appointment as 16 Apr. 1783, and say died at Sekundra, Aug. 1804.

306. Moirene, John. Asst. Surg. 1782. *d.* at Barrackpur, 13 Aug. 1784; S.A.L.M.B. and D. and M. also C.G. 19 Aug. 1784, where name is spelt Dr. Moraine). Probably the same as Alexander Morraine, No. 308.

1783

307. Wilson, Robert (b, c). C.C.S. 1776. Surg. 'Hawke,' 1779–80. Surgeon of 'Blandford,' 1781–83. Asst. Surg. 18 Jan. 1783. Surg. 18 Mar. 1802. S.S. 4 Jan. 1815. M.D. K.C. Ab. 1815. Retired, 6 June 1819. *d.* in London, 17 Apr. 1822 (A.J. May 1822).

* B. Mily. Cons. 14 Jan. 1783; John, corrected to Walter, Williams, 18 Dec.; T. L. Stokes, 19 Dec.; John Burgh, 20 Dec.

1783] INDIAN MEDICAL SERVICE

*308. Morine, or **Morraine,** or **Morris, Alexander** (b, c). Surgeon of ' Rochford,' 1780–83, where name is given as Alex. MacMorine. Asst. Surg. 10 Mar. 1783, where name is given as Alex. Morris. Leave to sea B. Mily. Cons. 2 Aug. 1784, where name is spelt Alex. Morine. Name in Genl. Stibbert's List of 12 Nov. 1783, where spelt Alex. Morine. No further information. Probably same as John Moirene, No. 306 ; the two names do not occur simultaneously in any record.

309. Orrock, or **Orrok, James** (b, c). b. 1758. Surgeon of ' Ganges,' 1779–82. Asst. Surg. 10 Mar. 1783 ; (B. Mily. Cons. 10 Mar. 1783, where name is spelt Orrock). d. at Chitpur, Calcutta, 25 June 1788 ; (tombstone in S. Park St., where name is spelt Orrok). S.A.L.M.B. and D. and M. give date of appointment as 15 Nov. 1784, and of death as 4 June 1789. C.G. of 3 July 1788, says d. " recently " in Genl. Hosp., and spells name Orrik.

310. Davidson, George (b, c). Surgeon of ' Seahorse,' 1768–69 ; of ' Lord Camden,' 1770–71 ; of ' Earl of Ashburnham,' 1772 ; of ' Lord Holland,' 1778–79 ; of ' Latham,' 1781–83. C.C.S. 1783. Asst. Surg. 10 Mar. 1783. Surg. 13 Mar. 1797. d. on board ' Huddart ' on passage to England, 8 Feb. 1814.

311. Campbell, James (c). M.D.St.A. 1781. Asst. Surg. 10 Mar. 1783. L.R.C.P. Ed. 1785. F.R.C.P. Ed. 1786. M.R.C.S. Surg. 14 Mar. 1797. d. at Barrackpur, 4 May 1817. S.A.L.M.B. gives date of commission as 18 Apr. 1783.

312. Russell, Alexander (b, c). C.C.S. 1780. Surgeon of ' Locke,' 1781–82 : (Proc. C.M.B. 21 Nov. 1795 ; in Hardy's Register of ships name is given as Robert Russell). Asst. Surg. 10 Mar. 1783. Surg. 30 Oct. 1797. S.S. 21 Dec. 1814. M.D. Mar. Coll. Ab. 1819. M.M.B. 17 Mar. 1823. Retired, 8 Mar. 1825. d. in London, 9 May 1826.

313. Cooper, William S (c, d). C.C.S. 1781. Asst. Surg. 10 Mar. 1783. S.A.L.M.B. and D. and M. give date of appointment as 15 Nov. 1784, and say " resigned," without any date. No further information. Name not in Genl. Stibbert's list of 12 Nov. 1783, where name of Wm. Smith is given in his place (No. 320, q.v.). Apparently never joined. Date of appointment given as 15 Nov. 1784 in S.A.L.M.B.

314. Jones, William (c). Asst. Surg. 10 Mar. 1783. Dismissed by Court Martial, 9 Oct. 1783. S.A.L.M.B. and D. and M. give no date of commission.

315. Wilkins, David, or **Thomas** (b, c). Surgeon of ' Ann and Emilia,' 1782–83. Asst. Surg. 10 Mar. 1783 ; (B. Mily. Cons. 10 Mar. 1783, where first name is given as Thomas). d. at Chunar, 27 Mar. 1792. S.A.L.M.B. and D. and M. give date of appointment as 20 Apr. 1783, and Christian name as David.

316. Davidson, William (b, c). Surg. Mate, ' Calcutta,' 1771–72. Surgeon of ' Calcutta,' 1774–76 and 1778–81. Asst. Surg. 10 Mar. 1783. Surg. 20 Oct. 1797. Gave up promotion to remain at Sylhet, and reverted to Asst. Surg. 27 Mar. 1799. Resigned, 7 Jan. 1803.

* B. Mily. Cons. 10 Mar. 1783, G.O. 16 Mar. 1783. The following persons, recommended by the Surg. Genl. to be appointed Asst. Surgeon, to rank after the Asst. Surgeons appointed by the Court this year, in the following order : Alex. Morris, Jas. Orrock, George Davidson, Jas. Campbell, Alex. Russell, Wm. Cooper, Wm. Jones, Thos. Wilkins, Wm. Davidson, Thos. Clarke, Wm. Cooke, Thos. Powles.

317. **Clarke, Thomas** (a, b, c). Surgeon of ' Earl of Chesterfield,' 1781–83. Asst. Surg. 10 Mar. 1783. Name in Genl. Stibbert's list of 12 Nov. 1783. Noted as dead in Proc. C.M.B. 8 July 1788. Perhaps same as T. Clarke, No. 371.

318. **Cooke, William** (b, c). *b.* 1760. Surgeon of ' Rodney,' 1781–82. Asst. Surg. 10 Mar. 1783. Surg. 7 Dec. 1797. *d.* on board ' Surrey,' on passage to England, 14 Feb. 1815. Third Maisur war, 1790–92.

319. **Powles, Thomas** (c). Asst. Surg. 10 Mar. 1783. Dismissed by Court Martial " for behaviour unbecoming the character of an officer and a gentleman "; (B. Mily. Cons. 30 May 1784). S.A.L.M.B. gives name as James Powles.

320. **Smith, William** (a). Asst. Surg. 10 Mar. 1783, to take place of Wm. Cooper; (B. Mily. Cons. 28 Apr. 1783). *d.* Feb. 1785; (Advt. of estate of late Asst. Surg. William Smith in C.G. of 10 Mar. 1785).

321. **MacEvoy, John** (a, b). Surg. ' Duke of Kingston,' 1780–81. Asst. Surg. 15 Mar. 1783, appointed by Court. Name not in Genl. Stibbert's list of 12 Nov. 1783. No further information. Doubtful if ever joined.

322. **Meik, James.** *b.* 1759. C.C.S. 1783. Asst. Surg. 16 Mar. 1783. Surg. 20 May 1796. S.S. 17 Dec. 1812. M.M.B. 21 Jan. 1819. President, 28 Feb. 1826. R. 21 Feb. 1829. *d.* in Calcutta, 25 Apr. 1837. D. and M. spell name Meick. S.A.L.M.B. spells Meek, also spelt Meek in Roll of Corp. Surg. Third Maratha or Pindari war, 1817–18, as S.S.

323. **Rankin, George.** C.C.S. 1782. Asst. Surg. 17 Mar. 1783. Surg. 21 May 1796. S.S. 30 Sept. 1814. R. 30 Apr. 1817. *d.* in Edinburgh, 17 Feb. 1819. Probably same as Asst. Surg. Rankin, who served at siege of Malie in 1779; (M. Mily. Cons. 22 Apr. 1779). Java war, 1811, capture of Java. M. No. 221.

324. **Corse, afterwards Corse Scott, John.** C.C.S. 1783. Hosp. Mate, H.M's. South Fencible Regt. 1 Sept. 1779 to Apr. 1783, also Ensign from 1781 to Apr. 1783, when regt. was disbanded; (Proc. C.M.B. 21 Aug. 1796). Asst. Surg. 18 Mar. 1783. Surg. 22 May 1796. R. 30 July 1800. F.R.S. 16 Jan. 1800. Afterwards took name of Corse-Scott. D. and M. say retired, 1801. Author of Observations on different species of Asiatic Elephants, 1799.

325. **Smith, John.** C.C.S. 1777. Asst. Surg. 19 Mar. 1783. Surg. 23 May 1796. R. 11 June 1806. *d.* 8 Mar. 1827.

326. **Pye, Richard.** Asst. Surg. 20 Mar. 1783. *d.* 23 Mar. 1792, at Fort Marlborough; (S. Cons. of that day). *d.* at Fort Marlborough, Bencoolen, 19 Aug. 1792; (M.S. casualty list, 1792). D. and M. say died at Bencoolen, 11 Sept. 1792.

327. **Wood, John.** C.C.S. 1783. Asst. Surg. 21 Mar. 1783. *d.* at Fatehgarh, 10 June 1791; (M.S. casualty list, 1791). S.A.L.M.B. and D. and M. give date of death as 10 June 1790.

328. **Smith, James** (b). Surgeon of ' Nassau,' 1778–80. Asst. Surg. 22 Mar. 1783. Surg. 24 May 1796. R. 22 Oct. 1806. *d.* 10 Feb. 1807; (C.G. 26 Nov. 1807). Second Maratha war, 1802–05, severely wounded in action near Sarsang Fort, 7 Jan. 1803.

329. Turnbull, Peter (a, b). C.C.S. 1780. Surg. Mate, ' Stormont,' 1777–78. Surg. of ' Ponsborne,' 1780–82. Asst. Surg. 23 Mar. 1783. *d.* 9 Sept. 1788 ; (S.A.L.M.B.).

330. Bright, Edward. Asst. Surg. 23 Mar. 1783. *d.* in Calcutta, 25 July 1789.

331. MacLeod, Gilbert. *b.* 1759. C.C.S. 1783. Asst. Surg. 24 Mar. 1783. Surg. 25 May 1796. Gave up promotion to remain at Tippera, and reverted to Asst. Surg. 2 Feb. 1799. Applied to retire on half pay, Jan. 1805, refused, as he had given up promotion ; (Cal. Pub. L. 18 Jan. 1805, paras. 321–324). Went to England on ' Marquis Wellesley.' 1805. *d.* in London, 6 Aug. 1818 ; (G.M. Oct. 1818).

332. Gardiner, William (a, b). Surg. ' Royal Charlotte,' 1781–82. Asst. Surg. 24 Mar. 1783. *d.* Nov. 1786 ; ("lately," C.G. of 30 Nov. 1786. where name is spelt Gardner).

333. Casement, Thomas (b). *b.* 1754. C.C.S. 1783. Surg. ' Lord North,' 1781–82. Asst. Surg. 25 Mar. 1783. Surg. 26 May 1796. R. 4 Dec. 1806 ; (C.G. 16 Nov. 1809). S.A.L.M.B. and D. and M. give date of retirement as 30 Jan. 1807.

334. Arthur, James, or **David** (a). C.C.S. 1783. Asst. Surg. 25 Mar. 1783. *d.* in Calcutta, 22 May 1786, aged 49 (De Rosario). In Cal. Cons. of 14 Feb. 1787, Christian name given as David.

335. Turner, Edward. C.C.S. 1783. Asst. Surg. 26 Mar. 1783. Surg. 27 May 1796. *d.* in England 30 Dec. 1810. Second Maratha war, 1803–05.

336. Fyffe, Charles. C.C.S. 1873. Asst. Surg. 27 Mar. 1783. Surg. 28 May 1796. Invalided, 28 Aug. 1806. *d.* in Calcutta, 28 May 1810. His name is also entered in S.A.L.M.B. as Charles Tyffe.

337. Toshach, George. Asst. Surg. 28 Mar. 1783. Surg. 29 May 1796. Lost on or about 14 Mar. 1809, in ' Lady Jane Dundas,' which parted company from homeward bound fleet on that day, and was not heard of again. Name spelt Toshech in S.A.L.M.M. Third Maisur war, 1791–92.

338. Nasmyth, James. C.C.S. 1783. M.D. Ed. 1783. Asst. Surg. 29 Mar. 1783. Surg. 30 May 1796. Furlough, Aug. 1797 ; (Mily. L. from B. 28 Aug. 1797, para. 92). Did not rejoin. Struck off, 8 Feb. 1808 ; (C.G. 9 Mar. 1808). Probably then dead. D. and M. say "out of service, having exceeded his period of furlough," without date.

339. Kearns, Michael. Asst. Surg. 30 Mar. 1783. Resigned, 1794.

340. Todd, Charles. C.C.S. 1783. Asst. Surg. 31 Mar. 1783. Surg. 31 May 1796. Gave up promotion to remain at Rungpur, and reverted to Asst. Surg. 27 Mar. 1799. Resigned, Feb. 1808.

341. Johnson, William. C.C.S. 1783. Asst. Surg. 1 Apr. 1783. Acted as Surgeon of ' Dutton,' on voyage to India, charged with mutiny on board ; (Cal. Cons. 27 Oct. and 22 Nov. 1785), presumably acquitted. *d.* Sept. 1795, on passage home on ' Hawkesbury ' ; (C.G. 10 Sept. 1795).

342. MacCulloch, Frederick (c). Went to India as Surgeon's Mate of 23rd, afterwards 19th Light Dragoons; (Proc. C.M.B. 21 Nov. 1795). Asst. Surg. 14 Apr. 1783; (B. Mily. Cons.). *d.* Sept. 1796 (?); (Advt. of estate of late Asst. Surg. Frederick. McCulloch in C.G. of 22 Sept. 1796). Second Maisur war, 1781–82, in 19th Light Dragoons.

343. Gray, Alexander (c). Served as Surgeon in R.N. for five years; (Proc. C.M.B. 25 Nov. 1794). Was Surgeon of H.M.S. 'Pondicherry'; (Bo. Cons. 5 Feb. 1783). A.S. 15 Apr. 1783. Surg. 17 June 1799. *d.* in Calcutta, 26 July 1807. Left £30,000 to town of Elgin; (G.M. Jan. 1810), which was used to found and endow Gray's Hospital, Elgin. v. Hist. of I.M.S. ii. 77. Second Maisur war, 1790–92. Second Rohilla war, 1794, battle of Bitaura, 26 Oct. 1794.

344. Gilpin, James (b, c). Surgeon of 'Ceres,' 1782–83. Asst. Surg. 16 Apr. 1783; (B. Mily. Cons. 15 Apr. 1783). Resigned, 17 Sept. 1792.

345. Boyd, William (b, c). M.D. Ed. 1780. Surgeon's Mate of 'Nassau,' 1780–82; (Proc. C.M.B. 21 Nov. 1795). Asst. Surg. 17 Apr. 1783; (B. Mily. Cons. 15 Apr. 1783). *d.* at Buxar, 25 June 1800. In Muster Roll of 1st Brigade for 1787, is said to have joined at Calcutta in 1778.

346. Ewart, Peter (b, c). Surgeon of 'Alfred,' 1782–83. Asst. Surg. 28 Apr. 1783; (B. Mily. Cons.). Surg. 29 Oct. 1801. R. 26 Aug. 1806; (C.G. 16 Nov. 1809). S.A.L.M.B. and D. and M. give date of retirement as 26 Nov. 1806.

347. Anderson, William (c). Ed. Univ. C.C.S. 1782. Asst. Surg. 2 June 1783; (B. Mily. Cons. 2 June 1783). Surg. 2 Jan. 1802. R. 18 Dec. 1802. *d.* 1 Jan. 1847. D. and M. give date of appointment as 28 Apr. 1783.

348. Gibb, Alexander (b, c). *b.* 1761. M.A. 1779; M.D. 1815; Mar. Coll. Ab. Surgeon of 'Dutton,' 1782–83. Asst. Surg. 30 June 1783; (B. Mily. Cons.). Surg. 15 Oct. 1802. S.S. 12 Dec. 1815. M.M.B. 8 Mar. 1825. President, 20 June 1828. *d.* in Calcutta, 3 June 1829; (tombstone in S. Park St.). D. and M. give name as Alex. Gibbs, and date of death as 3 June 1828. Nipal war, 1815, as S.S. Third Maratha or Pindari war, 1817–18, as S.S.

349. Turnbull, Gawen (b, c). C.C.S. 1776. Surgeon of 'Royal Henry,' 1777–81, of 'Rodney,' 1782–83. Asst. Surg. 17 July 1783; (B. Mily. Cons.). Resigned, 6 Feb. 1798; (S.A.L.M.B.). D. and M. give date of retirement as 6 Feb. 1789. He was granted leave to Europe, with permission to return, in B. Genl. L. of 22 Dec. 1788 para. 14; went home as Surg. of 'Phoenix,' and permitted to return to India, (Mily. L. from Court, 11 Mar. 1791, para. 5).

*350. Stewart, Henry (c). Asst. Surg. 7 Aug. 1783; (B. Mily. Cons. 21 Aug. 1783). *d.* at Dinapur, 25 July 1792.

351. Martin, Thomas (c). Asst. Surg. 8 Aug. 1783. Cashiered by Court Martial at Barhampur, 16 Feb. 1793; (G.O. 5 Mar. 1793, Proc. C.M.B. 20 Mar. 1793). v. Hist. of I.M.S. ii. 231, 232. S.A.L.M.B. and D. and M. give date of appointment as 1 May 1783.

* B. Mily. Cons. 21 Aug. 1783, G.O. 24 Aug. 1783. Asst. Surgeons appointed if found qualified on exam. by Surg. Genl. Hy. Stewart, 7 Aug.; Thos. Martin, 8 Aug.; Thos. Cooper, this day, 21 Aug.; Geo. Frazer, 22 Aug.

352. **Ross, James** (c). M.A. Mar. Coll. Ab. 1777. Surgeon R.N. before joining, Surg. H.M.S. 'Bountiful'; (Mad. Cons. 3 June 1783). Asst. Surg. 11 Aug. 1783; (B. Mily. Cons.). Surgeon. 31 Dec. 1802. R. 19 July 1804. d. at Exeter, 22 July 1831. Author of Translation of Gulistan, 1823.

353. **Cooper, Thomas** (a, b, c). Surgeon of 'Colebrooke,' 1771–72; of 'Royal Bishop,' 1782–83. Asst. Surg. 21 Aug. 1788. d. Oct. 1787; (Cal. Cons. 25 Oct. 1787).

354. **Frazer, or Fraser, George** (c). Asst. Surg. 22 Aug. 1783. d. at Shahabad, 5 Jan. 1800; (S.A.L.M.B.). D. and M. give same date of death, but place as Calcutta.

355. **Mowbray, William** (c). Asst. Surg. 28 Aug. 1783; (B. Mily. Cons.). d. at Ramgarh (Hazaribagh), 11 Oct. 1785. D. and M. give date of appointment as 1782.

356. **Barday, John.** (b, c). Surgeon of 'Duke of Grafton,' 1776–78. M.D. Ed. 1784. Asst. Surg. 29 Aug. 1783; (B. Mily. Cons. 28 Aug. 1783). d. at Buxar, 2 Dec. 1791.

357. **Alexander, John** (c). b. 1763. Asst. Surg. 4 Sept. 1783; (B. Mily. Cons.). d. at Midnapur, 1 Mar. 1792; (tombstone). D. and M. say died at Monghyr, 31 Jan. 1792.

358. **Church, Robert** (c). Asst. Surg. 16 Sept. 1783; (B. Mily. Cons.). Granted three years' leave to England without pay, 16 Feb. 1785; (B. Mily. Cons.). Went home as Surg. Mate of 'Marquis of Lansdowne.' Did not rejoin. Struck off, 1793. S.A.L.M.B. gives date of commission as 7 May 1783.

359. **Fontana, Nicolas** (c). Asst. Surg. 20 Oct. 1783; (B. Mily. Cons. which give initial as D.). R. 29 Oct. 1800. d. 1812. D. and M. give date of appointment as 8 May 1783, and say "not to be traced." His first name is given as Wm. in Fort Wm. Pub. L. of 30 Nov. 1783, para. 32, which reports his appointment; and surname is spelt Fontaine in Genl. Stibbert's list of 12 Nov. 1783. S.A.L.M.B. gives first name as Nicholas or William. Author of a work on poisons.

360. **Bingham, George** (c). Asst. Surg. 20 Oct. 1783; (B.M. Cons.). d. in Calcutta, 9 June 1793.

361. **Ferguson, Murdoch** (c). Asst. Surg. 20 Oct. 1783; (B.M. Cons.). d. at Chunargarh, 23 Aug. 1784. S.A.L.M.B. spells name Fergusson.

362. **Moore, William** (c). M.D. Ed. 1780. Asst. Surg. 5 Nov. 1783; (B. Mily. Cons.). d. at Barrackpur, 5 Apr. 1800. S.A.L.M.B. and D. and M. give date of appointment as 10 May 1783.

363. **Houston, Robert** (c). Asst. Surg. 13 Nov. 1783; (B. Mily. Cons.). d. at Cawnpur, 4 July 1793. D. and M. give date of appointment as 11 May 1783.

364. **Howison, James** (c). Asst. Surg. 13 Nov. 1783 (?). Surg. 5 Nov. 1802. R. 17 Sept. 1806; (C.G. 16 Nov. 1809). d. at Penang, May 1807; ("lately," C.G. 4 June 1807). S.A.L.M.B. and D. and M. give date of appointment as 12 May 1783, and of retirement, 3 Apr. 1807. Author of Malay Dictionary, 1801.

365. **Henderson, John** (e). Asst. Surg. 13 Nov. 1783 (?). Surg. 9 June 1803. R. 12 Aug. 1814. d. 26 May 1816. S.A.L.M.B. and D. and M. give date of appointment as 13 May 1783.

366. **Strahan, Alexander** (a, c). Asst. Surg. 8 Dec. 1783; (G.O. 11 Dec. 1783; Proc. C.M.B. 8 July 1788, which note " no account of him "). Noted as dead in M.S. Army List of 15 July 1788.

1784

367. **Kegan, Charles** (b, c). Surgeon of 'Major,' 1782, burned at Kalpi, 24 June 1782. Asst. Surg. 7 June 1784; (B.M. Cons.). Surg. 13 July 1803. R. 19 June 1807. d. at Bath, aged 72, 11 Mar. 1835; (A.J. Apr. 1835, p. 303). S.A.L.M.B. and D. and M. give date of appointment as 7 June 1783.

368. **D'Orival,** — (a). Asst. Surg. 24 June 1784. Appointed by Warren Hastings, at Lucknow, to Delhi Residency; (Cal. Cons. 3 Nov. 1785). No further information.

369. **Cooper, John.** b. 1762. C.C.S. 1787. A.S. Madras, 19 Aug. 1788 (M. Mily. Cons.). Transferred Bengal; (M. Mily. Cons. 20 Jan. 1789). A.S. Bengal, 29 Jan. 1789. d. at Barhampur, . . . 1795. M. No. 291.

1789

370. **Hamilton, John** (b, c). Surgeon of 'Ranger,' 1786–87; of 'Lord Hawkesbury,' 1788–89. C.C.S. 1789. A.S. 1 Jan. 1789. Surg. 27 Aug. 1803. S.S. 30 Jan. 1817. R.14 Oct. 1824. d. in England, 3 June 1828. D. and M. give date of retirement as 14 Oct. 1814.

371. **Clarke, Thomas** (d). A.S. 2 Jan. 1789. Ranked next Hamilton; (C.G. 24 Dec. 1795). D. and M. give date of appointment as 15 Nov. 1786. M.S. Army List of 1790 states " Appointed by Court, 1789, not arrived "; (Mily. L. from C. 8 Apr. 1789, paras. 120, 121). No further information. Apparently never joined.

372. **Desborough, Charles.** b. 1763. C.C.S. 1788. A.S. 3 Jan. 1789. Surg. 30 Sept. 1803. d. in Fort William, 30 Aug. 1816.

373. **Freeman, Daniel Spencer.** C.C.S. 1788. A.S. 4 Jan. 1789. d. at Cawnpur, 6 June 1799; (Proc. C.M.B. 7 Aug. 1799). D. and M. and S.A.L.M.B. give date of death as 8 June 1799.

374. **Robinson, John.** b. 1755. C.C.S. 1789. A.S. 5 Jan. 1789. R. on Ensign's half-pay, 25 Jan. 1804; (S.A.L.M.B.). d. 6 June 1819. Third Maisur war, 1791–92.

375. **Ogilvy, Alexander.** A.S. 6 Jan. 1789. C.C.S. 1790. Surg. 27 Aug. 1803. S.S. 1817. M.M.B. 28 Feb. 1826. President, 3 June 1829. R. 21 Jan. 1831. d. in London, 29 Nov. 1846. Third Maratha or Pindari war, 1817–18, as S.S.

376. **Yeld, Thomas.** b. 1767. C.C.S. 1789. A.S. 7 Jan. 1789. Surg. 30 Sept. 1803. Gave up promotion to remain at Benares, where he held appointment of Mint-Master. d. at Benares, 16 Sept. 1829; (v. A.J. Apr. 1830, p. 236).

377. **Stephens, Andrew.** b. 1760. Had served in R.N.; (tombstone in S. Park St.). A.S. 8 Jan. 1789. Surg. 30 Sept. 1803. d. in Calcutta, 26 Aug. 1806.

378. Robertson, James. M.D. Ed. 1788. C.C.S. 1789. A.S. 10 Jan. 1789. Surg. 13 Apr. 1804. S.S. 4 Sept. 1813. *d.* at Coolbarreah (Kulbaria, near Barhampur), 15 Sept. 1817; (C.G. 25 Sept. 1817). D. and M. give date of death as 6 Sept. 1817, also S.A.L.M.B.

379. Orr, John. C.C.S. 1789. A.S. 11 Jan. 1789. Surg. 12 Apr. 1804. *d.* at sea, 2 June 1813, on 'Chichester.' Capture of Colombo, 1796; Desp.; (Ceylon G.O. 13 Sept. 1803, A.J. 1803, Chronicle, p. 53, and Prize Rolls).

380. MacNab, James. A.S. 12 Jan. 1789. Surg. 30 May 1804. R. 12 Aug. 1818. S.A.L.M.B. spells name MacNabb.

381. Keys, Roger. *b.* 1763. C.C.S. 1789. A.S. 13 Jan. 1789. M.D. K.C. Ab. 1803. Surg. 30 May 1804. S.S. 29 Dec. 1815. *d.* at Mirat, 25 July 1823; (v. A.J. 1824, pp. 197, 211).

382. Inglis, Edward. C.C.S. 1789. A.S. 15 Jan. 1789. Surg. 21 Sept. 1804. *d.* at Nohmalla, Agra, 24 Sept. 1810.

*****383. Harper, William** (c). A.S. 16 Jan. 1789. Surg. 21 Sept. 1804. R. 17 Aug. 1807; (C.G. 16 Nov. 1809). D. and M. give date of retirement as 9 Sept. 1807.

384. Hare, James (c). M.D. Ed. 1782. A.S. 17 Jan. 1789. Surg. 21 Sept. 1804. Furlough, S.C. 1803. Struck off from 8 Feb. 1808; (C.G. 9 Mar. 1809), absent five years. Uncle of James M. Hare, No. 509.

†**385. Mercer, Graeme** (c). *b.* 4 July 1764. M.D. Ed. 1784. A.S. 18 Jan. 1789. Surg. 21 Sept. 1804. R. 30 Nov. 1814. *d.* at Mavisbank, Midlothian, 6 Oct. 1841. Third Maisur war, 1790–91. Second Maratha war, 1803–04. Resident with Scindia (Gwalior), 1807–10.

386. Morgan, Thomas (c). *b.* 1762. A.S. 19 Jan. 1789. Surg. 21 Sept. 1804. Gave up promotion and reverted to A.S. to remain at Nattore (Rajshahai); (C.G. 19 Dec. 1805). Name omitted from Army List in 1815.

387. Dow, Anthony (c). A.S. 20 Jan. 1789, to rank next Morgan; (Proc. C.M.B. 2 Dec. 1788). *d.* at Dinapur, 23 June 1791; (M.S. Army List, 1 Jan. 1792). S.A.L.M.B. and D. and M. give date of death as 23 June 1790, and date of appointment as 25 Jan. 1785.

388. Irving, Ralph (c). *b.* 1760. M.D. Ed. 1785. A.S. 20 Jan. 1789. *d.* at Monghyr, 1795; (tombstone). S.A.L.M.B. and D. and M. say, " died at sea, 1795."

389. Dyer, John (c). *b.* 1764. M.D. Mar. Coll. Ab. 1796. A.S. 21 Jan. 1789. Surg. 21 Sept. 1804. S.S. 1 June 1817. *d.* at Chauringhi, Calcutta, 16 Dec. 1820. Second Maratha war, 1803–04. Third Maratha or Pindari war, 1817–18.

390. Johnson, Daniel (c, e). *b.* 1767. A.S. 22 Jan. 1789. Surg. 11 Mar. 1805. R. 29 Apr. 1809. *d.* at Great Torrington, Devonshire, 19 Sept. 1835. Author of Sketches of Indian Field Sports, 1822; Observations on Cold, Fevers, and Other Diseases, 1823; and chapter on Customs of Natives of India in James Johnson's Influence of Tropical Climates on European Constitutions.

---

* Harper is stated to have been Surg. to a regiment of Light Dragoons; (Hickey's Memoirs, iii. 241). Name not in Johnston's Roll of R.A.M.C.

† It was while serving as Commandant of the Resident's (Mercer's) escort that Lieutenant, afterwards Colonel T. D. Broughton wrote the well-known Letters written in a Mahratta Camp.

391. **Howison, Nicholas** (b, c). Surg. ' Ganges,' 1783-84. A.S. 23 Jan. 1789, Sumatra, 27 Mar. 1789 ; (S. Cons.). *d.* at Fort Marlborough, 20 May 1793 ; (S. Cons.).

392. **Kennedy, John** (c). A.S. 24 Jan. 1789. *d.* in Calcutta, Dec. 1802 ; (tombstone in S. Park St.). D. and M. say *d.* 22 Nov. 1802, also S.A.L.M.B.

393. **Lewis, George** (b, c). *b.* 1750. C.C.S. 1782. Surgeon of ' Royal Charlotte,' 1784-87 ; of ' Dublin,' 1788-89. A.S. 27 Jan. 1879. *d.* in Calcutta, 17 Mar. 1790 ; (tombstone in S. Park St.). S.A.L.M.B. and D. and M. say *d.* 28 Feb. 1790.

394. **Denny, James.** C.C.S. 1782. Cadet, Bengal Inf., July 1783. Ensign, 21 Feb. 1785. A.S. 11 July 1789 ; (Mily L. from B. 10 Aug. 1789, where first name is given as Charles). Surg. 5 July 1805. R. 7 Oct. 1818. *d.* in London, 9 Mar. 1830. D. and M. give name both in Bengal Infantry and Medl. list.

395. **Drysdale, John.** C.C.S. 1789. A.S. 16 Dec. 1789. *d.* at Barhampur, 4 Sept. 1792 ; (M.S. casualty list for 1792). D. and M. give date of appointment as 1790, and of death as 11 Sept. 1792.

1790

396. **Fletcher, James** (a). C.C.S. 1790. M.D. Ed. 1790. A.S. 9 Jan. 1790. Furlough to England, 1797 ; (Mily. L. from B. 13 Mar. 1797, paras. 92-93). R. on half-pay, May 1800. *d.* 1800 ; (S.A.L.M.B.).

397. **Wood, David** (c). A.S. Madras, 18 June 1790 ; (Mad. Mily. Cons.). Confirmed by Court as A.S. Bengal from 3 Oct. 1790 ; (Mily. L. from C. 24 Mar. 1795, para. 83). *d.* at Boglepore (Bhagalpur), 5 Sept. 1796. D. and M. give name in Bengal, but not in Madras list. M. No. 322.

398. **Macdougal, James.** C.C.S. 1790. A.S. 10 Nov. 1790. *d.* at Goalpara, 14 June 1794.

1791

399. **Smith, John William.** A.S. 5 Jan. 1791. *d.* in Calcutta, 25 Sept. 1799. Name spelt Smyth in S.A.L.M.B., and date of commission given as 1790.

400. **Mitchell, Adam** (b). Surg. Mate, ' Dutton,' 1785-86. A.S. Madras, 2 Feb. 1791 ; (Mad. Mily. Cons.). A.S. Bengal, 30 Aug. 1791. Surg. 13 Dec. 1805. *d.* at Chunar, 23 Jan. 1809 ; (tombstone). S.A.L.M.B. and D. and M. say died in Bundlecund, Jan. 1809. Third Maisur war, 1791-92. M. No. 344.

401. **Wood, Robert** (a, b, d). A.S. 9 Feb. 1791. Never joined. ' Does not go " ; (Cadet Regr.). C.C.S. 1790. Surg. Mate, ' Exeter,' 1798-99.

402. **Clydsdale, James.** *b.* 1770. M.A. C.C.S. 1790. A.S. 9 Feb. 1791, in place of Robert Wood ; (Cadet Regr.). *d.* at Monghyr, 22 Aug. 1795 ; (tombstone, where name is spelt Clisdale). D. and M. give date of appointment as 1790, and say *d.* at Tanjepore, Aug. 1795. In S.A.L.M.B. name is spelt Clisdale, and date of appointment given as 1790 ; in Roll of Corp. Surg. spelt Clidsdale.

403. **Haig, Alexander** (b). Surgeon of ' Lord Macartney,' 1785-86 and 1788-90. A.S. 27 Aug. 1791. Surg. 4 Apr. 1805. Gave up promotion to remain at Nadiya, and reverted to A.S. ; (C.G. 10 Apr. 1806). R. 8 Jan. 1820 ; (C.G. 14 Dec. 1820 and E.I. Regr.). *d.* at Bath, 10 Nov. 1840. D. and M. give date of retirement as 8 Jan. 1830, also S.A.L.M.B.

404. Barnet, Henry (b). C.C.S. 1789. Surg. 'Busbridge,' 1789–90. A.S. 28 Aug. 1791. Surg. 23 Aug. 1805. Gave up promotion to remain at Baulea, Rajshahai, and reverted to A.S.; (C.G. 18 Jan. 1806). Omitted in list of 1816. Name spelt Barnett in S.A.L.M.B. and in Roll of Corp. Surg.

405. Allison, William (b). Surgeon of 'Pitt,' 1788–90. A.S. 27 Aug. 1791. R. on half-pay, 3 Aug. 1803. R. 15 June 1808; (E.I. Regr.).

406. De Vaumorel, John. C.C.S. 1790. A.S. 31 Aug. 1791. Surg. 9 Jan. 1806. *d.* in England, 22 Jan. 1809.

407. Campbell, Charles. A.S. Fort Marlborough Establishment, 1788. A.S. Bengal, 1 Sept. 1791. Surg. 27 May 1806. *d.* in Calcutta, 9 Jan. 1808. Third Maisur war, 1791–92.

408. Turnbull, David (b). *b.* 1768. Surg. Mate, 'Pitt,' 1788–90. C.C.S. 1790. A.S. 2 Sept. 1791. Declined promotion to remain at Mirzapur. On 27 Mar. 1809 was promoted to Surgeon, from 14 Jan. 1806. Again reverted to Asst. Surg. and reposted to Mirzapur; (C.G. 4 Mar. 1813). *d.* at Mirzapur, 14 Dec. 1822.

409. Powell, James. C.C.S. 1790. A.S. 3 Sept. 1791. *d.*, date unknown; (D. and M.). Sumatra, 1793. *d.* at Croee, Sumatra, May 1800; (S. Cons. 13 and 21 May 1800).

410. Thackeray, Henry. *b.* 1768. C.C.S. 1790. A.S. 4 Sept. 1801. Surg. 28 May 1806. Invalided, 28 July 1806. *d.* in Calcutta, 14 Aug. 1813. S.A.L.M.B. and D. and M. spell name Thackery.

411. Briars, John. C.C.S. 1787. A.S. 6 Sept. 1791. Became insane on voyage to India. Shown as insane in E.I. Regrs. up to 1804, name is omitted in 1805, probably dead. v. Hist. of I.M.S. i. 499. D. and M. spell name Briers, and say "left the Service, date not known."

1792

412. Whitefield, William (b). C.C.S. 1791. Surg. Mate, 'Triton,' 1790–91. A.S. 18 Feb. 1792. *d.* at Chunar, 13 Dec. 1793. Christian name given as William in S.A.L.M.B., also in Mily. L. from C. 14 Mar. 1792, para. 9, noting his appointment. D. and M. give first name as Thomas, and date of appointment as 1791. In S.A.L.M.B. both Thomas Whitefield, 1791, and William Whitfield, 1792, are given.

413. Deeks, John. A.S. 22 Feb. 1792. Transferred to Madras, in exchange with R. Riddick, No. 414; (Mily. L. from C. 12 Dec. 1792, para. 3). Arrived Madras, Dec. 1792; (Mad. Mily. Cons. 11 Dec. 1792). *d.* 1796. D. and M. give his name in Madras list, with date of appointment 22 Aug. 1792, but not in Bengal list. M. No. 360.

414. Riddick, Robert (b). C.C.S. 1789. Surg. Mate, 'Princess Amelia,' 1789–91. A.S. Madras, 22 Feb. 1792. Arrived Madras, 10 Aug. 1792; (Mad. Mily. Cons.). Transferred to Bengal in exchange with No. 413, John Deeks, to rank next to W. Whitefield; (Mily. L. from C. 12 Dec. 1792, para. 7). *d.* at Port Cornwallis, Andamans, Jan. 1796; (Proc. C.M.B. 10 Feb. 1796). D. and M. spell his name Reddick, include it in their Bengal, but not in Madras list, with date of appointment as 1791, and say "Died date not known." S.A.L.M.B. gives name twice, as Reddick, and as Robert Riddick; name spelt Reddick in Roll of Corp. Surg. M. No. 363.

415. **Ledlie, Thomas.** C.C.S. 1790. A.S. 15 July 1792. Surg. 11 Mar. 1806. R. 31 Dec. 1812. M.R.C.S. 1821. Third Maisur war, 1791–92.

416. **Ure, George** (b). Surgeon of snow, ' Intelligence,' 1785 ; of ' Melville Castle,' 1787–92. A.S. 10 Sept. 1792. Surg. 27 Aug. 1806. *d.* at Haidarabad, 11 Dec. 1806.

417. **Patch, John.** C.C.S. 1791. A.S. 11 Sept. 1792. Surg. 29 Aug. 1806. *d.* at Cuttack, 11 Apr. 1814.

418. **Moore, Ross** (b). *b.* 3 Aug. 1763. C.C.S. 1789. Surgeon of ' Carnatic,' 1788–89 ; of ' Triton,' 1790–91. A.S. 12 Sept. 1792. Surg. 29 Aug. 1806. *d.* at Midnapur, 16 Dec. 1806. Third Maisur war, 1791–92.

419. **Boutflower, Henry Johnson.** C.C.S. 1791. A.S. 14 Sept. 1792. Surg. 27 Aug. 1806. *d.* at Benares, 7 Nov. 1806. D. and M. give date of appointment as 4 Sept.

420. **O'Neal, William.** C.C.S. 1791. A.S. 15 Sept. 1792. Surg. 27 Aug. 1806. M.R.C.S. 1813. S.S. 24 Sept. 1817. *d.* on board ' Rockingham ' on passage to England, 14 Mar. 1819. Name spelt O'Neill in S.A.L.M.B., O'Neale in Roll of Corp. Surg.

421. **Reddie, George.** *b.* 1769. C.C.S. 1791. A.S. 16 Sept. 1792. Surg. 27 Aug. 1806. S.S. 23 June, 1818. *d.* at Cawnpur, 22 Sept. 1827. Was appointed to Medl. Board in 1827, but died before joining ; (G.M. Mar. 1828). Third Maratha or Pindari war, 1817–18 ; (P.R.). Bharatpur war, 1825–26, siege and storm of Bharatpur, as S.S. ; (P.R.).

422. **Dickson, Anthony.** C.C.S. 1792. A.S. 17 Sept. 1792. Surg. 29 Aug. 1806. S.S. 21 Jan. 1819. M.M.B. 20 June 1828. President, 21 Jan. 1831. R. 14 June 1832. *d.* at Plymouth, 22 Dec. 1855.

423. **Lowe, Robert.** C.C.S. 1792. A.S. 18 Sept. 1792. Surg. 17 Sept. 1806. S.S. 14 Mar. 1819. R. 29 June 1824. Java war, 1811, capture of Java, as Field Surgeon ; (P.R.).

424. **Richardson, Richard Samuel.** C.C.S. 1792. A.S. 19 Sept. 1792. Surg. 22 Oct. 1806. *d.* at Barrackpur, 21 Nov. 1818. Said to have been a native of India ; (Cadet Regr. ii. A) ; if so, was the first Indian appointed to the I.M.S. From his name, more probably an Eurasian. v. Hist. of I.M.S. i. 502.

425. **Williamson, Samuel** (a). A.S. 20 Sept. 1792. R. 23 Apr. 1802. In List of Asst. Surgeons, 1791–1814, date of appointment is given as 28 Feb. 1792, in S.A.L.M.B. as 20 Sept. 1791.

426. **Cheese, Michael.** *b.* 1757. C.C.S. 1790. A.S. 21 Sept. 1792. Surg. 8 Nov. 1806. *d.* in Fort William, 14 Jan. 1816. Originally appointed by Court to Bombay, in Mily. desp. of 4 Aug. 1791, but did not proceed ; (S.A.L.M. Bo.). Bo. No. 260.

427. **Law, John.** *b.* 1772. A.S. 22 Sept. 1792. Surg. 4 Dec. 1806. S.S. 17 Dec. 1820. *d.* at Barhampur, 22 Sept. 1828.

428. **Drury, James** (a). A.S. 1792 (?). Shown as A.S. Chunar in Muster Roll of Bengal Army for 1792. No further information.

429. **Hook, William** (a). A.S. 1792 (?). Shown as A.S. Batt. Sepoys, age 33, in Muster Roll of Bengal Army for 1793. No further information.

430. Burnett, Alexander (a). A.S. 1792 (?). Asst. Surg. Alex. Burnett permitted to return to duty; (Mily. L. from C. 4 June 1793, para. 7). No further information.

1794

431. Fraser, James (d). C.C.S. 1793. A.S. 19 Sept. 1794; (Mily. L. from C. 23 Apr. 1794, para. 6). Permitted to remain in England till next season; (Mily. L. from C. 11 June 1794, para. 5). Never joined.

432. Nisbett, or Nesbit, David. C.C.S. 1793. A.S. 20 Sept. 1794. Surg. 12 Dec. 1806. R. 12 July 1815. d. 13 Aug. 1865. D. and M. spell name Nesbit. S.A.L.M.B. spells it Nesbitt; also Roll of Corp. Surg.

433. Townsend, John. C.C.S. 1794. A.S. 21 Sept. 1794. d. in Hampshire, July 1806; (C.G. 2 July 1807).

434. Kean, Henry Bloomfield. C.C.S. 1794. Formerly Asst. Surg. R.N.; (Proc. C.M.B. 18 May 1795). A.S. 22 Sept. 1794. M.D. St. A. 1800. R. 9 Apr. 1802. d. 11 Nov. 1850.

435. Gardiner, James. Formerly Asst. Surg. British Army, for five months; (Proc. C.M.B. 18 May 1795). Name not in Johnston's Roll of R.A.M.C. A.S. 23 Sept. 1794. d. at Dinajpur, Sept. 1805. Name spelt Gardner in S.A.L.M.B.

*436. Robertson, Robert. C.C.S. 1793. A.S. 24 Sept. 1794. Surg. 17 Dec. 1806. d. at Ludhiana, 23 Aug. 1811; (from bite of a cobra, S.A.L.M.B.) S.A.L.M.B. and D. and M. give date of appointment as 24 Sept. 1793.

437. Muschet, Patrick. Glasgow Univ. M.F.P.S.G. 1790. C.C.S. 1793. A.S. 25 Sept. 1794. R. 14 Aug. 1805. M.D. St. A. 1815. d. at Stirling, 1837.

438. Buchanan, Francis, afterwards **Buchanan-Hamilton** (b, e). b. 15 Feb. 1762. M.A. Glasgow 1779. M.D. Ed. 1783. Surgeon of 'Duke of Montrose,' 1785–89; of 'Phoenix,' 1791–92; of 'Rose,' 1794. A.S. 26 Sept. 1794. Surg. 20 June 1807. R. 14 Aug. 1816. d. 15 June 1829. F.R.S. 1 May 1806. In 1818 took surname of Hamilton, on succeeding to his mother's property of Bardowie, on the death of his elder brother, Col. John Buchanan, and established his claim to the chieftainship of the Clan Buchanan in 1826. v. Life, by Lt.-Col. Sir D. Prain, No. 2188, and Hist. of I.M.S. ii. 62, 140. Author of A Journey from Madras, through Mysore, Canara and Malabar, 1808; Genealogies of Hindus, 1819; Kingdom of Nipal, 1819; Account of Ganges Fishes, 1822; Account of Dinajpur, 1833; and History, Antiquities, Topography, and Statistics of Eastern India, 1838, edited by and published under the name of Montgomery Martin. The MSS. both of Buchanan's great survey and report on Bihar and Northern Bengal, and of the daily journal from which the report was compiled, are among the India Office Records; Journal of Francis Buchanan, Survey of District of Patna and Gaya, edited by V. H. Jackson, 1927.

439. Morris, Robert (a, b, d). C.C.S. 1784. Surgeon of 'Essex,' 1785–86 and 1791–92; of 'Hawke,' 1787–88; of 'Wesley,' 1789–90; of 'Swallow,' 1792–94. A.S. 27 Sept. 1794; (Mily. L. from C. 3 July 1795, para. 5). Never joined. J. Shoolbred, No. 440, appointed in his place; (Mily. L. from C. 5 July 1797, para. 174). In list of Asst. Surgeons, 1791–1814, date of appointment is given as 20 Apr. 1795.

* The only case of death from snakebite recorded in the I.M.S.

440. Shoolbred, John (b). C.C.S. 1785. Surg. Mate, 'General Goddard, 1786–87; Surgeon 1789–90. A.S. 27 Sept. 1794. Surg. 27 July 1807. R. 17 Jan. 1821. *d.* 12 Oct. 1831; (C.G. 12 Mar. 1832).

441. Maclean, Hector (b, d). M.D. Mar. Coll. Ab. 1790. Surgeon of 'Airly Castle,' 1788–89; of 'Princess Amelia,' 1790–91; of 'Middlesex,' 1792–93. A.S. 28 Sept. 1794. Permitted to remain in England till next season; (Mily. L. from C. 11 June 1794, para. 3). Never joined. Appointed to A.M.D. Dy. Purveyor, St. Domingo, 1 June 1796. Asst. Inspector of Hosps., St. Domingo, 12 Oct. 1796. R. on half pay, 25 June 1802. *d.* 31 Aug. 1810. v. Johnston's Roll of R.A.M.C. No. 1504. Author of Mortality among troops at San Domingo, 1797.

442. Clunes, Archibald Campbell. C.C.S. 1793. A.S. 29 Sept. 1794. Drowned near Pattagottah (Purnea (?)). July 1805 (?). D. and M. give date of death as 15 Aug. 1805. The C.G. of 15 Aug. 1805, contains an advt. dated 25 July, of estate of late Asst. Surg. A. C. Clunes, Civil Surgeon, Purnea. The C.G. of 2 Oct. 1794, gives his name, on first appointment, as Andrew Carmichael Clunes.

443. Macaulay, Kenneth. C.C.S. 1793. A.S. 30 Sept. 1794. Surg. 17 Aug. 1807. *d.* at Gwalior, 17 Oct. 1813. Second Maratha war, 1803–04.

444. Jones, Springal. C.C.S. 1793. A.S. 1 Oct. 1794. *d.* in Bandalkund, 17 Sept. 1806.

445. Robinson, Charles. C.C.S. 1792. A.S. 2 Oct. 1794. Surg. 19 Aug. 1807. S.S. 3 Feb. 1822. M.M.B. 3 June 1829. President, 11 Mar. 1831. R. 1 Feb. 1834. *d.* at Stellenbosch, Cape Colony, 16 June 1835; (A.J. Nov. 1835, p. 132). Third Maratha or Pindari war, 1817–18; (P.R.).

446. Smith, John. C.C.S. 1793. A.S. 3 Oct. 1794. *d.* at Haidarabad, 29 Jan. 1798; (Bengal Directory, 1798). S.A.L.M.B. and D. and M. say *d.* at Shoopoorah, 29 Jan. 1798.

447. Durham, Samuel. C.C.S. 1794. A.S. 4 Oct. 1794. Surg. 1 Sept. 1807. S.S. 23 Feb. 1823. R. 28 July 1829. In C.G. of 2 Oct. 1794, his name, on appointment, is given as Samuel Durrand. Nipal war, 1815–16.

448. Fraser, Alexander (b). Surg. of 'Earl FitzWilliam,' 1790–91, of 'Duke of Montrose,' 1792–93. A.S. 5 Oct. 1794. Gave up promotion to remain at Gorakhpur; (C.G. 12 May 1808). Name shown in E.I. Regrs. as "at home" from 1820 to 1823, omitted in 1824.

449. Kelly, Alexander (d). A.S. 6 Oct. 1794. Appointment noted in Mily. L. from C. 23 Apr. 1794, where name is spelt Kellie. Never joined.

450. Macdowall, James. C.C.S. 1793. M.D. A.S. 7 Oct. 1794. Surg. 9 Sept. 1807. S.S. 5 Jan. 1823. M.M.B. 21 Jan. 1831. President, 1 Feb. 1834. R. 25 Feb. 1834. *d.* in London, 18 Mar. 1846. Third Maratha or Pindari war, 1817–18; (P.R.).

451. Hunter, Charles. *b.* 1772. C.C.S. 1793. A.S. 8 Oct. 1794. Surg. 5 Dec. 1807. S.S. 15 Feb. 1823. M.M.B. 11 Mar. 1831. *d.* in Calcutta, 6 May 1831. Nipal war, 1815–16. Third Maratha or Pindari war, 1817–18; (P.R.).

452. Lyon, Thomas (b, c). Surgeon of 'Earl of Wycombe,' 1787–90; of 'Woodford,' 1791–92; of 'Pigot,' 1793–94, taken by French off Bencoolen on 7 Feb. 1794, was a prisoner three months; (Proc. C.M.B. 4 Aug. 1794). A.S. 9 Oct. 1794. Second Maratha war, 1803–04, killed in battle of Dīg, 13 Nov. 1804.

1797

453. Tulloh, Hector (a, d). C.C.S. 1796. A.S. 24 Feb. 1797; (List of A.S. 1791–1814). Transferred to Bombay before arrival; (Mily. L. from C. 30 June 1797, para. 14). A.S. Bombay, 16 Sept. 1797. *d.* at Fort Gavilgarh, 1 Feb. 1804; (C.G. 10 Feb. 1804). D. and M. give his name in Bombay, but not in Bengal list, and say died at Daulatabad, 1 Jan. 1804. Bo. No. 278.

454. Dinmore, or **Gilmore, Richard** (a, d). C.C.S. 1796. A.S. 24 Feb. 1797; (List of A.S. 1791–1814, where his name is scratched out, with note, "v. separate list"). Appointment notified in Mily. L. from C. 1 Mar. 1797, para. 6. In C.G. of 8 Mar. 1798 name is given as Richard Gilmore, spelt Dinmore in Roll of Coll. Surg. Never joined. No further information. The London Medl. Journal of 1792, vol. xi. contains an article on "a case of monstrous birth," by Richard Denmore, Surgeon, Walton, Norfolk.

455. Cornish, Charles. C.C.S. 1796. A.S. 13 Mar. 1797. Surg. 8 Feb. 1808. R. 5 May 1813. *d.* 1818.

456. Roselle, James (a, c). A.S. 22 May 1797, to serve on 'Nonsuch'; (Proc. C.M.B. 22 May 1797). Apparently only a temporary appointment. *d.* in Calcutta, 23 Aug. 1815; (C.G. 31 Aug. 1815, where name is spelt Roselt).

457. Maxwell, Francis. M.D. Ed. 1795. C.C.S. 1796. A.S. 23 June 1797. *d.* on board 'Duchess of Gordon,' 30 Nov. 1805.

458. Balfour, John. *b.* 1778. C.C.S. 1796. A.S. 24 June 1797. Surg. 8 Feb. 1808. *d.* at Ludhiana, 20 May 1819.

459. Russell, William (e). *b.* 29 May 1773. M.D. Ed. 1793. A.S. 25 June 1797. Surg. 21 July 1808. Gave up promotion to S.S. to remain in Calcutta; (Mily. L. from B. 17 Feb. 1823, para. 8). R. 18 June 1831. Created Bart., 18 Feb. 1832, for services in London cholera epidemic of 1831. F.R.S. 5 Apr. 1832. L.R.C.P. Lond. 1832. *d.* at Charlton Park, Gloucestershire, 26 Sept. 1839.

460. Lauder, Hugh. C.C.S. 1796. A.S. 26 June 1797. Surg. 4 Sept. 1808. Gave up promotion to remain at Chapra, and reverted to A.S.; (C.G. 6 Mar. 1809). *d.* at Chapra, 17 Dec. 1809. Egypt, 1801.

461. Laing, James. C.C.S. 1796. A.S. 27 June 1797. Drowned bathing in river at Barhampur, Apr. 1798; (C.G. 26 Apr. 1798).

462. Waring, Henry. C.C.S. 1797. A.S. 28 June 1797. *d.* at Balambangan, Sulu Islands, Aug. 1805. Egypt, 1801.

463. Browne, John. *b.* 1765. A.S. 29 June 1797. Surg. 4 Sept. 1808. S.S. 25 July 1823. M.M.B. 6 May 1831. *d.* at Cuttack, 23 July 1833. Father of Genl. Sir Sam. Browne, V.C. Java, 1811, capture of Java. Burma, 1824–25, as S.S., capture of Rangoon; (P.R.).

464. Judson, Thomas. C.C.S. 1796. A.S. 1 July 1797. *d.* at Lucknow, 3 Mar. 1806. Egypt, 1801.

465. White, Thomas. A.S. 2 July 1797. Surg. 28 Sept. 1808. R. 4 Mar. 1813. *d.* at Bognor, 26 Dec. 1823.

466. Johnston, James (b). Surgeon of 'Valentine,' 1794–95. A.S. 3 July 1797. Surg. 20 Jan. 1809. R. 11 June 1826. *d.* in Edinburgh, 2 Feb. 1837. Third Maratha or Pindari war, 1817–18 ; (P.R.).

467. White, John Boddington. C.C.S. 1796. A.S. 4 July 1797. *d.* at Isle of France (Mauritius), Mar. 1805.

468. Robertson, Walter Holcombe. A.S. 5 July 1797. Surg. 24 Jan. 1809. *d.* in Java, 24 Aug. 1814. War with France, shown in E.I. Regr. of 1806 as "on furlough, a prisoner on parole." Java, 1811, capture of Java.

469. Stanton, Robert. C.C.S. 1793. A.S. 6 July 1797. Surg. 4 Mar. 1809. *d.* near Chittagong, 21 Jan. 1822.

470. Davis, Richard. *b.* 1773. C.C.S. 1796. A.S. 7 July 1797. Surg. 30 Apr. 1809. *d.* at Fatehgarh, 20 July 1818. Name spelt Davies in S.A.L.M.B.

471. Cooke, Edward. C.C.S. 1797. A.S. 8 July 1797. Surg. 30 Apr. 1809. *d.* on board 'Sir William Pulteney,' on passage to England, 16 Apr. 1810. Name spelt Cook in S.A.L.M.B. and D. and M.

472. Martin, John (b). Surgeon of 'Triton,' 1795–96, captured by French in Balasore Roads, 29 Jan. 1796. A.S. 9 July 1797. *d.* at Lakhipur, 18 Nov. 1807 ; (E.I. Regr.). S.A.L.M.B. and D. and M. give same date of death, but place as Calcutta. Probably same man as John Martin, No. 276, Bombay, 1796.

473. Julius, George. C.C.S. 1797. A.S. 10 July 1797. Surg. 30 Apr. 1809. R. 28 Apr. 1812. In C.G. of 8 Mar. 1798 name is given as George Jullings.

474. Sealy, John. C.C.S. 1796. A.S. 11 July 1797. Surg. 23 Jan. 1810. *d.* at Prince of Wales Island, 14 Feb. 1810.

475. Grant, William Lewis (b). C.C.S. 1793. Surgeon of 'Airlie Castle,' 1794–95. A.S. 12 July 1797. Surg. 23 Jan. 1810. S.S. 8 Mar. 1825. *d.* at Arakan, 8 Sept. 1825. Second Maratha war, 1804–05, with Bodyguard. Burma, 1824–25, as S.S., capture of Rangoon, desp. ; L.G. 1 Oct. 1825 ; (P.R.).

476. Wyatt, George Nevill. C.C.S. 1796. A.S. 13 July 1797. Gave up promotion to remain at Sitapur. *d.* at Sitapur, 8 Aug. 1817. Fourth Maisur war, 1799.

477. Ovington, John. C.C.S. 1796. A.S. 14 July 1797. Surg. 16 Apr. 1810. *d.* at Muttra, 18 Sept. 1818. Third Maratha or Pindari war, 1817–18 ; (P.R.).

478. Sproull, Thomas (a). A.S. 14 July 1797 ; (Mily. L. from C. 19 Apr. 1797, para. 6). Serving at Barhampur in 1800. Out of list in E.I. Regr. in 1802. No further information.

479. Fellowes, James. Had served at Cape of Good Hope with 84th Foot; (M.P.L. No. 524–106, 15–30 Apr. 1799). A.S. 15 July 1797. *d.* at Chicacole, 25 Nov. 1799; (S.A.L.M. Madras). S.A.L.M.B. and D. and M. say *d.* at Madras, no date. Capture of Cape of Good Hope. Fourth Maisur war, 1799.

480. Innes, Thomas (a.d.). A.S. 12 Oct. 1797; (List of A.S., 1791–1814). Apparently never joined. No further information. Called James Innes in S.A.L.M.B.

481. Lumsdaine, James (c). Officiating A.S. 10 Nov. 1797, appointed by Bengal Council, and posted to Fort Marlborough; (Proc. C.M.B. 20 Nov. 1797). "A Native, but well qualified"; (Proc. C.M.B. 14 July 1797). A.S. Bengal, 9 Sept. 1799. Surg. 17 Dec. 1812. R. 5 July 1825. v. Hist. of I.M.S. i. 502.

482. Tutin, William (b, c). *b.* 1759. Surgeon of 'Hinchinbrooke,' 1781–83 Officiating A.S. 22 Dec. 1797; (Mily. L. from B. 22 Dec. 1797, para. 48). Confirmed, 8 Sept. 1799. Surg. 28 Apr. 1812. *d.* at Dakka, 5 Dec. 1813.

1798

483. Shippard, — (a, c). Appointed temporary A.S. at Dinajpur, 7 Feb. 1798; (Proc. C.M.B.). No further information.

484. Leny, Robert (b). C.C.S. 1794. Surg. 'Thetis,' 1794–97. Asst. Surg. 5 Nov. 1798. Surg. 2 July 1810. *d.* in Fort William, 21 Mar. 1918.

485. Wallace, Alexander (a). C.C.S. 1797. Nominated 29 July 1799, (S.A.L.M.B.). Never joined Bengal. A.S. Bombay, 1 Aug. 1798. Surg. 22 Nov. 1804. Furlough, Feb. 1806. Did not rejoin. Reported to be practising in America, struck off, 1813. Bo. No. 290.

1799

486. Dumergue, Charles (a). C.C.S. 1797. A.S. 6 Feb. 1799; (List of A.S. 1791–1814). Resigned while on sick leave in England, 14 Dec. 1803; (C.G. 9 Aug. 1804). Afterwards in practice in London.

487. Hume, Joseph (b, e). *b.* 23 Jan. 1777. Surg. Mate, 'Hawke,' 1795–96. L.R.C.S. Ed. 1796. C.C.S. 1797. Surg. 'Hope,' 1798–99. M.D. Mar. Coll. Ab. 1799. A.S. 27 Aug. 1799. Resigned, Feb. 1808. M.P. for Weymouth, 1812; for Montrose Burghs, 1818–30; Middlesex, 1830–37; Kilkenny Town, 1837–41; Montrose Burghs, 1842–55. F.R.S. 2 Jan. 1818. Lord Rector, Ab. Univ. 1824–25 and 1828–29 *d.* at Burnley Hall, Norfolk, 20 Feb. 1855. Second Maratha war, 1803–05. Author of translation of Dante's Inferno, 1812.

488. Ridges, Josiah (b). Surgeon of 'Earl of Abergavenny,' 1793–94; of 'Canton,' 1796–98. A.S. 28 Aug. 1799. Surg. 25 Sept. 1810. S.S. 21 Jan. 1826. *d.* at Nasirabad, 21 Mar. 1826. Third Maratha or Pindari war, 1817–18; (P.R.).

489. Williamson, James. C.C.S. 1799. M.D. Mar. Coll. Ab. 1800. L.R.C.S. Ed. 1803. A.S. 29 Aug. 1799. Surg. 31 Dec. 1810. R. 29 June 1824. *d.* at Cheltenham, 18 Aug. 1850.

490. Rose, William. A.S. 31 Aug. 1799. Furlough, 1801; (Mily. L. from B. 30 Sept. 1801, paras. 133–137). M.R.C.S. 1802. Did not rejoin. Struck off, absent 7½ years; (C.G. 9 Mar. 1809).

491. **Evans, Samuel George** (b). Surgeon of 'Pitt,' 1796–98. A.S. 1 Sept. 1799. M.R.C.S. 1801. Surg. 19 Jan. 1811. d. at Bareli, 10 Aug. 1818.

492. **Nisbett, Charles James.** A.S. 2 Sept. 1799. Surg. 12 June 1811. d. on board 'Euphrates,' on passage home, 17 Oct. 1811. D. and M. give name as Nesbitt. Name corrected from Nesbitt to Nisbett in List of A.S. 1791–1814.

493. **Woolley, William.** C.C.S. 1799. A.S. 3 Sept. 1799. Surg. 24 Aug. 1811. Invalided, 1 June 1813. d. at Serampur, 6 Nov. 1863.

494. **Limond, Robert.** C.C.S. 1798. A.S. 4 Sept. 1799. Posted to Bombay, in Mily. L. from C. to Bombay, 5 Dec. 1798, paras. 5 and 6, but allowed to go to Bengal first. Transferred to Bengal; (G.O. 16 Aug. 1799). Surg. 18 Oct. 1811. S.S. 22 Jan. 1826. d. on board 'Oriental,' on passage to England, 2 Mar. 1832. In S.A.L.M.Bo. called Limond or Lemond. D. and M. give his name in Bengal, but not in Bombay List. Never joined Bombay. Burma, 1824–26, with Field Hosp.; (P.R.). Bo. No. 301.

495. **Grant, Samuel.** C.C.S. 1799. A.S. 5 Sept. 1799. Surg. 17 Dec. 1811. M.R.C.S. 1812. R. 23 May 1825. Third Maratha or Pindari war, 1817–18 (P.R.).

496. **Penrice, George** (b). Surg. 'Minerva,' 1796–97. C.C.S. 1798. A.S. 6 Sept. 1799. Resigned in India, 18 Dec. 1805; (E.I. Regr.). S.A.L.M.B. and D. and M. give date of Resignation as 19 Feb. 1806.

497. **Small, James** (b). Surgeon of 'General Elliott,' 1785–88. A.S. 7 Sept. 1799. d. in Calcutta, 30 May 1803. Egypt, 1801.

498. **Heriot, James** (b). b. 1759. Surg. Mate of 'Britannia,' 1787–88. Surg. 'Britannia,' 1788–95; of 'Neptune,' 1797–98. A.S. 10 Sept. 1799. d. at Penang, 27 Apr. 1807.

499. **Gibson, Henry.** A.S. Sept. 1799. Surg. 1 Jan. 1813. d. 19 July 1818. War with France, was on board the 'Kent' when she was taken by Surcouf in 'La Confiance,' in Bay of Bengal on 7 Oct. 1800, wounded; (C.G. 14 Oct. 1800).

500. **McMoody, John** (a, d). A.S. 12 Sept. 1799. Appointment noted in C.G. of 12 Mar. 1801, to rank, next H. Gibson. L. from C. of 28 Aug. 1800, quoted in Proc. C.M.B. 10 Mar. 1801, gives name as William Woody, rank next H. Gibson. Never joined. In C.G. of 26 Oct. 1809, it is stated that A.S. John Woody went back sick from the Cape to England in 1801, and made no further application. In S.A.L.M.B. Robert Woody is said to have been appointed A.S. on 12 Sept. 1799. List of A.S. 1791–1814, gives Robert Woody as appointed on 18 June 1800. Apparently same man as Robert Woody, No. 674, 1810.

501. **Carnegie, John.** A.S. 13 Sept. 1799. M.R.C.S. 1800. Surg. 20 Feb. 1813. R. 16 June, 1823.

502. **Wake, Charles.** A.S. 14 Sept. 1799. M.R.C.S. 1802. Granted furlough Mily. L. from B. 19 May 1806, paras. 333–338. Did not rejoin. Resigned, 30 Aug. 1809. Egypt, 1801; (P.R.).

503. **Holland, John** (or **James**). C.C.S. 1800. A.S. 15 Sept. 1799. d. at Ghazipur, 28 Dec. 1810. D. and M. give first name as James, but in E.I. Regr. and in S.A.L.M.B. it is given as John.

504. **Proctor, George.** A.S. 16 Sept. 1799. Surg. 5 Mar. 1813. *d.* in Calcutta, 22 July 1825. Egypt, 1801. Nipal war, 1815–16, as Field Surgeon.

505. **Langstaff, Joseph.** *b.* 1778. A.S. 18 Sept. 1799. M.R.C.S. 1800. Surg. 5 Mar. 1813. S.S. 24 June 1826. M.M.B. 23 July 1833. President, 25 Feb. 1834. R. 23 July 1838. F.R.C.S. original list, 1843. *d.* in London, 6 Dec. 1856. Third Maratha or Pindari war 1817–18 ; (P.R.).

506. **Assey, Charles Chaston.** *b.* 1779. A.S. 19 Sept. 1799. M.R.C.S. 1800. Surg. 1 June 1813. Chief Secretary to Government of Java, 1814–17. *d.* in Fort William, 21 Mar. 1821. Second Maratha war, 1803–05, battles of Delhi and Laswari, and Monson's retreat ; (A.J. Nov. 1821). Java, 1811, capture of Fort Cornelis ; (P.R.). Author of The Trade to China and the Indian Archipelago, 1819.

507. **Campbell, George.** M.D. Ed. 1798. A.S. 20 Sept. 1799. Surg. 3 June 1813. R. 19 June 1820. Knighted, 5 Mar. 1832, for services as County Magistrate in Fife. *d.* 20 May 1854 at Edenwood, Cupar, Fife. Elder brother of Lord Chancellor Campbell.

508. **Briggs, Robert** (b). Surgeon of 'Exeter,' 1798–99. A.S. 21 Sept. 1799. *d.* at Croee, Sumatra, 21 Sept. 1805 ; (E.I. Regr. and S. Cons.). S.A.L.M.B. and D. and M. give date of death as 21 Oct. 1805.

1801

*509. **Hare, James MacAdam** (c). M.D. Ed. 1796. C.C.S. 1797. Officiating A.S. 31 Mar. 1801. Confirmed, 4 Aug. 1802. Surg. 16 Dec. 1814. M.R.C.S. 1817. R. 6 June 1827. *d.* in Edinburgh, 12 Feb. 1831. Nephew of James Hare, No. 384, supra.

*510. **Reilly, Bernard** (b, c). Surg. 'Georgiana, 1800–01. Officiating A.S. 31 Mar. 1801. Confirmed, 5 Aug. 1802. Surg. 16 Dec. 1814. *d.* at Fatehgarh, 25 May 1816.

511. **Moffatt, Thomas** (a). M.D. Ed. 1800. Formerly in R.N. ; (G.M. Jan. 1803). A.S. 19 Aug. 1801. *d.* on board the 'Asia,' 25 Sept. 1802 ; (C.G. 28 Oct. 1802).

512. **Campbell, John** (a). *b.* 1779. M.D. Ed. 1800. M.R.C.S. 1800. A.S. 30 Aug. 1801. *d.* in Presy. Genl. Hosp. Calcutta, 19 Nov. 1803 ; (C.G. 24 Nov. 1803, tombstone in South Park St.).

513. **Mansell, William.** M.R.C.S. 1801. A.S. 20 Aug. 1801. Surg. 18 June 1813. R. 8 Aug. 1826. *d.* 10 Apr. 1869. Third Maratha or Pindari war, 1817–18 ; (P.R.).

514. **Gibb, James.** A.S. 21 Aug. 1801. Surg. 18 Oct. 1813. *d.* at Ghazipur, 24 Oct. 1825. D. and M. spell name Gibbs.

515. **Todd, David.** M.R.C.S. 1801. A.S. 22 Aug. 1801. Surg. 6 Dec. 1813. S.S. 1 Aug. 1826. R. 16 June 1831. *d.* at Winchmore Hill, 5 May 1839.

516. **Moscrop, Henry.** M.R.C.S. 1800. A.S. 23 Aug. 1801. Surg. 7 Feb. 1814. R. 14 Apr. 1825 ; (S.A.L.M.B.). *d.* at Newton Stewart, 21 June 1847. D. and M. give date of retirement as 14 Apr. 1823.

* The first appointment of Hare and Reilly is notified in Proc. C.M.B. 31 Mar. 1801, and Mily. L. from B. 28 May 1801, para. 253.

517. **Stewart, John** (a). A.S. 23 Aug. 1801. *d.* on board ' Curera,' on passage from Bengal to Mocha, Feb. 1802 ; (A.A. Regr. 1802, p. 121 ; and G.M. Jan. 1803). Name spelt Stuart in S.A.L.M.B. Egypt, 1801.

518. **Swiney, John.** M.R.C.S 1801. A.S. 24 Aug. 1801. M.D. St. A. 1811. Surg. 12 Apr. 1814. S.S. 26 Sept. 1828. M.M.B. 1 Feb. 1834. R. 31 Dec. 1837. *d.* at Cheltenham, 24 Dec. 1870. Second Maratha war, 1805–06. Author of A Medical Vocabulary.

519. **Ross, Samuel** (a). A.S. 24 Aug. 1801. *d.* in Calcutta, 7 Feb. 1804 ; (C.G. 16 Feb. 1804). Date of death given as 14 Feb. 1804 in S.A.L.M.B. Second Maratha war, 1803–04.

520. **Muston, William Pitts** (b). *b.* 20 Feb. 1779. Surg. Mate, ' Hillsborough,' 1797–98. A.S. 25 Aug. 1801. Surg. 12 Aug. 1814. S.S. 21 June 1833. Reverted from S.S. to Presy. Surgeon ; (G.O. 23 Oct. 1834). *d.* in Calcutta, 30 July 1837. Second Maratha war, 1805–06. Nipal, 1815–16.

521. **Thomas, George.** M.R.C.S. 1801. A.S. 26 Aug. 1801. Furlough, 1806 ; (Mily. L. from B. 19 May 1806, paras. 333–338). Did not rejoin, Struck off in 1813. D. and M. and S.A.L.M.B. say "struck off from 31 Aug. 1808." Egypt, 1801. Second Maratha war, 1805–06.

522. **Breton, Peter.** A.S. 27 Aug. 1801. Surg. 22 Aug. 1814. Gave up promotion to S.S. *d.* in Calcutta, 18 Nov. 1830. Supt. of first native medical school in Calcutta ; v. Hist. of I.M.S. i. 318, and ii. 119. Nipal war, 1815–16. Author of Vocabulary of Anatomical, Medical, and Technical Terms, in English, Arabic, Persian, Hindi, and Sanskrit. 1825 ; On the Native Method of Couching, 1826 ; On Gases, 1826 ; Lectures on Air, 1828 ; Medico-Topography of the Ceded Provinces, South-West Frontier, 1828.

1802

523. **Williams, Richard.** A.S. 28 July 1802. Surg. 25 Aug. 1814. S.S. 1 Aug. 1826. R. 19 Aug. 1829. *d.* at Newcastle, Bridgend, Glamorgan, 30 May 1837. Third Maratha or Pindari war, 1817–18 ; (P.R.). Bharatpur, 1825–26, as Field Surgeon, siege and storm of Bharatpur ; (P.R.).

524. **Phillott, George.** M.R.C.S. 1801. A.S. 29 July 1802. Surg. 30 Sept. 1814. *d.* at Kishenganj, Purnea, 14 Feb. 1823. Third Maratha or Pindari war, 1817–18 ; (P.R.).

525. **Porter, John** (a). M.R.C.S. 1802. A.S. 30 July 1802. *d.* at Madras, 3 June 1804 ; (S.A.L.M.B. and C.G. 28 June 1804).

526. **Hall, Grayson.** A.S. 31 July 1802. *d.* at Saharanpur, 13 Oct. 1812.

527. **Fullarton, John** (e). *b.* 1780. M.A. 1794 ; M.D. 1800 ; Glas. A.S. 1 Aug. 1802. Resigned, 21 Oct. 1812, and joined Banking house of Alexander and Co., Calcutta, as a partner. Left India, 1823. Sent by British Government on a special mission to China in 1834–38. *d.* 24 Oct. 1849. Author of On Regulation of Currencies, 1844.

528. **Hooper, Henry** (a). M.R.C.S. 1802. A.S. 2 Aug. 1802. Second Maratha war ; killed in action with Mir Khan Pindari, near Kunch in Bandalkund, 22 May 1804 ; (tombstone at Kunch, Jalaun).

529. **Young, Henry.** *b.* 1782. M.D. St. A. 1802. A.S. 3 Aug. 1802. Surg. 30 Nov. 1814. Gave up promotion and reverted to A.S. to remain in 24 Parganas ; (C.G. 2 June 1815). Struck off, on furlough, 23 July 1823. *d.* in London, 22 Sept. 1844. Second Maratha war, 1804–05 ; (Proc. C.M.B. 2 Nov. 1803).

1803

530. **Gregg, John.** M.R.C.S. 1801. A.S. 18 May 1803. *d.* in Calcutta, 1 Oct 1807. Second Maratha war, 1805–06.

531. **Ballard, George.** M.R.C.S. 1802. A.S. 19 May 1803. Gave up promotion to remain at Bauleah (Rajshahai) ; (C.G. 8 June 1815). R. 30 Oct. 1819. Joined house of Alexander and Co., Calcutta, as a partner ; (Mily. L. from B. 24 Dec. 1819, para. 559).

532. **Skipton, George.** *b.* 1782. M.R.C.S. 1802. A.S. 20 May 1803. Surg. 16 Dec. 1814. S.S. 1 Aug. 1826. M.M.B. 25 Feb. 1834. *d.* at the Cape of Good Hope, 3 Oct. 1835.

533. **Sawers, John.** A.S. 21 May 1803. Surg. 21 Dec. 1814. S.S. 20 June 1828. M.M.B. 3 Oct. 1835. President, 23 July 1838. R. 3 Oct. 1840. *d.* 17 May 1862. Second Maratha war, 1803–05 ; (Proc. C.M.B. 2 Nov. 1803). Third Maratha or Pindari war, 1817–18 ; (P.R.).

534. **Smith, Thomas.** A.S. 22 May 1803. Surg. 4 Jan. 1815. S.S. 9 Mar. 1827. M.M.B. 31 Dec. 1837. Phys. Genl. and Presd. 1 July 1842. R. 31 Dec. 1842. *d.* at Craigforth House, Stirling County, 25 Feb. 1856. Father of T. Smith, No. 1208, infra, 1831. Second Maratha war, 1803–05.

535. **MacWhirter, John.** A.S. 23 May 1803. Surg. 15 Feb. 1815. M.D. St. A. 1816. L.R.C.P. Ed. 1823. F.R.C.P. Ed. 1824. R. 11 May 1825. *d.* in Edinburgh, 13 Dec. 1853. First name given by D. and M. as George. Second Maratha war, 1803–05.

536. **Crawfurd, John** (e). *b.* 13 July 1783. Ed. Univ. A.S. 24 May 1803. M.R.C.S. 1815. Surg. 12 July 1815. R. 12 July 1827. *d.* in London, 11 May 1868. F.R.S. 7 May 1818. Political employ, Java, 1811–17 ; Embassy to Siam and Cochin China, 1820–23 ; succeeded Sir Stamford Raffles as Administrator of Singapur, 1823–26 ; Embassy to Ava, 1826–27. Second Maratha war, 1803–05. Java war, 1811, capture of Java. Author of History of the Indian Archipelago, 1820 ; Journal of Embassy to Ava, 1829 ; Journal of Embassy to Siam and Cochin China, 1830 ; Enquiry into Monopolies of E.I. Co., 1830 ; Letters from British Settlers in India, 1831 ; Historical and Descriptive Account of China (in collaboration), 1836 ; Appeal from inhabitants of British India, 1839 ; Grammar and Dictionary of Malay Language, 1852 ; Vital Statistics of a District in Java, 1849 ; Descriptive Dictionary of the Indian Islands, 1856. v. Hist. of I.M.S. ii. 129.

537. **Kennedy, Henry** (a). A.S. 15th E. Yorks Foot, 24 Sept. 1800. Surg. Royal North Down Militia, 5 June 1801 ; (Johnston's Roll of R.A.M.C.. No. 2038). A.S. Bengal, 25 May 1803. *d.* on board ' Euphrates ' at mouth of Ganges, 27 Aug. 1804 ; (G.M. Mar. 1805). Second Maratha war, 1803–04.

538. **Cotton, Samuel.** M.R.C.S. 1803. A.S. 26 May 1803. Transferred Madras, 1803. Pensioned in India, 19 June 1810. *d.* 12 Aug. 1811. D. and M. give name both in Bengal and Madras Lists. M. No. 498.

539. **Wilson, John Major** (b). *b.* 1770. Surgeon of ' Rose,' 1799–1800. A.S. 27 May 1803. M.D. Mar. Coll. Ab. 1812. Surg. 15 July 1815. *d.* in Calcutta, 24 May 1818.

540. **Patterson, John.** A.S. 28 May 1803. Surg. 1 Nov. 1815. *d.* in Calcutta, 9 Nov. 1827.

1804

541. **Phillott, Richard.** A.S. 15 Feb. 1804. Pensioned on Lord Clive's Fund, 9 Oct. 1811.

542. **Harley, Alexander.** A.S. 16 Feb. 1804. Surg. 12 Dec. 1815. Struck off in 1819, absent five years.

543. **Campbell, Colin.** M.D. Ed. 1801. A.S. 17 Feb. 1804. Surg. 15 Jan. 1816. S.S. 22 Sept. 1827. M.M.B. 23 July 1838. S.G. 1 July 1842. Phys. Genl. and Pres. 1 Jan. 1843. R. 23 July 1843. *d.* at Brighton, 1 Nov. 1858. Third Maratha or Pindari war, 1817–18 ; (P.R.). Bharatpur, 1825–26, siege and storm of Bharatpur ; (P.R.).

544. **Sewell, Barnaby.** M.R.C.S. 1803. A.S. 18 Feb. 1804. *d.* in Upper Provinces, Jan 1805 ; (E.I. Regr. and C.G. 7 Feb. 1805). D. and M. give date of death as Oct. 1804.

545. **Taylor, Alexander.** A.S. 19 Feb. 1804. *d.* at Delhi, 23 May 1807. Second Maratha war, 1805–06.

546. **Thomas, William** (b). C.C.S. 1799. Surg. ' True Briton,' 1799–1800 ; ' Wyndham,' 1801–02. A.S. 20 Feb. 1804. Surg. 26 May 1816. S.S. 1 Feb. 1829. R. 1 Aug. 1837 ; (G.O. No. 9 of 5 Jan. 1838). D. and M. give date of retirement as Sept. 1837. Second Maratha war, 1805–06. Burma, 1824–25 ; (P.R.).

547. **Impey, Elijah.** *b.* 1781. A.S. 27 Sept. 1804. M.R.C.S. 1807. Surg. 15 Aug. 1816. *d.* at Baliganj, Calcutta, 9 June 1821. Second Maratha war, 1805–06.

548. **Venour, Walter Askell.** M.R.C.S. 1804. A.S. 28 Sept. 1804. Surg. 31 Aug. 1816. S.S. 3 June 1829. R. 3 Jan. 1837.

549. **Patullo, George** (d). M.D. Ed. 1801. M.R.C.S. 1804. A.S. 29 Sept. 1804. *d.* on board ' Asia,' on passage to India, 31 Aug. 1804, before joining.

550. **Armstrong, Archibald.** M.R.C.S. 1803. A.S. 30 Sept. 1804. *d.* at Rewari, 28 Nov. 1810.

551. **Campbell, George Gunning.** M.R.C.S. 1800. A.S. 1 Oct. 1804. Surg. 29 Nov. 1816. S.S. 21 Jan. 1831. R. 1 Sept. 1835 ; (G.O. No. 36 of 12 Mar. 1838). F.R.C.S. original list, 1843. *d.* 7 May 1858. D. and M. give date of retirement as 1 Aug. 1837. Bharatpur, 1825–26, siege and storm of Bharatpur.

1805

552. **Ludlow, Samuel.** M.R.C.S. 1804. A.S. 18 Mar. 1805. Surg. 30 Jan. 1817. S.S. 11 Mar. 1831. M.M.B. Oct. 1840. R. 1 Jan. 1841. F.R.C.S. original list, 1843. *d.* at Bath, 17 Oct. 1853.

553. **Bunce, John.** M.R.C.S. 1803. A.S. 19 Mar. 1805. Surg. 10 Feb. 1817. *d.* at Dinapur, 8 Apr. 1819 ; (A.J. Nov. 1819). D. and M. and S.A.L.M.B. give date of death as 8 May 1819.

554. Tweedie, Thomas. A.S. 20 Mar. 1805. Surg. 22 Feb. 1817. S.S. 6 May 1831. M.M.B. 1 Jan. 1841. I.G. Hosps. 1 July 1842. S.G. 1 Jan. 1843. Phys. Genl. and Pres. 3 July 1843. R. 16 Feb. 1844. d. at Rachan House, Peebles, 12 Nov. 1855. Father of A. Tweedie, No. 1372, infra, 1841. Burma, 1824-25, with Field Hosp., Desp. L.G. 7 Oct. 1826.

555. Playfair, George (b). b. 1782. M.R.C.S. 1802. Surg. Mate, 'Ocean,' 1801-02 ; Surg. 'Ocean,' 1802-04. A.S. 21 Mar. 1805. Surg. 22 Feb. 1817. S.S. 20 Feb. 1832. M.M.B. and I.G. Hosps. 31 Dec. 1842. R. 1 Mar. 1843. d. at St. Andrews, 26 Nov. 1846. Father of Lyon Playfair, Lord Playfair ; of Lt.-Col. Sir Robert Playfair, of G. R. Playfair, No. 1459, and of W. S. Playfair, No. 1762, infra. Afghanistan, 1839-41. Author of Taleef Shareef, Indian Materia Medica, 1833.

556. Roe, William (a, b). Surg. Mate, 'Brunswick,' 1803-04. C.C.S. 1805. A.S. 22 Mar. 1805. d. at Dinajpur, 15 Aug. 1806 ; (C.G. 4 Sept. 1806, and S.A.L.M.B.).

557. Rutherford, Thomas. A.S. 23 Mar. 1805. Gave up promotion to remain at Moradabad. R. 12 May 1825 ; (C.G. 19 Dec. 1825). D. and M. and S.A.L.M.B. give date of retirement as 12 Jan. 1825.

558. Turner, William Henry (a). B.A. T.C.D. 1799. M.R.C.S. 1804. A.S. 24 Mar. 1805. d. in Calcutta, 7 Sept. 1806 ; (C.G. 11 Sept. 1806).

559. Ainslie, William. A.S. 25 Mar. 1805. Surg. 30 Apr. 1817. R. 13 Nov. 1819. Joined house of Colvin and Co., Calcutta, as a partner ; (Mily. L. from B. 24 Dec. 1819, para. 559).

560. Roberts, James. M.R.C.S. 1804. A.S. 26 Mar. 1805. d. in Java, 26 Dec. 1812. Java, 1811.

561. Reardon, Jeremiah. M.R.C.S. 1805. A.S. 27 Mar. 1805. d. at Cawnpur, 2 July 1809.

562. Childs, Christopher. A.S. 28 Mar. 1805. d. at Delhi, 26 Sept. 1816.

563. Durant, Henry (a). A.S. 29 Mar. 1805. Lost in the 'Earl of Abergavenny,' wrecked on the Shambles, Portland Island, 4 Feb. 1805, three days after leaving Portsmouth. His commission was dated nearly two months after his death, on duty.

564. Ramsay, Andrew Forbes. A.S. 29 Mar. 1805. Surg. 1 June 1817. M.D. St. A. 1820. R. 9 Aug. 1823. d. at Canterbury, 9 Feb. 1829.

565. MacKenzie, James Hector. b. Dec. 1787. L.R.C.S. Ed. A.S. 30 Mar. 1805. Surg. 21 Sept. 1817. d. at Kaitur, Hamirpur, 23 May 1828 ; (tombstone). Third Maratha or Pindari war, 1817-18 ; (P.R.). Bharatpur, 1825-27, siege and storm of Bharatpur ; (P.R.).

566. Marshall, John. b. 1783. M.R.C.S. 1805. A.S. 31 Mar. 1805. Surg. 22 Mar. 1818. S.S. 24 July 1833. M.M.B. and I.G. Hosps. 1 Mar. 1843. S.G. 23 July 1843. Phys. Genl. and Pres. 16 Feb. 1844. F.R.C.S. original list, 1844. R. 16 Feb. 1845. d. at Falmouth, 30 Aug. 1850.

567. Pearson, William. M.C.R.S. 1804. A.S. 1 Apr. 1805. Furlough, S.C. 1806. Struck off in 1813, from 30 Mar. 1809.

568. **Chalmers, William.** *b.* 1786. M.A. 1803; M.D. 1820; Mar. Coll. Ab. M.R.C.S., 1805. A.S. 2 Apr. 1805. Surg. 27 Mar. 1818. R. 6 Jan. 1825. M.F.P.S.G. 1828. Asst. Physn. Royal Infirmary, Glasgow, 1829–1832. *d.* at Brighton, 13 Oct. 1862. Father of No. 1359, infra, C. B. Chalmers, and of J. Chalmers, No. 945, M.

569. **Hough, Henry Francis** (b). *b.* 1781. M.R.C.S. 1803. Surg. 'Comet,' 1803. A.S. 3 Apr. 1805. Surg. 25 May 1818. S.S. 25 Feb. 1834. M.M.B. and I.G. Hosps. 23 July 1843. S.G. 16 Feb. 1844. F.R.C.S. original list, 1844. Phys. Genl. and Pres. 16 Feb. 1845. R. 24 July 1848. *d.* in London, 30 Oct. 1855. Cape of Good Hope, 1806, action at Blaubourg, 8 Jan. 1806.

570. **Panton, William.** M.R.C.S. 1804. A.S. 4 Apr. 1805. Surg. 23 June 1818. S.S. 1 Feb. 1834. M.M.B. and I.G. Hosps. 16 Feb. 1844. S.G. 16 Feb. 1845. Phys. Genl and Pres. 24 July 1848. R. 10 Feb. 1849. *d.* at Tunbridge Wells, 10 May 1858.

571. **Rixon, George** (a, b). C.C.S. 1798. Surg. ' Hugh Inglis,' 1800–04. A.S. 20 May 1805. *d.* in Calcutta, 9 Oct. 1806; (C.G. 16 Oct. 1806, and S.A.L.M.B.).

572. **Atkinson, James** (b, e). *b.* 1780. Surg. Mate, 'Lord Duncan,' 1802–03 ; Surg. ' United Kingdom,' 1804–05. Acting A.S. 23 May 1805 ; (C.G. 30 May 1805). Confirmed, 29 June 1807. Surg. 14 July 1820. S.S. 9 Dec. 1840. M.R.C.S. 1841. M.M.B. and I.G. Hosps. 16 Feb. 1845. R. 10 Apr. 1847. *d.* in London, 7 Aug. 1852. Father of R. J. Atkinson, No. 1468, infra. Afghanistan, 1839–41, as S.S. Army of Indus, capture of Ghuzni; (P.R.); Desp. L.G. 30 Oct. 1839. Order of Durani Empire, 3rd Class, 17 Dec. 1841. Author of Rodolfo, a poem, 1801; Sohrab, a poem, 1814; Hatim Taee, a romance, 1818; Aubid, an Eastern Tale, 1819; Translation of Foscolo's Ricciardo, 1823; The City of Palaces, and other poems, 1824; Translation of Tassoni's La Secchia Rapita, 1825; Description of the new process of perforating and destroying the Stone in the Bladder (his only professional work), 1831; Translation of Firdausi's Shahnama, 1832; Customs and Manners of the Women of Persia, 1832; Translation of Nizami's Layla and Majnun, 1836; The Expedition into Afghanistan, 1842; Sketches in Afghanistan, 1842; Medico-topographical account of Dacca. v. Hist. of I.M.S. ii. 158–161.

1806

573. **Anderson, James.** A.S. 28 Feb. 1806. *d.* in England, 21 Aug. 1814.

574. **Leake, Thomas** (b). L.R.C.S. Ed. Surg. ' Phoenix,' 1800–02 ; ' Lord Duncan,' 1802–04. A.S. 1 Mar. 1806. Surg. 1818. *d.* at Malda, 17 Sept. 1819.

575. **Leslie, William.** M.D. Ed. 1804. A.S. 2 Mar. 1806. *d.* at Prince of Wales Island, 7 Aug. 1814. S.A.L.M.B. gives his name as Leslie or Leyslie.

576. **Howell, John.** *b.* 5 Nov. 1781. M.R.C.S. 1800. M.D. Ed. 1805. A.S. 3 Mar. 1806. Surg. 1818. *d.* 28 June 1819.

577. **Findon, William Morris.** *b.* Mar. 1783. M.R.C.S. 1804. A.S. 4 Mar. 1806. Surg. 12 Aug. 1818. S.S. 23 Oct. 1834. R. 1 Jan. 1843. *d.* at Cheltenham, 14 Oct. 1849. Bharatpur, 1825–26; siege and storm of Bharatpur; (P.R.).

578. **Finn, John** (a). M.D. Ed. 1802. M.R.C.S. 1805. A.S. 5 Mar. 1806. d. at Dinapur, 21 Oct. 1806 ; (S.A.L.M.B.).

579. **Hunter, Oswald.** M.D. Ed. 1803. L.R.C.P. Ed. 1803. F.R.C.P. Ed. 1803. A.S. 6 Mar. 1806. Surg. 1818. d. at Karnal, 14 Jan. 1820.

580. **Anderson, Archibald.** b. 10 Jan. 1784. M.R.C.S. 1806. A.S. 7 Mar. 1806. Third Maratha or Pindari war, 1817–18. Killed at capture of Chanda Fort, 11 June 1818 ; (A.J. Dec. 1818). D. and M. give date of death as 11 May 1818, " Whilst on a survey with a reconnoitring party of the fort of Chanda, and its defences, Mr. A. Anderson, Assistant Surgeon on the Bengal Establishment. He was shot through the heart by the last gun that was fired ; " (Obituary in G.M. of May 1819, no date given).

581. **Noyes, William** (b). Surg. Mate, ' Berrington,' 1796–97 ; Surgeon of ' Preston,' 1799–1802 ; of ' Lady Castlereagh,' 1803–04 ; of ' William Pitt,' 1805–06. A.S. 8 Mar. 1806. d. at Radnagore (Radhanagar in Midnapur). 18 Nov. 1807.

582. **Bayldon, George.** b. 29 July 1782. M.R.C.S. 1805. A.S. 9 Mar. 1806. d. in Europe, 20 Feb. 1816.

583. **Renton, David.** b. 20 Aug. 1783. L.R.C.S. Ed. A.S. 10 Mar. 1806. Surg. 20 Aug. 1818. S.S. 25 Dec. 1836. d. at Benares, 13 July 1837.

584. **Crichton, Thomas** (b). Surg. Mate, ' Earl Spencer,' 1800–01 ; Surg. ' United Kingdom,' 1802–03 ; ' Lady Burges,' 1804–05. A.S. 11 Mar. 1806. Surg. 19 Sept. 1818. d. in London, 17 Sept. 1827.

585. **Stephens, John.** b. 18 Sept. 1782. M.R.C.S. 1805. A.S. 17 Sept. 1806. Surg. 7 Oct. 1818. Asst. to Agent to Govr. Genl., Sagar, 1824–27. Assassinated at Seoni, 17 Aug. 1827.

586. **Mellis, James** (b). b. 16 Nov. 1781. M.A. 1799. M.D. 1806. Mar. Coll. Ab. M.R.C.S. 1802. Surg. ' Fame,' 1804–05. A.S. 18 Sept. 1806. Surg. 25 Nov. 1818. L.R.C.P. Ed. 1826. F.R.C.P. Ed. 1827. S.S. 13 July 1837. F.R.C.S. original list, 1844. R. 1 Apr. 1845. d. in London, 17 Mar. 1846.

587. **Hall, Angus.** b. 3 Jan. 1784. L.R.C.S. Ed. A.S. 19 Sept. 1806. Surg. 21 Jan. 1819. Furlough, 26 Jan. 1827. Struck off from 21 May 1829, absent five years ; (C.G. 24 July 1832). Afterwards permitted to retire from that date ; (S.A.L.M.B.). d. . . . 1836.

588. **Halliday, Alexander.** b. Apr. 1786. M.D. Ed. 1805. A.S. 20 Sept. 1806. Surg. 14 Mar. 1819. S.S. 31 Dec. 1837. R. 31 Jan. 1844. d. 11 Nov. 1851.

589. **Barclay, James.** b. 16 Jan. 1784. M.D. Ed. 1805. A.S. 21 Sept. 1806. d. at Prince of Wales Island, 22 Oct. 1811. D. and M. give place of death as Prince William's Island.

590. **Adamson, William** (b). Surg. Mate, ' Boddam,' 1797–98 ; Surg. ' Herculean,' 1802–04. M.R.C.S. 1806. A.S. 22 Sept. 1806. Surg. 9 May 1819. R. 1 July 1823. d. at New York, 1846.

591. **Yeomans, Richard Rowland.** b. Mar. 1782. M.R.C.S. 1805. A.S. 23 Sept. 1806. Surg. May 1819. d. at Murshidabad, 30 Sept. 1819.

592. Jacob, George Ogle. *b.* Mar. 1786. M.R.C.S. 1806. A.S. 24 Sept. 1806. Surg. 21 May 1819. R. 5 June 1827. Father of W. A. Jacob, M. No. 1155. Java, 1811; capture of Java.

593. Scott, William Chisholme. *b.* 3 Aug. 1783. M.R.C.S. 1806. A.S. 25 Sept. 1806. Surg. 29 June 1819. Struck off, 14 July 1820, absent five years.

1807

594. King, George. *b.* 19 Dec. 1782. M.R.C.S. 1805. A.S. 28 Jan. 1807. Surg. 18 Sept. 1819. S.S. 3 Oct. 1840. R. 31 Jan. 1844. *d.* at Brighton, 9 Mar. 1845. Java, 1811, capture of Java; China, 1840–41, as S.S., Medal.

595. Adams, William. *b.* Jan. 1778. M.R.C.S. 1806. A.S. 29 Jan. 1807. *d.* in Fort William, 24 Oct. 1818.

596. Farquhar, William. M.D. Ed. 1803. A.S. 88th Foot, having previously served as Hosp. Mate, 24 May 1804. Resigned, 3 Feb. 1806. A.S. Bengal, 30 Jan. 1807. Surg. 20 Nov. 1819. R. 15 Apr. 1827. v. Johnston's Roll of R.A.M.C. No. 2374.

597. Gordon, George James. A.S. 31 Jan. 1807. Surg. 21 Nov. 1819. R. 15 Apr. 1820. *d.* in London, 26 Feb. 1853. Java, 1811, capture of Java, with Body Guard; (P.R.).

598. Adamson, David. L.R.C.S. Ed. A.S. 1 Feb. 1807. Struck off, absent over time, 10 Mar. 1812.

599. Nicolson, Simon. *b.* 5 July 1799. St. Georges. M.R.C.S. 1802. Originally nominated for Madras (A.S. Certs. vol. ii.), but posted to Bengal on arrival. A.S. 2 Feb. 1807. Surg. 8 Jan. 1820. S.S. 1839. Permitted to resign promotion and revert to Surgeon, to remain as Presy. Surg. Calcutta. F.R.C.S. original list, 1844. R. 1 Aug. 1855. *d.* in Calcutta, 8 Aug. 1855. His picture, in oils, is in the rooms of the Asiatic Society, Calcutta. v. Hist. of I.M.S. ii. 255–257

600. Baird, Andrew (b). M.D. K.C. Ab. 1800. Surg. of 'Culland's Grove,' 1802–03, taken by French, 22 July 1803, detained as prisoner of war in France till 1810, when he escaped, and proceeded to Bengal; (C.G. 20 Dec. 1810). M.R.C.S. 1810. A.S. (in absentia), 3 Feb. 1807. *d.* at Chittagong, 28 July 1812. Java, 1811, capture of Java. v. Hist. of I.M.S. ii. 202, 203.

601. Jameson, James. *b.* 10 June 1786. A.S. 25 June 1807. Surg. 15 Jan. 1820. First Supt. of Calcutta Native Medl. School, 1822. *d.* in Calcutta, 20 Jan. 1823. Author of Report on Epidemic Cholera in Bengal, 1817–19; 1820.

602. Matthew, Patrick. *b.* Aug. 1784. A.S. 26 June 1807. Surg. 16 Apr. 1820. *d.* at Cawnpur, 15 Aug. 1830. S.A.L.M.B. spells name Mathew. Java, 1811, capture of Java; (P.R.).

603. Gardner, Gilbert Ogilvy. *b.* 5 Feb. 1785. M.R.C.S. 1806. M.D. Glas. 1806. A.S. 27 June 1807. Surg. 19 June 1820. R. 23 Feb. 1826. Burma, 1824–25.

604. Robinson, James. *b.* 23 July 1785. M.R.C.S. 1806. A.S. 28 June 1807. *d.* in Calcutta, 23 June 1819.

605. Howden, Thomas (a, d). A.S. 23 July 1807. Resigned appointment, never joined ; (A.S. Certs. vol. ii.). G. MacCraken nominated in his place ; (A.S. Certs. vol. ii.). Afterwards in Royal Navy.

606. MacCraken, Gilbert. *b.* 11 July 1782. M.D. Ed. 1805. A.S. 23 July 1807. Appointed in place of T. Howden. *d.* in Java, 18 Oct. 1811. Java, 1811, capture of Java ; (P.R.).

607. Curran, William. *b,* 5 Sept. 1786. M.R.C.S. 1806. A.S. 24 July 1807. Resigned in England, 18 Jan. 1815.

608. MacGhee, John (b). Surg. of ' Indus,' 1806–07. A.S. 25 July 1807. *d.* Jan. 1810, on board ' Elizabeth,' on passage to England.

609. Castell, Jehosaphat (b). *b.* Apr. 1774. Surg. ' Duke of Montrose,' 1797–99. M.R.C.S. 1800. A.S. 26 July 1807. Surg. 17 Dec. 1820. R. 11 May 1830. *d.* in London, 6 July 1844. Third Maratha or Pindari war, 1817–18 ; (P.R.).

610. Fraser, Archibald (b). Surg. Mate, ' Dover Castle,' 1803–04. A.S. 4 Aug. 1807. Lost in ' Charger,' Gun brig in 1807. First name given as Alexander in S.A.L.M.B.

611. Goldie, Alexander Robert Bembridge. *b.* 30 Jan. 1786. A.S. 5 Aug. 1807. *d.* at Monghir, 17 Apr. 1809.

612. Brown, Andrew. *b.* 3 Nov. 1785. M.D. Ed. 1806. A.S. 6 Aug. 1807. Surg. 17 Jan. 1821. R. 25 Nov. 1824. *d.* at Stewarton, Ayrshire, 3 Nov. 1861.

613. Stuart, Charles. *b.* 28 Mar. 1782. M.R.C.S. 1806. A.S. 7 Aug. 1807. Surg. 22 Mar. 1821. R. 28 Aug. 1822. Entered a mercantile house ; (Mily. L. from B. 30 Nov. 1822, para. 335).

614. Gibson, John Jack. *b.* 1 May 1773. Surg. Loyal Inverness Regt. 21 Nov. 1794, afterwards Ensign and Lieut. in same regt. ; (S.A.L.M.B.) Surg. Dumfries, Roxburgh, and Selkirk Militia, 21 May 1803. A.S. 8 Aug. 1807. Surg. 10 June 1821. Surg. to King of Oudh. *d.* at Lucknow, 20 Aug. 1823 ; (A.J. 1824, p. 464).

615. Stewart, Walter. *b.* 22 Apr. 1785. A.S. 9 Aug. 1807. *d.* at Kalpi, 3 Sept. 1815.

616. Webb, George. *b.* Apr. 1787. M.R.C.S. 1807. A.S. 10 Aug. 1807. Surg. 22 Jan. 1822. R. 1 Jan. 1829. Bharatpur, 1825, siege and storm of Bharatpur ; (P.R.).

617. Hogg, Jonah John (b). *b.* 7 Aug. 1781. Surg. Mate, ' Worcester,' 1801–02. M.R.C.S. 1807. A.S. 11 Aug. 1807. R. 4 May 1822, and joined a mercantile house in Calcutta ; (Mily. L. from B. 31 Oct. 1822, para. 383).

618. Laurie, Adam. *b.* 21 Jan. 1785. M.R.C.S. 1806. A.S. 12 Aug. 1807. *d.* in Fort William, 26 Nov. 1813. Java, 1811, capture of Java ; (P.R.).

619. Adams, Joseph (b). *b.* 1775. C.C.S. 1798. Surg. of ' Manship,' 1799–1800 ; of ' Charlton,' 1801–06. A.S. 13 Aug. 1807. Surg. 23 Feb. 1822. R. 24 May 1829.

620. Phillips, Edward. *b.* July 1782. A.S. 11 Nov. 1807. Resigned, 9 Mar. 1808. Reappointed A.S. 10 Mar. 1809. Surg. 27 Sept. 1823. *d.* at Mullye (Mallai in Champarun), 23 Mar. 1828. Capture of Mauritius, 1810. Burma, 1824–25 ; (P.R.).

1808

621. Stubbs, Richmond Robert. *b.* Jan. 1782. M.R.C.S. 1806. A.S. 12 Mar. 1808. *d.* at Chittagong, 4 Oct. 1813.

622. Barnes, John (b). *b.* 29 Mar. 1781. Surg. of ' Comet,' 1801–03 ; of ' Warren Hastings,' 1803–06, severely wounded and captured when ' Warren Hastings ' was taken by French frigate ' Piémontaise,' on 21 June 1806 ; v. Hist. of I.M.S. ii. 201, and James' Naval History, iv, 346. M.R.C.S. 1807. A.S. 13 Mar. 1808. Resigned, 17 Oct. 1815 ; (C.G. 26 Oct. 1815). Restored to service, 25 June 1817 ; (C.G. 5 Mar. 1818). Surg. 4 May 1822. R. 14 July 1825. *d.* at Byfleet, 28 Jan. 1847. War with France.

623. Nicholetts, William Hole. *b.* 1 Oct. 1786. M.R.C.S. 1807. A.S. 14 Mar. 1808. *d.* in Calcutta, 9 Mar. 1816.

624. Jackson, Isaac. *b.* 6 Oct. 1784. M.R.C.S. 1807. A.S. 15 Mar. 1808. Surg. 28 Aug. 1822. R. 15 Oct. 1840. *d.* 26 Apr. 1868. Third Maratha or Pindari war, 1817–18 ; (P.R.).

625. Ledmon, William. A.S. 4th Dragoons, 18 Sept. 1806, previously Hosp. Mate. Resigned, 8 Oct. 1807. v. Johnston's Roll. of R.A.M.C. No. 2670. A.S. Bengal, 16 Mar. 1808. Surg. Jan. 1823. R. 29 Jan. 1823. *d.* at Maglass, Co. Kerry, 3 Jan. 1832. Third Maratha or Pindari war, 1817–18 ; (P.R.).

626. Tytler, Robert. *b.* 18 Nov. 1787. Served at Cape of Good Hope from 1800. A.S. 81st Foot, 25 June 1802. Resigned, 10 Sept. 1803. v. Johnston's Roll of R.A.M.C. No. 2160. M.D. Ed. 1807. A.S. Bengal, 17 Mar. 1808. Surg. 20 Jan. 1823. *d.* at Chouada, near Gwalior, 17 Mar. 1838. Java, 1811, capture of Java. Burma, 1824–25. Author of Budaic Sabism, 1817 ; Remarks on Morbus Oryzeus, 1820 ; Illustrations of Ancient Geography and History, 1826.

627. Savage, John (b). *b.* 20 Oct. 1770. C.C.S. 1796. Surg. of ' Melville Castle,' 1796–97. Asst. Surg. to Settlement of New South Wales, 1 July 1802 ; (S.A.L.M.B.). A.S. Bengal, 18 Mar. 1808. Surg. 29 Jan. 1823. R. 5 Aug. 1835.

628. Fair, Peter. *b.* 1 Feb. 1786. M.D. Ed. 1807. A.S. 19 Mar. 1808, *d.* in Edinburgh, 3 Feb. 1821 ; (A.J. Mar. 1821). S.A.L.M.B. and D. and M. give date of death as 3 Jan. 1821. Third Maratha or Pindari war, 1817–18 ; (P.R.).

629. Hodgson, John. *b.* Aug. 1786. A.S. 20 Mar. 1808. *d.* at Biabong, Java, 23 Nov. 1815 ; (C.G. 11 Apr. 1816). Java, 1811, capture of Java ; (P.R.).

630. Baillie, George. *b.* 4 Feb. 1787. A.S. 21 Mar. 1808. M.A. K.C. Ab. 1813. M.R.C.S. 1814. Surg. 14 Feb. 1823. R. 13 June 1840. Father of No. 1601, G. O. Baillie, and of No. 1726, N. B. Baillie, infra. Java, 1811, capture of Java ; (P.R.). Third Maratha or Pindari war, 1817–18 ; (P.R.).

631. Lewis, David. *b.* 7 Feb. 1784. A.S. 22 Mar. 1808. Furlough, 1819. M.D. St. A. 1820. R. 4 Jan. 1823.

632. Bellamy, Charles. *b.* Sept. 1787. A.S. 23 Mar. 1808. *d.* at Barrackpur, 3 Nov. 1822.

633. **Grierson, James.** *b.* 15 Oct. 1786. M.R.C.S. 1808. A.S. 24 Mar. 1808. Surg. 17 Mar. 1823. R. 18 Nov. 1829; (C.G. 26 Apr. 1830). *d.* at Beech Hill, Haddington, 14 Sept. 1861. D. and M. give date of retirement as 10 Nov. 1829. Burma, 1824–25, as Field Surgeon, Desp. L.G. 25 Dec. 1824.

634. **Heaslop, Richard** (b). *b.* 1772. M.R.C.S. 1801. Surg. of 'Isabella,' 1797–98; of 'Thames,' 1798–1800; of 'Nile,' 1801–03; of 'Ganges,' 1803–04; of 'Lord Duncan,' 1805–06. A.S. 25 Mar. 1808. R. 7 May 1823. *d.* in London, 1 Oct. 1846.

635. **Cocke, Archibald.** *b.* 16 Jan. 1786. M.R.C.S. 1807. A.S. 26 Mar. 1808. Surg. 16 June 1823. *d.* at Dinapur, 12 June 1827; (A.J. Feb. 1828, p. 266). D. and M. give date of death as 12 July 1827. Third Maratha or Pindari war, 1817–18; (P.R.).

636. **Lamb, George.** *b.* 26 Oct. 1787. M.A. Mar. Coll. Ab. 1801. A.S. 27 Mar. 1808. Surg. 1 July 1823. S.S. 1 Jan. 1841. M.M.B. and I.G. Hosps. 10 Apr. 1847. S.G. 24 July 1848. Phys. Genl. and Pres. 10 Feb. 1849. R. 10 Apr. 1852. *d.* at Cheltenham, 3 Feb. 1862. Name spelt Lambe in Army Lists, but his signature, in A.S. Certs. vol. iv. is Lamb, without final e. Capture of Mauritius, Dec. 1810; (P.R.).

637. **Davies, William Freeman.** *b.* 9 Nov. 1784. A.S. 14 Sept. 1808. *d.* in camp at Chanda, 20 May 1818; C.G. 18 June 1818). Third Maratha or Pindari war, 1817–18; (P.R.).

638. **Stiven, William Sutherland.** *b.* 31 Jan. 1787. A.S. 15 Sept. 1808. Surg. 11 July 1823. S.S. 11 Jan. 1842. M.M.B. and I.G. Hosps. 24 July 1848. S.G. 10 Feb. 1849. Phys. Genl. and Pres. 10 Apr. 1852. R. 16 May 1853. *d.* in Edinburgh, 13 July 1856. Father of No. 1503, infra, W. S. Stiven. Nipal 1815–16. Afghanistan, 1841–42, as S.S. of Genl. Pollock's force in advance on Kabul; Desp. L.G. 8 Nov. and 14 Nov. 1842. Central India, 1842.

639. **Babington, George.** *b.* 29 Dec. 1776. M.R.C.S. 1811. Surg. 3rd Foot Guards, 29 July 1795. Resigned, 25 May 1808; (Johnston's Roll of R.A.M.C., No. 1433). A.S. Bengal, 16 Sept. 1808. *d.* at Amboyna, 18 Nov. 1816; (tablet in church there, Times, 27 Dec. 1917). D. and M. give date of death as 18 Nov. 1817. Flanders, Helder, 1799, with Guards, severely wounded in charge at Akersloot. Java, 1811, capture of Java. Amboyna, 1816.

640. **Wilson, Horace Hayman** (e). *b.* 26 Sept. 1786. St. Thomas. M.R.C.S. 1805. A.S. 17 Sept. 1808. Surg. 11 July 1823. Dy. Assay Master, Calcutta Mint, 1808–16. Assay. Master, 1816–32. Secy. Asiatic Society, 1811–32. R. 28 Jan. 1834. M.A. Oxon. 1833. Boden Professor of Sanskrit, Oxford, 1832–60. F.R.S. 10 Apr. 1834. Librarian to E.I. Co. 1834–60. *d.* in London, 8 May 1860. Married a granddaughter of Mrs. Siddons, and managed Calcutta theatre for many years. Author of Translation of Kalidasa's Meghaduta, 1813; Sanskrit-English Dictionary, 1819; Theatre of Hindus, 3 vols., 1826–27; Documents illustrative of Burmese war, 1827; Catalogue of Mackenzie Collection of MSS., 1828; Review of external commerce of India, 1830; Notes on Indica of Ctesias, 1836; Sankhya Karika, 1837; Vishma Purana, translation, 6 vols., 1840; Lectures on Religious and Philosophical Systems of Hindus, 1840; Ariana Antiqua, 1841; Oriental Portfolio, 1841; Moorcroft's Travels in Himalayas (written from rough notes), 1841; Religious Sects of Hindus, 1846; Sanskrit Grammar,

1847; vols. vi. to ix. of Mill's History of India, 1848; Narrative of Burmese war of 1824-26, 1852; Glossary of Indian Judicial and Revenue Terms, 1855; translation of Rigveda Sanhita, 6 vols., 1850-58; Essays, 2 vols., 1862; Essays, 3 vols., 1862-64. Wilson's works, edited by Reinhold Rost, were published in 12 vols., by Trubner, London, 1862-1877.

641. **Shaw, Thomas Burke.** *b.* 20 Oct. 1784, in Jamaica. M.R.C.S. 1807. A.S. 18 Sept. 1808. *d.* in Major Bradshaw's camp on Nipal frontier, 29 Oct. 1814. Nipal war, 1814.

642. **Knight, Rice Davies.** M.R.C.S. 1808. A.S. 19 Sept. 1808. Surg. 11 July 1823. *d.* at Bareli, 12 Aug. 1828. He married the eldest daughter of Daniel Anthony Overbeek, the last Dutch Governor of Chinsura. Third Maratha or Pindari war, 1817-18; (P.R.).

643. **Welsh, William Simpson.** *b.* 11 July 1786. A.S. 20 Sept. 1808. *d.* at Jaunpur, 11 Feb. 1819. Java, 1811, capture of Java; (P.R.).

1809

644. **Ranken, James.** *b.* 24 Aug. 1788. M.D. Ed. 1808. M.R.C.S. 1808. A.S. 3 Feb. 1809. Surg. 11 July 1823. Postmaster-Genl. N.W.P. 1 Jan. 1841. F.R.C.S. original list, 1844. R. 18 Sept. 1845. *d.* at After Lodge, Ayrshire, 3 May 1848. D. and M. spell name Rankin. Third Maratha or Pindari war, 1817-18; (P.R.). Bharatpur, 1825-26, siege and storm of Bharatpur; (P.R.). Author of Report on Pali Plague, 1838.

645. **Darling, David** (b). *b.* 2 May 1772. Surg. Mate, 'Barwell,' 1793-94. C.C.S. 1795. Surg. of 'Fort William,' 1795-97; of 'David Scott,' 1806-07. A.S. 4 Feb. 1809. *d.* at sea, 22 Feb. 1819.

646. **Thornton, Henry.** *b.* 30 May 1786. A.S. 5 Feb. 1809. R. 6 July 1820.

647. **Napier, Adam.** *b.* 24 May 1782. Originally posted to Madras, arrived there, 12 Feb. 1809. Transferred to Bengal, 26 May 1809; (G.O. 26 May 1809, S.A.L.M.M.). A.S. Bengal, 6 Feb. 1809. Surg. 9 Aug. 1823. *d.* at Cape of Good Hope, 16 Apr. 1825. D. and M. give name in Bengal, but not in Madras List. M. No. 578.

648. **Prichard, Edward.** M.R.C.S. 1807. A.S. 7 Feb. 1809. *d.* at sea, 8 July 1819. Third Maratha on Pindari war, 1817-18; (P.R.).

649. **Kirchner, Benjamin** (a, d). *b.* 16 July 1780. A.S. 14 June 1809; (L. from C. 30 June 1809; C.G. 14 Dec. 1809). Name entered in A.S. Certs, vol. v. and erased. Never joined. Appointed Hosp. Mate. A.M.D. 8 July 1809. Name not in Johnston's Roll of R.A.M.C.

650. **MacDonald, Ewen.** *b.* 12 July 1788. A.S. 24 July 1809. Surg. 9 Aug. 1823. R. 1 May 1838. *d.* 19 Aug. 1840. Java, 1811, capture of Java; Bharatpur, 1825-26, siege and storm of Bharatpur; (P.R.).

651. **Hardtman, Benjamin.** *b.* 19 Nov. 1786, in St. Kitts, West Indies. M.D. Ed. 1807. A.S. 25 July 1809. Surg. 27 Sept. 1823. *d.* in Calcutta, 20 Jan. 1826. D. and M. spell name Hardman.

652. **Lamb, John.** *b.* 21 Jan. 1787. A.S. 26 July 1809. Gave up promotion to remain at Malda. *d.* in Edinburgh, 31 July 1854. Afterwards gazetted to retire from 15 Feb. 1856.

653. **Halket, Patrick.** *b.* 17 Jan. 1788. A.S. 27 July 1809. Surg. 27 Sept. 1823. R. 2 June 1828. Java, 1811, capture of Java. Third Maratha or Pindari war, 1817-18 ; (P.R.).

654. **Govan, George.** *b.* 15 Nov. 1787. M.D. Ed. 1806. A.S. 28 July 1809. Surg. 27 Sept. 1823. R. 24 Apr. 1834. *d.* at Whinfield, Kinross, 11 Oct. 1865. Father of G. M. Govan, No. 1756, infra.

655. **Calder, James.** *b.* 20 Feb. 1787. A.S. 29 July 1809. *d.* at Cawnpur, 6 Oct. 1816 ; (A.J. May 1817). S.A.L.M.B. and D. and M. give place of death as Allahabad, same date.

656. **Hopkins, David.** *b.* 25 Dec. 1772. M.R.C.S 1808. A.S. 30 July 1809. *d.* at Samarang, Java, 29 Dec. 1813 ; (G.M. Nov. 1814). Java, 1811.

657. **Wilson, Andrew.** *b.* 10 Dec. 1784. A.S. 1 Aug. 1809. *d.* at Dinapur, 31 Aug. 1810.

658. **Blair, Robert.** *b.* 7 Nov. 1788. A.S. 1 Aug. 1809. Struck off, 11 Aug. 1817. D. and M. say " pensioned," no date.

659. **Eckford, John** (b). *b.* 22 Jan. 1788. Surg. Mate, ' Henry Addington,' 1808-09. A.S. 11 Nov. 1809. Surg. 27 Sept. 1823. *d.* at Allahabad, 5 Sept. 1835. Java, 1811, capture of Java.

660. **Malcom, William.** *b.* 5 Jan. 1788. L.R.C.S. Ed. 1808. A.S. 12 Nov. 1809. Furlough, 1811. M.D. St. A. 1813. Pensioned on Lord Clive's Fund, 19 June 1816. Afterwards in practice at Perth. *d.* 20 Oct. 1854.

661. **Paterson, Robert.** *b.* 7 July 1782. M.D. Ed. 1803. A.S. 13 Nov. 1809. M.R.C.S. 1810. Surg. 27 Sept. 1823. *d.* in Calcutta, 9 Dec. 1829. Burma, 1824-25 ; (P.R.).

662. **Hogg, William** (b, c). Surg. Mate, ' Walthamstow,' 1803-04 ; Surg. ' Walthamstow,' 1806-07 ; of ' Streatham,' 1808-09. A.S. 14 Nov. 1809. M.D. K.C. Ab. 1816. *d.* at Hughli, 30 Sept. 1820. Anne Hogg, his wife, *d.* on 6 Oct. and was buried in the same grave ; (C.G. 12 and 26 Oct. 1820).

1810

663. **Wakeford, Thomas Huckell.** *b.* 19 Aug. 1788. M.R.C.S. 1809. A.S. 30 July 1810. *d.* in Genl. Hosp. Calcutta, 26 Sept. 1810 ; (C.G. 27 Sept. 1810).

664. **Compton, Thomas.** *b.* 24 Feb. 1787. M.R.C.S. 1809. A.S. 31 July 1810. Cashiered, 21 Dec. 1816 ; Sentence remitted on account of mental affection. Pensioned, 27 Dec. 1816. *d.* 1833 ; (Advt. of estate in C.G. of 5 Oct. 1833).

665. **Watson, John.** *b.* Sept. 1787. M.R.C.S. 1809. A.S. 1 Aug. 1810. *d.* at Cawnpur, 31 Dec. 1812.

666. **Meikle, David William.** *b.* 21 Sept. 1788. A.S. 2 Aug. 1810. *d.* at Kunch, Jalaun, 17 June 1814. War with France ; went out to India on the ' Astell,' which, with the ' Wyndham,' and ' Ceylon,' was attacked off Johanna by two French frigates and a corvette ; the ' Astell ' escaped, the two others were taken ; mentioned for services to the wounded in the action ; (A.A. Regr. 1810, pp. 107, 108).

667. **Lawson, George.** *b.* 16 Mar. 1788. M.R.C.S. 1809. A.S. 3 Aug. 1810. *d.* at sea, on Indiaman ' Pilot,' off Scilly, 6 Mar. 1821 ; (E.I. Regr.). S.A.L.M.B. and D. and M. give date of death as 6 Mar. 1820. Capture of Mauritius, 1810 ; (P.R.). Java, 1811, capture of Java.

668. **Muston, Edward.** *b.* Dec. 1788. M.R.C.S. 1809. A.S. 4 Aug. 1810. Surg. 27 Sept. 1823. R. 14 Nov. 1831. *d.* at Bordeaux, 5 Jan. 1864. Capture of Mauritius, 1810 ; (P.R.). Java, 1811, capture of Java.

669. **Fallowfield, Jonathan** (b). *b.* 28 May 1780. Surg. ' Northumberland,' 1808–09. A.S. 5 Aug. 1810. M.R.C.S. 1815. Surg. 27 Sept. 1823. R. 11 May 1830. *d.* 12 Apr. 1860. First name given as James in S.A.L.M.B. Java, 1811, capture of Java ; (P.R.). Third Maratha or Pindari war, 1817–18 ; (P.R.).

670. **Duncan, James Johnston** (a, d). *b.* 23 Aug. 1791. A.S. Madras, 22 Aug. 1810. Gazetted to Bengal in C.G. of 14 Nov. 1811, struck off Bengal list in C.G. of 7 May 1812. M.A. Mar. Coll. Ab. 1812. L.R.C.S. Ed. 18—. *d.* at Cannanore, 11 Nov. 1821. D. and M. give name in Madras, but not in Bengal list.

671. **Buchanan, Benjamin Bartlett.** *b.* June 1785. M.D. Ed. 1806. A.S. 3 Oct. 1810. Furlough, M.C. G.O. 27 Nov. 1810. L.R.C.P. Ed. 1812. F.R.C.P. Ed. 1813. Resigned, 17 Nov. 1813.

672. **Garrack, John** (b). *b.* 6 June 1783. M.D. Ed. 1805. M.R.C.S. 1805. Surg. ' Sir William Bensley,' 1808–09. A.S. 4 Oct. 1810. *d.* at Jumna Ghat, Allahabad, 1 Mar. 1811 ; (C.G. 14 Mar. 1811).

673. **Wingfield, Charles.** *b.* July 1787. A.S. 5 Oct. 1810. Furlough, 1813. Struck off in 1818, absent 2½ years ; (C.G. 13 Aug. 1818).

674. **Woody, Robert** (a, d). C.C.S. 1791. A.S. 8 Nov. 1810, gazetted in C.G. of that date. Never joined. Apparently same man as Robert MacWoody, No. 500, supra, 1799. T. C. Brown, No. 688, infra, nominated " in room of Robert Woody, who does not proceed " ; (A.S. Certs. vol. vii.). Was in practice at Shrewsbury, 1791.

675. **Thomson, James.** *b.* 8 Aug. 1789. M.R.C.S. 1806. A.S. 10 Nov. 1810. Surg. 27 Sept. 1823. S.S. 16 Mar. 1842, supy. for force in China ; (G.O. No. 69 of 16 Mar. 1842). S.S. 31 Dec. 1842. M.M.B. and I.G. Hosps. 10 Feb. 1849. S.G. 10 Apr. 1852. Phys. Genl. and Pres. 16 May 1853. *d.* in Calcutta, 25 Aug. 1853. K.C.B. 17 Aug. 1850, the first I.M.S officer to receive the Order of the Bath, Military Division, when extended to medical officers. v. Hist. of I.M.S. ii. 211. Java, 1811, capture of Java. Burma, 1824–25. Desp. L.G. 20 July 1825. Afghanistan, 1839–42, with 2nd Cavalry, and afterwards as S.S. Army of Indus, capture of Ghuzni ; (P.R.), medal. China, 1842–45, as S.S. capture of Nankin, medal.

676. **Thomson, Harvey.** *b.* 6 Nov. 1788. M.A. Mar. Coll. Ab. 1808. M.R.C.S. 1810. A.S. 11 Nov. 1810. Struck off from 31 Dec. 1818, remained as a merchant in Java ; (C.G. 17 Apr. 1823). Java, 1811, capture of Java ; (P.R.).

677. **Ramsay, Crichton.** *b.* 22 July 1787. A.S. 12 Nov. 1810. *d.* at Saharanpur, 22 July 1817. Java, 1811, capture of Java ; (P.R.).

678. **Morison, John.** *b.* 20 May 1790. M.D. Ed. 1808. A.S. 13 Nov. 1810. Drowned near Kedgeree (Khijri), at mouth of Hughli, 10 Oct. 1821. Java, 1811, capture of Java ; (P.R.). Nipal, 1815–16.

679. Irving, John Lowther. *b.* 4 Aug. 1790. L.R.C.S. Ed. A.S. 14 Nov. 1810. *d.* at Jabalpur, 4 Aug. 1822. Java, 1811, capture of Java; (P.R.). Third Maratha or Pindari war, 1817-18; (P.R.).

680. Dickson, Robert (a). *b.* 14 Nov. 1789. A.S. 15 Nov. 1810; (C.G. 30 Apr. 1812). *d.* at Batavia, Oct. 1811. Java, 1811, capture of Java.

681. Paterson, John James. *b.* 12 Dec. 1787. M.A. Mar. Coll. Ab. 1805. M.R.C.S. 1809. A.S. 16 Nov. 1810. M.D. K.C. Ab. 1820. Surg. 27 Sept. 1823. *d.* at Genl. Croxton's seat in Northamptonshire, 22 Mar. 1837. Java, 1811, capture of Java; (P.R.).

1811

682. Pollock, or **Pollok, William** (a, d). *b.* 5 Mar. 1784. M.D. Glas. 1803. Hosp. Mate, A.M.D. 8 Sept. 1803. A.S. 53rd Foot, 24 Oct. 1803. A.S. Bengal, 20 Feb. 1811; (C.G. 29 Aug. 1811). Declined appointment, and remained in A.M.D.; (C.G. 16 Apr. 1812). Surg. 53rd Foot, 8 Oct. 1818. R. on half-pay, 14 July 1825. Afterwards took name of Morris. v. Johnston's Roll of R.A.M.C. No. 2296, where name is spelt Pollok. Also spelt Pollok in A.S. Certs. vol. vii. 1811. Nipal, 1814-15.

683. Hanson, Richard Charles (a, d). M.R.C.S. 1809. A.S. 27 Mar. 1811. " Resigned without joining "; (List of A.S. 1791-1814). Afterwards in practice at Bristol. *d.* 1849; name omitted from Medical Directory in 1850.

684. Brown, Robert. *b.* 1 July 1790. A.S. 16 Aug. 1811. Surg. 27 Sept. 1823. S.S. 1 Jan. 1843. *d.* at Digha, near Dinapur, 15 Mar. 1853. Nipal, 1814-15, actions at Jitgarh and Mukwanpur. Third Maratha or Pindari war, 1817-18, capture of Mandla. Bharatpur, 1825-26, siege and storm of Bharatpur.

685. Spilsbury, George Green. *b.* 30 July 1786. M.D. Ed. 1807. A.S. 17 Aug. 1811. Surg. 27 Sept. 1823. S.S. 31 Jan. 1844. M.M.B. and I.G. Hosps. 10 Apr. 1852. S.G. 16 May 1853. Phys. Genl. and Pres. 26 Aug. 1853. *d.* in Calcutta, 6 July 1857. Nipal, 1814-16, medal. Third Maratha or Pindari war, 1817-18, siege and capture of Hathras in 1817, and of Asirgarh, 1819. Author of Hindustani translation of London Pharmacopœia, 1848.

686. Woolley, Joseph. *b.* 10 Feb. 1791. M.R.C.S. 1811. A.S. 18 Aug. 1811. Surg. 27 Sept. 1823. *d.* at Fatehgarh, 18 Apr. 1831; (A.J. Nov. 1831, p. 139). D. and M. give date of death as 18 Apr. 1830. Java, 1811, capture of Java. Bharatpur, 1825-26, siege and storm of Bharatpur; (P.R.).

687. Brown, Thomas Campbell. *b.* 16 Feb. 1788. M.D. Ed. 1808. M.R.C.S. 1811. A.S. 19 Aug. 1811. " Nominated in room of Robert Woody, who does not proceed "; (A.S. Certs. vol. vii.). Surg. 27 Sept. 1823. *d.* near Jodhpur, 22 Oct. 1839. Name spelt Browne in S.A.L.M.B. Java, 1811, capture of Java.

688. Murray, Andrew (b). *b.* Dec. 1788. Surg. Mate of 'Earl Howe, 1806-07. M.D. Ed. 1810. M.R.C.S. 1811. A.S. 20 Aug. 1811. Surg. 24 Mar. 1824. Furlough, 1 Feb. 1835, struck off in India, 1 Aug. 1837; (S.A.L.M.B.). *d.* in Edinburgh, 24 Apr. 1838. Java, 1811, capture of Java. Third Maratha or Pindari war, 1817-18; (P.R.).

689. **Hall, James.** *b.* 14 Nov. 1788. L.R.C.S. Ed. 1811. A.S. 20 Nov. 1811. Surg. 29 June 1824. R. 9 Feb. 1834. Third Maratha or Pindari war, 1817–18; (P.R.). Bharatpur, 1825–26, siege and storm of Bharatpur.

1812

690. **Hamilton, William.** L.R.C.S. Ed. ———. A.S. 13 Jan. 1812. *d.* at Bareli, 7 Dec. 1815.

691. **Harding, Daniel** (b). *b.* June 1787. M.R.C.S. 1810. Surg. of 'Larkins,' 1810–11. A.S. 30 July 1812. Surg. 29 June 1824. R. 2 Apr. 1838. *d.* 26 Oct. 1845. Bharatpur, 1825–26, siege and storm of Bharatpur; (P.R.).

692. **Marechaux, Joseph.** *b.* 27 Aug. 1764. M.R.C.S. 1811. A.S. 31 July 1812. Drowned, 5 Dec. 1814; (C.G. 8 Dec. 1814).

693. **Nicoll, John** (b). *b.* Sept. 1789. M.D. K.C. Ab. 1812. Surg. of 'Carmarthen,' 1812. A.S. 1 Aug. 1812. Surg. 4 Oct. 1824. *d.* at Nasirabad, 16 Sept. 1834. Third Maratha or Pindari war, 1817–18; (P.R.). Burma, 1824–25.

694. **Renny, Charles.** *b.* 11 May 1789. M.A. Mar. Coll. Ab. 1806. M.R.C.S. 1811. A.S. 2 Nov. 1812. Surg. 25 Nov. 1824. S.S. 1 Mar. 1843. M.M.B. and I.G. Hosps. 16 May 1853. S.G. 25 Aug. 1853. F.R.C.S. 1855. R. 10 Apr. 1857. *d.* at Exmouth, 25 Mar. 1876. D. and M. spell name Ranny. C.B. 17 Mar. 1850. Nipal, 1814–15, with Field Hosp., medal. Third Maratha or Pindari war, 1817–18. Afghanistan, 1839–42. Second Sikh or Panjab war, 1848–49, as S.S., battles of Ramnagar and Chilianwala, Desp. L.G. 3 Mar. 1849, and Gujrat, Desp. L.G. 18 Apr. 1849. Author, with J. MacRae, No. 1125, infra, of Report on Medical Arrangements of Field Hospital of Army of the Panjab, 1848–49; and of Report on Mahamurree in Garhwal, 1849–50, 1851.

695. **Clapperton, John Buncle.** *b.* 10 Feb. 1791. A.S. 19 Dec. 1812. Surg. 6 Jan. 1825. S.S. 23 July 1843. M.M.B. and I.G. Hosps. 26 Aug. 1853. S.G. 10 Apr. 1857. R. 13 Feb. 1858. *d.* 20 Jan. 1869.

696. **Primrose, Robert.** *b.* 27 Apr. 1774. C.C.S. 1796. A.S. 20 Dec. 1812. Surg. 23 May 1825. R. 16 June 1826. Third Maratha or Pindari war, 1817–18; (P.R.).

1813

697. **Kennedy, Gilbert MacClure** (b, c). Surg. of 'Ann,' 1810–11; of 'Harriet,' 1812–13. Officiating A.S. 2 Jan. 1813; (C.G.). Confirmed, 19 Nov. 1813. *d.* at Patna, 17 June 1824.

698. **Smith, John** (b, c). M.D. Ed. 1812. Surg. of 'Marquis Wellesley,' 1811–13. Officiating A.S. 7 Aug. 1813; (Mily. L. from C. 7 Aug. 1813, paras. 74, 75). Confirmed, 20 Nov. 1813. Surg. 5 May 1826. *d.* at Nimach, 24 July 1830.

699. **Patterson, David Aikman** (b). *b.* 16 Feb. 1782. Surg. Mate, 'Europa,' 1802–04; Surg. 'Henry Addington,' 1805–12. A.S. 10 Aug. 1813. Had originally been nominated in season, 1804–05, next James Roberts, No. 560, supra; (Lists of A.S. 1791–1814). *d.* in Genl. Hosp. Calcutta, 7 Apr. 1821.

700. Watson, William. *b.* 7 Mar. 1788. M.D. Mar. Coll. Ab. 1810. M.R.C.S. 1812. A.S. 11 Aug. 1813. Surg. 17 Apr. 1825. S.S. 16 Feb. 1844. F.R.C.S. original list, 1844. *d.* at Benares, 10 Aug. 1849.

701. Jack, William (b, e). *b.* 29 Jan. 1792. M.R.C.S. 1811. Surg. Mate, 'Neptune,' 1811. A.S. 12 Aug. 1813. *d.* on board the 'Layton' in Bencoolen Roads, 15 Sept. 1822; (C.G. 19 Dec. 1822). Nipal, 1814–16. Author of Papers on Malayan Plants, in Malayan Miscellanies, 2 vols., 1821–22.

702. Allan, John (b). *b.* Dec. 1788. Surg. Mate, 'Charles Grant,' 1810–11 A.S. 13 Aug. 1813. M.R.C.S. 1822. Surg. 11 May 1825. *d.* in Calcutta, 16 Oct. 1835. Third Maratha or Pindari war, 1817–18; (P.R.).

703. Luxmoore, Thomas. *b.* 13 Mar. 1774. A.S. 8 Sept. 1813. M.R.C.S. 1820. Surg. 23 May 1825. *d.* at Lucknow, 2 Oct. 1828.

704. Melville, Alexander (b). *b.* 14 Oct. 1790. Surg. Mate, 'Castlereagh,' 1807–08. Hosp. Mate, A.M.D. 10 Jan. 1811. Resigned, —; (v. Johnston's Roll of R.A.M.C. No. 3280). M.R.C.S. 1812. A.S. Bengal, 9 Sept. 1813. R. 28 May 1824. *d.* at Wimbledon, 16 Sept. 1840.

705. Tytler, John. *b.* 26 Sept. 1790. Barts. M.R.C.S. 1813. A.S. 7 Nov. 1813. Surg. 5 July 1825. *d.* at St. Helier's, Jersey, 5 Mar. 1837. Father of H. W. Tytler, No. 1401, infra. Author of Fusul-i Abkrat, or Aphorisms of Hippocrates, translated into Arabic, 1832; Anis-ul-Musharrahin, or Anatomist's Vademecum, translated into Arabic, 1835.

706. Jackson, William. *b.* 28 Oct. 1790. M.R.C.S. 1812. A.S. 8 Nov. 1813. Surg. 14 July 1825. F.R.C.S. original list, 1844. S.S. 15 Feb. 1845. R. 1 Aug. 1853. *d.* in Edinburgh, 30 Mar. 1854. S.A.L.M.B. gives date of retirement as 1 Mar. 1853. Father of J. R. Jackson, No. 1666, infra. Nipal, 1814–16. Third Maratha or Pindari war 1817–18, siege and capture of Hathras, 1817; (P.R.). Burma, 1824–25, capture of Rangoon; (P.R.).

707. Davies, Joseph. *b.* 26 May 1789. A.S. 9 Nov. 1813. *d.* at Murshidabad, 13 Feb. 1819.

708. Warner, Gregory (a, d). *b.* 13 Oct. 1779. M.R.C.S. 1805. A.S. 9 Nov. 1813. Sailed for India in 'Barosa'; (Genl. L. from C. 12 May 1813; C.G. 25 Nov. 1813). Apparently never joined. Name omitted from list in E.I. Regr. in 1816. No further information. Probably *d.* on 'Barosa,' during voyage to India, but her log for that voyage is not available.

709. Wills, William Inglis (b). Surg. Mate, 'Fairlie,' 1811–12. A.S. 10 Nov. 1813. *d.* at Sagar, 24 Oct. 1819. Third Maratha or Pindari war, 1817–18; (P.R.).

710. Evans, James. *b.* 4 Nov. 1790. M.R.C.S. 1812. A.S. 11 Nov. 1813. Surg. 22 July 1825. R. 24 Apr. 1834.

711. Ray, Charles. M.R.C.S. 1812. A.S. 12 Nov. 1813. Surg. 8 Sept. 1825. *d.* at Tannington, Suffolk, 4 Mar. 1830. Nipal, 1815–16. Third Maratha or Pindari war, 1817–18; (P.R.). Bharatpur, 1825–26, siege and storm of Bharatpur.

712. Stratton, Andrew (b). *b.* 19 June 1786. Surg. 'Northumberland,' 1810–12. A.S. 13 Nov. 1813. Surg. 24 Oct. 1825. *d.* at Karnal, 27 Sept. 1829. Name spelt Straton in E.I. Regr. but his signature, in A.S. Certs. vol. xiii. 1812–13, is Stratton. Nipal, 1814–16. Burma, 1824–25.

713. **Gray, John.** *b.* 30 Sept. 1790. A.S. 14 Nov. 1813. M.R.C.S. 1814. *d.* at Nagpur, 7 May 1822.

714. **Davidson, John Maxwell.** *b.* 9 Sept. 1792. M.R.C.S. 1812. A.S. 15 Nov. 1813. *d.* at Purnea, 17 Aug. 1819.

715. **Webb, William Taylor.** *b.* Feb. 1792. M.R.C.S. 1812. A.S. 16 Nov. 1813. Surg. 20 Jan. 1826. *d.* at Chunar, 14 Sept. 1828. Third Maratha or Pindari war, 1817–18 ; (P.R.).

716. **Watson, James.** *b.* 11 Sept. 1792. M.D. Ed. 1812. A.S. 17 Nov. 1813. Surg. 23 Feb. 1826. R. 30 July 1833. *d.* at Bath, 27 Sept. 1878.

717. **Darby, William.** *b.* 12 Nov. 1790. M.R.C.S. 1810. A.S. 18 Nov. 1813. Surg. 25 Mar. 1826. F.R.C.S. original list, 1844. S.S. 1 Apr. 1845. R. 31 Dec. 1849. *d.* in London, 10 Mar. 1867. Nipal, 1814–16, medal. Third Maratha or Pindari war, 1817–18 ; (P.R.). Afghanistan, 1841–42, as First Field Surgeon, medal.

1814

718. **Berger, John Francis** (a, d). *b.* at Geneva, 26 June 1778, a Swiss. M.D. Paris, 1806. L.R.C.P. Lond. 1809. Had previously served in A.M.D. ; (List of A.S. 1791–1814, but name not in Johnston's Roll of R.A.M.C.). Nominated A.S. Madras, 16 Feb. 1814, name subsequently transferred to Bengal ; (S.A.L.M.M.). Never joined. Gazetted Hosp. Asst. A.M.D. 10 Jan. 1814 ; appointment cancelled, L.G. 9 Apr. 1814. Afterwards in practice in London. M.R.C.P. Lond. 1859.

719. **Hastie, William.** *b.* 22 May 1791. A.S. 4 May 1814. Third Maratha or Pindari war, 1817–18. Accidentally killed in camp before Chanda, by explosion of his rifle when loading it, May 1818 ; (C.G. 4 June 1818).

720. **Leslie, William.** *b.* 2 July 1793. M.D. Ed. 1813. A.S. 5 May 1814. Surg. 5 May 1826. *d.* at Landour, 14 June 1831. Bharatpur, 1825–26, siege and storm of Bharatpur ; (P.R.).

721. **MacLean, Alexander.** *b.* Jan. 1785. A.S. 6 May 1814. *d.* at Cuttack, 29 Sept. 1831.

722. **Corbyn, Frederick.** *b.* 11 May 1791. C.C.S. 1813. A.S. 7 May 1814. Surg. 5 May 1826. M.R.C.S. 1841. S.S. 10 Mar. 1846. *d.* at Simla, 7 Oct. 1853. Father of F. Corbyn, No. 1554, and of J. C. Corbyn, No. 1583, infra. Nipal, 1814–16, actions of Samanpur and Makwanpur, medal. Third Maratha or Pindari war, 1817–20, capture of Mandla, 1818, of Asirgarh, 1819, and of Garha Kota, 1820. First Sikh or Sutlej war, 1845–46, as S.S. Genl. Littler's force. Second Sikh or Panjab war, 1848–49, as S.S. Panjab Division. Author of Management and Diseases of Infants in India, 2 vols. 1828 ; Treatise on Epidemic Cholera, 1832 ; Science of National Defence, with reference to India, 1840 ; Edited India Journal of Medical and Physical Science, 1836–1843.

723. **Sempill, Francis, the Hon.** *b.* 31 May 1791, second son of Hugh, 13th Baron Sempill. A.S. 8 May 1814. *d.* in Calcutta, 2 Jan. 1823. Third Maratha or Pindari war, 1817–18, with Body Guard ; (P.R.).

724. **Pears, Charles.** *b.* 17 Mar. 1774. M.D. A.S. 9 May 1814. Resigned in India, 13 Nov. 1819.

725. **Wallich, Nathaniel** (e). *b.* at Copenhagen, 28 Jan. 1786. Real name Nathan Wolff. Lic. Royal Acad. Surg. Copenhagen, 1806. Surgeon to Danish settlement of Serampur, 1807–08, taken by British in 1808. Appointed Asst. to Dr. Roxburgh, 1809; (Pub. L. from B. 30 June 1809, para. 210). v. Hist. of I.M.S. ii. 143, 144. A.S. 10 May 1814. M.D. Mar. Coll. Ab. 1819. Ph.D. Copenhagen, 1821. Surg. 5 May 1826. R. 9 Apr. 1846. *d.* in London, 28 Apr. 1854. Father of G. C. Wallich, No. 1287, and of N. D. S. Wallich, No. 1546, infra. Knight of Dannebrog, 1818. Silver Cross of Dannebrogsmund, 1829. F.R.S. 1829. Author of Tentamen Floræ Nipalensis, 2 vols. 1824–26; List of Specimens in E.I. Co.'s Museum, 1828; Plantæ Asiaticæ Rariores, 3 vols. 1830–32.

726. **Maxwell, Neil.** *b.* 11 Feb. 1792. M.D. Ed. 1812. A.S. 11 May 1814. Surg. 5 May 1826. R. 1 Feb. 1837. *d.* in Edinburgh, 24 Jan. 1861. Bharatpur, 1825–26, siege and storm of Bharatpur; (P.R.).

727. **Brown, Alexander.** *b.* 11 Nov. 1791. M.R.C.S. 1813. M.D. Glas. 1813. A.S. 11 May 1814. *d.* in Calcutta, 21 Aug. 1814.

728. **Casey, Thomas.** B.A. 1800; M.B. 1808; M.D. 1814; T.C.D. A.S. 12 May 1814. *d.* in Fort William, 15 Aug. 1817.

729. **Daniel Lewis** (b). *b.* 25 Mar. 1790. Surg. Mate, 'Hope,' 1810–12. M.R.C.S. 1812. A.S. 12 May 1814. *d.* at Gaya, 29 Jan. 1819; (tombstone). D. and M. and S.A.L.M.B. give date of death as 26 Jan. 1818.

730. **Lancaster, John.** *b.* 23 Nov. 1788. A.S. 12 Oct. 1814. *d.* at Bencoolen, 16 Sept. 1821.

731. **Hickman, Charles.** *b.* 28 Nov. 1791. M.R.C.S. 1812. A.S. 13 Oct. 1814. R. 10 May 1825. *d.* 21 Nov. 1866. Third Maratha or Pindari war, 1817–18; (P.R.). Author of A History of Cholera.

732. **Gibb, Francis Thomas.** *b.* May 1792. M.R.C.S. 1814. A.S. 14 Oct. 1814. Resigned in India, 6 Dec. 1816. Nipal, 1815–16, in Field Hosp.; (S.A.L.M.B.).

733. **Hayley, Thomas.** *b.* Sept. 1791. M.R.C.S. 1813. A.S. 15 Oct. 1814. Surg. 5 May 1826. Invalided, 7 Aug. 1829. R. 10 Jan. 1832. *d.* 2 Oct. 1845. S.A.L.M.B. gives date of invaliding as 7 Aug. 1830. Nipal, 1815–16.

734. **Baker, Thomas Eld.** *b.* 19 June 1791. St. Georges. M.R.C.S. 1813. A.S. 16 Oct. 1814. Surg. 5 May 1826. R. 3 Aug. 1838. *d.* in London, 23 July 1868. Nipal, 1814–16. Third Maratha or Pindari war, 1817–18; (P.R.). Bharatpur, 1825–26, siege and storm of Bharatpur. Author of The Art of Preserving Health in India, 1829.

735. **Manly, Joshua.** *b.* 22 May 1789. M.R.C.S. 1814. A.S. 25 Nov. 1814. Surg. 5 May 1826. R. 9 Apr. 1832. *d.* 14 Jan. 1879. Third Maratha or Pindari war, 1817–18; (P.R.).

736. **Fraser, John Munro.** *b.* Dec. 1791. M.R.C.S. 1814. A.S. 25 Nov. 1814. *d.* at Bettiah, Champarun, 29 Sept. 1815. First name given as James in S.A.L.M.B.

737. **Saunders, Henry Petrie.** *b.* Aug. 1791. M.R.C.S. 1813. A.S. 26 Nov. 1814. Surg. 5 May 1826. R. 3 July 1828. Burma, 1824–25; (P.R.).

738. **Gerard, James Gilbert** (e). b. 13 Feb. 1793. M.A. K.C. Ab. 1811. M.R.C.S. 1814. A.S. 27 Nov. 1814. Surg. 5 May 1826. d. at Sabathu, 31 Mar. 1835. Accompanied Sir Alex. Burnes on his journey to Bokhara and Central Asia.

739. **Duncan, Joseph.** b. Nov. 1790. A.S. 28 Nov. 1814. Surg. 5 May 1826. d. at Abernethy, Perthshire, 3 May 1837. Third Maratha or Pindari war, 1817–18; (P.R.).

740. **Rind, James Nathaniel.** b. 16 Oct. 1793. A.S. 29 Nov. 1814. Surg. 5 May 1826. Invalided, 13 June 1836. d. at sea, 27 Apr. 1840. Brother of T. Rind, No. 465, Bombay, 1820; and of No. 1158, infra, M. M. Rind, 1829.

741. **Stoddart, Thomas.** b. 29 Oct. 1792. M.D. Glas. 1813. A.S. 30 Nov. 1814. Surg. 5 May 1826. R. 5 Apr. 1838.

742. **Wardell, John.** b. 1787. M.R.C.S. 1808. A.S. 1 Dec. 1814. R. 1 Feb. 1825.

1815

743. **Scott, Robert** (a, b, c). M.R.C.S. 1814. Surg. Mate, 'Castlereagh,' 1814–15. Officiating A.S. Bengal, 24 Jan. 1815; (C.G. 2 Feb. 1815). Struck off, 1 Aug. 1817; (C.G. 6 Nov. 1817). Reappointed officiating A.S. 28 Oct. 1817; (C.G. 6 Nov. 1817). Officiating A.S. Madras, 2 Oct. 1819; (Madras G.O. 2 Oct. 1819). Confirmed as A.S. Madras, 24 Aug. 1821. Surg. 15 Sept. 1833. S.S. 2 Mar. 1847. R. 15 Dec. 1853. d. at Kensington, 10 June 1858. Name not in D. and M's. list, of either Bengal or Madras. S.A.L.M.B. gives name as Scott, Robert, or Scot, J. Third Maratha or Pindari war, 1817–18; (P.R.). M. No. 641.

744. **Barker, James** (b, c). b. May 1792. M.R.C.S. 1814. Surg. 'Coldstream,' 1814–15. Officiating A.S. 28 Jan. 1815; (C.G. 9 Feb. 1815). Struck off, 1 Aug. 1817; (C.G. 7 Aug. 1817). Reappointed officiating A.S. 28 Oct. 1817; (C.G. 6 Nov. 1817). Struck off, 30 Sept. 1820; (C.G. 12 Oct. 1820). A.S. 27 June 1821. Surg. 9 Feb. 1834. R. 1 Feb. 1845. Nipal, 1815–16.

*745. **Mendes, Matthew** (a, b, c). Surg. of E.I. Co.'s Cruiser 'Ariel,' 1814–15. Officiating A.S. 7 Feb. 1815; (C.G. 16 Feb. 1815). Struck off, 1 Aug. 1817; (C.G. 7 Aug. 1817). Reappointed officiating A.S. 28 Oct. 1817; (C.G. 6 Nov. 1817). Struck off, 30 Sept. 1820; (C.G. 12 Oct. 1820). Relieved and Discharged, 4 Nov. 1820. A.S. Madras, 5 May 1822. M.R.C.S. 1824. d. in London, 9 July 1828. Name given by D. and M. in Madras, but not in Bengal list. Apparently never joined appointment in Madras; (S.A.L.M.B.). Third Maratha or Pindari war, 1817–19, capture of Asirgarh, 1819, severely wounded. M. No. 642.

*746. **MacCowan, George** (b, c). b. 1790. M.R.C.S. 1814. Surg. 'Marchioness of Ely,' 1814–15. In the Marine Records his name is given as George Cowan. Officiating A.S. 15 Feb. 1815; (C.G. 23 Feb. 1815). Struck off, 1 Aug. 1817; (C.G. 7 Aug. 1817). Reappointed officiating A.S. 28 Oct. 1817; (C.G. 6 Nov. 1817). Struck off, 30 Sept. 1820; (C.G. 12 Oct. 1820). Relieved and discharged, 15 Oct. 1820. A.S. 21 Feb. 1824. d. in Fort William, 1 July 1824.

* In Mily. Letter from Bengal of 31 Mar. 1821, para. 84, are given the actual dates of relief and discharge of sixteen officiating Asst. Surgeons, who were ordered to be struck off in C.G. of 12 Oct. 1820: G. MacCowan, 15 Oct. 1820; W. Mitchelson, 15 Oct.; G. Craigie, 26 Oct.; J. Ronald, 2 Nov.; M. Mendes, 4 Nov.; J. Laing, 5 Nov.; J. P. Barnett, 12 Nov.; Turnbull, 4 Dec.; J. Sullivan, 21 Dec.; John Smith, 21 Dec.; R. Walker, 24 Dec.; P. I. de Joncourt, 5 Jan. 1821; J. Wilson, 15 Jan.; C. Wilkinson, 20 Jan.; J. King, 6 Feb.; J. P. Reynolds, 11 Feb.

747. **Rennick** or **Renneck, A.** — (a, c). M.R.C.S. 1815. Officiating A.S. 1815. Struck off, 30 Sept. 1820; (C.G. 12 Oct. 1820, where name is spelt Renneck). Reappointed officiating A.S. 6 Jan. 1826; (C.G. 16 Jan. 1826, where name is spelt Rennick, " formerly of Dromedary Corps "). Struck off, Oct. 1827. Afterwards in practice at Enniskillen. Third Maratha or Pindari war, 1817–18; (P.R.).

748. **Philan, Joseph.** *b.* 30 Mar. 1786. M.D. 18—. M.R.C.S. 18—. L.R.C.P. Lond. 18—. A.S. 21 Aug. 1815. *d.* in England, 24 Mar. 1822.

749. **Garden, Alexander.** *b.* Sept. 1794. M.A. 1813; M.D. 1835; K.C. Ab. M.R.C.S. 1813. A.S. 25 Aug. 1815. Surg. 5 May 1826. F.R.C.S. original list, 1844. *d.* in Calcutta, 24 Apr. 1845. Father of No. 1667, infra, A. M. Garden. Third Maratha or Pindari war, 1817–18; (P.R.).

750. **Urquhart, George Trail.** *b.* 3 Jan. 1791. M.R.C.S. 1814. A.S. 26 Aug. 1815. Surg. 5 May 1826. *d.* at Mirat, 16 Nov. 1840. Third Maratha or Pindari war, 1817–18; (P.R.).

751. **Mercer, Hugh Smyth.** *b.* 27 Feb. 1793. A.S. 22 Sept. 1815. Surg. 5 May 1826. R. 18 Apr. 1843. *d.* at Charlton Kings, Cheltenham, 22 May 1870. Third Maratha or Pindari war, 1817–18; (P.R.).

752. **Strong, Francis Pemble.** *b.* Oct. 1784. M.R.C.S. 1805. A.S. 23 Sept. 1815. Gave up promotion to remain in 24 Parganas, and held that Civil Surgeoncy for 35 years, 1822–57, without furlough. *d.* in London, 10 May 1858.

753. **Whitehead, James Towers.** *b.* 12 Mar. 1794. A.S. 24 Sept. 1815. *d.* in camp at Tanghi, near Chilka Lake, 12 Dec. 1817.

754. **Watson, John Alexander Davidson** (b). *b.* 14 Feb. 1791. M.R.C.S. 1809. Surg. Mate, ' Hugh Inglis,' 1810–11; Surg. ' Marquis of Wellington,' 1812–13. A.S. 25 Sept. 1815. Surg. 5 May 1826. *d.* at Garawari, 27 Dec. 1832. Bharatpur, 1825–26, siege and storm of Bharatpur; (P.R.).

755. **Pigott, William.** *b.* 25 Feb. 1775. M.R.C.S. 1815. A.S. 26 Sept. 1815. *d.* at Cuttack, 12 Dec. 1818.

756. **Everest, Charles Evereux.** *b.* Dec. 1790. M.R.C.S. 1815. A.S. 27 Sept. 1815. Surg. 5 May 1826. R. 11 Sept. 1830. *d.* in London, 2 Apr. 1857. Nipal, 1815–16.

757. **Woodburn, David.** *b.* 18 Nov. 1792. M.R.C.S. 1815. A.S. 28 Sept. 1815. Surg. 5 May 1826. *d.* at Masuri, 28 May 1844, from effect of a fall over a precipice, when delirious; (S.A.L.M.B.). Third Maratha or Pindari war, 1817–18; (P.R.).

758. **MacLeod, Bannatyne William.** *b.* 8 Mar. 1793. M.D. Ed. 1815. A.S. 29 Sept. 1815. Surg. 5 May 1826. S.S. 10 Apr. 1847. *d.* at Simla, 2 Oct. 1856. C.B. 17 Aug. 1850. Burma, 1824–25, with Chittagong column. Afghanistan, 1839–42, capture of Ghuzni, medal. First Sikh or Sutlej war, 1845–46, as officiating S.S., battle of Sobraon, Desp. L.G. 14 Feb. 1846, medal.

759. **Pennington, Richard Baggally.** *b.* 10 Apr. 1792. M.R.C.S. 1815. A.S. 30 Sept. 1815. Surg. 5 May 1826. *d.* at Masuri, 4 Sept. 1838. Third Maratha or Pindari war, 1817–18; (P.R.).

760. **Gerard, William** (b). b. 25 Apr. 1794. Surg. Mate, ' Thomas Grenville,' 1810–11. C.C.S. 1812. Surg. ' Marchioness of Exeter,' 1812–13. A.S. 1 Oct. 1815. d. at Sehore, 30 June 1819. Name spelt Gerard in birth cert., Gerrard in diploma.

761. **Jones, Griffith Bowen** (a, d). M.R.C.S. 1815. A.S. 1 Oct. 1815. Postponed to 1819, when he attended Gilchrist's lectures; (A.S. Certs. vol. x.) Finally did not join.

762. **Bain, James** (b). b. Dec. 1789. Surg. Mate, ' Hope,' 1812–13. M.R.C.S. 1815. A.S. 2 Oct. 1815. d. at Almora, 27 May 1818.

763. **Henderson, John.** b. July 1795. A.S. 3 Oct. 1815. Surg. 11 June 1826. d. at Ludhiana, 12 Mar. 1836. Author of Observations on Colonies of New South Wales and Van Diemen's Land.

764. **Angus, George.** b. 1 Aug. 1793. M.A. Mar. Coll. Ab. 1812. M.R.C.S. 1815. A.S. 4 Oct. 1815. L.S.A. 1825. Surg. 16 June 1826. S.S. 24 July 1848. R. 31. Dec 1854. Third Maratha or Pindari war, 1817–18; (P.R.).

765. **Row, John.** b. 20 July 1794. M.R.C.S. 1815. A.S. 5 Oct. 1815. Surg. 23 June 1826. S.S. 10 Feb. 1849. M.M.B. and I.G. Hosps. 10 Apr. 1857. I.G. Lower Provinces, 26 Jan. 1858. R. 1 Aug. 1859. d. 3 Apr. 1862. Third Maratha or Pindari war, 1817–18, siege and capture of Hathras, 1817. Bharatpur, 1825–26, siege and storm of Bharatpur, medal.

766. **Cooper, Henry.** b. 11 Aug. 1792. A.S. 6 Oct. 1815. Surg. 8 Aug. 1826. R. 12 Aug. 1839. d. at Norwich, 15 Oct. 1869.

767. **Thompson, Thomas.** b. 19 Dec. 1791. M.R.C.S. 1810. A.S. Madras, 7 Oct. 1815. Transferred to Bengal, 15 Mar. 1816; (C.G. 5 Sept. 1816). d. in Calcutta, 8 Dec. 1824. D. and M. give name in Bengal, but not in Madras list. M. No. 653.

768. **Charles, Thomas.** b. 2 Nov. 1794. M.D. Ed. 1815. A.S. 8 Oct. 1815. d. in Fort William, 27 Oct. 1816.

769. **Sloper, John Smith.** b. 29 Sept. 1786. St. Thomas. M.R.C.S. 1808. Enlisted in H.E.I. Co.'s Artillery, Feb. 1814, served as dresser in field under Surgeon William Scott; (A.S. Certs. vol. xi.). A.S. Madras, 1815. Transferred to Bengal, 1816; (Mily. Desp. to Madras, 12 June 1816, para. 160; S.A.L.M.M.). Resigned, 6 Feb. 1819. D. and M. give name in Bengal list, with only 1815 as date of commission, but not in Madras list.

1816

770. **Smith, Hugh.** b. 3 Feb. 1795. M.D. Ed. 1815. A.S. 28 Sept. 1816. d. 14 Feb. 1826. Bharatpur, 1825–26, as Surg. to Lord Combermere, Commander-in-Chief, siege and storm of Bharatpur; (P.R.).

771. **Turner, John** (b). b. 10 May 1788. Surg. Mate, ' Thames,' 1809; Surg. ' William Pitt,' 1809–10; ' Scaleby Castle,' 1811–14. A.S. 29 Sept. 1816. Surg. 14 Apr. 1827. R. 1 Mar. 1838. b. in London, 25 Oct. 1852. Burma, 1824–25; (P.R.).

772. **Warner, Allbrook** (a, d). A.S. 30 Sept. 1816. Originally appointed in season 1812, name erased in list of A.S. 1791–1814. The vacancy was given to G. N. Cheek.

773. **Cheek, George Nicholas.** *b.* 18 Nov. 1793. Hosp. Asst. A.M.D. 19 July 1813 ; half-pay, 25 Apr. 1816 (v. Johnston's Roll of R.A.M.C. No. 3638). A.S. Bengal, 30 Sept. 1816. Resigned A.M.D. 18 Nov. 1824. Gave up promotion to remain at West Bardwan (now Bankura). *d.* in Nilgiri Hills, 26 June 1859. Father of A. H. Cheek, No. 1339, and of G. N. Cheek, No. 1671, infra. Peninsula, 1813, capture of San Sebastian and Orthez, medal. Waterloo campaign, 1815, but not present at battle of Waterloo ; (A.S. Certs. vol. xi.). Third Maratha or Pindari war, 1817–18, siege and capture of Hathras, 1817.

774. **Wood, Andrew.** *b.* 6 Feb. 1796. A.S. 1 Oct. 1816. Surg. 14 Apr. 1827. S.S. 10 Aug. 1849. R. 1 Mar. 1854. *d.* in Edinburgh, 7 July 1879. Gwalior, 1843–44, as officiating S.S, battle of Maharajpur, Desp. L.G. 8 Mar. 1844, bronze star.

775. **Burnett, John.** *b.* 3 Feb. 1793. M.A. Mar. Coll. Ab. 1812. L.R.C.S. Ed. 1815. A.S. 2 Oct. 1816. *d.* at Agra, 9 Oct. 1825. Third Maratha or Pindari war, 1817–18 ; (P.R.).

776. **Scott, Alexander.** *b.* 15 Feb. 1796. A.S. 3 Oct. 1816. Surg. 5 June 1827. R. 8 July 1836. *d.* 6 July 1879. Bharatpur, 1825–26, siege and storm of Bharatpur ; (P.R.).

777. **Wray, Octavius.** *b.* Aug. 1793. M.R.C.S. 1815. A.S. 4 Oct. 1816. Surg. 6 June 1827. *d.* at Agra, 19 Mar. 1836.

778. **Curling, Charles Simons.** *b.* Feb. 1794. M.R.C.S. 1816. A.S. 5 Oct. 1816. Surg. 12 July 1827. S.S. 10 Apr. 1852. R. 1 Sept. 1858. *d.* at Cheltenham, 2 Oct. 1871. Third Maratha or Pindari war, 1817–18.

779. **Francis, Charles Bransby.** *b.* 29 July 1795. M.R.C.S. 1815. A.S. 6 Oct. 1816. Surg. 12 July 1827. S.S. 1 Mar. 1853. *d.* in Calcutta, 28 Sept. 1854. Father of C. R. Francis, No. 1447, infra. First Sikh or Sutlej war, 1845–46, battles of Mudki, Firuzshahr, Aliwal, and Sobraon ; medal with three clasps.

780. **Grant, John.** *b.* 28 Aug. 1794. A.S. 7 Oct. 1816. Surg. 17 Aug. 1827. S.S. 17 July 1852. R. 11 Sept. 1857. *d.* in London, 14 Apr. 1862. With J. T. Pearson, No. 1038, infra, started and edited India Journal of Medical Science, 1834–36 ; and with J. R. Martin, No. 797, infra, edited Jackson's Formation, Discipline, and Economy of Armies, and wrote Jackson's biography, 1845. (v. Roll of R.A.M.C., No. 1190.)

781. **Butter, Thomas.** *b.* 4 Sept. 1794. L.R.C.S. Ed. 1816. A.S. 8 Oct. 1816. *d.* at Indore, 4 Nov. 1821. Third Maratha or Pindari war, 1817–18, with Body-guard.

782. **Cathcart, Robert Moore.** *b.* 10 May 1796. L.R.C.S. Ed. 18—. A.S. 9 Oct. 1816, sent home mentally affected, 1819 ; (Mily. L. from B. 24 Dec. 1819, para. 546). Struck off in 1822, absent 2½ years, and not having reported arrival in England ; (C.G. 29 Jan. 1827). D. and M. and S.A.L.M.B. say " Struck off in 1824."

783. **Henderson, Thomas.** *b.* 6 Oct. 1794. M.D. Ed. 1814. L.R.C.S. Ed. 1816. A.S. 10 Oct. 1816. Surg. 17 Sept. 1827. R. 4 June 1829 ; (C.G. 24 Aug. 1833). *d.* in Edinburgh, 2 July 1858. D. and M. and S.A.L.M.B. give date of retirement as 4 June 1831.

784. **Gordon, James.** *b.* 18 May 1793. M.D. Ed. 1815. A.S. 11 Oct. 1816. Surg. 2 June 1828. *d.* in Edinburgh, 7 Mar. 1829.

785. **Hastie, David.** b. 29 Aug. 1795. M.D. Ed. 1816. A.S. 12 Oct. 1816. d. at Saharanpur, 5 Nov. 1818. D. and M. and S.A.L.M.B. give place of death as Sehampore.

786. **Munro, Thomas Munro.** b. 10 May 1795. M.D. 18—. A.S. 13 Oct. 1816. Surg. 9 Nov. 1827. R. 1 Mar. 1838. d. at Benrig, Roxburgh, 15 Mar. 1862.

787. **Adam, John.** b. 3 Jan. 1793. M.R.C.S. 1812. M.D. Ed. 1814. A.S. 14 Oct. 1816. Surg. 23 May 1828. d. at the Presidency (Calcutta), 29 July 1830.

788. **Dyer, William.** b. 8 Aug. 1795. L.S.A. 1816. A.S. 15 Oct. 1816. Surg. 23 May 1828. R. 16 Dec. 1839. d. 30 June 1877.

789. **Wardrop, Alexander.** b. 15 Dec. 1794. A.S. 16 Oct. 1816. Surg. 3 July 1828. d. in Calcutta, 6 July 1832. Third Maratha or Pindari war, 1817–18 ; (P.R.). Bharatpur 1825–26, siege and storm of Bharatpur ; (P.R.).

790. **Cussones, Roderick** (a, c).
791. **Frobisher, Thomas** (a, c).
792. **Herbert, —** (a, c).
793. **Morland, R. S. B.** (a, c).
794. **Picard, Edward C.** (a, c).

The names of these five officers are entered in S.A.L.M.B. with the same note in each case, " Dekkan war, 1817–18 ; (P.R.)." The Dekkan war is the third Maratha war. Apparently all five were temporary officiating Asst. Surgeons. None of the names appear in lists of the Sub-Medl. Dept. No further information about any of them.

1817

795. **Clarkson, Ebenezer.** b. 14 June 1796. M.D. Ed. 1816. A.S. 3 Sept. 1817. Surg. 2 June 1828. R. 6 Aug. 1840. d. in Edinburgh, 15 Nov. 1867.

796. **Duff, William** (b). b. 7 Jan. 1793. Surg. Mate, ' Devonshire,' 1812–13. M.R.C.S. 1816. A.S. 4 Sept. 1817. Surg. 14 Sept. 1828. Afghanistan, 1839–42, with 54th N.I. Permitted to retire from 15 Oct. 1841 ; (G.O. 22 Sept. 1841) ; but was unable to leave Kabul. Killed in retreat from Kabul, between Tehzin and Sah Baba, 10 Jan. 1842, having previously undergone amputation of arm for severe wounds.

797. **Martin, James Ranald** (e). b. 12 May 1796. St. George's and Windmill St. School. C.C.S. 1811. M.R.C.S. 1814. A.S. 5 Sept. 1817. Surg. 22 Sept. 1828. R. 20 May 1842. F.R.C.S. original list, 1844. Examining Phys. to Secy. of State for India, 1859–64. President, Medl. Board, India Office, 1864 (when Board was formed), to 1874. d. in London, 27 Nov. 1874. F.R.S. 1845. C.B. 25 Apr. 1860. Knighted, 1860. Hony. I.G. 1864. v. Life of Sir Ranald Martin, by Sir J. Fayrer, 1897. Author of Medical Topography of Calcutta, 1839 ; rewrote and edited 6th edition of James Johnson's Influence of Tropical Climates on European Constitutions, 1841, 8th edition, 1861 ; Naval, Military, and Commercial Advantages of reoccupation of Negrais Island, 1843 ; with J. Grant, No. 780, supra, edited D. I. G. Robert Jackson's Formation, Discipline, and Economy of Armies, with Biography of Jackson, 1845 ; On Fatty Degeneration of Heart ; Article on Hospitals in Holmes' System of Surgery, 1864.

798. **Newmarch, Henry.** *b.* 23 Feb. 1795. M.R.C.S. 1817. A.S. 6 Sept. 1817. Surg. 2 Oct. 1828. R. 11 Oct. 1841. *d.* at York, 22 June 1866. Third Maratha or Pindari war, 1817–18 ; (P.R.).

799. **Chisholme, William Henry Newton.** *b.* 24 Sept. 1797, in West Indies, M.R.C.S. 1817. A.S. 7 Sept. 1817. *d.* in Arakan, 21 June 1825. Burma, 1824–25 ; (P.R.).

800. **Ross, Andrew.** *b.* 20 Feb. 1796. M.D. St. A. 1817. A.S. 17 Sept. 1817. Surg. 12 Aug. 1828. R. 1 Oct. 1852. *d.* in London, 12 Feb. 1864. Bharatpur, 1825–26, siege and storm of Bharatpur ; (P.R.).

801. **MacLachlan, Colin** (a, b, c). Surg. Mate, 'William Pitt,' 1807–08. Officiating A.S. 11 Nov. 1817 ; (C.G. 20 Nov. 1817). Struck off 30 Sept. 1820 ; (C.G. 12 Oct. 1820). Appointed to Army of the Nizam, 24 Oct. 1820 ; (S.A.L.M.B.). *d.* at Hingoli, 14 Aug. 1845. Third Maratha or Pindari war, 1817–18 ; (P.R.).

802. **Fletcher, William** (a, c). M.R.C.S. 1816. Officiating A.S. 16 Nov. 1817 ; (G.O. 16 Nov. 1817). Struck off, 4 Aug. 1818 ; (C.G. 13 Aug. 1818).

803. **Sullivan, Joseph Stapleton** (c). M.R.C.S. 1815. Officiating A.S. 1817. Struck off, 30 Sept. 1820 ; (C.G. 12 Oct. 1820). Relieved and discharged, 21 Dec. 1820. A.S. 24 Apr. 1823. Surg. 1 May 1837. *d.* in Calcutta, 16 Feb. 1843.

804. **Ross, J—** (a, c). M.D. —. Officiating A.S. 1817 ; (appointment reported in Mily. L. from B. 21 July 1818, para. 227). No further information. Possibly same as Andrew Ross, No. 800, supra. If not, probably struck off before 30 Sept. 1820.

1818

805. **Forbes, Joseph James.** *b.* May 1795. M.D. Ed. 1816. A.S. 9 Mar. 1818. Surg. 7 Mar. 1829. *d.* at Batora, Jaunpur, 12 June 1829.

806. **Ramsay, David.** M.D. Ed. 1817. A.S. 10 Mar. 1818. Surg. 1 Jan. 1829. *d.* at Cawnpur, 13 July 1831.

807. **MacRa, James Malcolm.** *b.* Jan. 1796. A.S. 11 Mar. 1818. Surg. 1 Feb. 1829. *d.* at Balmanghati, Sinhbhum, 27 May 1832 ; (tombstone, Midnapur old cemetery).

808. **Heynes, Charles Stokes.** *b.* 30 Mar. 1796. M.R.C.S. 1816. L.S.A. 1816. A.S. 12 Mar. 1818. Surg. 24 May 1829. *d.* at Dinapur, 27 Nov. 1831.

809. **Beattie, David** (b). *b.* 1 Dec. 1795. M.R.C.S. 1815. Surg. Mate, 'Atlas,' 1815–16. A.S. 13 Mar. 1818. Sent home mentally affected, 1819 ; (Mily. L. from B. 26 June 1819, paras. 728–730). Pensioned in England, 23 July 1823.

810. **Inglis, Thomas.** *b.* 31 Mar. 1796. M.D. Ed. 1817. L.R.C.S. Ed. 18—. F.R.C.S. Ed. 18—. A.S. 14 Mar. 1818. Surg. 24 May 1829. R. 1 May 1839. *d.* at Eastbourne, 31 Mar. 1874. Burma, 1824–25.

811. **Carruthers, Peter.** *b.* 6 Dec. 1797. M.R.C.S. 1818. A.S. 14 Mar. 1818. Surg. 3 June 1829. R. 1 Jan. 1840. *d.* in Edinburgh, 12 Feb. 1886.

812. **Barker, Thomas Brown.** b. 16 June 1796. M.R.C.S. 1817. A.S. 14 Mar. 1818. Surg. 4 June 1829. d. on board the 'Gloriana' on way home, 16 Mar. 1848.

813. **Matthews, Francis Seymour** (b). b. 14 July 1787. M.R.C.S. 1808. Surg. Mate, 'Scaleby Castle,' 1808–09; Surg. 'Taunton Castle,' 1810–12; of 'Essex,' 1812–13; of 'Lord Melville,' 1815–16. A.S. 29 Mar. 1818. Surg. 28 July 1829. d. at Uitenhage, Cape of Good Hope, 2 Sept. 1835. Bharatpur, 1825–26, siege and storm of Bharatpur; (P.R.).

814. **Charters, William Seton.** b. 18 Nov. 1795. Hosp. Asst. A.M.D. 16 June 1815. H.P. 25 Nov. 1816. M.D. Ed. 1817; resigned, 27 Jan. 1824; (v. Johnston's Roll of R.A.M.C. No. 3902). A.S. Bengal 27 Apr. 1818. Surg. 28 July 1829. R. 1 Jan. 1841. d. at Trinity, Edinburgh, 20 Feb. 1868.

815. **MacQueen, Kenneth.** b. 27 Dec. 1797. A.S. 3 May 1818. Surg. 18 Sept. 1829. R. 5 Jan. 1839. d. 28 Oct. 1878.

816. **Coulter, John** (b). b. 29 Mar. 1790. M.R.C.S. 1818. Surg. Mate, 'Baring,' 1812–13. M.R.C.S. 1818. A.S. 3 May 1818. Surg. 19 Aug. 1829. d. at Subathu, 28 May 1835.

817. **Lignum, John** (a, b, c). Surg. Mate, 'Alfred,' 1806–07; of 'Admiral Gardner,' 1808–09; of 'City of London,' 1809–10; Surg. 'City of London,' 1812–13. M.R.C.S. 1812. Officiating A.S. 19 May 1818, to Sneyd's Corps of Frontier Cavalry; (C.G. 28 May 1818). Struck off, date not ascertained, earlier than orders of 12 Oct. 1820. Afterwards in practice at Manchester.

818. **Cameron, William.** b. 12 Aug. 1796. A.S. 30 May 1818. Surg. 16 Sept. 1829. d. in Calcutta, 2 Nov. 1846.

819. **Lamb, George** (a, b, c). Surg. 'Asia,' 1808–09, lost in Bengal river, 1 June 1809; of 'Prince Regent,' 1816–17. Officiating A.S. 2 June 1818, to do duty with the reformed corps, received into the service from the troops of Mir Khan; (C.G. 11 June 1818). Transferred to Nizam's regular forces, 31 July 1819; (C.G. 12 Aug. 1819).

820. **Knott, William** (a, c). b. 18 Oct. 1792. St. George's. M.R.C.S. 1811. Hosp. Asst. A.M.D. 16 June 1815. H.P. 25 Feb. 1816. Officiating A.S. Bengal, 3 July 1818; (G.O. 15 July 1818). Transferred to Ceylon Establishment, having been appointed by H.R.H. the Commander-in-Chief as Hosp. Asst. to the Forces, 14 Oct. 1819; (C.G. 14 Oct. 1819). A.S. 15th Foot, 5 May 1825, 6th Dragoons, 13 July 1826. R. on H.P. 4 Dec. 1835. Afterwards medical attendant to Household of Queen Dowager, Camford House, Dorset. d. 8 Jan. 1881. v. Johnston's Roll of R.A.M.C. No. 3910.

821. **Montgomerie, William** (c). b. 1797. M.D. Ed. 1817. Officiating A.S. 3 July 1818, confirmed, 12 May 1819. Surg. 9 Dec. 1829. S.S. 15 Mar. 1853. d. in Calcutta, 21 Mar. 1856. China, 1841–42. Burma, 1852–53, as Field Surgeon, Desp. L.G. 15 June 1852.

822. **Wilkinson, Charles** (a, c). M.R.C.S. 1816. L.S.A. 1816. Officiating A.S. 7 July 1818; (C.G.). Struck off, 30 Sept. 1820; (C.G. 12 Oct. 1820). Relieved and discharged, 20 Jan. 1821.

823. Reynolds, John Poat (c). *b.* 23 Apr. 1796. Officiating A.S. 7 July 1818, to do duty with troops proceeding to Ceylon, and to be borne on books of 2nd Batt. 20 N.I.; (C.G. 16 July 1818). Struck off, 30 Sept. 1820; (C.G. 12 Oct. 1820). Relieved and discharged, 11 Feb. 1821. A.S. 18 Feb. 1823. *d.* at Dinajpur, 12 Apr. 1827. Father of J. W. Reynolds, No. 765, Bo. 1845.

824. Martin, A. J. (a, c). Officiating A.S. 15 July 1818, to do duty with troops proceeding to Ceylon, and to be borne on books of 2nd Batt. 20 N.I.; (C.G. 23 July 1818). Struck off, date not ascertained, earlier than orders of 12 Oct. 1820.

825. Bell, Benjamin (c). M.R.C.S. 1817. Officiating A.S. 21 July 1818, to do duty with troops proceeding to Ceylon, and to be borne on books of 2nd Batt. 20 N.I.; (C.G. 30 July 1818). Struck off, 30 Sept. 1820; (C.G. 12 Oct. 1820). A.S. 31 Jan. 1821. Surg. 6 July 1832. R. 1 Aug. 1841. *d.* 3 May 1872. Burma, 1824–25.

826. Suter, Peter (b). *b.* 1793. Surg. Mate, 'William Pitt,' 1809–16. Officiating A.S. Bengal, July 1818; (Mily. L. from B. 21 July 1818, para. 22). A.S. Madras, 22 July 1818. Transferred to Bengal, 9 June 1819. Ranked as A.S. Bengal, from 24 May 1820; (G.O. 20 Jan. 1821). M.R.C.S. 1820. *d.* in Calcutta, 10 June 1821. D. and M. give name in both Bengal and Madras lists. D. and M. and S.A.L.M.B. give date of rank in Bengal as 9 June 1819. M. No. 688.

827. Fraser, Hector. *b.* 24 May 1798. M.R.C.S. 1818. A.S. 6 Aug. 1818. *d.* at Mhow, 12 Oct. 1824. D. and M. spell name Frazer.

*828. MacNally, Michael (a, c). Officiating A.S. 11 Aug. 1818; (G.O. 14 Aug. 1818). Struck off, 30 Sept. 1820; (C.G. 12 Oct. 1820).

829. De Joncourt, Peter Isaac (a, c). Tempy. A.S. Ordnance Medl. Dept. 29 June 1815. Second A.S. ditto, 26 Jan. 1816. R. on H.P. 1 May 1816. v. Johnston's Roll of R.A.M.C. No. 3987. Officiating A.S. Bengal, 14 Aug. 1818; (G.O. 14 Aug. 1818). Struck off, 30 Sept. 1820; (C.G. 12 Oct. 1820). Relieved and discharged, 5 Jan. 1821. Dead before Mar. 1828.

830. Hume, James. *b.* 29 Dec. 1796. M.R.C.S. 1818. A.S. 1818. *d.* at Comilla, 26 Sept. 1819. Nephew of Joseph Hume, No. 487, supra, 1799.

831. Powell, Morgan (b, c). M.R.C.S. 1817. L.S.A. 1817. Surg. of 'Dove,' permitted to remain in India; (Mily. L. from Madras, 20 Oct. 1818, para. 13). Officiating A.S. 1818. Struck off, date not ascertained, earlier than orders of 12 Oct. 1820. A.S. 21 Nov. 1821. Surg. 31 Mar. 1835. *d.* in Europe, 4 Dec. 1842.

832. Guthrie, Hugh (c). M.D. Ed. 1816. L.R.C.S. Ed. 1816. Officiating A.S. 24 Oct. 1818; (C.G. 29 Oct. 1818). Confirmed, 31 Dec. 1819. Surg. 15 Aug. 1830. S.S. 16 May 1853. R. 24 Feb. 1856. *d.* in London, 13 Apr. 1871. Third Maratha or Pindari war, 1817–18. Afghanistan, 1839–42, storm and capture of Ghuzni, medal.

---

* Military Letter from Bengal, 26 Dec. 1818, para. 385, reports the appointments of MacNally, de Joncourt, Davisson, Guthrie, Smith, and Craigie.

833. **Smith, John** (afterwards **Smyth, J.**) (c). Enlisted as a private in E.I. Co.'s army, served with Bengal Volunteers in Ceylon; (S.A.L.M.B.). Officiating A.S. 31 Oct. 1818; (C.G. 12 Nov. 1818). Struck off, 30 Sept. 1820; (C.G. 12 Oct. 1820). Relieved and discharged, 21 Dec. 1820. M.D. Ed. 1823. A.S. 21 Feb. 1824. Changed name to Smyth; (C.G. 3 Jan. 1838). Surg. 1 Mar. 1838. R. 10 Feb. 1847. d. 1870.

1819

834. **Stewart, Poyntz.** b. 15 Sept. 1797. M.R.C.S. 1817. M.D. Ed. 1818. A.S. 5 Feb. 1819. Appointed officiating A.S. in C.G. of 24 June 1819, but subsequently appointed by Court from 5 Feb. 1819. d. in Calcutta, 16 July 1827. Burma, 1824–25.

835. **Moncrieff, Robert** (a, c). Officiating A.S. 13 Mar. 1819; (C.G. 25 Mar. 1819). Resigned, 24 Apr. 1819; (C.G. 6 May 1819). d. in Calcutta, before 13 May 1819; (Advt. of Estate in C.G. 13 May 1819).

836. **MacKinnon, Charles.** b. 21 Jan. 1799. A.S. 14 Mar. 1819. M.R.C.S. 1820. Resigned in India, 1 May 1829.

837. **Clarke, James.** b. 16 Sept. 1796. M.A., K.C. Ab. 1814. M.R.C.S. 1816. A.S. 15 Mar. 1819. Surg. 27 Sept. 1829. d. at Landour, 11 Nov. 1836.

838. **Taylor, Whitney.** b. Oct. 1794. M.R.C.S. 1818. A.S. 15 Mar. 1819. d. at Cawnpur, 28 Oct. 1826.

839. **Colvin, John** (c.) b. 1794. M.D. 18—. M.R.C.S. 1816. Officiating A.S. 27 Mar. 1819; (C.G. 8 Apr. 1819). Struck off, 30 Sept. 1820; (C.G. 12 Oct. 1820), but serving up till Apr. 1821; (G.O. 19 Apr. 1821). A.S. 17 Jan. 1823. Surg. 3 Jan. 1837. d. in Calcutta, 3 Oct. 1839.

840. **Barnett, John Park** (b, c). b. 27 Sept. 1796. M.R.C.S. 1815. Surg. 'Lady Carrington,' 1818–19. Officiating A.S. 3 Apr. 1819; (C.G. 8 Apr. 1819). Discharged, and ordered to rejoin his ship, 6 May 1819; (C.G. 13 May 1819). Reappointed officiating A.S. 27 May 1819; (C.G.). Struck off, 30 Sept. 1820; (C.G. 12 Oct. 1820). Relieved and discharged, 12 Nov. 1820. A.S. 8 May 1822. d. in Calcutta, 31 July 1823.

841. **Hutchinson, James.** b. 6 May 1796. M.A. Mar. Coll. Ab. 1817. M.R.C.S. 1818. Nominated A.S. Madras, but did not join; (S.A.L.M.M.). A.S. Bengal, 6 Apr. 1819. Surg. 18 Nov. 1829. F.R.C.S. original list, 1844. R. 17 July 1845. d. at Wynberg, Cape Colony, 9 July 1870. D. and M. give name in Bengal, but not in Madras list. M. No. 697. Author of Observations on Cholera, 1832; Report on Indian Jails, 1835; Bengal Medical Code, 1838; The Sunyasi, and other poems, 1838.

842. **Davidson, John** (c). M.D. Ed. 1818. Officiating A.S. 1819. Struck off, 30 Sept. 1820; (C.G. 12 Oct. 1820). A.S. 19 Mar. 1822. Surg. 5 Sept. 1825. R. 26 Mar. 1854. d. 13 May 1876. First Sikh or Sutlej war, 1845–46.

843. **Craigie, George** (c). b. 28 Jan. 1795. M.R.C.S. 1814. Officiating A.S. 1819. Struck off, 30 Sept. 1820; (C.G. 12 Oct. 1820). Relieved and discharged, 26 Oct. 1820. M.D. Mar. Coll. Ab. 1823. A.S. 16 Sept. 1824. Surg. 4 Sept. 1838. d. in Calcutta, 16 Jan. 1853. Gwalior,

1843–44, bronze star. First Sikh or Sutlej war, 1845–46, battles of Badiwal, Aliwal, and Sobraon, medal with two clasps. Second Sikh or Panjab war, 1848–49, battles of Ramnagar, Sadullapur, Chilianwala, and Gujrat, medal with two clasps.

844. Wilson, James (a, c). Officiating A.S. 8 Apr. 1819; (C.G. 15 Apr. 1819). Struck off, 30 Sept. 1820; (C.G. 12 Oct. 1820). Relieved and discharged, 15 Jan. 1821.

845. Mitchelson, William (c). M.R.C.S. 1817. Officiating A.S. 8 Apr. 1819; (C.G. 15 Apr. 1819) Struck off, 30 Sept. 1820; (C.G. 12 Oct. 1820). Relieved and discharged, 16 Oct. 1820. A.S. 31 Jan. 1821. Surg. 27 Dec. 1832. F.R.C.S. original list, 1844. R. 1 Jan. 1846. *d.* 25 May 1866. Burma, 1824–25; (P.R.). Bharatpur, 1825–26, siege and storm of Bharatpur.

846. Stewart, James (b, c). *b.* 27 Sept. 1793. Surg. Mate, ' Carnatic,' 1812–13; Surg. same ship, 1815–16. A.S. 17 Apr. 1819. Appointed officiating A.S. in C.G. of 24 June 1819, but subsequently appointed by Court from 17 Apr. 1819. Had formerly been in service of King of Oudh; (S.A.L.M.B.). *d.* at Bhagalpur, 9 Oct. 1826. Bharatpur, 1825–26, siege and storm of Bharatpur; (P.R.).

847. Hickman, Edward. *b.* Feb. 1797. Guy's. M.R.C.S. 1817. A.S. 17 Apr. 1819. Resigned in India, 6 Oct. 1826. Afterwards in practice in London. *d.* in London, 14 Feb. 1859.

848. Brown, William (a, c). M.D. Ed. 1811. Hosp. Mate, A.M.D. 13 Feb. 1812. A.S. 24th Dragoons, 2 Apr. 1812. H.P. 25 May 1819. Officiating A.S. Bengal, 6 May 1819; (C.G. 13 May 1819). Struck off, 30 Sept. 1820; (C.G. 12 Oct. 1820), but continued to serve till 19 Apr. 1821, when he was ordered to join 87th Foot. A.S. 87th Foot, from 1 Nov. 1820. Surg. 45th Foot, 18 Jan. 1827; 52nd Foot, 23 Sept. 1833. *d.* at Newry, 7 Oct. 1839. v. Johnston's Roll of R.A.M.C. No. 3403.

849. MacLeod, Murdoch (b). *b.* 1794. M.D. Ed. 1813. Surg. 'Union,' 1815–17. A.S. 26 May 1819. *d.* at Midnapur, 18 May 1824. D. and M. and S.A.L.M.B. give date of appointment as 20 Apr. 1820, which is that of Charles M. MacLeod, No. 884, infra.

850. Welchman, Charles Walter. *b.* May 1797. M.D. Ed. 1817. A.S. 26 May 1819. M.R.C.S. 1828. Surg. 11 Apr. 1830. *d.* at Barrackpur, 3 July 1832.

851. Griffiths, John. *b.* 3 Apr. 1796. A.S. 26 May 1819. M.R.C.S. 1821. Surg. 11 May 1830. R. 10 Feb. 1841. *d.* 29 Sept. 1841. D. and M. spell name Griffith, but his signature, in A.S. Certs. vol. xiv. 1819, is Griffiths. It is spelt Griffiths in S.A.L.M.B.

852. Todd, John Mitchell. *b.* 17 Apr. 1797. M.R.C.S. 1819. A.S. 26 May 1819. Surg. 12 May 1830. *d.* in Calcutta, 19 Feb. 1838. D. and M. spell name Tod.

853. MacPherson, George Gordon. *b.* 2 June 1797. A.S. 29 May 1819. Surg. 24 July 1830. R. 17 Sept. 1842. *d.* in London, 8 Oct. 1875. D. and M. give date of appointment as 26 May 1818.

854. Shutter, Thomas. M.R.C.S. 1816. A.S. 9 June 1819. M.D. Glas. 1827. R. 4 June 1828. *d.* 25 June 1868.

855. **Turnbull, William** (a, c). M.D. Ed. 1814. M.R.C.S. 1814. Lt. Champarun Light Infy., appointed officiating A.S. 24 June 1819; (C.G.). Struck off, 30 Sept. 1820; (C.G. 12 Oct. 1820). Relieved and discharged, 4 Oct. 1820. *d.* on board S.S. ' Hindostan,' on passage to Ceylon, 14 Oct. 1846; (F.I. 12 Nov. 1846).

856. **Laing, James** (c). *b.* 24 June 1799. Officiating A.S. 24 June 1819; (C.G.). Struck off, 30 Sept. 1820; (C.G. 12 Oct. 1820). Relieved and discharged, 5 Nov. 1820. A.S. 19 Jan. 1822. *d.* in India, Jan. 1824; (Advt. of Estate in C.G. of 29 Jan. 1824).

857. **Ronald, James** (c). *b.* 1 Sept. 1796. Officiating A.S. 24 July 1819; (C.G. 29 July 1819). Struck off, 30 Sept. 1820; (C.G. 12 Oct. 1820). Relieved and discharged, 2 Nov. 1820. A.S. 14 May 1822. Surg. 15 Oct. 1835. R. 1 Mar. 1843. *d.* at Glasgow, 5 Apr. 1877. Burma, 1824-25, with Field Hosp.; (P.R.).

858. **MacTaggart, John** (a, c). Officiating A.S. 24 July 1819; (C.G. 29 July 1819). *d.* at Tangi, Cuttack, 9 Jan. 1820; (C.G. 20 Jan. 1820).

859. **King, James** (a, c). Officiating A.S. 31 July 1819; (C.G. 12 Aug. 1819). Struck off, 30 Sept. 1820; (C.G. 12 Oct. 1820). Relieved and discharged, 6 Feb. 1821.

860. **Gerard, John Mair** (a, c). Officiating A.S. 14 Aug. 1819; (C.G. 26 Aug. 1819). Struck off, 30 Sept. 1820; (C.G. 12 Oct. 1820).

861. **Nighland, Robert** (a, c). *b.* 1796. Apothecary in Sub. Medl. Dept. . . . Officiating A.S. 21 Aug. 1819; (C.G. 2 Sept. 1819). *d.* at Howrah, 20 Oct. 1820; (tombstone in N. Park St. cemetery).

862. **Royle, John Forbes** (e). *b.* 20 May 1798. M.R.C.S. 1819. A.S. 30 Sept. 1819. Surg. 29 July 1830. R. 25 Apr. 1837; (A.J. July 1837, p. 263). M.D. Munich, 1837. F.R.S. 1837. Prof. Mat. Med. King's College London, 1836–1856. Reporter on Economic Products, India Office, 1838–57. Officer, Legion of Honour, 1855. *d.* at Acton, 2 Jan. 1858. S.A.L.M.B. and D. and M. give date of retirement as 19 Sept. 1834. Author of Illustrations of Botany of Himalayas, 2 vols. 1834; Essay on Antiquity of Hindu Medicine, 1837; The Productive Resources of India, 1840; Production of Isinglas in India, 1842; Manual of Materia Medica and Therapeutics, 1847, sixth edition, edited by J. Harley, 1876; Report on Culture of China Tea Plant in Himalayas, 1849; On Culture and Commerce of Cotton in India, 1851; The Arts and Manufactures of India, 1852; The Fibrous Plants of India, 1855; The Culture of Cotton in India, 1857.

1820

863. **Harris, Henry** (c). *b.* 2 July 1792. C.C.S. 1813. Officiating A.S. 1 Jan. 1820; (C.G. 13 Jan. 1820). Struck off, 30 Sept. 1820; (C.G. 12 Oct. 1820). A.S. 14 Mar. 1823. *d.* at Dakka, 10 Jan. 1828. Father of No. 1531, infra, H. P. Harris, 1848, and of F. W. Harris, No. 769, Bombay, 1845.

864. **Graham, James.** *b.* 28 Jan. 1797. M.D. Ed. 1819. A.S. 9 Jan. 1820. Surg. 11 Sept. 1830. Killed by mutineers at Sialkot, 9 July 1857. Gwalior, 1843–44, battle of Paniar, bronze star. First Sikh or Sutlej war, 1845–46, battles of Sobraon and Firuzshahr, Desp. L.G. 1 Apr. 1846, medal with clasp. Second Sikh or Panjab war, 1848–49, siege of Multan.

865. **Forsyth, John** (b). b. 1799. L.R.C.S. Ed. 18—. Surgeon's Mate of 'Warren Hastings,' 1818-19. A.S. 10 Jan. 1820. Surg. 18 Nov. 1830. S.S. 26 Aug. 1853. I.G. and D.G. 12 Nov. 1857. R. 25 Apr. 1862. d. at Brighton, 14 Jan. 1883. Order of Durani Empire, 3rd Class, 13 Apr. 1849. Q.H.P. 6 Sept. 1861. C.B. civil, 29 Aug. 1862. K.C.S.I. 24 May 1881. Afghanistan, 1839-42, as Senior Surgeon with Shah Shuja's forces, storm and capture of Ghuzni, capture of Pachut; Served with Genl. Sale's brigade from Khurd Kabul pass to Jalalabad, affairs of Tazin, Jagdalak, and Manu Khel, defence of Jalalabad, action of 7 Apr. 1842, reoccupation of Kabul under Genl. Pollock, Desp. Sale's desp. of 16 Apr. 1842, thanks of Govt., three medals, Afghanistan, Ghuzni, and Jalalabad.

866. **Johnston, James** (b). b. 1797. Surg. 'Fairlie,' 1818-19. M.D. St. A. 1820. A.S. 14 Feb. 1820. Surg. 21 Jan. 1831. d. in Fort William, 6 Apr. 1846. S.A.L.M.B. and D. and M. spell name Johnstone, but his signature, in A.S. Certs. vol. xiv. 1819, is Johnston. Afghanistan, 1839-42, capture of Ghuzni and Kalat; (P.R.).

867. **Martin, John Woodhouse** (a, c). M.R.C.S. 1806. In Royal Cornwall Militia. Hosp. Asst. A.M.D. 29 Apr. 1809. A.S. 35th Foot, 27 July 1809; 22nd Foot, 18 Oct. 1810. Accompanied Marquis of Hastings, Governor Genl. to India. Officiating A.S. Bengal, 14 Feb. 1820; (C.G. 24 Feb. 1820). Struck off, 30 Sept. 1820; (C.G. 12 Oct. 1820). Half-pay, 22nd Foot, 29 June 1821. Appointed Surgeon to Raja of Nagpur, 1821. d. at Raipur, 11 Feb. 1825; (C.G. 7 Apr. 1825). v. Johnston's Roll of R.A.M.C. No. 3001. Walcheren, 1809.

868. **Walker, Richard** (a, c). Officiating A.S. Feb. 1820. Struck off, 30 Sept. 1820; (C.G. 12 Oct. 1820). Relieved and discharged, 24 Dec. 1820.

869. **Child, Thomas Smith.** b. 25 Aug. 1797. M.R.C.S. 1820. A.S. 21 Feb. 1820. Surg. 7 May 1831. R. 6 May 1833. d. at Wotton-under-Edge, Gloucestershire, 25 Mar. 1888.

870. **Beaty, John** (a, d). A.S. 21 Feb. 1820. Never joined; (A.S. Certs. vol. xv.). Entered as " deceased," and vacancy given to James Taylor, No. 975, infra, 1824; (Cadet Register, vol. vii.).

871. **Douglas, John** (a, c). Officiating A.S. 22 Feb. 1820; (C.G. 2 Mar. 1820). Struck off, 30 Sept. 1820; (C.G. 12 Oct. 1820). Reappointed officiating A.S. Mar. 1825. Struck off, 1827. Bharatpur, 1825-26, siege and storm of Bharatpur; (P.R.).

872. **Harding, Robert** (a, c). Officiating A.S. 26 Feb. 1820; (C.G. 2 Mar. 1820). Struck off, 30 Sept. 1820; (C.G. 12 Oct. 1820), but serving up to 22 Apr. 1821; (C.G. 7 June 1821). L.S.A. 1821.

873. **Le Cerf, George William** (a, c). b. 1790. Officiating A.S. 26 Feb. 1820; (C.G. 9 Mar. 1820). Struck off, 30 Sept. 1820; (C.G. 12 Oct. 1820), but served up to Aug. 1821; (C.G. 9 Aug. 1821). d. in Calcutta, 6 Dec. 1828; (C.G. 8 Dec. 1828).

874. **Tod, John Forrest.** b. 4 Apr. 1799. M.D. St. A. 1819. A.S. 4 Mar. 1820. d. at Dumdum, 5 Sept. 1821. S.A.L.M.B. and D. and M. spell name Todd, it is spelt Tod on tombstone.

875. **Johnston, James.** b. 25 Jan. 1796. A.S. 4 Mar. 1820. d. at Sambalpur, 21 Sept. 1821. D. and M. and S.A.L.M.B. spell name Johnstone, but his birth cert. in A.S. Certs. vol. xv. 1820, spells it Johnston.

876. **Morton, James.** *b.* 12 May 1797. M.R.C.S. 1819. A.S. 16 Mar. 1820. Surg. 7 May 1831. Senior Asst. Commission, Arakan, 1834; (G.O. 10 Oct. 1834). *d.* at Kyukphyu, 24 June 1845.

877. **Dempster, Charles.** *b.* 23 Sept. 1799. A.S. 16 Mar. 1820. *d.* at Patna, 5 Aug. 1822. Twin brother of T. E. Dempster, No. 886, infra.

878. **Nisbet, Matthew.** *b.* Dec. 1796. M.D. Glas. 1820. Surg. 14 June 1831. R. 31 Dec. 1849. *d.* at Cheltenham, 17 Jan. 1871. D. and M. spell name Nesbit. Name spelt Nisbet in birth cert., but his signature is Nesbit; (both A.S. Certs. vol. xv. 1820). Afghanistan, 1839–42, capture of Ghuzni; (P.R.).

879. **Jackson, Alexander Russell.** *b.* 6 Aug. 1798. M.D. Ed. 1819. M.R.C.S. 1820. A.S. 15 Apr. 1820. Surg. 18 June 1831. R. 29 Jan. 1839. Depot Surgeon, Chatham, Jan. 1841. F.R.C.S. original list, 1844. *d.* at Warley Barracks, Essex, 28 July 1855.

880. **Waddell, George** (b). *b.* 15 Aug. 1788. Surg. 'Surrey,' 1814–16; of 'Cabalva,' 1818, lost on Corgado shoal, Mauritius, 7 July 1818. M.D. Ed. 1820. A.S. 15 Apr. 1820. Surg. 14 July 1831. *d.* in Calcutta, 20 Sept. 1833. Burma, 1824–25, capture of Rangoon; (P.R.).

881. **Stewart, Charles.** *b.* 17 Aug. 1798. A.S. 20 Apr. 1820. *d.* at Nowgong (Nayagaon), Assam, 23 Nov. 1824. Burma war, 1824, in Assam, Desp. C.G. 20 Apr. 1825.

882. **Shuter, James** (a, d). *b.* 12 Sept. 1795. M.R.C.S. 1820. A.S. Bengal, 20 Apr. 1820; (A.S. Certs. vol. xv. 1820, and S.A.L.M.B.). Never joined. A.S. Madras, 21 Feb. 1821. *d.* at Heffleton, Wareham, 12 Oct. 1826. D. and M. give name in Madras, but not in Bengal list. M. No. 723.

883. **Davidson, Alexander.** *b.* 15 May 1797. M.A. Mar. Coll. Ab. 1816. M.R.C.S. 1818. M.D. Ed. 1819. A.S. 20 Apr. 1820. Surg. 13 July 1831. S.S. 25 Oct. 1853. R. 25 Mar. 1859. *d.* at Cheltenham, 31 Mar. 1883. Afghanistan, 1841–42, with Genl. Pollock's force, medal.

884. **MacLeod, Charles Murdock.** *b.* 10 Oct. 1793. A.S. 30 Apr. 1820. Surg. 14 Nov. 1831. Invalided, 23 Apr. 1832. R. 24 Aug. 1836.

885. **Toke, John Syme.** *b.* June 1797. M.R.C.S. 1820. A.S. 8 May 1820. Surg. 27 Nov. 1831. S.S. 1 Mar. 1854. *d.* at Dinapur, 8 Aug. 1854. First Sikh or Sutlej war, 1845–46, battles of Mudki, Aliwal, and Sobraon, medal with two clasps. Second Sikh or Panjab war, 1848–49, battles of Chilianwala and Gujrat, medal.

886. **Dempster, Thomas Erskine.** *b.* 23 Sept. 1799. A.S. 19 May 1820. Surg. 2 Mar. 1832. S.S. 1 Sept. 1854. R. 16 Sept. 1857. *d.* 15 Feb. 1883. Twin brother of Charles Dempster, No. 877, supra. First Sikh or Sutlej war, 1845–46, Sobraon, medal. Second Sikh or Panjab war, 1848–49, as S.S. Multan Field Force. Author of The test of organic disease of the Spleen to detect malarious localities, 1848.

887. **Hamilton, William.** M.D. Ed. 1819. A.S. 5 June 1820. Surg. 9 Apr. 1832. Resigned, 9 June 1833.

888. **Thomson, Richard Mowbray Martin.** *b.* 7 Apr. 1799. A.S. 8 June 1820. Surg. 23 Apr. 1832. *d.* in Calcutta, 23 Mar. 1839. Name spelt Thompson by D. and M., in S.A.L.M.B. Thomson, and his signature in A.S. Certs. vol. xv. 1820, is Thomson. Afghanistan. 1839–42, as Field Surgeon, capture of Ghuzni.

889. **MacCalman, Duncan.** A.S. 16 July 1820. *d.* at Fort Marlbro, 8 July 1822.

890. **Fraser, William.** *b.* 29 Apr. 1796. M.D. Ed. 1816. M.R.C.S. 1820. A.S. 3 Sept. 1820. *d.* on 'Caledonia,' on passage to Europe, 18 Aug. 1821. D. and M. spell his name Frazer, but his signature, in A.S. Certs. vol. xv. is Fraser.

891. **Paterson, George Murray.** *b.* 7 June 1796. M.D. Ed. 1817. M.R.C.S. 1820. A.S. 21 Sept. 1820. *d.* at Southampton, 9 Apr. 1829. Author of The Sacred Lemmas, being Analyses of Scripture, 1827.

892. **Hodges, Thomas.** *b.* 17 Sept. 1796. Surgeon, Sagar Island Establishment, 13 Oct. 1820. A.S. Bengal, 4 Dec. 1828. *d.* in Calcutta, 16 Dec. 1831. D. and M. gives 4 Dec. 1827 as date of Bengal commission.

893. **Drever, Thomas.** *b.* 12 Sept. 1797. M.D. Ed. 1818. A.S. 24 Nov. 1820. Surg. 27 May 1832. R. 1 Jan. 1840. *d.* at Glasgow, 1 Jan. 1857.

894. **Pringle, Anthony.** *b.* 1797. M.D. Ed. 1819. A.S. 24 Nov. 1820. Surg. 14 June 1832. *d.* at Agra, 3 Feb. 1844.

1821

895. **Grime, William.** M.R.C.S. 1816. A.S. 3 Jan. 1821. Surg. 3 July 1832. R. 9 Mar. 1839. *d.* on board 'Thomas Grenville,' on passage to Europe, 24 Apr. 1839. Burma, 1824–25; (P.R.).

896. **Paterson, John Cockerell.** *b.* 17 Apr. 1794. M.R.C.S. 1820. A.S. 16 Jan. 1821. *d.* in Calcutta, 10 Jan. 1827.

897. **Glass, Walter.** *b.* 10 Aug. 1800. M.D. Ed. 1819. A.S. 4 Feb. 1821. R. 28 Aug. 1833.

898. **Pullar, David** (b). *b.* 5 Feb. 1798. Surg. Mate, 'Waterloo,' 1819–20. A.S. 10 Feb. 1821. *d.* at Arakan, 3 Nov. 1825. Burma, 1824–25.

899. **MacKinnon, Charles.** *b.* 8 Feb. 1800. M.R.C.S. 1820. A.S. 9 Mar. 1821. Surg. 9 June 1833. S.S. 20 Oct. 1854. R. 31 Mar. 1859. *d.* at Millbrook, Southampton, 9 Jan. 1883. Bharatpur, 1825–26, siege and storm of Bharatpur, medal.

900. **Harrison, Thomas Charles.** *b.* 1 Sept. 1796. M.R.C.S. 1819. L.S.A. 1820. A.S. 9 Mar. 1821. *d.* at Arakan, 12 Dec. 1825. Burma, 1824–25.

901. **Gold, Francis.** *b.* 7 Feb. 1799. M.R.C.S. 1820. A.S. 21 Mar. 1821. *d.* in camp at Dougah, 21 Dec. 1832.

902. **Stenhouse, Alexander.** *b.* Feb. 1799. M.D. Ed. 1818. A.S. 4 Apr. 1821. Furlough, S.C. G.O. 24 Nov. 1826. Struck off from 22 May 1829, absent five years; (C.G. 24 July 1832).

903. **Burt, Benjamin.** *b.* 23 Apr. 1797. M.D. Ed. 1819. A.S. 4 Apr. 1821. Surg. 23 July 1833. R. 4 Aug. 1841. *d.* in Edinburgh, 18 July 1875. Burma, 1824–25.

904. **Buchanan, John Ruxton.** *b.* July 1798. M.R.C.S. 1821. A.S. 4 Apr. 1821. *d.* at Delhi, 7 Feb. 1827.

INDIAN MEDICAL SERVICE [1821

905. **Dalrymple, John.** b. Aug. 1798. M.R.C.S. 1820. A.S. 4 Apr. 1821. Surg. 30 July 1833. d. at Ambala, 27 Nov. 1844. Burma, 1824–25; (P.R.). Sind, 1843, as officiating S.S., actions of Miani and Dabha, Desp. L.G. 9 May 1843.

906. **Richardson, J. R.** (d). A.S. 4 Apr. 1821. Apparently never joined. Name omitted from list in 1823. No further information.

907. **Francis, Robert Bransby.** b. 30 July 1798. M.R.C.S. 1820. A.S. 15 Apr. 1821. Surg. Aug. 1833. d. at Jessore, 6 Oct. 1833.

908. **Butter, Donald.** b. 3 Oct. 1799. M.D. Ed. 1820. A.S. 5 May 1821. Surg. 28 Aug. 1833. Cashiered, 19 May 1850; (G.O. 7 May 1850). Reinstated, 8 Dec. 1852; (G.O. No. 140 of 16 Feb. 1853). v. Hist. of I.M.S. ii. 238. S.S. 31 Dec. 1854. R. 23 Apr. 1859. d. at Norwood, 24 Dec. 1877. Author of Outlines of Topography and Statistics of Southern District of Oudh, and of Cantonment of Sultanpore, 1839.

909. **Hewett, William Wrighte.** b. 5 Dec. 1795. L.S.A. 1817. M.D. Mar. Coll. Ab. 1821. M.R.C.S. 1821. A.S. 5 May 1821. Struck off in India, 16 Apr. 1830. Afterwards Apothecary to St. George's Hospital, and physician to H.M. King William IV. Father of Admiral Sir William Hewett. Name spelt Hewit by D. and M., Hewett by S.A.L.M.B. Signature, in A.S. Certs. vol. xvi. 1821, is Hewett.

910. **Hunter, George.** b. 5 Sept. 1798. A.S. 5 May 1821. d. at Nasirabad, 18 Apr. 1825.

911. **Dennis, Charles.** b. 26 Nov. 1798. M.R.C.S. 1821. A.S. 5 May 1821. Drowned at Sandoway, Arakan, 6 Mar. 1826. Burma, 1824–25.

912. **Cavell, William** (a). A.S. 23 May 1821 Passed, 23 May 1821. Went out to India in 'Andromeda'; (Cadet Regr. vol. vii.). No further information. Perhaps Christian name a mistake for Henry Cavell, No. 916, infra.

913. **Duncan, James.** M.D. Ed. 1821. A.S. 3 June 1821. Surg. 20 Sept. 1833. R. 1 Feb. 1842. d. 5 May 1853.

914. **Carte, William Edward.** b. 5 Feb. 1799. B.A. T.C.D. 1820. M.R.C.S. 1821. A.S. 3 June 1821. Surg. 7 Oct. 1833. Invalided, 1 Nov. 1842. Burma, 1824–25, with Chittagong column. Bharatpur, 1825–26, siege and storm of Bharatpur.

915. **Harpur, Edmund Tomkins.** b. Aug. 1798. M.R.C.S. 1820. A.S. 11 June 1821. Surg. 28 Jan. 1834. Afghanistan, 1839–42, with 5th Cavalry. Killed at Fatehabad, near Jalalabad, in retreat from Kabul, 14 Feb. 1842. v. Hist. of I.M.S. ii. 209. D. and M. spell name Harper, his signature in A.S. Certs. vol. xvi. 1821, is Harpur.

916. **Cavell, Henry.** b. Oct. 1797. M.R.C.S. 1818. A.S. 11 June 1821. d. at Subathu, 21 June 1827. Brother of Robert Cavell, No. 987, infra, 1825.

917. **Simson, Andrew.** b. 19 Dec. 1798. M.D. Ed. 1820. A.S. 25 June 1821. Surg. 1 Feb. 1834. R. 1 Feb. 1841. d. in Edinburgh, 30 Aug. 1843.

918. **Simms, George.** b. 22 Nov. 1796. M.R.C.S. 1820. A.S. Madras, 4 July 1821. Transferred to Bengal by Madras G.O. of 7 May 1822. R. 2 July 1828. d. in Dublin, 2 Dec. 1861. D. and M. give name in Bengal, but not in Madras list. M. No. 742.

919. **Barnard, Richard Nossiter.** *b.* Apr. 1800. M.R.C.S. 1820. L.S.A. 1820. A.S. 4 July 1821. Surg. 24 Apr. 1834. *d.* at Benares, 21 Mar. 1836.

920. **Turnbull, Gavin.** *b.* 25 Dec. 1800. A.S. 14 July 1821. Surg. 24 Apr. 1834. R. 31 Dec. 1852. *d.* in Jersey, 23 Oct. 1854. Second Sikh or Panjab war, 1848–49.

921. **Boyd, James Watson.** *b.* 2 Feb. 1800. A.S. 3 Sept. 1821. *d.* in Arakan, 18 Aug. 1825. Burma, 1824–25 ; (P.R.).

922. **MacDougal, Adam.** *b.* 30 Oct. 1792. M.D. Ed. 1813. A.S. 3 Sept. 1821. *d.* 5 Apr. 1824, on way from Cox's Bazar to Chittagong. v. Chevers, Diseases of India, p. 500.

923. **Lindesay, Alexander Kyd.** *b.* 8 Aug. 1801. A.S. 3 Sept. 1821. Surg. 24 Apr. 1834. R. 23 Nov. 1840. *d.* 22 Oct. 1878.

924. **Grahame, Robert.** *b.* 19 Feb. 1796. A.S. 20 Sept. 1821. Surg. 16 Sept. 1834. Invalided, 1 May 1837. *d.* at Landour, 17 Mar. 1841.

925. **Forrest, Thomas** (b). *b.* 21 Sept. 1799. Surg. Mate, ' Castle Huntly,' 1820–21. A.S. 29 Sept. 1821. Surg. 19 Sept. 1834. R. 28 Feb. 1843, *d.* 1 Jan. 1862. Burma, 1824–25, Desp. L.G. 25 Nov. 1824. Jhansi Field Force, 1839.

926. **Graham, William.** *b.* 12 Nov. 1795. M.R.C.S. 1821. A.S. 1 Dec. 1821. Resigned, 23 Mar. 1827. *d.* at Newington, Edinburgh, 14 Mar. 1843.

927. **Hoare, Charles Burton** (b). *b.* 25 Apr. 1798. Surg. Mate, ' General Hewitt,' 1818–21. M.R.C.S. 1821. A.S. 20 Dec. 1821. *d.* in Calcutta, 22 Mar. 1833.

1822

928. **Campbell, Donald.** *b.* 2 Jan. 1802. L.R.C.S. Ed. 18—. A.S. 19 Jan. 1822. Surg. 28 May 1835. R. 1 Jan. 1843. *d.* in London, 28 Jan. 1858.

929. **Clark, Hezekiah** (b). *b.* Dec. 1792. London Hosp. M.R.C.S. 1815. Surg. Mate, ' Wexford,' 1814–15 ; Surg. ' Thomas Grenville,' 1815–16 ; ' Waterloo,' 1816–20. A.S. 19 Jan. 1822. Surg. 1 Sept. 1835. R. 1 Feb. 1855. *d.* at Leamington, 23 Oct. 1868. Bharatpur, 1825–26, siege and storm of Bharatpur, medal.

930. **Leslie, John.** *b.* 12 Sept. 1801. A.S. 19 Jan, 1822. *d.* at Goalpara, Assam, 30 Mar. 1831.

931. **Morgan, Nathanial.** M.R.C.S. 1819. A.S. 16 Feb. 1822. Surg. 2 Sept. 1835. R. 12 Jan. 1843. Burma, 1824–25. Afghanistan, 1841–42.

932. **Mottley, Charles.** *b.* 3 July 1799. M.R.C.S. 1822. A.S. 31 Mar. 1822. Surg. 3 Oct. 1835. R. 1 May 1851.

933. **Corbet, William.** *b.* 23 Aug. 1797. M.A. Mar. Coll. Ab. 1816. M.R.C.S. 1821. A.S. 3 Apr. 1822. *d.* at Kotah, 20 Dec. 1827.

934. **Yeatman, Edward Jordan** (b). *b.* 10 Sept. 1797, at Philadelphia, U.S.A. Surg. Mate, ' Marquis of Huntly,' 1820–21. M.D. St. A. 1822. A.S. 14 May 1822. Surg. 12 Mar. 1836. R. 27 June 1845. First Sikh or Sutlej war, 1845–56.

935. **Innes, James.** *b.* 20 May 1796. M.D. 18—. A.S. 28 May 1822. Surg. 19 Mar. 1836. *d.* at Sekrol, Benares, 4 July 1846. D. and M. spell name Innis.

936. **Menzies, Alexander.** *b.* 22 Feb. 1789. M.D. 18—. Hosp. Mate. A.M.D. 9 Oct. 1807. A.S. 21st Dragoons, 4 Oct. 1810. H.P. 11 Sept. 1820; (v. Johnston's Roll of R.A.M.C. No. 3236). A.S. Bengal, 28 May 1822. *d.* at Hazaribagh, 25 Dec. 1823.

937. **MacGregor, James.** *b.* 27 Nov. 1797. M.D. Ed. 1820. A.S. June 1822. *d.* at Dinapur, 10 July 1823; (C.G. 6 Aug. 1823). S.A.L.M.B. and D. and M. give date of death as 10 July 1822.

938. **Jeffreys, Julius** (e). *b.* 14 Sept. 1800. M.R.C.S. 1822. A.S. 28 Sept. 1822. Invalided in India, 2 Apr. 1832. R. 21 Feb. 1838. *d.* at Richmond, 13 May 1877. Recommended formation of hill stations, and indicated Simla as a suitable locality. Inventor of the Respirator, patented, 23 Jan. 1836. F.R.S. 1840. v. Biography, by Lt.-Col. E. Jeffreys, 1855. Author of Dissertation on Climate of the Hill Provinces, 1824; On Construction and Use of the Respirator, 1836; Statics of the Chest, 1843; Atmospheric Treatment of the Chest, 1845; Climate, and Affections of the Throat and Lungs, 1849; The British Army in India, its Preservation, 1858.

939. **Smith, George.** *b.* 27 Sept. 1800. M.R.C.S. 1821. A.S. 11 Oct. 1822. Surg. 21 May 1836. *d.* at Guntur, 19 Nov. 1838. Bharatpur, 1825–26, siege and storm of Bharatpur; (P.R.).

940. **Steuart, James Frederick.** *b.* 13 Feb. 1801. M.D. 18—. A.S. 1 Nov. 1822. Surg. 8 July 1836. *d.* at Ludhiana, 2 Aug. 1846. D. and M. and E.I. Regr. spell name Stewart. S.A.L.M.B. spells it Steuart, and his signature, in A.S. Certs. vol. xvii. 1822, is Steuart. First Sikh or Sutlej war, 1845–46.

941. **Clark, Alexander Mackenzie.** *b.* 26 July 1793. M.R.C.S. 1821. A.S. 1 Nov. 1822. Surg. 11 Nov. 1836. R. 16 Dec. 1843. *d.* 27 Jan. 1865. D. and M. spell name Clarke. S.A.L.M.B. spells it Clark, and his signature, in A.S. Certs. vol. xvii. 1822, is Clark.

*942. **Wyatt, Arthur.** *b.* 12 Nov. 1796. M.R.C.S. 1821. A.S. 6 Dec. 1822. *d.* at Kissengunge (Kishanganj in Purnea), 22 May 1824; (D. and M.). The C.G. of 5 July 1824 states that he died at Kishorganj on 22 June 1824. This is evidently a mistake, there has never been any cantonment at Kishorganj, which is in Mymensinh district. Both the Bengal Obituary, and Wilson's Inscriptions on Tombs in Bengal state that there are two tablets to his memory in the cemetery at Rangpur, one of which gives the date of death as 22 June 1824, the other as 20 July 1824. Neither inscription states that Wyatt was actually buried at Rangpur. The E.I. Regr. for 1825 states that he died at Kissengunge on 22 May 1824.

* Wyatt's case illustrates the difficulty of ascertaining facts in India after the lapse of a century. Four records, which may all be considered more or less official—C.G.; E.I. Regr. Bengal Obituary, and Wilson's Inscriptions on Tombs, give three different dates, and three different places (if we count Rangpur). The latest date of death given, 20 July, cannot be correct, for the death had been reported earlier; in the C.G. of 5 July 1824. When I was stationed at Purnea, in 1890–92, there were many tombstones still to be seen in an old cemetery at Kishanganj, and a few others scattered about the cantonment, but the nameplates had all disappeared.—D.G.C.

1823

943. Paxton, George (b). *b.* 18 Dec. 1802. Surg. Mate, 'Phœnix,' 1818–19. M.D. K.C. Ab. 1822. A.S. 5 Jan. 1823. *d.* in Calcutta, 21 Dec. 1827. Bharatpur, 1825–26, siege and storm of Bharatpur; (P.R.).

944. Halkerston, John. *b.* 13 May 1800. M.D. Ed. 1821. A.S. 21 Jan. 1823. *d.* in Genl. Hosp. Calcutta, 10 June 1824. D. and M. give name as Hatherston. His signature in A.S. Certs. vol. xvii. 1822, is Halkerston.

945. Stevenson, William. L.S.A. 1820. A.S. 18 Feb. 1823. Surg. 1 Feb. 1837. R. 5 March 1846. *d.* 30 July 1854. Burma, 1824–25; (P.R.).

946. Bell, William. *b.* 18 Sept. 1798. L.S.A. 1821. M.R.C.S. 1822. M.D. Ed. 1823. A.S. 19 Feb. 1823. Surg. 5 Mar. 1837. R. 16 Apr. 1839. Name is in Medl. Directory, 1848, living in Cheltenham, omitted in 1851.

947. Thomson, David. *b.* 18 June 1801. A.S. 19 Feb. 1823. *d.* at Natal, Sumatra, 4 Sept. 1824.

948. Maysmor, Humphrey. *b.* 16 Jan. 1796. L.S.A. 1819. M.R.C.S. 1821. A.S. 19 Feb. 1823. Burma, 1824; Killed in action at Ramu, Chittagong frontier, 16 May 1824.

*949. Lawrie, James Adair. *b.* 25 June 1801. M.A. 1820; M.D. 1822; Glas. A.S. 12 Mar. 1823. M.P.F.S.G. 1830. Pensioned on Lord Clive's Fund, 18 June 1831. Prof. of Surgery, Anderson's College, Glasgow, 1829–52; ditto, Glas. Univ. 1852–59. *d.* at Bridge of Allan, 23 Nov. 1859. Name spelt Laurie by D. and M. but his signature in A.S. Certs. vol. xviii. 1823, is Lawrie.

950. Abel, Clarke (e). *b.* 5 Sept. 1789. C.C.S. 1813. Surgeon and Naturalist to Lord Macartney's mission to China, 1816–17. M.D. St. A. 1819. M.R.C.S. 1819. A.S. 15 Mar. 1823. *d.* at Cawnpur, 24 Nov. 1826. Author of Narrative of a journey to the interior of China, 1816–17; 1818.

951. Greig, John. *b.* 17 Sept. 1802. A.S. 24 Apr. 1823. Surg. 21 Mar. 1837. S.S. 24 Feb. 1856. R. 1 Dec. 1859. F.R.C.S. Ed. 1860. *d.* at Cheltenham, 27 Feb. 1883. Bhil Campaign, 1837. Afghanistan, 1839–42. Gwalior, 1843–44, action at Paniar, bronze star.

952. MacIsaac, Robert. *b.* 16 Jan. 1800. A.S. 8 May 1823. *d.* at Madras 25 Dec. 1830.

953. Grant, James William. *b.* 19 Feb. 1801. M.R.C.S. 1823. A.S. 8 May 1823. Surg. 3 May 1837. R. 10 Dec. 1851. *d.* in London, 29 Jan., 1873.

954. Shaw, Richard (b). *b.* 12 May 1793. M.R.C.S. 1815. Surg. Mate, 'Thomas Grenville,' 1815; Surg. same ship, 1816–1820. A.S. 14 June 1823. Surg. 13 July 1837. R. 27 Dec. 1848. *d.* at Southampton, 17 Jan. 1873.

955. Steart, Augustus William. *b.* 18 July 1798. M.R.C.S. 1821. L.S.A. 1821. A.S. 26 June 1823. Surg. 30 July 1837. R. 30 Mar. 1847. *d.* 20 Feb. 1869. Bharatpur, 1825–26, siege and storm of Bharatpur; (P.R.). First Sikh or Sutlej war, 1845–46.

---

* Lawrie's successor as Professor of Surgery at Glasgow was Mr., afterwards Lord Lister.

956. **Egerton, Charles Chandler** (e). *b.* Apr. 1798. Guy's and St. Thomas. M.R.C.S. 1819. A.S. 29 June 1823. Surg. 1 Aug. 1837. F.R.C.S. original list, 1844. R. 31 Jan. 1847. *d.* at Epping, Essex, 4 May 1885.

957. **Wilson, Jasper.** *b.* 22 Aug. 1802. C.M. Glas. 1823. A.S. 12 Aug. 1823. *d.* in Arakan, 23 June 1825. Burma, 1824-25 ; (P.R.).

958. **Menzies, John.** *b.* Apr. 1796. A.S. 19 Oct. 1823. Surg. 31 Dec. 1837. *d.* at Bhaga, Kangra District, 17 Feb. 1846. Bharatpur, 1825-26, siege and storm of Bharatpur ; (P.R.). First Sikh or Sutlej war, 1845-46, action at Aliwal, medal.

1824

959. **Wilson, Benjamin.** *b.* Apr. 1799. M.R.C.S. 1823. A.S. 18 Feb. 1824. Surg. 2 Feb. 1838. R. 1 Jan. 1845. *d.* 28 Apr. 1871. Afghanistan, 1839-42.

960. **MacGaveston, John.** *b.* 10 Mar. 1798. M.R.C.S. 1823. A.S. 21 Feb. 1824. Surg. 3 Feb. 1838. R. 9 Feb. 1843. Burma, 1824-25 : (P.R.). Afghanistan, 1838-39.

*961. **Walsh, Richard Fetnam** (a, c). *b.* 1799. M.D. Ed. 1820. M.R.C.S. 1823. Officiating A.S. 1 Apr. 1824 ; (C.G. 5 Apr. 1824). Struck off, Oct. 1827. Became an indigo planter. *d.* at Bogra, 22 Apr. 1831 ; (C.G. 2 May 1831). Burma, 1824-25 ; (P.R.), action at Kemmendine, wounded ; (C.G. 23 Dec. 1824).

962. **Rankine, Robert.** *b.* 25 Dec. 1794. C.C.S. 1811. M.R.C.S. 1814. A.S. 1 May 1824. Surg. 17 Mar. 1838. R. 30 Nov. 1841. *d.* in London, 21 Apr. 1875. Burma, 1824-25, wounded, medal. Author of Medical Topography of Sarun, 1839.

963. **Sully, Bishop Cranmer.** *b.* 2 Oct. 1796. M.D. Mar. Coll. Ab. 1823. M.R.C.S. 1824. A.S. 4 May 1824. R. 31 May 1834. Teacher in Oriental Seminary, Calcutta, 1835-48. *d.* in Calcutta, 11 Apr. 1848.

964. **Stevenson, William.** *b.* 23 Dec. 1799. M.D. 18—. A.S. 4 May 1824. Surg. 17 Mar. 1838. R. 31 Dec. 1841. *d.* at Crieff, 29 Oct. 1885. Burma, 1824-25 ; (P.R.).

965. **Thomson, William.** *b.* May 1801. M.A. Mar. Coll. Ab. 1822. M.D. Ed. 1824. A.S. 9 May 1824. Surg. 2 Apr. 1838. S.S. 21 Mar. 1856. R. 23 Mar. 1864. *d.* in London, 23 June 1889.

966. **Palsgrave, John Henry.** *b.* 2 May 1802. L.S.A. 1823. M.R.C.S. 1824. A.S. 16 May 1824. Surg. 5 Apr. 1838. R. 31 Jan. 1848. *d.* in London, 2 July 1880. First Sikh or Sutlej war, 1845-46.

967. **Taylor, Henry.** *b.* 1 Dec. 1800. M.R.C.S. 1823. A.S. 23 May 1824. Surg. 1 May 1838. R. 15 Dec. 1844. *d.* in London, 2 Dec. 1880. Afghanistan, 1842.

968. **Vignolet, Charles** (a, c). M.R.C.S. 1821. Officiating A.S. 31 May 1824 ; (C.G. 7 June 1824). *d.* at Bhagalpur, 21 May 1826 ; (C.G. 29 May 1826). Burma, 1824-25.

* In military Letter from Bengal, 16 June 1828, para. 28, it is stated that all Acting Asst. Surgeons were struck off in Oct. 1827.

969. **Temple, George** (b, c). *b.* 6 Dec. 1795. Surg. ' Rockingham,' 1822-24. Officiating A.S. 31 May 1824 ; (C.G. 7 June 1824). Resigned, 11 Feb. 1825 ; (C.G. 21 Feb. 1825). A.S. 4 Feb. 1826. *d.* in Calcutta, 3 Jan. 1840. Burma, 1824-25.

970. **Oliver, Edward** (a, c). Officiating A.S. 2 June 1824 ; (C.G. 7 June 1824). Struck off, Oct. 1827. *d.* 1833 ; (Advt. of estate in C.G. of 5 Oct. 1833).

971. **Miller, William** (b, c). Surg. ' David Scott,' 1809-12 ; ' Cabalva,' 1815-16. Officiating A.S. 24 June 1824 ; (C.G. 5 July 1824). Afterwards confirmed from same date. *d.* in Arakan, 27 Oct. 1825. Burma 1824-25 ; (P.R.).

972. **Clemishaw, Thomas** (b, c). Surg. Mate, ' Streatham,' 1810-11 ; ' Bridgwater,' 1812-13. M.R.C.S. 1815. Surg. ' Coldstream,' 1816-17. L.S.A. 1818. Surg. ' Warren Hastings,' 1819-20. Officiating A.S. 24 June 1824 ; (C.G. 5 July 1824). Confirmed from 9 Feb. 1825. *d.* at Sekror, Oudh, 25 Sept. 1834. Burma, 1824-25, with Sylhet column.

973. **Harlan, Josiah** (a, c). An American. Officiating A.S. 1 July 1824 ; (C.G. 5 July 1824, where name is spelt Harlem, corrected in C.G. of 7 Mar. 1825). Struck off, Oct. 1827. Afterwards in service, successively, of Ranjit Sinh, 1828-35 ; and of Dost Muhammad, 1836-38 ; v. Kaye's Afghan War, i. 135. Burma, 1824-25 ; (P.R.). Author of Memoir of India and Afghanistan, 1842. In this work is advertised another, as in preparation, Personal Narrative of eighteen years' residence in Asia, but apparently this was never published.

974. **Twining, William** (c, e). *b.* 1790, in Nova Scotia, M.R.C.S. 1860. Served two years in Royal Navy, Hosp. Mate, A.M.D. 6 Feb. 1812. A.S. Staff, 10 Mar. 1814. H.P. 25 Dec. 1823. Commuted H.P. 7 Dec. 1830. (v. Johnston's Roll of R.A.M.C. No. 3402). Went to Ceylon in 1821 as Surgeon to the Governor, General Sir Edward Paget, and accompanied him as Surgeon to India, when he was appointed Commander-in-Chief, in Jan. 1823. Officiating A.S. Bengal, 12 Aug. 1824 ; (C.G. 23 Aug. 1824). Confirmed from same date. *d.* in Genl. Hosp. Calcutta, 25 Aug. 1835. Peninsula, 1812-14, on Lord Hills' staff, present at entry of allies into Paris, Waterloo. Author of Diseases of the Spleen, 1828 ; Clinical Illustrations of Diseases of Bengal, 1832 ; Epidemic Cholera, 1833.

975. **Taylor, James.** *b.* 30 Mar. 1803. A.S. 15 Aug. 1824. Surg. 23 July 1838. R. 10 July 1846. *d.* at Easton, Elgin, 28 Dec. 1879. Author of Topography and Statistics of Dakka, 1840 ; The Cotton Manufacture of Dakka, 1841.

976. **Bousfield, Henry.** *b.* 10 Mar. 1802. M.R.C.S. 1824. A.S. 25 Aug. 1824. Surg. 3 Aug. 1838. R. 19 Sept. 1844. Burma, 1824-25 ; (P.R.).

977. **Walker, Andrew** (c). *b.* 1798. Officiating A.S. 2 Sept. 1824 ; (C.G. 6 Sept. 1824, where first name is given as Adam). Confirmed, 5 June 1825. Surg. Nov. 1839. *d.* at Kandahar, 21 Dec. 1839. Burma, 1824-25, with flotilla, Afghanistan, 1839, capture of Ghuzni ; (P.R.).

978. **Buchan, Robert.** *b.* 22 Feb. 1801. M.R.C.S. 1823. A.S. 13 Oct. 1824. *d.* at Cawnpur, 1 Sept. 1825.

979. **Glendinning,** — (a, c). Officiating A.S. Nov. 1824. Still serving in Feb. 1827; (B. Mily. Cons. 9 Feb. 1827, No. 16). *d.* Feb. 1827, name given in a list of officers recently deceased; (B. Mily Cons. 16 Feb. 1827, No. 210).

980. **Scott, George Milligan** (a, c). *b.* 13 May 1802. Officiating A.S. 2 Dec. 1824; (C.G. 6 Dec. 1824). Struck off, Oct. 1827. A.S. Madras, 8 Mar. 1830. *d.* at Trichinopoly, 4 May 1837. D. and M. give name in Madras, but not in Bengal list. M. No. 806. Burma, 1824–25; (P.R.).

981. **Boyd, J. W.** (a, c). *b.* 1791. Officiating A.S. 2 Dec. 1824; (C.G. 6 Dec. 1824). *d.* in Fort William, 18 May 1826; (C.G. 23 May 1826).

982. **Birmingham,** or **Bermingham, George** (a, c). Middlesex Hosp. Officiating A.S. 9 Dec. 1824; (C.G. 13 Dec. 1824). Struck off, Oct. 1827. M.R.C.S. 1829. Afterwards Surgeon in Portuguese Navy. In practice in London, 1840–77. F.R.C.S. 1853. *d.* 1877, name omitted from Medl. Directory of 1878. K.T.S. Burma, 1824–25; (P.R.).

983. **Logan, John** (c). Officiating A.S. 16 Dec. 1824. Confirmed 8 May 1827. *d.* on board ' Cæsar ' on passage to Europe in 1828; (C.G. 6 Oct. 1828). D. and M. give date of death as 1829. Burma, 1824–25; (P.R.).

984. **Chalmers, Alexander.** *b.* 14 Feb. 1796. M.D. Glas. 1824. A.S. 30 Dec. 1824. Surg. 19 Nov. 1838. *d.* in Calcutta, 28 Apr. 1851. Bharatpur, 1825–26, siege and storm of Bharatpur; (P.R.). Gwalior, 1843–44, battle of Maharajpur, Desp. L.G. 8 Mar. 1844, bronze star.

985. **Jones, Walter** (a, d). M.R.C.S. 1823. A.S. 1824. Relinquished appointment; (A.S. Certs. vol. xviii.). Never joined. No further information.

986. **Trigge, James** (a, c). Officiating A.S. 1824; (S.A.L.M.B.). Struck off, Oct. 1827. Burma, 1824–25, with Field Hosp.; (P.R.).

1825

987. **Cavell, Robert** (a). *b.* 8 Mar. 1799. M.R.C.S. 1824. A.S. 2 Feb. 1825. *d.* on passage to Europe, on board ' Katherine,' early in 1827; (C.G. 24 May 1827). Brother of Henry Cavell, No. 916, supra, 1821.

988. **Townsend, Edward Richard** (d). *b.* 31 July 1800. M.D. Ed. 1822. L.R.C.S.I. 1823. A.S. 9 Feb. 1825. Never joined. Went into practice at Cork. F.K.Q.C.P. 1863. *d.* at Queenstown, Cork, 6 Jan. 1878.

989. **Webster, Alexander Binney.** M.D. Ed. 1824. A.S. 9 Feb. 1825. Appointed officiating A.S. 27 May 1825; (C.G. 30 May 1825). Subsequently appointed by Court from 9 Feb. 1825. R. 14 Nov. 1836. *d.* in Edinburgh, 8 Jan. 1879. Bharatpur, 1825–26, with Field Hosp., siege and storm of Bharatpur.

990. **Barber, James** (c). *b.* Apr. 1802. L.S.A. 1824. Officiating A.S. 11 Feb. 1825; (C.G. 21 Feb. 1825). Confirmed 3 Feb. 1827. Surg. 1 Apr. 1843. *d.* at Lahore, 15 Sept. 1859. Christian name sometimes given as John in Gazettes. S.-W. Frontier, operations against Kols, 1825. Bharatpur, 1825–26, siege and storm of Bharatpur, central India, 1842, operations in Bandalkund. First Sikh or Sutlej war, 1845–46.

991. MacFarlane, Robert (a, c). Officiating A.S. 18 Feb. 1825; (C.G. 21 Feb. 1825). *d.* at Sagar, 28 Aug. 1826; (C.G. 2 Oct. 1826).

992. Pickthorn, Francis Peregrine Burrell (a, c). M.R.C.S. 1823. Officiating A.S. 25 Feb. 1825; (C.G. 7 Mar. 1825). Resigned, 7 Apr. 1825; (C.G. 11 Apr. 1825).

993. Kelly, James (a, c). M.D. Ed. 1817. Officiating A.S. 11 Mar. 1825; (C.G. 14 Mar. 1825). Struck off, Oct. 1827. Probably same man as James Kellie, A.S. Madras, 11 Mar. 1829. M. No. 876.

994. Douglas, John (a, c). Officiating A.S. 18 Mar. 1825; (B. Mily. Cons.). Struck off, Oct. 1827 Probably same man as No. 871, supra.

995. O'Dwyer, John. M.R.C.S. 1822. A.S. 18 Mar. 1825. Surg. 1 Jan. 1839. R. 6 July 1855. *d.* in London, 26 Feb. 1857. Burma, 1825–26, medal. First Sikh or Sutlej war, 1845–46. Second Sikh or Panjab war, 1848–49, medal.

996. Gray, Duncan MacQueen. *b.* 13 Mar. 1803. M.D. Glas. 1824. A.S. 20 Mar. 1825. Surg. 5 Jan. 1839. R. 12 Jan. 1844. *d.* in London, 14 Feb. 1870. Bharatpur, 1825–26, siege and storm of Bharatpur; (P.R.). China, 1841–42, medal.

997. Brown, George Gilbert. *b.* 9 Feb. 1800. M.A. 1817; M.D. 1825; Mar. Coll. Ab. A.S. 20 Mar. 1825. Surg. 29 Jan. 1839. S.S. 10 Apr. 1857. I.G. 1 Aug. 1859. R. 8 Nov. 1860. *d.* at Aberdeen, 24 Mar. 1873. Central India, 1842, operations in Bandalkund. Gwalior, 1843–44, bronze star. First Sikh or Sutlej war, 1845–46, Sobraon, medal. Second Sikh or Panjab war, 1848–49, medal.

998. Stewart, Duncan. *b.* 22 Feb. 1804. L.R.C.S. Ed. 1823. M.D. K.C. Ab. 1824. A.S. Bombay, 15 Apr. 1825. Transferred to Bengal, 5 Oct. 1825; (S.A.L.M.Bo.). A.S. Bengal, ranked from, 15 Apr. 1825. Surg. 9 Mar. 1839. R. 9 Oct. 1855. Staff Surg. Warley Depot, 2 Oct. 1855. M.R.C.P. Lond. 1860. *d.* at Tunbridge Wells, 26 Mar. 1875. D. and M. give name in Bengal, but not in Bombay list. Bo. No. 527. Author of Practical Arabic Grammar, 1841; Vaccination in Bengal, 1827–44; 1844.

999. Hardie, James (b, c). Surg. Mate, 'Sophia,' 1824–25. Officiating A.S. 15 Apr. 1825; (C.G. 18 Apr. 1825). Confirmed, 13 Feb. 1826. *d.* in Paris, 26 May 1834.

1000. Greenwell, Whitfield. M.R.C.S. —. Officiating A.S. Madras, 1817. Appointed A.S. Haidarabad Residency; (A.S. Certs. vol. xx.). A.S. Bengal, 15 Apr. 1825. Discharged by Court Martial, 1 Mar. 1827; (C.G. 5 Mar. 1827). D. and M. give Christian name as Whitford, and give name in Bengal, but not in Madras list. M. No. 677.

1001. Stewart, William (a, c). *b.* 1799. Officiating A.S. 22 Apr. 1825; (C.G. 25 Apr. 1825). Resigned, 8 Dec. 1826; (C.G.). Appointed to Nizam's service in 1827, but died at Ahmadnagar on his way to join, Apr. 1827; (C.G. 23 Apr. 1827). Burma, 1825–26; (P.R.).

1002. Spencer, Thomas Knyfton. *b.* 23 Nov. 1800. M.R.C.S. 1824. A.S. 29 Apr. 1825. *d.* at Barisal, 20 July 1826.

1003. **Thompson, Adam** (a, c). Officiating A.S. 6 May 1825; (C.G. 9 May 1825). Transferred to Prince of Wales Island Establishment, Oct. 1827; (Mily. L. from B. 14 June 1828, para. 117). Retransferred to Bengal, 7 Apr. 1830. R. 1 Aug. 1839. *d.* Aug. 1841. D. and M. give name in P.W.I. but not in Bengal list, and spell name Thomson, also spelt Thomson in S.A.L.M.B. P.W.I. No. 9.

1004. **Wilkie, George** (a, c). M.D. Ed. 1824. Officiating A.S. 13 May 1825; (C.G. 16 May 1825). Struck off, on account of ill-health, 9 Dec. 1825; (C.G. 12 Dec. 1825).

1005. **Evans, George** (a, c). *b.* 1798. M.R.C.S. 18—. Officiating A.S. 31 May 1825; (C.G. 6 June 1825). Resigned, 2 Dec. 1825; (C.G. 5 Dec. 1825). *d.* in London, 22 Oct. 1866; (Lancet, 27 Oct. 1826).

1006. **Tweddell, Hubbersty Maddison.** *b.* 28 Apr. 1799. L.S.A. 1823. M.R.C.S. 1824. A.S. 3 June 1825. Surg. 16 Apr. 1839. R. 10 Aug. 1861. *d.* 22 Aug. 1871. Central India, 1842–43, with Sagar and Narbada Field Force. Gwalior, 1843–44. First Sikh or Sutlej war, 1845–46, Firuzshahr, medal.

1007. **Magrath, John.** *b.* 2 Dec. 1800. M.R.C.S. 1824. A.S. 5 June 1825. Surg. 12 Aug. 1839. *d.* at Firuzpur, 6 July 1845. Afghanistan, 1839–42, with 37 N.I. Capture of Ghuzni; (P.R.); wounded and taken prisoner in retreat from Kabul, 10 Jan. 1842.

1008. **Mercer, Robert.** *b.* 1802. M.R.C.S. 1823. M.D. Glas. 1824. A.S. 5 June 1825. *d.* at Cawnpur, 8 Sept. 1826.

1009. **Foley, Robert.** *b.* 24 June 1798. M.D. Ed. 1824. A.S. 5 June 1825. Surg. 3 Oct. 1839. R. 1 Feb. 1843. *d.* 15 May 1845. Bharatpur, 1825–26, siege and storm of Bharatpur; (P.R.).

1010. **MacIntosh, Robert** (b). *b.* 23 Dec. 1799. Surg. Mate, ' Kellie Castle,' 1821–22. L.R.C.S. Ed. 18—. A.S. 6 June 1825. Surg. 16 Dec. 1839. *d.* at Delhi, 31 Oct. 1847. Bharatpur, 1825–26, siege and storm of Bharatpur; (P.R.). First Sikh or Sutlej war, 1845–46, Sobraon, medal.

1011. **Malcolm, Finlay.** *b.* 29 Sept. 1802. A.S. 19 June 1825. *d.* at Barrackpur, 25 Oct. 1839. S.A.L.M.B. gives date of commission as 19 July 1825.

1012. **Donaldson, Hugh Douglas** (c). *b.* 1803. M.D. Ed. 1824. Officiating A.S. 8 July 1825; (C.G. 18 July 1825). Confirmed, 30 Jan. 1826. *d.* in Calcutta, 19 Apr. 1839. Burma, 1825–26.

1013. **Beattie, Alexander** (c). M.R.C.S. 1823. M.A. Mar. Coll. Ab. 1824. Officiating A.S. 5 Aug. 1825; (C.G. 8 Aug. 1825). Confirmed, 23 Aug. 1826. Surg. 1 Feb. 1843. R. 18 Nov. 1848. M.D. K.C. Ab. 1848. Burma, 1825–26; (P.R.).

1014. **Worrall, Joseph.** M.R.C.S. 1823. M.D. Ed. 1825. A.S. 14 Aug. 1825. Surg. 21 Dec. 1839. R. 1 Apr. 1846. *d.* 6 Nov. 1849. D. and M. spell name Warrall. Afghanistan, 1839–42, capture of Ghuzni; (P.R.). First Sikh or Sutlej war, 1845–46.

1015. **Turkington, John H.** (a, c). *b.* 1802. M.R.C.S. 1824. Officiating A.S. 24 Aug. 1825; (C.G. 29 Aug. 1825). *d.* in Calcutta, 7 Dec. 1826; (C.G. 11 Dec. 1826). Burma, 1825–26; (P.R.).

1016. Jacob, William. A.S. 6 Sept. 1825. Surg. 1 Jan. 1840. *d.* at Kandahar, 13 Jan. 1842. Afghanistan, 1839–42, action at Kelat-i-Ghilzai, Desp. C.G. 7 July 1841. Author of A Short account of the District of Jessore, 1837.

1017. Laughton, Richard. *b.* 28 Aug. 1803, in Ceylon. A.S. 10 Sept. 1825. Surg. 1 Jan. 1840. Invalided in India, 16 Dec. 1840. R. 20 Sept. 1848.

1018. Bogie, William. *b.* 5 Nov. 1797. M.D. Ed. 1824. A.S. 10 Sept. 1825. Surg. 10 June 1840. R. on H.P. 21 Oct. 1841, with extra pension of £50, on account of blindness; (S.A.L.M.B.). *d.* in Edinburgh, 1 Aug. 1863.

1019. Christie, Alexander. *b.* 15 May 1803. A.S. 10 Sept. 1825. Surg. 6 Aug. 1840. R. 16 Jan. 1844. *d.* at St. Andrews, 13 Mar. 1885.

1020. Smith, Alexander. *b.* 1 Aug. 1802. M.R.C.S. 1822. L.R.C.S. Ed. 1824. M.D. Ed. 1825. A.S. 15 Sept. 1825. M.D. Jena, 1838. Surg. 3 Oct. 1840. R. 8 Apr. 1846.

1021. Brett, Frederick, Harrington. *b.* 12 Aug. 1803. M.R.C.S. 1824. A.S. 2 Sept. 1825. Surg. of 'Eliza,' 1828–29. Surg. 15 Oct. 1840. R. 23 Jan. 1844. L.R.C.P. Lond. 1844. *d.* 10 Dec. 1859. In 1854 was appointed Field Surgeon, to serve in Crimea, but apparently never went. Author of The Principal Surgical Diseases of India, 1840; The Gems of Tuscany, 1842.

1022. Wynne, Thomas Price (b). *b.* 4 Jan. 1799. M.R.C.S. 1819. Surg. Mate, 'Carnatic,' 1819–20. A.S. 22 Sept. 1825. *d.* at Patna, 25 July 1832.

1023. Fender, John (b). *b.* 13 Feb. 1798. Surg. Mate, 'Marquis of Huntly,' 1822–23, 'Duchess of Athol,' 1824–25. A.S. 25 Sept. 1825. *d.* on river Jumna, near Hamirpur, 8 Mar. 1837.

1024. Maxwell, Charles. *b.* 29 Aug. 1802. M.D. St. A. 1824. A.S. 12 Oct. 1825. Surg. 16 Nov. 1840. *d.* in camp at Bhundri, near Delhi, 26 Jan. 1843.

1025. Hoffbower, C. H. (a, c). A. Hanoverian. Officiating A.S. Fort Marlbro Establishment, for Natal garrison, Nov. 1824, transferred to Bengal, 1825; (Mily. L. from B. 16 June 1828, paras. 27–33). Officiating A.S. Bengal, 14 Oct. 1825; (G.O. 14 Oct. 1825). Struck off, Oct. 1827. *d.* in Genl. Hosp. Calcutta, 6 Nov. 1832; (Memoir in A. J. Feb. 1833, p. 80). Waterloo, with Hanoverian contingent. Burma, 1824–25; (P.R.).

1026. Brown, John (a, c). M.D. Ed. 1823. Officiating A.S. 2 Dec. 1825; (C.G. 5 Dec. 1825). Confirmed, 8 May 1826; (C.G.). Name omitted from list in 1827. No further information.

1027. Tritton, Edmund. *b.* 1801. L.S.A. 1823. M.R.C.S. 1824. A.S. 4 Dec. 1825. Surg. 23 Nov. 1840. S.S. 3 Oct. 1856. I.G. 12 Nov. 1857. *d.* at Simla, 15 June 1858. In S.A.L.M.B. date of death is given, erroneously, as 15 June 1859. C.B. 19 May 1858. Second Sikh or Panjab war, 1848–49, Sadullapur, Chilianwala, and Gujrat, medal with two clasps. Indian Mutiny, 1857–58, as S.S. siege and storm of Delhi, Desp. L.G. 24 Dec. 1857, medal, C.B.

1028. **Bowron, John.** *b.* Feb. 1799. Sub. Medl. Dept. 1813-25; Medical Pupil, 1 July 1813; Apothecary, 7 Sept. 1816. M.R.C.S. 1824. A.S. 20 Dec. 1825. Surg. 16 Dec. 1840. R. 31 Dec. 1851. *d.* at Hove, aged 100, 5 Mar. 1899. Second Sikh or Panjab war, 1848-49.

1029. **Spens, Thomas.** *b.* 12 Aug. 1803. M.D. Ed. 1824. A.S. 28 Dec. 1825. *d.* in Calcutta, 5 Jan. 1836.

1030. **MacRae, John** (c). *b.* 6 Sept. 1797. M.D. Ed. 1824. Officiating A.S. 11 Nov. 1825; (Army list). Confirmed, 27 June 1828. Surg. 24 June 1845. R. 31 Mar. 1851. *d.* at Monghyr, 1864. Son of John MacRae, No. 302, supra, 1782. In S.A.L.M.B. his name is given as John Macrae, and also as " James McRae, query John ? " Burma, 1825-26; (P.R.).

1826

1031. **Hartt, Falls** (c). *b.* 1798. Officiating A.S. 6 Jan. 1826; (C.G. 9 Jan. 1826). Confirmed, 20 Jan. 1829. *d.* in Calcutta, 12 May 1836.

1032. **Lee, John.** *b.* 15 May 1803. M.D. Ed. 1825. A.S. 12 Jan. 1826. Resigned, 4 July 1832.

1033. **Beadon, Hugh.** *b.* 31 Dec. 1801. M.R.C.S. 1825. A.S. 12 Jan. 1826. N.-E. Frontier, 1829, operations against Khasias, killed in action by an arrow, Nanklau, Khasia Hills, 28 May 1829.

1034. **MacKenna, John** (a, c). *b.* 31 Dec. 1802. L.R.C.S. Ed. 1824. M.D. 18—. Officiating A.S. 25 Jan. 1826; (C.G. 30 Jan. 1826). Struck off, Oct. 1827. A.S. Madras, 20 May 1828. Surg. 31 Dec. 1843. S.S. 8 Aug. 1857. R. 10 Oct. 1863. *d.* in London, 3 June 1874. D. and M. give name in Madras, but not in Bengal list. M. No. 816. Burma, 1826. Gumsur campaign, 1836-37.

1035. **Downes, Ezra Thomas.** *b.* 29 Oct. 1801. M.R.C.S. 1824. A.S. 30 Jan. 1826. Surg. 1 Jan. 1841. R. 31 May 1866. *d.* at St. Leonards, 2 July 1876.

1036. **MacDonnell, James** (d). *b.* 28 Feb. 1782. M.D. 18—. Hosp. Asst. A.M.D. Irish Establishment, 29 Nov. 1813 to 13 Dec. 1815. A.S. 84th Foot, 14 Dec. 1815; 50th Foot, 1 Jan. 1818; H.P. 25 Dec. 1818. F.P. 55th Foot, by exchange, 14 Jan. 1819. Gazetted A.S. Bengal, 30 Jan. 1826, but never joined. Returned to England with 55th Foot. L.R.C.P. Lond. 1829. Surg. 87th Foot, 21 Sept. 1830. R. on H.P. 1 Mar. 1839. *d.* at Bath, 31 July 1845. v. Johnston's Roll of R.A.M.C. No. 3969. D. and M. say " Resigned in England, 22 Apr. 1828."

1037. **Finch, Cuthbert.** *b.* 30 Oct. 1802. A.S. 4 Feb. 1826. Surg. 1 Jan. 1841. R. 1 June 1846. *d.* 19 Jan. 1850. Author of Effect of change of Climate on Health of Native Army.

1038. **Pearson, John Thomas.** *b.* 22 Aug. 1801. M.R.C.S. 1825. C.M. Glasgow, 1826. A.S. 4 Feb. 1826. Surg. 1 Feb. 1841. *d.* at Barrackpur, 5 Mar. 1851. Author of A Note on Darjeeling, 1839.

1039. **MacDonald, Colin John.** *b.* 18 Apr. 1794. Originally nominated to Madras in 1825; (Desp. to M. 23 Nov. 1825, para. 9); but permitted to proceed to Bengal instead; (S.A.L.M.M.). A.S. 5 Feb. 1826. Surg. 10 Feb. 1841. *d.* at Chunar, 19 Dec. 1844. M. No. 813. D. and M. give name in Bengal, but not in Madras list.

1040. Llewellyn, Charles. *b.* Mar. 1795. M.R.C.S. 1816. L.S.A. 1816. A.S. 11 Feb. 1826. Surg. 1 Aug. 1841. *d.* at Barrackpur, 11 Sept. 1849.

1041. Laing, William Christie. A.S. 13 Feb. 1826. Surg. 4 Aug. 1841. R. 15 Jan. 1848. *d.* 23 Nov. 1861.

1042. Carr, George (a). *b.* Nov. 1800. M.D. Ed. 1822. Originally nominated to Madras; (S.A.L.M.M.); but transferred to Bengal. A.S. 16 Feb. 1826. *d.* at Akyab, 15 Mar. 1829. M. No. 817.

1043. Furnell, Frederick. *b.* 14 Jan. 1800. M.R.C.S. 1822. A.S. 11 Mar. 1826. Surg. 11 Oct. 1841. R. 1 Jan. 1847.

1044. Grant, Charles Stuart. *b.* Feb. 1797. M.D. C.M. Glas. 1825. A.S. 11 Mar. 1826. *d.* at Mallai, Champarun, 14 Oct. 1838.

1045. Newton, Charles. *b.* 1796. M.R.C.S. 1820. L.S.A. 1821. A.S. 11 Mar. 1826. *d.* at Tamluk, Midnapur, 10 July 1836.

1046. Chapman, Henry. *b.* 6 May 1800. M.R.C.S. 1823. A.S. 11 Mar. 1826. Surg. 15 Oct. 1841. R. 31 Mar. 1854. *d.* at Canterbury, 28 Nov. 1873.

1047. Morice, James. *b.* 2 May 1801. London Hosp. L.R.C.S. Ed. 1821. M.D. K.C. Ab. 1826. A.S. 15 Mar. 1826. Surg. 21 Oct. 1841. R. 5 Dec. 1848. *d.* 15 Aug. 1868.

1048. Raleigh, Edward Ward Walter. *b.* 23 Nov. 1802. L.S.A. 1824. M.R.C.S. 1825. A.S. 15 Mar. 1826. Surg. 30 Nov. 1841. F.R.C.S. original list, 1844. R. 1 June 1846. *d.* 23 Jan. 1865. Author of Idiopathic Dysentery in Europeans in Bengal, 1842.

1049. Duncan, Alexander Campbell. *b.* 5 Feb. 1804. M.A. Mar. Coll. Ab. 1819. M.D. Ed. 1825. A.S. 15 Mar. 1826. Officiating A.S. 3 Apr. 1826; (C.G.); but subsequently appointed by Court from 15 Mar. 1826. Surg. 30 Dec. 1841. R. 1 Jan. 1848. *d.* in Edinburgh, 10 Dec. 1877. Author of Tentamen Medicum Inaugurale de Cholera, 1825.

1050. MacGregor, William Lewis. *b.* Dec. 1801. M.D. Ed. 1825. A.S. 15 Mar. 1826. Surg. 13 Jan. 1842. *d.* at Dinapur, 7 Sept. 1853. First Sikh or Sutlej war, 1845–46, Firuzshahr, Sobraon, medal and clasp. Author of Observations on Diseases of European and Native Soldiers, 1843; History of the Sikhs, 1846; Medical Topography of Loodiana.

1051. MacLean, Hugh. *b.* 5 Dec. 1803. M.A. Mar. Coll. Ab. 1821. A.S. 15 Mar. 1826. Surg. 14 Jan. 1842. R. 1 Dec. 1848. *d.* 8 Apr. 1885. First Sikh or Sutlej war, 1845–46, Mudki, Firuzshahr, and Sobraon, medal with three clasps.

1052. Seton, George Somner. *b.* 4 Dec. 1802. M.D. Ed. 1823. A.S. 15 May 1826. *d.* at Balua, Noakhali, 11 May 1828. D. and M. spell name Seaton.

1053. Wardlaw, David Brown (b). *b.* Jan. 1803. Surg. Mate, 'Kent,' 1822–23. M.R.C.S. 1826. A.S. 15 Apr. 1826. Furlough S.C. 1829. Pensioned on Lord Clive's Fund, 16 Dec. 1831. *d.* 19 Aug. 1867.

1054. Murray, Adam. M.R.C.S 1821. M.D. Ed. 1824. A.S. 5 May 1826. Surg. 1 Feb. 1842. R. 31 Dec. 1847. *d.* at Londonderry, 28 Mar. 1868.

1055. Hart, Thomas Barnard. *b.* 14 May 1803. M.R.C.S. 1825. A.S. 15 May 1826. B.A. T.C.D. 1838. Surg. 20 May 1842. R. 1 Jan. 1848. Gwalior, 1843–44, Maharajpur, bronze star. First Sikh or Sutlej war, 1845–46, Aliwal, medal.

1056. Duncan, Robert Barclay. *b.* 6 Jan. 1802. M.A. Mar. Coll. Ab. 1818. M.R.C.S. 1822. A.S. 15 May 1826. Surg. 17 Sept. 1842. *d.* at Dakka, 17 Oct. 1843.

1057. Dollard, William. *b.* May 1800. M.R.C.S. 1825. A.S. 21 May 1826. Surg. 15 Nov. 1842. F.R.C.S. original list, 1844. *d.* at Delhi, 4 Oct. 1845. Author of Medical Topography of Kalee Kumaon and Shere Valley, 1840.

1058. Davidson, Isaac (b). *b.* 5 Aug. 1803. Surg. Mate, ' Marquis of Huntly,' 1824–25. A.S. 21 May 1826. *d.* at Wigton, 25 June 1833. D. and M. misprint Wigton as Wiglon.

1059. MacLeod, Donald Alexander. *b.* 19 Dec. 1801. M.A. K.C. Ab. 1819. Hosp. Asst. A.M.D. 1 Dec. 1825. Resigned, 25 Jan. 1826. v. Johnston's Roll of R.A.M.C. No. 4118. A.S. Bengal, 21 May 1826. Surg. 4 Dec. 1842. R. 5 June 1847. *d.* at Dalvey, Elgin, 22 Sept. 1872. Author of Medical Topography of Bishnath, 1837.

1060. Brander, James Mainwaring. *b.* 15 Jan. 1796. A.S. 21 May 1826. Surg. 31 Dec. 1842. R. 16 Dec. 1852. *d.* at Clifton, 12 Apr. 1856.

1061. Bell, Henry Peile. *b.* 29 Sept. 1797. M.D. Glas. 1826. A.S. 22 May 1826. *d.* in Calcutta, 28 Sept. 1840.

1062. Roe, Henry. *b.* Apr. 1803. M.R.C.S. 1825. A.S. 22 May 1826. Resigned, 6 Mar. 1837.

1063. Warlow, William. *b.* 18 May 1803. M.R.C.S. 1824. A.S. 22 May 1826. Furlough, S.C. 9 Sept. 1832. Pensioned on Lord Clive's Fund, 31 Jan. 1835. Practising at Haverfordwest, Pembroke, in 1851. *d.* 22 May 1865. D. and M. give date of retirement as 21 Jan. 1835.

1064. Gale, Alfred Athelstan Wilkins (a, d). *b.* 29 Oct. 1802. M.R.C.S. 1825. L.S.A. 1825. A.S. 22 May 1826. Declined appointment, never joined. In practice at Shepton Mallet, Somerset, in 1848.

1065. Woodhouse, Charles Theodore. *b.* 22 Feb. 1802. M.R.C.S. 1824. L.S.A. 1825. A.S. 22 May 1826. *d.* at Sagar, 12 Nov. 1831.

1066. Carnie, James. *b.* 28 July 1801. M.D. Ed. 1822. A.S. 24 May 1826. *d.* at Titalya, 25 Nov. 1827.

1067. Gordon, Archibald Campbell. *b.* 29 May 1804. M.D. C.M. Glas. 1826. A.S. 13 June 1826. Surg. 1 Jan. 1843. *d.* at Jalandhar, 30 Nov. 1849. Afghanistan, 1842, with Genl. Pollock's Force.

1068. Goss, James. *b.* 28 Sept. 1800. M.R.C.S. 1822. L.S.A. 1822. A.S. 19 June 1826. R. 22 July 1841. *d.* 18 July 1879.

1069. Leese, John Vaux. *b.* 9 Feb. 1802. M.R.C.S. 1826. A.S. 27 June 1826. Surg. 26 Jan. 1843. R. 30 Nov. 1846. *d.* at Ryde, Isle of Wight, 2 Jan. 1853.

1070. Crawford, William Henry (a, d). M.D. Ed. 1823. Hosp. Asst. A.M.D. 6 Oct. 1825. v. Johnston's Roll of R.A.M.C. No. 4096. A.S. Bengal, 28 June 1826. Declined appointment, never joined.

1071. **Rogers, William Henry.** *b.* June 1803. M.R.C.S. 1825. A.S. 30 June 1826. *d.* at Jodhpur, 23 Nov. 1835.

1072. **Babington, Henry.** *b.* 28 Oct. 1802. M.R.C.S. 1824. L.S.A. 1824. A.S. 12 July 1826. *d.* at the Cape of Good Hope, 11 Apr. 1833.

1073. **Burgoyne, Joseph** (b). *b.* 6 Apr. 1794. M.R.C.S. 1815. Surg. Mate of ' Bombay,' 1821–22. A.S. 13 July 1826. *d.* at Sitapur, 27 May 1832.

1074. **Ransford, John.** *b.* 7 Feb. 1801. L.S.A. 1823. M.R.C.S. 1825. A.S. 16 July 1826. Surg. 13 Jan. 1843. R. 31 Dec. 1859. *d.* 27 Mar. 1869.

1075. **Forbes, George.** *b.* 19 Aug. 1801. M.R.C.S. 1825. M.D. 18—. A.S. 17 July 1826. *d.* at Hijli (Hidgellee), 23 Oct. 1837. D. and M. say died at Contai, same date.

1076. **Small, Beaumont Dixie.** *b.* 30 Apr. 1803. M.R.C.S. 1825. L.S.A. 1825. A.S. 21 July 1826. *d.* at Nasirabad, 3 Sept. 1831.

1077. **O'Donoghue, Mathew.** *b.* 15 Dec. 1793. M.D. T.C.D. 18—. A.S. 8 Aug. 1826. *d.* in Genl. Hosp. Calcutta, 24 May 1830; (C.G.). D. and M. and E.I. Regr. for 1831, give date of death as 23 Aug. 1829.

1078. **Rose, William Kenneth MacLeay** (b). *b.* 22 Mar. 1803. Surg. Mate, ' Princess Charlotte of Wales,' 1825–26. A.S. 13 Aug. 1826. Surg. 9 Feb. 1843. *d.* at Cawnpur, 25 Sept. 1843. Central India, 1842, operations in Bandalkund.

1079. **Gilmore, Allan.** *b.* 10 Apr. 1804. M.D. Ed. 1826. A.S. 25 Aug. 1826. *d.* in Calcutta, 9 June 1837.

1080. **Heath, William.** *b.* Dec. 1803. A.S. 23 Aug. 1826. Drowned in the Hughli, Calcutta, 28 May 1827.

1081. **Elliot, Thomas Curry.** *b.* 5 Oct. 1798. M.D. Ed. 1820. M.R.C.S. 1826. A.S. 1 Sept. 1826. Surg. 9 Feb. 1843. *d.* at Mirat, 14 Nov 1849. First Sikh or Sutlej war, 1845–46, with 48 N.I. Second Sikh or Panjab war, 1848–49, with 6th Light Cavalry.

1082. **Dunlap, William Lemon.** *b.* Jan. 1804. M.R.C.S. 1824. A.S. 9 Sept. 1826. *d.* at Nimach, 31 May 1839. Name given as Dunlop in Army Lists, but his signature, in A.S. Certs. vol. xxi. 1826, is Dunlap.

1083. **Spencer, William.** *b.* Mar. 1795. M.R.C.S. 1824. A.S. 12 Sept. 1826. Surg. 16 Feb. 1843. R. 3 Feb. 1850. *d.* at Bath, 3 July 1863. First Sikh or Sutlej war, 1845–46, Mudki, Aliwal, and Sobraon, medal with two clasps. Second Sikh or Panjab war, 1848–49.

1084. **Burt, Thomas Williams.** *b.* Oct. 1797. M.R.C.S. 1824. L.S.A. 1824. A.S. 12 Sept. 1826. Surg. 28 Feb. 1843. L.R.C.P. Lond. 1843. R. 22 Dec. 1849.

1085. **MacKinnon, Kenneth MacKenzie.** *b.* 8 Aug. 1804. M.D. Ed. 1826. A.S. 19 Nov. 1826. Surg. 1 Mar. 1843. R. 11 Jan. 1857. *d.* in Edinburgh, 13 Feb. 1861. Author of Medical Topography of Tirhut, 1839; A Treatise on Public Health, Climate, Hygiene, and Diseases of Bengal, and N.W.P. 1848. Brother of C. MacKinnon, 13,826, *supra*.

1086. **Cameron, Lachlan John.** *b.* 20 Oct. 1803. M.D. Ed. 1825. A.S. 19 Nov. 1826. *d.* in England, 3 Feb. 1830.

1087. **Buchanan, William Miller.** *b.* 22 Jan. 1801. M.D. Glas. 1826. A.S. 15 Dec. 1826. R. 20 July 1839. *d.* 1 Jan. 1893.

1827

1088. **Stokes, James.** *b.* 11 Feb. 1804. M.D. Ed. 1806. A.S. Bombay, 7 Jan. 1827. Originally nominated to Bombay, transferred to Bengal; (Bo. G.O. 14 June 1827). A.S. Bengal, from same date, 7 Jan. 1827. Surg. 1 Mar. 1843. R. 31 Jan. 1852. *d.* in London, 1 Feb. 1880. D. and M. give name in Bengal, but not in Bombay list. S.A.L.M.Bo. gives date of commission as 1826. Bo. No. 545.

1089. **Nisbet, James** (b). *b.* 9 Mar. 1803. Surg. 'Childe Harold,' 1825–26. A.S. 16 Jan. 1827. *d.* in Fort William, 17 Apr. 1828. D. and M. and S.A.L.M.B. spell name Nisbett, but his signature, in A.S. Certs. vol. xxii. 1827, is Nisbet.

1090. **Willan, Joseph.** *b.* 29 Oct. 1791. M.R.C.S. 1817. A.S. 21 Jan. 1827. Discharged by Court Martial, 3 Jan. 1831.

1091. **Bryce, Alexander.** *b.* 24 Dec. 1804. M.D. Ed. 1826. A.S. 13 Feb. 1827. Afghanistan, 1839–42, with Artillery, killed in retreat from Kabul, near Tezin, 10 Jan. 1842.

1092. **Gullan, David.** *b.* 6 Mar. 1796. A.S. 10 Mar. 1827. Surg. 23 July 1843. R. 1 Feb. 1845. *d.* in London, 28 May 1868.

1093. **Wilson, Andrew.** *b.* 5 July 1802. A.S. 10 Mar. 1827. Surg. 25 Sept. 1843. D.I.G. 30 July 1858. R. 31 Mar. 1863. *d.* at Cheltenham, 23 Oct. 1868.

1094. **Morgan, Tom Trafford.** *b.* 18 July 1802. M.R.C.S. 1824. A.S. 17 Mar. 1827. *d.* at sea, on the 'Neptune,' on passage to England, 25 Feb. 1828.

1095. **Baker, John.** *b.* Oct. 1789. M.R.C.S. 1826. A.S. 23 Mar. 1827. Surg. 17 Oct. 1843. R. 6 Feb. 1846. *d.* 20 Dec. 1852.

1096. **Woodburn, David.** *b.* 8 Mar. 1805. M.D. Ed. 1824. M.R.C.S. 1826. A.S. 6 Apr. 1827. Surg. 16 Dec. 1843. R. 18 July 1856. *d.* at Ayr, 13 Apr. 1888. Father of Sir John Woodburn, K.C.S.I. B.C.S. Lieut.-Governor of Bengal, 1898–1902.

1097. **Spry, Henry Harpur.** *b.* 6 Jan. 1804. M.R.C.S. 1827. A.S. 10 Apr. 1827. M.D. Erlangen, 1837. *d.* in Calcutta, from effects of a carriage accident, 4 Sept. 1842. F.R.S. 1841. Author of Modern India, 1837.

1098. **Corbet, James.** *b.* Mar. 1804. C.M. Glas. 1826. M.R.C.S. 1826. L.A.H. Dublin, 1827. A.S. 10 Apr. 1827. Surg. 12 Jan. 1844. R. 31 Mar. 1849.

1099. **Campbell, Archibald.** *b.* 20 Apr. 1805. M.D. Ed. 1826. A.S. 8 May 1827. Surg. 16 Jan. 1844. R. 8 Feb. 1862. *d.* 5 Nov. 1884. Supt. Darjiling, 1840–62. N.-E. Frontier of India, Sikkim, 1860–61; v. Hooker's Himalayan Journals, chaps. 25, 26. Author of Routes from Darjiling to Thibet, 1848; Papers on Sikkim Morang, and Kooch Behar, 1851.

1100. **Lovell, Matthew** (b). *b.* 1795. Surg. Mate, 'Winchelsea,' 1814–17; 'Windsor,' 1819–20; Surg. 'Princess Charlotte of Wales,' 1821–26. A.S. 25 May 1827. Surg. 23 May 1844. R. 1 Feb. 1845. *d.* in London, 8 Mar. 1860. Afghanistan, 1842.

1101. Agnew, Edward Jones. *b.* 11 Mar. 1805. C.M. Glas. 1827. A.S. 25 May 1827. R. 22 Apr. 1840. *d.* 11 Feb. 1848.

1102. Wyatt, John Hindes (a). *b.* 10 Aug. 1804. M.R.C.S. 1827. A.S. 10 July 1827. *d.* in a boat on river Ganges, near Ghazipur, Apr. 1830; (" lately," C.G. 15 Apr. 1830). S.A.L.M.B. gives date of death as Apr. 1829.

1103. Fleming, Frederick. *b.* 1790. A.S. 10 July 1827. Surg. 31 Jan. 1844. R. 15 May 1850. *d.* in Edinburgh, 3 Nov. 1859.

1104. Vans Dunlop, Andrew. *b.* 8 Feb. 1805. M.D. Ed. 1826. L.R.C.S. Ed. 1826. A.S. 11 July 1827. Surg. 31 Jan. 1844. R. 1 May 1851. *d.* in Edinburgh, 27 Feb. 1880. Founder of Vans Dunlop Scholarships at Edin. Univ.

1105. Wise, Thomas Alexander. *b.* 13 June 1802. M.D. Ed. 1824. M.R.C.S. 1824. L.S.A. 1826. A.S. 13 Aug. 1827. Surg. 2 Feb. 1844. R. 11 Feb. 1851. F.R.C.S. Ed. 1852. F.R.C.S. Eng. 1859. *d.* at Norwood, 23 July 1889. Father of J. F. N. Wise, No. 1730, infra. Author of The Pathology of the Blood, 1831; The Barah Bheyas of Eastern Bengal; The Hindu System of Medicine, 1845; Diseases of the Eye, 1847; Cholera, 1864; Review of the History of Medicine, 1867.

1106. Gordon, William. *b.* 26 Oct. 1804. M.A. Mar. Coll. Ab. 1821. M.D. Ed. 1827. A.S. 13 Oct. 1827. Surg. 16 Feb. 1844. R. 10 Oct. 1849. *d.* 1 Nov. 1881. First Sikh or Sutlej war, 1845–46.

1107. MacAndrew, Aeneas. *b.* 8 Dec. 1803. M.A. Mar. Coll. Ab. 1820. M.D. Ed. 1824. A.S. 13 Oct. 1827. *d.* at Mirat, 29 June 1830.

1108. Holmes, Samuel. *b.* 2 May 1803. M.R.C.S. 1826. A.S. 4 Nov. 1827. Surg. 28 May 1844. *d.* on board the 'Alfred,' near the Cape of Good Hope, 16 Apr. 1855.

*1109. Boswell, John Campbell (a). *b.* 17 Nov 1796. A.S. P.W.I. Establishment, 15 Nov. 1827. Transferred to Bengal, 7 Apr. 1830. *d.* at Penang, 28 Oct. 1841. D. and M. give name in P.W.I. but not in Bengal list.

*1110. Oxley, Thomas. *b.* May 1805. M.D. Mar. Coll. Ab. 1823. M.R.C.S, 1827. A.S. P.W.I. Establishment, 1827. Transferred to Bengal. 7 Apr. 1830. Surg. 1 Jan. 1847. R. 20 Jan. 1857. *d.* at Southampton, 6 Mar. 1886. D. and M. give name in both P.W.I. and Bengal lists. China, 1841–42.

1828

1111. Inglis, John. *b.* 13 Apr. 1805. M.D. Ed. 1827. L.R.C.S. Ed. 1827. A.S. 3 Jan. 1828. Surg. 19 Sept. 1844. R. 31 Dec. 1853. *d.* 15 June 1873.

---

* The small Presidency, named Prince of Wales Island, including Prince of Wales Island, Penang, Malacca, and Singapur, was abolished from 1 May 1830, and included under the Bengal Presidency. The senior officers were pensioned, and the juniors transferred to the Bengal Establishments. Four medical officers were thus transferred, A. Thompson, No. 1003, supra, J. C. Boswell, T. Oxley, and J. J. Boswell, No. 1163, infra. These dependencies were officered from Bengal, until Apr. 1867, when they were removed from the control of the Government of India, and incorporated into a Crown Colony, under the name of Straits Settlements. Oxley survived his original service by nearly sixty years.

1112. Osborn, Robert Farquhar (a, d). A.S. 11 Jan. 1828. Declined appointment. Never joined.

1113. Thorburn, David James. *b.* 31 Dec. 1805. A.S. 19 Jan. 1828. Furlough, S.C. 28 Jan. 1830. Pensioned on Lord Clive's Fund, 28 June 1832.

1114. Fulton, Henry. *b.* 3 Apr. 1793. M.D. Ed. 1824. A.S. 19 Jan. 1828. Resigned, 17 July 1829.

1115. Shelton, Charles Robert. *b.* 3 May 1803. A.S. 3 Feb. 1828. *d.* at Mhau, 1 Nov. 1829.

1116. Grierson, William (b). *b.* 15 Feb. 1803. Surg. Mate, 'Marchioness of Ely,' 1824–25. A.S. 22 Feb. 1828. Surg. 27 Nov. 1844. R. 31 Dec. 1853. *d.* at Smallholm, Dumfrieshire, 12 June 1878. First Sikh or Sutlej war, 1845–46, Firuzshahr, medal.

1117. Walker, Andrew. *b.* 8 Feb. 1806. A.S. 23 Feb. 1828. *d.* at Katwa, Bardwan, 18 Nov. 1844 ; (tombstone).

1118. Berwick, George Jackson. *b.* 23 Aug. 1799. A.S. 23 Feb. 1828. Surg. 15 Dec. 1844. R. 6 Dec. 1852. *d.* at St. Helen's, Isle of Wight, 30 May 1873. Surgeon to Sir William MacNaghten's Embassy to Kabul, detailed to attend on sick and wounded prisoners ; v. Kaye's Afghan war, ii. 325. Afghanistan, 1839–42.

1119. Colquhoun, Archibald. *b.* 1804. L.R.C.S. Ed. 18—. A.S. 26 Feb. 1828. Surg. 19 Dec. 1844. R. 31 Dec. 1847. *d.* in Edinburgh, 25 Apr. 1890. Afghanistan, 1839–42, with Shah Shuja's Force, capture of Ghuzni, actions on Helmund river, and at Zamindawan, Desp. C.G. 11 Aug. 1841 and 22 Sept. 1841. First Sikh or Sutlej war, 1845–46, Firuzshahr and Sobraon, medal.

1120. Dickson, John Burnie (b). *b.* 5 Jan. 1806. Surg. 'Winchelsea,' 1825–27. A.S. 26 Feb. 1828. Surg. 1 Jan. 1845. D.I.G. 30 July 1858. I.G. 25 Apr. 1862. R. 31 Mar. 1864. *d.* in London, 11 June 1884. First Sikh or Sutlej war, 1845–46. Indian Mutiny, 1857–58.

1121. Spurgeon, Astley Cooper. *b.* 30 Aug. 1804. M.R.C.S. 1827. A.S. 26 Feb. 1828. Resigned, 17 Jan. 1833.

1122. Steel, James. *b.* 16 June 1797. M.D. 18—. A.S. 11 Apr. 1828. Surg. 1 Feb. 1845. R. 10 Feb. 1866. *d.* at Cheltenham, 14 Dec. 1874. First Sikh or Sutlej war, 1845–46, as Field Surgeon, Firuzshahr and Sobraon, Desp. L.G. 1 Apr. 1846, medal.

1123. Fullarton, Robert. *b.* 16 Mar. 1806. M.D. Ed. 1827. A.S. 16 Apr. 1828. *d.* at Cawnpur, 20 July 1837. Had held a commission in Militia ; (A.S. Certs. vol. xxiii. 1827–28).

1124. Cumberland, Robert Bakewell. *b.* 9 Feb. 1804. M.R.C.S. 1827. A.S. 16 Apr. 1828. Surg. 1 Feb. 1845. R. 20 Jan. 1854. *d.* at Crediton, 17 Dec. 1876. Author of Stray Leaves from the Diary of an Indian Officer (published under pseudonym of Carlisle), 1865 ; Medical and Statistical Report on District of Puri.

1125. MacRae, James. *b.* 5 Sept. 1803. A.S. 10 May 1828. Surg. 1 Feb 1845. *d.* in Calcutta, 6 Sept. 1856. Gwalior, 1843–44, Maharajpur, bronze star. First Sikh or Sutlej war, 1845–6, Mudki, Aliwal, and

Firuzshahr, medal with two clasps. Second Sikh or Panjab war, 1848–49, Ramnagar, Chilianwala, and Gujrat, Desp. L.G. 3 Mar. and 19 Apr. 1849, medal. Author, with C. Renny, No. 694, supra, of Reports on Field Hospital of Army of Panjab, 1850.

1126. **Garbett, Christopher.** b. 20 June 1806. M.R.C.S. 1828. A.S. 23 May 1828. Surg. 5 Feb. 1845. Second Sikh or Panjab war, 1848–49. Indian Mutiny, 1857, d. June 1857, in Genl. Wheeler's Entrenchment at Cawnpur. Lancet of 14 Nov. 1857 states that he died of wounds.

1127. **Cumming, William Fullerton.** b. 6 Oct. 1804. M.D. Ed. 1827. A.S. 2 June 1828. Furlough, S.C. 27 Apr. 1830. Pensioned on Lord Clive's Fund, 23 Sept. 1832. d. at Loch Baa, Mull, Argyll, 27 July 1892. Author of Notes of a Wanderer in search of Health, through Italy, Egypt, Greece, Turkey, up the Danube and down the Rhine, 1839.

1128. **Sill, Henry.** b. Apr. 1806. A.S. 10 June 1828. Surg. 1 Apr. 1845. d. at Nowgong (Nayagaon), Assam, 20 Feb. 1852. Central India, 1842, operations in Bandalkund.

1129. **Griffiths, Charles.** b. 29 Aug. 1805. M.R.C.S. 1828. A.S. 18 June 1828. Surg. 24 Apr. 1845. R. 14 Sept. 1850. d. 15 June 1875. Mission to Bhutan, 1838–39.

1130. **Webster, William Binny.** b. 24 June 1806. A.S. 19 July 1828. Surg. 27 June 1845. R. 6 Mar. 1846. d. in London, 13 May 1862.

1131. **Anderson, George.** b. 24 Nov. 1803. M.R.C.S. 1827. A.S. 21 July 1828. d. at Masuri, 28 June 1841. Afghanistan, 1839–40, capture of Ghuzni; (P.R.).

1132. **Eccles, John.** b. 27 June 1798. M.D. Ed. 1828. A.S. 8 Aug. 1828. d. at Sagar, 11 Oct. 1839.

1133. **Davies, Samuel.** b. 5 Oct. 1794. M.R.C.S. 1828. A.S. 8 Aug. 1828. Surg. 6 July 1845. R. 20 Feb. 1846. d. at Cheltenham, 2 Oct. 1852.

1134. **Fuller, Charles Wray.** b. 16 Oct. 1805. M.R.C.S. 1827. A.S. 12 Sept. 1828. Surg. 17 July 1845. R. 2 Mar. 1851.

1135. **Davenport, James.** b. 12 July 1806. M.D. Ed. 1827. M.R.C.S. 1828. A.S. 12 Sept. 1828. Surg. 4 Oct. 1845. R. 22 Sept. 1850. d. in Guernsey, 16 Mar. 1898.

— **Hodges, Thomas.** A.S. 4 Dec. 1828. v. No. 892, supra.

1136. **Lightfoot, Samuel** (a). M.D. St. A. 1825. Hosp. Asst. A.M.D. 27 Apr. 1826. A.S. 47th Foot, 28 Sept. 1826; 14th Foot, by exchange, 13 Dec. 1828. (v. Johnston's Roll of R.A.M.C. No. 4156.) A.S. Bengal, 4 Dec. 1828. Invalided, 20 Mar. 1846. d. at Bhowanipur, Calcutta, 29 Jan. 1848.

1829

1137. **Irvine, Robert Hamilton.** b. 7 Mar. 1806. M.D. Ed. 1828. A.S. 15 Jan. 1829. Surg. 1 Jan. 1846. R. 9 July 1857. S.A.L.M.B. gives date of retirement as 2 May 1857. Son of William Irvine, A.M.D. Physician to the Forces; (Johnston's Roll of R.A.M.C. No. 2768). First Sikh or Sutlej war, 1845–46. Author of Medical Topography of Ajmeer, 1841; Native Materia Medica of Patna, 1848.

1138. **Andrew, William Peter.** *b.* Oct. 1806. M.D. Ed. 1828. A.S. 15 Jan. 1829. R. 6 July 1838.

1139. **Fisher, Frederick Horatio** (b). *b.* 28 Dec. 1805. Surg. 'Orient,' 1825–26. A.S. 15 Jan. 1829. *d.* at Quebec, 15 Jan. 1835.

1140. **MacKenzie, Hugh.** *b.* 1 June 1794. Ensign, 57th Foot, 24 Feb. 1813; Lieut. 25 Feb. 1814; H.P. 24 Feb. 1816. Lieut. Lanark Militia, 5 July 1820. M.D. Glas. 1823. A.S. 15 Jan. 1829. *d.* at Sandoway, Arakan, 24 Dec. 1831. Peninsula, 1813–14, battles of Vittoria, Nive, and Nivelle.

1141. **MacAnally, Acheson Archibald.** *b.* Oct. 1803. M.R.C.S. 1828. A.S. 20 Jan. 1829. Surg. 6 Feb. 1846. R. 27 Jan. 1853. *d.* 19 Mar. 1859, at Warrenpoint, Co. Down. Afghanistan, 1839–42, capture of Ghuzni; (P.R.).

1142. **Storm, Alexander.** *b.* 28 Oct. 1800. M.R.C.S. 1828. A.S. 20 Jan. 1829. *d.* at Agra, 5 June 1835; (A.J. Jan. 1836, p. 39). E.I. Regr. states died at Delhi, same date.

1143. **Blackwood, James.** *b.* 20 Mar. 1805. A.S. 7 Feb. 1829. *d.* at Cawnpur, 30 Sept. 1833.

1144. **Kent, Matthew Salmon.** *b.* 18 Oct. 1805. A.S. 7 Mar. 1829. *d.* at Moradabad, 13 Dec. 1836.

1145. **Dwyer, Francis.** *b.* May 1797. M.R.C.S. 1819. A.S. 7 Mar. 1829. *d.* in Calcutta, 18 Dec. 1829. S.A.L.M.B. gives date of death as 18 Dec. 1830.

1146. **Bacon, John Ferguson.** *b.* 29 Oct. 1806. M.R.C.S. 1828. A.S. 28 Mar. 1829. Surg. 17 Feb. 1846. R. 8 May 1853. *d.* at Exeter, 14 July 1854. First Sikh or Sutlej war, 1845–46.

1147. **Baddeley, Paul Frederick Henry.** *b.* June 1806. M.R.C.S. 1828. A.S. 28 Mar. 1829. Surg. 20 Feb. 1846. R. 1 Feb. 1855. *d.* at Eastbourne, 26 Jan. 1882. Afghanistan, 1839–42, capture of Ghuzni; (P.R.). Author of Investigation of the Duststorms and Whirlwinds of India, 1860; Cyclone Compass, with Diagrams, 1860.

1148. **Brown, David** (a). *b.* 29 Nov. 1798. A.S. 9 May 1829. *d.* at Maybole, 29 May 1837.

1149. **Duncan, James** (a). *b.* 28 Aug. 1806. M.D. Ed. 1827. A.S. 9 May 1829. Surg. 5 Mar. 1844. *d.* at Wynberg, Cape Colony, 6 Mar. 1848. Firsh Sikh or Sutlej war, 1845–46.

1150. **Edmonds, Byrt Dyneley** (a). *b.* 13 Sept. 1806. A.S. 27 May 1829. *d.* on board the Juliana, on passage to England, 16 Apr. 1830.

1151. **Galt, Hugh Montgomery** (a). *b.* 12 July 1805. A.S. 7 June 1829. *d.* at Mirat, 1 May 1836.

1152. **Dicken, William Stephens** (a). *b.* 30 Sept. 1804. L.S.A. 1826. M.R.C.S. 1828. A.S. 17 June 1829. Surg. 6 Mar. 1846. D.I.G. 30 July 1858. *d.* at Sialkot, 15 Dec. 1861. Indian Mutiny, 1857–58, recapture of Gorakhpur, final siege and capture of Lucknow, Mar. 1858, medal and clasp.

1153. Bruce, James. *b.* 14 Nov. 1796. M.D. Ed. 1827. A.S. 9 July 1829. Surg. 20 Mar. 1846. R. 1 Mar. 1847. *d.* in Edinburgh, 27 Oct. 1865. Originally appointed in 1828, appointment cancelled for not joining; (A.S. Certs. vol. xxiii. 1827–28).

1154. Stuart, Andrew MacDouall. *b.* Jan. 1805. A.S. 29 Aug. 1829. Surg. 1 Apr. 1846. *d.* at Cherrapunji, Assam, 5 June 1851. Name spelt Stewart in birth certificate, but his signature in A.S. Certs. vol. xxiv. 1828–29, is Stuart.

1155. Bramley, Mountford Joseph. *b.* 16 Apr. 1803. M.R.C.S. 1825. Hosp. Asst. A.M.D. 24 Nov. 1825. A.S. Rifle Brigade, 5 Jan. 1826, Resigned, 11 June 1829; (v. Johnston's Roll of R.A.M.C. No. 4113. where his name is given as Joseph Mountford Bramley). A.S. Bengal, 29 Aug. 1829. First Principal of Medl. College, Calcutta, on its foundation, Jan. 1835. *d.* in Calcutta, 19 Jan. 1837. Author of Dictionary of Terms and Technicalities in Anatomy, Pathology, Physiology, and Surgery, 1836.

1156. Burnie, John. *b.* Nov. 1806. A.S. 28 Aug. 1829. *d.* at Allahabad, 17 Oct. 1830.

1157. Harvey, James. M.R.C.S. 1829. A.S. 2 Oct. 1829. *d.* in Ireland, 21 May 1837. In S.A.L.M.B. name is spelt Hervey.

*1158. Rind, Malcolm MacNeil. *b.* 12 Aug. 1807. L.R.C.S. Ed. 18—. A.S. 10 Oct. 1829. Surg. 6 Apr. 1846. S.M. 1 Feb. 1859. D.I.G. 21 June 1861. *d.* in Calcutta, 17 Dec. 1863. Brother of No. 740, supra, J. N. Rind; and of T. Rind, No. 465, Bo.

1159. Serrell, John Halkett. *b.* 27 Aug. 1806. M.R.C.S. 1829. A.S. 10 Oct. 1829. *d.* at Mainpuri, 2 Feb. 1845. Afghanistan, 1839–42, wounded in action in Haft Kotal pass, 14 Oct. 1842; (C.G. 23 Nov. 1842).

1160. Rhodes, William. *b.* 14 Jan. 1804. M.R.C.S. 1825. A.S. 25 Nov. 1829. *d.* at Bareli, 30 May 1836.

1161. MacCallum, Peter (a, b). *b.* 4 Sept. 1807. Surg. 'Abberton,' 1825–26. A.S. 22 Dec. 1829. *d.* in Calcutta, 27 Oct. 1830.

1162. Washbourn, Robert (b). *b.* 5 Feb. 1806. M.R.C.S. 1827. Surg. 'Malcolm,' 1828–29. A.S. 22 Dec. 1829. Furlough, S.C. 1832. Pensioned on Lord Clive's Fund, 15 Dec. 1834. *d.* at Stroud, 28 Dec. 1837. D. and M. spell name Washburn, but his signature, in A.S. Certs. vol. xxiv. 1828–29, is Washbourn.

1163. Boswell, John James. *b.* 8 Dec. 1794. A.S. P.W.I. Establishment, 1829. Transferred to Bengal, 1 May 1830. R. 6 Dec. 1836. D. and M. give name in both Bengal and P.W.I. lists.

1830

1164. MacDonald, Alexander. *b.* 9 July 1827. M.D. Ed. 1829. A.S. 3 Jan. 1830. *d.* at Barrackpur, 23 Aug. 1832.

1165. Richardson, Mark. *b.* 6 Nov. 1805. M.D. Ed. 1826. A.S. 3 Jan. 1830. Surg. 8 Apr. 1846. R. 31 Mar. 1852. *d.* in London, 28 Feb. 1880. First Sikh or Sutlej war, 1845–46, Sobraon, medal.

---

* By clause 9 of the Warrant of 1 Feb. 1859, the title of Surgeon Major and rank of Lieut.-Colonel was granted to all medical officers, at twenty years' service.

1166. **Allingham, Edward Herrick.** *b.* 25 Oct. 1805. L.R.C.S.I. 1829. A.S. 12 Jan. 1830. Struck off from 9 Dec. 1839, absent on sick leave since 1 Feb. 1831; (G.O. No. 212 of 9 Dec. 1839). Afterwards in practice at Dromehair, Leitrim. *d.* at Dromehair, 1857.

1167. **MacIntyre, Coll.** *b.* 16 Nov. 1803. C.M. Glas. 1822. A.S. 5 Feb. 1830. Surg. 9 Apr. 1846. R. 1 Mar. 1848. *d.* at Portobello, 8 Nov. 1867.

1168. **MacNab, David.** *b.* 8 May 1797. A.S. 5 Feb. 1830. Surg. 1 June 1846. R. 28 Feb. 1848. *d.* at Auchadeshenaig, Mull, 5 June 1850.

1169. **Hope, John.** *b.* 18 Feb. 1807. M.R.C.S. 1829. A.S. 5 Feb. 1830. Surg. 1 June 1846. R. 5 June 1847. *d.* at Henley-on-Thames, 23 May 1876. Author of The House of Scindia, 1863.

1170. **Thornton, Henry John.** *b.* 28 Aug. 1806. M.R.C.S. 1829. A.S. 5 Feb. 1830. Surg. 4 July 1846. S.M. 1 Feb. 1859. R. 16 Feb. 1860. *d.* at Brighton, 22 Sept. 1868. Indian Mutiny, 1857-58.

1171. **MacDonald, John Bannatyne.** *b.* 27 Nov. 1807. A.S. 27 Feb. 1830. Surg. 10 July 1846. *d.* at Lucknow, 8 Aug. 1857. S.-W. Frontier, operations against Kols, 1832. First Sikh or Sutlej war, 1845-46; Mudki, Firuzshahr, and Sobraon, medal with two clasps. Indian Mutiny, 1857. Defence of Lucknow, Desp. L.G. 17 Feb. 1858.

1172. **Stewart, James.** *b.* 1 Feb. 1802. M.R.C.S. 1831. A.S. 28 Mar. 1830. *d.* at Banda, 17 Aug. 1833.

1173. **MacKinnon, Campbell.** *b.* 27 Sept. 1806. M.D. Glas. 1829. A.S. 30 Mar. 1830. Surg. 2 Aug. 1846. D.I.G. 30 July 1858. I.G. 27 Aug. 1858. R. 6 Aug. 1862. *d.* 4 Mar. 1871. C.B. 1 Mar. 1861. Q.H.P. 6 Sept. 1861. Afghanistan, 1839-42, capture of Ghuzni, operations in Bamian and Kohistan, defence of Kelat-i-Ghilzai, advance on Kabul under Genl. Nott, second capture of Ghuzni, three medals. Second Sikh or Panjab war, 1848-49, Ramnagar, Chilianwala, and Gujrat, medal. Indian Mutiny, 1857-58, as S.S., siege and storm of Delhi, Desp. L.G. 15 Dec. 1857, medal with clasp, C.B.

1174. **Falconer, Hugh** (e). *b.* 29 Feb. 1808. M.A. K.C. Ab. 1826. M.D. Ed. 1829. A.S. 7 Apr. 1830. Surg. 2 Nov. 1846. R. 3 Sept. 1855. *d.* in London, 31 Jan. 1865. F.R.S. 1845. v. Palæontological Memoirs, by C. Murchison, 1868. Author, with P. Cautley, of Fauna Antiqua Sivalensis, 1845-49.

1175. **MacClelland, John.** *b.* 17 Nov. 1800. M.R.C.S. 1828. A.S. 7 Apr. 1830. Surg. 30 Nov. 1846. S.M. 1 Feb. 1859. D.I.G. 1 Aug. 1859. I.G. 8 Nov. 1860. Principal I.G. 25 Apr. 1862. R. 24 Nov. 1865. *d.* at St. Leonards, 31 July 1883. Author of Geology of Kumaon, 1835; Report on Assam Tea plant, 1837; The Teak Forests of Pegu, 1855; Medical Topography of Bengal and N.W.P. 1859. Also edited Calcutta Journal of Natural History, 1841-47. Also edited posthumous works of W. Griffith (M. No. 929); Icones Plantanum Asiaticarum, 1847-51; Notulæ ad Plantas Asiaticas, 4 vols. 1847-1854; Palms of British India, 1850.

1176. **Handyside, Charles Baird.** *b.* 19 June 1804. M.D. Ed. 1827. A.S. 12 May 1830. Surg. 31 Jan. 1847. R. 31 Mar. 1851. *d.* at Boulogne, 2 Feb. 1859. First Sikh or Sutlej war, 1845-46, Firuzshahr, Aliwal, medal. Second Sikh or Panjab war, 1848-49, Chilianwala, Gujrat, medal.

1177. **Russell, David.** *b.* 7 July 1806. M.D. Ed. 1827. A.S. 13 May 1830. *d.* at Nimach, 11 Sept. 1837.

1178. **Brien, James Richard.** *b.* 1806. M.R.C.S. 1829. A.S. 13 May 1830. *d.* at St. Helena, 16 Dec. 1835, on passage to England.

1179. **Green, William Abbott.** *b.* 28 Feb. 1808. L.S.A. 1829. M.R.C.S. 1830. A.S. 6 June 1830. L.R.C.P. Lond. 1843. Surg. 5 Feb. 1847. D.I.G. 30 July 1858. M.R.C.P. Lond. 1861. I.G. 31 Mar. 1864. Senior I.G. 1 Sept. 1866. R. 31 Mar. 1869. *d.* at Norwood, 21 July 1887. Q.H.S. 6 Sept. 1861. Indian Mutiny, 1857–58, with Naval Brigade at Dakka, wounded.

1180. **Jackson, John.** *b.* 17 Nov. 1804. Univ. Coll. Lond. St. Catherine's College, Cambridge. M.B. 1829, M.D. 1855, Cantab. A.S. 27 June 1830. F.R.C.S. original list, 1844. Surg. 1 Mar. 1847. R. 31 Dec. 1855. M.R.C.P. Lond. 1856. F.R.C.P. Lond. 1859. *d.* at Brighton, 31 Mar. 1887. Author of Forms of Tetanus in India, 1856.

1181. **Laing, Alexander.** *b.* 25 Nov. 1807. M.D. Ed. 1828. A.S. 27 June 1830. *d.* at Dakka, 11 Sept. 1831.

1182. **Minto, Alexander Muir MacKenzie.** *b.* 25 Nov. 1806. A.S. 20 July 1830. Surg. 30 Mar. 1847. R. 27 Dec. 1854. *d.* 1 Oct. 1882.

1183. **Winbolt, Samuel.** *b.* 8 Dec. 1801. M.R.C.S. 1825. A.S. 24 July 1830. Surg. 10 Apr. 1847. R. 31 July 1850. *d.* in London, 25 Sept. 1865. Gwalior, 1843–44, Maharajpur, bronze star. First Sikh or Sutlej war, 1845–46, Sobraon, medal.

1184. **Bruce, Henry Alexander.** *b.* 9 Apr. 1806. M.D. Ed. 1829. L.R.C.S. Ed. 18—. A.S. 17 Aug. 1830. Surg. 5 June 1847. S.M. 1 Feb. 1859. D.I.G. 1 May 1859. I.G. 8 Aug. 1862. Principal I.G. 24 Nov. 1865. R. 1 Sept. 1866. *d.* at Burntisland, Fife, 8 May 1894. Afghanistan, 1839–42, capture of Ghuzni, battle of Bamian, medal with clasp. First Sikh or Sutlej war, 1845–46, Aliwal, Sobraon, medal with two clasps.

1185. **Keir, Adam.** *b.* 4 July 1806. M.D. Ed. 1830. A.S. 30 Aug. 1830. Surg. 5 June 1847. R. 10 Mar. 1855. *d.* at West Norwood, 24 Mar. 1897.

1186. **Ginders, Thomas.** *b.* 22 July 1805. M.R.C.S. 1829. A.S. 30 Sept. 1830. *d.* at sea, on board 'Hindostan,' on passage to England, 23 Mar. 1844. Central India, 1840–41, operations in Bandalkund, capture of Fort Chargong, Desp. C.G. 12 May 1841.

1831

1187. **Scott, William.** *b.* 8 Feb. 1807. A.S. 21 Jan. 1831. *d.* at Dinapur, 12 Aug. 1834.

1188. **Watson, William Errington.** *b.* 15 June 1802. L.S.A. 1823. M.R.C.S. 1824. A.S. 22 Jan. 1831. Resigned, 1 Dec. 1836; (G.O. No. 200 of 10 Oct. 1836). S.A.L.M.B. and D. and M. give date of resignation as 4 Nov. 1836. Afterwards in practice at Brighton.

1189. **Foley, Roger.** *b.* Feb. 1803. A.S. 22 Jan. 1831. *d.* at Kotah, 29 Aug. 1838.

1190. **Stott, Thomas.** *b.* 18 Sept. 1807. M.R.C.S. 1830. A.S. 29 Jan. 1831. Surg. 31 Oct. 1847. *d.* at Delhi, 19 Jan. 1850.

1191. **MacCosh, John.** *b.* 5 Mar. 1805. A.S. 2 Feb. 1831. M.D. Ed. 1841. Surg. 31 Dec. 1847. R. 31 Jan. 1856. *d.* in London, 16 Jan. 1885. Was the only passenger who survived the wreck of the barque 'Lady Munro,' on island of Amsterdam, 11 Oct. 1833. v. Hist. of I.M.S. ii. 253. Brother of D. MacCosh, No. 937, Bombay, 1859. S.-W. Frontier, operations against Kols, 1832–33. Gwalior, 1843–44, Maharajpur, bronze star. Second Sikh or Panjab war, 1848–49, Sadullapur, Chilianwala, and Gujrat, medal with two clasps. Burma 1852–54, capture of Rangoon and Bassein, operations in Pegu; Desp. L.G. 24 Aug. 1852 and 15 Feb. 1853, medal. Author of Narrative of the Loss of the 'Lady Munro,' 1835; Topography of Assam, 1837; Medical Advice to the Indian Stranger, 1841; Advice to Officers in India, 1843; Nuova Italia, a poem, 1873, ditto, second series, 1875; Grand Tour in Many Lands, a poem, 1881.

1192. **Henderson, Francis Charteris.** *b.* 24 July 1808. M.D. Ed. 1829 A.S. 10 Feb. 1831. Surg. 31 Dec. 1847. R. 4 Oct. 1851. *d.* in Edinburgh, 3 Sept. 1881. Afghanistan, 1839–42, capture of Ghuzni, medal. Gwalior, 1843–44, Maharajpur, bronze star. First Sikh or Sutlej war, 1845–46, Aliwal and Badiwal, capture of Kot Kangra, medal.

1193. **Esdaile, James** (a, e). *b.* 8 Feb. 1808. M.D. Ed. 1829. A.S. 10 Feb. 1831. Surg. 1 Jan. 1848. R. 11 Oct. 1853. *d.* at Sydenham, 10 Jan. 1859. Was the first to demonstrate the possibility of and to practice surgical operations under anæsthesia caused by mesmerism. v. Hist. of I.M.S. ii. 153–156. Author of Letters from the Red Sea, Egypt, and the Continent, 1830; Mesmeric Facts, 1845; Mesmerism in India, and its practical application to Surgery and Medicine, 1846; Record of Cases treated in the Mesmeric hospital, from Nov. 1846 to Dec. 1847, 1847; A Review of my Reviewers, 1848; Introduction of Mesmerism as an Anæsthetic and Curative Agent into Hospitals of India, 1852; Natural and Mesmeric Clairvoyance, with the practical application of Mesmerism in Surgery and Medicine, 1852.

1194. **Christopher, George Eumenes.** *b.* 7 Apr. 1806. M.R.C.S. 1828. A.S. 10 Feb. 1831. *d.* at Wiesbaden, 7 May 1842.

1195. **Crighton, Alexander.** *b.* 29 Dec. 1808. M.D. Ed. 1830. A.S. 10 Feb. 1831. *d.* on board the 'Adelaide,' in Sagar Roads, 19 Aug. 1837.

1196. **Drummond, Andrew.** *b.* 15 Aug. 1806. A.S. 13 Apr. 1831. Discharged by Court Martial at Hazaribagh, 6 Mar. 1839. Granted a compassionate allowance of £50 per annum, 1842; (S.A.L.M.B.).

1197. **Goodeve, Henry Ives Hurry.** *b.* 13 May 1807. M.R.C.S. 1828. M.D. Ed. 1829. A.S. 16 Apr. 1831. F.R.C.S. original list, 1844. Surg. 1 Jan. 1848. R. 9 Sept. 1853. M.R.C.P. Lond. 1860. F.R.C.P. Lond. 1860. *d.* at Cook's Folly, near Bristol, 17 June 1884. Was on special duty with Bengali medical students, in London, 19 Feb. 1845 to 7 Mar. 1848. Brother of No. 1373, infra, E. Goodeve, 1841. S.-W. Frontier, operations against Kols, 1832. Author of Hints on Children in India, 1844. The fifth edition was edited by S. C. G. Chuckerbutty, the sixth, in 1872, by J. Ewart, the seventh, in 1879, by E. A. Birch. The name of Goodeve has since been dropped. In 1918 was published the fifth edition of Birch, and eleventh of Goodeve, edited by C. R. M. Green and V. A. Green Armytage.

1198. **MacCheyne, William Oswald Hunter.** *b.* 19 Jan. 1809. L.R.C.S. Ed. 1830. A.S. 25 Apr. 1831. R. 1 Nov. 1838. *d.* in Edinburgh, 24 Oct. 1892.

1199. Phillipson, Richard (b). b. Sept. 1804. L.S.A. 1825. M.R.C.S. 1826. Surgeon's Mate, ' Minerva,' 1829–30. A.S. 7 May 1831. Surg. 15 Jan. 1848. R. 10 Apr. 1855. Afghanistan, 1839–42, capture of Ghuzni ; (P.R.), medal.

1200. Madden, Charles. b. 15 Mar. 1809. A.S. 15 May 1831. Surg. 31 Jan. 1848. R. 27 Apr. 1854. d. at Brighton, 10 Sept. 1876. Staff Surg. Warley, 1845–49. Afghanistan, 1839, capture of Ghuzni (P.R.).

1201. Rankin, George Campbell. b. 14 Dec. 1801. Surgeon 1st Regiment York Militia, Upper Canada, 1828–30. A.S. 1 June 1831. Surg. 28 Feb. 1848. R. 17 Dec. 1852. d. in London, 2 Jan. 1880. S.-W. Frontier, operations against Kols, 1832. China, 1840–41, medal. Second Sikh or Panjab war, 1848–49, siege and capture of Multan, battle of Gujrat, medal.

1202. Reid, Alexander. b. 3 Apr. 1808. A.S. 10 June 1831. Surg. 1 Mar. 1848. d. at Douglas, Isle of Man, 28 Mar. 1858.

1203. Henderson, Andrew. b. 11 Oct. 1800. A.S. 12 June 1831. d. at Chaibasa, 18 July 1840.

1204. Shirreff, William. b. 6 May 1809. L.F.P.S.G. 1829. A.S. 16 June 1831. d. at Dumdum, 9 July 1840.

1205. MacDonald, Anthony MacTier. b. 10 May 1809. A.S. July 1831. d. at Dumdum, 7 June 1832.

1206. Davies, William Bolton. b. 15 Jan. 1809. L.R.C.S. Ed. 1830. M.R.C.S. 1830. A.S. 10 Aug. 1831. d. at Rangpur, 22 Feb. 1837. Son of W. A. Davis, No. 319, Bombay, 1799. Though his father's name is given as Davis, his signature, in A.S. Certs. vol. xxv. 1830–31, is Davies.

1207. Kean, Archibald. b. 18 Aug. 1799. M.D. Ed. 1827. A.S. 20 Oct. 1831. Surg. 6 Mar. 1848. d. at sea, on board S.S. ' Bentinck,' 17 May 1855. First Sikh or Sutlej war, 1845–46.

1208. Smith, Thomas. b. 15 July 1809. M.D. Ed. 1831. L.R.C.S. Ed. 1831. A.S. 22 Oct. 1831. Surg. 16 Mar. 1848. Invalided, 15 Mar. 1853. Killed by mutineers at Meerut, 10 May 1857. Son of T. Smith, No. 534, supra, 1803. First Sikh or Sutlej war, 1845–46.

1832

1209. Mitchell, Ebenezer. b. 21 Oct. 1809. A.S. 8 Feb. 1832. Surg. 17 Apr. 1848. Invalided, 13 Aug. 1850. d. in Calcutta, 9 May 1855.

1210. Bryce, James. b. 19 Jan. 1810. M.D. Ed. 1830. A.S. 10 Feb. 1832. d. at Kyukphyu, Arakan, 8 Aug. 1834.

1211. Griffith, Samuel Moody. b. Feb. 1800. M.R.C.S. 1830. A.S. 12 Feb. 1832. Surg. 17 Apr. 1848. d. on board the ' Mary Anne,' off Madras, 5 Nov. 1852. Persia, 1833. First Sikh or Sutlej war, 1845–46.

1212. Login, John Spence. b. 9 Nov. 1809. L.R.C.S. Ed. 1828. M.D. Ed. 1831. A.S. 5 Mar. 1832. Surg. 17 Apr. 1848. R. 15 Apr. 1858. d. at Felixstowe, 18 Oct. 1863. Tutor to Maharaja Dulip Sinh, 1849–58. Knighted, 14 Nov. 1854. v. Memoir, Sir John Login and Dulip Sinh, by Lady Login, 1890. Brother of No. 1412, infra, J. N. D. Login.

Operations against Bhils, with Nizam's forces, 1835. Afghanistan, 1839–42, with D'Arcy Todd at Herat. Second Sikh or Panjab war, 1848–49. Author of Memoir on Field Carriage of Sick and wounded Soldiers in Bengal Army ; Political Relations with Herat, 1837–41.

1213. **Pagan, James.** *b.* Oct. 1809. A.S. 7 Mar. 1832. *d.* in Calcutta, 28 Dec. 1843.

1214. **Russell, Thomas** (b). *b.* 24 May 1807. M.R.C.S. 1826. Surgeon's Mate, ' Charles Grant,' 1829–30. A.S. 22 Mar. 1832. Surg. 17 Apr. 1848. *d.* at Aberdeen, 28 Sept. 1856. First Sikh or Sutlej war, 1845–46. Second Sikh or Panjab war, 1848–49 ; action of Ramnagar, passage of Chenab, battles of Sadullapur, Chilianwala, and Gujrat, taking of Kot Kangra, medal.

1215. **MacKean, Archibald.** *b.* 5 May 1808. A.S. 27 Mar. 1832. *d.* at Masuri, 7 Mar. 1843.

1216. **Chapman, Thomas.** *b.* 2 Dec. 1802. M.D. Ed. 1826. A.S. 9 June 1832. *d.* at Penzance, 7 Feb. 1838.

1217. **Brassey, Richard John.** *b.* 12 May 1810. L.R.C.S. Ed. 18—. A.S. 9 June 1832. Surg. 17 Apr. 1848. R. 8 Apr. 1852. *d.* 16 Apr. 1888.

1218. **Rait, William.** *b.* 2 Aug. 1808. A.S. 16 June 1832. *d.* at Nasirabad, 23 Aug. 1837.

1219. **Green, Henry Mark.** *b.* July 1807. M.R.C.S. 1830. A.S. 28 July 1832. *d.* at Mhau, 7 Sept. 1836.

1220. **Murray, John** (b). *b.* Nov. 1809. M.A. Mar. Coll. Ab. 1828. M.D. Ed. 1831. Surgeon's Mate, ' Repulse,' 1830–31. A.S. 6 Aug. 1832. Surg. 17 Apr. 1848. D.I.G. 30 July 1858. I.G. 24 Nov. 1865. R. 1 Jan. 1871. *d.* at Sherringham, Norfolk, 27 July 1898. First Sikh or Sutlej war, 1845–46, as Field Surg. battle of Aliwal, Desp. L.G. 27 Mar. 1846, medal. Author of Topography of Meerut, 1839 ; Topography of Fatehpur Sikri, 1853 ; Treatment of Epidemic Cholera, 1869 ; Pathology and Treatment of Cholera, 1874.

1221. **Vos, James Gregory.** M.D. Ed. 1830. A.S. 16 Sept. 1832. Surg. 17 Apr. 1848. R. 15 Oct. 1850. *d.* at Southampton, 28 Apr. 1860. v. Hist. of I.M.S. i. 502, 503. S.A.L.M.B. spells name Voss. S.-W. Frontier, operations against Kols, 1832. First Sikh or Sutlej war, 1845–46. Author of Vaccine Lymph, 1832.

1222. **Waugh, John Hugh Wharrie.** *b.* 8 Feb. 1810. M.A. St. A. 1828. L.R.C.S. Ed. 1832. A.S. 2 Dec. 1832. Furlough, S.C. 13 Mar. 1837. R. 11 Sept. 1839. *d.* at Lanark, 27 June 1895. Author of Essay on Proximate Causes of Fever ; Mathematical Essays on Differential and Integral Calculus.

1223. **Nash, Davyd William.** *b.* 28 Oct. 1810. M.R.C.S. 1832. A.S. 8 Dec. 1832. Recommended for commission by London University as the most distinguished student of his year ; (S.A.L.M.B.). Resigned in England, 14 June 1838. Afterwards in practice at Leatherhead.

1833

1224. **Dallas, James Henry.** *b.* 18 Nov. 1807. M.D. Ed. 1828. A.S. 13 Jan. 1833. *d.* at Bilsa, 10 Jan. 1836.

1225. **Wilkie, John.** *b.* 22 Dec. 1810. M.D. Ed. 1831. A.S. 26 Feb. 1833. Surg. 17 Apr. 1848. D.I.G. 3 Sept. 1858. R. 1 Feb. 1867. *d.* at Naini Tal, 23 May 1870. Indian Mutiny, 1857–58.

1226. **Anderson, James.** *b.* May 1809. M.D. Ed. 1828. M.R.C.S. 1831. A.S. 18 Apr. 1833. Surg. 17 Apr. 1848. S.M. 1 Feb. 1859. D.I.G. 21 May 1859. R. 8 Nov. 1866. *d.* in London, 3 Jan. 1891. S.-W. Frontier, operations against Kols, 1832. Second Sikh or Panjab war, 1848–49; Ramnagar, Sadullapur, Chilianwala, and Gujrat, medal with two clasps.

1227. **Thompson, Francis.** *b.* 2 Nov. 1808. M.R.C.S. 1832. A.S. 18 Apr. 1833. Surg. 24 July 1848. R. 14 July 1856. *d.* at Braunton, 22 Aug. 1904.

1228. **Smith, John Colpoys.** *b.* Aug. 1810. A.S. 18 Apr. 1833. Surg. 18 Nov. 1848. R. 6 Dec. 1855. *d.* at Rydal, 28 June 1864.

1229. **MacCurdy, Charles.** *b.* 9 June 1806. A.S. 6 May 1833. *d.* at Jalandhar, 15 Oct. 1847.

1230. **Christie, Robert.** *b.* 8 June 1811. M.R.C.S. . . . A.S. 27 June 1833. Surg. 1 Dec. 1848. R. 29 Oct. 1858. *d.* at Brixton, 14 July 1870. First Sikh or Sutlej war, 1845–46.

1231. **Clarributt, Edward William.** *b.* June 1810. M.R.C.S. 1832. A.S. 8 Aug. 1833. *d.* at Akyab, 6 Mar. 1841.

1232. **O'Shaughnessy, William Brooke** (e). *b.* Oct. 1808. M.D. Ed. 1829, A.S. 8 Aug. 1833. Surg. 5 Dec. 1848. S.M. 1 Feb. 1859. R. 10 Oct. 1861. *d.* at Southsea, 8 Jan. 1889. F.R.S. 1843. D.G. Telegraphs. 1852–61. Knighted, 28 Oct. 1856. Changed name to O'Shaughnessy-Brooke in 1861. Author of Manual of Chemistry, 1837; Report on Poisoning, 1841; Lectures on Galvanic Electricity, 1841; Bengal Dispensatory, 1841; Bengal Pharmacopœia, 1844; Electric Telegraph Manual, 1853; and of many official reports on the introduction and construction of Electric Telegraphs in India.

1233. **Davidson, Charles James.** *b.* 30 Sept. 1811. A.S. 23 Nov. 1833. Surg. 27 Dec. 1848. R. 22 Sept. 1855. *d.* in London, 26 July 1875.

1234. **MacDonell, James.** *b.* 1807 in Jamaica. A.S. 23 Nov. 1833. *d.* at Dinapur, 25 Aug. 1835. Son of Surg. A. S. MacDonell, A.M.D. 28th Foot; (Johnston's Roll of R.A.M.C. No. 4278).

1834

1235. **Dunbar, William.** *b.* 11 Aug. 1810. M.D. Ed. 1831. A.S. 14 Jan. 1834. *d.* at sea, on passage to Europe, 16 Dec. 1845. S.A.L.M.B. gives date of commission as 14 July, 1834.

1236. **Scott, Keith MacAlister.** *b.* 16 Sept. 1809. A.S. 25 Apr. 1834. Surg. 10 Feb. 1849. *d.* at Barrackpur, 8 Oct. 1855.

1237. **Leckie, Thomas** (b). *b.* 20 Oct. 1806. L.R.C.S. Ed. 1829. Surg. Mate, 'Sir David Scott,' 1830–31; 'Edinburgh,' 1831–32. A.S. 25 Apr. 1834. M.D. Ed. 1847. Surg. 23 Mar. 1849. S.M. 1 Feb. 1859. R. 23 Feb. 1859. M.R.C.P. Lond. 1860. *d.* in London 18 Nov. 1878. China, 1841–42.

1238. **Hunter, Thomas Christopher.** *b.* 19 Apr. 1810. M.R.C.S. 1834. A.S. 24 July 1834. Surg. 31 Mar. 1849. *d.* at Cawnpur, 28 Mar. 1858. Indian Mutiny, 1857–58, siege and storm of Delhi.

1239. **MacConnochie, Richard Campbell** (b). *b.* 15 Nov. 1805. Surgeon's Mate, ' Castle Huntly,' 1826–29 ; Surgeon, ' Castle Huntly,' 1830–31 ; ' Reliance,' 1831–32. A.S. 8 Sept. 1834. *d.* on the river, off Dakka, 7 Dec. 1843.

1240. **Knight, John Williams.** *b.* 9 Aug. 1815. M.R.C.S. 1834. A.S. 5 Oct. 1834. *d.* at Dehra Dun, 22 Nov. 1838.

1241. **Sutherland, John Stewart.** *b.* 24 Jan. 1812. L.R.C.S. Ed. 1834. A.S. 16 Nov. 1834. M.D. St. A. 1838. R. 20 July 1846. Author of Mercury in Fevers, Dysentery, and Hepatitis, as they occur in India, 1846 ; Health, Disease, and Homœopathic Treatment ; Topography and Medical Statistics of Upper Sind.

1835

1242. **Paton, George.** *b.* 23 Mar. 1812. M.A. Mar. Coll. Ab. 1831. M.D. Ed. 1833. A.S. 21 Jan. 1835. Surg. 10 Aug. 1849. S.M. 1 Feb. 1859. R. 22 Sept. 1864. *d.* in London, 13 Jan. 1889. Postmaster Genl., N.W.P. 1854–56. D.G. Post Office, India, Mar. 1856. Afghanistan, 1839–42, capture of Ghuzni ; (P.R.), operations in Khaibar Pass. First Sikh or Sutlej war, 1845–46.

1243. **Bond, Harman Read.** *b.* 1 Mar. 1841. A.S. 24 Feb. 1835. Surg. 11 Sept. 1849. S.M. 1 Feb. 1859. R. 25 Sept. 1860. *d.* at Teignmouth, Devon, 7 Apr. 1884.

1244. **Webb, Allan.** *b.* July 1808. L.S.A. 1832. M.R.C.S. 1833. A.S. 20 Mar. 1835. Surg. 10 Oct. 1849. S.M. 1 Feb. 1859. F.R.C.S. 1861. M.R.C.P. Lond. 1861. M.D. . . . *d.* at Clevedon, 15 Sept. 1863. Author of Pathologica Indica, 3 vols. 1844–48 ; Historical Relations of Ancient Greek with Hindu Medicine, 1850 ; Ready Rules for Operations in Surgery, 1855.

1245. **Brydon, William** (e). *b.* 9 Oct. 1811. M.R.C.S. 1834. A.S. 9 July 1835. Surg. 14 Nov. 1849. S.M. 1 Feb. 1859. R. 1 Nov. 1859. *d.* at Westfield, Ross-shire, 20 Mar. 1873. C.B. 16 Nov. 1858. Afghanistan, 1839–42, with 5 N.I. Sole survivor of retreat from Kabul, Jan. 1842 ; (Commemorated in Lady Butler's picture, in Tate Gallery, London, " The Remnants of an Army ") ; defence of Jalalabad, advance on Kabul under General Pollock in 1842, wounded ; Afghanistan and Jalalabad medals. Burma, 1852–53, capture of Rangoon. Indian Mutiny, 1857–58, defence of Lucknow, severely wounded, Desp. of Genl. Inglis, 26 Sept. 1857 ; L.G. 16 Jan. 1858 ; medal and clasp, C.B. one year extra service.

1246. **Wrightson, Robert White** (b). *b.* 2 Dec. 1807. M.R.C.S. 1832. Surgeon, ' Severn,' 1832–33. A.S. 22 Aug. 1835. Surg. 30 Nov. 1849. *d.* on board ' Alfred,' off Sagar, on passage to Cape of Good Hope, 13 Feb. 1853. China, 1840–41, medal. Second Sikh or Panjab war, 1848–49.

1247. **Stewart, Alexander.** *b.* 17 Apr. 1807. M.D. Ed. 1830. A.S. 21 Sept. 1835. *d.* at Barrackpur, 25 Aug. 1840.

1836

1248. Marshall, Robert. *b.* 21 Feb. 1813. M.D. Ed. 1834. A.S. 6 Feb. 1836. Surg. 22 Dec. 1849. *d.* at Allahabad, 23 Mar. 1857. S.-W. Frontier, operations against Kols, 1836–37. First Sikh or Sutlej war, 1845–46, Sobraon. Second Sikh or Panjab war, 1848–49, Chilianwala and Gujrat, medal. Burma, 1852–53, medal.

1249. Dodgson, George. *b.* 23 Dec. 1813. A.S. 6 Feb. 1836. *d.* at Nimach, 21 Dec. 1839.

1250. Wood, John. *b.* 18 Oct. 1806. L.R.C.S. Ed. 1828. A.S. 8 Mar. 1836. Surg. 31 Dec. 1849. S.M. 1 Feb. 1859. R. 7 May 1859. *d.* in New Zealand, 23 Apr. 1888. First Sikh or Sutlej war, 1845–46. Second Sikh or Panjab war, 1848–49, Sadullapur, Chilianwala, and Gujrat, medal.

1251. Sibbald, Thomas (b). *b.* 16 June 1812. Surgeon's Mate, 'Duke of Sussex,' 1830–33. A.S. 19 Mar. 1836. *d.* at Kyukphyu, Arakan, 28 Aug. 1837.

1252. Batson, Stanlake Henry. *b.* 3 Apr. 1810. M.R.C.S. 1834. A.S. 22 Apr. 1836. Surg. 31 Dec. 1849. S.M. 1 Feb. 1859. R. 24 Aug. 1862. *d.* at Dinapur, 27 Aug. 1869. Was rejected for Madras in 1835; (A.S. Certs. No. 13, cancelled). First Sikh or Sutlej war, 1845–46, Aliwal, medal. Indian Mutiny, 1857–58, at Delhi when troops there mutinied, 11 May 1857, volunteered to carry despatches to Mirat; siege and storm of Delhi, as Field Surgeon, medal and clasp.

1253. Gibbon, Alexander. *b.* 5 Dec. 1810. M.A. Mar. Coll. Ab. 1828. M.R.C.S. 1830. A.S. 15 June 1836. Surg. 19 Jan. 1850. S.M. 1 Feb. 1859. D.I.G. 21 May 1859. R. 24 May 1861. *d.* at Aberdeen, 3 Apr. 1890. Sind, 1843, Miani and Dabha, medal.

1254. Tucker, Henry John. *b.* 3 Sept. 1811 at Sandys, Bermuda. M.D. Ed. 1835. A.S. 20 June 1834. *d.* at Barhampur, 19 Feb. 1843.

1255. Brown, John Campbell. *b.* 13 May 1813. A.S. 5 July 1836. Surg. 3 Feb. 1850. S.M. 1 Feb. 1859. D.I.G. 1 Dec. 1859. I.G. 24 Nov. 1870. R. 15 Feb. 1876. *d.* in Edinburgh, 27 July 1890. C.B. 24 Mar. 1858. Q.H.S. 6 Sept. 1861. G.S.P. 13 Dec. 1867. K.C.B. 29 May 1875. Afghanistan, 1840–42, defence of Jalalabad, actions against Akbar Khan, 7 Apr. and 13 Sept. 1842, Desp. of Genl. Sale, 16 Apr. 1842, L.G. 9 Aug. 1842, Afghanistan and Jalalabad medals. First Sikh or Sutlej war, 1845–46, Aliwal and Sobraon, medal with clasp. Second Sikh or Panjab war, 1848–49. Indian Mutiny, 1857–58, action at Badli-ka-Sarai, siege and storm of Delhi, Desp. G.G.O. No. 111 of 1858; with Sir Hope Grant's flying column, actions at Bulandshahr, Aligarh, and Agra, affairs at Kanauj and Banthora; Relief of Lucknow, Desp. G.G.O. No. 1546 of 10 Dec. 1857; battle of Cawnpur, Desp. G.G.O. No. 1649 of 24 Dec. 1857, affair at Khudaganj, reoccupation of Fatehgarh; siege and capture of Lucknow, Desp. L.G. 16 and 27 Jan. 1858, G.G.O. No. 54 of 5 Apr. 1858; medal with three clasps; C.B.

1256. Sealy, William Fulford. *b.* 5 July 1814. M.R.C.S. 1836. *d.* at Rampur Boalia, 11 Feb. 1843. China, 1840–42.

1257. Baines, Philip Ottley Egerton (b, d). *b.* 1812. Late Surg. of 'Falcon'; (S.A.L.M.B.). M.R.C.S. 1836. A.S. 17 Dec. 1836. Relinquished appointment; (G.O. No. 95 of 25 June 1838). **Never joined.** L.S.A. 1839. *d.* at Cheltenham, 19 Feb. 1856.

1258. Drummond, John. A.S. 18 Dec. 1836. Resigned, 22 Mar. 1843. Formerly Surg. R.N. ; (S.A.L.M.B.).

1259. Balfour, John. b. 8 July 1809. L.R.C.S. Ed. 1829. A.S. 18 Dec. 1836. Surg. 15 May 1850. S.M. 1 Feb. 1859. D.I.G. 8 Nov. 1860. R. 31 Mar. 1863. d. at Leven, Fife, 13 Dec. 1886. Afghanistan, 1841. Burma, 1852, capture of Rangoon and Pegu, Desp. G.O.C.C. 18 Jan. 1852, medal. Indian Mutiny, 1857–58.

1837

1260. Kelly, Luke (d). M.D. Ed. 1825. Colonial, A.S. 3 Dec. 1833. A.S. Bengal, 8 Jan. 1837. Relinquished appointment, having been appointed A.S. in H.M.'s Forces ; (G.O. No. 95 of 25 June 1838). Never joined. A.S. A.M.D. 5 May 1837. d. in Ceylon, 14 Oct. 1842. v. Johnston's Roll of R.A.M.C. No. 4480.

1261. Loch, William James. b. 6 May 1812. M.R.C.S. 1836. L.S.A. 1836. A.S. 8 Jan. 1837. Surg. 19 May 1850. R. 6 June 1857. d. at St. Leonards, 4 Nov. 1891. Afghanistan, 1839–42, advance on Kabul, capture of Setalif, medal. Gwalior, 1843–44, Maharajpur, bronze star. First Sikh or Sutlej war, 1845–46.

1262. Staig, James Anderson. b. 15 Apr. 1813. M.R.C.S. 1835. A.S. 10 Jan. 1837. Surg. 21 July 1850. S.M. 1 Feb. 1859. R. 20 Apr. 1859. d. in London, 8 Jan. 1864.

1263. Anderson, Francis. b. Dec. 1813. M.R.C.S. 1834. M.D. Ed. 1835. A.S. 15 Jan. 1837. Surg. 13 Aug. 1850. S.M. 1 Feb. 1859. D.I.G. 20 Dec. 1861. R. 1 Jan. 1866. d. in London, 10 Feb. 1898. Marwar Field Force, 1839. First Sikh or Sutlej war, 1845–46, Mudki, Firuzshahr, and Sobraon, medal with two clasps.

1264. Freeth, Henry. b. Oct. 1806. M.R.C.S. 1834. A.S. 15 Jan. 1837. d. on the Brahmaputra, below Gauhati, 12 Dec. 1838.

1265. Donaldson, James. A.S. 15 Feb. 1837. d. at Benares, 15 Dec. 1837.

1266. Macansh, James (b). b. 15 July 1813. Surg. Mate, 'Prince Regent,' 1832–33. A.S. 24 Feb. 1837. Surg. 14 Sept. 1850. d. at Simla, 29 Sept. 1858. Son of Surg. John Macansh, R.N.

1267. Foaker, Edward. b. May 1814. M.R.C.S. 1836. A.S. 24 Feb. 1837. d. at sea, on board the 'Maidstone,' 11 Feb. 1847.

1268. Morison, Alexander Cushnie. b. 19 Feb. 1813. M.R.C.S. 1835. A.S. 7 Mar. 1837. Surg. 15 Oct. 1850. S.M. 1 Feb. 1859. R. 20 Feb. 1859. d. in Edinburgh, 5 Feb. 1861.

1269. Wilson, Thomas Watkins. b. 20 Dec. 1812. M.D. Ed. 1834. A.S. 14 Mar. 1837. Surg. 22 Dec. 1850. S.M. 1 Feb. 1859. R. 19 Dec. 1869. d. in London, 15 Jan 1897. Author of Guide to Health on board Troop and Emigrant Vessels, 1854.

1270. Rae, George. b. 30 Jan. 1811. L.R.C.S. Ed. 1836. A.S. 14 Mar. 1837. Surg. 1 Jan. 1851. S.M. 1 Feb. 1859. R. 9 Feb. 1859. d. 25 Apr. 1884. Afghanistan, 1839–42, with Shah Shuja's Forces, capture of Ghuzni ; (P.R.). Desp. C.G. 20 Sept. 1841, medal.

1271. **Guise, Richard Charles.** *b.* 3 Aug. 1814. A.S. 14 Mar. 1837. Surg. 1 Jan. 1851. S.M. 1 Feb. 1859. R. 31 Jan. 1863. *d.* at Blackheath, 19 June 1889. Brother of No. 1291, infra, J. A. Guise. First Sikh or Sutlej war, 1845–46, Mudki, Firuzshahr, and Sobraon, medal with two clasps. Second Sikh or Panjab war, 1848–49, medal with clasp.

1272. **Nightingale, Manby.** *b.* Mar. 1813. M.R.C.S. 1837. A.S. 15 Mar. 1837. *d.* at Masuri, 10 Apr. 1850. Afghanistan, 1839–42, capture of Ghuzni, action at Bamian, medal. Gwalior, 1843–44, battle of Paniar, bronze star. First Sikh or Sutlej war, 1845–46, Sobraon, medal.

1273. **Donaldson, Archibald.** *b.* 15 Dec. 1814. M.D. C.M. Glas. 1836. A.S. 2 June 1837. Furlough, S.C. 4 Aug. 1841. R. 6 Mar. 1844.

1274. **Watson, Lewis Thackeray.** *b.* 5 Sept. 1808. M.R.C.S. 1837. A.S. 28 June 1837. *d.* at Agra, 27 Dec. 1838.

1275. **Cardew, George Schuyler.** *b.* Mar. 1815. M.D. Ed. 1837. L.R.C.S. Ed. 1837. A.S. 18 Aug. 1837. Surg. 3 Mar. 1851. S.M. 1 Feb. 1859. D.I.G. 25 Apr. 1862. R. 31 Mar. 1868. *d.* 10 Sept. 1894. Father of Major G. S. Cardew, R.A.M.C. (Johnston's Roll of R.A.M.C. No. 7127). Gwalior 1843–44, bronze star. Indian Mutiny, 1857–58, Delhi Field Force, medal.

1276. **Arnott, John.** *b.* 9 May 1813. M.D. Ed. 1835. A.S. 22 Aug. 1837. *d.* at Dibrugarh, 30 June 1845. Brother of F. S. Arnott, No. 592, Bo. 1829; Father of J. Arnott, No. 967, Bo. 1867.

1277. **Davies, Elliot Voyle.** *b.* 1813. M.R.C.S. 1836. L.S.A. 1836. A.S. 27 Aug. 1837. M.D. Mar. Coll. Ab. 1844. Surg. 5 Mar. 1851. Dismissed by Court Martial, 7 Aug. 1857. *d.* at Barrackpur, 22 Oct. 1857. First Sikh or Sutlej war, 1845–46. Second Sikh or Panjab war, 1848–49. N.-W. Frontier, Kohat Pass, 1850.

*1278. **Dunbar, James Alexander.** *b.* 20 Oct. 1815. M.D. 18—. L.R.C.S. Ed. 18—. A.S. 12 Dec. 1857. Surg. 31 Mar. 1851. S.M. 1 Feb. 1859. D.I.G. 6 Aug. 1862. R. 1 Nov. 1868. *d.* at Clapham, 6 June 1901. Gwalior, 1843–44, bronze star. First Sikh or Sutlej war, Aliwal and Sobraon, medal. Second Sikh or Panjab war, 1848–49.

1838

1279. **Faithfull, Richard William.** *b.* 8 June 1815. M.R.C.S. 1837. A.S. 10 Feb. 1838. Surg. 31 Mar. 1851. S.M. 1 Feb. 1859. D.I.G. 31 Mar. 1863. *d.* at Masuri, 9 Sept. 1863. Afghanistan, 1842, advance on Kabul under Genl. Pollock. First Sikh or Sutlej war, 1845–46, Mudki, Firuzshahr, and Sobraon, medal with two clasps.

1280. **Boult, Edward.** *b.* 3 Jan. 1815. M.R.C.S. 1836. A.S. 1 Feb. 1838. R. 5 July 1844. F.R.C.S. 1846. Surgeon to Bath Infirmary after retirement. *d.* at Bath, 24 Jan. 1863.

1281. **Eddy, Henry Charles.** *b.* Apr. 1815. M.R.C.S. 1837. A.S. 18 Feb. 1838. *d.* at Bareli, 19 Aug. 1842. Afghanistan, 1839–42, battle of Parwandara.

---

* D. and M. give no date of commission for the last 23 officers in their Bengal list, No. 1278, J. A. Dunbar, to No. 1300, K. W. Kirk, inclusive, the dates of their commissions not having appeared in the Army list when D. and M.'s list was published. K. W. Kirk is the last name entered in D. and M.'s Bengal list.

1282. **Veal, William.** *b.* Mar. 1813. L.S.A. 1837. M.R.C.S. 1838. A.S. 1 Mar. 1838. *d.* at Ambala, 9 Apr. 1850.

1283. **Bowling, Henry Hawkins.** *b.* 7 Mar. 1814. L.S.A. 1837. M.R.C.S. 1838. A.S. 1 Mar. 1838. Surg. 28 Apr. 1851. Killed by mutineers at Shahjahanpur, 31 May 1857. Brother of J. P. Bowling, No. 1584, infra. Afghanistan, 1838–39, Army of Indus. Burma, 1852–53. Indian Mutiny.

1284. **Paton, Andrew.** *b.* 13 Aug. 1814. A.S. 1 Mar. 1838. Surg. 1 May 1851. *d.* at Mian Mir, 21 Dec. 1858. Afghanistan, 1839–42, capture of Ghuzni ; (P.R.).

1285. **Greig, Alexander.** *b.* 1 Jan. 1815. M.D. Ed. 1837. A.S. 10 Mar. 1838. Surg. 5 June 1851. *d.* at Mian Mir, 27 July 1852.

1286. **Murray, Thomas.** *b.* 11 Mar. 1816. M.D. 18—. A.S. 6 May 1838. Surg. 4 Oct. 1851. *d.* in Calcutta, 11 Jan. 1852. Son of Patrick Murray, Surg. E.I. Co.'s Marine Service.

1287. **Wallich, George Charles** (e). *b.* 16 Nov. 1815. M.D. Ed. 1836. L.R.C.S. Ed. 1837. A.S. 27 May 1838. Surg. 10 Dec. 1851. S.M. 1 Feb. 1859. R. 1 Sept. 1859. *d.* 31 Mar. 1899. Son of No. 725, supra, N. Wallich. Brother of No. 1546, infra, N. D. S. Wallich. Served on the ' Bulldog,' 1860–62, on Survey of Atlantic bed for proposed cable. Linnean Society's Gold Medal for Zoology, 1898. First Sikh or Sutlej war, 1845–46, Sobraon, medal. Second Sikh or Sutlej war, 1848–49, medal. Sonthal rebellion, 1857, as Field Surgeon. Author of Notes on the presence of Animal Life at vast depths in the Ocean, 1860 ; the North Atlantic Seabed, 1862.

1288. **Cheyne, George Macartney.** *b.* 22 Jan. 1810. M.R.C.S. 1837. A.S. 27 May 1838. Surg. 31 Dec. 1851. *d.* on board the ' Cyclone,' between Calcutta and Australia, 22 Oct. 1854. Son of John Cheyne, Phy. Genl. A.M.D. (v. Johnston's Roll of R.A.M.C. No. 1708).

1289. **Wethered, Thomas Allman.** *b.* 12 June 1814, at Antigua. M.R.C.S. 1837. A.S. 27 May 1838. L.S.A. 1840. Surg. 11 Jan. 1852. S.M. 1 Feb. 1859. R. 16 Aug. 1862. *d.* in Paris, 17 Oct. 1897. First Sikh or Sutlej war, 1845–46. Second Sikh or Panjab war, 1848-49. Indian Mutiny, 1858–59, as P.M.O. of force under Genl. Sir Hope Grant, operations in Oudh and Trans Gogra, medal.

1290. **Strover, Thomas Rogers.** *b.* 25 July 1814. M.R.C.S. 1838. A.S. 27 May 1838. Surg. 31 Jan. 1852. S.M. 1 Feb. 1859. R. 20 Feb. 1860. F.R.C.S. 1860. *d.* at St. Helier's, Jersey, 8 Jan. 1870. Second Sikh or Panjab war, 1848–49.

1291. **Guise, James Alexander.** *b.* 16 Apr. 1816. A.S. 30 May 1838. Surg. 20 Feb. 1852. S.M. 1 Feb. 1859. D.I.G. 27 May 1863. R. 31 Mar. 1869. *d.* at Clifton, 4 Oct. 1884. Brother of No. 1271, supra, R. C. Guise. Indian Mutiny, 1857–58.

1292. **Evans, Arthur Benoni.** *b.* 18 July 1813. M.R.C.S. 1835. L.S.A. 1836. A.S. 30 May 1838. Lost in the ' Protector,' wrecked in Sagar Roads, 17 Oct. 1838. D. and M. give name as B. A. Evans.

1293. **Edge, John.** *b.* Jan. 1816. M.R.C.S. 1838. A.S. 16 June 1838. *d.* at Rangpur, 2 Sept. 1843.

1294. Shillito, William. *b.* Mar. 1816. M.R.C.S. 1838. A.S. 7 July 1838. Surg. 31 Mar. 1852. F.R.C.S. 1857. S.M. 1 Feb. 1859. R. 23 July 1863. *d.* at Putney, 5 Jan. 1903. Afghanistan, 1839–42.

1295. Shuter, Richard Valpy. *b.* Jan. 1814. L.S.A. 1837. M.R.C.S. 1838. A.S. 18 July 1838. *d.* at Gauhati, 11 Jan. 1843.

1296. Gerrard, Mark Anthony Biscoe. *b.* 6 Aug. 1815. M.R.C.S. 1838. A.S. 19 July 1838. *d.* at Dinapur, 17 Dec. 1846. Afghanistan, 1840–42, at Kandahar.

1297. MacIntire, John. *b.* 4 Apr. 1816. M.D. Glas. 1837. M.R.C.S. 1838. A.S. 20 July 1838. Surg. 8 Apr. 1852. S.M. 1 Feb. 1859. D.I.G. 10 June 1863. *d.* at Peshawur, 21 June 1867. Nominated in place of Luke Kelly, who declined appointment; (A.S. Certs. vol. xxviii.). v. No. 1260, supra.

1298. Jameson, William (e). *b.* 25 May 1815. L.R.C.S. Ed. 1836. A.S. 30 Aug. 1838. Surg. 10 Apr. 1852. S.M. 1 Feb. 1859. R. 31 Dec. 1875. *d.* at Dehra Dun, 13 Mar. 1882. C.I.E. 1 Jan. 1878. Author of Report on cultivation of Tea in Kumaon and Garhwal, 1845; On Importation of teamakers, implements, and seeds, from China into N.W.P. 1852; Report on Saharanpur Botanical Gardens, 1855; Cultivation and Manufacture of Flax in the N.W.P. 1861; Government Tea Plantations, 1862; Plantation of Canal banks in N.W.P., and cultivation of Timber Trees, 1876.

1299. Andrews, Charles Gould. *b.* 2 June 1813. M.R.C.S. 1838. A.S. 15 Sept. 1838. Surg. 27 July 1852. S.M. 1 Feb. 1859. R. 19 Dec. 1863. *d.* 11 Nov. 1874. Burma, 1852–52, capture of Donabew, Desp. L.G. 24 June 1853, medal. Indian Mutiny, 1857–58, medal.

1300. Kirk, Kinloch Winlaw. *b.* 24 Dec. 1814. M.D. Ed. 1835. A.S. 2 Oct. 1838. Surg. 1 Oct. 1852. Killed by mutineers at Gwalior, 13 June 1857. Central India, 1842, operations in Bandalkund. Sind, 1843. Indian Mutiny, 1857. Author of Topography of Upper Sind, 1847.

1301. Collyer, Nathaniel. *b.* 6 Aug. 1806. L.S.A. 1833. M.R.C.S. 1834. A.S. 1 Nov. 1838. Surg. 5 Nov. 1852. Killed at Cawnpur, 27 June 1857. Indian Mutiny, 1857.

1302. Henderson, Charles Murray. *b.* 26 Apr. 1814. M.D. Ed. 1838. A.S. 1 Nov. 1838. Surg. 6 Dec. 1852. S.M. 1 Feb. 1859. R. 11 Mar. 1864. *d.* in London, 28 Mar. 1877. First Sikh or Sutlej war, 1845–46, Sobraon, medal. Indian Mutiny, 1857–58, Central India Field Force, capture of Kotghar, affair at Bharucha, medal.

1303. Haig, James Swiney. *b.* 15 Aug. 1815. A.S. 1 Nov. 1838. *d.* at Kotah, 9 Apr. 1840.

1304. Cumberbach, William Suker. *b.* 25 Sept. 1810. M.R.C.S. 1834. A.S. 22 Dec. 1838. Surg. 16 Dec. 1852. *d.* at Cape of Good Hope, 10 June 1853. Sind, 1843–44, severely wounded in action, Aug. 1844; (G.O. 27 Sept. 1844).

1839

1305. Irwin, Henry. *b.* 29 Aug. 1816. M.R.C.S. 1839. F.R.C.S.I. 18—. A.S. 13 Jan. 1839. Surg. 17 Dec. 1852. S.M. 1 Feb. 1859. R. 24 Aug. 1862. *d.* 31 Jan. 1883. Afghanistan, 1842, forcing of the Khaibar Pass, medal.

1306. Hinton, Henry Benjamin. *b.* 7 Mar. 1813. M.R.C.S. 1835. A.S. 14 Jan. 1839. Surg. 31 Dec. 1852. S.M. 1 Feb. 1859. R. 7 Mar. 1868. Hony. F.R.C.S. Eng. 1913. *d.* at Adelaide, aged 103, 14 May 1916. Gwalior war, 1843–44. First Sikh or Sutlej war, 1845–46, Aliwal, Badiwal, and Sobraon, medal with clasp. Second Sikh or Panjab war, 1848–49, Gujrat, medal. China, 1859–60.

1307. MacRae, Alexander Charles. *b.* 21 Dec. 1816 in Demerara. M.D. Ed. 1838. L.R.C.S. Ed. 1838. A.S. 24 Jan. 1839. Surg. 15 Jan. 1853. S.M. 1 Feb. 1859. R. 28 Jan. 1865. *d.* at Eastbourne, 20 July 1908. First Sikh or Sutlej war, 1845–46.

1308. MacRae, Duncan. *b.* 8 Oct. 1816. L.R.C.S. Ed. 18—. A.S. 24 Jan. 1839. Surg. 27 Jan. 1853. S.M. 1 Feb. 1859. D.I.G. 9 June 1863. R. 21 Dec. 1868. *d.* at Port Bannatyne, Argyllshire, 14 Dec. 1898. Afghanistan, 1839–42, medal. Sind, Bagti campaign, 1846. Second Sikh or Panjab war, 1848–49, siege of Multan, battle of Gujrat, medal with two clasps. Indian Mutiny, 1857–58, siege and capture of Delhi, medal with clasp.

1309. Pitt, William. *b.* Sept. 1816. M.R.C.S. 1838. A.S. 24 Jan. 1839. Surg. 13 Feb. 1853. S.M. 1 Feb. 1859. R. 22 Sept. 1859. *d.* in London, 27 Oct. 1887. Burma, 1852–53, capture of Rangoon. Indian Mutiny, 1857–58, defence of Lucknow, medal.

1310. Edlin, Edward. *b.* 19 Dec. 1814. L.S.A. 1836. M.D. St. A. 1837. M.R.C.S. 1838. A.S. 24 Jan. 1839. *d.* in Calcutta, 6 Apr. 1850. First Sikh or Sutlej war, 1845–46, Sobraon, medal. Second Sikh or Panjab war, 1848–49, as Field Surg. medal. Edited Indian Register of Medical Science, 1848.

1311. Kinsey, Robert Bancroft. *b.* 24 May 1816, at ·sea. L.S.A. 1838. M.R.C.S. 1838. A.S. 17 Feb. 1839. Surg. 15 Mar. 1853. F.R.C.S. 1857. S.M. 17 Feb. 1859. D.I.G. 17 Dec. 1863. *d.* in Calcutta, 1 Apr. 1865. Indian Mutiny, 1857–58.

1312. Turner, George. *b.* Jan. 1815. M.R.C.S. 1837. A.S. 24 Feb. 1839. *d.* on S.S. 'Benares,' near Monghir, 1 Oct. 1848. First Sikh or Sutlej war, 1845–46.

1313. Hare, Edward. *b.* 26 Apr. 1812. Caius Coll. Camb. Middlesex Hosp. and King's Coll. London. M.R.C.S. 1838. L.S.A. 1838. A.S. 24 Feb. 1839. Surg. 15 Mar. 1853. S.M. 24 Feb. 1859. D.I.G. 23 Mar. 1864. R. 10 Dec. 1866. *d.* at Bath, 13 Feb. 1897. Father of No. 2231, infra, E. C. Hare. C.S.I. 16 Sept. 1867. Afghanistan, 1840–42, defence of Jalalabad, advance on Kabul under Genl. Pollock, Desp. L.G. 9 Aug. 1842, Afghan and Jalalabad medals. Burma, 1852–54, recapture of Pegu, medal. Indian Mutiny, 1857–58, action at Badli-ki-Sarai, siege and capture of Delhi, Desp. L.G. 15 Dec. 1857, medal. Author of Improved Treatment of Fever and Dysentery, 1847; Diet in Health and Disease, 18—; Treatment and Disposal of Sewage, 18—; Health Primer for Soldiers in India, 18—; Treatment of wounds by gum resin and essential oils, 18—; Treatment of Tropical Dysentery by Enemata of Tepid Water, 1849; Malarious Fever, 1864; Life of William Lambe, M.D. 1897. v. Memoirs of Edward Hare, C.S.I. by E. C. Hare, No. 2231, infra, 1900.

1314. Martin, William. *b.* Mar. 1814. L.S.A. 1835. M.R.C.S. 1836. A.S. 9 Mar. 1839. Surg. 8 May 1853. F.R.C.S. 1857. R. 7 Aug. 1859. *d.* in London, 16 Mar. 1879. Author of The Operation of Bronchotomy, 1853; Cases in Calcutta Eye Infirmary, 1857; Illustrations of Use of Ophthalmoscope, 1859.

1315. **Pringle, William.** *b.* 18 Feb. 1816. M.D. Ed. 1837. A.S. 26 Mar. 1839. *d.* at Gwalior, 5 Oct. 1845. China, 1840–41.

1316. **Walker, Henry.** *b.* 10 Apr. 1803. St. Thomas', Guy's, Webb St. School, and Berlin. L.S.A. 1824. M.R.C.S. 1835. A.S. 5 May 1839. Surg. 16 May. 1853 *d.* at Hendon, 22 May 1857. Gwalior war, 1843–44, with Bodyguard, Maharajpur, bronze star. First Sikh or Sutlej war, 1845–46, as Surgeon to Govr. Genl. Lord Hardinge, Mudki (horse shot under him), Firuzshahr, and Sobraon, Desp. L.G. 1 Apr. 1846, medal with two clasps.

1317. **Grahame, William** (b). *b.* 3 Oct. 1797. Surgeon's Mate, ' Buckinghamshire,' 1820–30 ; Surgeon, ' Thomas Grenville,' 1830–34. A.S. 5 May 1839. *d.* at Hongkong, 5 Nov. 1843. China, 1841–43.

1318. **Ross, William Hamilton Brown.** *b.* 11 June 1816. L.R.C.S. Ed. 1836. A.S. 13 July 1839. Surg. 12 June 1853. S.M. 13 July 1859, R. 25 Sept. 1859. *d.* at Brighton, 19 July 1871.

1319. **Durant, May Osmund Alonzo** (d). *b.* May 1816. M.R.C.S. 1839. A.S. 17 July 1839 ; (A.S. Certs. vol. xxix). Never joined. J. G. da C. Denham, No. 1349, infra, got the vacancy. Practising at Ashton, Manchester, in 1851.

1320. **Harper, George.** *b.* 13 June 1810. A.S. 23 July 1839. Surg. 25 Aug. 1853. S.M. 23 July 1859. R. 1 Aug. 1865. Afghanistan, 1841–42, forcing of Khaibar Pass, and advance on Kabul under Genl. Pollock, medal. Second Sikh or Panjab war, 1848–49, medal. Gujrat, clasp.

1321. **Mann, George Smyth.** *b.* 24 Dec. 1816. M.R.C.S. 1839. A.S. 22 Aug. 1839. Surg. 7 Sept. 1853. S.M. 22 Aug. 1859. F.R.C.S. 1859. D.I.G. 31 Mar. 1864. *d.* at Dakka, 31 Oct. 1864. China, 1841–42, medal. N.-W. Frontier of India, Ranizai, 1852. Indian Mutiny, 1857–58.

1322. **Rothney, James Hay.** *b.* 26 June 1817. M.R.C.S. 1839. L.S.A. 1839. A.S. 4 Sept. 1839. *d.* at Karnal, 3 Mar. 1843.

1323. **Cantor, Theodore.** *b.* 6 Feb. 1809, at Copenhagen. A Dane. M.D. Copenhagen . . . Uncovd. Medical Service, Surgeon to Bengal Marine Survey, 1837–39. M.R.C.S. 1839. A.S. 12 Sept. 1839. Surg. 9 Sept. 1853. S.M. 12 Sept. 1859. *d.* at sea, 26 Mar. 1860. China, 1841–42, medal. First Sikh or Sutlej war, 1845–46, medal. Second Sikh or Panjab war, 1848–49, Ramnagar, Chilianwala, and Gujrat, medal. Author of Spicilegium Serpentum Indicorum, 1839 ; Catalogue of Mammalia inhabiting the Malayan Peninsula and Islands, 1846.

1324. **Morton, Alexander Ross.** *b.* 3 Sept. 1817. M.D. Ed. 1837. A.S. 28 Sept. 1839. *d.* at Darjiling, 6 July 1841. China, 1840–41.

1325. **Metcalfe, Francis Ralph.** *b.* 3 May 1814. M.D. Glas. 1839. M.R.C.S. 1839. A.S. 8 Oct. 1839. Afghanistan, 1839–42, with the 5th Light Cavalry. Killed at Gandamak, in retreat from Kabul, 13 Jan. 1842. Son of Sir Charles Theophilus Metcalfe, B.C.S.

1326. **Hutchinson, Theodosius Cayley.** *b.* Feb. 1817. M.R.C.S. 1839. L.S.A. 1839. A.S. 16 Oct. 1839. Surg. 7 Oct. 1853. S.M. 16 Oct. 1859. R. 3 Jan. 1866. China, 1840–43, capture of Chusan, Amoy, Chinhai, recapture of Chusan, and occupation of Ningfu, medal.

1327. **Shurlock, William.** *b.* Aug. 1816. M.R.C.S. 1839. A.S. 16 Oct. 1839. Surg. 11 Oct. 1853. S.M. 16 Oct. 1859. R. 24 Oct. 1860. *d.* in London, 14 Apr. 1889. China, 1840-41, capture of Chusan, medal, Indian Mutiny, 1857-58.

1328. **Campbell, Edward.** *b.* Mar. 1815. M.R.C.S. 1837. A.S. 14 Nov. 1839. Surg. 15 Nov. 1853. S.M. 14 Nov. 1859. R. 11 July 1864. *d.* in London, 16 Jan. 1890. Afghanistan, 1840-42, storming of Istalif; detailed to attend on sick and wounded prisoners, when army retreated from Kabul, Jan. 1842, Desp. L.G. 24 Nov. 1842, medal. v. Kaye's Afghan war, II, 325. Gwalior war, 1843-44, Maharajpur, bronze star. First Sikh or Sutlej war, 1845-46, with Bodyguard; Mudki, Firuzshahr, Aliwal, and Sobraon, medal with three clasps. Crimea, 1855, as D.I.G. with Turkish contingent, 17 Apr. to 1 Sept. 1855, medal. Sonthal rebellion, 1855.

1329. **Cardew, Edward Rotherham.** *b.* 23 May 1817. M.D. Ed. 1839. L.R.C.S. Ed. 18—. A.S. 23 May 1839. Afghanistan, 1840-42, with 27th N.I. Killed near Kabul, in retreat from Kabul, 10 Jan. 1842.

1330. **MacPherson, John** (e). *b.* 20 May 1817. King's Coll. Ab., St. George's, and Vienna. M.A. 1833; M.D. 1845; K.C. Ab. M.R.C.S. 1839. A.S. 1 Dec. 1839. Surg. 1 Dec. 1853. S.M. 1 Dec. 1859. R. 29 Mar. 1866. *d.* in London, 17 Mar. 1890. First Sikh or Sutlej war, 1845-46. Author of Bengal Dysentery, 1850; Insanity among Europeans in Bengal, 1853; Mineral Waters of India, 1854; Quinine and Antiperiodics, 1856; Cholera in its home, 1866; Baths and Wells of Europe, 1869; Our Baths and Wells, the Mineral Waters of the British Islands, 1871; Annals of Cholera, 1872; Articles on Baths (Vol. 3) and on Mineral Waters (Vol. 16), in 9th edition of Encyc. Britannic, 1875-89; Articles on Baths and on Inflamation of Liver in Quain's Dict. of Med., 1st edition, 1882; and on Baths in 3rd edition, 1902; Essay on Celtic Names.

1331. **Turner, Gurney.** *b.* 13 May 1813. M.R.C.S. 1836. A.S. 18 Dec. 1839. *d.* at Puri, 20 Nov. 1848. First Sikh or Sutlej war, 1845-46. Author of First Impressions, or a Day in India, 1841.

1332. **Davidson, Richard Owen.** *b.* Mar. 1817. M.R.C.S. 1839. A.S. 18 Dec. 1839. *d.* at Sukkur, Sind, 29 Dec. 1842.

1333. **Crozier, Alexander William.** *b.* 3 Nov. 1816, at Cape Town. M.R.C.S. 1839. A.S. 19 Dec. 1839. Surg. 1 Dec. 1853. F.R.C.S.I. 18—. S.M. 19 Dec. 1859. *d.* at Dehra Dun, 7 Mar. 1863. China, 1841-43, capture of Amoy, recapture of Chusan, occupation of Ningfu, medal. Gwalior, 1843-44, Panniar, bronze star. First Sikh or Sutlej war, 1845-46, Badiwal and Aliwal, medal. Indian Mutiny, 1857-58, actions at Agra against Nasirabad and Nimach rebels (horse shot under him), operations against Gwalior rebels, operations in Etawa and Manipuri, medal.

1334. **Thomson, Thomas** (e). *b.* 4 Dec. 1817. M.D. Glas. 1839. A.S. 21 Dec. 1839. Surg. 1 Dec. 1853. S.M. 21 Dec. 1859. R. 25 Sept. 1863. *d.* in London, 18 Apr. 1878. F.R.S. 1855. Afghanistán, 1839-42, capture of Ghuzni, 1839, taken prisoner at Ghuzni, Mar. 1842, released, 21 Sept. 1842. First Sikh or Sutlej war, 1845-46, Firuzshahr, medal. Second Sikh or Panjab war, 1848-49, medal. Author of Western Himalaya and Thibet, 1852; (with Sir J. Hooker), Introductory Essay to Flora Indica, 1855.

1840

1335. Jones, Juxon Henry. b. Sept. 1815. M.R.C.S. 1839. A.S. 3 Jan. 1840. Surg. 1 Dec. 1853. S.M. 1 Jan. 1860. R. 31 Mar. 1867. d. at Eastbourne, 8 Mar. 1875. Sind, operations in 1845.

1336. Butler, James Henry. b. Jan. 1813. M.R.C.S. 1839. A.S. 3 Jan. 1840. F.R.C.S 1851. Surg. 1 Dec. 1853. S.M. 3 Jan. 1860. D.I.G. 31 Oct. 1864. d. at Dalhousie, 2 June 1865. Author of Risaleh Beech Biyan Amali Juraheeke (translation into Urdu of Cooper's Surgery), 1848.

1337. Mouat, Frederic John. b. 18 May 1816. Ed. Univ., Univ. Coll. Lond., and Paris. M.R.C.S. 1838. M.D. Ed. 1839. A.S. 3 Jan. 1840. F.R.C.S. original list, 1844. Surg. 1 Dec. 1853. S.M. 3 Jan. 1860. R. 3 Dec. 1870. Medl. Inspr. Local Govt. Board, 1874–87; (v. Hist. of I.M.S. ii. 177). d. in London, 12 Jan. 1897. LL.D. Ed. 1886. Son of Surgeon James Mouat, A.M.D. 25th Dragoons (Johnston's Roll of R.A.M.C. No. 3458). Brother of I.G., Sir James Mouat, V.C., K.C.B., A.M.D. (Johnston's Roll of R.A.M.C. No. 4530). Author of Nosological Arrangement of Bengal Medical Returns, 1845; Hindustani version of London Pharmacopœia, 1845; Atlas of Anatomical Plates, 1846; Manual of Anatomy, 1849; Rough notes of a Trip to Reunion, Mauritius, and Ceylon, 1852; The British Soldier in India, 1859; (with T. G. Heathcote, No. 1418, infra, and G. R. Playfair, No. 1459, infra), The Andaman Islands, with notes on Barren Island, 1859; Adventures and Researches among the Andaman Islanders, 1863; Prison Statistics and Discipline in Lower Bengal, 1867; Value of European Life in India, 1873; The Death Tribute of England to India, 1875; (with H. S. Snell), Hospital Construction and Management, two vols, 1883–84.

1338. Freeman, Joseph Hammond. b. Feb. 1817. M.R.C.S. 1839. A.S. 3 Jan. 1840. d. on board S.S. 'Enterprise' at Kyukphyu, 23 Apr. 1846.

1339. Cheek, Alfred Howarth. b. 11 Dec. 1815. M.R.C.S. 1839. A.S. 3 Jan. 1840. Surg. 1 Dec. 1853. S.M. 3 Jan. 1860. D.I.G. 7 Feb. 1865. R. 18 Jan. 1867. d. 7 Feb. 1868. Son of G. N. Cheek, No. 773, supra; and brother of G. N. Cheek, No. 1671, infra. Central India, 1841–42, operations in Bandalkund, capture of Chirgong.

1340. Gerrard, William Ricketts. b. 6 Aug. 1815. M.R.C.S. 1839. A.S. 3 Jan. 1840. d. at Fatehgarh, 16 May 1854.

1341. Fogarty, George Taylor Cornelius. b. 16 Mar. 1813. M.R.C.S. 1834. A.S. 8 Feb. 1840. Surg. 1 Dec. 1853. d. at Ambala, 3 Sept. 1854. Second Sikh or Panjab war, 1848–49, Ramnagar, Chilianwala, and Gujrat, pursuit to Peshawar, medal with two clasps.

1342. Beale, Anthony. b. 24 Nov. 1817, at St. Helena. M.R.C.S. 1840. A.S. 8 Feb. 1840. Surg. 1 Dec. 1853. S.M. 8 Feb. 1860. R. 17 Sept. 1862. d. at Cheltenham, 25 Oct. 1880. Central India, 1842, operations in Bandalkund. First Sikh or Sutlej war, 1845–46, Firuzshahr, medal.

1343. Koe, Herbert. b. 8 Oct. 1817. M.R.C.S. 1839. L.S.A. 1839. A.S. 15 Feb. 1840. d. in camp at Kirta, Bolan Pass, 19 Nov. 1841. Afghanistan, 1840–41.

1344. **Elderton, Charles Augustus.** *b.* 2 June 1815. M.R.C.S. 1839. A.S. 24 Feb. 1840. Surg. 1 Dec. 1853. *d.* at Marri, 3 Oct. 1854. Afghanistan, 1841–42, with force under Genl. Pollock, medal. First Sikh or Sutlej war, 1845–46.

1345. **Brougham, James Peter.** *b.* 8 June 1816. M.D. Ed. 1839. M.R.C.S. 1839. A.S. 8 Mar. 1840. Surg. 31 Dec. 1853. S.M. 8 Mar. 1860. R. 1 Oct. 1871. *d.* at Inverness, 27 May 1890. S.-W. Frontier, operations in Gumsur, 1846, occupation of Sambalpur, 1848. Indian Mutiny, 1857–58, action at Badli-ki-Sarai, siege and capture of Delhi, Desp. G.O. 5 Nov. 1857, L.G. 15 Dec. 1857; operations in Oudh, 1857, advance on Lucknow by Lord Clyde, siege and capture of Lucknow, Mar. 1858; severely wounded, 29 Oct. 1858, medal with two clasps.

1346. **Deane, William Charles.** *b.* 27 Feb. 1813. A.S. 8 Mar. 1840. Drowned bathing in river Hughli at Katwa, Bardwan, 25 Sept. 1840. Name spelt Dean in S.A.L.M.B. His signature, in A.S. Certs. vol. xxx. 1839, is Deane.

1347. **Naismith, John.** *b.* 26 Jan. 1818. M.D. Glas. 1838. A.S. 12 Mar. 1840. Surg. 20 Jan. 1854. S.M. 12 Mar. 1860. D.I.G. 23 June 1865. *d.* at Agra, 5 June 1868. Bhutan, 1865–66, as P.M.O., medal.

1348. **Comon, John Rawdon.** *b.* 9 Jan. 1816. M.D. Ed., 1837. A.S. 21 Mar. 1840. *d.* on board S.S. 'Goomtee,' near Rampur Boalia, 11 Feb. 1848. China, 1841–42.

1349. **Denham, James George da Cruz.** *b.* 12 Dec. 1817. M.R.C.S. 1838. L.S.A. 1838. A.S. 14 Apr. 1840, in place of M. A. O. Durant, No. 1319, supra, who never joined. *d.* at Puri, 18 Sept. 1852. First Sikh or Sutlej war, 1845–46.

1350. **Wells, Warwick Walter.** *b.* Mar. 1807. M.R.C.S. 1835. A.S. 10 May 1840. Surg. 1 Mar. 1854. F.R.C.S. 1853. R. 6 Oct. 1859. *d.* at Cheltenham, 9 Apr. 1892. Originally appointed in 1828; "forfeited appointment, 21 May 1828"; (A.S. Certs. vol. xxx. 1839). Indian Mutiny, 1857–58, Defence of Lucknow, Desp. L.G. 17 Feb. 1858, medal.

1351. **Grant, George.** *b.* 6 June 1811. L.S.A. 1839. M.R.C.S. 1840. A.S. 4 June 1840. Surg. 26 Mar. 1854. *d.* at Firuzpur, 19 Apr. 1855. Second Sikh or Panjab war, 1848–49.

1352. **Bowhill, John.** *b.* 9 Oct. 1814. L.R.C.S. Ed. 18—. L.S.A. 1837. Surg. 'Stratheden,' 1835–37; 'Marquis Camden,' 1839–40, wrecked near Manilla. A.S. 4 June 1840. Surg. 31 Mar. 1854. M.D. K.C. Ab. 1856. S.M. 4 June 1860. D.I.G. 29 Mar. 1866. R. 26 Jan. 1867. *d.* 2 Sept. 1868. C.B. 13 Mar. 1867. Indian Mutiny, 1857–58, siege and capture of Delhi, actions at Bulandshahr, 30 Sept. 1857, and Agra, 10 Oct. 1857; relief of Lucknow, Nov. 1857; Action at Cawnpur, 6 Dec. 1857; siege and capture of Lucknow, Mar. 1858; operations in N.W.P. in 1858, medal with three clasps.

1353. **Lacy, Thomas Saumarez.** *b.* 19 June 1816, at St. Peter's Port, Guernsey. M.R.C.S. 1838. L.S.A. 1838. A.S. 1 July 1840. Surg. 27 Apr. 1854. S.M. 1 July 1860. R. 1 Jan. 1866. *d.* in Guernsey. 18 Dec. 1884. Second Sikh or Panjab war, 1848–49, Chilianwala, Gujrat, and pursuit to Peshawar, medal with two clasps.

1354. Douglas, Charles. *b.* 16 May 1818. M.D. Ed. 1839. L.R.C.S. Ed. 18—. A.S. 4 July 1840. Surg. 16 May 1854. R. 4 June 1859. *d.* at Kelso, 26 Mar. 1901. Brother of F. Douglas, No. 1465, infra. First Sikh or Sutlej war, 1845–46, Badiwal, Aliwal, and Sobraon, medal with clasp. Second Sikh or Panjab war, 1848–49, medal.

1355. Bird, Richard Herbert Lewis. *b.* 1816. M.R.C.S. 1840. A.S. 31 July 1840. *d.* at Darjiling, 20 Apr. 1847. Afghanistan, 1841–42.

1356. Thomson, George Ferguson. *b.* 26 Jan. 1816. M.D. Ed. 1837. A.S. 19 Aug. 1840. *d.* at Lahore, 27 Aug. 1849. First Sikh or Sutlej war, 1845–46, Aliwal and Sobraon, medal with clasp.

1357. Jowett, Joseph. *b.* 23 Apr. 1814. M.R.C.S. 1838. L.S.A. 1838. A.S. 20 Oct. 1840. Surg. 8 Aug. 1854. S.M. 20 Oct. 1860. R. 10 Jan. 1866. *d.* at Beckenham, 3 Oct. 1884. China, 1841–45, medal. First Sikh or Sutlej war, 1845–46.

1358. Grant, Alexander. *b.* 22 Jan. 1817. L.R.C.S. Ed. 1838. A.S. 11 Nov. 1840. Surg. 3 Sept. 1854. S.M. 11 Nov. 1860. F.R.C.S. Ed. 1861. R. 23 Aug. 1863. *d.* in London, 3 Jan. 1900. Q.H.S. 6 Sept. 1861. Surgeon to Govr. Genl. Lord Dalhousie. v. Biography, Physician and Friend, by George Smith, LL.D., 1902. China, 1841–44, capture of Amoy, Chusan, and Chefu, storm of Woosung, occupation of Shanghai, assault and capture of Chingkiangfu, investment of Nankin, medal. First Sikh or Sutlej war, 1845–46. Author of Guide to Domestic medicine chest in India, 1852; Remarks on Hill Diarrhœa and Dysentery, 1853; Edited Annals of Military and Naval Surgery, and Tropical Medicine and Hygiene, 1863.

1359. Chalmers, Charles Bonnor. *b.* 3 Dec. 1818, at sea, in Straits of Malacca. M.R.C.S. 1840. A.S. 4 Dec. 1840. Surg. 28 Sept. 1854. S.M. 4 Dec. 1860. D.I.G. 23 Dec. 1866. R. 30 Sept. 1871. *d.* at Brisbane, 24 June 1889. Son of W. Chalmers, No. 568, supra. v. Hist. of I.M.S. ii. 252. Brother of J. Chalmers, No. 945, Madras, 1833. Indian Mutiny, 1857–58.

1360. Campbell, John. *b.* Apr. 1817. A.S. 22 Dec. 1840. M.D. K.C. Ab. 1853. Surg. 3 Oct. 1854. S.M. 22 Dec. 1860. R. 24 Sept. 1864. *d.* at Looe, Cornwall, 26 Aug. 1904. C.B. 16 Nov. 1858. Afghanistan, 1842, with force under General Pollock, medal. Sind, 1845–46. Indian Mutiny, 1857–58, defence of Lucknow, Desp. L.G. 10 and 16 Jan. 1858, medal with clasp, C.B., and one year's extra service.

1361. Rolfe, William Amys. *b.* Apr. 1815. M.R.C.S. 1838. L.S.A. 1839. A.S. 22 Dec. 1840. Surg. 22 Oct. 1854. *d.* in Calcutta, 4 Aug. 1857.

1362. Keates, William. *b.* Apr. 1817. M.R.C.S. 1840. A.S. 25 Dec. 1840. Surg. 27 Dec. 1854. S.M. 25 Dec. 1860. D.I.G. 23 Dec. 1866. *d.* in Calcutta, 19 Apr. 1869. Indian Mutiny, 1857–58, siege and capture of Delhi.

1363. Whittall, Richard. *b.* Apr. 1818. M.R.C.S. 1840. L.S.A. 1840. A.S. 25 Dec. 1840. Surg. 31 Dec. 1854. S.M. 25 Dec. 1860. R. 15 May 1863. *d.* at Dehra Dun, 15 Sept. 1890. Afghanistan, 1842, with force under Genl. Pollock, forcing of Khaibar Pass, actions at Mannu Khel, Jagdalak, and Tazin, capture of Istalif, medal. First Sikh or Sutlej war, 1845–46, Sobraon, medal.

1364. Pollard, William Ellis. *b.* Apr. 1817. M.R.C.S. 1840. A.S. 25 Dec. 1840. *d.* at Sukkur, Sind, 5 Nov. 1843. Afghanistan, 1841–42.

1365. **Diaper, Herbert.** b. Oct. 1818. L.S.A. 1839. M.R.C.S. 1840. A.S. 25 Dec. 1840. Surg. 1 Feb. 1855. F.R.C.S. 1855. S.M. 25 Dec. 1860. d. at Chunar, 27 July 1863. Central India, 1842, Operations in Bandalkund. Indian Mutiny, 1857–58, Field Surgeon to Cawnpur Field Force.

1366. **Rumley, Henry William.** b. 20 Sept. 1817. M.R.C.S. 1839. A.S. 25 Dec. 1840. Surg. 1 Feb. 1855. d. in Paris, 10 Dec. 1859. First Sikh or Sutlej war, 1845–46. Mudki (horse shot), Firuzshahr, and Sobraon, medal with two clasps. Second Sikh or Panjab war, 1848–49, Ramnagar, Sadullapur, Chilianwala, and Gujrat, medal.

1367. **Seely, George Bebb.** b. Mar. 1817. M.R.C.S. 1840. A.S. 25 Dec. 1840. d. at Peshawar, 16 Feb. 1855.

1841

1368. **Hilliard, John.** b. June 1810. M.R.C.S. 1832. A.S. 8 Jan. 1841. M.D. St. A. 1853. F.R.C.S. 1853. Surg. 10 Mar. 1855. S.M. 8 Jan. 1861. R. 23 July 1868. d. in London, 2 Oct. 1876. Central India, 1842, Operations in Bandalkund. Sonthal Rebellion, 1856. Indian Mutiny, 1857–58, Central India, medal.

1369. **White, Archibald.** b. 19 Sept. 1818. M.D. Ed. 1839. L.R.C.S. Ed. 1839. A.S. 30 Jan. 1841. Surg. 10 Apr. 1855. S.M. 30 Jan. 1861. R. 7 Mar. 1864. d. in Edinburgh, 15 Mar. 1882. Afghanistan, 1842, with force under Genl. Pollock, forcing of Khaibar Pass, medal. First Sikh or Sutlej war, 1845–46, Sobraon, medal with clasp. Burma, 1852–53, medal with clasp. Indian Mutiny, 1857–58, operations in Oudh, medal with clasp. When on furlough in 1851 volunteered to serve in expedition in search of Sir John Franklin; permission refused; (S.A.L.M.B.).

1370. **Sutherland, John.** b. 30 Nov. 1813. L.R.C.S. Ed. 1834. M.D. St. A. 1838. A.S. 4 Feb. 1841. Surg. 16 Apr. 1855. S.M. 4 Feb. 1861. D.I.G. 23 Dec. 1866. R. 3 Jan. 1870. d. at Lee, Kent, 23 Feb. 1882. First Sikh or Sutlej war, 1845–46. Author of Route from N.W.P. to Upper Scinde, 1844.

1371. **Morton, George Edward.** b. 8 Feb. 1819. M.D. Ed. 1840. A.S. 27 Feb. 1841. Surg. 19 Apr. 1855. S.M. 27 Feb. 1861. D.I.G. 18 Jan. 1867. R. 12 Mar. 1872. d. at Stroud, 28 Dec. 1884. Second Sikh or Panjab war, 1848–49, Chilianwala and Gujrat, medal with two clasps. Indian Mutiny, 1857–58, capture of Lucknow, medal with clasp. N.-W. Frontier of India, Hazara, 1868.

1372. **Tweedie, Alexander.** b. 25 Oct. 1808. Guy's. M.R.C.S. 1831. A.S. 8 Mar. 1841. Killed by a shooting accident at Benares, 14 Sept. 1841. Son of T. Tweedie, No. 554, supra, 1805.

*1373. **Goodeve, Edward.** b. 27 Jan. 1816. Bristol and Bart's. M.R.C.S. 1840. M.B. Lond. 1840. A.S. 8 Mar. 1841. Surg. 17 May. 1855. S.M. 8 Mar. 1861. R. 13 Oct. 1866. d. at Drinagh, Bristol, 27 Oct. 1880. Brother of H. H. I. Goodeve, No. 1197, supra, 1831. First Sikh or Sutlej war, 1845–46, medal. Second Sikh or Panjab war, 1848–49, Ramnagar, Chilianwala, and Gujrat, medal with two clasps. Author of articles on Epidemic Cholera, Diarrhœa, Jaundice, Biliary Calculi, Cirrhosis of Liver, and Acute Yellow Atrophy of Liver, in J. Russell Reynolds' System of Medicine, 1866.

* E. Goodeve, No. 1373, appears to have been the first to enter the service with a London University degree.

1374. **Eales, Henry Travers.** *b.* 3 Nov. 1816. M.R.C.S. 1840. A.S. 8 Mar. 1841. *d.* on board S.S. 'Carnatic' in Bay of Bengal, 16 Mar. 1842.

1375. **Forbes, Charles.** *b.* 13 Feb. 1818. A.S. 8 Mar. 1841. *d.* at Rawal Pindi, 21 Aug. 1854. Brother of G. F. Forbes, No. 712, Bombay, 1841.

1376. **Nugent, Henry Nicholas.** *b.* 25 Feb. 1811. A.S. 21 Apr. 1841. Retired, 28 Oct. 1851.

1377. **Thring, Edward Brouncker.** *b.* 22 Mar. 1819. L.S.A. 1840. M.R.C.S. 1841. A.S. 24 Apr. 1841. Surg. 6 July 1855. S.M. 24 Apr. 1861. D.I.G. 20 Jan. 1867. R. 16 Dec. 1871. *d.* 30 Jan. 1882. China, 1841-42. Indian Mutiny, 1857-58.

1378. **Eatwell, William Coverdale Beattie.** *b.* 20 Mar. 1819. Univ. Coll. London, Montpelier, and Giessen. M.B. C.M. Glas. 1840. A.S. 11 June 1841. Surg. 1 Aug. 1855. M.R.C.P. Lond. 1860. S.M. 11 June 1861. R. 24 Feb. 1863. F.R.C.P. Lond. 1873. *d.* at Norwood, 7 Aug. 1899. China, 1842-44. First Sikh or Sutlej war, 1845-46. Author of Poppy Cultivation and the Benares Opium Agency, 1851.

1379. **MacRae, John.** *b.* 20 Sept. 1817. M.D. Ed. 1840. A.S. 13 June 1841. Surg. 3 Sept. 1855. *d.* at Cawnpur, 21 Jan. 1857. First Sikh or Sutlej war, 1845-46.

1380. **Collins, John Hammett.** Middlesex Hosp. and St. Georges. M.R.C.S. 1839. Tempy. Asst. Surg. for China war, 14 July 1841; (S.A.L.M.B., B. Mily. Cons. 14 July 1841, No. 106). Medl. Officer transport 'Sylvia,' Discharged . . . 1842. Afterwards Medl. Officer East Indian Railway. F.R.C.S. 1866. *d.* at Portishead, 13 July 1871. China, 1841-42, medal.

1381. **Bedborough, Henry.** *b.* Jan. 1819. M.R.C.S. 1840. A.S. 15 July 1841. Resigned, 8 Jan. 1844.

1382. **Cox, Charles Lindsay.** *b.* May 1813. B.A. 18—. M.R.C.S. 1838. A.S. 27 July 1841. Surg. 22 Sept. 1855. F.R.C.S. 1860. S.M. 27 July 1861. D.I.G. 22 June 1867. R. 1 Dec. 1873. *d.* at Clifton, 23 May 1886. China, 1841-43, medal. Second Sikh or Panjab war, 1848-49, medal.

1383. **Boyes, William Robert.** *b.* Oct. 1816. M.D. 18—. M.R.C.S. 1838. L.S.A. 1838. A.S. 1 Aug. 1841. Surg. 8 Oct. 1855. Indian Mutiny, 1857. Killed at Cawnpur, 27 June 1857.

1384. **Biden, —.** Tempy. A.S. for China war, 7 Aug. 1841; (S.A.L.M.B., Mily. L. from B. 28 Feb. 1842, para. 27). Late Surgeon of 'Hastings.' Discharged, . . . 1843. China, 1841-42.

1385. **Lunn, G.** Tempy. A.S. for China war, 19 Aug. 1841; served with 37 N.I., discharged end of Mar. 1842; (S.A.L.M.B., Mily. Cons. June 1843, No. 142). China, 1841-42.

1386. **Boileau, John Theophilus.** *b.* Mar. 1819. B.A. T.C.D. 1841. A.S. 20 Aug. 1841. *d.* at Hongkong, 27 Nov. 1842. China, 1841-42.

1387. **Crommelin, Henry Blyth.** *b.* 13 Jan. 1806. M.R.C.S. 1840. A.S. 20 Aug. 1841. R. on half-pay, 1 July 1850. *d.* 28 Jan. 1883. China, 1842.

1388. **Finch, C.** Tempy. A.S. for China, 31 Aug. 1841. Surgeon of transport 'Thomas Grenville'; (order of Sir Hugh Gough, Amoy Castle, 31 Aug. 1841, F.I. 3 Mar. 1842). Discharged 1843. China 1841-43.

1389. Goodridge, William Gastwycke. *b.* 10 Nov. 1819. M.R.C.S. 1839. A.S. 11 Sept. 1841. *d.* at Mirat, 27 Aug. 1846. China, 1841–43, medal.

1390. Kemp, Andrew John. *b.* 22 Oct. 1819. M.D. Glas. 1840. A.S. 22 Nov. 1841. *d.* at Akyab, 14 Apr. 1844.

1391. O'Shaughnessy, Richard. *b.* 1812. M.R.C.S. 1835. Uncovd. Medl. Service, 1 Feb. 1837 to 3 Dec. 1841. A.S. 4 Dec. 1841. F.R.C.S. 1844. Surg. 9 Oct. 1855. R. 4 May 1860. *d.* 13 Apr. 1889. First Sikh or Sutlej war, 1845–46. Author of Diseases of the Jaws, 1844.

1392. Robertson, James. Tempy. A.S. for China war . . . 1841. Served with 98th Foot. Discharged . . . 1843. China, 1841–43.

1842

1393. O'Callaghan, Daniel James. *b.* 31 Aug. 1814. M.R.C.S. 1839. A.S. R.N. 1839–41. A.S. Bengal, 8 Jan. 1842. Surg. 6 Dec. 1855. S.M. 8 Jan. 1862. D.I.G. 31 Mar. 1868. R. 28 Oct. 1872. *d.* in London, 12 Aug. 1900. First Sikh or Sutlej war, 1845–46. Indian Mutiny, 1857–58, siege and capture of Delhi, medal with clasp. China, 1860–61, capture of Pekin, medal with clasp. Author of The Fatal Falter at Meerut, 1881.

1394. Oakley, Richard Henry. *b.* May 1819. M.R.C.S. 1841. L.S.A. 1841. A.S. 8 Jan. 1842. Surg. 31 Dec. 1855. S.M. 8 Jan. 1862. R. 24 May 1865. *d.* 11 Dec. 1900. Second Sikh or Panjab war, 1848–49. Chilianwala and Gujrat, medal with clasp. Indian Mutiny, 1857–58, siege and capture of Delhi, medal with clasp. (In Lancet of 26 Sept. 1857, the names of R. H. Oakley and J. Fayrer are erroneously included in a list of medical officers killed in the Mutiny.)

1395. Harland, Charles. *b.* 7 Jan. 1809. M.R.C.S. 1831. A.S. 8 Jan. 1842. Surg. 31 Jan. 1856. R. 23 Feb. 1860. *d.* 7 Aug. 1861. First Sikh or Sutlej war, 1845–46.

1396. MacDonald, James Thomas Fraser. *b.* 15 Feb. 1810. A.S. 25 Jan. 1842. *d.* at Ghazipur, 1 June 1844.

1397. Hinton, Thomas Lambert. *b.* 1 May 1808. Oxford and Paris. M.R.C.S. 1833. L.S.A. 1833. A.S. 30 Jan. 1842. Resigned, 24 Oct. 1845. For many years Surgeon to Reading Dispensary. *d.* at St. Leonards, aged 100, 14 June, 1908. v. Hist. of I.M.S. ii. 360.

1398. Lacon, Graham. *b.* Jan. 1818. M.D. Ed. 1840. M.R.C.S. 1841. A.S. 3 Feb. 1842. Surg. 31 Jan. 1856. *d.* at Aligarh, 13 Feb. 1857. First Sikh or Sutlej war, 1845–46, Aliwal, medal.

1399. Archer, Charles. *b.* 13 Mar. 1818. M.D. 18—. M.R.C.S. 1839. A.S. 10 Feb. 1842. Surg. 24 Feb. 1856. S.M. 10 Feb. 1862. D.I.G. 6 June 1868. R. 25 Sept. 1873. *d.* 17 Mar. 1884.

1400. Withecombe, John Rees. *b.* 21 Nov. 1816. Guy's. M.R.C.S. 1841. L.S.A. 1841. M.D. St. A. 1841. A.S. 15 Feb. 1842. Surg. 21 Mar. 1856. F.R.C.S. 1857. M.R.C.P. Lond. 1859. R. 10 July 1859. Master, Apothcary's Society, London, 1893. *d.* at Richmond, 1 Feb. 1904. Sind, 1843. Second Sikh or Panjab war, 1848–49, Ramnagar, Chilianwala, and Gujrat, medal with two clasps.

1401. **Tytler, Henry William.** b. 30 Apr. 1819. A.S. 23 Feb. 1842. Surg. 14 July 1856. S.M. 23 Feb. 1862. d. at Hampstead, 25 May 1863. Son of John Tytler, No. 705, supra. Second Sikh or Panjab war, 1848–49.

1402. **Veitch, —.** Tempy. A.S. for China war, 2 Mar. 1842; (S.A.L.M.B., B. Mily. Cons. 2 Mar. 1842, No. 101). Served with Bengal Volunteer Regt. Discharged . . . 1843. China, 1842–43.

1403. **Shaw, James Barron.** M.R.C.S. 1836. M.D. Glas. 1836. Tempy. A.S. for China war, 2 Mar. 1842; (S.A.L.M.B.). Served with Bengal Volunteer Regt. Discharged . . . 1843. Afterwards in practice in London. China, 1842–43.

1404. **Barlas, James.** M.D. Ed. 1837. Tempy. A.S. for China war, 2 Mar. 1842; (S.A.L.M.B.). Served with Bengal Volunteer Regt. Name also given as Burlas in S.A.L.M.B. Discharged . . . 1843. d. in Australia, 1 Oct. 1871. China, 1842–43.

1405. **Falloon, Edward Leslie.** b. 1819. T.C.D. and Stevens Hosp. Dublin. M.R.C.S. 1840. Tempy. A.S. for China war, 2 Mar. 1842; (S.A.L.M.B.). Served with Bengal Volunteer Regt. Discharged . . . 1843. Afterwards in practice at Everton, Liverpool. L.R.C.S. Ed. 1863. d. at Liverpool, 13 Sept. 1872. China, 1842–43.

1406. **Homan, Samuel Adamson.** b. 27 Nov. 1818. M.R.C.S. 1841. A.S. 3 Mar. 1842. Surg. 18 July 1856. S.M. 3 Mar. 1862. R. 23 Dec. 1873. d. 10 Mar. 1895. Second Sikh or Panjab war, 1848–49, siege of Multan, battle of Gujrat, medal with two clasps.

1407. **Le Dieu, D.** Tempy. A.S. for China war, 6 Mar. 1842; (S.A.L.M.B.). Served in transports 'Chio' and 'Flowers of Ugia.' Discharged . . . 1843. China, 1842–43.

1408. **Irons, George Robert.** M.R.C.S. 1841. Tempy. A.S. for China war, 16 Mar. 1842; (S.A.L.M.B.). Served with 55th Foot. Discharged . . . 1843. Afterwards in practice at Newcastle-on-Tyne. d. at Newcastle, Sept. 1853. China, 1842–43.

1409. **Innis, Thomas.** M.R.C.S. 1840. Tempy. A.S. for China war, Mar. 1842; (S.A.L.M.B.). Served on transport 'Gertrude.' Discharged . . . 1843. China, 1842–43.

1410. **Harrison, James.** b. 13 Mar. 1820. M.D. Ed. 1841. M.R.C.S. 1842. A.S. 5 Apr. 1842. Surg. 6 Sept. 1856. F.R.C.S. 1861. S.M. 5 Apr. 1862. d. at Uxbridge, 26 Oct. 1862. First Sikh or Sutlej war, 1845–46, Firuzshahr, medal. Second Sikh or Panjab war, 1848–49, siege of Multan, battles of Sadullapur, Chilianwala, and Gujrat, medal with clasp. Author of Origin and Progress of the Bengal Medical College, 1857.

1411. **Littler, John Harry.** b. 6 June 1809. Guy's. L.S.A. 1829. M.R.C.S. 1830. M.D. Glas. 1837. A.S. 17 Apr. 1842. Surg. 28 Sept. 1856. S.M. 17 Apr. 1862. R. 27 July 1865. d. 22 Oct. 1883. Son of Genl. Sir J. H. Littler, G.C.B. Indian Mutiny, 1857–58.

1412. **Login, James Neil Dryburgh.** b. 1 May 1817. M.D. Ed. 1840. A.S. 6 May 1842. d. at Dinapur, 13 Nov. 1849. Brother of J. S. Login, No. 1212, supra. First Sikh or Sutlej war, 1845–46.

1413. **Newenham, Arthur Wellesley Robert.** *b.* 21 Aug. 1812. M.R.C.S. 1842. M.D. Heidelberg, 18—. A.S. 11 May 1842. Surg. 3 Oct. 1856. Killed at Cawnpur, 27 June 1857. First Sikh or Sutlej war, 1845-46. Indian Mutiny, 1857.

1414. **Kelly, John Price.** *b.* 27 June 1820. M.R.C.S. 1842. A.S. 8 June 1842. Surg. 11 Jan. 1857. S.M. 8 June 1862. R. 19 Sept. 1869. *d.* in London, 2 Aug. 1881.

1415. **Mauger, Oliver.** *b.* 18 Mar. 1817, at St. Peter Port, Guernsey. Westminster. L.S.A. 1839. M.R.C.S. 1839. A.S. Royal Guernsey Militia, 3 June 1841. A.S. Bengal, 24 June 1842. *d.* at Hackney, 10 Apr. 1849.

1416. **Horton, Charles.** *b.* 21 May 1813. M.D. Ed. 1840. M.R.C.S. 1841. A.S. 25 July 1842. Cashiered by Court Martial, 10 July 1853. Burma, 1852, medal.

1417. **Saunders, George.** *b.* Dec. 1819. M.R.C.S. 1842. A.S. 28 July 1842. Surg. 20 Jan. 1857. S.M. 28 July 1862. D.I.G. 20 July 1868. R. 7 July 1874. *d.* at Ryde, 7 Jan. 1894. Asst. Surg. Warley Depot, Feb. 1853 to Nov. 1854.

1418. **Heathcote, Thomas Godfrey.** *b.* Feb. 1818. M.R.C.S. 1841. L.S.A. 1841. A.S. 12 Aug. 1842. Surg. 21 Jan. 1857. Indian Mutiny, 1857, killed at Cawnpur, 15 July 1857. Author (with F. J. Mouat, No. 1337, supra, and G. R. Playfair, No. 1459, infra), of The Andaman Islands, with notes on Barren Island, 1859.

1419. **Grant, James.** *b.* 22 Oct. 1812. M.R.C.S. 1832. M.D. Ed. 1841. A.S. 9 Sept. 1842. *d.* on the river, near Tippera, 26 Mar. 1853. First Sikh or Sutlej war, 1845-46, Firuzshahr and Sobraon, medal with clasp.

1420. **Lay, Peter Goodall.** *b.* 10 Sept. 1819. M.R.C.S. 1841. A.S. 9 Sept. 1842. Surg. 21 Mar. 1857. F.R.C.S. 1857. S.M. 9 Sept. 1862. R. 15 Oct. 1863. *d.* at Cairo, 21 Nov. 1892.

1421. **Hastings, Thomas.** *b.* 13 Jan. 1819. M.R.C.S. 1840. L.S.A. 1840. A.S. 9 Sept. 1842. Surg. 21 Mar. 1857. F.R.C.S. 1857. S.M. 9 Sept. 1862. R. 1 Jan. 1874. *d.* at Brighton, 27 Jan. 1897. Author of Observations on the Nature and Treatment of Cholera, 1840.

1422. **Crozier, William.** *b.* Sept. 1816. Barts. M.R.C.S. 1839. A.S. 18 Sept. 1842, gained commission as a prize from Royal College of Surgeons, nomination given by Sir J. Lushington. Surg. 10 Apr. 1857. S.M. 18 Sept. 1862. *d.* on board S.S. 'Simla,' in Red Sea, on passage to England, 12 Nov. 1862. First Sikh or Sutlej war, 1845-46, Mudki, Aliwal, and Firuzshahr, medal with two clasps.

1423. **MacPherson, Hugh Martin.** *b.* 30 Aug. 1820. M.D. K.C. Ab. 1837. M.R.C.S. 1842. A.S. 18 Sept. 1842. Surg. 22 May 1857. S.M. 18 Sept. 1862. F.R.C.S. 1867. R. 16 Mar. 1870. *d.* in London, 4 Apr. 1902.

1424. **Roper, George Trevor.** Manchester. M.R.C.S. 1842. Tempy. A.S. for China war, 20 Dec. 1842 ; (Mily. L. from Madras, No. 58 of 20 Dec. 1842). Discharged . . . 1844. L.R.C.P. Ed. 1860. Afterwards changed name to Trevor-Roper. In practice at Tranmere, Cheshire, in 1848, at Rockferry, Cheshire, in 1870. China, 1842-44.

1425. **Bryden, William Alexander.** Tempy. A.S. for China war, . . . 1842 ; (S.A.L.M.B. ; Mily. L. from B. 19 July 1843). Served as Surgeon to barque ' Haskery ' and transport ' Sophia.' Discharged . . . . 1843. M.D. Ed. 1845. L.S.A. 1847. China, 1842-43.

1426. Coles, William Carey. *b.* 25 July 1817. Univ. Coll. Lond. L.S.A. 1839. M.R.C.S. 1840. Tempy. A.S. for China war, 1842. Served with 5th N.I. Discharged . . . 1843. M.D. Ed. 1844. A.S. Bombay, 1 Mar. 1845. F.R.C.S. 1857. M.R.C.P. London, 1860. Surg. 27 Oct. 1861. S.M. 1 Mar. 1865. R. 14 July 1867. *d.* at Bourton-on-the-Water, Gloucestershire, 17 May 1888. China, 1842–43, capture of Canton, medal. Bo. No. 761.

1843

1427. Learmonth, John (d). M.D. Ed. 1834. A.S. 2 Jan. 1843. Never joined, struck off ; (G.O. No. 235 of 16 Aug. 1844).

1428. Craddock, William. *b.* July 1818. M.R.C.S. 1840. L.S.A. 1840. A.S. 30 Jan. 1843. Surg. 31 May 1857. F.R.C.S. 1859. L.R.C.P. Ed. 1859. M.D. St. A. 1859. S.M. 30 Jan. 1863. R. 25 Dec. 1870. *d.* on board S.S. ' Scotland,' off Cape St. Vincent, 18 Apr. 1872. First Sikh or Sutlej war, 1845–46. China, 1858–59.

1429. Harrison, John Barton. *b.* 15 Apr. 1817. M.R.C.S. 1841. M.D. St. A. 1842. A.S. 1 Feb. 1843. Surg. 31 May 1857. S.M. 1 Feb. 1863. R. 31 Mar. 1875. *d.* in London, 9 Oct. 1875. First Sikh or Sutlej war, 1845–46. N.-W. Frontier, Sheorani, 1851.

1430. Miller, James. *b.* 20 June 1818. M.D. Ed. 1841. M.R.C.S. 18—. A.S. 14 Jan. 1843. Resigned, 2 Apr. 1845. M.R.C.P. London, 1846.

1431. Glennie, William Ritchie. *b.* 18 Apr. 1819. M.D. Ed. 1840. M.R.C.S. 1840. A.S. 20 Feb. 1843. *d.* at Gorakhpur, 4 Oct. 1849. Gwalior, 1843–44, Maharajpur, bronze star. First Sikh or Sutlej war, 1845–46, Firuzshahr, medal.

1432. Bell, Adam. *b.* 29 Oct. 1809. M.D. Ed. 1834. A.S. 1 Mar. 1843. *d.* at Venice, 9 July 1854.

1433. Clifford, Frederick Morrison. *b.* 16 Feb. 1820. M.R.C.S. 1842. A.S. 4 Apr. 1843. Surg. 6 June 1857. S.M. 4 Apr. 1863. R. 31 Mar. 1871. *d.* in London, 15 June 1898. Sind, 1844–45. Indian Mutiny, 1857–58.

1434. Gray, Thomas Alexander. *b.* 4 Aug. 1819. A.S. 23 Apr. 1843. *d.* in Fort William, 9 Mar. 1844.

1435. Sprenger, Aloys (e). A Swiss. *b.* 3 Sept. 1813, at Nassreuth, Tyrol. Vienna and Leyden. M.D. Leyden, 1841. M.R.C.S. 1843. A.S. 12 May 1843. Surg. 15 June 1857. R. 10 Mar. 1859. Professor, Oriental Languages, Berne, 1858–81. *d.* at Heidelberg, 19 Dec. 1893. Author of De Originibus Medicinæ Arabicæ sub Khalifatu (thesis for degree), Leyden, 1841 ; Meadows of Gold and Mines of Gems from the Arabic, 1841 ; Technical terms of the Sufees, 1844 ; Selections from Arabic Authors, 1845 ; History of Mahmud Ghuznah, 1847 ; Translation of Gulistan of Sadi, 1851 ; Life of Muhammad, 1851 ; Catalogue of Arabic, Persian, and Hindustani Manuscripts in the Libraries of the King of Oudh, 1854 ; Catalogue of Bibliotheca Orientalis Sprengeriana, Giessen, 1857 ; Leben under Lehre des Mohamed, 3 vols, Berlin, 1861–65 ; Die Porte und Reiserouten des Orients, Leipsic, 1864 ; Die Alte Geographia Arabica, Berne, 1875 ; Muhammad und der Koran, Hamburg, 1889 ; Muhammad's journey to Syria.

1436. Rose, Joseph. *b.* 25 Dec. 1820. A.S. 25 May 1843. Surg. 27 June 1857. S.M. 25 May 1863. D.I.G. 16 Mar. 1870. R. 31 Mar. 1872. *d.* 10 Dec. 1875.

1437. **Hay, John MacDowall.** *b.* 2 Feb. 1819. M.D. Ed. 1840. A.S. 29 May 1843. Killed by mutineers, Bareli, 31 May 1857. Son of Surg. John Hay, No. 404, Madras, 1797. Gwalior, 1843–44, Maharajpur, bronze star. Indian Mutiny, 1857.

1438. **Beatson, John Fullarton.** *b.* 11 Mar. 1818. M.A. 1839, M.D. 1842, Glas. A.S. 16 June 1843. Surg. 27 June 1857. S.M. 16 June 1863. D.I.G. 3 May 1869. S.G. 24 Nov. 1875. R. 29 Mar. 1880. *d.* in London, 29 July 1898. C.I.E. 1 Jan. 1878. G.S.P. 22 Dec. 1878. First Sikh or Sutlej war, 1845–46, Firuzshahr, medal. Second Sikh or Panjab war, 1848–49, medal.

1439. **Hathaway, Charles.** *b.* Mar. 1817. Guy's and St. Thomas. M.R.C.S. 1839. L.S.A. 1839. M.D. K.C. Ab. 1842. A.S. 10 Aug. 1843. Surg. 27 June 1857. S.M. 10 Aug. 1863. Private Secretary to Govr. Genl. Lord Laurence, 1864–69. R. 14 Feb. 1866. *d.* at St. Leonards, 29 Aug. 1903. Author of Panjab Jail Manual, 1858.

1440. **Elton, Henry Nathaniel.** *b.* 11 Mar. 1819. M.R.C.S. 1840. A.S. 9 Sept. 1843. Surg. 27 June 1857. S.M. 9 Sept. 1863. R. 1 Mar. 1872. *d.* 28 Oct. 1907. First Sikh or Sutlej war, 1845–46. Indian Mutiny, 1857–58.

1441. **Howden, William Marcus.** *b.* 23 Mar. 1819. A.S. 9 Sept. 1843. *d.* at Allahabad, 15 July 1847.

1442. **Maltby, Samuel.** *b.* Sept. 1820. St. Thomas. M.R.C.S. 1842. L.S.A. 1842. A.S. 31 Oct. 1843. Surg. 9 July 1857. Killed by mutineers at Cawnpur, 15 July 1857. Sind, 1845. Indian Mutiny, 1857.

1443. **Scott, Walter.** *b.* 10 July 1817. M.D. Ed. 1841. A.S. 1 Dec. 1843. *d.* at Allahabad, 15 Aug. 1844.

1444. **Cape, Henry.** *b.* June 1817. M.R.C.S. 1840. L.S.A. 1841. A.S. 30 Dec. 1843. Surg. 9 July 1857. F.R.C.S. 1860. S.M. 30 Dec. 1863. *d.* at Sagauli, Champarun, 27 Sept. 1866. Indian Mutiny, 1857–58, operations in Oudh, medal with clasp.

1445. **Warneford, Charles Francis.** *b.* 9 Aug. 1821. M.D. Ed. 1842. A.S. 30 Dec. 1843. Surg. 11 July 1857. S.M. 30 Dec. 1863. R. 14 June 1865. *d.* in England, 10 July 1901. First Sikh or Sutlej war, 1845–46. Second Sikh or Panjab war, 1848–49, Ramnagar and Gujrat, medal with clasp. Indian Mutiny, 1857–58.

1844

1446. **Fletcher, John William.** *b.* Apr. 1818. Univ. Coll. Lond. M.R.C.S. 1839. A.S. 1 Jan. 1844. F.R.C.S. 1847. Surg. 12 July 1857. R. 25 July 1859. *d.* in London, 2 Dec. 1859. First Sikh or Sutlej war, 1845–46.

1447. **Francis, Charles Richard.** *b.* 12 Jan. 1821. Middlesex Hosp. M.R.C.S. 1843. L.S.A. 1843. M.B. Lond. 1843. A.S. 16 Jan. 1844. Surg. 4 Aug. 1857. S.M. 16 Jan. 1864. D.I.G. 16 Mar. 1870. R. 16 Mar. 1875. M.R.C.P. Lond. 1878. *d.* in London, 10 Aug. 1901. Son of C. B. Francis, No. 779, supra. Author of Sketches of Native Life in India, 1848; Army Hospital Equipment for India, 1867; Indian Medical Officer's Vademecum, 1874; Endemic Plague in India, 1880; List of Professional publications in vernacular languages of Bengal, 18—; Anglo-Urdu medical handbook, 1895; The Indian Medical Service (pamphlet), 1898; Edited Indian Medical Gazette, 1868.

1448. Graham, John Colin. *b.* 24 Nov. 1819. M.D. Ed. 1840. A.S. 16 Jan. 1844. Killed by mutineers, Sialkot, 9 July 1857. Second Sikh or Panjab war, 1848–49, siege and capture of Multan, action at Surajkund, battle of Gujrat, and pursuit to Peshawar, medal with two clasps. Indian Mutiny, 1857.

1449. Morrieson, James Stuart. *b.* 12 May 1821. M.D. Ed. 1842. L.R.C.S. Ed. 1843. A.S. 27 Jan. 1844. Surg. 7 Aug. 1857. S.M. 27 Jan. 1864. R. 1 Feb. 1871. *d.* at Ealing, 11 Jan. 1892. G.S.P.

1450. Young, John. *b.* Nov. 1818. M.R.C.S. 1841. A.S. 4 Feb. 1844. *d.* at Bombay, 30 Nov. 1851. First Sikh or Sutlej war, 1845–46. Second Sikh or Panjab war, 1848–49, siege and capture of Multan, medal.

1451. Simpson, Alexander. *b.* Feb. 1819. M.A. 1838, M.D. 1841, Mar. Coll. Ab. A.S. 28 Feb. 1844. Surg. 8 Aug. 1857. F.R.C.S. Ed. 1861. S.M. 28 Feb. 1864. *d.* at Dakka, 14 Nov. 1864. First Sikh or Sutlej war, 1845–46. Indian Mutiny, 1857–58.

1452. Cole, George. *b.* 10 Nov. 1821. M.R.C.S. 1842. A.S. 29 Feb. 1844. F.R.C.S. 1854. Surg. 15 Sept. 1857. *d.* on board S.S. 'Indus' in Red Sea, on passage to Europe, 15 June 1858. Second Sikh or Panjab war, 1848–49, siege and capture of Multan, medal.

1453. Mawe, Thomas. *b.* 19 Aug. 1816. M.R.C.S. 1838. A.S. 4 Mar. 1844. *d.* at Manipur, Banda, 28 June 1857, of fatigue and exposure, after escape from massacre at Jhansi. Second Sikh or Panjab war, 1848–49, siege and capture of Multan, action at Surajkund, battle of Gujrat, medal with two clasps. Indian Mutiny, 1857.

1454. Buckle, Henry Bruges. *b.* Dec. 1815. M.R.C.S. 1840. L.S.A. 1840. A.S. 18 Mar. 1844. Surg. 16 Sept. 1857. S.M. 18 Mar. 1864. D.I.G. 4 Oct. 1870. *d.* in London, 12 Dec. 1874. C.B. 29 May 1865. G.S.P. 4 Oct. 1872. Second Sikh or Panjab war, 1848–49, Chilianwala and Gujrat, pursuit to Peshawar, medal with two clasps. Indian Mutiny, 1857–58, siege and capture of Delhi, medal with clasp. N.-W. Frontier, 1859–60, Mahsud Waziri. N.-E. Frontier, 1871–72, Lushai, as P.M.O., medal.

1455. Nisbet, James Anderson. *b.* 18 Feb. 1822. M.D. Glas. 1843. A.S. 2 Apr. 1844. *d.* at Multan, 9 Mar. 1858.

1456. Bedford, Joseph Richard. *b.* 24 Dec. 1815. Guy's. M.R.C.S. 1840. A.S. 21 Apr. 1844. *d.* on board S.S. 'Alma,' in Sagar Roads, 9 Oct. 1856. First Sikh or Sutlej war, 1845–46. Author of Notes on Vaccination and Epidemic Disease, 1851 ; Vital and Medical Statistics of Chittagong, 1852 ; (with N. Chevers, No. 1538, infra), Public Health in India, 1854.

1457. Symons, John Stephens Croft. *b.* Sept. 1817. M.R.C.S. 1839. A.S. 25 May 1844. *d.* at Mirat, 4 Apr. 1851.

1458. Allan, James. *b.* 29 Aug. 1821. M.R.C.S. 1843. A.S. 3 July 1844. F.R.C.S. 1856. Surg. 10 Mar. 1858. R. 5 Sept. 1862. *d.* at St. Leonards, 2 Jan. 1892.

1459. Playfair, George Rankin. *b.* 13 Nov. 1816. M.D. Ed. 1838. L.R.C.S. Ed. 18—. A.S. Indian Navy, 1841–44. A.S. Bengal, 3 Nov. 1844. Surg. 28 Mar. 1858. S.M. 3 Nov. 1864. D.I.G. 29 Mar. 1871. R. 31 Mar. 1872. *d.* in London, 4 Oct. 1881. Son of G. Playfair, No. 555, supra, and brother of W. S. Playfair, No. 1762, infra. China, 1841–42, capture of Chusan, taking of Amoy and Woosung, assault and capture of Ching Kiangfu, medal. Indian Mutiny, 1857–58, operations in Oudh, medal. Author (with F. J. Mouat, No. 1337, and T. S. Heathcote, No. 1418, supra) of the Andaman Islands, 1859.

1460. **MacTier, William Fullerton.** *b.* 1 Oct. 1822. M.D. Ed. 1843. A.S. 3 Dec. 1844. Surg. 29 Mar. 1858. S.M. 3 Dec. 1864. R. 24 Sept. 1866. *d.* at St. Andrews, 19 June 1915. First Sikh or Sutlej war, 1845–46, Mudki, Aliwal, and Firuzshahr, medal with two clasps. Second Sikh or Panjab war, 1848–49, Ramnagar, Sadullapur and Chilianwala, medal. Indian Mutiny, 1857–58, siege and capture of Delhi, Desp. L.G. 24 Nov. and 15 Dec. 1857, medal.

1461. **Johnston, Maxwell.** Bapt. 1820. A.S. 29 Dec. 1844. *d.* at sea on board the 'Tudor,' 28 Feb. 1848.

1845

1462. **Lee, James.** *b.* 2 May 1814. M.D. Ed. 1814. A.S. 10 Jan. 1845. Surg. 16 Apr. 1858. S.M. 10 Jan. 1865. R. 21 Dec. 1867. *d.* in Edinburgh, 10 July 1870. First Sikh or Sutlej war, 1845–46. Indian Mutiny, 1857–58.

1463. **Banister, George.** *b.* 17 Oct. 1820. M.R.C.S. 1840. A.S. 12 Jan. 1845. Surg. 16 June 1858. F.R.C.S. 1860. S.M. 12 Jan. 1865. D.I.G. 10 May 1871. R. 6 Dec. 1876. *d.* at Eastbourne, 6 Dec. 1884, Nominated in place of J. Learmonth, No. 1427, supra. Indian Mutiny, 1857–59, siege and capture of Delhi, operations in Rajputana, and final campaign in Oudh, medal with clasp.

1464. **Kemp, James George.** *b.* 1 Oct. 1818. M.D. Ed. 1840. A.S. 18 Jan. 1845. *d.* at sea, on S.S. 'Khersonese,' 11 May 1858. First Sikh or Sutlej war, 1845–46, Aliwal and Badiwal, medal. Second Sikh or Panjab war, 1848–49, medal.

1465. **Douglas, Francis.** *b.* 14 Mar. 1815. M.D. Ed. 1836. A.S. 18 Jan. 1845. Surg. 16 June 1858. S.M. 18 Jan. 1865. R. 25 July 1865. *d.* at Kelso, 7 Mar. 1886. Brother of Charles Douglas, No. 1354, supra. First Sikh or Sutlej war, 1845–46, Aliwal, Badiwal, and Sobraon, medal with clasp. Second Sikh or Panjab war, 1848–49, Ramnagar, Chilianwala, and Gujrat, medal with clasp. Indian Mutiny, 1857–58, siege and capture of Lucknow in Mar. 1858, medal with clasp.

1466. **Ross, Alexander.** *b.* 9 Aug. 1821. A.S. 20 Jan. 1845. *d.* at Sydney, 27 Dec. 1846.

1467. **Hodgson, Robert.** *b.* 24 Dec. 1821. A.S. 24 Jan. 1845. *d.* at Ashford, 14 Oct. 1854. First Sikh or Sutlej war, 1845–46, Mudki, Badiwal, Aliwal, and Firuzshahr, medal with two clasps. Second Sikh or Panjab war, 1848–49, medal with two clasps.

1468. **Atkinson, Robert James.** *b.* 23 Mar. 1812. M.R.C.S. 1834. A.S. 24 Jan. 1845. Surg. 2 Sept. 1858. F.R.C.S. 1861. S.M. 24 Jan. 1865. R. 29 May 1870. *d.* at Agra . . . 1879. Son of James Atkinson, No. 572, supra. First Sikh or Sutlej war, 1845–46.

1469. **Turnbull, Francis.** *b.* 1 July 1821. M.D. Ed. 1843. A.S. 11 Feb. 1845. Surg. 30 Sept. 1858. S.M. 11 Feb. 1865. R. 11 Dec. 1872. *d.* in London, 7 Mar. 1902. First Sikh or Sutlej war, 1845–46, siege and capture of Multan, battle of Gujrat, medal with two clasps. Indian Mutiny, 1857–58, siege and capture of Lucknow in Mar. 1858, capture of Bareli and operations in Oudh, medal with clasp.

1470. **Garner, Hartwell Samuel.** *b.* July 1821. A.S. 11 Feb. 1845. Killed by mutineers at Saganli, 23 July 1857. First Sikh or Sutlej war, 1845–46. Second Sikh or Panjab war, 1848–49. Indian Mutiny, 1857.

1471. Tresidder, John Nicholas. *b.* 10 Jan. 1819. M.R.C.S. 1840. L.S.A. 1842. A.S. 1 Mar. 1845. Surg. 30 Oct. 1858. S.M. 1 Mar. 1865. D.I.G. 31 Mar. 1872. R. 31 Mar. 1877. *d.* at Dulwich, 27 May 1889. First Sikh or Sutlej war, 1845–46, medal with clasp. Second Sikh or Panjab war, 1848–49, Chilianwala and Gujrat, medal with two clasps. Indian Mutiny, 1857–58.

1472. Tucker, St. George Wade. *b.* 14 Jan. 1820, at St. George, Bermuda. M.D. Ed. 1843. L.R.C.S. Ed. 1843. A.S. 14 Mar. 1845. Surg. 22 Dec. 1858. S.M. 14 Mar. 1865. R. 16 Nov. 1870. *d.* at Bournemouth, 12 Jan. 1885. First Sikh or Sutlej war, 1845–46, Sobraon, medal. Indian Mutiny, 1857–58.

1473. Smith, Charles Manners. *b.* Mar. 1822. M.R.C.S. 1843. L.S.A. 1844. A.S. 19 Mar. 1845. Surg. 21 Feb. 1859. F.R.C.S. 1864. S.M. 19 Mar. 1865. D.I.G. 31 Mar. 1872. R. 31 Mar. 1877. *d.* 22 Apr. 1883, in London. Second Sikh or Panjab war, 1848–49, siege and capture of Multan, action at Surajkund, battle of Gujrat, medal with two clasps. Indian Mutiny, 1857–58.

1474. Allan, Robert Dallas Dove. *b.* Apr. 1819. M.R.C.S. 1840. M.D. K.C. Ab. 1842. A.S. 20 Mar. 1845. Killed by mutineers at Cawnpur, 27 June 1857. First Sikh or Sutlej war, 1845–46, Mudki, Aliwal, and Firuzshahr, medal with two clasps. Second Sikh or Panjab war, 1848–49, medal with two clasps. Indian Mutiny, 1857.

1475. MacAulay, Robert Welbank. *b.* 4 Mar. 1823. M.D. Ed. 1844. A.S. 20 Mar. 1845. Surg. 21 Feb. 1859. *d.* on board S.S. 'Mauritius,' at Talienwan, China, 15 July 1860. Indian Mutiny, 1857–58, siege and capture of Delhi. China, 1859–60.

1476. Walker, James Pattison. *b.* 17 Mar. 1823. M.D. K.C. Ab. 1842. M.R.C.S. 1844. A.S. 5 Apr. 1845. Surg. 24 Feb. 1859. S.M. 5 Apr. 1865. D.I.G. 22 June 1872. R. 22 June 1877. *d.* at Clacton-on-Sea, 11 Feb. 1906. First Supt. of Andaman Islands, 1858–59, opened out settlements at Port Blair. Second Sikh or Panjab war, 1845–46, Gujrat, medal. Indian Mutiny, 1857–58, defence of Agra, medal. (v. B.M.J. 21 Apr. 1906.)

1477. Thring, Richard Southby Otto. *b.* Jan. 1818. M.D. Ed. 1840. M.R.C.S. 1841. A.S. 20 Apr. 1845. Surg. 11 Mar. 1859. S.M. 20 Apr. 1865. R. 10 Apr. 1868. *d.* at Batheaston, 2 Sept. 1875. First Sikh or Sutlej war, 1845–46, Firuzshahr, medal. Second Sikh or Panjab war, 1848–49, siege and capture of Multan, battle of Gujrat, and pursuit to Peshawar, medal with two clasps.

1478. Squire, John. *b.* July 1822. M.R.C.S. 1844. A.S. 30 Apr. 1845. Surg. 1 Apr. 1859. S.M. 30 Apr. 1865. R. 28 Dec. 1871. *d.* 8 Feb. 1905. First Sikh or Sutlej war, 1845–46. Indian Mutiny, 1857–58, operations in N.W.P. and Oudh, Desp. G.O. 21 Apr. 1858, medal.

1479. Watson, James Cock. *b.* July 1822. M.A. M.D. Ed. 1844. A.S. 20 May 1845. *d.* in London, 27 Jan. 1857. Second Sikh or Panjab war, 1848–49, Chilianwala and Gujrat, medal.

1480. Sissmore, Charles Nicol. *b.* 11 Nov. 1819. M.R.C.S. 1841. L.S.A. 1842. A.S. 20 May 1845. R. 13 June 1854. *d.* 27 May 1871, in London. First Sikh or Sutlej war, 1845–46.

1481. **Glover, Joseph Tuthill.** *b.* 10 July 1817. M.R.C.S. 1842. M.D. Glas. 1844. A.S. 14 June 1845. Surg. 21 Apr. 1859. F.R.C.S. 1861. Invalided, 25 July 1862. *d.* at Rathmines, Dublin, 29 Nov. 1873. Burma, 1852–53, medal.

1482. **Ross, James Tyrrell Carter.** *b.* 5 Apr. 1823. St. George's. M.R.C.S. 1845. A.S. 26 July 1845. F.R.C.S. 1857. Surg. 24 Apr. 1859. S.M. 26 June 1865. D.I.G. 10 Dec. 1872. S.S.C. Cantab. 1878. R. 10 Dec. 1879. *d.* 27 Apr. 1897. C.I.E. 1 Jan. 1878. First Sikh or Sutlej war, 1845–46. Second Sikh or Panjab war, 1848–49, medal. N.-W. Frontier, Miranzai and Ranizai, 1851–52. Indian Mutiny, 1857–58, operations in N.W.P., medal. N.-E. Frontier, Daphla, 1874–75. Edited I.M.G. 1869–70.

1483. **Fleming, Andrew.** *b.* 7 Mar. 1822. M.A. K.C. Ab. 1838. M.D. Ed. 1843. L.R.C.S. Ed. 18—. A.S. 20 Sept. 1845. Surg. 26 Apr. 1859. S.M. 20 Sept. 1865. R. 27 Jan. 1873. *d.* in Edinburgh, 25 Mar. 1901. First Sikh or Sutlej war, 1845–46. Author of Report on the Geology and mineral wealth of the Salt Range in the Panjab, 1853.

1484. **Smith, Nicholas Skottowe.** *b.* 2 Nov. 1820. M.R.C.S. 1843. A.S. 1 Oct. 1845. *d.* at Cork, 19 May 1853.

1485. **Scott, David.** *b.* 9 Sept. 1823. M.D. Ed. 1844. A.S. 20 Dec. 1845. Surg. 8 May 1859. S.M. 20 Dec. 1865. *d.* at Ambala, 15 Sept. 1867. Second Sikh or Panjab war, 1848–49, Ramnagar, Sadullapur, Chilianwala, and Gujrat, medal with clasp. N.-W. Frontier, Yusufzai, 1849. Indian Mutiny, 1857–58, siege of Delhi, Desp. L.G. 15 Dec. 1857, medal and one year's service.

1846

1486. **Maxwell, Thomas.** *b.* 6 Nov. 1823. M.D. Glas. 1844. A.S. 26 Jan. 1846. Surg. 6 June 1859. S.M. 26 Jan. 1866. R. 23 Jan. 1868. F.R.C.S. Ed. 1873. *d.* at Guildford, 24 Apr. 1908. Second Sikh or Panjab war, 1848–49, Ramnagar, Sadullapur, Chilianwala, and Gujrat, medal with two clasps. Indian Mutiny, 1857–58, siege and capture of Lucknow, Mar. 1858, campaign in Rohilkand, actions at Bareli, Aliganj, Mohanpur (slightly wounded), and Pilibhit, medal with clasp.

1487. **Palmer, Charles.** *b.* 30 Jan. 1824. M.D. Ed. 1844. M.R.C.S. 1846. L.S.A. 1846. A.S. 20 Feb. 1846. Surg. 11 July 1859. S.M. 20 Feb. 1866. R. 31 Mar. 1879. Member, Medl. Board, India Office, 1879–81. *d.* in London, 22 Sept. 1901. Author (with Capt. W. G. Murray, R. E. and V. Ball), of Report on hill Mohendragiri and native port of Barwah, in Ganjam District, as sanitaria for Calcutta, 1870.

1488. **Walter, James King.** *b.* 1 June 1805. M.R.C.S. 1835. A.S. 20 Feb. 1846. Surg. 26 July 1859. S.M. 20 Feb. 1866. R. 6 Aug. 1868. *d.* at Hampstead, 28 May 1884. Carlist war in Spain, 1835–38, relief of San Sebastian, capture of Venta and Hernani, action at Andoia, storm and capture of Irun, Spanish medal.

1489. **Williams, St. George.** *b.* 25 July 1824. Peter St. School, Dublin Officiating A.S. 28 Mar. 1846; (G.O. 28 Mar. 1846), to 19 June 1848. Confirmed, 20 June 1848. Appointment cancelled, and name struck off, 9 June 1849; (G.O. 9 June 1849). A.S. Madras, 25 May 1850. *d.* at Kurnul, 2 May 1859. Crimea, 1855–56, with Turkish contingent, medal. M. No. 1126.

1490. Baillie, Herbert. b. Jan. 1819. M.R.C.S. 1842. L.S.A. 1843. A.S. 20 Apr. 1846. F.R.C.S. 1858. Surg. 2 Aug. 1859. M.D. St. A. 1862. S.M. 20 Apr. 1866. R. 1 Sept. 1870. d. at Cheltenham, 25 Dec. 1890.

1491. Ainger, Major. b. Oct. 1820. M.R.C.S. 1842. L.S.A. 1842. A.S. 15 May 1846. F.R.C.S. 1854. Surg. 8 Aug. 1859. d. in London, 10 Feb. 1861. Medjidie, 4th Class, 1858. Crimea, with Turkish contingent, 30 Apr. 1855 to 20 June 1856, medal, Medjidie, 4th Class.

1492. MacDonald, Donald. b. 26 Feb. 1822. M.A. 1841; M.D. 1846; K.C. Ab. A.S. 20 May 1846. Surg. 2 Sept. 1859. S.M. 20 May 1866. D.S.G. 8 July 1873. d. at Shillong, 19 Aug. 1874. Second Sikh or Panjab war, 1848–49, medal. N.-W. Frontier, Ranizai, 1852.

1493. Cannon, Henry Mills. b. May 1820. King's Coll. London. M.R.C.S. 1843. M.B. Lond. 1844. A.S. 1 June 1846. Surg. 16 Sept. 1859. M.R.C.P. Lond. 1860. S.M. 1 June 1866. D.S.G. 20 Aug. 1873. R. 1 Jan. 1879. d. in London, 13 Oct. 1892. G.S.P. 10 Mar. 1878. Second Sikh or Panjab war, 1848–49, in medl. charge of headquarters staff of Commander-in-Chief, Lord Gough, battles of Ramnagar, Chilianwala, and Gujrat, medal with three clasps. Indian Mutiny, 1857–59, operations in Rohilkand and Oudh, medal; was recommended for promotion to Brevet-Surgeon, but got the step by seniority earlier.

1494. Clemenger, William George Ward. b. Dec. 1821. BA. M.B. T.C.D. 1843. A.S. 18 June 1846. Surg. 23 Sept. 1859. S.M. 18 June 1866. R. 24 Sept. 1867. d. at Carnarvon, 26 July 1891.

1495. Webb, Charles Knight. b. Apr. 1823. M.R.C.S. 1845. A.S. 1 July 1846. Surg. 25 Sept. 1859. S.M. 1 July 1866. R. 7 Jan. 1871. d. 7 Apr. 1909. Indian Mutiny, 1857–58, operations in Rohilkand, capture of Bareli. N.-W. Frontier, Mahsud Waziri, 1860.

1496. Campbell, Arthur Lewis Stuart. b. Mar. 1822. M.D. St. A. 1843. A.S. 11 July 1846. Surg. 7 Oct. 1859. S.M. 11 July 1866. d. at Fatehpur, 11 Sept. 1868. Second Sikh or Panjab war, 1848–49, siege and capture of Multan, battle of Gujrat, medal with two clasps. N.-W. Frontier, Bari Khel Afridi, 1855.

1497. Tucker, Samuel Reeve. b. 19 June 1824, at Bermuda. M.D. Ed. 1845. A.S. 15 July 1846. d. in Edinburgh, 10 May 1857. Second Sikh or Panjab war, 1848–49, Ramnagar, Chilianwala, and Gujrat, medal with two clasps.

1498. Givins, George Edward. b. 24 Apr. 1819, at Toronto. M.R.C.S. 1844. A.S. 25 July 1846. Surg. 2 Nov. 1859. S.M. 25 July 1866. R. 24 July 1867. d. 14 Mar. 1885. Second Sikh or Panjab war, 1848–49. Indian Mutiny, 1857–60, operations in Oudh, medal.

1499. Oldfield, Henry Ambrose. b. 18 May 1822. Guy's. M.R.C.S. 1845. M.D. St. A. 1845. A.S. 25 July 1846. Surg. 2 Dec. 1859. S.M. 25 July 1866. R. 10 Nov. 1868. d. 14 Mar. 1885. Second Sikh or Panjab war, 1848–49. Author of Sketches from Nipal, 1880.

1500. Crawford, John Duncan. b. 20 Apr. 1824. B.A. M.B. T.C.D. 1846. A.S. 11 Aug. 1846. Surg. 11 Dec. 1859. S.M. 11 Aug. 1866. d. at Dharmsala, 16 May 1871.

1501. **Atkinson, Alexander Russell.** *b.* 20 Sept. 1823. M.D. Ed. 1844. A.S. 11 Aug. 1846. Surg. 1 Jan. 1860. S.M. 11 Aug. 1866. *d.* at Hounslow, 25 Sept. 1866. Son of H. Atkinson, No. 563, Madras, 1807; brother of J. J. Atkinson, No. 667, Bombay, 1837. Second Sikh or Panjab war, 1848–49, siege and capture of Multan, battle of Gujrat, medal with clasp. N.-W. Frontier, Kohat, 1850.

1502. **Basse, Charles Ferdinand.** *b.* 8 July 1822, at Frankfort. M.R.C.S. 1846. M.D. 18—. A.S. 11 Aug. 1846. *d.* at Ludhiana, 22 Oct. 1848.

1503. **Stiven, William Sutherland.** *b.* 30 Sept. 1818. M.D. Ed. 1839. M.R.C.S. 1846. A.S. 10 Sept. 1846. *d.* at Allahabad, 27 Feb. 1858. Son of No. 638, *supra*, W. S. Stiven, 1808. Second Sikh or Panjab war, 1848–49. Indian Mutiny, 1857–58. Author of Notes on Papermaking in India, 1856.

1504. **Wrench, Thomas George.** *b.* 24 Aug. 1824. St. Thomas'. L.S.A. 1845. M.R.C.S. 1846. A.S. 20 Sept. 1846. R. 12 Oct. 1857. *d.* 24 Sept. 1858.

1505. **Brown, James Bannatyne Samuel.** *b.* 9 Aug. 1823. St. George's. M.R.C.S. 1846. A.S. 20 Oct. 1846. Surg. 17 Feb. 1860. S.M. 20 Oct. 1866. R. 9 Aug. 1881. *d.* at Snettisham, King's Lynn, Norfolk, 7 Oct. 1908. Indian Mutiny, 1857, advance on Cawnpur, medal.

1506. **Mountjoy, John William.** *b.* 23 Aug. 1820. Univ. Coll. London. M.R.C.S. 1842. L.S.A. 1845. A.S. 20 Oct. 1846. Surg. 21 Feb. 1860. R. 7 Apr. 1864. *d.* at Akyab, 28 Oct. 1879.

1507. **Small, David Henry.** *b.* 5 Oct. 1824. L.R.C.S. Ed. 1845. A.S. 21 Nov. 1846. Surg. 24 Feb. 1860. R. 1 Jan. 1866. *d.* at Upper Norwood, 28 Mar. 1914.

1508. **Mathias, Charles.** *b.* 23 Sept. 1817. M.R.C.S. 1839. L.S.A. 1846. A.S. 20 Dec. 1846. Surg. 27 Feb. 1860. R. 24 Mar. 1865. *d.* at Penally, Pembroke, 13 Apr. 1888. Indian Mutiny, 1857–58, capture of Kotah.

1847

1509. **Ray, George Hutchinson.** *b.* 14 Feb. 1823. M.D. Ed. 1845. A.S. 3 Jan. 1847. Surg. 5 May 1860. S.M. 3 Jan. 1867. D.S.G. 21 Dec. 1873. R. 17 Dec. 1879. *d.* at Eastbourne, 12 Dec. 1908. Second Sikh or Panjab war, 1848–49, Ramnagar, passage of Chenab, Chilianwala, medal with clasp. N.-W. Frontier, Ambeyla, 1863, medal with clasp.

1510. **Nichol, Robert.** *b.* 22 Dec. 1824. St. Thomas'. M.R.C.S. 1846. L.S.A. 1846. A.S. 20 Jan. 1847. M.D. K.C. Ab. 1853. Resigned, 5 Jan. 1854. Pensioned on Lord Clive's Fund, G.O. 24 Jan. 1856. *d.* in London, 13 Oct. 1873.

1511. **Thorp, Edward Courtenay.** *b.* 4 July 1821. M.D. St. A. 1846. M.R.C.S. 1846. A.S. 20 Jan. 1847. Surg. 16 July 1860. S.M. 20 Jan. 1867. D.S.G. 20 Apr. 1874. R. 20 Oct. 1879. *d.* at Folkestone, 9 Apr. 1892. Second Sikh or Panjab war, 1848–49, siege and capture of Multan, action at Surajkund, battle of Gujrat, medal with clasp. N.-E. Frontier, Kuki, 1860–61.

1512. **Cockburn, Robert.** *b.* 25 Nov. 1824. M.R.C.S. 1846. A.S. 20 Jan. 1847. Surg. 25 Sept. 1860. S.M. 20 Jan. 1867. D.S.G. 20 Aug. 1874. R. 20 Aug. 1879. *d.* in London, 30 Apr. 1899. Second Sikh or Panjab war, 1848–49.

1513. Moore, Thomas. An American. *b.* 28 Nov. 1819. M.R.C.S. 1843. B.A. M.D. 18—. Uncovd. Medl. Service, Gwalior contingent, 21 Nov. 1845; (G.O. 21 Nov. 1845). A.S. 20 Jan. 1847. Killed by mutineers, en route from Cuttack to Sambalpur, 17 Nov. 1857. First Sikh or Sutlej war, 1845-46. Indian Mutiny, 1857. Author of Selections from my Medical Notebooks, Observations on Village Cholera, 1852.

1514. Grayling, Hosier Gell. *b.* June 1824. M.R.C.S. 1847. A.S. 26 Feb. 1847. *d.* at Lahore, 27 Sept. 1848.

1515. Leathes, George Cerjat. *b.* Oct. 1824. M.R.C.S. 1846. A.S. 1 Mar. 1847. *d.* in England, 21 July 1858. Second Sikh or Panjab war, 1848-49, siege and capture of Multan, battle of Gujrat, medal with clasp.

1516. White, John. *b.* 11 Jan. 1820. M.D. Ed. 1842. A.S. 9 Mar. 1847. Surg. 26 Sept. 1860. S.M. 9 Mar. 1867. *d.* at Barhampur, 29 June 1871. Second Sikh or Panjab war, 1848-49, Chilianwala and Gujrat, and pursuit to Peshawar, medal with two clasps. Indian Mutiny, 1857-58.

1517. MacEgan, William Barker. *b.* 30 May 1817. M.R.C.S. 1840. L.R.C.P. Lond. 1845. A.S. 9 Mar. 1847. Killed by mutineers at Jhansi, 7 June 1857. Dekkan, 1850-51, in Hingoli Field Force (horse shot under him), siege of forts Raiman and Dhaur. Crimea, 1855-56, served with Turkish contingent, 26 Mar. 1855 to 1 Mar. 1856; (S.A.L.M.B.). Indian Mutiny, 1857.

1518. Irving, James. *b.* 24 June 1822. M.D. Ed. 1843. L.R.C.S. Ed. 1843. A.S. 27 May 1847. Surg. 9 Nov. 1860. S.M. 27 May 1867. D.S.G. 13 Dec. 1874. R. 13 Dec. 1879. *d.* at Clifton, 3 May 1898. Indian Mutiny, 1857-58. Author of Report on Palsy from use of Kesari Dal as food, 1860.

1519. Williams, John. *b.* Dec. 1820. M.R.C.S. 1841. A.S. 19 June 1847, gained commission as a prize at R.C.S. on nomination of Sir J. Hogg. F.R.C.S. 1859. Surg. 11 Feb. 1861. S.M. 19 June 1867. R. 23 Dec. 1870. *d.* at Redlands, Bristol, 21 May 1878. Second Sikh or Panjab war, 1848-49, siege and capture of Multan, medal with clasp.

1520. Cole, John Jones. *b.* 16 Mar. 1817. Guy's. M.R.C.S. 1845. A.S. 21 June 1847. M.D. St. A. 1852. *d.* at Marri, 24 Apr. 1855. Second Sikh or Panjab war, 1848-49, siege and capture of Multan, Desp. L.G. 7 and 23 Mar. 1849. Author of A Sketch of the siege of Multan, 1849; Military Surgery, experience of field practice in India in 1848-49, 1852.

1521. Atchison, Thomas. *b.* 14 Oct. 1823, at Valetta, Malta. Univ. Coll Lond. M.R.C.S. 1845. L.S.A. 1846. A.S. 26 June 1847. Surg. 25 May 1861. S.M. 26 June 1867. R. 3 Sept. 1867. *d.* in London, 9 June 1874. Second Sikh or Panjab war, 1848-49, siege and capture of Multan, action at Surajkund, battle of Gujrat, medal with clasp. N.-W. Frontier, Momund, 1863-64, medal.

1522. Stewart, Haldane. *b.* Apr. 1825. A.S. 23 July 1847. Surg. 11 Aug. 1861. S.M. 23 July 1867. *d.* in London, 5 Feb. 1870. Second Sikh or Panjab war, 1848-49, siege and capture of Multan, battle of Ramnagar, medal with clasp. Indian Mutiny, 1857-58, action at Badli-ki-Sarai, siege and capture of Delhi, medal with clasp.

1523. Lyell, Robert. *b.* 30 May 1825. M.D. Ed. 1847. A.S. 25 Sept. 1847. Killed by mutineers in a riot at Patna, 3 July 1857. Second Sikh or Panjab war, 1848–49, Ramnagar, Chilianwala, and Gujrat, and pursuit to Peshawar, medal. N.-W. Frontier, Sheorani, 1853; (v. Hist. of I.M.S. ii. 206). Indian Mutiny, 1857. Author of Notes on Patna Opium Agency, 1857.

1524. Ebden, Henry Anderson. *b.* 15 June 1824. Guy's. M.R.C.S. 1845. M.D. St. A. 1845. A.S. 7 Oct. 1847. Surg. 11 Oct. 1861. R. 10 Aug. 1863. *d.* at Rondebosch, Cape Colony, 14 June 1886. Second Sikh or Panjab war, 1848–49, Ramnagar, Chilianwala, and Gujrat, and pursuit to Peshawar, medal.

1525. Farquhar, Thomas. *b.* 8 Oct. 1825. M.D. K.C. Ab. 1846. L.R.C.S. Ed. 1847. A.S. 20 Oct. 1847. Surg. 16 Dec. 1861. S.M. 30 Oct. 1867. R. 14 Mar. 1871. *d.* at Aberdeen, Jan. 1891. Second Sikh or Panjab war, 1848–49. Indian Mutiny, 1857–58, defence of Agra.

1526. Bogle, Alexander Laing. *b.* 11 May 1823. M.D. Ed. 1845. L.R.C.S. Ed. 1845. A.S. 20 Oct. 1847. Surg. 9 Feb. 1862. S.M. 20 Oct. 1867. R. 7 Nov. 1872. *d.* at St. Leonard's, 23 May 1898.

1527. Delpratt, William. *b.* 19 July 1822, in Jamaica. M.R.C.S. 1846. A.S. 20 Nov. 1847. Resigned . . . 1861. Brother of No. 1638, infra, S. Delpratt. Second Sikh or Panjab war, 1848–49, siege and capture of Multan.

1528. Buckell, Robert Kemp. *b.* June 1823. M.R.C.S. 1846. L.S.A. 1847. A.S. 20 Nov. 1847. Surg. 13 May 1862. S.M. 20 Nov. 1867. R. 8 Dec. 1871. *d.* 16 Mar. 1880. Burma, 1852–54, medal. Indian Mutiny, 1857–58, relief of Lucknow, Nov. 1857, action at Cawnpur, medal.

1529. Collins, John Charles. *b.* Aug. 1822. M.R.C.S. 1845. L.S.A. 1846. A.S. 22 Dec. 1847. Surg. 26 July 1862. M.D. St. A. 1865. S.M. 22 Dec. 1867. R. 22 Aug. 1871. *d.* at Stroud, 20 Aug. 1893.

1848

1530. Pemberton, George Richard. *b.* 28 Feb. 1823. M.D. Ed. 1847. M.R.C.S. 1847. A.S. 20 Jan. 1848. Surg. 7 Aug. 1862. S.M. 20 Jan. 1868. R. 1 Jan. 1876. *d.* in London, 28 Oct. 1890. Second Sikh or Panjab war, 1848–49, Chilianwala, Gujrat, and pursuit to Peshawar, medal with two clasps. Indian Mutiny, 1857–58.

1531. Harris, Horatio Philip. *b.* 11 July 1823, at sea, near Ceylon. M.R.C.S. 1847. A.S. 7 Apr. 1848. Killed by mutineers at Cawnpur, 12 June 1857. Son of H. Harris, No. 863, supra. Brother of F. W. Harris, No. 769, Bombay, 1845. Second Sikh or Panjab war, 1848–49. Indian Mutiny, 1857.

1532. Lee, Thomas Masson. *b.* 24 Dec. 1815. M.D. Ed. 1844. A.S. 20 Apr. 1848. *d.* on board S.S. 'Princess Charlotte,' between Hong Kong and Singapur, 30 Nov. 1858. Second Sikh or Panjab war, 1848–49.

1533. Bow, John Campbell. *b.* 3 Nov. 1825. M.D. Ed. 1846. A.S. 20 Apr. 1848. Surg. 17 Aug. 1862. S.M. 20 Apr. 1868. D.S.G. 16 Mar. 1875, *d.* in Edinburgh, 29 Sept. 1877. Second Sikh or Panjab war, Ramnagar, Chilianwala, Gujrat, and pursuit to Peshawar, medal with two clasps.

1534. Johnson, Cavendish. *b.* 25 Dec. 1825. St. George's. M.R.C.S. 1848. A.S. 26 June 1848. Surg. 25 Aug. 1862. S.M. 26 June 1868. R. 1 Dec. 1872. *d.* in London, 14 Aug. 1875.

1535. Pearson, Francis. b. 8 Apr. 1826. M.R.C.S. 1848. A.S. 2 July 1848. Surg. 25 Aug. 1862. R. 1 Jan. 1879. d. in London, 28 Nov. 1882. Author of Report on Mahamurree and Smallpox in Garhwal, 1861.

1536. White, William. b. 22 July 1814. Bart's. M.R.C.S. 1836. M.D. 18—. A.S. 4 July, 1848. F.R.C.S. 1859. Surg. 4 Sept. 1862. S.M. 4 July 1868. R. 20 Aug. 1871. d. at Penrhôs, Carnarvon, 12 Dec. 1875. Second Sikh or Panjab war, 1848–49, Gujrat, medal. Burma, 1852, capture of Rangoon, medal.

1537. Hayter, Henry William Goodenough. b. 15 June 1822. A.S. 21 July 1848. d. at Ludhiana, 10 Apr. 1849.

1538. Chevers, Norman. b. 27 Apr. 1818. Guy's. M.D. Glas. 1839. L.S.A. 1839. M.R.C.S. 1841. A.S. 1 Aug. 1848. Surg. 18 Sept. 1862. S.M. 1 Aug. 1868. R. 31 Mar. 1876. F.R.C.S. 1878. d. in London, 2 Dec. 1886. Son of Surgeon F. M. Chevers, R.N. C.I.E. 24 May 1881. Author of Medical Jurisprudence for India, 1854, reprinted 1856 and 1870; Morbid conditions of pulmonary artery, 1851; Diseases of the Heart and Aortic Aneurism, 1851; Removable and mitigable causes of death, 1852; (with J. R. Bedford, No. 1456, supra); On Public Health in India, 1854; On preserving health of European Soldiers in India, 4 parts, 1858–60; On preservation of health of seamen, 1864; Commentary on Diseases of India, 1886.

1539. Wilson, Aylmer St. Aubyn. b. 25 June 1825. M.D. Ed. 1847. A.S. 20 Aug. 1848. d. at Simla, 28 Sept. 1849. Second Sikh or Panjab war, 1848–49, Chilianwala, medal.

1540. MacLean, Alexander. b. 24 June 1826. M.A. M.D. K.C. Ab. 1848. A.S. 1 Sept. 1848. d. at Dibrugarh, 8 Aug. 1854. N.-E. Frontier, Naga, 1850, capture of Konoma.

1541. Bousfield, Sydney George. b. Aug. 1826. Middlesex Hosp. M.R.C.S. 1847. A.S. 10 Nov. 1848. Surg. 17 Oct. 1862. R. 12 Oct. 1863. Indian Mutiny, 1857–58.

1542. Allen, Frederick Freeman. b. 18 Mar. 1825. M.R.C.S. 1846. L.S.A. 1847. A.S. R.N. 25 July 1847 to 6 Sept. 1848. A.S. Bengal, 20 Nov. 1848. Surg. 13 Nov. 1862. S.M. 20 Nov. 1868. D.S.G. 6 Dec. 1876. R. 31 Aug. 1880. d. at Tunbridge, 28 Dec. 1888. C.B. 10 Sept. 1872. Q.H.P. 27 Oct. 1880. Central India, 1851, operations in Bandalkund. Indian Mutiny, 1857–58, siege and capture of Delhi, operations in Oudh, medal with clasp. N.-W. Frontier, Momund, 1863–64, action at Shabkadr, medal; Hazara, 1868; N.-E. Frontier, Lushai, 1871–72, as P.M.O. right column, Desp. C.B. Afghanistan, 1878–79, P.M.O. in Kurram Valley.

1543. Morris, William Gardiner. b. 12 Sept. 1826, in Pennsylvania. M.D. Ed. 1847. A.S. 20 Nov. 1848. d. at Delhi, 13 Jan. 1858. Indian Mutiny, 1857, siege and capture of Delhi.

1544. Payne, Arthur James. b. 21 Oct. 1826. King's Coll. Lond. M.R.C.S. 1847. B.A. M.D. Lond. 1848. A.S. 20 Dec. 1848. Surg. 1 Feb. 1863. S.M. 20 Dec. 1868. D.S.G. 13 Sept. 1879. R. 1 Feb. 1885. d. at South Kensington, 21 May 1915.

1545. Waugh, John Neill (d). b. 1818. Bart's. M.R.C.S., 1840. A.S. 20 Dec. 1848. Never joined. Name struck off by G.O. 21 Feb. 1853. L.S.A. 1856. M.D. St. A. 1856. d. at Brisbane, Oct. 1900.

1546. **Wallich, Nathaniel David Scott.** *b.* June 1825. Bart's. M.R.C.S. 1847. A.S. 20 Dec. 1848. Surg. Feb. 1863. *d.* at Dagshai, 9 June 1863. Son of N. Wallich, No. 725, supra, brother of G. C. Wallich, No. 1287, supra. N.-W. Frontier, Sheorani, 1853; Miranzai, 1855; Kurram Valley, 1856.

1849

1547. **Parker, Robert.** *b.* Aug. 1825. M.D. 18—. A.S. 1 Jan. 1849. Surg. 28 Feb. 1863. R. 24 June 1865. Indian Mutiny, 1857–58, siege and capture of Delhi, medal with clasp.

1548. **Hansbrow, George.** *b.* 6 Feb. 1823. M.R.C.S. 1845. A.S. 4 Feb. 1849, gained commission as a prize at R.C.S. England, on nomination of Sir J. Lushington. Killed by mutineers at Bareli, 31 May 1857. Indian Mutiny, 1857.

1549. **Miles, Richard Davidson.** *b.* 6 Apr. 1826. M.R.C.S. 1847. A.S. 20 Mar. 1849. *d.* at Naini Tal, 14 Aug. 1855.

1550. **Gee, Adolphus John.** *b.* Nov. 1823. M.R.C.S. 1847. A.S. 11 Apr. 1849. *d.* at Lucknow, 5 Dec. 1858. Indian Mutiny, 1857–58, operations in Gorakhpur and Oudh.

1551. **Stokes, John MacDonough.** *b.* Aug. 1816. A.S. 5 May 1849. *d.* at Rawal Pindi, 22 Oct. 1859.

1552. **Peskett, William.** *b.* Dec. 1821. Guy's. M.R.C.S. 1842. L.S.A. 1850. M.D. St. A. 18—. A.S. 26 June 1849. Surg. 3 Apr. 1863. S.M. 26 June 1869. *d.* in Calcutta, 11 Mar. 1870.

1553. **Morgan, David.** *b.* Aug. 1827. M.R.C.S. 1843. L.S.A. 1849. A.S. 9 Aug. 1849. *d.* at Naini Tal, 21 June 1850.

1554. **Corbyn, Frederick.** *b.* 20 Feb. 1827. M.D. Ed. 1849. A.S. 20 Sept. 1849. Surg. 16 May 1863. *d.* at Cheltenham, 5 Feb. 1868. Son of F. Corbyn, No. 722, supra, brother of J. C. Corbyn, No. 1583, infra. Indian Mutiny, 1857–58, relief of Lucknow, battle of Cawnpur, final siege and capture of Lucknow, Mar. 1858, medal with two clasps.

1555. **Lowdell, Charles.** *b.* 18 Mar. 1824. M.R.C.S. 1849. A.S. 20 Oct. 1849. Surg. 25 May 1863. S.M. 20 Oct. 1869. R. 24 Nov. 1870. *d.* at St. Leonards, 29 May 1898. Father of C. W. G. Lowdell, Bombay, No. 1051. Indian Mutiny, 1857–58, operations at Agra, medal.

1556. **Clark, Stewart.** *b.* 26 Mar. 1814. St. Thomas'. Mar. Coll. Ab. M.R.C.S. 1834. A.S. 24 Nov. 1849. Surg. 28 May 1863. S.M. 24 Nov. 1869. R. 29 July 1873. *d.* 25 Mar. 1897. Indian Mutiny, 1857–58, operations round Aligarh, medal. Author of Jail Manual for N.W.P. 1863; Hygiene of Army of India, 1864. See Stewart Clark, one of Nature's Noblemen, by S. E. S. C. (his widow), 1898.

1850

1557. **Hooper, John.** *b.* Jan. 1825. M.D. 18—. A.S. 16 Feb. 1850. Surg. 10 June 1863. *d.* at Lalitpur, 5 Aug. 1866. Indian Mutiny, 1857–58, with Jhind force, siege and capture of Delhi, medal with clasp.

1558. Young, David. *b.* 10 Sept. 1816. L.R.C.S. Ed. 18—. M.D. Glas. 1849. A.S. 20 Mar. 1850. F.R.C.S. Ed. 1860. Surg. 24 July 1862. S.M. 20 Mar. 1870. R. 6 Sept. 1876. *d.* in London, 18 June 1898. Indian Mutiny, 1858–59, with Naval Brigade, operations in Bihar against Koer Sinh.

1559. Mayne, Edgar William. *b.* 22 May 1822, at Boulogne. M.R.C.S. 1849. A.S. 25 Mar. 1850. *d.* at Jhilam, 2 Aug. 1851.

1560. Camplin, John Mussendine. *b.* 5 July 1825. M.R.C.S. 1847. L.S.A. 1848. A.S. 15 June 1850. Furlough S.C., G.O. 13 May 1853. Resigned, 9 Nov. 1856.

1561. Collins, Alfred. *b.* 1 July 1826. M.R.C.S. 1850. A.S. 26 June 1850. *d.* at Lahore, 16 June 1851. Son of Robert Collins, No. 233, supra (1780).

1562. Fayrer, Joseph. *b.* 6 Dec. 1824. Charing Cross Hosp. M.R.C.S. 1847. A.S. R.N. 12 Aug. 1847, resigned, 15 Sept. 1847. M.D. Rome, 1849. A.S. Ordnance Medl. Dept., 6 Dec. 1849, resigned, 1850. A.S. Bengal, 29 June 1850. Bt.-Surg. 7 Sept. 1858. M.D. Ed. 1859. F.R.C.S. Ed. 1859. M.R.C.P. Lond. 1860. Surg. 28 July 1863. S.M. 29 June 1870. F.R.C.P. Lond. 1872. R. with rank of D.S.G. 1 Dec. 1873. Member, Medl. Board, India Office, Feb. 1873; President, 8 Dec. 1873 to 6 Jan. 1895. F.R.C.S. 1878. S.G. 12 Jan. 1895. *d.* at Falmouth, 21 May 1907. Father of Lt.-Col. Sir Joseph Fayrer, R.A.M.C. (Johnston's Roll, No. 7168), and of Lt.-Col. F. D. S. Fayrer, I.M.S. 1898, Genl. List, No. 35. Accompanied Duke of Edinburgh in 1870, and Prince of Wales in 1875–76, on tours in India. Hony. Physn. to Prince of Wales, 12 May 1876. Physn. Extraordinary to King, Mar. 1901. C.S.I. 8 Dec. 1868. Q.H.P. 22 July 1871. Medjidie, 3rd Class, 26 Oct. 1875. K.C.S.I. 6 Mar. 1876. Star of Concepcion of Portugal, 6 May 1876. F.R.S. 19 Apr. 1877. LL.D. Ed. 1878. Cons. Physn. and Life Governor, Charing Cross Hosp. 1878. LL.D. St. A. 1890. F.C.P. Philadelphia, 1891. Phil. Doc. Padua, 1892. Bart. 7 Feb. 1896. G.S.P. 25 Oct. 1898. Sicilian revolution, 1848, operations at Palermo between Neapolitan and Sicilian troops, and attack on city of Rome by French troops under Genl. Oudinot. Burma, 1852–53, capture of Rangoon, medal with clasp. Indian Mutiny, 1857–58, defence of Lucknow, action at Cawnpur, Desp. of Sir J. Inglis, 26 Sept. 1857, and of Sir J. Outram, 25 Nov. 1857, L.G. 16 Jan. 1858, medal with clasp, Brevet-Surgeon, and one year's service for defence of Lucknow. Author of Clinical Surgery in India, 1866; European Child-life in Bengal, 1873; Clinical and Pathological Observations in India, 1873; The Royal Bengal Tiger, 1875; With the Princes in India, 1879; Tropical Dysentery and Chronic Diarrhœa, 1881; Climate and Fevers of India (Croonian Lectures), 1882; Thanatophidia of India, 1884; Life of Sir James Ranald Martin, 1897; Recollections of my Life, 1900; and of articles on Beriberi, Delhi Sore, Dengue, Elephantiasis, Sunstroke, and Venomous Animals, in Quain's Dictionary of Medicine, 1882; on Tropical Diarrhœa, Liver Abscess, and Sunstroke, in Davidson's Diseases of Warm Climates, 1893; on Sunstroke and Climate and Fevers of India, in Allbutt's system of Medicine, 1896–97.

1563. Owen, William Charles. *b.* May 1823. M.D. Ed. 1849. M.R.C.S. 1850. A.S. 17 July 1850. *d.* at Midnapur, 24 May 1853.

1564. Watkins, John. *b.* 20 May 1828. M.R.C.S. 1850. A.S. 11 Aug. 1850. *d.* at Jhang, 20 Aug. 1861.

1565. **Adley, William Henry.** *b.* 20 Apr. 1827, at Jaffna, Ceylon. M.R.C.S. 1850. A.S. 2 Sept. 1850. Surg. 24 Aug. 1863. S.M. 2 Sept. 1870. D.S.G. 22 June 1877. R. 1 Apr. 1882. *d.* at Haverfordwest, 18 June 1898. N.-W. Frontier, Ranizai, 1852; Buri Pass, Nov. 1853; Bussy Khel Afridi, 1855. Indian Mutiny, 1857-58, operations in Rohilkand, medal. N.-E. Frontier, Bhutan; 1865-66, clasp.

1566. **Cathcart, John Edwin.** *b.* 29 Aug. 1828. M.D. Ed. 1849. M.R.C.S. 1850. A.S. 30 Sept. 1850. *d.* at Kohat, 1 Apr. 1854.

1567. **Williams, Henry Francis.** *b.* 26 Feb. 1821. M.R.C.S. 1843. M.D. Glas. 1844. A.S. R.N. 1845-50. A.S. Bengal, 20 Nov. 1850. M.R.C.P. Lond. 1860. Surg. 10 Sept. 1863. S.M. 20 Nov. 1870. R. 5 Jan. 1878. *d.* at Southsea, 27 Apr. 1884.

1568. **Vivian, Edward John.** *b.* 17 Aug. 1825. M.R.C.S. 1849. L.S.A. 1849. A.S. 20 Nov. 1850. Surg. 16 Sept. 1863. S.M. 20 Nov. 1870. R. 1 Dec. 1872. *d.* at Folkestone, 23 Oct. 1888. Indian Mutiny, 1857-58.

1569. **Hutchinson, James Alexander Caldwell.** *b.* Feb. 1828. M.R.C.S. 1849. A.S. 20 Nov. 1850. Surg. 25 Sept. 1863. S.M. 20 Nov. 1870. D.S.G. 31 Mar. 1877. R. 28 Sept. 1884. *d.* at Bedford, 26 Oct. 1895. Brother of R. F. Hutchinson, No. 1614, infra. Father of F. H. G. Hutchinson, Genl. list, I.M.S. No. 15.

1570. **Locock, Henry Smyth.** *b.* 12 Jan. 1827. A.S. 20 Nov. 1850. *d.* at Thayetmyo, 31 July 1855. Burma, 1852-53, medal.

1851

1571. **Scriven, John Barclay.** *b.* Apr. 1828. Univ. Coll. Lond. M.B. Lond. 1849. M.R.C.S. 1850. A.S. 11 Jan. 1851. Surg. 12 Oct. 1863. S.M. 11 Jan. 1871. R. 13 June 1881. *d.* in London, 22 July 1905. Burma, 1852-53, capture of Tonghu, medal.

1572. **Amesbury, Joseph Walter Raleigh.** *b.* 31 Dec. 1828. M.R.C.S. 1850. A.S. 11 Jan. 1851. Bt.-Surg. 14 Aug. 1860. Surg. 18 Dec. 1863. S.M. 11 Jan. 1871. *d.* at Masuri, 6 Oct. 1881. Brother of S. C. Amesbury, No. 1668, infra. Burma, 1852-53, medal. Indian Mutiny, 1857-58, Commanded a troop of 3rd Oudh Irregular Cavalry, in advance on Cawnpur (horse shot under him), appointed acting A.D.C. to Genl. Neill, raised and horsed Volunteer Cavalry under Neill; action of 2 Mar. 1858, attack on Belwar Fort, actions at Amara, 5 Mar., Thelga, 17 Apr., Amara, 25 Apr., capture of Fort Nagar; medal, Brevet-Surgeon.

1573. **Stewart, Charles.** *b.* 30 Oct. 1821. M.A. M.D. Ed. 1843. A.S. 26 Feb. 1851. Surg. 20 Dec. 1863. *d.* at Jhansi, 6 Aug. 1864. Burma, 1852-54, relief of Pegu, medal.

1574. **MacKellar, Edward.** *b.* 28 May 1827. Univ. Coll. Lond. M.R.C.S. 1849. A.S. 9 July 1851. Surg. 20 Dec. 1863. M.D. St. A. 1870. S.M. 9 July 1871. R. 31 Mar. 1877. *d.* at Brighton, 27 Oct. 1914. Burma, 1852-53, capture of Martaban, operations at Rangoon, capture of Prome, medal with clasp. Indian Mutiny, 1857-58, operations at Agra, and in N.W.P. and Oudh, medal. Abyssinia, 1868, medal.

1575. **Allen, James Bedford.** *b.* Jan. 1828. M.R.C.S. 1850. A.S. 25 July 1851. Surg. 8 Mar. 1864. *d.* at Bankipur, Patna, 11 July 1870. Indian Mutiny, 1857–58, medal.

1576. **De Renzy, Annesley Charles Castriot.** *b.* 7 Apr. 1828. B.A. T.C.D. 1851. M.R.C.S. 1851. A.S. 29 July 1851. Surg. 12 Mar. 1864. S.M. 29 July 1871. D.S.G. 12 Nov. 1877. R. 9 Dec. 1882. *d.* at Ealing, 24 Dec. 1914. C.B. 22 Feb. 1881. G.S.P. 14 Jan. 1882. K.C.B. 29 June 1902. Burma, 1852–54, capture of Martaban, Rangoon, and Prome, medal with clasp. Indian Mutiny, 1857–58, Mutiny at Nasirabad, siege and capture of Lucknow, Mar. 1858, medal with clasp. N.-E. Frontier, Naga, 1879–80, Desp. medal with clasp, C.B. Author of Remarks on Report of Sany. Commr. on Cholera Epidemic of 1872, in N. India, 1874.

1577. **Brown, Alexander.** *b.* 21 Dec. 1828. M.D. Ed. 1849. L.S.A. 1851. M.R.C.S. 1852. A.S. 26 Aug. 1851. *d.* at Peshawar, 4 Oct. 1852.

1578. **Umphelby, Joseph Edmond.** *b.* 22 Sept. 1826. M.R.C.S. 1851. A.S. 26 Aug. 1851. Dismissed by Court Martial, 23 Apr. 1856. Brother of A. Umphelby, No. 1186, Madras, 1854. Burma, 1852–53.

1579. **Tait, Dalhousie.** *b.* 23 July 1829. M.D. Ed. 1850. A.S. 17 Sept. 1851. *d.* in Medl. Coll. Hosp. Calcutta, 20 May 1853. Burma, 1852–53, capture of Rangoon.

1580. **Christison, Alexander.** *b.* 26 Aug. 1828. M.D. Ed. gold medal, 1850. A.S. 20 Oct. 1851. Surg. 24 Mar. 1864. S.M. 20 Oct. 1871. D.S.G. 31 Mar. 1877. R. 24 Nov. 1882. *d.* in Edinburgh, 14 Oct. 1918. Succeeded his father, Sir Robert Christison, as second baronet, 23 Jan 1882. Burma, 1852–53, capture of Rangoon, medal with clasp. Indian Mutiny, 1857–58, operations near Agra, action at Sasia, capture of Gwalior, medal with clasp.

1581. **Keith, David.** *b.* 9 May 1829. M.A. Mar. Coll. Ab. 1847. M.D. Ed. 1851. A.S. 3 Nov. 1851. *d.* at Abbottabad, 11 July 1853.

1582. **Cuningham, James MacNabb.** *b.* 2 June 1829, at Cape of Good Hope. M.D. Ed. 1851. A.S. 20 Nov. 1851. Surg. 1 Apr. 1864. S.M. 20 Nov. 1871. S.G. 29 Mar. 1880. R. 29 Mar. 1885. *d.* in London, 26 June 1905. C.S.I. 16 June 1885. Q.H.S. 15 Aug. 1888. LL.D. Ed. 1892. Indian Mutiny, 1857–58. Author of Sanitary Primer for Indian Schools, 1879; Cholera, what can the State do to prevent it? 1884; Sanitary Primer for Burmese Schools, 1886.

1583. **Corbyn, Joseph Christian.** *b.* Aug. 1829. M.D. 18—. A.S. 24 Nov. 1851. Surg. 8 Apr. 1864. S.M. 24 Nov. 1871. R. 1 Jan. 1879. *d.* at Cheltenham, 24 Oct. 1912. Son of F. Corbyn, No. 722, supra, and brother of F. Corbyn, No. 1554, supra. Indian Mutiny, 1857–58, Siege and capture of Delhi, siege and capture of Lucknow, Mar. 1858, operations against Koer Sinh in Bihar, two medals with clasps.

1584. **Bowling, John Pierce.** *b.* Mar. 1825. M.R.C.S. 1847. L.S.A. 1847. A.S. 20 Dec. 1851. Killed by mutineers, Cawnpur, 27 June 1857. Brother of H. H. Bowling, No. 1283, supra. Kafir war, 1850, as a volunteer. Burma, 1852–53, capture of Rangoon, medal. Indian Mutiny, 1857.

1585. Govan, George Moncrieff. b. 3 Mar. 1829. M.D. Ed. 1851. L.R.C.S. Ed. 1851. A.S. 20 Dec. 1851. Surg. 1 Apr. 1864. S.M. 20 Dec. 1871. R. 3 Mar. 1887. d. at Almora, 1 Apr. 1898. Son of G. Govan, No. 654, supra. Burma, 1852-53, capture of Rangoon, medal with clasp. Indian Mutiny, 1859, operations near Delhi, 1859. N.-E. Frontier, Bhutan, 1865-66, capture of Buxa and Tazagaon, clasp.

1852

1586. Perkins, Richard Henry. b. 23 July 1824, in Brussels. A.S. 20 Apr. 1852. Surg. 15 June 1864. S.M. 20 Apr. 1872. D.S.G. 10 Dec. 1877. R. 4 May 1884. d. in London, 16 Jan. 1888. Afghanistan, 1880; P.M.O. 1st Division, Northern Afghanistan Field Force, medal.

1587. Townsend, Stephen Chapman. b. Dec. 1826. M.R.C.S. 1851. L.S.A. 1851. A.S. 1 June 1852. Surg. 15 June 1864. S.M. 1 June 1872. D.S.G. 18 Dec. 1878. R. 18 Dec. 1883. d. at Exeter, 9 Feb. 1901. C.B. 22 Feb. 1881. G.S.P. 1 Mar. 1882. Burma, 1852-53, medal. Afghanistan, 1878-80, as P.M.O. in Kurram Valley, affair of Hazar Dirakht defile, severely wounded, Desp. medal with clasp, C.B.

1588. Haynes, William. b. 2 Aug. 1829. M.R.C.S. 1852. A.S. 15 June 1852. d. at Donabue, Burma, 24 Apr. 1853. Burma, 1852-53.

1589. Beatson, William Burns. b. May 1825. Guy's. M.R.C.S. 1846. L.S.A. 1846. M.D. St. A. 1852. A.S. 30 June 1852, gained commission as a prize at Guy's, on nomination of J. Masterman. Surg. 15 June 1864. F.R.C.S. 1867. S.M. 30 June 1872. D.S.G. 20 Dec. 1878. R. 20 Dec. 1883. M.R.C.P. Lond. 1884. F.R.C.P. Lond. 1901. d. at Eastbourne, 26 Apr. 1911. Burma, 1852-53, medal with clasp. Author of The Indian Medical Service, past and present, 1902.

1590. Silver, Ebenezer David. b. Dec. 1820. Guy's. M.D. K.C. Ab. 1848. M.R.C.S. 1848. Colonial Surgeon, Gold Coast, 1849-50. A.S. 20 July 1852. R. 23 Aug. 1858. d. at Sutton-at-Hone, Kent, 26 Jan. 1911. Author of A treatise on Diseases of the Rectum and Anus, 1868.

1591. Paske, Charles Thomas. b. 10 Apr. 1830. Middlesex Hosp. M.R.C.S. 1852. A.S. 26 Aug. 1852. Surg. 15 June 1864. S.M. 26 Aug. 1872. R. 1 Jan. 1879. d. 10 Apr. 1920. Burma, 1853, medal. Indian Mutiny, 1857-58, actions at Ghaga, Kudwa, and Chanda, medal. N.-E. Frontier, Bhutan, 1865-66, clasp. Author of Myamma; Life and Travel in Lower Burma, 1892; (with F. G. Aflalo), The Sea and the Rod, a handbook to British and other Seafishing, 1892.

1592. Dalzel, William Frederick Blyth. b. 6 June 1823. M.D. Ed. 1850. A.S. 20 Sept. 1852. Surg. 15 June 1864. S.M. 20 Sept. 1872. R. 14 Mar. 1873. d. in London, 19 June 1897. Indian Mutiny, 1857-58, operations near Agra, relief of Lucknow, Nov. 1857, action at Cawnpur, final siege and capture of Lucknow, Mar. 1858; capture of Kalpi. Central Indian campaign, capture of rebel leader, Tantia Topi; medal with three clasps.

1593. Partridge, Samuel Bowen. b. Nov. 1828. King's Coll. Lond. M.R.C.S. 1851. L.S.A. 1851. A.S. 12 Oct. 1852. Bt.-Surg. 7 Sept. 1858. F.R.C.S. Ed. 1858. Surg. 15 June 1864. F.R.C.S. 1871. S.M. 12 Oct. 1872. R. 1 Jan. 1880. Member, Medl. Board, India Office, 1876–79 and 1889–93. d. at Anerley, Kent, 7 May 1898. Q.H.S. 23 June 1883. C.I.E. 3 June 1893. Burma, 1853, medal. Indian Mutiny, 1857–58, defence of Lucknow, action at Cawnpur, final siege and capture of Lucknow, Mar. 1858; Desp. L.G. 16 Jan. 1858; medal with three clasps, Brevet-Surgeon, and one year's service for defence of Lucknow.

1594. Skinner, George Robert. b. 16 Sept. 1825. M.R.C.S. 1847. F.R.C.S. 1852. A.S. 20 Dec. 1852. Nominated by Sir J. M. Hogg, on recommendation of Royal College of Surgeons. d. at Bath, 26 Mar. 1856.

1853

1595. *Knight, Richard Chalmers (b). M.D. —. Surgeon's Mate 'General Kyd,' 1829–30; Surgeon, same ship, 1830–31. Officiating A.S. Bombay, 27 Aug. 1840; (Bo. G.O. 27 Aug. 1840); struck off 21 Aug. 1841; (Bo. G.O. 21 Aug. 1841). Uncovd. Medical Service, Bengal, 1850–53. A.S. Bengal, 4 Feb. 1853. d. at Bijnor, 14 June 1860. Afghanistan, 1840, with Sind Field Force; Desp. Bo. G.O. 20 Apr. 1841. Indian Mutiny, 1857–58. Bo. No. 690.

1596. Butt, William Boyne. b. Dec. 1825. M.R.C.S. 1850. A.S. 20 Mar. 1853. Surg. 15 June 1864. d. on board S.S. 'St. Lawrence,' on passage to Europe, 14 Apr. 1865.

1597. Murchison, Charles (e). b. 26 July 1830, at Vere, Jamaica. L.R.C.S. Ed. 1850. M.D. Ed. with honours, 1851. A.S. 4 Apr. 1853. Resigned, Oct. 1855. M.R.C.P. Lond. 1855. F.R.C.P. Lond. 1859. Physn. and Lect. on Medicine, Middlesex Hospital, 1860–71; ditto, St. Thomas', 1871–79. d. in London, 23 Apr. 1879. F.R.S. 1866. LL.D. Ed. 1870. Burma, 1853–54, medal. Author of Treatise on Continued Fevers of Great Britain, 1862, 3rd ed. 1884; Diseases of the Liver, 1867, 4th ed. 1894; Palæontological Memoirs of the late H. Falconer, 1868; and translated, for the New Sydenham Society, Frerichs' Diseases of the Liver, two vols. 1861–62.

1598. Duthoit, Thomas James. b. 9 Mar. 1828. Bart's. M.B. Lond. 1849. M.R.C.S. 1850. L.S.A. 1850. A.S. 20 Apr. 1853, gained commission as a prize at Bart's, on nomination of J. Masterman. d. at Allahabad, 18 Sept. 1858. Indian Mutiny, 1857–58.

1599. Clarke, John James. b. 27 June 1827. MR.C.S. 1853. A.S. 14 May 1853. Surg. 15 June, 1864. M.D. St. A. 1872. S.M. 14 May 1873. D.S.G. 20 Apr. 1879. R. 14 Jan. 1884. d. at Melbourne, 23 Feb. 1895. G.S.P. 9 Dec. 1882. Indian Mutiny, 1857–58, advance on and relief of Lucknow, Sept. 1857; second defence of Lucknow, Sept. to Nov. 1857; final siege and capture of Lucknow, Mar. 1858; operations in Oudh; medal with two clasps. N.-E. Frontier, Akha, 1883–84, as P.M.O.

---

* R. C. Knight was the last officer who had served as Surgeon of one of the Company's fleet of Indiamen, abolished in 1834.

1600. Baillie, George Olans. *b.* 11 Aug. 1830. M.B. M.D. 1852, Mar. Coll. Ab. M.R.C.S. 1853. A.S. 14 May 1853. Surg. 15 June 1864. S.M. 14 May 1873. R. 18 June 1874. *d.* at Dover, 27 Aug. 1881. Son of George Baillie, No. 630, supra (1808). Brother of N. B. Baillie, No. 1726, infra. Burma, 1853-54, operations in Tharawadi.

1601. Tuson, John Edward. *b.* 3 July 1829. St. George's and Middlesex Hosp. M.R.C.S. 1851. A.S. 17 June 1853. M.D. St. A. 1862. F.R.C.S. 1863. Surg. 15 June 1864. S.M. 17 June 1873. D.S.G. 20 Aug. 1879. R. 8 Sept. 1884. *d.* at Eastbourne, 24 Dec. 1908. N.-W. Frontier, Miranzai, 1855. Indian Mutiny, 1857-58, capture of Najibabad, action at Nagina, medal. N.-W. Frontier, Mahsud Waziri, 1860, Desp., medal with clasp.

1602. MacNamara, Francis Nottidge. *b.* 11 Apr. 1831. King's Coll. Lond. M.R.C.S. 1852. M.D. St. A. 1852. A.S. 18 June 1853, gained commission as a prize at King's College, on nomination of W. A. C. Plowden. Surg. 15 June 1864. S.M. 18 June 1873. R. 14 Feb. 1876. Examiner Medl. Stores, India Office, 1876-99. *d.* in London, 5 Mar. 1899. Author of Climate and Medical Topography of Himalayan India, 1880 ; Article on Goitre in Davidson's Diseases of Warm Climates, 1893.

1603. Chaldecott, Frederick James. *b.* Oct. 1825. M.R.C.S. 1851. M.D. St. A. 1853. A.S. 1 July 1853. Dismissed by Court Martial, 16 May 1856. *d.* at Sydney, 22 Dec. 1862.

1604. Tierney, John Francis. *b.* 19 Feb. 1830. M.R.C.S. 1851. A.S. 26 July 1853. *d.* at Barhampur, 6 Apr. 1849. Sonthal Insurrection, 1855-56.

1605. Taylor, Edward. *b.* Feb. 1825. M.R.C.S. 1852. A.S. 1 Aug. 1853. Surg. 11 July 1864. S.M. 1 July 1873. R. 15 Mar. 1880. *d.* at Stevenage, Herts., 26 July 1906. Indian Mutiny, 1857-58, Central India Campaign, medal with clasp. N.-E. Frontier, Bhutan, 1865-66, medal. Abyssinia, 1868, medal with clasp. Afghanistan, 1878-80, medal.

1606. Jeston, Richard Pope. *b.* 17 June 1826. King's Coll. Lond. M.R.C.S. 1849. L.S.A. 1849. A.S. 11 Aug. 1853. Resigned, 20 Aug. 1857. *d.* at Henley-on-Thames, 11 Oct. 1901.

1607. Spry, Henry William. *b.* 25 Aug. 1831. M.R.C.S. 1852. A.S. 20 Oct. 1853. Surg. 7 Aug. 1864. S.M. 1 July 1873. *d.* at Firuzpur, 3 Nov. 1883.

1608. Dale, Alfred James. *b.* 27 Dec. 1830. London Hosp. M.R.C.S. 1852. L.S.A. 1853. A.S. 20 Oct. 1853, gained commission as a prize at London Hosp. on nomination of R. Ellis. Surg. 26 Sept. 1864. S.M. 1 July 1873. B.S. 27 Nov. 1879. D.S.G. 3 Aug. 1882. R. 23 July 1886. *d.* in London, 24 Nov. 1903. Burma, 1854. Afghanistan, 1879, in Kurram Valley, medal.

1609. Young, Arthur. *b.* 21 Dec. 1816. M.R.C.S. 1838. Officiating A.S. Bombay, 5 Dec. 1846. Uncovd. Medl. and Civil Officer, Sind, 1846-53. A.S. Bengal, 20 Oct. 1853. Surg. 4 Oct. 1864. R. 26 Mar. 1872. *d.* in Tasmania, 27 Mar. 1906. Served in Oudh Commission, 1861-72. Bo. No. 798.

1610. Simpson, Benjamin. *b.* 31 Mar. 1831. B.A. T.C.D. 18—. M.R.C.S. 1852. M.D. St. A. 1853. A.S. 20 Oct. 1853. Surg. 26 Sept. 1864. S.M. 1 July 1873. B.S. 27 Nov. 1879. D.S.G. 21 Mar. 1882. S.G. 29 Mar. 1885. R. 29 Mar. 1890. *d.* in London, 27 June 1923. G.S.P. 20 Dec. 1885. K.C.I.E. 15 Feb. 1887. N.-E. Frontier, Bhutan, 1865–66, medal with clasp.

1611. Daly, George Hickie. *b.* Apr. 1831. Medl. Coll. Calcutta ; Univ. Coll. London ; and Barts. M.R.C.S. 1853. M.D. St. A. 1853. A.S. 4 Nov. 1853. Surg. 15 Nov. 1864. S.M. 1 July 1873. R. 6 Aug. 1875. *d.* at Chippenham, 25 July 1889. Indian Mutiny, 1857–58, medal. China, 1860–61, medal with two clasps. Abyssinia, 1868, medal.

1612. O'Brien, Peter. *b.* 19 Nov. 1806. Medl. Coll. Calcutta, and St. Georges. L.M.S. Calcutta. Apothecary, 7 Oct. 1825–46. M.R.C.S. 1843. Uncovd. Medl. Service, Gwalior contingent, 2 Mar. 1846 to 19 Nov. 1853. A.S. 20 Nov. 1853. F.R.C.S. 1859. Surg. 15 Nov. 1864. R. 6 July 1866. *d.* at St. Heliers, Jersey, 24 Mar. 1882. Central India, 1844–50, minor operations. Burma, 1852–53, capture of Ava. Indian Mutiny, 1857–58, Central India campaign, actions at Madanpur and Betwa, siege and storm of Jhansi, action at Kunch, capture of Lahuri and Kalpi, medal with clasp.

1613. Barnard, George. *b.* Nov. 1829. M.R.C.S. 1853. A.S. 25 Nov. 1853. Surg. 15 Nov. 1864. S.M. 1 July 1873. R. 31 Jan. 1879. *d.* at Norwood, 13 Mar. 1882. Author of Cholera Maligna an Acute Specific Inflammation, 1869.

1614. Hutchinson, Robert Faure. *b.* 17 Nov. 1831. M.D. Ed. 1853. L.R.C.S. Ed. 1853. A.S. 3 Dec. 1853. Surg. 27 Jan. 1865. S.M. 1 July 1873. B.S. 27 Nov. 1879. D.S.G. 24 Oct. 1882. R. 9 Dec. 1887. *d.* in London, 11 Jan. 1894. Brother of J. A. C. Hutchinson, No. 1569, supra. Afghanistan, 1879–80, medal. Author of Glossary of Medical and Medico legal terms, 1873.

1615. Currie, James Allan. *b.* 30 Dec. 1827. M.A. M.D. Ed. 1853. M.R.C.S. 1853. A.S. 4 Dec. 1853. *d.* at Agra, 15 June 1861.

1616. Picthall, John. *b.* 10 Aug. 1828. M.R.C.S. 1853. A.S. 14 Dec. 1853. L.R.C.P. Lond. 1862. M.D. St. A. 1862. Surg. 15 Apr. 1865. S.M. 1 July 1873. B.S. 27 Nov. 1879. R. 1 Dec. 1882. *d.* in London, 17 July 1893. Sonthal Insurrection, 1856. Indian Mutiny, 1857–58.

1617. Crewe, Alfred Godley. *b.* July 1831. St. George's. M.R.C.S. 1853. A.S. 14 Dec. 1853. Surg. 24 May 1865. R. 2 Apr. 1867. M.D. Philadelphia, 1870. *d.* at Milton, Hants, 2 Apr. 1894.

1618. Grant, Nathaniel James. *b.* 13 June 1831. M.R.C.S. 1852. A.S. 18 Dec. 1853. Surg. 3 June 1865. S.M. 1 July 1873. R. 27 Apr. 1877. *d.* 27 Nov. 1914. N.-W. Frontier, Aka Khel and Bussy Khel, 1854–55. Indian Mutiny, 1857–58, operations in Bihar, dangerously wounded at Rohni, June 1857, medal. Abyssinia, 1868, capture of Magdala, medal.

1619. Mott, Marcus William. *b.* Mar. 1830. M.R.C.S. 1853. A.S. 20 Dec. 1853. M.D. St. A. 1859. Surg. 14 June 1865. R. 25 Aug. 1867. *d.* 27 July 1899.

1620. Ewart, Joseph. *b.* 30 Sept. 1831. Guy's. M.R.C.S. 1853. M.D. St. A. 1853. A.S. 20 Dec. 1853, gained commission as a prize at Guy's, on nomination of J. H. Astell. Surg. 19 July 1865. S.M. 1 July 1873. M.R.C.P. Lond. 1876. R. 31 Jan. 1879. F.R.C.P. Lond. 1881. *d.* at Brighton, 9 Jan. 1896. Mayor of Brighton, 1891–94. Knighted, 24 May 1895. Indian Mutiny, 1857–58. Author of The Vital Statistics of the European and Native armies in India, 1859 ; Sanitary Condition of Indian Gaols, 1860 ; Catalogue of pathological preparations in Calcutta Medical College Museum, 1865 ; (with MacKenzie), Indian and Australian Snake poisoning, 1875 ; The poisonous Snakes of India (an abridgment of Fayrer's Thanatophidia), 1878 ; Article on Dysentery in Quain's Medical Dictionary, 1882 ; edited 6th edition of Goodeve's Hints on Children, 1872.

1621. Moir, Robert. *b.* 23 Oct. 1831. L.R.C.S. Ed. 1851. M.D. Ed. 1853. A.S. 20 Dec. 1853. F.R.C.P. Ed. 1859. Surg. 27 July 1865. S.M. 1 July 1873. R. 16 June 1877. *d.* at St. Andrews, 7 June 1899. Father of D. M. Moir, No. 2271, infra, 1888.

1622. MacLagan, James MacGrigor. *b.* 18 May 1830. M.D. Ed. 1851. L.R.C.S. Ed. 1851. A.S. 20 Dec. 1853. Resigned, 1 Dec. 1857. After retirement in practice at Rotherham, Sheffield. *d.* at Riding Mill-on-Tyne, Northumberland, 15 Dec. 1891.

1854

1623. Duka, Theodore. A Hungarian. *b.* 24 June 1825, at Dukasaln, Hungary. St. George's and Paris. M.D. St. A. 1853. M.R.C.S. 1853. A.S. 4 Jan. 1854. Surg. 1 Aug. 1865. F.R.C.S. 1866. S.M. 1 July 1873. R. 27 Mar. 1877. M.D. Buda-Pest, 1899. *d.* at Bournemouth, 5 May 1908. Hungarian Order of Valour, 1849. Knight of Iron Crown of Hungary, 1883. Hungarian revolution, 1848–49, A.D.C. to Genl. Görgey, commander of 7th Army Corps of Hungarian Army ; battle of Komoru, 26 Apr. 1849, Order of Valour ; taken prisoner when Hungarians surrendered to Russians at Villagos, 13 Aug. 1849. Author of Life of Semmelweiss, 1882 ; Essay on Brahui grammar, 1885 ; Life of Alexander Csoma-de Koros, 1885 ; Childbed Fever, 1888 ; Kossuth and Görgëi, recollections of a stormy period, 1899.

1624. Currie, George Vernon. *b.* Mar. 1828. A.S. 14 Jan. 1854. Surg. 24 Nov. 1865. S.M. 1 July 1873. B.S. 27 Nov. 1879. R. 10 Apr. 1884. *d.* in London, 3 Dec. 1900. Son of Physn. Genl. Claud Currie, M. No. 549, 1806. Brother of C. D. Currie, M. No. 1031, W. F. Currie, M. No. 1091, and A. O. Currie, M. No. 1122. Indian Mutiny, 1858. N.-W. Frontier, Yusufzai, 1866. Afghanistan, 1879, medal.

1625. MacLean, Lachlan John Hector. *b.* Mar. 1827. M.R.C.S. 1853. A.S. 14 Jan. 1854. M.D. Heidelberg, 1865. Surg. 1 Jan. 1866. R. 24 Sept. 1867. M.R.C.P. Lond. 1880. *d.* 10 Apr. 1884.

1626. O'Donel, Francis Hugh. *b.* 28 Dec. 1829. M.D. Ed. 1853. A.S. 14 Jan. 1854. Surg. 1 Jan. 1866. S.M. 1 July 1873. *d.* at Mian Mir, 18 Jan. 1879. Indian Mutiny, 1857–59, relief of Lucknow, Nov. 1857, action at Cawnpur, final siege and capture of Lucknow, Mar. 1858, operations in Oudh, medal with two clasps.

1627. Lawrence, John James Trevor. b. 30 Dec. 1831. Bart's. M.R.C.S. 1853. A.S. 20 Jan. 1854. Surg. 1 Jan. 1866. Resigned, 24 Feb. 1866. d. at Burford House, Dorking, 22 Dec. 1913. Succeeded his father, Sir William Lawrence, as second Baronet, 5 July 1867. M.P. Mid-Surrey, 1875–85; Reigate Division of Surrey, 1885–92. Treasurer, St. Bart's., 1892–1904. K.C.V.O. 9 Nov. 1902.

1628. Greenhow, Henry Martineau. b. 6 Sept. 1829. Newcastle and Univ. Coll. Lond. M.R.C.S. 1853. A.S. 20 Jan. 1854. Brevet-Surg. 5 Sept. 1858. F.R.C.S. 1859. F.R.C.S. Ed. 1859. Surg. 1 Jan. 1866. S.M. 1 July 1873. R. 20 Aug. 1876. d. at Esher, Surrey, 26 Nov. 1912. Indian Mutiny, 1857–58, defence of Lucknow, operations in Oudh, Desp. L.G. 16 Jan. 1858, medal with two clasps, Brevet-Surgeon, and one year's service for defence of Lucknow. Author of The Bow of Fate, 1893; The Tower of Ghilzean, 1896; Brenda's Experiment, 1896; Amy Vivian's Ring, 1897; The Emperor's Design, 1901; Leila's Lovers, 1902; (all novels).

1629. Morgan, Robert Bond. b. 26 June 1830. M.R.C.S. 1852. A.S. 4 Feb. 1854. d. at Cawnpur, 12 Jan. 1855.

1630. Graham, Henry William. b. 17 Sept. 1827. M.R.C.S. 1853. A.S. 14 Feb. 1854. Surg. 1 Jan. 1866. S.M. 1 July 1873. R. 6 June 1884. d. at Barnes, 1 June 1894.

1631. Lamb, Martin Brydon. b. 24 Nov. 1826. M.D. Ed. 1847. M.R.C.S. 1851. L.S.A. 1851. A.S. 14 Feb. 1854. d. at Landour, 21 June 1860. Indian Mutiny, 1857–58, operations in Oudh.

1632. Elliot, John. b. 17 Apr. 1830. M.D. Ed. 1852. A.S. 20 Feb. 1854. Surg. 1 Jan. 1866. S.M. 1 July 1873. d. in Calcutta, 7 Jan. 1878. Author of Report on Epidemic remittent and intermittent fevers, occurring in parts of Burdwan and Nuddea Divisions, 1863.

1633. Farncombe, Thomas Beard. b. July 1830. M.R.C.S. 1851. L.S.A. 1852. A.S. 20 Feb. 1854. Surg. 8 Jan. 1866. S.M. 1 July 1873. R. 16 Feb. 1875. d. 16 May 1923. Sonthal Insurrection, 1855–56. N.-E. Frontier, Bhutan, 1865–66.

1634. James, Edward. b. May 1831. L.S.A. 1852. M.R.C.S. 1853. A.S. 20 Mar. 1854. Resigned, 19 Aug. 1858. Afterwards in practice at Exeter, living 1870; (Med. Dir. 1871).

1635. Earle, Frederick John. b. 6 Jan. 1827. L.S.A. 1848. M.R.C.S. 1849. A.S. 20 Mar. 1854. M.D. St. A. 1862. Surg. 14 Feb. 1866. S.M. 1 July 1873. R. 31 Mar. 1877. d. in London, 28 Feb. 1881.

1636. Dopping, Anthony. b. 6 Aug. 1830. B.A. M.D. T.C.D. 1853. A.S. 4 Apr. 1854. Killed by mutineers, Delhi, 11 May 1857. Indian Mutiny, 1857.

1637. Ringer, Theobald. b. Oct. 1826. Guy's. M.R.C.S. 1849. L.S.A. 1849. M.D. St. A. 1853. A.S. 17 Apr. 1854. M.R.C.P. Lond. 1860. Surg. 27 Feb. 1866. S.M. 1 July 1873. B.S. 27 Nov. 1879. R. 21 Sept. 1881. d. at Cheltenham, 12 June 1906. Indian Mutiny, 1857–58, final siege and capture of Lucknow, Mar. 1858; operations in Oudh and Rohilkand, capture of Bareli, medal with clasp.

INDIAN MEDICAL SERVICE   [1854

1638. **Delpratt, Samuel.** *b.* 1 Nov. 1828, in Jamaica. M.R.C.S. 1853. A.S. 6 May 1854. Surg. 29 Mar. 1866. S.M. 1 July 1873. *d.* in England, 17 Feb. 1875. Brother of W. Delpratt, No. 1527, supra. Indian Mutiny, 1857-58, operations in Bihar, medal.

*1639. **Sutherland, Philip Warren.** *b.* 10 Jan. 1832. King's Coll. Lond. M.R.C.S. 1853. A.S. 6 May 1854. Surg. 6 May 1866. S.M. 1 July 1873. B.S. 27 Nov. 1879. D.S.G. 18 Dec. 1883. R. 5 Feb. 1889. *d.* in London, 6 June 1925. Indian Mutiny, 1857-58, medal.

1640. **Anderson, Thomas** (e). *b.* 5 Feb. 1832. M.D. Ed. 1853. A.S. 20 May 1854. Surg. 20 May 1866. *d.* in Edinburgh, 26 Oct. 1870. Indian Mutiny, 1857-58, siege and capture of Delhi, medal with clasp. Author of Catalogue of Plants in Royal Botanical Garden, Calcutta, 1865.

1641. **Eteson, Alfred.** *b.* 29 Apr. 1832. Bart's. M.R.C.S. 1854. A.S. 20 May 1854. Surg. 20 May 1866. S.M. 1 July 1873. M.D. St. A. 1878. B.S. 27 Nov. 1879. D.S.G. 20 Dec. 1883. R. 13 Jan. 1889. *d.* in London, 15 Feb. 1910. C.B. 28 June 1907. Indian Mutiny, 1857-59, relief of Arrah, capture of Jagdespur, actions at Almora and Khiri. Desp. L.G. 13 Oct. 1857, 31 Jan. and 22 Feb. 1859, medal. Afghanistan, 1879, medal. N.-E. Frontier, Akha, 1883-84.

1642. **Jones, Hugh Davies.** *b.* Mar. 1828. M.R.C.S. 1854. L.S.A. 1854. A.S. 20 May 1854. Surg. 20 May 1866. *d.* at Barrackpur, 16 Sept. 1868. Indian Mutiny, 1857-58.

1643. **Jones, Arthur Trefusis.** *b.* 11 Aug. 1831, at Malta. M.D. Ed. 1853. M.R.C.S. 1853. A.S. A.M.D. 1853-54. A.S. Bengal, 1 June 1854. Resigned, Sept. 1855 ; (G.O. 21 Aug. 1855).

1644. **Clark, William Falconer.** *b.* 8 Apr. 1830. King's Coll. Lond. M.R.C.S. 1853. L.S.A. 1854. A.S. 4 June 1854. Resigned, 13 Dec. 1864. *d.* at Dorking, 13 Feb. 1906. N.-W. Frontier, Miranzai, 1854 ; Bozdar, 1857. Indian Mutiny, 1857-58, siege and capture of Delhi, actions at Najafgarh, Bulandshahr, and Agra, second relief of Lucknow, Nov. 1857, action at Cawnpur, final siege and capture of Lucknow, Mar. 1858, medal with three clasps.

1645. **Halls, John James.** *b.* 1 Sept. 1820. B.A. Cantab. 18—. M.R.C.S. 1846. F.R.C.S. 1850. A.S. 10 June 1854. *d.* on board S.S. ' Ceylon,' on passage to Europe, 6 Nov. 1860. Indian Mutiny, 1857-58, defence of Arrah, medal. Author of Two Months in Arrah in 1857, 1860.

1646. **Waghorn, Albert Richard.** *b.* Aug. 1829. M.R.C.S. 1854. A.S. 22 June 1854. Surg. 31 May 1866. L.S.A. 1872. M.D. St. A. 1873. S.M. 1 July 1873. R. 1 Mar. 1876. *d.* at Redhill, 6 Feb. 1895. Indian Mutiny, 1857-58, siege and capture of Delhi, medal with clasp. N.-E. Frontier, Bhutan, 1865-66, medal.

1647. **Dukes, Frederick Farmer.** *b.* 2 Jan. 1821. M.R.C.S. 1843. A.S. 24 June 1854. *d.* at Raniganj, 19 Mar. 1860.

* P. W. Sutherland was the last I.M.S. survivor who had served in the Mutiny.

1648. **Dillon, Thomas.** *b.* Feb. 1829. M.B. Mar. Coll. Ab. 1854. L.R.C.S. Ed. 18—. A.S. 28 June 1854. Surg. 28 June 1866. *d.* at Allahabad, 3 June 1869. Indian Mutiny, 1857-58, medal.

1649. **Bizzett, William Weddel.** *b.* 5 June 1832, at Port Royal, Jamaica. M.D. Ed. 1853. M.R.C.S. 1854. A.S. 20 July 1854. *d.* at Mian Mir, 24 Aug. 1856.

1650. **Watson, William.** *b.* 19 Mar. 1832. M.A. 1850; M.B. 1853; Mar. Coll. Ab. A.S. 1 Aug. 1854. Surg. 1 Aug. 1866. M.D. Ab. 1870. S.M. 1 July 1873. B.S. 27 Nov. 1879. R. 21 Dec. 1883. *d.* at Corstorphine, Midlothian, 16 June 1912. Indian Mutiny, 1857-58, operations at Agra, wounded slightly in head at Sasia. Author of Plants of Kumaon.

1651. **Cowie, Alexander John.** *b.* 12 May 1832. St. George's. M.R.C.S. 1854. A.S. 4 Aug. 1854. Surg. 4 Aug. 1866. S.M. 1 July 1873. B.S. 27 Nov. 1879. D.S.G. 19 Apr. 1884. R. 9 Apr. 1889. *d.* in London, 6 Apr. 1890.

1652. **Wilson, Charles Cooper Watson.** *b.* Dec. 1830. M.R.C.S. 1854. L.S.A. 1854. A.S. 26 Aug. 1854. Surg. 26 Aug. 1866. *d.* at Agra, 15 Jan. 1873. N.-W. Frontier, Miranzai, 1855.

1653. **Bellew, Patrick Francis.** *b.* 12 Aug. 1832. M.R.C.S. 1854. L.S.A. 1854. A.S. 6 Sept. 1854. Surg. 6 Sept. 1866. S.M. 1 July 1873. R. 1 Dec. 1882. *d.* 16 May 1909. Brother of H. W. Bellew, No. 1706, infra. Sonthal Insurrection, 1855-56.

1654. **Robinson, Henry William.** *b.* Jan. 1830. B.A., T.C.D., 1852. L.R.C.S.I. 1854. A.S. 7 Sept. 1854. Resigned, 28 Dec. 1863. Afterwards in practice in London, till 1871 at least. *d.* at Forest Gate, Essex, 10 Feb. 1883. China, 1860-61.

1655. **Palmer, William John.** *b.* May 1826. King's Coll. Lond. M.R.C.S. 1853. A.S. 7 Sept. 1854. Gained commission as a prize at King's Coll. on nomination of W. B. Bayley. Surg. 7 Sept. 1866. F.R.C.S. 1868. M.D. St. A. 1868. S.M. 1 July 1873. R. 10 June 1881. *d.* in London, 26 Aug. 1896. Author of Rough Notes on Skin diseases met with in Calcutta, 1873; Dhatura and Aconite.

1656. **Tomkyns, Alexander Pakyngton.** *b.* 29 May 1832. M.R.C.S. 1853. A.S. 20 Sept. 1854. Surg. 20 Sept. 1866. S.M. 1 July 1873. *d.* at Bareli, 7 Nov. 1877. Indian Mutiny, 1857-58, with Hariana Field Force under Genl. Van Cortlandt, medal.

1657. **Pringle, Robert.** *b.* 15 Feb. 1832. M.D. Ed. 1854. L.R.C.S. Ed. 1854. A.S. 4 Oct. 1854. Surg. 4 Oct. 1866. S.M. 1 July 1873. R. 8 Dec. 1884. *d.* at Blackheath, 13 Jan. 1899. Author of Enteric Fever in India, 1891; Efficient Vaccination, 1892.

1658. **FitzGerald, Augustin Ernest.** *b.* 29 Mar. 1820. M.R.C.S. 1849. A.S. 3 Nov. 1854. F.R.C.S. Ed. 1859. Surg. 3 Nov. 1866. R. 6 Jan. 1871. *d.* at Brighton, 5 Apr. 1888. Indian Mutiny, 1857-58, advance on Cawnpur, relief of Lucknow, second defence of Lucknow, Sept. to Nov. 1857.

1659. **MacNamara, Nottidge Charles.** *b.* 14 Oct. 1832. M.R.C.S. 1854. A.S. 4 Nov. 1854. Surg. 4 Nov. 1866. S.M. 1 July 1873. F.R.C.S. 1875. R. 15 Apr. 1876. F.R.C.S.I. 1877. Surgeon and Lecturer on Clinical Surgery, Westminster Hospital, 1874 ; Surgeon Westminster Ophthalmic Hospital, 1875 ; Member of Council, R.C.S. England, 1885–1901 ; Vice-President, 1893 and 1896. *d.* at Rickmansworth, 21 Nov. 1918. Sonthal Insurrection, 1855–56. Author of Lectures on Diseases of the Eye, 1866, 4th edition, 1882, as Manual of Diseases of the Eye ; Asiatic Cholera, 1870 ; History of Asiatic Cholera, 1876, (with Supplement up-to-date, 1892) ; Lectures on Diseases of Bone, 1878, became Diseases of Bones and Joints, 3rd edition, 1887 ; Physical defects which disqualify candidates for Government Service, 1894 ; The Story of an Irish Sept. 1900 ; Origin and character of the British People, 1900 ; Craniology, the Hunterian Oratim, 1901 ; Human Speech, 1908 ; Evolution and Function of purposive living matter, 1910 ; Instinct and Intelligence, 1915 ; Articles on Cholera and Leprosy in Davidson's Diseases and Hygiene of Warm Climates, 1893 ; and on Cholera Asiatica, Choleraic Diarrhœa, and Tetanus, in Quain's Dictionary of Medicine, 1882 ; edited Indian Medical Gazette, 1871–73.

1660. **Clark, John Andrew.** *b.* 20 Sept. 1826. M.R.C.S. 1852. A.S. 4 Dec. 1854. Resigned, 25 Oct. 1858. L.R.C.P. Ed. 1860. Afterwards in practice in London. *d.* at Ayr, 3 Mar. 1887. Indian Mutiny, 1857–58, Rajputana Field Force.

1661. **Loch, James Henry.** *b.* 21 Sept. 1832. M.D. Ed. 1853. A.S. 20 Dec. 1854. Surg. 20 Dec. 1866. S.M. 1 July 1873. B.S. 27 Nov. 1879. D.S.G. 1 Jan. 1884. R. 1 Jan. 1889. *d.* at Guildford, 9 Apr. 1918. Father of E. A. Loch, I.M.S. 1902, Genl. List, No. 189. Indian Mutiny, 1857–58, operations in Bihar, relief of Azamgarh, medal.

1662. **Rouse, Robert.** *b.* 6 Nov. 1832. St. George's. M.R.C.S. 1854. A.S. 20 Dec. 1854. Surg. 20 Dec. 1866. S.M. 1 July 1873. B.S. 27 Nov. 1879. R. 1 Sept. 1885. *d.* at Reigate, 20 Jan. 1910.

1663. **Smith, Clement Madeley.** *b.* Dec. 1827. M.R.C.S. 1849. L.S.A. 1849. M.D. St. A. 1849. A.S. 20 Dec. 1854. Resigned, 25 Aug. 1861. *d.* at Torquay, 22 Mar. 1907.

1664. **Annesley, John Charles.** *b.* July 1832. St. George's. M.R.C.S. 1854. A.S. 30 Dec. 1854, gained commission as a prize at St. George's, on nomination of R. D. Mangles. Surg. 30 Dec. 1866. S.M. 1 July 1873. *d.* at Cheltenham, 8 Feb. 1874.

1665. **Clarke, Thomas Fernandez** (d). *b.* 9 Aug. 1828. Charing Cross. M.R.C.S. 1853. L.S.A. 1853. M.D. St. A. 1853. A.S. 30 Dec. 1854. Never joined. Forfeited appointment, struck off, 1855 ; (A.S. Certs. vol. xxxviii). G. K. Poole, No. 1681, infra, got his place. Subsequently in practice at Wantage, Berks., and Medl. Officer, Wantage Union.

1855

1666. **Jackson, James Rawlinson.** *b.* 22 Dec. 1832. M.D. Ed. 1854. A.S. 4 Jan. 1855. Took place of J. N. Waugh, No. 1545, supra, who declined appointment. Surg. 4 Jan. 1867. S.M. 1 July 1873. B.S. 27 Nov. 1879. R. 3 Dec. 1883. Killed by a shooting accident at Kirkbuddo, Forfarshire, 1 Sept. 1887. Son of W. Jackson, No. 706, supra, 1813. N.-W. Frontier, Miranzai, 1855 ; Kurram Valley, 1856 ; Bozdar, 1857 ; Waziri, 1859. Indian Mutiny, 1857–58, siege and capture of Delhi, operations in Rohilkand, capture of Barcli, medal with clasp.

1667. Garden, Archibald MacDonald. b. 26 May 1832. M.R.C.S. 1854. M.D. 18—. A.S. 11 Jan. 1855. Surg. 11 Jan. 1867. S.M. 1 July 1873. B.S. 27 Nov. 1879. R. 26 Jan. 1881. d. at Guildford, 17 Dec. 1887. Son of A. Garden, No. 749, supra, 1815.

1668. Amesbury, Samuel Cornwallis. b. 21 Nov. 1832. Middlesex Hosp. and King's Coll. Lond. M.R.C.S. 1854. A.S. 14 Jan. 1855. L.R.C.P. Ed. 1860. F.R.C.S. Ed. 1866. Surg. 11 Jan. 1867. S.M. 1 July 1873. B.S. 3 Dec. 1883. R. extra pension, 30 Apr. 1890. d. at Dehra Dun, 8 Nov. 1916. Brother of J. W. R. Amesbury, No. 1572, supra. N.-W. Frontier, Hazara, 1868. Author of Manual of Treatment of Children in India.

1669. Bartrum, Robert Henry. b. 16 Aug. 1831. Guy's. M.R.C.S. 1854. L.S.A. 1854. A.S. 14 Jan. 1855; gained commission as a prize at Guy's, on nomination of J. Masterman. Indian Mutiny, 1857, Relief of Lucknow, killed in action, 26 Sept. 1857, the day on which the Residency was relieved. His wife was in the Residency throughout the siege, and published an account of the siege entitled, A Widow's Reminiscences of the siege of Lucknow, 1858.

1670. Hadow, Gilbert Bethune. b. 15 Aug. 1832. M.R.C.S. 1854. A.S. 20 Jan. 1855. Surg. 20 Jan. 1867. S.M. 1 July 1873. d. at Aligarh, 31 July 1876. Indian Mutiny, 1857-58, Defence of Lucknow, Desp. L.G. 17 Feb. 1858, medal with clasp, and one year's service.

1671. Cheek, George Nicholas. b. 20 Dec. 1831. Guy's. M.R.C.S. 1854. A.S. 20 Jan. 1855. Surg. 20 Jan. 1867. d. at Norwood, 16 Oct. 1869. Son of G. N. Cheek, No. 773, supra, 1816; and brother of A. H. Cheek, No. 1339, supra, 1840. Indian Mutiny, 1857-58, Central India campaign, capture of Kalpi and Gwalior, medal.

*1672. Chuckerbutty, Soorjo Coomar Goodeve. b. 1826. Calcutta and Univ. Coll. Lond. L.M.S. Calcutta. M.R.C.S. 1848. M.B. and M.D. Lond. 1849. Uncovd. Medl. Service, Bengal, 10 May 1850 to 1854. A.S. 24 Jan. 1855. Surg. 24 Jan. 1867. S.M. 1 July 1873. d. in London, 29 Sept. 1874. Author of Pathology of Dysentery, 1865; Lectures on subjects of Indian interest, 1870; edited 4th edition of Goodeve's Hints on Children in India.

1673. Brake, John. b. 6 Dec. 1827. St. Thomas'. M.R.C.S. 1853. L.S.A. 1853. A.S. 24 Jan. 1855. Surg. 24 Jan. 1867. S.M. 1 July 1873. B.S. 27 Nov. 1879. D.S.G. 29 Mar. 1885. R. 2 Sept. 1886. d. at Southsea, 8 Feb. 1893. Indian Mutiny, 1857-59, siege and capture of Delhi, operations in Oudh and Rohilkand, action at Biswa, pursuit of Firuzshah; Desp. L.G. 25 July 1859, wounded.

1674. Hill, Marcus George. b. 1829. St. George's. M.R.C.S. 1853. L.S.A. 1853. A.S. 24 Jan. 1855. Indian Mutiny, 1857, killed by mutineers, Sitapur, 2 June 1857.

1675. Mantell, Alfred Adams. b. 1830. London Hosp. M.R.C.S. 1852. M.D. St. A. 1852. L.S.A. 1852. A.S. 24 Jan. 1855. Surg. 24 Jan. 1867. S.M. 1 July 1873. R. 5 Jan. 1877. d. at Bathampton, Bath, 22 Aug. 1911.

---

* S. C. G. Chuckerbutty was the first Indian to enter the Service. He was also the first man appointed to Bengal by competitive exam., passing second, in the first competitive exam. held, in Jan. 1855. George Marr, who passed first, went to Madras; (M. No. 1203). A few appointments by nomination continued to be made, during the next 3½ years; M.S. Scaulan, No. 1802, infra, being the last, on 11 Aug. 1858.

1676. **Collison, John Bowmer.** *b.* 1829. St. George's. M.R.C.S. 1854. A.S. 24 Jan. 1855. Surg. 24 Jan. 1867. S.M. 1 July 1873. R. 5 Apr. 1875. *d.* 5 Sept. 1883. Indian Mutiny, 1857–58, second relief of Lucknow, Nov. 1857, action at Cawnpur, operations in Oudh, medal.

1677. **King, John Bishop.** *b.* 1829. Guy's. M.R.C.S. 1853. L.S.A. 1853. M.D. St. A. 1855. A.S. 24 Jan. 1855. Surg. 24 Jan. 1867. S.M. 1 July 1873. R. 26 Apr. 1874. *d.* 27 Jan. 1900.

1678. **Morgan, Arthur.** *b.* 1828. L.R.C.S.I. 18—. L.A.H. 18—. A.S. 24 Jan. 1855. *d.* at Barrackpur, 10 Nov. 1861. Sonthal Insurrection, 1855–56. Indian Mutiny, 1857–58.

1679. **Brown, John.** *b.* 1829. M.D. Ed. 18—. L.R.C.S. Ed. 18—. A.S. 24 Jan. 1855. *d.* in Calcutta, 13 Nov. 1863; (Army List, tombstone in Scottish burial-ground gives date as 1 Nov. 1863). Indian Mutiny, 1857–58, advance on Cawnpur, first relief of Lucknow, Sept. 1857 second defence of Lucknow, Sept. to Nov. 1857, final siege and capture of Lucknow, Mar. 1858 Desp., medal with two clasps.

1680. **Reed, Augustus Keppel.** *b.* 7 Oct. 1832. Asst. Surg. R.N. 9 Mar. 1854 to 14 Feb. 1855. A.S. Bengal, 28 Feb. 1855. Surg. 28 Feb. 1867. S.M. 1 July 1873. *d.* at Jhilam, 7 June 1881. Baltic, 1854, as Asst. Surg. H.M.S. 'Conflict.' Indian Mutiny, 1857, medal.

1681. **Poole, George Kenneth.** *b.* Mar. 1832. London Hosp. M.R.C.S. 1855. A.S. 14 Mar. 1855. Took the place of T. F. Clarke, No. 1666, supra. M.D. Erlangen, 1863. Surg. 14 Mar. 1867. S.M. 1 July 1873. R. 7 Mar. 1876. *d.* at Upper Norwood, 19 Dec. 1919.

1682. **Edwards, Thomas Nelson.** *b.* Dec. 1831. Bart's. M.R.C.S. 1854. L.S.A. 1854. A.S. 14 Mar. 1855. *d.* in Presy. Genl. Hosp. Calcutta, 16 June 1855.

1683. **Garden, Alexander.** *b.* 18 Mar. 1833. St. George's. M.R.C.S. 1854. M.D. St. A. 1854. A.S. 28 Mar. 1855. Surg. 28 Mar. 1867. S.M. 1 July 1873. B.S. 27 Nov. 1879. R. extra pension, 18 Apr. 1888. *d.* at Hampstead, 14 Sept. 1889. Indian Mutiny, 1857–58, with Bengal Yeomanry Cavalry, final siege and capture of Lucknow, March 1858.

1684. **Wylie, John Dick.** *b.* 23 Nov. 1825. Charing Cross Hosp. M.D. St. A. 1847. A.S. 4 Apr. 1855. *d.* at Naini Tal, 19 Feb. 1866.

1685. **Walker, William.** *b.* 28 Nov. 1832. M.A. 1853; M.D. 1855; Mar. Coll. Ab. L.R.C.S. Ed. 1855. A.S. 4 Aug. 1855. Surg. 4 Aug. 1867. F.R.C.S. Ed. 1870. S.M. 1 July 1873. B.S. 27 Nov. 1879. D.S.G. 24 Oct. 1882. R. 31 Oct. 1889. *d.* at Dulwich, 10 Oct. 1893. LL.D. Ab. 1885. G.S.P. 21 Aug. 1887. Q.H.P. 10 Sept. 1890. Indian Mutiny, 1857–58, operations against Nimach and Indore mutineers, medal. Author of Angling in the Kumaon Lakes.

1686. **Brettingham, Charles.** *b.* 12 Oct. 1829. M.R.C.S. 1850. L.S.A. 1851. A.S. 4 Aug. 1855. Resigned, 4 July 1863.

1687. **Watson, George Alder.** *b.* 18 June 1831. Guy's. M.R.C.S. 1853. L.S.A. 1853. Acting A.S. A.M.D. 1854–55. A.S. 4 Aug. 1855. Surg. 4 Aug. 1867. S.M. 1 July 1873. B.S. 27 Nov. 1879. R. 7 Dec. 1885. *d.* at Cheltenham, 12 Jan. 1915. Crimea, 1854–55. Indian Mutiny, 1857–58, operations in Central India, medal with clasp. Afghanistan, 1879, advance on Kandahar and Kelat-i-Ghilzai, medal.

1688. Kendall, Bernard. b. 21 June 1831. M.R.C.S. 1853. L.S.A. 1853. A.S. 4 Aug. 1855. Surg. 4 Aug. 1867. S.M. 1 July 1873. R. 22 Sept. 1879. d. at Upper Norwood, 3 Sept. 1912. Indian Mutiny, 1857–58.

1689. Stewart, John Lindsay. b. 13 Dec. 1831. M.D. Glas. 1853. L.R.C.S. Ed. 18—. A.S. 4 Aug. 1855. Surg. 4 Aug. 1867. S.M. 1 July 1873. d. at Dalhousie, 5 July 1873. Indian Mutiny, 1857–58, siege and capture of Delhi, medal. Author of Panjab Plants, 1869; Report on Deodar tracts of the Bias, 1865; Report on Deodar Forests of Bissahir, 1865; Report on Deodar Forests on Chenab and Ravi, 1866: Report on Forests in Panjab, 1868; Forest Flora of North West and Central India, 1874.

1690. Mathew, Theobald Mark. b. 25 Apr. 1833. B.A., T.C.D., 1854. L.R.C.S.I. 18—. A.S. 4 Aug. 1855. Surg. 4 Aug. 1867. S.M. 1 July 1873. B.S. 27 Nov. 1879. R. 24 Apr. 1884. d. at Bruges, 22 Mar. 1887. Father of C. M. Mathew, M. No. 1546. Author of Hills and Plains (a novel), 1861.

*1691. Fairweather, James. b. 19 Oct. 1828. M.D. Ed. 1851. L.R.C.S. Ed. 1851. A.S. 4 Aug. 1855. Surg. 4 Aug. 1867. S.M. 1 July 1873. B.S. 27 Nov. 1879. R. extra pension, 19 Oct. 1886. d. at St. Heliers, Jersey, 29 Apr. 1917. N.-W. Frontier, Bozdar, 1857; Yusufzai, 1857. Indian Mutiny, 1857–58, siege and capture of Delhi; actions at Bulandshahr, Aligarh, and Agra; second relief of Lucknow, Nov. 1857; action at Cawnpur, final siege and capture of Lucknow, Mar. 1858; operations in Rohilkand, action of Aliganj, capture of Bareli, medal with three clasps.

1692. Hayes, John Boon. b. 19 Aug. 1826. M.D. K.C. Ab. 1852. M.R.C.S. 1848. A.S. 4 Aug. 1855. d. in Calcutta, 18 July 1856.

1693. Hood, David. b. 9 Feb. 1831. M.R.C.S. 18—. M.D. Ed. 1853. A.S. 4 Aug. 1855. d. in London, 2 June 1867. Indian Mutiny, 1857–58. Author of Report on Typhoid Continued Fever in Boolundshuhur, 1862.

*1694. Jackson, Charles Julian Joseph. b. 21 Apr. 1831. King's Coll. Lond. M.R.C.S. 1853. A.S. 4 Aug. 1855. Surg. 4 Aug. 1867. S.M. 1 July 1873. B.S. 10 Jan. 1881. R. extra pension, 31 Mar. 1887. d. at Nice, 16 Jan. 1895. Indian Mutiny, 1857–58, operations in Oudh.

1695. Kirk, John. b. 17 Dec. 1830. M.D. Ed. 1852. L.R.C.S. Ed. 18—. A.S. 4 Aug. 1855. d. at Attock, 21 July 1857.

1696. Bird, Robert. b. 17 July 1832. M.D. Ed. 1854. L.R.C.S. Ed. 18—. A.S. 4 Aug. 1855. Brevet-Surgeon, 7 Sept. 1858. Surg. 4 Aug. 1867. S.M. 1 July 1873. B.S. 26 Jan. 1881. R. 12 May 1881. d. at Cobham, Virginia, U.S.A. 31 Oct. 1890. Indian Mutiny, 1857, defence of Lucknow, Desp. of Brig.-Genl. Inglis, 26 Sept. 1857, L.G. 16 Jan. 1858, medal with clasp, Brevet-Surgeon, and one year's service for defence of Lucknow.

1697. Duncan, Archibald Alexander. b. 14 Feb. 1830. B.A., M.B., T.C.D. 1854. L.R.C.S.I. 18—. A.S. 4 Aug. 1855. d. at sea, on board S.S. 'Calcutta,' 13 Mar. 1858.

---

* J. Fairweather and C. J. J. Jackson were the first two officers to receive " extra compensation pensions " on retirement. These pensions were given by I.A.C., June 1886, clause 91, with effect from the financial year, 1886–87, as compensation for loss of promotion, when the Sanitary Deputy Surgeon Generalships were abolished. Four were given each year, two in Bengal, one each in Madras and Bombay. Only officers who entered the Service before the end of the year 1889 were eligible for these pensions. v. Hist. of I.M.S. i. p. 451.

1698. **Coates, John Martin.** *b.* 6 July 1832. Q.C. Belfast, M.D. Q.U.I. 1855. L.F.P.S.G. 18—. A.S. 4 Aug. 1855. Surg. 4 Aug. 1867. S.M. 1 July 1873. B.S. 12 May 1881. R. extra pension, 6 July 1890. *d.* in Calcutta, 18 July 1895. Indian Mutiny, 1857, operations in Bihar, medal. Author of Vocabulary of seven Languages or Dialects of Chota Nagpore, 1875.

1699. **Thom, Henry.** *b.* 14 July 1831. M.D. Ed. 1852. L.R.C.S. Ed. 18—. A.S. 4 Aug. 1855. Surg. 4 Aug. 1867. S.M. 1 July 1873. *d.* at Lahore, 11 Nov. 1879. N.-W. Frontier, Bozdar, 1857. Indian Mutiny, 1857–58, operations in Oudh, medal.

1700. **Sillifant, Francis Synge.** *b.* 2 July 1832. M.R.C.S. 1854. A.S. 4 Aug. 1855. Surg. 4 Aug. 1867. S.M. 1 July 1873. R. 1 July 1874. *d.* in England, 26 July 1894. Indian Mutiny, 1857–58, medal. N.-E. Frontier, Khasia and Jainthia Hills, 1863.

1701. **Penhall, John Thomas.** *b.* 28 Mar. 1833. St. Thomas'. M.R.C.S. 1855. L.S.A. 1855. A.S. 4 Aug. 1855. Resigned, 5 Mar. 1856. F.R.C.S. 1873. M.D. St. A. 1876. In practice at St. Leonard's, and Surgeon, East Sussex Infirmary. *d.* at Broadway, Worcestershire, 14 July 1916.

1702. **MacAuley, Daniel.** *b.* 1 Aug. 1830. Q.C. Belfast. M.D. Q.U.I. 18—. L.R.C.S. Ed. 18—. A.S. 4 Aug. 1855. Indian Mutiny, 1857; killed by mutineers, Cawnpur, 15 July 1857.

*1703. **Planck, Charles.** *b.* 1 Mar. 1831. Guy's. M.R.C.S. 1855. L.S.A. 1855. A.S. 4 Aug. 1855. Surg. 4 Aug. 1867. S.M. 1 July 1873. D.S.G. 4 Aug. 1881. F.R.C.S. Ed. 1881. R. 4 Aug. 1886. M.R.C.P. Lond. 1888. *d.* at Edenbridge, Kent, 23 Aug. 1918. Name spelt Plank in S.A.L.M.B. Indian Mutiny, 1857–58, second relief of Lucknow, Nov. 1857, action at Cawnpur, medal.

1704. **Carter, Frederick.** *b.* 25 Mar. 1830. M.R.C.S. 1852. A.S. 4 Aug. 1855. Surg. 4 Aug. 1867. S.M. 1 July 1873. R. 25 Apr. 1877. *d.* at Marden Ash, Ongar, 24 Jan. 1916. Indian Mutiny, 1857, medal.

1705. **Hayes, William Henry.** *b.* 27 Nov. 1833. M.R.C.S. 1855. A.S. 4 Aug. 1855. Surg. 4 Aug. 1867. S.M. 1 July 1873. R. 16 Apr. 1878. *d.* at Farnham, Surrey, 8 Sept. 1914. Served in Bengal Commission, 1858–78. Indian Mutiny, 1857–58, Kol rising, operations in Chota Nagpur, wounded near Chaibasa, 14 Jan. 1858.

*1706. **Bellew, Henry Walter** (e). *b.* 30 Aug. 1833. St. George's. M.R.C.S. 1854. L.S.A. 1854. Acting A.S. A.M.D. 24 Nov. 1854. A.S. 12 Jan. 1855. Resigned, 6 Oct. 1855. A.S. Bengal, 14 Nov. 1855. Surg. 14 Nov. 1867. S.M. 1 July 1873. D.S.G. 14 Nov. 1881. R. 14 Nov. 1886. *d.* at Farnham Royal, Bucks., 26 July, 1892. Brother of P. F. Bellew, No. 1653, supra. C.S.I. 6 Feb. 1873. Crimea, 1854–55. N.-W. Frontier, second Yusufzai, Ambeyla, 1863–64. Afghanistan, 1878–79, attack on Sherpur, medal with clasp. Author of Journal of a Political Mission to Afghanistan under Col. Lumsden in 1857, 1862; Report on the Eusufzais, 1864; Pukhto Grammar, 1867; Pukhto Dictionary, 1867; Our Punjab Frontier (anonymous, by a Punjab official), 1868; The Mission to Seistan under Genl. Pollock, 1873; From Indus to Tigris, 1874; Kashmir and Kashgar, 1875; General description of Karhgaria, 1875; History of Kashgaria, 1875; Afghanistan and the Afghans, 1879; The races of Afghanistan, 1880; A new Afghan Question, are the Afghans Israelites? 1881; History of Cholera in India, 1862 to 1881, 1882; Nature, Causes, and treatment of Cholera, 1887; Ethnography of Afghanistan, 1891.

* C. Planck and H. W. Bellew were the only two " Sanitary Deputy Surgeons General " in Bengal.

1707. Smith, David Boyes. *b.* 19 Nov. 1833. M.D. Ed. 1835. L.R.C.S. Ed. 1835. A.S. 28 Nov. 1855. Surg. 28 Nov. 1867. S.M. 1 July 1873. M.R.C.P. Lond. 1877. R. 1 Mar. 1882. F.R.C.P. Lond. 1885. Professor of Military Medicine Army Medl. School, Netley, 1885–89. *d.* at Woolstone, Southampton, 3 June 1889. Indian Mutiny, 1857–59; present at Meerut at first outbreak of Mutiny, 10 May 1857; actions of Hindun Nadi and Badli-ka-Sarai, siege and capture of Delhi; final siege and capture of Lucknow, Mar. 1858; operations in Rohilkand, capture of Bareli, actions at Mohumdi and Sasia Ghat, medal with two clasps. Author of The Pilgrimage to Juggernauth in 1868, 1869; The Drainage and Conservancy of Calcutta, 1869; first editor of Indian Medical Gazette, 1866.

1856

1708. Gayer, Edward John. *b.* 22 Dec. 1833. L.R.C.S.I. 18—. A.S. 2 Jan. 1856. Surg. 2 Jan. 1868. S.M. 1 July 1873. *d.* in Calcutta, 12 Aug. 1878. Indian Mutiny, 1857–58, advance on Cawnpur, first relief of Lucknow, Sept. 1857; second defence of Lucknow, Sept. to Dec. 1857, action at Cawnpur, medal with clasp.

1709. Thornton, James Howard. *b.* 7 Jan. 1834. King's Coll. Lond. B.A. 1854; M.B. 1855, Lond. M.R.C.S. 1855. A.S. 9 Jan. 1856, gained commission as a prize at King's College on nomination of Hon. W. H. L. Melville. Surg. 9 Jan. 1868. S.M. 1 July 1873. B.S. 1 Mar. 1882. D.S.G. 30 June 1886. R. 13 Aug. 1891. *d.* at Hove, 6 Jan. 1919. C.B. 25 Aug. 1885. G.S.P. 8 Dec. 1886. K.C.B. 24 June 1904. Indian Mutiny, 1857–59, Action of Benares, relief of Arrah, capture of Jagdespur; action of Surajpur, defence of Alambagh, final siege and capture of Lucknow, Mar. 1858, operations in Oudh and Gorakhpur; Desp. L.G. 13 Oct. 1857, medal with two clasps, one year's service for Lucknow. China, 1860, action of Sinho, capture of Taku forts, occupation of Pekin, medal with two clasps. N.-E. Frontier, Khasia and Jainthia Hills, 1862–63, capture of several stockades, wounded; Bhutan, 1865–66, forcing of Duranga pass, capture and recapture of Dewangiri, medal with clasp. Egypt, 1882, medal, bronze star. Sudan, 1885; Suakin, as P.M.O. of Indian contingent, Desp. L.G. 25 Aug. 1885, clasp, C.B. N.-W. Frontier, Hazara, 1888, as P.M.O. Desp. clasp. Author of Memories of Seven Campaigns, 1895.

*1710. Steuart, James Frederick. *b.* 2 Oct. 1832. M.D. Ed. 1853. Acting A.S. A.M.D. 7 Apr. 1854. Resigned, 23 Feb. 1856. A.S. Bengal, 20 Feb. 1856. *d.* at Agra, 21 July 1861. Name given as Stewart in his birth cert., but his signature is Steuart; (A.S. Certs. vol. xxxix. 1854). Crimea, 1854–55, with 28th Foot. Indian Mutiny, 1857–58.

1711. Darby, Edmund. *b.* 2 May 1833. M.R.C.S. 1854. M.D. St. A. 1855. A.S. 20 Feb. 1856. Indian Mutiny, 1857; first and second defence of Lucknow, Desp. of Brig.-Genl. Inglis, 27 Sept. 1857, L.G. 16 Jan. 1858. *d.* of wounds of head in Residency, Lucknow, 27 Oct. 1857.

1712. Powell, Frank. *b.* 30 Oct. 1830. Bart's. L.S.A. 1853. M.R.C.S. 1854. M.B. Lond. 1855. A.S. 20 Feb. 1856. Surg. 20 Feb. 1868. S.M. 1 July 1873. R. 12 May 1874. *d.* at Redhill, 9 May 1912. Indian Mutiny, 1857–59, Bozdar campaign, operations in Gorakhpur, medal.

* This officer's name, including the uncommon spelling Steuart, is exactly the same as that of No. 940, supra, 1822, James Frederick Steuart. The former, however, was not the son of the latter; he may have been a nephew. His father was Robert Steuart, writer to the Signet, Edinburgh.

1713. **Dixon, Edward Livesey.** *b.* 14 Feb. 1831. St. Thomas'. M.R.C.S. 1854. L.S.A. 1854. A.S. 20 Feb. 1856. Resigned, 19 Nov. 1859. L.R.C.P. Lond. 1862. M.R.C.P. Lond. 1876. M.D. St. A. 1876. In practice at Preston, and Hony. Medl. Officer, Preston and County of Lancs. Royal Infirmary. *d.* at Preston, 31 Mar. 1890.

1714. **Ince, John.** *b.* 10 Mar. 1830. Guy's. M.R.C.S. 1854. L.S.A. 1854. M.D. St. A. 1855. A.S. 20 Feb. 1856. Surg. 20 Feb. 1868. S.M. 1 July 1873. R. 31 Mar. 1878. *d.* at Swanley, Kent, 23 Aug. 1911. Indian Mutiny, 1857–58, Sagar Field Force, pursuit of Tantia Topi, operations in Central India, medal. N.-W. Frontier, second Yusufzai, 1863–64, third Yusufzai, 1866. Author of Kashmir Handbook, 1867, fourth edition, revised by J. Duke (No. 1996, infra), 1888; fifth edition, rewritten by A. Neve, 1899; Murree Directory, 1869; Murree Handbook, 1870.

1715. **Pettingal, Frederick James.** *b.* 16 Mar. 1828. L.M.S. Calcutta, 1848. Sub-Asst. Surg. Bengal, 1 Nov. 1848–56. M.R.C.S. 1855. A.S. 20 Feb. 1856. Surg. 20 Feb. 1868. *d.* at Clapham, 24 Jan. 1869. Second Sikh or Panjab war, 1848–49, battle of Chilianwala, medal with clasp.

1716. **Jones, John.** *b.* 17 Jan. 1830. M.R.C.S. 1853. M.D. St. A. 1856. A.S. 20 Feb. 1856. M.R.C.P. Lond. 1860. Surg. 20 Feb. 1868. S.M. 1 July 1873. B.S. 1 Apr. 1882. Member Medl. Board, India Office, 18 July 1882 to 31 Dec. 1884. R. 17 Jan. 1885. *d.* in London, 8 Aug. 1911. Indian Mutiny, 1857–58.

1717. **Browne, James.** *b.* 18 Aug. 1828. T.C.D. and Park St. School, Dublin. L.R.C.S.I. 1853. B.A. 1850; M.D. 1873; T.C.D. A.S. 20 Feb. 1856. Surg. 20 Feb. 1868. S.M. 1 July 1873. B.S. 3 Aug. 1882. R. 18 Aug. 1886. *d.* at Shanklin, Isle of Wight, 9 Mar. 1908. Indian Mutiny, 1857–58. Afghanistan, 1878–79, medal.

1718. **Bateson, Robert Sander.** *b.* 13 Nov. 1832. St. Thomas' and King's Coll. London. M.R.C.S. 1854. L.S.A. 1854. A.S. 20 Feb. 1856. Surg. 20 Feb. 1868. S.M. 1 July 1873. B.S. 24 Oct. 1882. R. 1 Sept. 1886. *d.* at Lancaster, 24 Oct. 1895. Indian Mutiny, 1857–58, operations at Agra and against Tantia Topi, medal.

1719. **James, William Henry.** *b.* 9 Nov. 1829. M.D. 18—. F.R.C.S.I. 18—. A.S. 20 Feb. 1856. Indian Mutiny, 1857; killed by mutineers at Agar, Central India, 4 July 1857.

1720. **Wright, Thomas Pettit.** *b.* 23 Oct. 1828. M.R.C.S. 1849. L.S.A. 1849. A.S. 20 Feb. 1856. Surg. 20 Feb. 1868. S.M. 1 July 1873. *d.* at Baksa, Bhutan, 28 May 1881. Indian Mutiny, 1857–59, operations on Nipal frontier and in N.W.P., defence of Azamgarh, Desp. medal.

1721. **Chavasse, William Boyle.** *b.* 10 July 1827. M.R.C.S. 1851. L.S.A. 1851. A.S. 20 Feb. 1856. *d.* at Mirat, 2 Nov. 1857. Indian Mutiny, 1857, siege and capture of Delhi.

1722. **Dallas, Alexander Morrison.** *b.* 5 July 1830. Guy's. M.R.C.S. 1855. A.S. 20 Feb. 1856. Surg. 20 Feb. 1868. S.M. 1 July 1873. B.S. 1 Dec. 1882. D.S.G. 9 Sept. 1884. R. extra pension, 2 Apr. 1889. *d.* at Ealing, 9 Nov. 1912. C.I.E. 29 May, 1886. Father of S. A. C. Dallas, M. No. 1527.

1723. **Kilkelly, Charles.** b. 14 Jan. 1830. L.R.C.S.I. 1853. B.A. M.B. T.C.D. 1854. F.R.C.S.I. 1855. A.S. 20 Feb. 1856. Surg. 20 Feb. 1868. S.M. 1 July 1873. B.S. 9 Dec. 1882. R. 14 Oct. 1884. d. in Dublin, 26 July 1907. Father of P. P. Kilkelly, Bo. No. 1118. Indian Mutiny, 1857–58, relief of Lucknow, medal.

1724. **Woodward, Thomas Hewlett.** b. 5 Dec. 1832. L.S.A. 1854. M.R.C.S. 1855. A.S. 20 Feb. 1856. Indian Mutiny, siege of Delhi, killed in action before Delhi, 31 Aug. 1857.

1725. **Poole, Charles Andrew.** b. 22 Sept. 1827. M.R.C.S. 1849. A.S. 18 Mar. 1856. d. at Peshawar, 13 Nov. 1867. Originally passed in list of 4 Aug. 1855, between MacAuley and Planck, but not gazetted till 18 Mar. 1856. Indian Mutiny, 1857–59, operations in Oudh and Rohilkand, reoccupation of Moradabad, capture of Bareli; Desp. 1 Apr. 1859, medal.

1726. **Baillie, Neil Benjamin.** b. 31 Mar. 1834. M.R.C.S. 1855. L.S.A. 1855. A.S. 8 Apr. 1856. Surg. 8 Apr. 1868. S.M. 1 July 1873. d. in London, 28 Jan. 1877. Son of G. Baillie, No. 630, supra, 1808. Brother of G. O. Baillie, No. 1600, supra. Indian Mutiny, 1857–58, siege and capture of Delhi, operations in Oudh and Rohilkand, medal with clasp.

1727. **Wilson, John.** b. 9 Apr. 1834. M.R.C.S. 1855. A.S. 7 May 1856. d. at Rawal Pindi, 27 Mar. 1862. Indian Mutiny, 1858–59, pursuit of Tantia Topi.

1728. **Shircore, Sarkies Michael.** b. 21 Mar. 1827. Calcutta. M.R.C.S. 1848. A.S. 2 July 1856. Surg. 2 July 1868. S.M. 1 July 1873. B.S. 18 Dec. 1883. R. 21 Mar. 1885. d. at Isleworth, 12 Nov. 1900.

1729. **MacKay, Alexander Lockhart.** b. 19 Apr. 1833. Ed. Univ. Bonn, Paris, and Berlin. L.R.C.S. Ed. 1854. A.S. 9 July 1856. Resigned, 24 Mar. 1857. Afterwards in United States and in practice at Achinduich, Ardgay, Scotland. American Civil war, as senior medical officer of Artillery, Army of Tennessee, Confederate States Army; battles of Chickamauga, Atlanta, Jonesborough, Franklin, Nashville, siege of Moville and Spanish Fort; Med. Dir., 1871, where name spelt Mackaye.

1730. **Wise, James Fownes Norton.** b. 18 June 1834. M.D. Ed. 1855. L.R.C.S. Ed. 18—. A.S. 16 July 1856. Surg. 16 Feb. 1868. S.M. 1 July 1873. R. 1 Jan. 1877. d. at Ramsgate, 11 July 1886. Son of T. A. Wise, No. 1105, supra, 1827. Indian Mutiny, 1857–58, siege and capture of Delhi, medal. Author of Notes on the Races, Castes, and Trades of Eastern Bengal, 1883.

1731. **Eddowes, William.** b. 10 Sept. 1827. M.R.C.S. 1850. L.S.A. 1850. A.S. 4 Aug. 1856. Surg. 4 Aug. 1868. S.M. 1 July 1873. d. at Sandymount, 17 Jan. 1880.

1732. **Bryden, James Lumsdaine.** b. 27 June 1833. M.D. Ed. gold medal, 1855. L.R.C.S. Ed. 18—. A.S. 4 Aug. 1856. Surg. 4 Aug. 1868. S.M. 1 July 1873. d. at Norwood, 18 Nov. 1880. Indian Mutiny, 1857–58, siege and capture of Delhi, relief of Lucknow, medal with two clasps. Author of Vital Statistics of the Bengal Presidency; and of numerous reports on Cholera.

1733. **Fryer, Robert.** *b.* 9 Jan. 1834. M.R.C.S. 1856. A.S. 4 Aug. 1856. *d.* in Edinburgh, 28 June 1865. Indian Mutiny, 1857–58, advance on Cawnpur, action of Cawnpur, medal.

1734. **Sherlock, Thomas Travers.** *b.* 16 Apr. 1830. M.R.C.S. 1852. B.A. T.C.D. 1856. A.S. 4 Aug. 1856. Surg. 4 Aug. 1868. S.M. 1 July 1873. R. 13 Feb. 1880. *d.* 5 Dec. 1882. Indian Mutiny, 1857–58, relief of Lucknow, medal.

1735. **Shaw, William Joseph.** *b.* 29 July 1833. M.R.C.S. 1855. A.S. 4 Aug. 1856. Indian Mutiny, 1857, second relief of Lucknow, Dec. 1857. *d.* at Dilkusha, Lucknow, 27 Nov. 1857.

1736. **Kirton, William Henry.** *b.* 1829. M.R.C.S. 1854. A.S. 4 Aug. 1856. Surg. 4 Aug. 1868. S.M. 1 July 1873. B.S. 20 Dec. 1883. R. 7 Dec. 1884. *d.* 17 Dec. 1900.

1737. **Westcott, Robert.** *b.* 21 July 1829. M.R.C.S. 1852. L.S.A. 1853. A.S. 4 Aug. 1856. *d.* at Fatehpur, 1 Oct. 1861. Indian Mutiny, 1857–58, operations in Rohilkand, capture of Bareli, operations in Bandalkund 1859, medal.

1738. **Farrell, George Elias.** *b.* 22 Oct. 1831. Stevens' Hosp., Dublin. F.R.C.S.I. 1856. A.S. 4 Aug. 1856. Surg. 4 Aug. 1868. S.M. 1 July. 1873. B.S. 21 Dec. 1883. D.S.G. 2 Sept. 1886. R. 28 Sept. 1893. *d.* in Dublin, 28 Apr. 1899. C.B. 29 May 1886. G.S.P. 20 Jan. 1889. Indian Mutiny, 1857–58, with Naval Brigade of H.M.S. 'Shannon,' second relief of Lucknow, Nov. 1857, action at Cawnpur, medal with clasp. N.-W. Frontier, Jowaki, 1877–78. Afghanistan, 1879–80, with Kuram Field Force. Burma, 1886–87, Desp. medal.

1739. **Ireland, William Wotherspoon** (e). *b.* 27 Oct. 1832. Ed. Univ. and Paris. M.D. Ed. 1855. A.S. 4 Aug. 1856. Resigned, 1 Aug. 1861. Supt. of Scottish National Institution for imbecile children at Larhert, 1869–79; afterwards Supt. of Asylums at Stirling, Prestonpans, and Polton, successively. *d.* at Musselburgh, 7 May 1909. Indian Mutiny, 1857, actions at Najafgarh and Badli-ki-Sarai, dangerously wounded, was shot through the head, and reported killed; shown as killed in action in the E.I. Regr. and Army List for Jan. 1858; medal with clasp, and three years' leave counted as service. The Lancet of 7 Nov. 1857, states: " A ball had entered the eye, and passed below the brain, coming out near the ear. . . . He had a second wound, though of a less serious character, a ball having entered the shoulder, which was found lodged in his back." Author of History of the Siege of Delhi, 1861; Randolph Methyl (a novel), 1863; What food to eat, 1865; Studies of a wondering Observer, 1867; Idiocy and Imbecility, 1877, enlarged and republished as The Mental Affections of Children, Idiocy, Imbecility and Insanity, 1898; The Blot on the Brain, Studies in History and Psychology, 1885; Through the Ivory Gate, 1889; Golden Bullets, a story in the days of Akbar and Elizabeth, 1890; The Life of Sir Harry Vane the Younger, 1905; and several articles in Hack Tuke's Dictionary of Psychological Medicine.

1740. **Bensley, Charles Egbert Wimond.** *b.* 19 May 1834. M.R.C.S. 1856. M.D. St. A. 1856. A.S. 4 Aug. 1856. Surg. 4 Aug. 1868. S.M. 1 July 1873. R. 8 Dec. 1882. *d.* at North Kensington, 5 Dec. 1909. Father of C. N. Bensley, No. 2226, infra, 1886. Brother of E. C. Bensley, No. 1807, infra, 1859. Indian Mutiny, 1857–58, medal.

1741. FitzPatrick, Thomas. *b.* 10 Feb. 1832. B.A. M.B. C.M. 1856; M.D. 1862; M.A. 1864; T.C.D. A.S. 4 Aug. 1856. Resigned, 24 July 1859. Afterwards in practice in London. M.D. Cantab. 1867. M.R.C.P. Lond. 1868. *d.* in London, June 1900. Author of Chronic Diseases of Liver, 1856; An Autumn Cruise in the Ægean, 1886; A Transatlantic Holiday, 1891; The FitzPatrick Lectureship in History of Medicine in the Royal College of Physicians, London, was founded in his memory by his widow in 1901.

1742. Daniell, Hickman Rose. *b.* 16 July 1819. M.R.C.S. 1842. A.S. 21 Sept. 1856. *d.* at Gorakhpur, 11 Sept. 1862. Indian Mutiny, 1858–59, operations in Chota Nagpur.

1743. Sewell, James Arthur. *b.* 27 Aug. 1834, at Quebec. M.D. Ed. 1856. L.R.C.S. Ed. 1856. A.S. 24 Sept. 1856. Resigned, 19 May 1864. *d.* at Mentone, 2 Jan. 1899. Indian Mutiny, 1857–58, operations round Agra and in Rohilkand, capture of Bareli, medal.

1744. Duff, Alexander Groves. *b.* 19 July 1834. Ed. Univ. and Paris. M.D. Ed. 1856. L.F.P.S.G. 1856. A.S. 1 Oct. 1856. Resigned, 30 Sept. 1862. *d.* at Palmerston, New Zealand, 25 Sept. 1909. Son of Rev. Alexander Duff, D.D., of Calcutta. Indian Mutiny, 1857–59, outbreak at Mirat, action at Hindun River, siege and capture of Delhi, final siege and capture of Lucknow, Mar. 1858, operations in Oudh and on Nipal frontier, medal with two clasps.

1745. Morice, John Charles. *b.* 7 July 1834. St. George's. M.R.C.S. 1856. A.S. 8 Oct. 1856. Surg. 8 Oct. 1868. S.M. 1 July 1873. B.S. 18 Jan. 1884. D.S.G. 21 Oct. 1887. R. 24 Oct. 1892. *d.* in London, 23 June 1898. G.S.P. 2 Sept. 1891. Indian Mutiny, 1857–59, second relief of Lucknow, Nov. 1857, action at Cawnpur, final siege and capture of Lucknow, Mar. 1858, operations in Rohilkand, medal with clasp, one year's service for relief of Lucknow. N.-W. Frontier, Hazara, 1868, medal with clasp. Sudan, 1885, Desp. L.G. 25 May 1885, medal with clasp.

1746. Charles, Thomas Edmonstone. *b.* 17 Oct. 1834. Ed. Univ. Paris, and Berlin. M.D. Ed. 1855. L.R.C.S. Ed. 1855. A.S. 22 Oct. 1856. M.R.C.P. Lond. 1866. Surg. 22 Oct. 1868. S.M. 1 July 1873. F.R.C.P. Lond. 1876. R. 18 Sept. 1882. *d.* at Flushing, Cornwall, 2 Mar. 1906. Q.H.P. 23 June 1883. LL.D. Ed. 1895. Indian Mutiny, 1857–58, action at Badli-ki-Sarai, siege and capture of Delhi, operations in Duab, actions at Gangeri, Patiali, and Mainpuri, relief of Lucknow, operations in Oudh, medal with two clasps. Author of Dengue, its history, symptoms, and treatment, 1872.

*1747. Rice, William Roche. *b.* 6 Jan. 1833. M.D. Q.U.I. 1856. M.R.C.S. 1856. A.S. 20 Nov. 1856. Surg. 20 Nov. 1868. S.M. 1 July 1873. B.S. 10 Apr. 1884. D.S.G. 9 Dec. 1887. S.G. 29 Mar. 1890. R. 29 Mar. 1895. *d.* at Brighton, 27 Mar. 1903. G.S.P. 26 July 1891. C.S.I. 25 May 1892. Q.H.P. 22 Apr. 1896. Indian Mutiny, 1857, at Indore, medal.

*1748. Bushman, Frederick Christian. *b.* 26 March 1833. M.R.C.S. 1856. A.S. 4 Dec. 1856. Died at Barkatha, 20 Jan. 1858. Indian Mutiny, 1857–58.

* Rice, Cary, Bushman, and Abbott, all passed for the Service in the list of 4 Aug. 1856. Rice next to Sherlock, Bushman next Rice, Abbott next Farrell, and Cary next Abbott.

*1749. Cary, Henry Thomas. b. 27 July 1833. M.B. T.C.D. 1856. A.S. 4 Dec. 1856. Indian Mutiny, 1857, killed by mutineers, Mehidpur, 8 Nov. 1857.

*1750. Abbott, Richard Theophilus. b. 20 Aug. 1833. Glas. Univ. and Carmichael School, Dublin. L.R.C.S.I. 1855. M.D. Glas. 1856. A.S. 10 Dec. 1856. Surg. 10 Dec. 1868. S.M. 1 July 1873. d. at Bray, Co. Wicklow, 11 Apr. 1881. Indian Mutiny, 1858–59, operations in Bandalkund, medal. Author of Jail Manual for Central Provinces, 1867.

1857

1751. Cayley, Henry. b. 20 Dec. 1834. King's Coll. Lond. M.R.C.S. 1855. A.S. 29 Jan. 1857. Surg. 29 Jan. 1869. S.M. 1 July 1873. B.S. 19 Apr. 1884. Member, Medl. Board, India Office, 7 Jan. 1855 to 22 Feb. 1887. F.R.C.S. 1886. R. 29 Apr. 1887. Professor Mily. Medicine, Army Medl. School, Netley, 1889–97. d. at Weybridge, 19 Mar. 1904. Q.H.S. 11 July 1900. C.M.G. 27 Sept. 1901. Indian Mutiny, 1857–58, operations in N.W.P. medal. South Africa, 1901, as Supt. Scottish Hospital, medal, C.M.G. Author of Report on route to Karakash River, 1868; Article on Tropical Diseases of Liver, in Davidson's Diseases and Hygiene of Warm Climates, 1893; Health Guide to Travellers, 1896.

1752. Best, Alexander Vans. b. 29 Dec. 1834. M.B. 1855; M.D. 1857; Mar. Coll. Ab. M.R.C.S. 1856. A.S. 29 Jan. 1857. F.R.C.S. 1868. Surg. 29 Jan. 1869. R. 4 Nov. 1869. d. at Hyères, 25 Mar. 1875. Indian Mutiny, 1857–58, with Naval Brigade, medal. China, 1860–61.

1753. Gillet, Thomas Carthew. b. 6 Dec. 1834. M.R.C.S. 18—. L.S.A. 1856. A.S. 29 Jan. 1857. d. in Calcutta, 13 Feb. 1858.

1754. White, James Henry. b. 14 Dec. 1883. L.R.C.S.I. 18—. A.S. 29 Jan. 1857. d. at Barrackpur, 2 Oct. 1866. China, 1857–58. Indian Mutiny, 1859, operations in Rohilkand.

1755. Penny, James Champion. b. 11 Mar. 1830. St. George's. M.R.C.S. 1853. M.D. St. A. 1855. A.S. 29 Jan. 1857. Surg. 29 Jan. 1869. S.M. 1 July 1873. B.S. 24 Apr. 1884. R. 3 June 1887. d. in London, 3 Apr. 1902. Indian Mutiny, 1857–58, second relief of Lucknow, Nov. 1857, action at Cawnpur, medal with clasp.

1756. Hilson, Archibald Hamilton. b. 3 Jan. 1835. L.R.C.S. Ed. 1855. M.D. Ed. 1857. A.S. 29 Jan. 1857. Surg. 29 Jan. 1869. S.M. 1 July 1873. B.S. 9 Sept. 1884. D.S.G. 20 Dec. 1888. R. 1 Apr. 1893. d. at Norwood, 4 Jan. 1894. G.S.P. 14 Dec. 1891. C.I.E. 3 June 1893. Indian Mutiny, 1857–58, with Peel's Naval Brigade and with Nipalese troops, operations in N.W.P. and Bihar, severely wounded in face by musket ball, medal. N.-E. Frontier, Bhutan, 1865–66, medal.

1757. Carny, John. b. 11 Mar. 1835. L.R.C.S. Ed. 18—. M.D. Mar. Coll. Ab. 1857. A.S. 29 Jan. 1857. d. in Calcutta, 12 Oct. 1858.

1758. Dickinson, James Charles. b. 17 Jan. 1829. King's Coll. Lond. M.B. Lond. 1849. M.R.C.S. 1851. Acting Asst. Surg. A.M.D. 26 May 1855. A.S. Bengal, 29 Jan. 1857. Resigned, 12 Mar. 1865. Crimea, 1854–55, medal. Indian Mutiny, 1857–58, operations in Gorakhpur and Saran, medal.

* *Vide* note to Rice, No. 1747, p. 156.

1759. **Smith, William Caldwell** (afterwards **Caldwell, William Smith**). *b.* 18 Apr. 1833. M.D. Glas. 1834. L.R.C.S. Ed. 18—. A.S. 29 Jan. 1857. Surg. 29 Jan. 1869. S.M. 1 July 1873. R. 4 July 1881. *d.* at Stranraer, 21 Sept. 1913. Changed name to W. S. Caldwell in 1875. Indian Mutiny, 1857–59, operations in Bihar and Rohilkand.

1760. **Raddock, Charles Edwin.** *b.* 28 Aug. 1830. Calcutta. L.M.S. Cal. 18—. Sub-Asst. Surg. Bengal, 19 June 1850 to Jan. 1857. M.R.C.S. 1856. A.S. 29 Jan. 1857. Surg. 29 Jan. 1869. S.M. 1 July 1873. B.S. 14 Oct. 1884. R. 6 Aug. 1887. *d.* at Norwood, 5 Jan. 1901. Indian Mutiny, 1857–58, second relief of Lucknow, Nov. 1857, action at Cawnpur, final siege and capture of Lucknow Mar. 1858, operations in Oudh, medal with clasp. N.-E. Frontier, Bhutan, 1865–66, medal with clasp. Afghanistan, 1879–80, with Khaibar Field Force. N.-W. Frontier, Mahsud Waziri, 1881.

1761. **Sheil, John.** *b.* 19 Sept. 1833. B.A. M.B. T.C.D. 18—. L.R.C.S.I. 18—. A.S. 29 Jan. 1857. Resigned, 10 Feb. 1860. Indian Mutiny, 1857–58, relief of Lucknow.

1762. **Playfair, William Smoult** (e). *b.* 27 July 1835. Ed. Univ. and Paris. M.D. Ed. 1856. L.R.C.S. Ed. 1857. A.S. 4 Aug. 1857. F.R.C.S. Ed. 1861. M.R.C.P. Lond. 1863. Resigned, 20 Oct. 1864. Asst. Physn. King's College Hosp. London, 1863–73. Physn. and Lecturer on Obstetric Medicine, 1873–98. F.R.C.P. Lond. 1870. *d.* at St. Andrews, 13 Aug. 1903. Son of G. Playfair, No. 555, supra, 1805, and brother of G. R. Playfair, No. 1459, supra, 1844. LL.D. St. A. 1885. LL.D. Ed. 1898. Grand Officer of Crown of Rumania. Indian Mutiny, 1857–58, operations in Oudh. Author of Handbook of Obstetric Operations, 1865; Treatise on Science and Practice of Midwifery, 1876, 9th edition, 1898; Treatment of Nerve Prostration and Hysteria, 1882; Articles on Neurasthenia and Diseases of Womb in Quain's Dictionary of Medicine, 1882 (also the latter article in second and third editions); Article on Treatment of Functional Neuroses in Dictionary of Psychological Medicine, 1892; Articles on Puerperal Septic Disease (Vol. I.) and Abdominal Diagnosis (Vol. III.), in Allbutt's System of Medicine, 1895–99; joint editor with T. C. Allbutt of A System of Gynæcology, 1896.

1763. **Clark, Hugh.** *b.* 19 Apr. 1835. M.D. Ed. 1856. L.R.C.S. Ed. 18—. A.S. 4 Aug. 1857. Surg. 4 Aug. 1869. R. on half-pay, 14 Mar. 1871. *d.* 23 Jan. 1876.

1764. **Sutherland, George Sackville.** *b.* 1 Dec. 1833, at St. Vincent, West Indies. L.R.C.S. Ed. 1855. Acting Asst. Surg. A.M.D. 19 Sept. 1855. M.D. Ed. gold medal, 1857. A.S. Bengal, 4 Aug. 1857. Surg. 4 Aug. 1869. S.M. 1 July 1873. B.S. 7 Dec. 1884. R. extra pension, 26 June 1888. *d.* in London, 19 May 1908. Medjidie, 5th Class, 2 Mar. 1856. Crimea, 1854–55, with Turkish contingent in Turkey and in Crimea, Turkish medal, Medjidie. Indian Mutiny, 1858–59, final siege and capture of Lucknow, Mar. 1858, operations in Oudh, medal with clasp.

1765. **Caird, William Edward.** *b.* 21 Apr. 1833. M.R.C.S. 1857. L.S.A. 1857. A.S. 4 Aug. 1857. Surg. 4 Aug. 1869. S.M. 1 July 1873. R 5 June 1879. *d.* at St. Leonard's, Apr. 1907. Indian Mutiny, 1858–59, operations in Oudh. N.-E. Frontier, Bhutan, 1865–66, capture of Dewangiri.

1766. **Banbury, Richard.** *b.* 8 Apr. 1830. M.R.C.S. 1852. L.S.A. 1854. Acting Asst. Surg. A.M.D. 25 Apr. 1855. A.S. Bengal, 4 Aug. 1857. *d.* at Hazaribagh, 25 Aug. 1866. Crimea, 1855–56, with Turkish contingent in Turkey and in Crimea, Turkish medal. Indian Mutiny, 1857–58, operations in Bihar, medal. China, 1860–61.

1767. **Bremner, James.** *b.* 17 Aug. 1835. M.A. 1850; M.D. 1856; K.C. Ab. L.R.C.S. Ed. 18—. A.S. 4 Aug. 1857. *d.* 23 Nov. 1860, at Huntly, Aberdeenshire.

1768. **Bonavia, Emanuel.** *b.* at Malta, 16 July 1833. Malta Univ. and Ed. Univ. M.D. Malta, 18—. M.R.C.S. 1857. A.S. 4 Aug. 1857. Surg. 4 Aug. 1869. S.M. 1 July 1873. B.S. 17 Jan. 1885. R. 26 Apr. 1888. *d.* at Worthing, 14 Nov. 1908. Indian Mutiny, 1857–58, final siege and capture of Lucknow, Mar. 1858, operations in Trans-Gogra country, medal with clasp. Author of The Future of the Date Palm in India, 1885; The Cultivated Oranges and Lemons of India and Ceylon, 1890, with Atlas of plates, 1897; Flora of Assyrian Monuments, 1894; Studies in the Evolution of Animals, 1895.

1769. **Taylor, Adam.** *b.* 11 Oct. 1834. M.R.C.S. 1856. L.S.A. 1857. A.S. 4 Aug. 1857. Surg. 4 Aug. 1869. S.M. 1 July 1873. *d.* at Delhi, 21 Oct. 1881.

1770. **Dickson, Lindsay Frederick.** *b.* 26 Oct. 1834. King's Coll. London. M.R.C.S. 1856. L.S.A. 1856. A.S. 4 Aug. 1857. Surg. 4 Aug. 1869. S.M. 1 July 1873. R. 27 Nov. 1882. *d.* in British Columbia, 25 Apr. 1908. Indian Mutiny, 1857–58, with Peel's Naval Brigade, final siege and capture of Lucknow, Mar. 1858, operations on Nipal frontier and in Shahabad, medal with clasp.

1771. **Daly, Denis Bowes.** *b.* 28 Feb. 1831. L.R.C.S.I. 18—. M.R.C.S. 18—. M.D. St. A. 1857. A.S. 4 Aug. 1857. Resigned, 27 Sept. 1868.

1772. **Marshall, Alfred.** *b.* 12 May 1834. M.R.C.S. 1855, L.S.A. 1856. A.S. 4 Aug. 1857. *d.* on board S.S. 'United Kingdom,' 26 Sept. 1858.

1773. **Pemberton, John MacLeod.** *b.* 8 Nov. 1835. M.D. Ed. 1857. M.R.C.S. 1857. A.S. 9 Dec. 1857. *d.* at Haidarabad, 30 June 1867.

1858

1774. **Colles, John Armstrong Purefoy.** *b.* 15 Sept. 1834. Stevens' Hosp., Dublin. L.R.C.S.I. 1854. M.D. St. A. 1857. A.S. 27 Jan. 1858. F.R.C.S.I. 1869. L.K.Q.C.P. 1870. Surg. 27 Jan. 1870. *d.* at Dinapur, 8 Feb. 1873. Indian Mutiny, 1858–59, operations in Trans-Gogra district. Edited Ind. Medl. Gazette, 1867.

*1775. **Haig, William James.** *b.* 7 Jan. 1836. L.R.C.S. Ed. 1856. M.D. Ed. 1857. A.S. 27 Jan. 1858. Resigned, 24 Jan. 1861. Afterwards settled at Dollar. Father of P. B. Haig, No. 2320, infra, 1892.

1776. **Campbell, Alexander Dugald.** *b.* 19 June 1833. L.R.C.S. Ed. 18—. M.D. Ed. 1857. A.S. 27 Jan. 1858. Surg. 27 Jan. 1870. S.M. 1 July 1873. R. 20 Oct. 1881. *d.* at Kensington, 8 Oct. 1911.

1777. **Courtney, Sydney Charles.** *b.* 3 Apr. 1835. St. George's and Mar. Coll. Ab. M.R.C.S. 1856. L.S.A. 1856. M.D. Mar. Coll. Ab. 1857. A.S. 27 Jan. 1858. Surg. 27 Jan. 1870. S.M. 1 July 1873. *d.* at Peshawar, 10 Feb. 1879.

---

* One of the Haigs of Bemersyde. v. The Haigs of Bemersyde, by John Russell, 1881, p. 450; P. de H. Haig, No. 2057, infra, 1875, was also one of the same family (p. 453).

1778. Prentis, Charles. b. 17 Apr. 1835. Bart's. M.R.C.S. 1857. A.S. 27 Jan. 1858. Surg. 27 Jan. 1870. S.M. 1 July 1873. L.R.C.P. Lond. 1877. R. 9 Jan. 1887. d. in Presy. Genl. Hosp. Calcutta, 14 Jan. 1887. Indian Mutiny, 1857–58, operations in N.W.P. and on Nipal frontier, medal.

1779. Chandra, Rajendra Chandra. b. 18 Oct. 1833. Calcutta. M.R.C.S. 1857. A.S. 27 Jan. 1858. Surg. 27 Jan. 1870. S.M. 1 July 1873. B.S. 28 Feb. 1890. R. 18 Oct. 1891. d. in London, 20 Dec. 1895. His first wife was a sister of Sir Hardinge Giffard, Solicitor-General, afterwards Lord Chancellor Lord Halsbury. Indian Mutiny, 1858–59, operations in N.W.P. N.-E. Frontier, Kuki, 1861; Khasia and Jainthia Hills, 1862–63.

1780. Lidderdale, Robert. b. 16 Apr. 1835. M.D. Ed. 1857. L.R.C.S. Ed. 1857. A.S. 27 Jan. 1858. Surg. 27 Jan. 1870. S.M. 1 July 1873. B.S. 21 Mar. 1885. R. 27 Jan. 1889. d. at Torquay, 9 Sept. 1908. N.-W. Frontier, 1854, medal. Indian Mutiny, 1857–58, medal with clasp.

1781. Aitchison, James Edward Tierney. b. 28 Oct. 1835. M.D. Ed. 1858. L.R.C.S. Ed. 1858. A.S. 27 Jan. 1858. F.R.C.S. Ed. 1863. M.R.C.P. Ed. 1868. Surg. 27 Jan. 1870. S.M. 1 July 1873. B.S. 29 Mar. 1885. R. 14 May 1888. d. at Kew, 30 Sept. 1898. Stood, unsuccessfully, as a Liberal Unionist, for Clackmannan and Kinross, 1892. C.I.E. 1 Jan. 1883. F.R.S. 7 June 1883. LL.D. Ed. 1889. Afghanistan, 1878, capture of Peiwar Kotal, medal. Author of Classified List of Diseases, English and Urdu, 18—; Flora of the Jhelum district, 1863; Catalogue of Plants of Punjab and Sindh, 1869; Handbook of Trade products of Leh, 1874; Flora of the Kuram Valley and of Afghanistan, 1880; Botany of the Afghan Delimitation Commission, 1888; Zoology of the Afghan Delimitation Commission, 1889; Products of Western Afghanistan and of North Eastern Persia, 1890.

1782. Lees, Leonard Horner. b. 12 Sept. 1835. M.D. Ed. 1856. L.R.C.S. Ed. 1856. A.S. 27 Jan. 1858. Surg. 27 Jan. 1870. d. at Brighton, 19 June 1873. China, 1860, action at Sinho, capture of Taku forts, occupation of Tientsin and Pekin, medal with two clasps. Author of Report on the probable causes of the sparseness of population of Burma and Akyab, 1864.

1783. Veale, Thomas Stick. b. 25 Mar. 1831. Univ. Coll. Lond. M.R.C.S. 1854. L.S.A. 1855. Civil Surgeon, Crimean war, 1854–55. A.S. 27 Jan. 1858. Surg. 27 Jan. 1870. M.D. St. A. 1872. S.M. 1 July 1873. R. 22 Feb. 1885. d. at Croydon, 1 Dec. 1912. Crimean war, 1854–55, in Army Civil Hosp. Dardanelles. Indian Mutiny, 1858, medal. N.-E. Frontier, Bhutan, 1865–66, medal. Afghanistan, 1879–80, medal with clasp.

1784. Switzer, Bamlet Walker. b. 19 July 1834. L.R.C.S.I. 1857. A.S. 27 Jan. 1858. F.R.C.S.I. 1863. Surg. 27 Jan. 1870. M.D. 18—. R. on half-pay, 13 Jan. 1873. Name omitted from Indian Army List, Jan. 1875.

1785. Daniell, Cyrus Octavius. b. 22 Nov. 1833. M.R.C.S. 1854. Asst. Surgeon. A.M.D. 27 Feb. 1855 to 25 Aug. 1857. M.D. St. A. 1857. A.S. Bengal, 27 Jan. 1858. Surg. 27 Jan. 1870. S.M. 1 July 1873. d. in London, 28 Mar. 1874. Crimea, 1854–56, with Royal Artillery, siege and capture of Sebastopol, medal with clasp, and Turkish medal.

1786. **Wright, Daniel.** *b.* 18 Dec. 1833. M.A. M.D. Ed. 1857. A.S. 28 May 1858. Surg. 28 May 1870. S.M. 1 July 1873. R. 1 Feb. 1876. *d.* at Aberdeen, 15 Jan. 1902. Author of Sketch of portion of Nepal open to Europeans, 1872 ; History of Nepal, 1877.

1787. **Cutcliffe, Henry Charles.** *b.* 31 Aug. 1832. M.R.C.S. 1854. L.S.A. 1854. F.R.C.S. 1857. A.S.28 May 1858. Surg. 28 May 1870. S.M. 1 July 1873. *d.* in Calcutta, 24 Oct. 1873.

1788. **Brown, Thomas Edwin Burton.** *b.* 8 Feb. 1833. Guy's. M.R.C.S. 1854. L.S.A. 1854. M.B. 1856; M.D. 1857; Lond. A.S. 23 July 1858. Surg. 23 July 1870. S.M. 1 July 1873. B.S. 1 Sept. 1885. R. extra pension, 1 Oct. 1889. *d.* in London, 28 July 1911. Father of F. H. Burton-Brown, No. 2307, infra, 1891, and of A. T. Brown, Madras, 1891, No. 1525. C.I.E. 1 Jan. 1891. Author of Symptoms and Treatment of Poisons principally used in the Panjab, 1863.

1789. **Potter, Henry.** *b.* 2 Nov. 1833. L.R.C.S.I. 1855. M.D. St. A. 1858 (honours). A.S. 23 July 1858. Surg. 23 July 1870. S.M. 1 July 1873. F.R.C.S.I. 1880. B.S. 7 Dec. 1885. R. extra pension, 2 Nov. 1891. *d.* in England, 9 Oct. 1904. Indian Mutiny, 1858–59, operations in N.W.P. and in Trans-Gogra tracts, medal. Egypt, 1882, medal, bronze star. Burma, 1886–87, medal with two clasps.

1790. **Stephen, Alexander.** M.A. 1850 ; M.D. K.C. Ab. 1857. A.S. 23 July 1858. Resigned, 5 Jan. 1859.

1791. **Verchere, Albert Marc.** *b.* 27 Aug. 1832. B.A. 18—. M.R.C.S. 1857. L.S.A. 1857. A.S. 23 July 1858. Surg. 23 July 1870. S.M. 1 July 1873. *d.* at Aden, 29 Sept. 1878. Indian Mutiny, 1858–59, action at Dariabad, medal. N.-W. Frontier, Mahsud Waziri, 1860.

1792. **Hatchell, Charles.** *b.* 24 Feb. 1835. Calcutta and King's Coll. Lond. M.R.C.S. 1857. A.S. 23 July 1858. Surg. 23 July 1870. S.M. 1 July 1873. R. 20 Oct. 1888. *d.* in London, 2 Apr. 1907. Name spelt Hatchett in S.A.L.M.B. N.-E. Frontier, Bhutan, 1865–66, medal.

1793. **Byrne, Oscar.** *b.* 16 Feb. 1831. M.R.C.S. 1853. L.S.A. 1855. M.D. 18—. A.S. 23 July 1858. *d.* at Buxar, 25 Nov. 1864.

1794. **Whishaw, John Charles.** *b.* 17 Jan. 1833. M.R.C.S. 1857. A.S. 23 July 1858. M.D. St. A. 1860. Surg. 23 July 1870. S.M. 1 July 1873. R. 15 Feb. 1886. *d.* at Mentone, 20 Jan. 1895.

1795. **De Fabeck, Frederick William Alexander.** *b.* 1 Feb. 1830. Paris. L.R.C.S. Ed. 1858. A.S. 23 July 1858. Surg. 23 July 1870. S.M. 1 July 1873. R. 24 Apr. 1884. *d.* at Alassio, Italy, 5 May 1912. Brother of W. F. de Fabeck, M. No. 1260.

1796. **White, John Berry.** *b.* 5 June 1834. M.R.C.S. 18—. L.S.A. 18—. A.S. 23 July 1858. Surg. 23 July 1870. S.M. 1 July 1873. R. 15 July 1882. *d.* in London, 19 Nov. 1896. Founded, by a legacy, J. B. White Medical School at Dibrugarh. N.-E. Frontier, Abor, 1859.

1797. **Brown, Robert.** *b.* 9 Dec. 1833. M.R.C.S. 1853. A.S. 23 July 1858. Surg. 23 July 1870. S.M. 1 July 1873. *d.* at Manipur, 18 Aug. 1876. Author of Report on the Exploration of the Angami Naga country in 1873–74, 1874 ; Statistical Account of the Native State of Manipur, 1874.

1798. **Richmond, Archibald Fullerton.** *b.* 15 Jan. 1836. L.R.C.S. Ed. 1857. A.S. 27 July 1858. Surg. 27 July 1870. S.M. 1 July 1873. *d.* at Baksa, Bhutan, 16 Feb. 1874.

1799. **Crosbie, Pierce Maurice.** *b.* 3 Apr. 1834. B.A. 1857, T.C.D. M.R.C.S. 1857. A.S. 23 July 1858. *d.* at Agra, 9 Aug. 1862. Indian Mutiny, 1858–59, pursuit of Tantia Topi, medal.

1800. **MacDermott, John Joseph.** *b.* 13 Jan. 1834. L.R.C.S.I. 1858. M.D. St. A. 1858. A.S. 23 July 1858. F.R.C.S.I. 1864. Surg. 23 July 1870. S.M. 1 July 1873. R. 31 Jan. 1879.

1801. **Harris, Worsley Poulett.** *b.* 17 Apr. 1833. M.R.C.S. 1856. M.D. St. A. 1856. L.S.A. 1856. A.S. 23 July 1858. Surg. 23 July 1870. S.M. 1 July 1873. *d.* at Blackheath, 16 Sept. 1882. China, 1860–61, capture of Taku forts, medal with clasp. Author of Lithotomy, and the extraction of stone from the Bladder, Prostate, and Urethra, 1876.

*1802. **Scanlan, Michael Stack.** *b.* 1 May 1814. T.C.D. M.R.C.S. 1843. Uncovd. Medl. Service, Gwalior contingent, 17 Dec. 1845; (C.G. 17 Dec. 1845) to 1853. A.S. 11 Aug. 1858. Resigned, 1862. *d.* 1 Sept. 1878, at Tullykinill, Co. Kerry.

1859

1803. **Allen, William Edward.** *b.* 23 Sept. 1834. Univ. Coll. Lond. M.R.C.S 1858. L.S.A. 1858. A.S. 10 Feb. 1859. F.R.C.S. 1870. Surg. 10 Feb. 1871. S.M. 1 July 1873. R. 5 Nov. 1884. *d.* at Romford, 15 May 1885.

1804. **Maingay, Alexander Carroll.** *b.* 25 Oct. 1836. M.D. Ed. gold medal, 1858. M.R.C.S. 1859. A.S. 10 Feb. 1859. Murdered in Rangoon Central Jail, 15 Nov. 1869. China, 1860–62, medal.

1805. **Mantell, Riners.** *b.* 15 Feb. 1834. London Hosp. M.R.C.S. 1855. M.D. Lond. 1855. L.S.A. 1856. A.S. 10 Feb. 1859. Surg. 10 Feb. 1871. S.M. 1 July 1873. R. 16 July 1884. *d.* at Hastings, 9 Nov. 1910.

1806. **Thomson, William John.** *b.* 5 Apr. 1832. L.R.C.S. Ed. 1858. A.S. 10 Feb. 1859. *d.* at Gurgaon, 10 Nov. 1862.

1807. **Bensley, Edwin Clement.** *b.* 17 Aug. 1836. St. Thomas'. M.R.C.S. 1858. A.S. 10 Feb. 1859. F.R.C.S. 1868. L.R.C.P. Ed. 1868. Surg. 10 Feb. 1871. S.M. 1 July 1873. R. 15 Nov. 1885. *d.* in London, 20 Mar. 1923. Brother of C. E. W. Bensley, No. 1740, supra, 1856, and father of C. H. Bensley, No. 2376, infra, 1895. Author of The Diarrhœa of Infants in India, 1867.

1808. **Fawcus, James.** *b.* 19 Apr. 1833. Univ. Coll. Lond., Paris, and Vienna. M.R.C.S. 1855. L.S.A. 1855. Acting Asst. Surg. A.M.D. 1855–56. M.D. Lond. 1859. A.S. Bengal, 10 Feb. 1859. Surg. 10 Feb. 1871. *d.* at North Shields, 11 Nov. 1871. Crimea, 1855–56, at hospital at Renkioi in Dardanelles, and in Crimea with Light Division and Land Transport Corps, medal. China, 1859–60, medal.

* M. S. Scanlan was the last man nominated to the Bengal Medical Service. The nomination, which was given by Russell Ellice, Chairman of the Court of Directors, was given to three men in succession. (1) George Tranter, nominated to Madras, 7 Nov. 1855, died at Mehidpur, 10 Dec. 1855, before joining. (2) William Johnston Long, nominated to Madras, 2 Jan. 1856, died in Calcutta, 27 Jan. 1856, before joining. (3) M. S. Scanlan, 11 Aug. 1858. All three were Uncovd. Medl. Officers in Bengal; in all three cases the column in the Cadet Register headed "by whom recommended" is filled in with the words "his services." (Cadet Regr. vol. xv. A.S. Certs. vol. xxxix.) Scanlan's is the last Bengal name in A.S. Certs. vol. xxxix.

1809. **Bremner, George.** *b.* 26 Oct. 1836. L.R.C.S. Ed. 1858. M.D. St. A. 1858. A.S. 10 Feb. 1859. *d.* in Europe, 20 Feb. 1868.

1810. **Sheppard, Thomas William.** *b.* 25 June 1837. M.R.C.S. 1858. A.S. 10 Feb. 1859. Surg. 10 Feb. 1871. L.R.C.P. Lond. 1872. S.M. 1 July 1873. *d.* at Gulzarbagh, Patna, 1 Oct. 1885.

1811. **Ellis, John.** *b.* 10 Jan. 1833. MA. M.B. 1858; M.D. M.Ch. 1871. T.C.D. A.S. 10 Feb. 1859. Surg. 10 Feb. 1871. S.M. 1 July 1873. *d.* on Indian Ocean, two days out from Bombay, on passage to Europe, on P. and O. S.S. 'Oriental,' 31 Mar. 1889.

1812. **Selous, Edric.** *b.* 2 Apr. 1836. M.R.C.S. 1858. A.S. 10 Feb. 1859. Surg. 10 Feb. 1871. S.M. 1 July 1873. R. 1 Feb. 1882. *d.* at Sydenham, 5 May 1891.

1813. **Costello, Charles Peter.** *b.* 28 June 1835. Carmichael School, Dublin, L.A.H. 1856. L.R.C.S. Ed. 1858. A.S. 10 Feb. 1859. Surg. 10 Feb. 1871. S.M. 1 July 1873. F.R.C.S. Ed. 1881. B.S. 30 June 1886. D.S.G. 1 Jan. 1889. R. 1 Jan. 1894. *d.* at Wimbledon, 1 Apr. 1915. N.-W. Frontier, second Yusufzai, Ambeyla, 1863–64, forcing Ambeyla pass, medal with clasp. Afghanistan, 1878–80, Hirsarah and Khagman Valley expeditions, medal. N.-E. Frontier, 1891, Manipur, Desp. G.G.O. No. 585 of 1891.

1814. **Durant, James John.** *b.* 11 Dec. 1831. Sub-Asst. Surg. 27 Apr. 1850–1853. M.R.C.S. 1858. A.S. 10 Feb. 1859. Surg. 10 Feb. 1871. S.M. 1 July 1873. R. 1 July 1883. *d.* at Crouch Hill, 14 May 1913.

1815. **Odevaine, Ferdinand.** *b.* 1 May 1836. L.R.C.S.I. 1855. Acting Asst. Surg. A.M.D. 1855–56. A.S. Bengal, 10 Feb. 1859. Surg. 10 Feb. 1871. S.M. 1 July 1873. F.R.C.S.I. 1875. R. 29 Apr. 1884. *d.* at Rathgar, Dublin, 20 Mar. 1910. Medjidie, 1856. Crimea, 1855–56, with Turkish contingent, 7 May 1855 to 15 June 1856, Turkish medal, Medjidie.

1816. **Rhind, Robert.** *b.* 9 Mar. 1832. L.R.C.S. Ed. 18—. A.S. 10 Feb. 1859. *d.* in Fort William, 24 Apr. 1863.

1817. **Grant, George.** *b.* 6 Aug. 1834. M.D. K.C. Ab. 1858. L.R.C.S. Ed. 1858. A.S. 10 Feb. 1859. Surg. 10 Feb. 1871. S.M. 1 July 1873. R. 30 Oct. 1885. *d.* at Bickley, Kent, 2 Oct. 1911.

1818. **Nichol, William** (d). *b.* 21 Mar. 1836. M.D. Ed. 1857. L.R.C.S. Ed. 18—. A.S. 10 Feb. 1859. Never joined. *d.* in Europe, 1859.

1819. **Chesnaye, George Cochet.** *b.* 29 Sept. 1837. Carmichael School, Dublin. L.R.C.S.I. 1857. A.S. 10 Feb. 1859. F.R.C.S.I. 1866. L.K.Q.C.P. 1866. Surg. 10 Feb. 1871. S.M. 1 July 1873. M.K.Q.C.P. 1881. B.S. 18 Aug. 1886. D.S.G. 9 Jan. 1889. R. 17 Apr. 1894. *d.* at Bournemouth, 12 Apr. 1904. G.S.P. 1 Jan. 1894. N.-W. Frontier, Hazara, 1868, medal with clasp. N.-E. Frontier, Lushai, 1891–92, clasp. Afghanistan, 1878–80, capture of Ali Musjid, expedition to Sherpur, Dec. 1879, action at Zahidabad, operations in Kohistan, march under Genl. Roberts from Kabul to Kandahar, battle of Kandahar, Desp. G.G.O. No. 566 of 1880, medal with three clasps, bronze star.

1820. Duncan, John. b. 4 Nov. 1834. M.D. K.C. Ab. 1858. L.R.C.S. Ed. 18—. A.S. 10 Feb. 1859. Surg. 10 Feb. 1871. S.M. 1 July 1873. B.S. 1 Sept. 1886. R. 16 June 1889. d. in England, 19 June 1902.

1821. Tandy, Edward Ord. b. 8 June 1835. T.C.D. L.R.C.S.I. 1857. A.S. 10 Feb. 1859. Surg. 10 Feb. 1871. S.M. 1 July 1873. B.S. 2 Sept. 1886. D.S.G. 2 Apr. 1889. R. 2 Apr. 1894. d. at Northam, North Devon, 10 Apr. 1916. G.S.P. 5 Jan. 1894. N.-E. Frontier, Sikkim, 1861. N.-W. Frontier, second Yusufzai, Ambeyla, 1863, forcing of Ambeyla pass, medal; Bezoti Afridi, 1868. Afghanistan, 1879-80, medal.

1822. Guenther, Henry (d). M.D. Rostock, 18—. M.R.C.S. 1858. Passed as A.S. 10 Feb. 1859; never joined

1823. Purefoy, James Robert. b. 5 Nov. 1838. L.R.C.S.I. 18—. M.D. St. A. 1858. A.S. 10 Feb. 1859. d. in Calcutta, 16 Feb. 1868.

1824. Parsons, Francis. b. 19 July 1836. Bristol. M.R.C.S. 1858. A.S. 10 Feb. 1859. Surg. 10 Feb. 1871. S.M. 1 July 1873. R. 20 July 1885. d. name omitted from Army List 1895. China, 1860, action of Sinho, capture of Taku forts, occupation of Pekin, medal with two clasps. N.-W. Frontier, second Yusufzai, Ambeyla, 1863, medal with clasp.

1825. Constant, Frederick George. b. 7 Nov. 1834. M.R.C.S. 1856. L.S.A. 1856. A.S. 10 Feb. 1859. Surg. 10 Feb. 1871. S.M. 1 July 1873. R. 17 Jan. 1882. d. at Eastbourne, 19 Feb. 1925. Abyssinia, 1867-68.

1826. Condon, James Hunt. b. 1 Mar. 1833. Ledwich School, Dublin. M.R.C.S. 1856. A.S. 10 Feb. 1859. Surg. 10 Feb. 1871. S.M. 1 July 1873. L.S.A. 1880. M.D. St. A. 1880. B.S. 19 Oct. 1886. R. 1 Mar. 1891. d. in Dublin, 19 July 1905.

1827. Hooper, William Roe. b. 12 Jan. 1837. M.R.C.S. 1858. A.S. 10 Feb. 1859. Surg. 10 Feb. 1871. S.M. 1 July 1873. B.S. 1 Mar. 1887. R. extra pension, 12 Jan. 1895. President, Medl. Board, India Office, 12 Jan. 1895 to 31 Dec. 1903. Surg. Col., 12 Jan. 1895. S.M.G. 14 Aug. 1895. C.S.I. 22 June 1897. K.C.S.I. 1 Jan. 1903. K.H.S. 6 Aug. 1904. d. at Aldeburgh, 29 Sept. 1921.

1828. Lackersteen, Mark Henry. b. 25 May 1835. King's Coll. Lond. M.R.C.S. 1858. A.S. 10 Feb. 1859. M.R.C.P. Lond. 1870. Surg. 10 Feb. 1871. S.M. 1 July 1873. Removed from list, 27 Nov. 1873.

1829. Smith, Henry Seymour. b. 23 Dec. 1833. B.A. M.B. T.C.D. 1858. L.R.C.S. Ed. 18—. A.S. 10 Feb. 1859. Surg. 10 Feb. 1871. S.M. 1 July 1873. d. at Allahabad, 18 Apr. 1884.

1830. Wallis, Edward. b. 15 Dec. 1834. M.R.C.S. 1856. A.S. 27 July 1859. d. at Tientsin, China, 20 Dec. 1860. China, 1860.

*1831. Cameron, Charles. b. 18 Aug. 1836. M.R.C.S. 1859. A.S. 27 July 1859. L.R.C.P. Lond. 1864. Surg. 27 July 1871. S.M. 1 July 1873. Surg. Lt.-Col. 12 Dec. 1891. R. 21 Sept. 1892. d. 26 June 1917. N.-E. Frontier, Bhutan, 1865-66, medal.

---

* The "compound titles" were introduced by the Royal Warrant of 12 Dec. 1891, when Surgeon-Majors became Surg. Lt.-Cols. at twenty years' service. At the same time, all Surgeon-Generals became Surgeon Major-Generals; Deputy Surgeon-Generals became Surgeon-Colonels; Surgeons became Surgeon-Captains, and the rank of Surgeon-Lieutenants was introduced, for officers under three years' service.

1832. **Cameron, John MacLeod.** *b.* 19 Nov. 1836. M.D. Ed. 18—. L.R.C.S. Ed. 1859. A.S. 27 July 1859. *d.* in Calcutta, 26 July 1870. Father of K. M. Cameron, R.A.M.C. (Johnston's Roll of R.A.M.C. No. 7414.) China 1860.

1833. **Richardson, John.** *b.* 26 Feb. 1837. K.C. Ab. and Univ. Coll. Lond. M.A. 1856; M.B. 1859; K.C. Ab. L.R.C.S. Ed. 18—. L.R.C.P. Ed. 18—. A.S. 27 July 1859. Surg. 27 July 1871. S.M. 1 July 1873. S.S.C. Cantab. 1883. B.S. 29 Apr. 1887. D.S.G. 19 May 1889. R. 19 May 1894. Member, Army Sany. Commission, July 1896 to July 1906. *d.* at Totland. Isle of Wight. 13 Aug. 1913. K.H.P. 26 Sept. 1903. N.-E. Frontier, Bhutan, 1865–66, capture of Baksa and Bala Pass, medal with clasp.

1834. **Holmes, Arthur Parker.** *b.* 17 Mar. 1835. L.R.C.S.I. 1858. M.D. Q.U.I. 18—. A.S. 27 July 1859. Surg. 27 July 1871. S.M. 1 July 1873. *d.* at San Remo, 1 Jan. 1887. N.-W. Frontier, second Yusufzai, Ambeyla, 1863, medal with clasp; Daur Valley, 1872; Jowaki, 1877–78, clasp. Afghanistan, 1878–79, medal with clasp. N.-W. Frontier, Mahsud Waziri, 1881, Desp. 20 June 1881.

1835. **Perreau, Montague James Sutherland.** *b.* 25 Oct. 1837. Westminster. M.R.C.S. 1859. A.S. 27 July 1859. *d.* at Dalimkot, Bhutan, 12 Aug. 1865. N.-E. Frontier, Bhutan, 1865.

1836. **Gray, Robert.** *b.* 3 Nov. 1833. M.A. 1853; M.D. 1859; K.C. Ab. L.R.C.S. Ed. 18—. A.S. 27 July 1859. Surg. 27 Feb. 1871. S.M. 1 July 1873. B.S. 3 June 1887. R. extra pension, 3 Apr. 1891. *d.* at Aberdeen, 28 Dec. 1918.

1837. **Fleming, Joseph MacNaghten.** *b.* 5 Sept. 1836. M.D. Glas. 1857. L.F.P.S.G. 1857. A.S. 27 July 1859. Surg. 27 July 1871. S.M. 1 July 1873. B.S. 6 Aug. 1887. R. extra pension, 9 Apr. 1892. *d.* 31 Aug. 1898. Father of A. M. Fleming, I.M.S. 1899 (Genl. list, No. 61). N.-E. Frontier, Bhutan, 1865–66, recapture of Diwangiri, medal with clasp. Afghanistan, 1879–80, medal. Author of Notes on Carbolic Treatment of Leprosy.

1838. **Oldham, Charles Frederick.** *b.* 2 Mar. 1832. St. George's. M.R.C.S. 1858. L.R.C.P. Ed. 1859. A.S. 27 July 1859. Surg. 27 July 1871. S.M. 1 July 1873. B.S. 24 Oct. 1887. R. 28 Feb. 1890. *d.* at Great Bealings, Suffolk, 25 Mar. 1913. Perak, 1875–76, medal with clasp. Afghanistan, 1879–80, Thal Chotiali Field Force, medal. Author of What is Malaria? 1871; The Sun and the Serpent, 1905.

1839. **FitzGerald, Edward Ambrose.** *b.* 22 Aug. 1834. M.R.C.S. 1856. A.S. 27 July 1859. Surg. 27 July 1871. S.M. 1 July 1873. B.S. 9 Dec. 1887. R. 18 Mar. 1890. *d.* in London, 9 Mar. 1902. Author of Nature, Treatment, and Prevention of Cholera, 1867; Sanitary Primer, 1879.

1840. **Henderson, George.** *b.* 30 Nov. 1836. K.C. Ab. and Paris. M.D. K.C. Ab. 1858. L.R.C.S. Ed. 1858. A.S. 27 July 1859. Surg. 27 July 1871. S.M. 1 July 1873. R. 20 Nov. 1889. *d.* at Inverness, 23 June 1929. Author of Catalogue of plants in the Royal Botanic Gardens, Calcutta, 1873; (with A. O. Hume), Lahore to Yarkand, 1873.

1841. **Reid, John.** *b.* 23 Dec. 1836. Calcutta. M.R.C.S. 1859. A.S. 27 July 1859. Surg. 27 July 1871. R. 27 July 1871. *d.* in London, 6 Mar. 1903. China, 1860–61.

1842. **Cullen, Peter.** *b.* 2 Aug. 1835. Calcutta and Ab. Univ. M.R.C.S. 1859. A.S. 27 July 1859. M.B. C.M. Ab. 1867. Surg. 27 July 1871. S.M. 1 July 1873. Cert. Pub. Health. R.C.P. Ed. 1886. B.S. 28 Apr. 1888. R. extra pension, 1 June 1892. *d.* at Jabalpur, 21 July 1920. Ordained Deacon, 10 Mar. 1900, Priest, 1900. K.-i-H. 3 June 1916. China, 1860.

1843. **Johnson, James Richard.** *b.* 19 Jan. 1838. L.R.C.S.I. 18—. A.S. 27 July 1859. Surg. 27 July 1871. S.M. 1 July 1873. *d.* at Abbottabad, 20 May 1878. N.-W. Frontier, Mahsud Waziri, 1860.

1844. **Newton, Isaac.** *b.* 9 Jan. 1838. Leeds and Paris. M.R.C.S. 1859. A.S. 27 July 1859. Surg. 27 July 1871. S.M. 1 July 1873. R. 6 July 1877. *d.* at Broadlands, Cheltenham, 28 Mar. 1922. China, 1860–61. Author of On Vaccination.

1860

1845. **Brotchie, Alexander Rainy.** *b.* 26 June 1838. M.A. 1856; M.D. 1859; K.C. Ab. L.R.C.S. Ed. 1859. A.S. 20 Jan. 1860. *d.* at Shahpur, 19 July 1861.

1846. **Emanuel, Leonard.** *b.* 26 Jan. 1835. Univ. Coll. Lond. M.R.C.S. 1859. A.S. 20 Jan. 1860. L.R.C.P. Lond. 1863. L.S.A. 1863. *d.* in London, May 1864.

1847. **Jameson, George William.** *b.* 11 Feb. 1835. M.R.C.S. 1859. L.S.A. 1859. A.S. 20 Jan. 1860. Surg. 20 Jan. 1872. S.M. 1 July 1873. R. 4 Apr. 1882. *d.* at Blackheath, 14 Nov. 1899.

1848. **Cookson, Henry.** *b.* 10 Feb. 1833. Ed. Univ., Leeds, and St. Thomas'. M.R.C.S. 1856. Asst. Surg. R.N. 1856–59. L.R.C.P. Ed. 1859. A.S. Bengal, 20 Jan. 1860. F.R.C.S. 1870. Surg. 20 Jan. 1872. S.M. 1 July 1873. R. 20 May 1880. D.P.H. 1882. *d.* at Cheltenham, 21 Apr. 1921. N.-W. Frontier, Jowaki, 1877–78, Desp. G.G.O. No. 738 of 1878, medal. Afghanistan, 1878–79, capture of Ali Musjid, Desp. G.O.C.C. of 14 Oct. 1879, medal with clasp.

1849. **Cunningham, Robert Wiseman.** *b.* 30 Dec. 1838. M.D. St. A. 1860. A.S. 20 Jan. 1860. Surg. 20 Jan. 1872. S.M. 1 July 1873. *d.* in Edinburgh, 19 Dec. 1881. N.-W. Frontier, second Yusufzai, Ambeyla, 1863, medal with clasp. Afghanistan, 1878–80, actions of Ahmad Khel and Arzu, march from Kabul to relief of Kandahar under Genl. Roberts, battle of Kandahar, Desp. medal with two clasps, bronze star. N.-W. Frontier, Mahsud Waziri, 1881.

1850. **Carter, Robert.** *b.* 22 Oct. 1835. Univ. Coll. Lond. M.R.C.S. 1859. A.S. 20 Jan. 1860. *d.* in Calcutta, 27 May 1860.

1851. **Moir, William.** *b.* 17 Nov. 1833. M.A. M.B. K.C. Ab. 1859. L.R.C.S. Ed. 18—. A.S. 20 Jan. 1860. Surg. 28 Jan. 1872. S.M. 1 July 1873. B.S. 26 Apr. 1888. R. 1 Apr. 1891. *d.* in Edinburgh, 10 Apr. 1902.

1852. **Skardon, Thomas Gray.** *b.* 7 June 1836. M.R.C.S. 1859. A.S. 20 Jan. 1860. Surg. 20 Jan. 1872. S.M. 1 July 1873. R. 31 Oct. 1884. *d.* at Paignton, Devon, 21 Jan. 1912.

1853. **O'Brien, Daniel.** *b.* 18 Oct. 1832. M.R.C.S. 1859. A.S. 20 Jan. 1860. Resigned, 1 Feb. 1861.

1854. **Schmitz, Charles Theodore.** *b.* 1837. M.D. Ed. 1856. A.S. 20 Jan. 1860. *d.* at Cape Town, 23 Dec. 1862.

1855. **Hoskins, Edmund John.** *b.* 1836. Bart's. M.R.C.S. 1858. L.S.A. 1859. M.D. St. A. 1860. A.S. 1 Oct. 1860. Surg. 1 Oct. 1872. S.M. 1 July 1873. R. 7 Apr. 1879. *d.* in London, 22 Jan. 1916.

1856. **Shaw, John Cardy.** *b.* 28 July 1836. L.R.C.S. and P. Ed. 1859. A.S. 1 Oct. 1860. Surg. 1 Oct. 1872. S.M. 1 July 1873. *d.* at Bankipur, Patna, 27 Sept. 1885. N.-E. Frontier, Bhutan, 1865–66, medal with clasp.

1857. **Johnston, John Wilson.** *b.* 31 Oct. 1836. L.R.C.S. Ed. 1858. M.D. Ed. 1859. A.S. 1 Oct. 1860. Surg. 1 Oct. 1872. S.M. 1 July 1873. R. 4 Feb. 1891. *d.* at Oxton, Cheshire, 7 July 1902. N.-W. Frontier, Jowaki, 1877–78, medal with clasp. Afghanistan, 1878–80, occupation of Kandahar and Kelat-i-Ghilzai, actions of Shahjui, Ahmad Khel, and Arzu (wounded), medal with clasp. Burma, 1885–86, clasp.

1858. **Cameron, John.** *b.* 23 Dec. 1832. L.F.P.S.G. 1858. M.D. Glas. 1859. A.S. 1 Oct. 1860. Surg. 1 Oct. 1872. S.M. 1 July 1873. *d.* at Adelaide, 27 Sept. 1885.

1859. **Pilcher, Jesse Griggs.** *b.* 25 Mar. 1839. L.R.C.S. Ed. 1858. L.A.H. 1858. M.R.C.S. 1860. A.S. 1 Oct. 1860. F.R.C.S. 1869. Surg. 1 Oct. 1872. S.M. 1 July 1873. B.S. 14 May 1888. D.S.G. 29 Mar. 1890. R. 29 Mar. 1895. *d.* in London, 3 July 1917.

1860. **Mackertich, Simon Nierses.** *b.* 1837. King's Coll. Lond. M.R.C.S. 1860. A.S. 1 Oct. 1860. M.D. St. A. 1861. Surg. 1 Oct. 1872. S.M. 1 July 1873. R. 6 Sept. 1881. *d.* in London, 17 Oct. 1881.

1861. **Neil, Alexander.** L.R.C.S. Ed. 1857. M.R.C.S. 1860. A.S. 1 Oct. 1860. Surg. 1 Oct. 1872. S.M. 1 July 1873. *d.* at Lahore, 22 July 1879.

1862. **French, John Gay.** *b.* 27 June 1839. Q.C. Galway, T.C.D., and Ledwich School, Dublin. M.R.C.S. 1859. L.K.Q.C.P. 1860. A.S. 1 Oct. 1860. M.D. M.Ch. Q.U.I. 1870. F.R.C.S. 1870. Surg. 1 Oct. 1872. S.M. 1 July 1873. *d.* at Ballingar, Galway, 28 July 1885. N.-E. Frontier, 1865–66, recapture of Diwangiri, medal with clasp. Author of Endemic Fever in Lower Bengal, 1873; edited Indian Medical Gazette, 1875–76.

1863. **Lyons, Richard Thomas.** *b.* 24 Nov. 1834. Bart's. M.R.C.S. 1860. M.D. St. A. 1860. A.S. 1 Oct. 1860. Surg. 1 Oct. 1872. S.M. 1 July 1873. R. 9 Feb. 1886. *d.* at Cambridge, Apr. 1903. N.-W. Frontier, second Yusufzai, Ambeyla, 1863, forcing of Ambeyla Pass, defence of Eagle's Crag picquet, Desp. G.G.O. No. 716 of 1864, medal. Afghanistan, 1878–79, operations in Khost Valley, medal. Author of A Treatise on Relapsing or Famine Fever, 1872.

1865

1864. MacLeod, Kenneth. *b.* 23 July 1840. M.A. Mar. Coll. Ab. 1857. M.D. Ed. 1861. L.R.C.S. Ed. 1864. A.S. 1 Apr. 1865. Surg. 1 July 1873. S.M. 1 Apr. 1877. F.R.C.S. Ed. 1860. B.S. 26 June 1888. R. 16 Apr. 1892. Member Medl. Board, India Office, 28 June 1893–97. Professor of Mily. Medicine, Army Medl. School, Netley, 1897–1905. Hony. F.R.C.S. 1900. LL.D. Ab. 1892. K.H.P. 2 May 1906. Col. 2 May 1906. *d.* at West End, Hants, 17 Dec. 1922. Author of Manual of Diseases of Cattle, 1869; Sanitary Treatment of Epizootics, 1869; Report on Medicolegal returns of 1868 and 1869, 1870, expanded into Medicolegal experiences in Bengal Presidency, 1875; History of the Medical Schools of the Bengal Presidency, 1872; Report on establishment of a Veterinary School in Bengal, 1883; Operative Surgery in the Calcutta Medical College Hospital, 1885; Articles on Delhi Boil and Scrotal Elephantiasis in Heath's Dictionary of Surgery, 1886; Articles on Cholera and Epidemic Dropsy in Allbutt's System of Medicine, 1896–99; Articles on Cholera, Choleraic Diarrhœa, Sunstroke, and Epidemic Dropsy in Quain's Dictionary of Medicine, 3rd ed. 1902; Indian Medical Memories, 1909; edited Indian Medical Gazette, 1871–91.

*1865. Cleghorn, James. *b.* 19 May 1841. Ed. Univ. and Vienna. M.D. St. A. 1862. L.R.C.S. Ed. 1863. A.S. on probation for A.M.D. Feb.-Mar. 1865. A.S. Bengal 1 Apr. 1865. Surg. 1 July 1873. S.M. 1 Apr. 1877. B.S. 19 Dec. 1886. D.S.G. 13 Aug. 1891. S.M.G. and D.G. 29 Mar. 1895. R. 25 Oct. 1898. *d.* at Haslemere, Surrey, 14 June 1920. G.S.P. 2 Apr. 1894. C.S.I. 22 June 1897. Q.H.S. 5 Oct. 1898. N.-E. Frontier, Bhutan, 1865–66, medal.

*1866. Harvey, Robert. *b.* 10 Mar. 1842. Ab. and Glas. Univ. M.B.C.M. (Honours) 1863; M.D. 1883; Ab. A.S. on probation for A.M.D. Feb.-Mar. 1865. A.S. Bengal, 1 Apr. 1865. Surg. 1 July 1873. S.M. 1 Apr. 1877. B.S. 1 Jan. 1889. M.R.C.P. Lond. 1889. D.S.G. 2 Sept. 1891. F.R.C.P. Lond. 1894. S.M.G. 1 Apr. 1895. D.G. 25 Oct. 1898. *d.* at Simla, 1 Dec. 1901. D.S.O. 19 Nov. 1891. G.S.P. 17 Jan. 1894. LL.D. Ab. 1895. C.B. 21 May 1898. N.-E. Frontier, Bhutan, 1865–66, medal with clasp; Lushai, 1871–72, Desp. G.G.O. No. 480 of 1872, clasp. N.-W. Frontier, 1st and 2nd Miranzai, 1891, as P.M.O., Desp. G.G.O. No. 632 of 1891, clasp; Hazara, 1891, as P.M.O. clasp; Isazai, 1892, as P.M.O. Author of Report on the Medicolegal returns of 1870–72, 1876; On the improvement of Military Medical Arrangements in India, since 1871, as illustrated by the Lushai campaign of 1871, and the Miranzai expeditions of 1891.

1867. Reid, Robert. *b.* 15 Mar. 1837. B.A. Q.U.I. 1854. L.R.C.S. Ed. 1857. L.K.Q.C.P. 1865. A.S. 1 Apr. 1865. Surg. 1 July 1873. S.M. 16 Nov. 1880; dropped 3½ years by refusing to undergo exam. for promotion to Surgeon Major, promoted when exam. was abolished in 1880. R. 25 Apr. 1887. *d.* at Ballymullen, Lisburn, County Down, 26 Mar. 1907.

---

* No new officers were admitted to the I.M.S. for four years, 1861–64, while the question of amalgamation with the A.M.D. was under consideration. When the service was again thrown open to competition, early in 1865, among the successful candidates were six officers who had just gone through the Netley course on probation for the A.M.D.; J. Cleghorn, R. Harvey, J. Bennett, H. Cook, J. T. Welsh, and A. Barry. The three last were posted to Bombay. Harvey passed out of Netley for A.M.D. second, Cleghorn fourth, Bennett eighth, Cook tenth, Welsh forty-fourth, and Barry sixtieth, out of a total of seventy-six.

1868. **Knowles, Benjamin.** *b.* Dec. 1842. M.B. C.M. (Honours), 1864; M.D. 1865, Ab. A.S. 1 Apr. 1865. *d.* at Kohat, 29 June 1866.

1869. **Skeen, Andrew.** *b.* 27 Feb. 1842. M.A. 1861; M.B. C.M. (Honours), 1864, Ab. S.S.C. Cantab. 18—. A.S. 1 Apr. 1865. Surg. 1 July 1873. S.M. 1 Apr. 1877. *d.* at Kasauli, 10 June 1885.

*1870. **Bennett, John.** *b.* 7 Aug. 1839. L.R.C.S. Ed. 1861. M.D. Ab. 1862. L.S.A. 1863. A.S. on probation for A.M.D. Feb.–Mar. 1865. A.S. Bengal, 1 Apr. 1865. Surg. 1 July 1873. S.M. 1 Apr. 1877. B.S. 13 Jan. 1889. R. 26 Sept. 1890. *d.* in Jersey, 23 June 1899.

1871. **Thomson,** Robert Bremner. *b.* 25 Nov. 1842. M.D. Ed. (Gold medal), 1864. L.R.C.S. Ed. 1864. A.S. 1 Apr. 1865. *d.* at Dalhousie, 13 Aug. 1869.

1872. **MacIver, James Robertson.** *b.* 30 Jan. 1841. M.D. Ed. 1862. L.R.C.S. Ed. 1862. A.S. 1 Apr. 1865. *d.* at Sialkot, 11 Dec. 1869. N.-W. Frontier, Bezoti Afridi, 1868–69.

1873. **Gardner, Edward Barton.** *b.* 4 Aug. 1840. St. Thomas'. M.R.C.S. 1861. L.S.A. 1861. L.R.C.P. Ed. 1864. A.S. 1 Apr. 1865. Surg. 1 July 1873. S.M. 1 Apr. 1877. Killed at polo, at Bareli, 17 June 1886.

1874. **Kelly, James.** *b.* 25 Sept. 1841. M.D. Q.U.I. 1864. M.R.C.S. 1864. A.S. 1 Apr. 1865. Surg. 1 July 1873. S.M. 1 Apr. 1877. R. 12 Mar. 1886. *d.* at Kingstown, Dublin, 3 Dec. 1907. N.-W. Frontier, Bezoti Afridi, 1868-69. Afghanistan, 1879–80, action at Shergash, Desp., medal.

1875. **Spencer, Lionel Dixon.** *b.* 16 June 1842. Newcastle. M.D. St. A. 1862. M.R.C.S. 1864. L.S.A. 1865. A.S. 1 Apr. 1865. Surg. 1 July 1873. S.M. 1 April 1877. B.S. 27 Jan. 1889. S. Col. 24 Oct. 1892. S.M.G. 25 Oct. 1898. R. 16 June 1902. *d.* in London, 22 Sept. 1915. G.S.P. 29 Mar. 1895. C.B. 27 Aug. 1895. K.H.S. 27 Jan. 1906. K.C.B. 25 June 1909. N.-W. Frontier, Waziristan, 1894–95, as P.M.O. Desp. G.G.O. No. 473 of 1895, medal with clasp, C.B.

1876. **King, George** (e). *b.* 12 Oct. 1840. M.B. C.M. (Honours), Ab. 1865. A.S. 1 Oct. 1865. Surg. 1 July 1873. S.M. 1 Oct. 1877. B.S. 2 Apr. 1889. R. extra pension, 28 Feb. 1898. *d.* at San Remo, 13 Feb. 1909. Supt. Botanical Gardens, Calcutta, Mar. 1871-98. Director, Royal Botanical Gardens, Kew, 1893–1905. LL.D. Ab. 1884. F.R.S. 1887. C.I.E. 1 Jan. 1890. K.C.I.E. 1 Jan. 1898. Linnæan Society's Gold Medal for Botany, 1901. Author of Manual of Cinchona Cultivation in India, 1876; Glossary of Indian Plants, contributed to U.C. Datta's Materia Medica of the Hindus, 1877; Monograph of Species of Ferns of India and China, 18—; Materials for a Flora of the Malay Peninsula, 1889; Annals of the Royal Botanic Gardens, Calcutta, 7 vols. 1889; (with D. Prain, No. 2188, infra), Directions for drying plants for a Herbarium, 1893; Guide to Royal Botanic Garden, Calcutta, 1895.

1877. **Wilson, Henry Octavius.** *b.* 8 Oct. 1839, Bristol. M.R.C.S. 1861. L.S.A. 1861. A.S. 1 Oct. 1865. Resigned, 19 Aug. 1870. Afterwards in practice at Birkenhead. *d.* at Claughton, Birkenhead, 10 Nov. 1874.

1878. **Center, William.** *b.* 7 Sept. 1838. M.A. K.C. Ab. 1857. M.B. C.M. (Honours) Ab. 1865. A.S. 1 Oct. 1865. Surg. 1 July 1873. S.M. 1 Oct. 1877. B.S. 19 Apr. 1889. R. extra pension, 2 Apr. 1893. *d.* at Ealing, 16 May 1902.

* *Vide* note on p. 168.

1879. **Purves, Henry Black.** *b.* 2 July 1843. L.R.C.P. and S. Ed. 1864. A.S. 1 Oct. 1865. Surg. 1 July 1873. S.M. 1 Oct. 1877. B.S. 16 June 1889. R. extra pension, 4 Dec. 1895. *d.* at Malvern, 14 Aug. 1915.

1880. **Orton, Theodore.** *b.* 1 May 1834. King's Coll. London. M.R.C.S. 1860. L.S.A. 1861. A.S. 1 Oct. 1865. *d.* at Faizabad, 9 June 1870.

1881. **Deacon, Robert.** *b.* 1 Mar. 1838. Ledwich School, Dublin. L.R.C.S.I. 1863. L.R.C.P. Ed. 1864. A.S. 1 Oct. 1865. Surg. 1 July 1873. *d.* at Hazaribagh, 29 Jan. 1874.

1882. **Heffernan, Patrick Joseph.** *b.* 17 Mar. 1840. L.R.C.S.I. 1861. L.R.C.P. Ed. 1864. A.S. 1 Oct. 1865. Surg. 1 July 1873. *d.* at Malta, 2 Feb. 1876. Brother of J. J. Heffernan, M. No. 1242, 1856.

1883. **Massy, Dawson Godfrey.** *b.* 25 Jan. 1840. L.M. L.Ch. T.C.D. 1865. A.S. 1 Oct. 1865. *d.* in Fort William, 20 July 1866.

1884. **Thomson, George.** *b.* 14 May 1843. M.B. C.M. Ab. 1864. A.S. 1 Oct. 1865. Surg. 1 July 1873. S.M. 1 Oct. 1877. B.S. 1 Oct. 1889. S. Col. 1 Apr. 1893. R. 6 July 1898. *d.* at Norwood, Dec. 1903. C.B. 21 Jan. 1896. K.C.B. 20 May 1898. Afghanistan, 1878–79, Desp. medal. N.-W. Frontier, Chitral, 1895; P.M.O. Lines of Communication, Desp. G.G.O. No. 998 of 1895, medal with clasp. C.B.; Tirah, 1897–98, P.M.O. of force, Desp. G.G.O. No. 244 of 1898, two clasps, K.C.B.

1885. **Jameson, Robert.** *b.* 20 Nov. 1842. M.D. Glas. 1865. L.R.C.S. Ed. 1865. A.S. 1 Oct. 1865. Surg. 1 July 1873. S.M. 1 Oct. 1877. B.S. 1 Mar. 1891. R. 15 Apr. 1896. *d.* at Tighnabruaich, Argyllshire, 21 Nov. 1908. Abyssinia, 1868, medal.

1886. **Mathew, Robert George.** *b.* 29 June 1841. Q.C. Cork and Ledwich School, Dublin. L.R.C.S.I. 1864. L.R.C.P. Ed. 1864. A.S. 1 Oct. 1865. Surg. 1 July 1873. S.M. 1 Oct. 1877. B.S. 18 Mar. 1890. R. 11 Aug. 1891. *d.* in London, 21 Sept. 1903.

1887. **Duncan, William.** *b.* 1 Jan. 1843. M.B. C.M. (Honours) Ab. 1865. A.S. 1 Oct. 1865. Surg. 1 July 1873. S.M. 1 Oct. 1877. R. 4 Dec. 1890. *d.* 27 Aug. 1921. Afghanistan, 1878–79, medal.

1888. **Chapman, Henry Theodore** (d). *b.* 2 Nov. 1842. Guy's. L.K.Q.C.P. 1865. L.R.C.S.I. 1865. A.S. on probation 1 Oct. 1865. Resigned from Netley. A.S. A.M.D. 1 Mar. 1866. M.R.C.S. 1868. Surg. 1 Mar. 1873. S.M. 31 Mar. 1878. R. 18 Aug. 1886; (Johnston's Roll of R.A.M.C. No. 6280). *d.* at Budleigh Salterton, Devon, 27 Nov. 1906.

1889. **Walsh, David John.** *b.* 29 Oct. 1840. Q.C. Cork. B.A. Q.U.I. 1862. L.R.C.P. and S. Ed. 1864. A.S. 1 Oct. 1865. *d.* at Chunar, 20 Aug. 1871.

1890. **Milne, Robert Moir.** *b.* 12 June 1843. M.B. C.M. Ab. 1865. A.S. 1 Oct. 1865. Surg. 1 July 1873. *d.* at Benares, 11 Aug. 1875. Father of C. J. R. Milne, No. 2374, infra, 1895.

1891. **Massy, George.** *b.* 17 Mar. 1842. M.R.C.S. 1864. L.R.C.S.I. 1864. L.K.Q.C.P. 1865. A.S. 1 Oct. 1865. Surg. 1 July 1873. S.M. 1 Oct. 1877. B.S. 29 Mar. 1890. R. 9 Sept. 1896. *d.* at Bath, 14 May 1906.

1892. **Ross, George Cumberland.** *b.* 21 Dec. 1842. L.R.C.S.I. 1864. L.K.Q.C.P. 1865. A.S. 1 Oct. 1865. Surg. 1 July 1873. S.M. 1 Oct. 1877. B.S. 30 Apr. 1890. S. Col. 1 Jan. 1894. R. 1 Oct. 1897. *d.* at Milan, 26 Feb. 1921. Father of Staff Surg. G. C. C. Ross, R.N. lost on H.M.S. ' Hawke,' 15 Oct. 1914.

1893. **Power, Richard.** *b.* 30 Sept. 1842. L.R.C.S.I. 1863. L.R.C.P. Ed. 1864. A.S. 1 Oct. 1865. Surg. 1 July 1873. S.M. 1 Oct. 1877. R. 1 Jan. 1896. *d.* in Australia, 21 Oct. 1924. N.-W. Frontier, Hazara, 1868, occupation of Black Mountain, medal with clasp; Jowaki, 1877–78, clasp. Afghanistan, 1879–80, capture of Ali Musjid, medal.

1894. **Knox, James.** *b.* 31 Aug. 1842. Ledwich School, Dublin. L.R.C.S.I. 1863. L.R.C.P. Ed. 1863. A.S. 1 Oct. 1865. *d.* at Mian Mir, 27 Dec. 1870.

1866

1895. **Griffith, Griffith.** *b.* 13 Jan. 1844. Liverpool and Univ. Coll. London. L.S.A. 1865. M.R.C.S. 1866. A.S. 31 Mar. 1866. Surg. 1 July 1873. S.M. 31 Mar. 1878. B.S. 6 July 1890. R. 1 May 1893. *d.* 25 Oct. 1924, at Hendrefeinws, Chwilog, North Wales. Abyssinia, 1867–68, medal. Afghanistan, 1879–80, medal. N.-W. Frontier, Mahsud Waziri, 1881.

1896. **Cameron, Lewis,** *b.* 18 June 1842. M.D. Ed. 1863. L.R.C.S. Ed. 1863. A.S. 31 Mar. 1866. Surg. 1 July 1873. S.M. 31 Mar. 1878. R. 9 Aug. 1891. *d.* at St. Heliers, Jersey, 17 Oct. 1927.

1897. **Raye, Daniel O'Connell.** *b.* 4 Aug. 1842. Q.C. Galway, R.C.S.I. Paris and Vienna. M.D. Q.U.I. 1865. L.R.C.S.I. 1865. A.S. 31 Mar. 1866. Surg. 1 July 1873. F.R.C.S.I. 1874. S.M. 31 Mar. 1878. B.S. 26 Sept. 1890. S. Col. 2 Apr. 1894. R. 2 Apr. 1899. Hony. F.R.C.S. 1900. *d.* 29 Dec. 1926, Lacks Yews, Mattingley. Nephew of Daniel O'Connell, the Liberator. N.-E. Frontier, Daphla, 1874–75.

1898. **Gage, James Thomas.** *b.* 14 Aug. 1842. M.D. C.M. (Honours) Ab. 1865. A.S. 31 Mar. 1866. *d.* in camp at Mirat, 8 Sept. 1867.

1899. **Warburton, William Pleace.** *b.* 17 Aug. 1843, at Halifax, Prince Edward Island. M.B. C.M. 1865; M.D. 1885, Ed. A.S. 31 Mar. 1866. Surg. 1 July 1873. S.M. 31 Mar. 1878. B.S. 1 Apr. 1891. S. Col. Jan. 1894. R. 9 Jan. 1899. Supt. Royal Infirmary, Edinburgh, Dec. 1899 to 31 July 1911. *d.* at Lowestoft, 18 Oct. 1911. Brother of G. A. Warburton, No. 2051, infra, 1875. C.S.I. 1 Jan. 1899.

1900. **Birch, Edward Alfred.** *b.* 24 Sept. 1840. L.R.C.S.I. 1861. A.S. R.N. 1861–65. L.K.Q.C.P. 1865. F.R.C.S.I. 1866. A.S. Bengal, 31 Mar. 1866. Surg. 1 July 1873. S.M. 31 Mar. 1878. S.S.C. Cantab, 1878. M.D. Brux, 1879. M.R.C.P. Lond. 1886. B.S. 3 Apr. 1891. R. 4 Oct. 1893. F.R.C.P. Lond. 1902. *d.* in London, 27 Nov. 1912. China, 1861, as A.S. R.N.; actions of Kagosima and Simonosaki, Desp. medal. Author of Management and Treatment of Children in India, 1879, the seventh edition of Goodeve's Hints on Children; fifth edition (eleventh of Goodeve), edited by C. R. M. Green, No. 2229, infra, 1886, and V. B. Green Armytage, 1913; contributed article on Influence of Warm Climates on the Constitution to Davidson's Hygiene and Diseases of Warm Climates, 1893.

1901. Palmer, Dean Philip. *b.* 31 Oct. 1843. L.R.C.S.I. 1863. M.D. Q.U.I. 1864. A.S. 31 Mar. 1866. Surg. 1 July 1873. *d.* at Allahabad. 4 Sept. 1876.

1902. Keegan, Denis Francis. *b.* 17 Dec. 1840. M.R.C.S. 1861. M.B. 1862; B.A., M.D. 1865, T.C.D. A.S. 31 Mar. 1866. Surg. 1 July 1873. S.M. 31 Mar. 1868. B.S. 11 Aug. 1891. F.R.C.S. 1891. R., extra pension, 1 Apr. 1894. *d.* at Killiney, Co. Dublin, 1 Jan. 1920. Afghanistan, 1879–80, march under Genl. Roberts from Kabul to Kandahar, battle of Kandahar, medal with clasp, bronze star. Author of Litholapaxy, 1887; Rhinoplastic Operations, 1900.

1903. Galloway, William Walker. *b.* 6 July 1841. M.B. C.M. Ab. 1865. A.S. 31 Mar. 1866. Surg. 1 July 1873. S.M. 31 Mar. 1878. *d.* at Rawal Pindi, 21 July 1879. Abyssinia, 1867–68, medal.

1904. Eades, Lewis Edward. *b.* 10 Sept. 1843. Stevens' Hosp. Dublin. L.R.C.S.I. 1864. L.R.C.P. Ed. 1865. A.S. 31 Mar. 1866. Surg. 1 July 1873. F.R.C.S.I. 1874. S.M. 31 Mar. 1878. R. 13 Oct. 1895. *d.* 11 Dec. 1898.

1905. MacKenzie, Stephen Coull. *b.* 5 Apr. 1842. M.D. Ed. 1864. L.R.C.P. and S. Ed. 1864. A.S. 31 Mar. 1866. M.R.C.P. Ed. 1870. Surg. 1 July 1873. F.R.C.S. Ed. 1874. S.M. 31 Mar. 1878. F.R.C.P. Ed. 1881. B.S. 13 Aug. 1891. *d.* at Darjiling, 1 Oct. 1893. Author of Medicolegal Experiences in Calcutta, 1891.

1906. MacDonnell, Joseph (d). *b.* 15 Sept. 1841. L.R.C.P. and S. Ed. 1864. A.S. on probation, 31 Mar. 1866. Never joined. Resigned, 20 June 1866. Afterwards Medl. Officer, Dunmore District, Co. Galway. L.R.C.P.I. 1879. Name omitted from Medl. Regr. 1924.

1907. Stewart, William Day. *b.* 1 May 1840. Madras. Hosp. Apprentice, Madras, 1 Nov. 1857. Asst. Apothecary, 9 Nov. 1858. Resigned, 1865. L.R.C.P. and S. Ed. 1866. A.S. 1 Oct. 1866. Surg. 1 July 1873. S.M. 1 Oct. 1878. M.D. St. A. 1889. F.R.C.S. Ed. 1889. *d.* at Cuttack, 23 Nov. 1890. Father of G. H. Stewart, I.M.S. 1899 (Genl. List, No. 93).

1908. Dutt, Omesh Chunder. *b.* Jan. 1840. Calcutta. L.M.S. Calcutta, 1863. L.R.C.P. and S. Ed. 1866. A.S. 1 Oct. 1866. *d.* in Univ. Coll. Hosp. London, 8 Feb. 1870.

1909. May, William Gormley. *b.* 4 Oct. 1837. Q. C. Galway. B.A. Q.U.I. 1859. L.R.C.S.I. 1861. L.R.C.P. Ed. 1866. A.S. 1 Oct. 1866. *d.* at Kasauli, 12 May 1872.

1910. Compigné, Horatio David Steel. *b.* 11 Jan. 1844. M.D. Ed. 1865. L.R.C.S. Ed. 1865. A.S. 1 Oct. 1866. Surg. 1 July 1873. S.M. 1 Oct. 1878. R. 13 Nov. 1884. D.P.H. Cantab, 1889. ——————. Afghanistan, 1879–80, with Kurram Field Force.

1911. Metcalfe, Fenwick. *b.* 13 June 1840. King's Coll. London. M.R.C.S. 1864. L.S.A. 1864. A.S. 1 Oct. 1866. Killed by a fall over precipice with horse, at Landour, 13 Oct. 1871.

1912. **Mullen, Thomas French** (afterwards **french-Mullen, Thomas**). *b.* 11 Aug. 1841. Q.C. Galway. M.D. 1864; M.Ch. 1865; Q.U.I. A.S. 1 Oct. 1866. Surg. 1 July 1873. S.M. 1 Oct. 1878. B.S. 2 Sept. 1891. R. 12 Aug. 1896. *d.* in London, 12 Oct. 1896. Signature on entry is Thomas french-Mullen. Brother of D. french-Mullen, No. 2087 infra, 1877, and of J. french-Mullen, No. 2103, infra, 1878. Took name of french-Mullen in 1890.

1913. **Gaffney, John Burke.** *b.* 22 Oct. 1839. Richmond Hosp. Dublin. L.A.H. 1861. L.R.C.S. Ed. 1864. Acting A.S. A.M.D. 9 Aug. 1864 to 31 Jan. 1865. A.S. Bengal, 1 Oct. 1866. Surg. 1 July 1873. S.M. 1 Oct. 1878. B.S. 18 Oct. 1891. R. 22 Oct. 1894. *d.* 5 Mar. 1913.

1914. **Curran, Richard Henry.** *b.* Mar. 1843. Ledwich School, Dublin. L.R.C.S.I. 1865. L.K.Q.C.P. 1865. A.S. 1 Oct. 1866. Surg. 1 July 1873. Killed by a fall from horse, at Rampur Boalia, 26 Sept. 1874.

1915. **MacKenna, Cornelius John.** *b.* 1 June 1841. Cecilia St. School, Dublin. L.R.C.P. and S. Ed. 1866. A.S. 1 Oct. 1866. Surg. 1 July 1873. S.M. 1 Oct. 1878. R. 16 Dec. 1891. *d.* at Bayonne, France, 4 July 1902. Afghanistan, 1879, medal. Burma, 1885–86, capture of Minhla and occupation of Mandalai, medal with clasp.

1916. **Wood, Julius John.** *b.* 10 Apr. 1842. M.B. C.M. Ed. 1865. A.S. 1 Oct. 1866. Surg. 1 July 1873. S.M. 1 Oct. 1878. R. 15 Feb. 1892. *d.* at Twickenham, 29 Oct. 1924. Author of Plants of Chutia Nagpur, 1902.

1917. **Finden, Woodforde.** *b.* 28 July 1844. King's Coll. Lond. and Paris. M.R.C.S. 1865. L.R.C.P. Ed. 1866. A.S. 1 Oct. 1866. Surg. 1 July 1873. S.M. 1. Oct. 1878. B.S. 2 Nov. 1891. R. 21 Dec. 1896. *d.* at Harrow, 27 Apr. 1916. Afghanistan, 1878–80, march under Genl. Roberts from Kabul to Kandahar, battle of Kandahar, Desp. G.G.O. No. 566 of 1880, medal with clasp, bronze star. Burma, 1887–88, medal. N.-W. Frontier, second Miranzai, 1891, clasp.

1918. **Paterson, Andrew MacMaster.** *b.* 5 July 1841. Madras and Ed. Univ. L.R.C.P. and S. Ed. 1866. A.S. 1 Oct. 1866. Surg. 1 July 1873. S.M. 1 Oct. 1878. R. 1 Nov. 1894. *d.* in England, 22 Apr. 1904. Afghanistan, 1879–80, Desp. medal. N.-W. Frontier, Zhob Valley, 1890. N.-E. Frontier, Manipur, 1891, medal with clasp.

1919. **MacMaster, Andrew** (d). *b.* 8 Apr. 1841. L.R.C.S.I. 1864. L.R.C.P. Ed. 1866. A.S. on probation, 1 Oct. 1866. Removed from Netley, 31 Oct. 1866. Never joined. Afterwards in practice at Omagh, Tyrone, and Bangor, Down. Name omitted from Medl. Regr. 1923.

1867

1920. **Lethbridge, Alfred Swaine.** *b.* 30 Sept. 1844. Calcutta, King's Coll. Lond. and Ab. Univ. M.B. C.M. 1865; M.D. 1867, Ab. M.R.C.S. 1865. A.S. 30 Sept. 1867. Surg. 1 July 1873. S.S.C. Cantab. 1876. S.M. 30 Sept. 1879. B.S. Lt.-Col. 9 Apr. 1892. Additional Member, Leg. Council, India, Feb. 1893. R. extra pension, 1 Apr. 1898. *d.* at Burlesdon, Hants, 11 Mar. 1917. C.S.I. 21 May 1890. K.C.S.I. 20 May 1897.

1921. Stephen, Arthur. b. 27 Dec. 1843. M.A. 1864 ; M.B. C.M. (Honours), 1867, Ab. A.S. 30 Sept. 1867. Surg. 1 July 1873. S.M. 30 Sept. 1879. B.S. Lt.-Col. 16 Apr. 1892. S. Col. 17 May 1894. R. 19 May 1899. d. at Ealing, 22 Apr. 1927. Abyssinia, 1868, medal.

1922. Newman, John Henry. b. 9 Dec. 1844. Q.C. Cork. M.D. M.Ch. Q.U.I. 1865. A.S. 30 Sept. 1867. Surg. 1 July 1873. S.M. 30 Sept. 1879. B.S. Lt.-Col. 1 June 1892. S. Col. 29 Mar. 1895. R. 14 July 1900. d. at Killinardrish, Co. Cork, 30 Nov. 1913. G.S.P. 1 Apr. 1900. Abyssinia, 1868, medal. Afghanistan, 1878–79, two Bazar Valley expeditions, medal.

1923. Johnstone, Hugh. b. 9 Apr. 1842. M.A. 1862 ; M.B. C.M. (Honours), 1867, Ab. A.S. 30 Sept. 1867. Surg. 1 July 1873. S.M. 30 Sept. 1879. R. 9 Apr. 1897. d. at Southsea, 11 Dec. 1898.

1868

1924. Cunningham, David Douglas. b. 29 Sept. 1843. Ed. Univ. and Munich. M.D. C.M. Ed. 1867. A.S. 1 Apr. 1868. Surg. 1 July 1873. S.M. 1 Apr. 1880. B.S. Lt.-Col. 24 Oct. 1892. R. extra pension, 26 June 1898. d. at Torquay, 31 Dec. 1914. F.R.S. 6 June 1889. C.I.E. 3 June 1893. K.H.P. 4 Dec. 1907. Col. 4 Dec. 1907, on appointment as K.H.P. Author (with Surg.-Major T. R. Lewis, A.M.D.) of article on Fungus Disease of India, in Quain's Dictionary of Medicine, 1882 ; of Physiological and Pathological Researches, 1888 ; and of many other scientific reports ; also author of Some Indian Friends and Acquaintances, 1903 ; Plagues and Pleasures of Life in Bengal, 1907.

1925. Whitwell, Henry. b. 23 Mar. 1843. Madras. Passed Hosp. Apprentice, Madras, 25 Apr. 1862. Asst. Apothecary, 26 June 1862. Resigned, 15 Nov. 1866. L.R.C.P. and S. Ed. 1867. A.S. 1 Apr. 1868. Surg. 1 July 1873. S.M. 1 Apr. 1880. d. from effects of an explosion of chemicals, Bankipur, 6 July 1887. Brother of R. R. H. Whitwell, No. 2138, infra, 1880.

1926. Cameron, Archibald. b. 13 Dec. 1845. M.B. C.M. Glas. 1867. A.S. 1 Apr. 1868. Surg. 1 July 1873. S.M. 1 Apr. 1880. B.S. Lt.-Col. 1 Apr. 1893. R. extra pension, 1 Apr. 1895. d. in London, 1 Aug. 1896.

1927. Evers, Benjamin. b. 28 Nov. 1841. L.R.C.P. and S. Ed. 1867. A.S. 1 Apr. 1868. Surg. 1 July 1873. M.B. C.M. 1878 ; M.D. 1879, Ab. S.M. 1 Apr. 1880. S.S.C. Cantab, 1885. R. 20 Apr. 1896. d. at West Kensington, 29 Mar. 1904.

1928. Carmichael, James Charles Gordon. b. 23 Apr. 1845. M.B. C.M. (Honours), 1867 ; M.D. 1889, Ab. A.S. 1 Apr. 1868. Surg. 1 July 1873. S.M. 1 Apr. 1880. B.S. Lt.-Col. 2 Apr. 1893. S. Col. 29 Mar. 1895. R. 2 May 1900. d. at Ealing, 23 Oct. 1905. Father of J. C. G. Carmichael and D. G. Carmichael, R.A.M.C. N.-W. Frontier, Mahsud Waziri, 1881. Egypt, 1882, battle of Tel-el-Kebir, medal with clasp, bronze star. Burma, 1886–87, Desp. G.G.O. No. 434, of 1887, medal with clasp. N.-W. Frontier, Malakand 1897–98, as P.M.O. of force ; Buner, as P.M.O. of force, capture of Tanga Pass, Desp. G.G.O. No. 1317 of 1897 and No. 217 of 1898, medal with clasp.

1929. **Harvey, William.** *b.* 23 Dec. 1840. Charing Cross Hosp. M.R.C.S. 1862. L.S.A. 1862. A.S. R.N. 13 May 1862 to 25 Jan. 1868. A.S. Bengal, 1 Apr. 1868. F.R.C.S. 1872. Surg. 1 July 1873. R. 6 Apr. 1879. Afterwards M.O.H. Newton Abbot and Dawlish, Devon. *d.* 28 Nov. 1922. Author of Science and Practice of Surgery (in Urdu).

1930. **Grant, Alexander Gibb.** *b.* 11 May 1841. M.B. C.M. Ab. 1865. A.S. 1 Apr. 1868. Surg. 1 July 1873. S.M. 1 Apr. 1880. R. 18 Aug. 1886. *d.* at Hove, 5 Oct. 1895. Afghanistan, 1879–80, with Kandahar Field Force, medal.

1931. **Jackson, Warwick.** *b.* 20 June 1841. L.R.C.P. and S. Ed. 1867. A.S. 1 Apr. 1868. Surg. 1 July 1873. S.M. 1 Apr. 1880. R. 8 Apr. 1888. *d.* 5 Apr. 1901. Afghanistan, 1878–79, capture of Peiwar Kotal, medal with clasp. N.-W. Frontier, Mahsud Waziri, 1881.

1932. **MacLaren, George Gilbert.** *b.* 11 Sept. 1845. M.B. C.M. Ed. 1886. A.S. 1 Apr. 1868. Surg. 1 July 1873. S.M. 1 Apr. 1880. B.S. Lt.-Col. 1 May 1893. R. 27 June 1893. *d.* at Blairgowrie, Perthshire, 17 Nov. 1922. Brother of J. F. MacLaren, No. 2166, infra, 1881.

1933. **Monteath, Joseph Johnstone.** *b.* 27 Mar. 1843. Q.C. Belfast. M.D. Q.U.I. 1867. L.R.C.S. Ed. 1867. A.S. 1 Apr. 1868. Surg. 1 July 1873. S.M. 1 Apr. 1880. *d.* at Chinsura, Hugli, 1 Sept. 1888. N.-E. Frontier, Lushai, 1871–72, medal.

1934. **Stevens, Richard Havell.** *b.* 16 July 1843. Ed. Univ. and King's Coll. Lond. M.B. C.M. Ed. 1867. M.R.C.S. 1867. A.S. 1 Apr. 1868. Surg. 1 July 1873. R. 11 Dec. 1875. *d.* 22 Mar. 1877.

1935. **Downie, Kenneth MacKenzie.** *b.* 15 July 1845. Ed. Univ. Vienna, and Munich. M.B. C.M. 1866. M.D. 1875, Ed. A.S. 1 Oct. 1868. Surg. 1 July 1873. Resigned, 14 Feb. 1875. S.S.C. Cantab. 1876. Reappointed, 15 May 1879, dropping 4¼ years. S.M. 29 Dec. 1884. S. Lt.-Col. 29 Dec. 1892. R. 1 Apr. 1893. *d.* at Cannes, 17 Feb. 1912. Burma, 1885–87, Ruby Mines Expedition, medal with clasp. N.-W. Frontier, Hazara, 1888, action of Kotkai, clasp.

1936. **MacKenzie, Frederic Morell.** *b.* Dec. 1843. London Hosp. M.R.C.S. 1866. L.S.A. 1868. A.S. 1 Oct. 1868. Surg. 1 July 1873. R. 3 Aug. 1877. Afterwards in practice in London. *d.* in London, 30 Jan. 1927.

1937. **MacGregor, John.** *b.* 1 Aug. 1841. M.A. St. A. 18—. L.R.C.P. and S. Ed. 1868. A.S. 1 Oct. 1868. Surg. 1 July 1873. S.M. 1 Oct. 1880. *d.* at Drumglass, Perthshire, 22 June 1881. Father of R. D. MacGregor, No. 330, Genl. List, I.M.S. 1904.

1938. **Hutcheson, George.** *b.* 27 June 1844. L.R.C.P. and S. Ed. 1868. A.S. 1 Oct. 1868. M.B. C.M. 1869; M.D. 1871, Glas. Surg. 1 July 1873. S.M. 1 Oct. 1880. B.S. Lt.-Col. 27 June 1893. S. Col. 1 Oct. 1897. R. 1 Oct. 1902. *d.* 21 May 1928. Father of Lt.-Col. G. Hutcheson, I.M.S. Gen. List, No. 41. Author of Cholera, its dissemination, 1885.

1939. **Johnson, Edward Reginald.** *b.* 23 Jan. 1846. Bart's. M.R.C.S. 1867. L.R.C.P. Ed. 1868. L.S.A. 1868. A.S. 1 Oct. 1868. Surg. 1 July 1873. S.M. 1 Oct. 1880. R. 2 Jan. 1894. ———. N.-E. Frontier, Lushai, 1871–72, Desp. medal with clasp; Akha, 1883–84, Desp.

1869

1940. Calthrop, Christopher William (afterwards **C. W. Carr-Calthrop**). b. 28 July 1844. Charing Cross Hosp. and Heidelberg. M.R.C.S. 1867. L.R.C.P. Lond. 1868. L.S.A. 1868. M.D. Heidelberg, 1869. A.S. 1 Apr. 1869. Surg. 1 July 1873. S.M. 1 Apr. 1881. B.S. Lt.-Col. 29 Mar. 1895. Col. 2 Apr. 1899. R. 2 Apr. 1904. C.B.E. 1 Jan. 1920. Took name of Carr-Calthrop in 1898. ———. Afghanistan. 1879–80, affair at Ali Khel, operations at and around Kabul, wounded, medal with clasp. Soudan, 1896, Dongola expedition as P.M.O., medal and Khedive's medal. War of 1914–18, C.B.E. Author of Assam Pharmacopœia, 1900; Notes on Families of Calthorpe and Calthrop, 1905.

1941. Wood, Alexander. b. 18 Jan. 1847. M.B. C.M. 1868. M.D. 1871, Ab. L.S.A. 1869. A.S. 1 Apr. 1869. Surg. 1 July 1873. d. in London, 16 July 1878.

1942. Sanders, Richard Careless. b. 13 July 1845. London Hosp. M.R.C.S. 1867. L.S.A. 1867. A.S. 1 Apr. 1869. Surg. 1 July 1873. S.M. 1 Apr. 1881. F.R.C.S. Ed. 1882. M.D. Durham, 1882. B.S. Lt.-Col. 4 Oct. 1893. R. 13 July 1900. d. at Faversham, 31 Dec. 1914.

1943. Sanders, Edwin. b. 15 July 1845. Bart's. M.R.C.S. 1868. L.S.A. 1869. A.S. 1 Apr. 1869. Surg. 1 July 1873. S.M. 1 Apr. 1881. R. 1 Jan. 1891. ———.

1944. Franklin, Benjamin. b. 30 Apr. 1844. Univ. Coll. Lond. and Paris. M.R.C.S. 1867. L.S.A. 1869. A.S. 1 Apr. 1869. Surg. 1 July 1873. S.M. 1 Apr. 1881. B.S. Lt.-Col. 1 Jan. 1894. S. Col. 25 Oct. 1897. S.G. and D.G. 2 Dec. 1901. R. 1 Jan. 1905. d. at East Sheen, Surrey, 15 Feb. 1917. C.I.E. 20 May. 1896. Q.H.P. 22 Mar. 1898. K.C.I.E. 1 Jan. 1903.

1945. Edis, Frederick Pooley. b. June 1843. Westminster Hosp. Dublin, and Vienna. M.B. Lond. 1864. M.R.C.S. 1864. F.R.C.S. 1868. A.S. 1 Apr. 1869. Surg. 1 July 1873. S.M. 1 Apr. 1881. d. at Santa Barbara, California, 9 Oct. 1881.

1946. Wright, Robert Temple. b. 2 Apr. 1843. King's Coll. Lond. and Ed. Univ. M.D. Ed. 1866. M.R.C.S. 1866. M.R.C.P. Lond. 1868. F.R.C.S. 1869. A.S. 1 Apr. 1869. Surg. 1 July 1873. S.M. 1 Apr. 1881. B.S. Lt.-Col. 2 Jan. 1894. R. 20 June 1894. d. at Bedford, 27 Aug. 1902. Afghanistan, 1880–81, medal. Author of Health Resorts during sick leave, 1877.

1947. Davis, George MacBride. b. 29 Mar. 1846. Q.C. Belfast. M.D. M.Ch. Q.U.I. 1866. L.A.H. 1866. A.S. 1 Apr. 1869. Surg. 1 July 1873. S.M. 1 Apr. 1881. B.S. Lt.-Col. 17 Jan. 1894. S. Col. 25 Oct. 1897. R. 25 Oct. 1902. d. at Wimbledon, 4 Oct. 1909. D.S.O. 27 Aug. 1895. C.B. 20 May 1898. G.S.P. 14 July 1900. N.-W. Frontier, Mahsud Waziri, 1881; first Miranzai, 1891; Hazara, 1891. medal with clasp; Waziristan Delimitation Escort, 1894, as P.M.O. Desp. G.G.O. No. 268 of 1895, action at Wana, 3 Nov. 1894; Waziristan 1894–95, clasp, D.S.O.; Tirah, 1897–98, as P.M.O., 2nd Division, actions of Dargai and of Sampagha and Arhanga Passes, operations in Bara Valley, Desp. G.G.O. No. 244 of 1898, medal with two clasps, C.B. China, 1900, as P.M.O. of force, Desp. L.G. 13 Sept. 1901, medal. N.-W. Frontier, Waziristan, 1901–02, as P.M.O., Desp. L.G. 8 Aug. 1902, clasp.

INDIAN MEDICAL SERVICE [1869

1948. Gupta, Kali Pada. *b.* 28 June 1843. Calcutta and Ed. Univs. M.A. (Honours), 1866; M.B. (Honours), 1868, Calcutta. L.R.C.P. and S. Ed. 1868. A.S. 1 Apr. 1869. Surg. 1 July 1873. F.R.C.S. Ed. 1879. S.M. 1 Apr. 1881. S.S.C. Cantab. 1884. R. 27 June 1898. *d.* in Calcutta, 28 Aug. 1911. Author of Elements of Sanitary Science and Practical Hygiene, 1901.

1949. Linton, Henry James. *b.* 18 Jan. 1844. T.C.D. and Westminster Hosp. M.R.C.S. 1867. L.R.C.P. Ed. 1868. A.S. 1 Apr. 1869. Surg. 1 July 1873. S.M. 1 Apr. 1881. *d.* at Peshawar, 4 Apr. 1892. Afghanistan, 1878–80, second Bazar Valley expedition, march under Genl. Roberts from Kabul to Kandahar, battle of Kandahar, medal with clasp, bronze star.

1950. Duke, Olliver Thomas. *b.* 14 Nov. 1848. Guy's. M.R.C.S. 1864. L.S.A. 1867. M.B. Lond. 1867. A.S. 1 Oct. 1869. Surg. 1 July 1873. S.M. 1 Oct. 1881. R. 22 Feb. 1887. *d.* at Folkestone, 29 Jan. 1914. Stood unsuccessfully, as Liberal Unionist, for South Beds, Luton division, in 1892 (twice), and in 1895; and for Stirling Burghs in 1900. Brother of J. Duke, No. 1996, infra, 1872. Afghanistan, 1878–80, Asst. to Govr. Genls. Agent for Biluchistan, action of Syad But, Desp. G.G.O. No. 610 of 1879, medal.

1951. Nicholson, Francis Cobham. *b.* 2 Nov. 1845, at Melbourne. M.B. C.M. Ed. 1869. A.S. 1 Oct. 1869. Surg. 1 July 1873. S.M. 1 Oct. 1881. B.S. Lt.-Col. 1 Apr. 1894. R. extra pension, 2 Apr. 1896. *d.* in London, 24 Dec. 1896. Father of M. A. Nicholson, No. 518, Genl. List, I.M.S. 1909. N.-E. Frontier, Lushai, 1871–72, medal with clasp.

1952. Gunn, John Sutherland. *b.* 20 Feb. 1845. M.B. C.M. Ab. 1868. A.S. 1 Oct. 1869. Surg. 1 July 1873. *d.* at Clarens, Switzerland, 11 May 1881.

1953. Hendley, Thomas Holbein. *b.* 21 Apr. 1847. Bart's. M.R.C.S. 1869. L.R.C.P. Lond. 1869. L.S.A. 1869. A.S. 1 Oct. 1869. Surg. 1 July 1873. S.M. 1 Oct. 1881. B.S. Lt.-Col. 2 Apr. 1894. S. Col. 2 Apr. 1898. R. 10 Apr. 1903. *d.* in London, 2 Feb. 1917. C.I.E. 1 Jan. 1891. V.D. 18 June 1896. Brother of H. Hendley, No. 2183, infra, 1884. Author of Jeypore Guide, 1876; Handbook on Jeypore and its Arts, 18—; Memorials of the Jeypore Exhibition of 1883, 1883; (with Lt.-Col. S. S. Jacob) Jeypore Enamels, 1886; Handbook of Jeypore Courts, London Indo-Colonial Exhibition of 1886, 1886; Ulwar and its Art Treasures, 1888; Damascening on Steel or Iron as practised in India, 1892; Medico-topographical account of Jeypore, 1895; Handbook to the Jeypore Museum, 1895; Asian Carpets, 1895; The Rulers of India and the Chiefs of Rajputana, 1897; Instructions for Hospital Assistants in Jeypore State, 1898; General Medical History of Rajputana, 1900; The Rajputs and the History of Rajputana, 1905; Indian Jewellery, 1906–07.

1954. Gregg, William Henry. *b.* 30 Jan. 1845. B.A. M.B. M.Ch. T.C.D. 1869. A.S. 1 Oct. 1869. Surg. 1 July 1873. S.M. 1 Oct. 1881. S.S.C. Cantab. 1886. M.R.C.P. Lond. 1887. B.S. Lt.-Col. 20 June 1894. R. 4 Dec. 1899. *d.* in London, 6 Nov. 1913. N.-E. Frontier, Lushai, 1871–72, medal with clasp. Author of Textbook of Botany, 1883.

1869] INDIAN MEDICAL SERVICE

1955. Seaman, Albert Baird. *b.* 11 Dec. 1842. King's Coll. Lond. M.R.C.S. 1865. L.R.C.P. Ed. 1868. A.S. 1 Oct. 1869. Surg. 1 July 1873. S.M. 1 Oct. 1881. B.S. Lt.-Col. 22 Oct. 1894. R. extra pension, 1 Oct. 1896. ———. Burma, 1885–86, medal with clasp. N.-E. Frontier, Lushai, 1889, Desp. G.G.O. No. 592 of 1889. N.-W. Frontier, Waziristan, 1894, action at Wano, clasp.

1956. Ghose, Fokeer Chunder. *b.* 25 Dec. 1845. M.B. Calcutta, 1868. L.R.C.S. and P. Ed. 1868. A.S. 1 Oct. 1869. Surg. 1 July 1873. R. 12 Mar. 1879. ———.

1957. Smyth, Frederick Augustus. *b.* 27 July 1842. L.M. L.Ch. T.C.D. 1868. L.R.C.S.I. 1868. A.S. 1 Oct. 1869. Surg. 1 July 1873. S.M. 1 Oct. 1881. B.S. Lt.-Col. 12 Jan. 1895. R. 27 July 1898. ———. Burma, 1885–86, medal with two clasps. N.-W. Frontier, 1897, defence of Malakand, Desp. G.G.O. No. 1089 of 1897, medal.

1958. Boyd, Herbert. *b.* 22 May 1847, at St. John's, New Brunswick. Harvard, St. Mary's, and Paris. M.D. Harvard 18—. M.R.C.S. 1868. L.S.A. 1868. A.S. 1 Oct. 1869. Surg. 1 July 1873. S.M. 1 Oct. 1881. R. 15 Jan. 1895. *d.* at Birchington, 22 Apr. 1922. N.-W. Frontier, Jowaki, 1877–78, medal with clasp. Afghanistan, 1878–80, capture of Ali Musjid, operations in Khaibar Pass, medal with clasp. N.-W. Frontier, Hazara, 1888, clasp.

1959. Lloyd, John. *b.* 16 Jan. 1847. Q.C. Cork. M.D. M.Ch. Q.U.I. 1868. L.K.Q.C.P. 1869. A.S. 1 Oct. 1869. Surg. 1 July 1873. S.M. 1 Oct. 1881. *d.* at Sitapur, 11 Aug. 1885.

1960. Courtney, William Michael. *b.* 29 Sept. 1845. Ledwich School, Dublin. L.R.C.S.I. 1868. L.A.H. 1868. A.S. 1 Oct. 1869. Surg. 1 July 1873. S.M. 1 Oct. 1881. F.R.C.S.I. 1888. R. 7 Dec. 1895. *d.* 2 Dec. 1928. N.-E. Frontier, Daphla, 1873–74. Burma, 1886–87, medal with clasp. N.-E. Frontier, Chin Lushai, 1889–90, clasp.

1961. Ruttledge, Edward Butler. *b.* 29 Apr. 1844. London Hosp. M.R.C.S. 1865. L.S.A. 1866. A.S. 1 Oct. 1869. Surg. 1 July 1873. S.M. 1 Oct. 1881. R. 1 Oct. 1895. *d.* at Woking, 5 Dec. 1914.

1962. Robinson, Thomas. *b.* 15 May 1844. B.A. 1867. M.B. B.Ch. 1869, T.C.D. A.S. 1 Oct. 1869. Surg. 1 July 1873. S.M. 1 Oct. 1881. R. 30 Mar. 1895. *d.* 3 Oct. 1908. Afghanistan 1879, Chakmani and Zaimukht expeditions, capture of Zawa, medal. N.-W. Frontier, Mahsud Waziri, 1881–82; Zhob Valley, 1884, 1st Miranzai, 1891.

1963. Martin, Daniel Nicholas. *b.* 4 Aug. 1844. Q.C. Cork. B.A. M.D. M.Ch. Q.U.I. 1869. A.S. 1 Oct. 1869. Surg. 1 July 1873. S.M. 1 Oct. 1881. B.S. Lt.-Col. 28 Feb. 1898. R. extra pension, 1 May 1899. *d.* at Rowland's Castle, Hants., 8 Oct. 1929. Afghanistan. 1879–80, medal. N.-W. Frontier Mahsud Waziri, 1881.

1964. Strahan, Alexander Bannerman. *b.* 5 July 1842. M.B. C.M. Ab. 1865. A.S. 1 Oct. 1869. Surg. 1 July 1873. S.M. 1 Oct. 1881. R. 11 Feb. 1895. *d.* at Glenesk, Forfarshire, 8 June 1907. Afghanistan, 1879–80, operations at and around Kabul, in Dec. 1879, Hissarak expedition, medal with clasp. Burma, 1886–89, Desp. G.G.O. No. 782 of 1889, medal with two clasps.

1965. **Roe, William Alexander Crawford.** *b.* 4 Mar. 1847. T.C.D. L.R.C.P. and S. Ed. 1868. A.S. 1 Oct. 1869. Surg. 1 July 1873. S.M. 1 Oct. 1881. F.R.C.S. Ed. 1883. D.P.H. Cantab. 1892. B.S. Lt.-Col. 29 Mar. 1895. R. extra pension, 27 Feb. 1900. Representative of India Office on War Office Advisory Board, 1902. *d.* 19 Feb. 1915.

1966. **Kelly, Ambrose Hamilton.** *b.* 30 Sept. 1845. Stevens' Hosp. Dublin. L.K.Q.C.P. 1869. L.R.C.S.I. 1869. A.S. 1 Oct. 1869. Surg. 1 July 1873. Killed at Kabul, in the defence of the Residency, with Sir Louis Cavagnari, 3 Sept. 1879. N.-W. Frontier, Jowaki, 1877–78, medal. Afghanistan, 1878–79, medal.

1967. **Meadows, Charles John Walford.** *b.* 14 Jan. 1844. Guy's and Westminster Hosp. L.S.A. 1866. M.R.C.S. 1867. A.S. 1 Oct. 1869. Surg. 1 July 1873. S.M. 1 Oct. 1881. S.S.C. Cantab. 1882. B.S. Lt.-Col. 1 Apr. 1895. R. 9 June 1897. *d.* at Norwood, 2 Aug. 1899, from effects of an accident, knocked down by a bicycle. N.-E. Frontier, Lushai, 1871–72, Desp. G.G.O. No. 480 of 1872, medal with clasp.

1968. **Keefer, William Napier.** *b.* 17 Dec. 1844, at Thorold, Ontario. Toronto and MacGill Univ. B.A. Toronto, 1864. M.D. C.M. MacGill, 1869. L.R.C.S. Ed. 1869. L.S.A. 1869. A.S. 1 Oct. 1869. Surg. 1 July 1873. S.M. 1 Oct. 1881. R. 18 Dec. 1889. *d.* at Toronto, 27 Dec. 1922. Osmanieh, 4th Class, 1882. N.-E. Frontier, Lushai, 1871–72, medal with clasp. N.-W. Frontier, Jowaki, 1877–78, clasp. Afghanistan, 1878–80, capture of Ali Musjid, Laghman Valley and Zaimukht expeditions, capture of Zawa, Desp. medal with clasp. Egypt, 1882, action at Kassassin, battle of Tel-el-Kebir, medal with clasp, bronze star, Osmanieh.

1969. **Deane, Andrew.** *b.* 2 Dec. 1846. Ledwich School, Dublin. L.A.H. 1866. L.R.C.S.I. 1869. A.S. 1 Oct. 1869. Surg. 1 July 1873. S.M. 1 Oct. 1881. F.R.C.S.I. 1882. M.D. Durham, 1882. B.S. Lt.-Col. 4 Dec. 1895. R. extra pension, 1 Apr. 1900. Supt. Royal Victoria Hosp. Belfast, Dec. 1901 to Oct. 1920. *d.* at Westcliff-on-Sea, 29 Nov. 1922. Brother of W. Deane, No. 2157, infra, 1880.

1970. **Murray, William Flood.** *b.* 12 Apr. 1845. B.A. (Honours), M.B. M.Ch. T.C.D. 1868. A.S. 1 Oct. 1869. Surg. 1 July 1873. S.M. 1 Oct. 1881. B.S. Lt.-Col. 2 Apr. 1896. R. 18 Dec. 1899. ———.

1870

1971. **MacConnell, James Frederick Parry.** *b.* 13 Jan. 1848. Ab. Univ. and St. George's. M.B. C.M. 1869; M.D. 1882; Ab. A.S. 1 Apr. 1870. Surg. 1 July 1873. S.M. 1 Apr. 1882. M.R.C.P. Lond. 1883. F.R.C.P. Lond. 1888. *d.* in Calcutta, 24 Aug. 1896. Author of Catalogue of Calcutta Medical College Museum, 1881.

1972. **O'Brien, Joseph.** *b.* 8 Jan. 1844. Q.C. Cork and Ledwich School, Dublin. M.A. 1869; M.D. 1870; Q.U.I. M.R.C.S. 1869. L.R.C.P. and S. Ed. 1870. A.S. 1 Apr. 1870. Surg. 1 July 1873. S.M. 1 Apr. 1882. F.R.C.S. Ed. 1887. B.S. Lt.-Col. 4 May 1896. R. extra pension, 19 Aug. 1898. *d.* at Instow, Devon, 29 Dec. 1921. Brother of B. O'Brien, No. 2008, infra, 1872. N.-E. Frontier, Naga Hills, 1879–80, action of Konoma, Desp. G.G.O.s No. 123 and 405 of 1880, medal with clasp.

1973. MacDonnell, James O'Malley. b. 25 Mar. 1845. Q.C. Galway, St. Thomas', and Dublin. M.D. M.Ch. (Honours), 1869, Q.U.I. A.S. 1 Apr. 1870. Surg. 1 July 1873. M.R.C.S. 1880. F.R.C.S. 1880. S.M. 1 Apr. 1882. R. 29 July 1895. d. 9 Dec. 1918.

1974. Reid, James. b. 26 July 1844. M.B. C.M. Glas. 1868. A.S. 1 Apr. 1870. Surg. 1 July 1873. S.M. 1 Apr. 1882. R. 7 Apr. 1894. Examr., Medl. Stores, India Office, 1900–11. d. at Glasgow, 25 Apr. 1914.

1975. MacKenzie, Gilbert Proby. b. 15 Aug. 1847, in Demerara. M.B. C.M. Ed. 1869. L.R.C.S. Ed. 1869. A.S. 1 Apr. 1870. Surg. 1 July 1873. S.M. 1 Apr. 1882. d. on board P. and O. S.S. ' Peshawar,' off Sokotra, on passage to Europe, 2 Mar. 1890.

1872*

1976. Crombie, Alexander. b. 12 Dec. 1845. M.B. (Honours), 1867 ; M.D. 1870; Ed. L.R.C.S. Ed. 1867. L.S.A. 1870. A.S. A.M.D. 1 Apr. 1871 to 29 Mar. 1872; (Johnston's Roll of R.A.M.C. No. 6468). A.S. Bengal, 30 Mar. 1872. Surg. 1 July 1873. S.M. 30 Mar. 1884. S. Lt.-Col. 30 Mar. 1892. B.S. Lt.-Col. 11 Aug. 1896. R. 7 Apr. 1898. Lecturer, Tropical Diseases, Middlesex Hosp. 1899. Member Medl. Board, India Office, 1900–02. d. in King Edward's Hosp. London, 29 Sept. 1906. C.B. Civil, 22 Aug. 1902. Author of Articles on Sprue, Hill Diarrhœa, and Hepatic Abscess, in Allchin's Manual of Medicine, vol. v, 1903 ; Article on Tropical Fevers in Watson's Encyclopædia Medica, vol. ii, 1902 ; edited Indian Medical Gazette, 1892–93.

1977. Murphy, William Reid. b. 23 Oct. 1849. Meath Hosp. Dublin. L.R.C.S.I. 1871. L.K.Q.C.P. 1872. A.S. 30 Mar. 1872. Surg. 1 July 1873. S.M. 30 Mar. 1884. S. Lt.-Col. 30 Mar. 1892. B.S. Lt.-Col. 1 Oct. 1896. R. 15 July 1899. d. London, 7 Aug. 1927. D.S.O. 25 July 1890. G.S.P. 6 July 1918. Afghanistan, 1878–80, action of Saifudin and occupation of Kandahar ; battle of Ahmed Khel, actions of Arzu and Pathao Shana ; Desp. L.G. 22 Oct. 1878, medal with clasp. N.-W. Frontier, Hazara, 1888, Desp. G.G.O. No. 78 of 1888, medal with clasp. N.-E. Frontier, Lushai, 1889, clasp ; Chin Lushai, 1889–90, Desp. L.G. 12 Sept. 1890, clasp, D.S.O. N.-W. Frontier, Chitral, 1895, with relief force, medal with clasp. N.-W. Frontier, Samana, 1897, clasp. Tirah, 1897–98, with Kurram Kohat force, action in Ublan Pass, Desp. L.G. 11 Feb. 1898, and 5 Apr. 1898 ; P.M.O. Kurram movable column, two clasps.

1978. Joubert, Charles Henry. Full name Joubert de la Ferté, dropped the de la Ferté in 1869, resumed it after retirement, 20 Apr. 1906. b. 2 Mar. 1846. St. Mary's. M.R.C.S. 1868. M.B. Lond. 1870. F.R.C.S. 1872. A.S. 30 Mar. 1872. Surg. 1 July 1873. S.M. 30 Mar. 1884. S. Lt.-Col. 30 Mar. 1892. B.S. Lt.-Col. 9 Sept. 1896. Col. 31 Mar. 1900. R. 29 Mar. 1905. ———.

1979. Russell, Ebenezer Geer. Changed first name to Edgar in 1881. b. 7 Nov. 1848. Guy's. L.S.A., 1870. M.R.C.S., 1872. B.Sc. (Honours), 1872 ; M.B. 1872 ; Lond. A.S. 30 Mar. 1872. Surg. 1 July 1873. S.M. 30 Mar. 1884. S. Lt.-Col. 30 Mar. 1892. B.S. Lt.-Col. 30 Dec. 1896. R. 27 Aug. 1900. d. 8 Nov. 1920. Author of Malaria and the Spleen, 1880.

* Admission to Service closed for two years, Apr. 1870 to Mar. 1872.

INDIAN MEDICAL SERVICE [1872

1980. Scully, John. *b.* 3 Dec. 1846. Middlesex Hosp. M.R.C.S. 1871. L.R.C.P. Lond. 1871. L.D.S. R.C.S. 18—. A.S. 30 Mar. 1872. Surg. 1 July 1873. S.M. 30 Mar. 1884. S. Lt.-Col. 30 Mar. 1892. B.S. Lt.-Col. 9 Apr. 1897. R. extra pension, 8 Apr. 1899. *d.* at Eastbourne, 31 Aug. 1912.

1981. Hall, Geoffrey Craythorne. *b.* 27 Aug. 1848, at Grahamstown, South Africa. Guy's. M.R.C.S. 1871. L.R.C.P. Ed. 1871. A.S. 30 Mar. 1872. Surg. 1 July 1873. S.M. 30 Mar. 1884. S. Lt.-Col. 30 Mar. 1892. F.R.C.S. 1894. B.S. Lt.-Col. 1 Oct. 1897. Col. 2 Dec. 1901. R. 1 Nov. 1902. *d.* at Bexhill, 27 Oct. 1923. Franco-German war, 1870–71, with a Field Ambulance, German medal. Author of Causes of Blindness in India, 1879; Eye Diseases of Children, 1884; Complications of Cataract Operations, 1886; The crooked backed old man, 18—; Senile Cataract, 1899; When to wear glasses, 1900.

1982. Roy, Gopal Chunder. *b.* 16 May 1844. Cal. and Glas. Univ. L.M.S. Cal. 1865. Lecturer, Nagpur Medl. School, 1865–67. M.R.C.S. 1870. F.R.C.S. 1870. M.D. Glas. 1871. A.S. 30 Mar. 1872. Surg. 1 July 1873. S.M. 30 Mar. 1884. *d.* in Calcutta, 4 Feb. 1887. Burma, 1886, medal. Author of Causes, Symptoms, and treatment of Bardwan Fever, 1876.

1983. Reid, Adam Scott. *b.* 4 Apr. 1848. M.B. C.M. Ed. 1869. A.S. 30 Mar. 1872. Surg. 1 July 1873. S.M. 30 Mar. 1884. S. Lt.-Col. 30 Mar. 1892. B.S. Lt.-Col. 9 June 1897. Col. 19 May 1899. S.G. 16 June 1902. R. 25 Mar. 1907. *d.* in London, 2 Feb. 1918. G.S.P. 2 Dec. 1901. C.B. 26 June 1903. K.C.B. 19 June 1911. Afghanistan, 1879–80, medal. N.-E. Frontier, Chin Lushai, 1889–90, Burma column, medal with clasp. N.-W. Frontier, 1897–98, relief and defence of Malakand, relief of Chakdara, Malakand, operations in Bajaur and in Momand country, Desp. G.G.O. No. 178 of 1898, medal with two clasps. Author of Chin Lushai Land, 1893.

1984. Watson, George. *b.* 5 Sept. 1844. M.D. Ed. 1866. L.R.C.S. Ed. 1868. A.S. 30 Mar. 1872. Surg. 1 July 1873. *d.* at Peiwar Kotal, Afghanistan, 27 May 1880. Afghanistan, 1879–80.

1985. Fasken, William Andrew Durnford. *b.* 5 Apr. 1848. Ab. Univ. and Guy's. M.R.C.S. 1870. M.B. 1871; M.D. 1874; Ab. A.S. on probation, A.M.D. Oct. 1871 to Feb. 1872. A.S. Bengal, 30 Mar. 1872. Surg. 1 July 1873. S.M. 30 Mar. 1884. S. Lt.-Col. 30 Mar. 1872. *d.* at Fatehgarh, 1 Feb. 1897.

1986. Lawrie, Edward. *b.* 17 May 1846. Ed. Univ. and Paris. M.B. C.M. Ed. 1867. M.R.C.S. 1867. A.S. 30 Mar. 1872. Surg. 1 July 1873. S.M. 30 Mar. 1884. S. Lt.-Col. 30 Mar. 1892. R. 17 May 1901. Rejoined for service in war of 1914–18, 1 Dec. 1914. *d.* at Hove, 22 Aug. 1915. House Surg. to Syme in Ed. Royal Infy. Author of Results of Hyderabad Chloroform commission, 1894; Chloroform, a manual for Students and practitioners, 1901.

1987. Wilson, Joseph. *b.* 11 June 1848. Q.C. Cork. M.D. M.Ch. Q.U.I. 1871. A.S. 30 Mar. 1872. Surg. 1 July 1873. S.M. 30 Mar. 1884. S. Lt.-Col. 30 Mar. 1892. R. 24 Nov. 1894. *d.* at Southsea, from accidental burns, 13 Dec. 1897. N.-E. Frontier, Daphla, 1874–75.

1988. Lang, John Alfred Thomas. *b.* 19 Mar. 1849. L.S.A. 1870. M.R.C.S. 1871. A.S. 30 Mar. 1872. Surg. 1 July 1873. Drowned in river Baraki, Kachar, 12 Sept. 1873.

1989. Mulvany, Edward. *b.* 21 Nov. 1849. Catholic Univ. Dublin. L.R.C.S.I. 1871. L.K.Q.C.P. 1872. A.S. 30 Mar. 1872. Surg. 1 July 1873. S.M. 30 Mar. 1884. S. Lt.-Col. 30 Mar. 1892. R. 11 July 1892.

1990. Zorab, John (christened **Johannes**) **Manuk.** *b.* 9 Oct. 1846. Cal. and Ed. Univs. M.B. C.M. Ed. 1869. A.S. 30 Mar. 1872. Surg. 1 July 1873. S.M. 30 Mar. 1884. S. Lt.-Col. 30 Mar. 1892. R. 9 Oct. 1901. *d.* in Calcutta, 2 July 1904. Father of A. B. Zorab (I.M.S. Genl. List. No. 443).

1991. Dutt, Russick Lall. *b.* 26 Aug. 1845. Cal. and Ab. Univs. L.S.A. 1869. M.R.C.S. 1870. M.D. Ab. 1871. A.S. 30 Mar. 1872. Surg. 1 July 1873. S.M. 30 Mar. 1884. S. Lt.-Col. 30 Mar. 1892. B.S. Lt.-Col. 1 Apr. 1898. R. 31 Oct. 1899. *d.* in Calcutta, 3 Apr. 1924.

1992. Daphtary, Girdharlal Ratanlal. *b.* 4 Aug. 1845. Bombay and Glas. Univs. L.M.S. Bo. 1867. Sub. Asst. Surg. Bombay Civil Medl. Dept. 16 Dec. 1867. Travelling Fellow, Bombay Univ. 1871. A.S. 30 Mar. 1872. Surg. 1 July 1873. S.M. 30 Mar. 1884. R. 17 Feb. 1890. *d.* at Hammersmith, London, 26 May 1917. Afghanistan, 1879-80, medal.

1993. Bookey, John Thomas Brownrigg. *b.* 10 Dec. 1846. T.C.D. L.R.C.S.I. 1871. L.R.C.P. Ed. 1871. A.S. 30 Mar. 1872. Surg. 1 July 1873. S.M. 30 Mar. 1884. S. Lt.-Col. 30 Mar. 1892. B.S. Lt.-Col. 25 Oct. 1897. Col. 2 May 1900. R. 16 June 1905. *d.* at Bournemouth 19 Nov. 1921. C.B. 29 Nov. 1900. G.S.P. 16 June 1902. N.-W. Frontier, Jowaki, 1877-78, medal; Mahsud Waziri, 1881. Burma, 1886-87, operations of 2nd and 5th Brigades, Wuntho expedition, Desp. G.G.O. No. 434 of 1887, two clasps. N.-W. Frontier, Hazara, 1888, Desp. G.G.O. No. 978 of 1888, clasp; Second Miranzai, 1891, Desp. G.G.O. No. 632 of 1891, clasp; Waziristan, 1894-95, Desp. G.G.O. No. 473 of 1895, clasp; Malakand, 1897, Desp. L.G. 5 Nov. 1897, medal. China, 1900, Desp. L.G. 14 May 1901, medal with clasp, C.B. N.-W. Frontier, 1902, operations against Darwesh Khel Waziris, Desp. L.G. June 1903, clasp.

1994. MacGregor, Alexander. *b.* 9 Nov. 1846. Bart's. M.R.C.S. 1867. L.R.C.P. Ed. 1868. A.S. 30 Mar. 1872. Surg. 1 July 1873. S.M. 30 Mar. 1884. S. Lt.-Col. 30 Mar. 1892. R. 11 Apr. 1893. *d.* in London, 4 Jan. 1897. N.-W. Frontier, Hazara, 1888, Desp. medal.

1995. Young, James. *b.* 5 Aug. 1845. M.B. C.M. Ed. 1868. A.S. 30 Mar. 1872. Surg. 1 July 1873. S.M. 30 Mar. 1884. S. Lt.-Col. 30 Mar. 1892. B.S. Lt.-Col. 25 Oct. 1897. R. extra pension, 31 Mar. 1902. *d.* at Bedford, 13 July 1922. Burma, 1885-86, occupation of Mandalai, medal with clasp.

1996. Duke, Joshua. *b.* 14 June 1847. Guy's. M.R.C.S. 1868. L.S.A. 1868. A.S. 30 Mar. 1872. Surg. 1 July 1873. S.M. 30 Mar. 1884. S. Lt.-Col. 30 Mar. 1892. B.S. Lt.-Col. 2 Apr. 1898. R. extra pension, 1 Nov. 1902. Rejoined for service in war of 1914-18, 3 Dec. 1914 to 1917. *d.* at Rohais, Guernsey, 13 Feb. 1920. Brother of O.T. Duke, No. 1950, supra, 1869. Afghanistan, 1879-80, action at Charasiah, operations at and round Kabul, march under Genl. Roberts from Kabul to Kandahar, battle of Kandahar, operations against Marris, Desp. G.G.O. No. 137 of 1880, medal with two clasps, bronze star. Author of Banting in India, 1877; Queries at a Mess-table, 1878; Recollections of the Kabul campaign, 1883; Ince's Kashmir Handbook, revised and enlarged, 1888; the Prevention of Cholera, 1900; Kashmir and Jammu, 1903.

INDIAN MEDICAL SERVICE [1872

1997. **Gupta, Banka Bihari.** *b.* 25 Jan. 1845. Cal. and Glas. Univs. M.B. Cal. 1870. L.R.C.P. Ed. 1872. L.F.P.S.G. 1872. A.S. 30 Mar. 1872. Surg. 1 July 1873. S.M. 30 Mar. 1884. *d.* at Chinsura, Hugli, 18 Mar. 1892.

1998. **MacConaghey, John.** *b.* 8 Jan. 1849. Q.C. Galway and Belfast. M.D. M.Ch. Q.U.I. 1871. A.S. 30 Mar. 1872. Surg. 1 July 1873. S.M. 30 Mar. 1884. S. Lt.-Col. 30 Mar. 1892. B.S. Lt.-Col. 7 Apr. 1898. Col. 16 June 1902. R. 12 July 1905. *d.* at Exmouth, 18 Mar. 1907. Brother of W. MacConaghey, Bo. No. 997, 1869. Of three signatures in his application to appear for exam. two have an e before the y in his name, and one has not.

1999. **Palmer, Edward.** *b.* 8 Oct. 1846. Q.C. Galway and Guy's. L.R.C.S.I. 1869. L.K.Q.C.P. 1870. A.S. 30 Mar. 1872. Surg. 1 July 1873. S.M. 30 Mar. 1884. S. Lt.-Col. 30 Mar. 1892. B.S. Lt.-Col. 28 June 1898. R. extra pension, 31 Mar. 1901. *d.* 23 July 1906. Afghanistan, 1878–80, march under Genl. Roberts from Kabul to Kandahar, battle of Kandahar, Desp. 1 Jan. 1880, medal with clasp, bronze star. N.-W. Frontier, Hazara, 1891, Desp. G.G.O. No. 816 of 1891, medal. Chitral, 1895, relief of Chitral, medal with clasp.

2000. **Williams, Alfred Henry.** *b.* 20 Dec. 1846. Ab. Univ. and St. Thomas. M.B. C.M. Ab. 1871. M.R.C.S. 1872. A.S. 30 Mar. 1872. Surg. 1 July 1873. S.M. 30 Mar. 1884. S. Lt.-Col. 20 Mar. 1892. R. 4 July 1897. *d.* Eastbourne, 20 May 1925. Afghanistan, 1880, medal.

2001. **Holmes, Robert Andrew King.** *b.* 16 Sept. 1844. Q.C. Belfast and Dublin. B.A. 1866; M.B. 1870; Q.U.I. M.R.C.S. 1871. A.S. 30 Mar. 1872. Surg. 1 July 1873. S.M. 30 Mar. 1884. S. Lt.-Col. 30 Mar. 1892. R. 20 Mar. 1899. *d.* in London, 28 Jan. 1912.

2002. **Ferris, John Edward Charnock.** *b.* 6 Mar. 1849. Durham Univ. and St. George's. M.R.C.S. 1872. L.S.A. 1872. A.S. 30 Mar. 1872. Surg. 1 July 1873. S.M. 30 Mar. 1884. S. Lt.-Col. 30 Mar. 1892. R. 4 Aug. 1892. ———. Afghanistan, 1879–80, medal.

2003. **Lombard, David Edward Tyrrell.** *b.* 20 Dec. 1845. Q.C. Cork and Dublin. L.R.C.S.I. 1869. L.K.Q.C.P. 1870. A.S. 30 Mar. 1872. *d.* at Rawal Pindi, 15 Apr. 1873.

2004. **Brereton, Samuel.** *b.* 1845. Dublin and Paris. L.R.C.S.I. 1871. L.K.Q.C.P. 1872. A.S. 1 Oct. 1872. Surg. 1 July 1873. *d.* at Baghdad, 9 June 1880. Afghanistan, 1878–80, Kandahar Force, medal.

2005. **Moriarty, Mathew Denis.** *b.* 26 Jan. 1849. B.A. 1869; M.B. 1872; M.D. 1891; T.C.D. Medical Travelling Prizeman, T.C.D. 1872. L.R.C.S.I. 1872. A.S. 1 Oct. 1872. Surg. 1 July 1873. F.R.C.S.I. 1883. S.M. 1 Oct. 1884. S. Lt.-Col. 1 Oct. 1892. B.S. Lt.-Col. 27 July 1898. Col. 25 Oct. 1902. R. 26 Oct. 1905. *d.* at Guildford, 24 May 1925.

2006. **Price, Gordon.** *b.* 29 July 1848. Q.C. Belfast. M.D. M.Ch. Q.U.I. 1868. A.S. R.N. 1869–71. A.S. Bengal, 1 Oct. 1872. Surg. 1 July 1873. S.M. 1 Oct. 1884. S. Lt.-Col. 1 Oct. 1892. R. 16 Jan. 1898. *d.* at Utakamand, 7 Apr. 1912.

2007. Bovill, Edward. b. 9 Nov. 1846. Ab. Univ. and Guy's. M.B. C.M. 1871; M.D. 1891; Ab. A.S. 1 Oct. 1872. Surg. 1 July 1873. F.R.C.S. 1873. S.M. 1 Oct. 1884. S. Lt.-Col. 1 Oct. 1892. B.S. Lt.-Col. 19 Aug. 1898. R. extra pension, 9 Nov. 1901. Member Medical Board, India Office, 1905–07. d. in London, 1 Mar. 1908. N.-E. Frontier, Daphla, 1874–75.

2008. O'Brien, Bartholomew. b. 26 May 1848. Q.C. Cork. M.D. M.Ch. Q.U.I. 1872. A.S. 1 Oct. 1872. Surg. 1 July 1873. S.M. 1 Oct. 1884. S. Lt.-Col. 1 Oct. 1892 * Selected list, 2 Apr. 1899. Col. 1 Nov. 1902. R. 3 Dec. 1904. d. at Bognor, 1 Apr. 1905. Brother of J. O'Brien, No. 1972, supra, 1870.

2009. Dundas, George Albert. b. 9 July 1849. Guy's. M.R.C.S. 1872. L.R.C.P. Lond. 1872. A.S. 1 Oct. 1872. Surg. 1 July 1873. S.M. 1 Oct. 1884. d. at Mian Mir, 23 Oct. 1887.

2010. Hill, Henry Walter. b. 23 Aug. 1847. M.B. C.M. Ed. 1870. A.S. 1 Oct. 1872. Surg. 1 July 1873. S.M. 1 Oct. 1884. S. Lt.-Col. 1 Oct. 1892. d. at St. Helier's, Jersey, 22 Nov. 1892.

2011. Ahmed, Zainoor Allee. b. 19 July 1848. Cal. and Glas. Univs. L.M.S. Cal. 1871. M.B. 1872; M.D. 1873; Glas. L.R.C.P. Lond. 1872. L.F.P.S.G. 1872. A.S. 1 Oct. 1872. Surg. 1 July 1873. S.M. 1 Oct. 1884. S. Lt.-Col. 1 Oct. 1892. S. List, 3 Apr. 1899. R. extra pension, 19 July 1903. Rejoined for service in India, in war of 1914–18, 26 July 1915 to 1919. ———. N.-W. Frontier, Hazara, 1891, medal with clasp; Malakand, 1897–98, operations in Bajaur and in Momand country, Desp. G.G.O. No. 178 of 1898, medal with clasp; Tirah, 1897–98, operations in Bara Valley, clasp.

2012. Gilligan, William Arthur. b. 6 May 1845. Ledwich School, Dublin, T.C.D., and Univ. Coll. London. L.R.C.P. and S. Ed. 1872. A.S. 1 Oct. 1872. Surg. 1 July 1873. S.M. 1 Oct. 1884. S. Lt.-Col. 1 Oct. 1892. d. at Lahore, 15 Aug. 1893.

2013. Griffiths, William Edwin. b. 25 June 1849. Middlesex Hosp. L.S.A. 1871. M.R.C.S. 1872. A.S. 1 Oct. 1872. Surg. 1 July 1873. S.M. 1 Oct. 1884. S. Lt.-Col. 1 Oct. 1892. R. 6 Jan. 1903. d. at Florence, 14 May 1907. Brother of G. S. Griffiths, No. 2075, infra, 1876. Afghanistan, 1878–80, affairs at Matun and at Shutargardan pass, medal. N.-W. Frontier, Mahsud Waziri, 1894, action at Wana, medal with clasp.

1873

2014. Wilkie, David. b. 27 June 1849. Glas. and Berlin Univs. M.B. C.M. (Honours), Glas. 1871. A.S. 1 Apr. 1873. Surg. 1 July 1873. S.M. 1 Apr. 1885. S. Lt.-Col. 1 Apr. 1893. S. List, 1 May 1899. Col. 2 Apr. 1904. R. 2 Apr. 1909. d. at Falmouth, 6th Feb. 1930. G.S.P. 1 Oct. 1908.

---

* Under Royal Warrant of 26 Aug. 1898 the rank of Brigade-Surgeon-Lieutenant-Colonel was abolished, and its place taken by Lieutenant-Colonel " specially selected for increased pay under Article 6."

2015. **Battersby, William Edward.** *b.* 24 May 1847. B.A. 1867, M.B. 1869; M.Ch. 1870; T.C.D. M.R.C.S. 1870. A.S. 1 Apr. 1873. Surg. 1 July 1873. *d.* in England, 20 Feb. 1880.

2016. **Wall, Alfred John.** *b.* 21 Aug. 1847. St. Mary's. M.R.C.S. 1869. L.R.C.P. Lond. 1869. M.B. 1871; B.S. 1872; M.D. 1873; Lond. F.R.C.S. 1872. A.S. 1 Apr. 1873. Surg. 1 July 1873. T.H.P. 26 July 1882. R. 26 Feb. 1884. *d.* at Guildford, 29 Apr. 1898. Author of Indian Snake Poisons, 1883; Asiatic Cholera, 1893.

2017. **Moodie, Robert.** *b.* 23 Apr. 1845. Ed. and Vienna Univs. M.B. C.M. 1869; M.D. gold medal, 1881; B.Sc. 1882; Ed. A.S. 1 Apr. 1873. Surg. 1 July 1873. Resigned, 2 Jan. 1880. *d.* in Edinburgh, 7 Mar. 1898. Afghanistan, 1878–79, medal.

2018. **Tuohy, Francis Joseph.** *b.* 14 Sept. 1849. Q.C. Cork and Univ. Coll. Lond. M.D. M.Ch. 1871, Q.U.I. A.S. 1 Apr. 1873. Surg. 1 July 1873. T.H.P. 21 Nov. 1884. D.P.H. R.C.P. Lond. 1885. R. 21 Nov. 1886. M.A.O. R.U.I. 1889. *d.* at Cork, 10 Feb. 1894. Afghanistan, 1878–79, at Kandahar and Kelat-i-Ghilzai, medal.

2019. **Moynan, William Edward Bonsall.** *b.* 11 Feb. 1851. Q.C. Galway, and Carmichael School, Dublin. M.D., M.Ch., Q.U.I. 1872. A.S. 1 Apr. 1873. Surg. 1 July 1873. S.M. 1 Apr. 1885. *d.* at Kolaba, Bombay, 6 Oct. 1891. Burma, 1886–87, medal with clasp.

2020. **MacDonald, Denis Peter.** *b.* 19 Dec. 1848. Q.C. Cork and Catholic Univ. Dublin. M.D., M.Ch., Q.U.I. 1872. L.R.C.S.I. 1872. A.S. 1 Apr. 1873. Surg. 1 July 1873. S.M. 1 Apr. 1885. S. Lt.-Col. 1 Apr. 1893. S. List, 19 May 1899. R. extra pension, 6 July 1903. *d.* in England, 23 Mar. 1918. N.-W. Frontier, Jowaki, 1877–78, medal with clasp. Afghanistan, 1878–80, medal. N.-E. Frontier, Chin Lushai, 1889–90, clasp.

2021. **Baker, Oswald.** *b.* 21 Nov. 1847. London Hosp. L.R.C.P. and S. Ed. 1869. A.S. 1 Apr. 1873. Surg. 1 July 1873. S.M. 1 Apr. 1885. S. Lt.-Col. 1 Apr. 1893. R. 6 July 1898. M.D. Durham, 1899. Afterwards in practice in London. Outpatient Physn. Seamen's Hosp. London, 1899. ———. Translator of Leprosy, by E. Besnier, 1899.

2022. **Mallins, Henry.** *b.* 12 Feb. 1851. B.A. 1871; M.B. M.Ch. 1872; T.C.D. A.S. 1 Apr. 1873. Surg. 1 July 1873. Resigned, 25 July 1881. Afterwards in practice at Wotton, Norfolk. ———. Brother of C. Mallins, No. 1436, Madras, 1878. Afghanistan, 1878–79, with Khaibar force, actions at Ali Musjid and Fatehabad, medal with clasp.

2023. **Wright, Frederick William.** *b.* 7 Dec. 1850. M.B. C.M. Ed. 1872. A.S. 1 Apr. 1873. Surg. 1 July 1873. S.M. 1 Apr. 1885. S. Lt.-Col. 1 Apr. 1893. R. 7 Dec. 1905. *d.* at Bournemouth, 9 Sept. 1927. D.S.O. 1 July 1887. G.S.P. 4 Jan. 1919. Afghanistan, 1878–80, affairs at and near Jagdalak, action of Chihildakhteran, march under Genl. Roberts from Kabul to Kandahar, battle of Kandahar, operations against Marris, medal with clasp, bronze star. Burma, 1886–88, operations of 3rd and 4th Brigades, Desp. G.G.O. No. 434 of 1887, medal with two clasps, D.S.O. China, 1900, medal. N.-W. Frontier, Waziristan, 1901–02, medal with clasp.

2024. **Willcocks, Alexander John.** *b.* 15 May 1851. Ab. Univ. and Guy's. M.B. C.M. 1873; M.D. 1883; Ab. M.R.C.S. 1873 * Surg. 30 Sept. 1873. S.M. 30 Sept. 1875. S. Lt.-Col. 30 Sept 1893. S. List, 15 July 1899. R. 1 Apr. 1901. Member, Medl. Board, India Office, 1903–05. Rejoined for service in war of 1914–18. *d.* at Dehra Dun, 14 Jan. 1929. Brother of Genl. Sir James Willcocks, K.C.B., and of Sir William Willcocks, K.C.M.G. War of 1914–19, Egypt, Desp. L.G. 6 July 1917.

2025. **Moloney, Timothy.** *b.* 4 Dec. 1850. M.D. M.Ch. Q.U.I. 1872. Surg. 30 Sept. 1873. S.M. 30 Sept. 1885. *d.* at Glendarg, Co. Limerick, 21 Apr. 1890. N.-W. Frontier, Jowaki, 1877–78, medal with clasp. Afghanistan, 1879–80, defence of Sherpur, medal with clasp.

2026. **Deakin, Charles Washington Shirley.** *b.* 16 June 1849, at Hobart Town, Tasmania. Birmingham and Univ. Coll. Lond. M.R.C.S. 1872. L.R.C.P. Lond. 1873. L.S.A. 1873. Surg. 30 Sept. 1873. F.R.C.S. 1876. S.S.C. Cantab. 1876. S.M. 30 Sept. 1885. *d.* at Jhilam, 17 Sept. 1889. N.-W. Frontier, Hazara, 1888, action at Kotkai, medal. Author of The Contagious Diseases Acts, 1872.

2027. **MacKay, Henry Kellock.** *b.* 4 Dec. 1850, at Quebec. Guy's. M.R.C.S. 1873. L.S.A. 1873. Surg. 30 Sept. 1873. S.M. 30 Sept. 1885. S. Lt.-Col. 30 Sept. 1893. S. List, 30 Oct. 1899. Col. 3 Dec. 1904. R. 3 Dec. 1909. *d.* at Hythe, 14 Mar. 1930. C.I.E. 1 Jan. 1899. C.B. 29 June 1906. G.S.P. 2 Apr. 1909. N.-E. Frontier, Naga, 1875, Desp. G.G.O. No. 574 of 1875. Afghanistan, 1878–80, medal. N.-W. Frontier, Mahsud Waziri, 1881.

2028. **Swaine, Frederick Robert.** *b.* 20 Apr. 1851. M.B. C.M. Ab. 1872. Surg. 30 Sept. 1873. S.M. 30 Sept. 1885. S. Lt.-Col. 30 Sept. 1893. R. 1 Nov. 1904. *d.* at Ranchi, 14 July 1917. Brother of D. L. Swaine, M. No. 1415, 1876.

1874

2029. **Corbett, John Lane.** *b.* 8 Jan. 1852. Q.C. Cork. M.D. M.Ch. Q.U.I. 1873. Surg. 31 Mar. 1874. *d.* 24 Mar. 1886 at Montreux.

2030. **Browne, Samuel Haslett.** *b.* 19 Jan. 1850. Q.C. Belfast and Vienna. M.D. M.Ch. Q.U.I. 1870. A.S. R.N. 1870–72. Surg. Bengal, 31 Mar. 1874. S.M. 31 Mar. 1876. S. Lt.-Col. 31 Mar. 1894. M.R.C.P. Lond. 1896. S. List, 4 Dec. 1899. Col. 10 Apr. 1903. R. 29 Apr. 1906. ———. C.I.E. 1 Jan. 1896. Afghanistan, 1878–80, Desp. G.O.C.C. 14 Oct. 1879, medal.

2031. **Mair, Edward.** *b.* 3 July 1847. M.B. C.M. (Honours), Ab. 1870. Surg. 31 Mar. 1874. S.M. 31 Mar. 1886. S. Lt.-Col. 31 Mar. 1894. R. extra pension, 3 July 1902. ———.

2032. **Armstrong, James.** *b.* 28 Oct. 1846. B.A. M.B. M.Ch. T.C.D. 1871. Surg. 31 Mar. 1874. S.M. 31 Mar. 1886. S. Lt.-Col. 31 Mar. 1894. R. 17 Oct. 1899. *d.* in London, 25 Jan. 1923.

2033. **Dawson, Louis Richard.** *b.* 25 June 1851. Q.C. Belfast. M.D. (Honours), M.Ch. Q.U.I. 1873. Surg. 31 Mar. 1874. S.M. 31 Mar. 1886. *d.* at Gujrat, 20 Dec. 1889.

* Rank of Asst. Surgeon abolished, from 1 July 1873, by Royal Warrant of 10 May 1873.

2034. **Shircore, John** (christened **Johannes**) **Catchick Michael.** *b.* 10 Feb. 1850. M.B. C.M. Ed. 1871. Surg. 31 Mar. 1874. *d.* at Sultanpur, 5 Oct. 1882.

2035. **Malcolm-Smith, George John.** *b.* 3 Jan. 1850, at Galt, Canada. Ed. Univ. and Paris, M.B. C.M. 1871 ; M.D. 1874 ; Ed. M.R.C.S. 1871. Surgeon, 31 Mar. 1874. Resigned, 13 Mar. 1875. *d.* at Hurstpierpoint, Feb. 1896.

2036. **Yeld, Horace Parr.** *b.* 11 Sept. 1847. Glas. Univ. L.R.C.P. and S. Ed. 1870. Surg. 31 Mar. 1874. S.M. 31 Mar. 1886. S. Lt.-Col. 31 Mar. 1894. R. 15 Nov. 1894. *d.* at Harrogate, 28 June 1913. Afghanistan, 1878–79, with Thal Chotiali and Vitakri Field Force, medal.

2037. **Fullerton, John Campbell.** *b.* 3 Aug. 1850. B.A. M.B. M.Ch. T.C.D. 1872. Surg. 31 Mar. 1874. S.M. 31 Mar. 1886. S. Lt.-Col. 31 Mar. 1894. S. List, 27 Feb. 1900. R. extra pension, 25 June 1904. *d.* 11 Nov. 1928. Afghanistan, 1878–80, action at Saifudin, advance from Quetta to Kandahar, medal. N.-W. Frontier, Zhob Valley, 1890.

2038. **Warden, Charles James Hislop.** *b.* 23 Feb. 1851. M.R.C.S. 1872. L.R.C.P. Lond. 1873. Surg. 31 Mar. 1874. F.R.C.S. Ed. 1884. M.D. Brux, 1886. S.M. 31 Mar. 1886. S. Lt.-Col. 31 Mar. 1894. R. 4 June 1900. Examr. Medl. Stores, India Office, 1899–1900. *d.* at Highbury, London, 18 July 1900. Author, with W. Dymock and D. Hooper, of Pharmacographia Indica, 1893.

2039. **Stoker, Richard Nugent.** *b.* 31 Oct. 1851. L.R.C.S.I. 1873. L.K.Q.C.P. 1874. Surg. 30 Sept. 1874. S.M. 30 Sept. 1886. S. Lt.-Col. 30 Sept. 1894. R. 2 Apr. 1900. ———. Afghanistan, 1879, medal. N.-E. Frontier, Sikkim, 1888, forcing of Jelapla Pass, medal.

2040. **Bomford, Gerald.** *b.* 19 July 1851. King's Coll. Lond. L.S.A. 1872. L.R.C.P. Lond. 1873. M.R.C.S. 1873. M.B. 1874 ; Lond. Surg. 30 Sept. 1874. S.M. 30 Sept. 1886. S. Lt.-Col. 30 Sept. 1894. S. List, 29 Mar. 1900. S.G. and D.G. 1 Jan. 1905. R. 1 Jan. 1910. *d.* in London, 12 Apr. 1915. C.I.E. 1 Jan. 1903. Hony. F.R.C.S. Ed. 1905, G.S.P. 20 June 1905. Hony. M.D. Cal. 1908. K.C.I.E. 1 Jan. 1909. Perak, 1875–76, medal with clasp.

2041. **Barclay, Arthur.** *b.* 3 Aug. 1852. Glas. and Warburg Univs. M.B. C.M. Glas. 1874. Surg. 30 Sept. 1874. S.M. 30 Sept. 1886. *d.* at Simla, 2 Aug. 1891. Son of D.I.G. C. Barclay, M. No. 1028, 1839. Afghanistan, 1879–80, capture of Ali Musjid, medal with clasp. Author of reports on Rabies and on Vaccination, 1889.

2042. **Gray, Henry Alfred Chatham.** *b.* 26 Oct. 1849. Madras and Ed. Univs. M.B. C.M. Ed. 1873. Surg. 30 Sept. 1874. *d.* at Peshawar, 3 July 1879.

2043. **MacCartie, Charles Joseph.** *b.* 30 Mar. 1851. B.A. M.D. 1873 ; M.Ch. 1874 ; Q.U.I. Surg. 30 Sept. 1874. S.M. 30 Sept. 1886. S. Lt.-Col. 30 Sept. 1894. R. 25 June 1900. G.S.P. 10 Sept. 1927. Afghanistan, 1878–80, actions at Saifudin and Shahjui, Desp. 24 Oct. 1879, severely wounded near Kandahar, medal. Burma, 1891–92, medal with clasp. N.-W. Frontier, Chitral, 1895, relief of Chitral, medal with clasp ; Tirah, 1898, clasp ; Mohmand, Malakand ; operations in Bajaur, clasp. Author of a new system of Field Hospitals and Ambulance for Hill Warfare, 1898.

1875

2044. Ranking, George Spiers Alexander. *b.* 9 Jan. 1852. Bart's. and Cambridge. B.A. (Honours), 1873; M.B. 1875; M.D. 1879; Cantab. M.R.C.S. 1874. L.S.A. 1874. Surg. 31 Mar. 1875. S.M. 31 Mar. 1887. S. Lt.-Col. 31 Mar. 1895. S. List, 1 Apr. 1900. R. extra pension, 31 May 1905. Persian Lecturer, Oxford, 1905. Lt.-Col. R.A.M.C. T.F. and O.C. 3rd Southern (Oxford) Genl. Hosp. 15 Mar. 1909. Rejoined for service in war of 1914–18, 5 Aug. 1914–19. R. 19 Sept. 1923. ———. C.M.G. 26 July 1917. T.D. Dec. 1923. Examr. in Languages to Govt. of India, 17 June 1894–1905. Author of Hidayat-ul-Hukuma, 18—; Arabic and Persian Prosody, 1885; Talim-i-Zaban-i-Urdu, 1889; Glossary to Bagh-o-Bahar, 1902; On preservation of health in India, 1903; English-Hindustani Dictionary, 1905; edited and translated Tarikh-i-Budaoni, 1898; and Descriptio Imperii Moslemici of Al Mugadassi (with S. F. Azoo), 1897. War of 1914–19, Desp. L.G. 27 July 1917, C.M.G.

2045. Murray, Robert Davidson. *b.* 30 Aug. 1851. M.B. C.M. (Honours), Ed. 1873. Surg. 31 Mar. 1875. S.M. 31 Mar. 1887. S. Lt.-Col. 31 Mar. 1895. S. List, 2 May 1900. Col. 29 Mar. 1905. R. 29 Mar. 1910. *d.* in London, 12 Jan. 1920. Burma, 1886–87, operations of 1st Brigade, Desp. G.G.O. No. 434 of 1887, medal with clasp.

2046. Comins, Denis Wood Deane. *b.* 18 Jan. 1852. Bart's. M.R.C.S. 1873. L.R.C.P. Lond. 1874. Surg. 31 Mar. 1875. S.M. 31 Mar. 1887. S. Lt.-Col. 31 Mar. 1895. R. 16 July 1900. *d.* in London, 20 June 1902. Afghanistan, 1878–79, with Kandahar Field Force, action at Charasiah, capture of Kabul, affair at Latabund, relief of Sherpur, Desp. twice, medal with two clasps. Author of Diary of a Tour in Surinam or Dutch Guiana, 1892; Notes on Emigration from India to Jamaica, St. Lucia, Surinam, British Guiana, and Trinidad, 5 vols. 1892–93.

2047. O'Connor, Patrick Fenelon. *b.* 17 Mar. 1850. B.A. 1871; M.D. M.Ch. 1874; Q.U.I. Surg. 31 Mar. 1875. S.M. 31 Mar. 1887. S. Lt.-Col. 31 Mar. 1895. S. List, 13 July 1900. R. 13 July 1905. ———. C.B. 27 June 1902. G.S.P. 11 Jan. 1919. Afghanistan, 1878–80, battle of Ahmed Khel, actions of Urzu and Patkao Shana, Desp. G.G.O. No. 493 of 1880, medal with clasp. Egypt, 1882, action of Tel-el-Kebir, medal with clasp, bronze star. Burma, 1886–87, operations of 2nd Brigade, Wuntho expedition, Desp. G.G.O. No. 434 of 1887, medal with two clasps. N.-W. Frontier, Chitral 1895, relief of Chitral, action of Malakand Pass, Desp. G.G.O. No. 998 of 1895, medal with clasp; Malakand, 1897–98, operations in Bajaur and in Momand country, Utman Kbel, Buner, action of Tanga Pass, Desp. G.G.O. No. 178 of 1898, clasp. China, 1900, Desp. L.G. 21 Nov. 1902, medal, C.B.

2048. Moran, James. *b.* 3 July 1848. Q.C. Cork. B.A. 1869; M.D. 1873; M.Ch. 1874; Q.U.I. Surg. 31 Mar. 1875. S.M. 31 Mar. 1887. S.Lt.-Col. 31 Mar. 1895. S. List, 27 Aug. 1900. *d.* in London, 21 Sept. 1901. Afghanistan, 1878–79, medal.

2049. Beatson, William. *b.* 20 Oct. 1848. Guy's. M.R.C.S. 1870. L.R.C.P. Lond. 1871. Surg. 31 Mar. 1875. S.M. 31 Mar. 1887. *d.* at Gaya, 15 Oct. 1891.

INDIAN MEDICAL SERVICE [1875

2050. Simmonds, William Allason. *b.* 10 Sept. 1850. Guy's. M.R.C.S. 1874. L.R.C.P. Lond. 1874. L.S.A. 1874. Surg. 31 Mar. 1875. S.M. 31 Mar. 1887. S. Lt.-Col. 31 Mar. 1895. S. List, 31 Mar. 1901. R. 9 Aug. 1901. ———. G.S.P. 8 July 1923. Afghanistan, 1878–80, action at Charasiah, occupation of Kabul, operations at and around Kabul, medal with two clasps. Burma, 1885–86, occupation of Mandalai, operations round Shwebo, medal with clasp. N.-W. Frontier Isazai, 1892; Chitral, 1895, relief of Chitral, Desp. G.G.O. No. 998 of 1895, medal with clasp; Tochi, 1897–98, Desp. G.G.O. No. 1432 of 1897, clasp; Tirah, 1897–98, operations in Bazar Valley, clasp.

2051. Warburton, George Arthur. *b.* 28 Mar. 1850. M.B. C.M. Ed. 1873. Surg. 31 Mar. 1875. Resigned, 20 June 1883. Brother of W. P. Warburton, No. 1899, supra, 1866.

2052. MacRae, Roderick. *b.* 25 May 1850. M.B. C.M. Ed. 1873. Surg. 31 Mar. 1875. S.M. 31 Mar. 1887. S. Lt.-Col. 31 Mar. 1895. S. List. 1 Apr. 1901. Col. 12 Feb. 1905. R. 23 Feb. 1910. *d.* in Edinburgh, 5 Dec. 1915. G.S.P. 3 Dec. 1909. C.I.E. 24 June 1910. Afghanistan, 1878–80, affair at Jagdalak, operations at Sherpur, Kohistan, Logar, and Maidan Valley, medal with clasp.

2053. Bate, Thomas Elwood Lindesay. *b.* 29 July 1852. Adelaide Hosp. Dublin. L.R.C.S.I. 1870. L.K.Q.C.P. 1870. Surg. 31 Mar. 1875. S.M. 31 Mar. 1887. S. Lt.-Col. 31 Mar. 1895. S. List, 9 Aug. 1901. Col. 13 July 1905. R. 12 July 1910. ———. C.I.E. 26 June 1902. C.B.E. 7 Jan. 1918. Afghanistan, 1878–80, medal.

2054. Borah, Shibram. *b.* 10 Sept. 1849. Cal. and Glas. Univs. and Guy's. L.M.S. Cal. 1871. L.R.C.S. Ed. 1873. L.F.P.S.G. 1873. M.B. C.M. Glas. 1875. Surg. 31 Mar. 1875. S.M. 31 Mar. 1887. S. Lt.-Col. 31 Mar. 1895. R. 10 Sept. 1904. *d.* in Calcutta, 14 Apr. 1907. N.-E. Frontier, Naga Hills, 1879–80, medal with clasp.

2055. Weir, Patrick Alexander. *b.* 4 June 1851. Ab. Univ. and Guy's. M.A. (Honours), 1872; M.B. C.M. (Honours), 1874; Ab. Surg. 30 Sept. 1875. S.M. 30 Sept. 1887. S. Lt.-Col. 30 Sept. 1895. S. List, 21 Sept. 1901. Col. 26 Oct. 1905. R. 26 Oct. 1910. *d.* at Farnham Common, Bucks, 20 Apr. 1922. Brother of R. R. Weir, No. 2177, infra, 1882. Afghanistan, 1878–80, medal. Author (with J. Crofts, No. 2094, infra, 1877) of A Medico topographical account of Kota and Jhalawar.

2056. Freyer, Peter Johnston. *b.* 2 July 1851. Q.C. Galway, Stevens' Hosp. Dublin, and Paris. B.A. (Honours), 1872; M.D. M.Ch. (Honours), 1874; Q.U.I.; M.A. R.U.I. 1886. Surg. 30 Sept. 1875. S.M. 30 Sept. 1887. S. Lt.-Col. 30 Sept. 1895. R. 3 May 1896. Surgeon to St. Peter's Hosp. for stone, London, 1897. Rejoined for service in war of 1914–18, 1 Dec. 1914 to 10 May 1919. Tempy. Col. A.M.S. 10 Apr. 1918 to 10 May 1919. Hony. Col. I.M.S. 10 May 1919. *d.* in London, 9 Sept. 1921. Arnott Memorial Medal, 1904. C.B. 1 Jan. 1917. K.C.B. 4 June 1917. Author of Litholopaxy, 1885; enlarged editions, 1886 and 1896; Stone in the Bladder, 1900; Stricture of the Urethra and Enlargement of the Prostate, 1901, 3rd ed. 1906; Surgical Diseases of Urinary Organs, 1908; and articles on Diseases of Prostate and Vesical Calculus in Burghard's Operative Surgery, vol. iii, 1907.

2057. **Haig, Percy de Haga.** *b.* 25 June 1850. Bart's. M.R.C.S. 1873. L.R.C.P. Lond. 1873. Surg. 30 Sept. 1875. S.M. 30 Sept. 1887. S. Lt.-Col. 30 Sept. 1895. R. 15 Feb. 1901. *d.* at Monte Carlo, 9 Sept. 1920. Afghanistan, 1878–80, with Peshawar Valley Field Force, expedition to Tonk frontier, medal. N.-W. Frontier, Waziristan, 1894–95, action at Wana, severely wounded, medal with clasp.

2058. **Lewtas, John.** *b.* 13 Dec. 1851. Liverpool, St. Thomas, Ed. Univ. and Paris. M.R.C.S. 1873. L.S.A. 1873. M.B. 1873; M.D. 1887; Lond. Surg. 30 Sept. 1875. S.M. 30 Sept. 1887. S. Lt.-Col. 30 Sept. 1895. S. List, 9 Nov 1901. R. extra pension, 21 Nov. 1905. *d.* in London, 23 Sept. 1920. C.B.E. 7 Jan. 1918. Afghanistan, 1878–80, action at Ali Musjid, two Bazar Valley expeditions, action at Fatehabad, operations at and around Kabul, Desp. G.G.O. No. 328 of 1880, medal with clasp.

2059. **O'Neill, John.** *b.* 31 July 1848. Q.C. Cork. M.D. M.Ch. Q.U.I. 1870. Surg. R.N. 1872–75. Surg. Bengal, 30 Sept. 1875. S.M. 30 Sept. 1887. S. Lt.-Col. 30 Sept. 1895. R. 7 Apr. 1896. *d.* in London, 15 Oct. 1913. Ashanti, 1873–74, medal.

1876

2060. **Tomes, Arthur.** *b.* 18 Feb. 1851. Middlesex Hosp. M.R.C.S. 1873. L.S.A. 1873. S.S.C. Cantab, 1876. Surg. 31 Mar. 1876. M.D. Brux, (Honours), 1885. S.M. 31 Mar. 1888. S. Lt.-Col. 31 Mar. 1896. R. 13 Oct. 1897. *d.* Exmouth, 1 Nov. 1926.

2061. **Meredith, Edward Bishopp.** *b.* 8 Nov. 1853. T.C.D. L.R.C.S.I. 1875. L.K.Q.C.P. 1876. Surg. 31 Mar. 1876. *d.* at Port Blair, 19 Aug. 1878.

2062. **Mawson, William Arthur.** *b.* 29 Sept. 1850. Leeds. M.R.C.S. 1872. L.R.C.P. Lond. 1874. Surg. 31 Mar. 1876. S.M. 31 Mar. 1888. S. Lt.-Col. 31 Mar. 1896. S. List, 1 Jan. 1902. T.H.P. 1 June 1904. F.P. 15 Oct. 1904. R. 14 July 1906. Rejoined for service in war of 1914–18, 14 Nov. 1914–19. D. Cobham, Exeter, 9 June 1925. Afghanistan, 1878–80; actions of Ali Musjid and Charasiah; operations at and around Kabul; medal with three clasps. N.-W. Frontier, Tochi, 1897–98, medal with clasp; Waziristan, 1901–02, Desp. G.G.O. No. 611 of 1902, clasp.

2063. **Peevor, George Hamilton.** *b.* 29 Mar. 1852. Bart's. M.R.C.S. 1875. L.R.C.P. Lond. 1875. Surg. 31 Mar. 1876. S.M. 31 Mar. 1888. *d.* at Bakloh, 24 July 1893. N.-E. Frontier, Naga 1879–80, medal with clasp; Sikkim, 1888, forcing of the Jelapla Pass, clasp.

2064. **Dantra, Sorabji Hormasji.** *b.* 13 Sept. 1848. Bombay and Ab. Univs. M.B. C.M. 1874; M.D. 1877, Ab. Surg. 31 Mar. 1876. S.M. 31 Mar. 1888. S. Lt.-Col. 31 Mar. 1896. S. List, 31 Mar. 1902. R. 10 July 1903. ———.

2065. **MacDonald, Donald John.** *b.* 3 Apr. 1850. M.B. C.M. Ab. 1874. Surg. 31 Mar. 1876. Dismissed, 11 May 1880, G.O.C.C. 11 May 1880. Afterwards in practice at Walsall and Manchester. Name dropped out of Medl. Directory, 1900. Afghanistan, 1879–80.

2066. **Hamilton, Henry.** *b.* 7 Apr. 1851. Q.C. Belfast. B.A. 1872; M.D. M.Ch. 1875; Q.U.I. Surg. 31 Mar. 1876. S.M. 31 Mar. 1888. S. Lt.-Col. 31 Mar. 1896. B.S. Lt.-Col. 20 May 1898, special promotion for Tirah campaign. Col. 1 Oct. 1902. S.G. 24 Mar. 1907. R. 7 Apr. 1911. ———. G.S.P. 25 Oct. 1902. C.B. 24 June 1904. K.C.B. 3 June 1913. Afghanistan, 1878–80, action at Charasiah, operations at and around Kabul, affair at Shekhabad, march under Genl. Roberts from Kabul to Kandahar, battle of Kandahar, Desp. G.G.O. No. 582 of 1880, medal with three clasps, bronze star. N.-W. Frontier, Chitral, 1895, medal with clasp; 1897–98, operations in Samana and in Kurram Valley, Desp. G.G.O. No. 304 of 1898, two clasps; Tirah, 1897–98, Desp. G.G.O. No. 244 of 1898, promoted Brig. Surg. Lt.-Col., clasp. China, 1900, medal.

2067. **Halpin, Nicholas John.** *b.* 12 Sept. 1851. B.A. M.B. B.Ch. 1875; M.D. 1879; T.C.D. Surg. 31 Mar. 1876. L.K.Q.C.P. 1881. Killed by a fall from horse, Arrah, 21 Oct. 1882. N.-W. Frontier, Jowaki, 1877–78, medal.

2068. **Doyle, Bernard.** *b.* 16 Sept. 1850. M.B. B.Ch. T.C.D. 1875. Surg. 31 Mar. 1876. S.M. 31 Mar. 1888. S. Lt.-Col. 31 Mar. 1896. R. 30 July 1902. *d.* in London, 28 Nov. 1921. Afghanistan, 1878–80, medal.

2069. **Cobb, Robert.** *b.* 10 May 1852. Univ. Coll. Lond. M.R.C.S. 1874. L.R.C.P. Lond. 1875. Surg. 31 Mar. 1876. M.D. Brux, 1886. S.M. 31 Mar. 1888. S. Lt.-Col. 31 Mar. 1896. S. List, 16 June 1902. R. 10 Oct. 1906. Afterwards in service of British North Borneo Co. 1915. P.M.O. Sandakan, 1917–19. *d.* at Lincoln, 15 Jan. 1921.

2070. **Stephens, Augustus Edward Richard.** *b.* 5 Oct. 1850. Charing Cross. M.R.C.S. 1873. L.R.C.P. Lond. 1874. Surg. 31 Mar. 1876. S.M. 31 Mar. 1888. S. Lt.-Col. 31 Mar. 1896. R. 25 Apr. 1897. *d.* in London, 29 Jan. 1926. Afghanistan, 1878–80, action of Ahmed Khel, medal with clasp. N.-W. Frontier, Hazara, 1888, medal with clasp.

2071. **Cadge, William Hotson.** *b.* 11 Aug. 1853. St. George's. M.R.C.S. 1875. L.R.C.P. Lond. 1875. Surg. 31 Mar. 1876. S.M. 31 Mar. 1888. S. Lt.-Col. 31 Mar. 1896. R. 15 Nov. 1899. *d.* Lowestoft, 9 July 1926. O.B.E. 18 Feb. 1919. Afghanistan, 1879, with Peshawur Valley Field Force, Desp. medal.

2072. **Moorhead, James.** *b.* 4 Aug. 1850. Q.C. Belfast. B.A. Honours and Gold medal, 1871; M.A. Honours and Gold medal, 1872; M.D. Honours and Gold medal; 1875, Q.U.I. M.R.C.S. 1876. Surg. 30 Sept. 1876. S.M. 30 Sept. 1888. S. Lt.-Col. 30 Sept. 1896. R. 20 May 1898. Lecturer, Trop. Med. Q.C. Belfast, 1898. Afterwards in practice in London. *d.* at Boscombe, Bournemouth, 23 July 1918.

2073. **Beatson, Charles Henry.** *b.* 27 Mar. 1851, in Table Bay, Cape of Good Hope. Ed. and Glas. Univs. L.R.C.P. and S. Ed. 1873. Surg. 30 Sept. 1876. T.H.P. 8 May 1882. F.P. 21 Dec. 1882. S.M. 30 Sept. 1888. S. Lt.-Col. 30 Sept. 1896. S. List, 4 July 1902. Col. 16 June 1905. R. 27 Mar. 1911. Rejoined for service in war of 1914–18, 14 Oct. 1914–16. ———. Son of Surg. Genl. G. S. Beatson, C.B. A.M.D. (Johnston's Roll of R.A.M.C. No. 4517). C.B. 28 June 1907. Afghanistan, 1878–79, medal. N.-E. Frontier, Manipur, 1891, Desp. G.G.O. No. 585 of 1891, medal.

2074. Owen, Charles William. b. 28 Jan. 1853. St. Thomas, Paris and Brussels. M.R.C.S. 1874. L.R.C.P. Lond. 1874. M.A. Paris, 1875. Surg. R.N. Vol. Artillery, 1875–76. Surg. Bengal, 30 Sept. 1876. S.M. 30 Sept. 1888. S. Lt.-Col. 30 Sept. 1896. R. 15 Mar. 1902. Rejoined for service in war of 1914–18, Surg. Major, Sussex R.A.M.C. Vols. 1915 to 27 Mar. 1920. d. at Hankham, Sussex, 23 May 1922. C.I.E. 24 May 1881. C.M.G. 15 Feb. 1887. Harmat (Afghanistan), 1886. G.S.P. 29 Apr. 1918. Afghanistan, 1879–80, action at Charasiah, operations at and around Kabul, wounded, Desp. G.G.O. No. 137 of 1880, medal with clasp. Afghan Boundary Commission, 1885–87. N.-W. Frontier, Mohmund, 1895, medal with clasp. Author of Catalogue of Jeypoor Exhibits at Calcutta International Exhibition, 1883.

2075. Griffiths, Gilbert Saunders. b. 3 May 1854. Middlesex Hosp. M.R.C.S. 1876. L.S.A. 1876. Surg. 30 Sept. 1876. S.M. 30 Sept. 1888. S. Lt.-Col. 30 Sept. 1896. S. List, 1 Oct. 1902. R. extra pension, 1 June 1904. d. at Gibraltar, 1 Jan. 1930. Brother of W. E. Griffiths, No. 2013, supra, 1872. Afghanistan, 1878–80, Arambi Karez expedition, action at Bhagao, medal. N.-W. Frontier, Zhob Valley, 1884. N.-E. Frontier, Sikkim, 1888, medal with clasp.

2076. Grant, Peter MacPherson. b. 20 Aug. 1848. Ed. Univ. Paris, and Vienna. M.B. C.M. 1870; B.Sc. 1877; Ed. S.S.C. Cantab. 18— Surg. 30 Sept. 1876. d. at Agar, Central India, 22 July 1883. N.-W. Frontier, Jowaki, 1877–78, medal. Afghanistan, 1880, medal.

2077. Griffiths, Cecil Neil. b. 5 Feb. 1853. M.R.C.S. 1874. L.R.C.P. Ed. 1875. Surg. 30 Sept. 1876. Arrived at Fort William, 17 May 1877. Resigned soon after. Name never appeared in Army List. Afterwards in practice at Cheltenham. d. at Cheltenham, 10 Mar. 1894.

1877

2078. Owen, William. b. 21 Mar. 1852. B.A. 1873; M.B. 1874; T.C.D. L.R.C.S.I. 1873. Surg. 31 Mar. 1877. F.R.C.S.I. 1888. S.M. 31 Mar. 1889. S. Lt.-Col. 31 Mar. 1897. S. List, 25 Oct. 1902. R. 24 Mar. 1903. d. at Weston-super-Mare, 13 Nov. 1912. Afghanistan, 1878–80, actions of Ahmed Khel, and Urzu, medal with clasp. Egypt, 1882, battle of Tel-el-Kebir, medal with clasp, bronze star.

2079. Gillies, Walter. b. 21 Mar. 1854. M.B. C.M. Ed. 1875. Surg. 31 Mar. 1877. d. in London, 15 Oct. 1883. Afghanistan, 1878–80, medal. Egypt, 1882, medal with clasp, bronze star.

2080. Jack, David Morton. b. 11 Nov. 1853. M.B. C.M. Ed. 1875. Surg. 31 Mar. 1877. S.M. 31 Mar. 1889. d. at Sitapur, 13 Sept. 1890. Father of W. A. M. Jack, I.M.S. Genl. List, No. 508, 1909.

2081. Conry, Walter. b. 22 Apr. 1849. B.A. 1875; M.B. 1876; T.C.D. L.R.C.P. and S. Ed. 1875. Surg. 31 Mar. 1877. S.M. 31 Mar. 1889. S. Lt.-Col. 31 Mar. 1897. R. 28 Nov. 1898. d. at Caversham, 15 July. 1910. Burma, 1885–87, medal with clasp.

2082. Kellie, George Jerome. b. 15 Mar. 1854. King's Coll. Lond. M.R.C.S. 1876. L.R.C.P. Ed. 1876. Surg. 31 Mar. 1877. S.M. 31 Mar. 1889. D.P.H. R.C.S.I. 1889. S. Lt.-Col. 31 Mar. 1897. S. List, 1 Nov. 1902. Col. 16 Oct. 1905. R. 15 Oct. 1908. ——. Son of Asst. Surg. James Kellie, A.M.D; (Johnston's Roll of R.A.M.C. No. 4965). Burma, 1888–89, medal with clasp. N.-W. Frontier, Tirah, 1897–98, action of Arhanga pass, operations in Bara Valley, medal with two clasps.

2083. **Hancock, John Gatchell.** *b.* 5 Feb. 1853. King's Coll. Lond. and Paris. M.R.C.S. 1875. M.B. Lond. 1876. Surg. 31 Mar. 1877. T.H.P. 27 Sept. 1888. R. 27 Sept. 1890. *d.* at Taunton, 25 June 1893. Afghanistan, 1878–80, actions at Matun and Charasiah, operations at and around Kabul, medal with two clasps.

2084. **Basu, Dharmadas.** *b.* 26 Nov. 1851. L.M.S. Cal. 1873. Civil Asst. Surg. Bengal, 10 May 1873 to 20 June 1875. L.R.C.P. Ed. 1876. L.F.P.S.G. 1876. Surg. 31 Mar. 1877. S.M. 31 Mar. 1889. S. Lt.-Col. 31 Mar. 1897. R. 7 July 1902. *d.* Sept. 1926. Author of Hygiene and Public Health (in Bengal), two vols, 1885 and 1888.

2085. **MacKenzie, Alexander William.** *b.* 23 Oct. 1853. M.A. 1874; M.B. C.M. 1876; Ab. Surg. 31 Mar. 1877. S.M. 31 Mar. 1889. S. Lt.-Col. 31 Mar. 1897. R. 31 Jan. 1903. *d.* at Plymouth, 11 May 1913. Afghanistan, 1878–80, action at Chihil Dakhteran; march under Genl. Roberts from Kabul to Kandahar, battle of Kandahar, medal with two clasps, bronze star. N.-W. Frontier, Mahsud Waziri, 1881; first and second Miranzai, 1891, medal with clasp; Waziristan, 1894–95, clasp.

2086. **Mullane, Jeremiah.** *b.* 4 Mar. 1850. Q.C. Cork. M.D. (Honours), M.Ch. Q.U.I. 1876. Surg. 31 Mar. 1877. S.M. 31 Mar. 1889. S. Lt.-Col. 31 Mar. 1897. *d.* at Dibrugarh, 10 Nov. 1897. Brother of P. Mullane, No. 2164, infra, 1881. Afghanistan, 1878–80, advance on Ghazni, actions of Ahmed Khel and Arzu, march under Genl. Roberts from Kabul to Kandahar, battle of Kandahar, medal with two clasps, bronze star.

2087. **Mullen, Douglas** (afterwards **ffrench-Mullen, Douglas**). *b.* 21 July 1852. Q.C. Galway, and Stevens' Hosp. Dublin. M.D. 1872; M.Ch. 1873; Q.U.I. Surg. 31 Mar. 1877. S.M. 31 Mar. 1889. S. Lt.-Col. 31 Mar. 1897. S. List, 24 Mar. 1903. Col. 21 Mar. 1907. R. 25 Mar. 1912. *d.* at Hollywood, Rochester, 2 Apr. 1920. Took name of ffrench-Mullen in 1890. Brother of T. ffrench-Mullen, No. 1912, supra, 1866, and of J. ffrench-Mullen, No. 2103, infra, 1878. Author, with P. D. Pank, No. 2144, infra, 1880, of A Medico Topographical Account of Ajmere, Rajputana, 1900.

2088. **Taaffe, Robert James.** *b.* 21 Nov. 1851. B.A. 1873; M.B. B.Ch. 1875; T.C.D. Surg. A.M.D. 30 Sept. 1875 to 11 Oct. 1876. Surg. Bengal, 31 Mar. 1877. Resigned, 18 May 1886. Afterwards in practice at Kingston, County Dublin. Name omitted from Medl. Regr. 1927. N.-W. Frontier, Mahsud Waziri, 1881.

2089. **Robinson, Ernest Lawrie.** *b.* 11 Jan. 1855. St. George's. M.R.C.S. 1876. L.R.C.P. Lond. 1876. Surg. 31 Mar. 1877. T.H.P. 14 Jan. 1881. R. 19 Jan. 1887. Afterwards in practice in Guernsey, Surgeon St. Peter Port Hosp. ———. Author of Lectures for Nurses.

2090. **Nelis, James Alexander.** *b.* 23 May 1854. B. A., M.B., L.Ch., T.C.D. 1876. Surg. 31 Mar. 1877. S.M. 31 Mar. 1889. S. Lt.-Col. 31 Mar. 1897. R. 4 July 1902. *d.* in Dublin, 2 Jan. 1917. Afghanistan, 1878–80, advance on Ghazni, actions at Ahmed Khel and Arzu; march under Genl. Roberts from Kabul to Kandahar, battle of Kandahar; Aitchakzai expedition; operations against Marris, medal with two clasps, bronze star, N.-W. Frontier, Mahsud Waziri, 1881; Hazara, 1888, medal with clasp; second Miranzai, 1891, clasp; Isazai, 1892; Tirah, 1897–98, operations against Khanni Khel Chamkannis, operations in Bazar Valley, medal with two clasps.

2091. Smyth, William Beatty. b. 12 May 1850. B.A. 1872; M.B. 1875; T.C.D. L.R.C.S.I. 1875. Surg. 31 Mar. 1877. Murdered at Chapri, Thal, Kurram Valley, 25 June 1879. Afghanistan, 1878–79.

2092. Crofts, Aylmer Martin. b. 24 May 1854. Q.C. Cork L.R.C.S. Ed. 1876. L.R.C.P. Ed. 1877. Surg. 31 Mar. 1877. S.M. 31 Mar. 1889. S. Lt.-Col. 31 Mar. 1897. S. List, 10 Apr. 1903. Col. 15 Oct. 1908. S.G. 7 Apr. 1911. R. 25 May 1914. d. in London, 12 Apr. 1915. Brother of J. Crofts, No. 2094, infra, 1877. C.I.E. 24 May 1900. Knight's Cross of Philip the Magnanimous, of Hesse, 1904. K.H.S. 2 Mar. 1913. Afghanistan, 1878–80, with Kandahar and Khaibar Field Forces, affairs with Ghilzais at Jagdalak, medal. Egypt, 1882, actions at Kassassin and Tel-el-Kebir, medal with clasp, bronze star. N.-W. Frontier, Zhob Valley, 1884. China, 1900, medal.

2093. MacCarthy, Michael Joseph (d). b. 1854. Q.C. Cork. M.D. M.Ch. Q.U.I. 1876. Passed for I.M.S. 31 Mar. 1887. Never joined. Surg. R.N. Aug. 1877. Staff-Surg. 1889, Fleet-Surg. 1898. R. 23 Jan. 1899. d. at Torquay, 24 Oct. 1899. Soudan, 1884, medal and bronze star.

2094. Crofts, James. b. 13 May 1852. Q.C. Cork and T.C.D. M.B. M.Ch. T.C.D. 1874. Surg. 31 Mar. 1877. S.M. 31 Mar. 1889. S. Lt.-Col. 31 Mar. 1897. R. 15 July 1905. d. at Cork, 7 May 1913. Brother of A. M. Crofts, No. 2092, supra, 1877. Afghanistan, 1878–80, affair of Ali Khel, medal. Author (with P. A. Weir, No. 2055, supra, 1875), of A Medico topographical account of Kota and Jhalawar.

2095. Coates, William. b. 19 Jan. 1852. M.D. M.Ch. Q.U.I. 1876. Surg. 31 Mar. 1877. S.M. 31 Mar. 1889. S. Lt.-Col. 31 Mar. 1897. S. List, 6 July 1903. R. 4 July 1907. Rejoined for service in war of 1914–18, 1 Dec. 1914 to 31 Dec. 1915. G.S.P. 8 Aug. 1927. d. at Hove, 13 Feb. 1930. Afghanistan, 1878–80, actions of Ali Musjid and Charasiah, operations at and around Kabul, march under Genl. Roberts from Kabul to Kandahar, battle of Kandahar, Desp. G.G.O. No. 137 of 1880, medal with four clasps, bronze star. N.-W. Frontier, Mahsud Waziri, 1881.

2096. Blood, Joseph FitzGerald. b. 16 Mar. 1853. B.A. M.B. M.Ch. 1875; M.A. M.D. 1892; T.C.D. Surg. 31 Mar. 1877. S.M. 31 Mar. 1889. T.H.P. 21 Dec. 1890. R. 21 Dec. 1892. Afterwards Lecturer in Liverpool School, Trop. Med., and Surgeon and Cons. Surg. Birkenhead Boro. hospital. d. at Birkenhead, 29 July 1924. Afghanistan, 1878–79, with Kandahar and Thal Chotiali Field Forces, medal.

2097. Thom, Alexander (d). b. Aug. 1853. M.A. St. A. 1873. M.B. C.M. 1876; M.D. (Honours), 1882; Ed. Surg. on probation, 1 Oct. 1877. Resigned from Netley, 31 Jan. 1878. D.P.H. R.C.S. Ed. 1890. Afterwards in practice at Crieff. d. in Edinburgh, 16 Jan. 1906.

2098. Thomson, Samuel John. b. 17 Jan. 1853. M.R.C.S. 1874. L.S.A. 1874. Surg. 1 Oct. 1877. S.M. 1 Oct. 1889. S. Lt.-Col. 1 Oct. 1897. S. List. 10 July 1903. R. extra pension, 17 Jan. 1908. Rejoined for service in war of 1914–18, 20 June 1915–1919. Bt.-Col. 1 Jan. 1918. ———. C.I.E. 1 Jan. 1898. C.B.E. 3 June 1919. Afghanistan, 1880, medal. South Africa, 1902, Director of Burgher Camps, Transvaal, medal with two clasps. Author of Sanitary Principles for India, 1883; The Transvaal Burgher Camps, 1904; The Silent India, 1913; The Real Indian People, 1914.

2099. **Campbell, Robert Neil.** b. 24 Sept. 1854. M.B. C.M. Ed. 1876. Surg. 1 Oct. 1877. S.M. 1 Oct. 1889. S. Lt.-Col. 1 Oct. 1897. S. List, 19 July 1903. Col. 2 Apr. 1909. R. 2 Apr. 1914. Rejoined for service in war of 1914–18, 26 Nov. 1914–18. In command, Pavilion Hosp. Brighton. d. at Lahore, 18 Feb. 1928. K.-i-H. 1st class, 23 May 1900. C.I.E. 25 June 1909. C.B. 14 June 1912. G.S.P. 22 Sept. 1913. K.C.M.G. 4 June 1917. N.-E. Frontier, Naga Hills, 1879–80, Desp. G.G.O. No. 123 of 1880, medal with clasp. War of 1914–19, Desp. L.G. 27 July 1917, K.C.M.G.

2100. **Brander, Edward Salisbury.** b. 13 Sept. 1854. L.R.C.P. and S. Ed. 1876. M.B. C.M. Ed. 1877. Surg. 1 Oct. 1877. F.R.C.S. Ed. 1880. S.M. 1 Oct. 1889. S. Lt.-Col. 1 Oct. 1897. d. at Shahjahanpur, 3 Nov. 1902. Afghanistan, 1879–80, with Khaibar Field Force, medal.

2101. **Chatterjee, Fakir Chandra.** b. 27 July 1852. L.M.S. Cal. 1875. Civil Asst. Surg. Bengal, Mar. 1876 to Sept. 1877. M.B. C.M. Glas. 1877. Surg. 1 Oct. 1877. S.M. 1 Oct. 1889. S. Lt.-Col. 1 Oct. 1897. d. at Azamgarh, 11 Sept. 1898. Burma, 1886–87, operations of 1st Brigade, medal with clasp.

2102. **Emerson, George Augustus.** b. 30 Sept. 1852. M.B. C.M. Ed. 1876. Surg. 1 Oct. 1877. S.M. 1 Oct. 1889. S. Lt.-Col. 1 Oct. 1897. S. List, 2 Apr. 1904. R. 2 Apr. 1908. d. at Parkstone, Dorset, 17 Dec. 1924. Afghanistan, 1878–80, medal with clasp. Sudan, 1885, Suakin, medal with two clasps, bronze star.

1878

2103. **Mullen, Jarlath Joseph** (afterwards ffrench-Mullen, Jarlath). b. 7 Aug. 1855. Q.C. Galway. M.D. M.Ch. Q.U.I. 1873. Colonial Surgeon, Jamaica, 1874–77. Surg. A.M.D. 5 Aug. 1877 to 22 Jan. 1878. Surg. Bengal, 30 Mar. 1878. S.M. 30 Mar. 1890. S. Lt.-Col. 30 Mar. 1898. R. 25 May. 1908. d. 4 June 1928. Changed name to ffrench-Mullen in 1890. Brother of Staff Surg. St. L. ffrench-Mullen, R.N. of T. ffrench-Mullen, No. 1912, supra, 1866, and of D. ffrench-Mullen, No. 2087, supra, 1877. Author of Eastern Sunsets, 1903; White Roses, 1905; (both books of poems, under pseudonym of Iahrflaith).

2104. **Cretin, Eugéne.** b. 6 Jan. 1851, in Mauritius. Bart's. L.S.A. 1874. L.R.C.P. Lond. 1875. M.R.C.S. 1875. M.B. Lond. (Honours), 1875. F.R.C.S. 1876. Surg. 30 Mar. 1878. S.M. 30 Mar. 1890. S. Lt.-Col. 30 Mar. 1898. R. 31 Dec. 1905. d. at Felsted, 10 Sept. 1908. Afghanistan, 1880, action on Gara Heights, operations in Hisarak district, medal. Burma, 1885–87, operations of 2nd and 5th Brigades, medal with clasp. Soudan, 1896, Dongola expedition, medal. N.-W. Frontier, Tochi, 1897–98, medal with clasp.

2105. **Duncan, Andrew.** b. 10 Apr. 1850. King's Coll. Lond., Vienna and Strasburg. L.S.A. 1872. M.R.C.S. 1872. M.B. gold medal, 1874; M.D. 1875; B.S. (Honours), 1876; Lond. F.R.C.S. 1877. Surg. 30 Mar. 1878. Parkes Memorial Prize, 1885. M.R.C.P. Lond. 1890. S.M. 30 Mar. 1890. S. Lt.-Col. 30 Mar. 1898. R. 1 Feb. 1900. Physn. to Seamen's Hosp. London, 1899. Lect. Trop. Dis. Westminster Hosp. 19—. F.R.C.P. Lond. 1907. d. in London, 18 Oct. 1912. Afghanistan, 1878–80, actions at Matun and Charasiah (severely wounded), Desp., medal with clasp. N.-W. Frontier, Hazara, 1891, medal with clasp. Author of The Unsanitary tendencies of State Sanitation, 1885; Prevention of Disease in tropical and subtropical campaigns (Parkes Memorial Prize Essay), 1888; (with J. W. Carr, T. P. Pick, and A. H. G. Doran), The Practitioner's Guide, 1902; Guide to sick nursing in the tropics, 1908; articles on Dysentery and Kala Azar, in 3rd ed. of Quain's medical Dictionary, 1902; Article on Military Surgery in Treves' System of Surgery, vol. i, 1895.

2106. **Nicholson, George Frederick.** b. 7 Mar. 1855. M.D. Q.U.I. 1875. L.R.C.S.I. 1875. Surg. 30 Mar. 1878. S.M. 30 Mar. 1890. S. Lt.-Col. 30 Mar. 1898. R. 23 Feb. 1899. ———.

2107. **Hemsted, Arthur.** b. 13 Apr. 1852. Univ. Coll. Lond. M.R.C.S. 1877. L.R.C.P. Lond. 1877. Surg. 30 Mar. 1878. Resigned, 12 Sept. 1880. d. at Freshwater Bay, Isle of Wight, 21 June 1893.

2108. **Cones, George Augustus.** b. 17 Dec. 1850. St. George's. B.A. Cal. 1871. M.R.C.S. 1877. L.R.C.P. Lond. 1877. Surg. 30 Mar. 1878. T.H.P. 1 May 1885. F.P. 12 Jan. 1886. S.M. 30 Mar. 1890. R. 21 Oct. 1892. d. 12 Mar. 1915. Afghanistan, 1878–80, medal. Burma, 1889, medal with clasp.

2109. **Bigger, Samuel Ferguson.** b. 4 Oct. 1854. Liverpool and Univ. Coll. Lond. M.R.C.S. 1875. L.S.A. 1877. Surg. 30 Mar. 1878. S.M. 30 Mar. 1890. S. Lt.-Col. 30 Mar. 1898. R. 1 Sept. 1903. ———. Afghanistan, 1879–80, Zaimukht expedition, action of Zawa, medal. N.-E. Frontier, Chin Lushai, 1889–90, Desp. G.G.O. No. 677 of 1890, medal with clasp. N.-W. Frontier, Waziristan, 1894–95, clasp; Tirah, 1897–98, action of Dargai, Desp. G.G.O. No. 244 of 1898, medal with two clasps.

2110. **Robertson, George Scott** (e). b. 22 Oct. 1852. Westminster. L.S.A. 1876. M.R.C.S. 1877. Surg. 30 Mar. 1878. S.M. 30 Mar. 1890. S. Lt.-Col. 30 Mar. 1898. R. 12 Oct. 1899. Stood as Liberal, unsuccessfully, for Stirling County, 1900; M.P. Central Bradford (Liberal), 1906 to Jan 1916. d. in London, 2 Jan. 1916. C.S.I. 25 May 1892. K.C.S.I. 17 July 1895. D.C.L. Toronto, 18—. Afghanistan, 1879–80, operations at and round Kabul, affair at Shekhabad, operations in Kohistan, medal with clasp. N.-W. Frontier, Hunza-Nagar, 1891–92, as Chief Political Officer, Desp. G.G.O. No. 397 of 1892, medal; Chitral, 1895, as British Agent, defence of Fort of Chitral (wounded), Desp. G.G.O. No. 531 of 1895, medal with clasp, K.C.S.I. Author of The Kafirs of the Hindukush, 1896; Chitral, the story of a minor siege, 1898.

2111. **Biale, John Seton.** b. 16 Nov. 1855. St. George's. M.R.C.S. 1877. L.S.A. 1877. Surg. 30 Mar. 1878. d. at Prome, 17 Sept. 1879.

2112. **Walsh, John Edward.** b. 2 May 1855. M.D. M.Ch. Q.U.I. 1877. Surg. 30 Mar. 1878. d. at Kandahar, 23 July 1879. Afghanistan, 1878–79.

2113. **Nixon, George Michael.** b. 16 Feb. 1852. B.A. M.B. 1874; B.Ch. 1875; T.C.D. Surg. 30 Mar. 1878. S.M. 30 Mar. 1890. d. at Jhansi, 17 Aug. 1896. Afghanistan, 1879–80, with Kurram Field Force, medal. Burma, 1886–87, pursuit of Hla Oo, operations of 6th Brigade, medal with clasp.

2114. **Sweeny, Terence Humphreys.** *b.* 15 July 1856. St. Vincent's Hosp. Dublin. L.R.C.S.I. 1877. L.K.Q.C.P. 1878. F.R.C.S.I. 1879. Surg. 30 Sept. 1878. S.M. 30 Sept. 1890. Lt.-Col. 30 Sept. 1898. S. List, 21 June 1904. R. extra pension, 1 Mar. 1909. Rejoined for service in war of 1914–18, 30 Nov. 1914 to 31 Dec. 1915. *d.* at Cheltenham, 15 Nov. 1922. C.M.G. 4 June 1917. Afghanistan, 1879–80, operations at and around Kabul, defence of Sherpur, medal with clasp. War of 1914–19, Desp. L.G. 27 July 1917, C.M.G.

2115. **Barry, Daniel Francis.** *b.* 27 Jan. 1855. Q.C. Cork. M.D. M.Ch. Q.U.I. 1877. Surg. 30 Sept. 1878. S.M. 30 Sept. 1890. Lt.-Col. 30 Sept. 1898. R. 10 Dec. 1903. *d.* 13 July 1914. N.-E. Frontier, Naga Hills, 1879–80, medal with clasp. Sonthal operations, 1881.

2116. **Harris, George Francis Angelo.** *b.* 29 Feb. 1856. St. George's. M.R.C.S. 1878. L.R.C.P. Lond. 1878. Surg. 30 Sept. 1878. S.M. 30 Sept. 1890. M.R.C.P. Lond. 1893. Lt.-Col. 30 Sept. 1898. M.D. Dunelm, 1902. F.R.C.P. Lond. 1903. S. List, 3 Dec. 1904. Col. 28 Feb. 1910. S.G. 1 Apr. 1912. R. 1 Apr. 1915. Rejoined for service in war of 1914–18, 1915–1917. ———. C.S.I. 11 Dec. 1911. G.S.P. 25 May 1914. Afghanistan, 1880, on Khaibar line, medal. Author of The Bengal Medical Service, 1885.

2117. **Anderson, John.** *b.* 4 Aug. 1855. M.B. C.M. Ed. 1878. Surg. 30 Sept. 1878. S.M. 30 Sept. 1890. Lt.-Col. 30 Sept. 1898. S. List, 1 Jan. 1905. R. extra pension, 1 Apr. 1910. Member, Medl. Board, India Office, 28 Feb. 1913 to 4 Aug. 1920. ———. C.I.E. 4 June 1917. Afghanistan, 1878–80, action at Jagdalak, medal.

2118. **Bamber, Charles James.** *b.* 14 July 1855. Bart's. M.R.C.S. 1878. L.R.C.P. Lond. 1878. Surg. 30 Sept. 1878. S.M. 30 Sept. 1890. D.P.H. Cantab. 1892. Lt.-Col. 30 Sept. 1898. S. List, 12 Feb. 1905. Col. 12 July 1910. R. 12 July 1915. ———. M.V.O. 11 Dec. 1911. N.-W. Frontier, Mahsud-Waziri, 1881. Burma, 1886–87, operations 1st Brigade, medal with clasp. N.-W. Frontier, Malakand, 1897–98, medal with clasp. Author of Plants of the Panjab, 1917.

2119. **O'Dwyer, Malachi.** *b.* 15 July 1856. T.C.D. Meath, and St. Mark's Hosps. Dublin. B.A. M.B. B.Ch. T.C.D. 1877. Surg. 30 Sept. 1878. S.M. 30 Sept. 1890. Lt.-Col. 30 Sept. 1898. R. 30 Nov. 1898. ———. Brother of Sir Michael O'Dwyer, K.C.S.I., I.C.S. Afghanistan, 1879, medal.

2120. **Dumbleton, Edgar Hunt.** *b.* 15 Dec. 1855. M.R.C.S. 1877. L.R.C.P. Lond. 1878. Surg. 30 Sept. 1878. *d.* at Ali Khel, 5 Oct. 1879. Afghanistan, 1879.

1879

2121. **Perry, Francis Frederick.** *b.* 26 Dec. 1854. Univ. Coll. Lond. and Vienna. M.R.C.S. 1876. L.R.C.P. Lond. 1876. Surg. 31 Mar. 1879. S.M. 31 Mar. 1891. Lt.-Col. 31 Mar. 1899. S. List, 29 Mar. 1905. R. extra pension, 14 June 1909. Rejoined for service in war of 1914–18, Nov. 1914–1916. ———. C.I.E. 26 June 1908. C.M.G. 4 June 1917. War of 1914–19, Desp. L.G. 27 July 1917. C.M.G.

2122. **Dalzell, Pulteney William.** b. 16 Dec. 1856. M.B. C.M. Ed. 1878. Surg. 31 Mar. 1879. S.M. 31 Mar. 1891. d. at Isle of Sanday, Orkney, 29 Sept. 1894.

2123. **Little, Stephen.** b. 8 Jan. 1857. Q.C. Belfast and Bart's. M.D. (Honours), M.Ch. Q.U.I. 1878. Surg. 31 Mar. 1879. M.R.C.P. Lond. 1888. S.M. 31 Mar. 1891. Lt.-Col. 31 Mar. 1899. S. List, 30 May 1905. R. extra pension, 22 June 1909. ———. Afghanistan, 1879–80, Hissarak expedition, medal. N.-W. Frontier, Mahsud Waziri, 1881.

2124. **Gimlette, George Hart Desmond.** b. 8 Sept. 1855. St. Thomas'. M.R.C.S. 1877. L.S.A. 1877. M.D. M.Ch. Q.U.I. 1879. Surg. 31 Mar. 1879. S.M. 31 Mar. 1891. Lt.-Col. 31 Mar. 1899. S. List, 16 June 1905. R. extra pension, 1 Apr. 1910. Rejoined for service in war of 1914–18, 11 Sept. 1914–21 to Apr. 1919. ———. Son of Asst. Surg. G. H. D. Gimlette, R.N. C.I.E. 9 Nov. 1901. Egypt, 1882, action at Tel-el-Kebir, and pursuit to Zagazig, medal with clasp, bronze star. Was in charge of the Residency at Katmandu, Nipal, as Asst. Resident, during the absence of the Resident, at the time of the revolution in Nipal in 1885; (v. I.M.G. Apr. 1910, p. 142). Author of A Postscript to the Records of the Indian Mutiny, 1927.

2125. **Hunter, Christian Bernard.** b. 8 Dec. 1851. Univ. Coll. Lond. M.R.C.S. 1877. L.R.C.P. Lond. 1878. Surg. 31 Mar. 1879. S.M. 31 Mar. 1891. Lt.-Col. Mar. 1899. R. 15 Apr. 1900. d. at Pewsey, Wilts, 13 Nov. 1929. Afghanistan, 1878–80, medal. N.-W. Frontier, Zhob Valley, 1890; first and second Miranzai, 1891, medal with clasp.

2126. **Gaisford, Martin.** b. 9 July 1855. King's Coll. Lond. M.R.C.S. 1876. L.R.C.P. Lond. 1877. Surg. 31 Mar. 1879. d. at Kathgodam, U.P., 29 Mar. 1889. 1880.

2127. **Murray, Charles Herbert.** b. 3 Feb. 1855. B.A. 1872; M.A. 1876; M.D.; McGill. L.S.A. 1877. M.R.C.S. 1878. Surg. 31 Mar. 1879. d. at Peshawar, 10 July 1880. Afghanistan, 1879–80.

2128. **Smith, Julian Carter Carrington.** b. 7 Aug. 1854. M.B. C.M. Ed. 1878. Surg. 31 Mar. 1879. S.M. 31 Mar. 1891. Lt.-Col. 31 Mar. 1899. R. 7 Aug. 1909. Rejoined for service in war of 1914–19. d. at Edinburgh, 19 Dec. 1929. O.B.E. 3 June 1919. Afghanistan, 1878–80, medal. Burma, 1886–88, operations of 6th Brigade, medal with two clasps.

2129. **Dennys, George William Patrick.** b. 28 Apr. 1857. Bart's. M.R.C.S. 1878. L.R.C.P. Lond. 1878. Surg. 31 Oct. 1879. S.M. 31 Oct. 1891. Lt.-Col. 31 Oct. 1899. S. List, 21 Oct. 1906. Col. 16 June 1910. R. 10 Jan. 1917. d. at Milford-on-Sea, Hants, 30 July 1924. C.I.E. 1 Jan. 1915. Afghanistan, 1878–80, medal.

2130. **MacNamara, John William Unthank.** b. 12 July 1853. B.A. 1873; M.D. (Honours), 1879; Q.U.I. M.A. R.U.I. 1880. L.R.C.S.I. 1878. L.A.H. 1879. Surg. 31 Oct. 1879. S.M. 31 Oct. 1891. Lt.-Col. 31 Oct. 1899. R. 12 July 1908. ———. Brother of R. J. MacNamara, No. 2221, infra, 1886.

2131. **Stuart, Henry Ogilvy.** b. 25 Feb. 1857. Guy's. M.R.C.S. 1878. L.S.A. 1878. Surg. 31 Oct. 1879. Resigned, 31 Mar. 1881. Surg. A.M.D. 4 Feb. 1882. S.M. 4 Feb. 1894. d. in Middlesex Hosp. London, 11 May. 1896. Afghanistan, 1880–81, medal. Sudan, 1884, battles of El Teb and Tamai, Desp. medal with clasp, bronze star. Sudan, 1885, Nile expedition, action at Kirbekan, two clasps.

2132. **Sykes, Joseph.** *b.* 19 Apr. 1854. Madras and Glas. Univs. Hosp. App. S.M.D. Madras, 29 June 1874 to 23 Sept. 1876. L.R.C.P. Ed. 1879. L.F.P.S.G. 1879. Surg. 31 Oct. 1879. S.M. 31 Oct. 1891. Lt.-Col. 31 Oct. 1899. S. List, 25 Mar. 1907. R. 14 Dec. 1909. *d.* at Folkestone, 5 May 1925. N.-W. Frontier, Mahsud-Waziri, 1881. Egypt, 1882, actions of Tel-el-Kebir and Kassassin, medal with clasp, bronze star.

2133. **Stewart, John MacDougal.** *b.* 3 June 1857. Middlesex Hosp. M.R.C.S. 1878. L.S.A. 1878. Surg. 31 Oct. 1879. Resigned, 20 May 1880. Surg. A.M.D. 3 Feb. 1883. *d.* in Jersey, 26 Apr. 1891. Sudan, 1884–85, medal, bronze star.

2134. **Tuohy, John Francis.** *b.* 23 Apr. 1854. Q.C. Cork, Dublin, and Vienna. M.D. (Honours), 1878; M.Ch. 1879; Q.U.I. Surg. 31 Oct. 1879. M.A.O. R.U.I. 1889. S.M. 31 Oct. 1891. Lt.-Col. 31 Oct. 1899. R. 24 June 1900. *d.* at Brighton, 22 Feb. 1909. Afghanistan, 1880–81, medal.

2135. **Daubeny, Charles Alexander.** *b.* 5 Apr. 1852. Bart's. M.R.C.S. 1875. L.R.C.P. Ed. 1875. Surg. A.M.D. 30 Sept. 1875 to 8 Oct 1878. Surg. Bengal, 31 Oct. 1879. *d.* at Peshawar, 25 Aug. 1880. Afghanistan, 1880.

1880

2136. **Simpson, James** (d). *b.* 1 Jan. 1853. M.B. C.M. (Honours), 1876; M.D. Gold Medal, 1878; Ab. Surgeon, 31 Mar. 1880. Never joined in India. *d.* at Aberdeen, 10 Sept. 1880.

2137. **Lukis, Charles Pardey.** *b.* 9 Sept. 1857. Bart's. M.R.C.S. 1879. L.S.A. 1879. Surg. 31 Mar. 1880. M.B. 1889; M.D. 1894; Lond. F.R.C.S. 1890. S.M. 31 Mar. 1892. Lt.-Col. 31 Mar. 1900. S. List, 12 July 1905. S.G. and D.G. 1 Jan. 1910. Acting D.M.S. India, 15 Apr. 1916 to July 1916. Rank of Lt.-Gen. 22 Sept. 1916. *d.* at Simla, 21 Oct. 1917. G.S.P. 1 Jan. 1910. C.S.I. 24 June 1910. Member, Imperial Legislative Council, 1910. K.C.S.I. 11 Dec. 1911. K.H.S. 20 Feb. 1913. V.D. 30 Jan. 1915. N.-W. Frontier, Mahsud Waziri, 1881; Zhob Valley, 1894. Author of Practical Surgery in Urdu, 1903; Elementary manual of Midwifery, 1904; (with Major R. J. Blackham, R.A.M.C.), Tropical Hygiene for Anglo-Indians, 1911; edited first three editions of R. Ghosh's Maleria Medica, 1903–06; and sixth edition of Waring's Bazar Medicines of India, 1907.

2138. **Whitwell, Robert Richard Harvey.** *b.* 6 Oct. 1855. M.B. C.M. 1879; B.Sc. 1880; Ed. Surg. 31 Mar. 1880. S.M. 21 Mar. 1892. Lt.-Col. 31 Mar. 1900. S. List, 13 July 1905. R. 17 Sept. 1905. District Medl. Offr. Cyprus, 1916–17. ———. Brother of H. Whitwell, No. 1925, supra, 1868.

2139. **Waddell, Laurence Augustine** (afterwards **Laurence Austin Waddell**). *b.* 29 May 1854. M.B.C.M. (Honours), Glas. 1878. Surg. 31 Mar. 1880. Changed second name to Austin in 1881. S.M. 31 Mar. 1892. Lt.-Col. 31 Mar. 1900. S. List, 17 Sept. 1905. R. 21 Oct. 1906. Prof. of Tibetan, Univ. Coll. Lond. 1906. ———. LL.D. Glas. 1895. C.I.E. 24 July 1901. C.B. 16 Dec. 1904. Burma, 1886–87, operations of 2nd Brigade, Wuntho expedition, medal with clasp. N.-W. Frontier, Chitral, 1895, relief of Chitral, medal with clasp.

China, 1900, S.M.O. at base, and later at Pekin, Desp. L.G. 14 May 1901, medal with clasp, C.I.E. N.-W. Frontier, Waziristan, 1901–02, clasp. Tibet, 1904, as P.M.O., occupation of Lhasa, Desp. L.G. 13 Dec. 1904, medal with clasp, C.B. Author of Some new and little known hot springs in South Behar, 1890; Discovery of site of Asoka's classic capital of Pataliputra, 1892; The Buddhism of Thibet, 1895; Among the Himalayas, 1899; The tribes of the Brahmaputra Valley, 1900; Report on the excavations at Pataliputra, 1903; Lhasa and its mysteries, 1905; edited 2nd, 3rd and 4th editions of Lyon's Medical Jurisprudence for India, 1902, 1904, 1909; edited Indian Medical Gazette, 1884–85 and 1897–99; The Indo-Sumerian Seals deciphered, 1925; The Phœnician Origin of Britons, 1926; Sumer-Aryan Dict., Part I, 1927.

2140. Shewan, George (afterwards **Money-Shewan, George**). b. 20 Jan. 1857. M.B. C.M. Ed. 1879. Surg. 31 Mar. 1880. S.M. 31 Mar. 1892. d. at Trieste, 31 Dec. 1897. Took name of Money-Shewan in 1895. Son of Surg. A. Shewan, No. 885, Madras, 1829. Egypt, 1882, battle of Tel-el-Kebir, medal with clasp, bronze star. Burma, 1886–87. Ruby Mines expedition, operations 1st Brigade, medal with clasp. N.-W. Frontier, 1897, medal.

2141. Spencer, Dhanjibhai Barjoeji. b. 20 Feb. 1857. Bombay Univ. L.S.A. 1879. L.F.P.S.G. 1879. Surg. 31 Mar. 1880. S.M. 31 Mar. 1892. Lt.-Col. 31 Mar. 1900. S. List, 16 Oct. 1905. R. 17 May 1910. ———. Sudan, 1885, Suakin, actions of Hashin, Tofrek, and Tamai, medal with two clasps, bronze star. Burma, 1886–88, operations of 2nd Brigade, medal with two clasps. N.-E. Frontier, Lushai, 1892. China, 1900, S.M.O. Tientsin, Desp. L.G. 14 May 1901, medal. Author of A Record of Indian Fevers, 1899.

2142. Clarke, James. b. 8 Apr. 1855. Q.C. Belfast. M.D. (Honours), M.Ch. Q.U.I. 1877. Surg. 31 Mar. 1880. S.M. 31 Mar. 1892. F.R.C.S.I. 1893. D.P.H. Cantab. 1893. Lt.-Col. 31 Mar. 1900. d. at Sialkot, 15 Feb. 1901. N.-E. Frontier, Akha, 1883–84.

2143. Vaid, Cowasjee Cavasjee. b. 8 Apr. 1855. Bombay Univ. L.M.S. Bo. 1878. L.R.C.P. Ed. 1878. L.F.P.S.G. 1878. Surg. 31 Mar. 1880. S.M. 31 Mar. 1892. Lt.-Col. 31 Mar. 1900. R. 18 May 1905. d. 2 Mar. 1928. N.-W. Frontier, Mahsud Waziri, 1881. Burma, 1885–87, capture of Minhla, medal with clasp.

2144. Pank, Philip Durrell. b. 2 Oct. 1853. St. Thomas'. L.R.C.P. and S. Ed. 1879. Surg. 31 Mar. 1880. S.M. 31 Mar. 1892. Lt.-Col. 31 Mar. 1900. S. List, 26 Oct. 1905. R. 17 May 1910. Rejoined for service in war of 1914–18, 11 Apr. 1915–18. d. in London, 19 Mar. 1930. N.-W. Frontier, Mahsud Waziri, 1881. Author (with D. ffrench-Mullen, No. 2087, supra) of Medico Topographical Account of Rajputana, 1900.

2145. Mulroney, Thomas Richard. b. 23 June 1853. Bombay and Malta Univs. Asst. Apy. S.M.D. Bombay 27 Sept. 1873 to 30 Mar. 1880. M.D. C.M. Malta, 1879. L.R.C.P. and S. Ed. 1879. M.R.C.S. 1880. Surg. 31 Mar. 1880. S.M. 31 Mar. 1892. Lt.-Col. 31 Mar. 1900. F.R.C.S. 1990. R. 13 Aug. 1909. ———.

2146. **MacDonald, Thomas Rankin.** *b.* 17 May 1853. Ed. Univ. and Vienna. L.R.C.S. Ed. 1875. M.A. M.B. C.M. Ed. 1876. M.R.C.S. 1880. Surg. 31 Mar. 1880. S.M. 31 Mar. 1892. F.R.C.S. Ed. 1899. Lt.-Col. 31 Mar. 1900. R. 20 June 1900. *d.* at Inverness, 8 May 1921. Egypt, 1882, action of Tel-el-Kebir, medal with clasp, bronze star.

2147. **Giles, George Michael James.** *b.* 20 Dec. 1853. St. Mary's. L.S.A. 1876. M.R.C.S. 1876. M.B. (Honours), 1877. Cert. San. Science, 1880, Lond. F.R.C.S. 1880. Civil Surgeon, South Africa, 1878–79, Surg. 2 Oct. 1880. S.M. 2 Oct. 1892. Lt.-Col. 2 Oct. 1900. R. 15 Jan. 1901. *d.* at Plymouth, 24 Aug. 1916. South Africa, operations against Galekas, 1878 ; Zulu war, 1879, medal with clasp. Author of Report on Natural History collections of Chitral-Kafiristan Mission, 1889 ; Report on Kala Azar and Beri Beri, 1890 ; Tea Garden Sanitation, 1891 ; Qawaid-i-Jarahat-i-Jahida, Antiseptic Surgery in Urdu, 1897 ; Handbook of Gnats or Mosquitos, 1900 ; Notes on collecting and preserving Mosquitos, 1900 ; Climate and Health in Hot Countries, 1904 ; General Sanitation and Anti-Malarial measures in Sekondi, the Goldfields, and Kumasi, 1905.

2148. **Sedgfield, Arthur Robert Wyatt.** *b.* 6 May 1854. King's Coll. Lond. M.R.C.S. 1876. M.B (Honours), Lond. 1877. Surg. 2 Oct. 1880. S.M. 2 Oct. 1892. Lt.- Col. 2 Oct. 1900. *d.* at Sanawar, 8 Feb. 1902.

2149. **Dobson, Edwin Francis Horatio.** *b.* 21 Sept. 1853. Ab. Univ. and Middlesex Hosp. M.B. C.M. Ab. 1878. Surg. 2 Oct. 1880. S.M. 2 Oct. 1892. Lt.-Col. 2 Oct. 1900. S. List, 21 Nov. 1905. R. 27 Nov. 1910. Lost in S.S. ' Hirano Maru,' torpedoed and sunk off North Coast of Ireland, 5 Oct. 1918.

2150. **Shearer, Johnston.** *b.* 22 Oct. 1852. M.A. (Honours), 1873 ; M.B. C.M. (Honours), 1877 ; D.P.H. 1897 ; Ab. Surg. 2 Oct. 1880. S.M. 2 Oct. 1892. Lt.-Col. 2 Oct. 1900. S. List, 14 July 1906. Bt.-Col. 11 Nov. 1910. R. 6 Dec. 1910. *d.* at Bridge of Allan, 6 Feb. 1917. D.S.O. 20 May 1898. C.B. 26 June 1908. Egypt, 1882, medal, bronze star. Burma, 1887–88, operations of 1st and 3rd Brigades, Southern Shan column, medal with two clasps. N.-W. Frontier, Hazara, 1891, clasp ; second Miranzai, 1891, clasp ; Waziristan, 1894–95, Desp. G.G.O. No. 473 of 1895, clasp ; Tirah, 1897–98, Desp. L.G. 5 Apr. 1898, medal with two clasps, D.S.O.

2151. **Hassan, Syed.** *b.* 23 Mar. 1855. M.B. Cal. 1878. M.R.C.S. 1879. L.R.C.P. Lond. 1879. Surg. 2 Oct. 1880. S.M. 2 Oct. 1892. D.P.H. Cantab. 1894. R. 1 Jan. 1899. M.D. Dunelm, 1899. ———. Burma, 1886–87, medal with clasp. N.-E. Frontier, Chin Lushai, 1889–90, clasp. N.-W. Frontier, first Miranzai, 1891 ; Malakand, 1897, defence of Malakand, Desp. G.G.O. No. 1089 of 1897, medal.

2152. **Polden, Robert James.** *b.* 3 Apr. 1855. B.A. 1874 ; M.B. B.Ch. 1880 ; Dip. State Med. and Sany. Science, 1881 ; T.C.D. Surg. 2 Oct. 1880. Parkes Memorial prize, 1882. *d.* at Daudkandi, Tippera, 2 Dec. 1888. Egypt, 1882, medal, bronze star.

2153. **Banerjee, Hem Chandra.** *b.* 23 Nov. 1852. Cal. and Glas. Univs. L.R.C.P. Ed. 1878. L.F.P.S.G. 1878. Surg. 2 Oct. 1880. S.M. 2 Oct. 1892. Lt.-Col. 20 Oct. 1900. R. 1 Feb. 1906. *d.* 17 Sept. 1906. Burma, 1886–87, medal with clasp.

2154. **Nandi, Shambhu Chandra.** *b.* 20 Apr. 1857. M.B. C.M. Glas. 1879. Surg. 2 Oct. 1880. S.M. 2 Oct. 1892. Lt.-Col. 2 Oct. 1900. R. 6 Dec. 1905. ———. Burma, 1886–88, operations of 4th Brigade, medal with two clasps. N.-W. Frontier, first Miranzai, 1891 ; Tirah, 1897–98, medal with two clasps. China, 1900, medal. N.-W. Frontier, Waziristan, 1901–02, clasp.

2155. **Pierson, Alfred Henry.** *b.* 9 Dec. 1857. Guy's. M.R.C.S. 1879. L.R.C.P. Lond. 1879. L.S.A. 1879. Surg. 2 Oct. 1830. *d.* at Shelabagh, Baluchistan, 29 Jan. 1891.

2156. **Peck, Francis Samuel.** *b.* 1 Apr. 1858. Bristol and St. Thomas'. M.R.C.S. 1879. L.R.C.P. Ed. 1880. Surg. 2 Oct. 1880. S.M. 2 Oct. 1892. Lt.-Col. 2 Oct. 1900. S. List, 10 Oct. 1906. *d.* on board P. and O. S.S. 'Persia,' in Mediterranean, on passage to Europe, 9 Apr. 1908. Brother of E. S. Peck, No. 2359, infra, 1894. Burma, 1886–87, operations, 5th Brigade, pursuit of Hla Oo, medal with clasp.

2157. **Deane, William.** *b.* 28 Mar. 1856. Peter St. and Meath Hosps. Dublin. L.R.C.S.I. 1879. L.R.C.P. Ed. 1879. Surg. 2 Oct. 1880. S.M. 2 Oct. 1892. F.R.C.S.I. 1892. *d.* at Naini Tal, 7 May 1895. Brother of A. Deane, No. 1969, supra, 1869. N.-E. Frontier, Akha, 1883–84. Burma 1886–87, medal with clasp.

2158. **De Conceiçao, Philip.** *b.* 1 Jan. 1853. Bo. Univ. L.M.S. Bo. 1876. Civil Asst. Surg. Bombay, 1878–80. L.S.A. 1879. L.F.P.S.G. 1879. Surg. 2 Oct. 1880. *d.* in London, 29 June 1889. Burma, 1884–87, Desp. medal.

1881

2159. **Griffiths, Herbert Tyrrell.** *b.* 10 Aug. 1853. Cambridge (Trinity Coll.), and St. George's. M.A. 1879 ; M.B. 1881 ; M.D. 1884 ; Cantab. M.R.C.S. 1879. L.S.A. 1879. L.R.C.P. Lond. 1881. Surg. 2 Apr. 1881. Resigned, 15 June 1883. M.R.C.P. Lond. 1885. Physn. to Seamen's Hosp. Greenwich, 1886. *d.* at Preston Candover, 3 Nov. 1905.

2160. **Hawkins, Frederick Daly Cæsar.** *b.* 18 Nov. 1858. St. George's, M.R.C.S. 1880. L.R.C.P. Ed. 1880. Surg. 2 Apr. 1881. S.M. 2 Apr. 1893. Lt.-Col. 2 Apr. 1901. R. 26 Oct. 1901. ———.

2161. **Cunningham, John Adams.** *b.* 29 Apr. 1858. M.D. M.Ch. R.U.I. 1880. Surg. 2 Apr. 1881. S.M. 2 Apr. 1893. Lt.-Col. 2 Apr. 1901. S. List, 17 Jan. 1908. Col. 27 Nov. 1910. *d.* in Calcutta, 31 Dec. 1910. N.-W. Frontier, Tirah, 1897–98, medal with clasp.

2162. **Hudson, Harry Chalmers.** *b.* 17 Sept. 1858, at Port Elizabeth, Cape Colony. Richmond Hosp. Dublin. L.R.C.S.I. 1879. L.K.Q.C.P. 1880. Surg. 2 Apr. 1881. S.M. 2 Apr. 1893. *d.* in London, 8 Feb. 1901. Sudan, 1885, medal with clasp, bronze star. Burma, 1886–88, Ruby Mines expedition, Maniloung expedition, Northern Shan column, medal with two clasps. N.-E. Frontier, Manipur, 1891, Desp. G.G.O. No. 585 of 1891, clasp. N.-W. Frontier, Waziristan, 1894–95, action at Wana, clasp ; Tochi, 1897–98, Desp. G.G.O. No. 1432 of 1897, medal with clasp.

2163. **Silcock, Alexander.** *b.* 22 Sept. 1856. T.C.D. King's Coll. and Univ. Coll. Lond. B.A. M.B. B.Ch. 1880; M.D. 1892; T.C.D. Surg. 2 Apr. 1881. S.M. 2 Apr. 1893. D.P.H. Cantab. 1893. Lt.-Col. 2 Apr. 1901. S. List, 2 Apr. 1908. R. extra pension, 25 Mar. 1909. ————.

2164. **Mullane, Patrick.** *b.* 12 Mar. 1854. Q.C. Cork. M.D. M.Ch. R.U.I. 1880. Surg. 2 Apr. 1881. S.M. 2 Apr. 1893. Lt.-Col. 2 Apr. 1901. R. 1 Nov. 1901. *d.* 13 June 1926. Brother of J. Mullane, No. 2086, supra, 1877. Burma, 1886–87, operations of 2nd and 3rd Brigades, medal with two clasps. N.-W. Frontier, first Miranzai, 1891; Chitral, 1895, relief of Chitral, medal with clasp; Tirah, 1897–98, actions of Dargai and of Sampagha and Arhanga Valley, two clasps.

2165. **Rodgers, John William.** *b.* 3 Sept. 1856. L.R.C.P. and S. Ed. 1880. Surg. 2 Apr. 1881. S.M. 2 Apr. 1893. Lt.-Col. 2 Apr. 1901. S. List, 15 Oct. 1908. R. extra pension, 5 July 1911. *d.* 26 Sept. 1913. N.-W. Frontier, Hazara, 1888, medal with clasp; Chitral, 1895, relief of Chitral, medal with clasp. East Africa, Somaliland, 1903–04, medal with clasp.

2166. **MacLaren, James Farquharson.** *b.* 22 Oct. 1854. M.B. C.M. Ed. 1877. Surg. 2 Apr. 1881. S.M. 2 Apr. 1893. Lt.-Col. 2 Apr. 1901. S. List, 15 Oct. 1908. R. 24 June 1911. ————. Brother of G. G. MacLaren, No. 1932, supra, 1868. V.D. 21 June 1901. Sudan, 1885, actions of Hashin and Tamai, medal with clasp, bronze star.

2167. **Young, Louis Tarleton.** *b.* 26 July 1859. L.M. L.Ch. 1881; B.A. M.B. M.Ch. 1882; M.D. 1892; T.C.D. Medl. Travelling Prizeman, T.C.D. 1881. Surg. 1 Oct. 1881. S.M. 1 Oct. 1893. R. 29 Apr. 1899. *d.* 20 Mar. 1904. N.-E. Frontier, Akha, 1883–84. Author of Carlsbad treatment for tropical ailments, 1895.

2168. **Gibbons, James Barry.** *b.* 13 Jan. 1859. St. Vincent's Hosp. Dublin. L.R.C.S.I. 1878. L.K.Q.C.P. 1880. Surg. 1 Oct. 1881. S.M. 1 Oct. 1893. Lt.-Col. 1 Oct. 1901. R. 17 Feb. 1908. Rejoined for service in war of 1914–18, 19 Oct. 1914 to 1918. ————. Author of Manual of Medical Jurisprudence for India, 1904.

2169. **Shand, George Jolly.** *b.* 25 Nov. 1853. M.B. C.M. 1879; M.D. 1881; Ab. Surg. 1 Oct. 1881. *d.* at Chinawan, Panjab, 1 Apr. 1887.

2170. **Grant, Donald St. John Dundas.** *b.* 10 May 1858. B.A. M.B. B.Ch. T.C.D. 1881. Surg. 1 Oct. 1881. S.M. 1 Oct. 1893. Lt.-Col. 1 Oct. 1901. S. List, 1 Mar. 1909. Col. 1 Jan. 1911. R. 14 Mar. 1917. ————. N.-E. Frontier, Akha, 1883–84.

2171. **Crawford, Dirom Grey.** *b.* 21 July 1857, at Chinsura, son of J. A. Crawford, B.C.S. M.B. C.M. Ed. 1881. Surg. 1 Oct. 1881. S.M. 1 Oct. 1893. Lt.-Col. 1 Oct. 1901. S. List, 25 Mar. 1909. R. extra pension, 5 Dec. 1911. Rejoined for service in war of 1914–18, 7 Nov. 1914 to 29 Mar. 1919. ————. Brother of J. M. Crawford, No. 2299 infra, 1891. War of 1914–18, Hosp. ships, 'Glenart Castle' and 'Syria,' Desp. L. G. 24 Feb. 1917, star, two medals. Author of A Brief History of the Hughli District, 1903; Hughli Medical Gazetteer, 1903; History of the Indian Medical Service, 1915; History of Midnapur Zamindari Company, 1928; Roll of Indian Medical Service.

1882

2172. Charles, Richard Henry Havelock. b. 10 Mar. 1858. Q.C. Cork, Univ Coll. Lond., Paris, Berlin, and Vienna. M.D. (Honours and Gold Medal), B.Ch. R.U.I. 1881. Surg. 1 Apr. 1882. F.R.C.S.I. 1894. S.M. 1 Apr. 1894. Lt.-Col. 1 Apr. 1902. Hony. F.R.C.S. 1906. Gold Medal of R.C.S. Eng. 1906. Physn. in Ordinary to H.R.H. the Prince of Wales, 1906. Member, Medl. Board, India Office, Dec. 1907 to Feb. 1913; President, 28 Feb. 1913–23. Sergeant-Surgeon to H.M. George V, 1910. Hony. Surg.-Genl. 28 Feb. 1913. Dean, London School of Trop. Medicine, 1916. Medl. Adviser to Secy. of State for India, June 1916 to Aug. 1923, LL.D. Belfast, 1923. ———. K.C.V.O. 19 Mar. 1906. G.C.V.O. 4 Feb. 1912. G.S.P. 22 Oct. 1917. K.C.S.I. 1 Jan. 1923. Bart. 2 Jan. 1928. Served with Afghan Boundary Commission, 1884–86. Author of Report on Hospital Service of Afghan Boundary Commission, 1886.

2173. Duncan, George. b. 16 Aug. 1856. L.R.C.S. Ed. 1877. M.B. C.M. Ed. 1878. Surg. 1 Apr. 1882. S.M. 1 Apr. 1894. Lt.-Col. 1 Apr. 1902. d. at Dera Ismail Khan, 3 Feb. 1904. N.-W. Frontier, Hazara, 1888; Hazara, 1891, medal with two clasps; Waziristan, 1894–95, action at Wana, clasp; Chitral, 1895, relief of Chitral, medal with clasp.

2174. Sykes, William Ainley. b. 22 July 1857. Bart's. M.R.C.S. 1879. L.R.C.P. Lond. 1879. M.B. Lond. 1881. Surg. 1 Apr. 1882. S.M. 1 Apr. 1884. Lt.-Col. 1 Apr. 1902. S. List, 2 Apr. 1909. R. extra pension, 18 July 1912. Rejoined for service in war of 1914–18, Nov. 1914–1918. ———. Sudan, 1885, Suakin, medal with two clasps, bronze star. Burma, 1885–89, Ruby Mines expedition, Desp. G.G.O. No. 434 of 1887, medal with two clasps, D.S.O. N.-W. Frontier, Zhob Valley, 1890; Waziristan, 1894–95, clasp; Malakand, 1897–98, operations in Bajaur and in Mamund country; Buner, action of Tanga Pass, Desp. G.G.O. No. 217 of 1898, medal with clasp. China, 1900, medal.

2175. Leahy, Albert William Denis. b. 20 July 1855. Charing Cross Hosp., Vienna, Strasburg, and Paris. L.S.A. 1877. M.R.C.S. 1878. F.R.C.S. 1881. Lecturer on Anatomy, School of Medicine for Women, and Asst. Surg. Westminster Ophthalmic Hosp. 1880–82. Surg. 30 Sept. 1882. S.M. 30 Sept. 1894. M.D. Dunelm, 1893. Lt.-Col. 30 Sept. 1902. R. 5 June 1903. d. in London, 19 July 1917.

2176. Webb, William Wilfrid. b. 28 Nov. 1857. Ab. Univ. and Charing Cross Hosp. L.S.A. 1878. M.R.C.S. 1880. M.B. C.M. (Honours), 1881; M.D. 1894; Ab. Surg. 30 Sept. 1882. T.H.P. 22 Aug. 1892. R. 22 Aug. 1894. Secy. Army Medl. School, Netley, 1 Mar. 1893 till school closed on 31 Mar. 1905. Major, 20 June 1900. d. at Exeter, 18 Oct. 1911. Author of Vaccination Manual, in Hindi, 1886; Jail Manual, Bikanir State, 1888; The Indian Medical Service, a guide to intending candidates, 1890; The Currencies of the Hindu States of Rajputana, 1893; and of 38 articles in Dict. Nat. Biography, vols. xi. and later.

2177. Weir, Richard Rose. b. 21 Feb. 1855. M.B. C.M. Ab. 1882. Surg. 30 Sept. 1882. S.M. 30 Sept. 1894. Lt.-Col. 30 Sept. 1902. S. List, 14 June 1909. R. 21 Feb. 1910. ———. Brother of P. A Weir, No. 2055, supra, 1875.

1883

2178. Young, John More. b. 7 Mar. 1857. M.A. 1877, M.B. C.M. (Honours, and Brunton Scholarship), 1881, Glas. M.R.C.S. 1883. Surg. 31 Mar. 1883. d. at Gorakhpur, 23 Apr. 1885.

2179. Jameson, Granville. b. 8 Apr. 1856. M.B. C.M. Ed. 1882. M.R.C.S. 1882. Surg. 31 Mar. 1883. S.M. 31 Mar. 1895. d. at Krishnagarh, 3 July 1897. Brother of J. B. Jameson, No. 1108, Bombay, 1890. Sudan, 1885, Suakin, medal with clasp.

2180. Pratt, James John. b. 12 June 1860. Westminster Hosp. M.R.C.S. 1881. L.R.C.P. Ed. 1881. Surg. 29 Sept. 1883. S.M. 29 Sept. 1895. Lt.-Col. 29 Sept. 1903. S. List, 22 June 1909. R. extra pension, 27 Dec. 1912. F.R.C.S. 1912. Lecturer, Trop. Diseases, Westminster Hosp. 1913. Surg. Seamen's Hosp., Albert Docks, and Lecturer London School of Tropical Medicine, 1914. Rejoined for service in war of 1914–18, 2 Dec. 1914–1919. Bt.-Col. 1 Jan. 1918. Examr. Surg. Stores, India Office, 1919. War of 1914–19, Brevet of Colonel. ———. N.-W. Frontier, Zhob Valley, 1884.

2181. Shore, Robert. b. 10 Nov. 1856. M.A. 1877; M.D. 1881; R.U.I. L.F.P.S.G. 1881. Surg. 29 Sept. 1883. S.M. 29 Sept. 1885. Lt.-Col. 29 Sept. 1903. S. List, 2 Dec. 1909. R. 25 Dec. 1911. Rejoined for service in India in war of 1914–18, 5 Feb. 1915–20. ———. K.-i-H. 1st class, 1 Jan. 1906.

1884

2182. Walsh, John Henry Tull. b. 6 July 1859. Westminster Hosp. M.R.C.S. 1881. L.R.C.P. Lond. 1883. Surg. 1 Apr. 1884. F.R.C.S. 1895. S.M. 1 Apr. 1896. Lt.-Col. 1 Apr. 1904. R. 21 July 1905. Rejoined for service in war of 1914–18, 20 Jan. 1915, invalided July 1915. ———. Burma, 1885–87, expedition up Chindwin river, medal with clasp. Author of History of Murshidabad district, 1902; edited 7th ed. of Moore's Family Medicine for India, 1903.

2183. Hendley, Harold. b. 16 Apr. 1861. Bart's. M.R.C.S. 1882. L.R.C.P. Lond. 1882. L.S.A. 1883. Surg. 1 Apr. 1884. D.P.H. Cantab. 1894. S.M. 1 Apr. 1896. Lt.-Col. 1 Apr. 1904. M.D. Dunelm, 1904. S. List, 14 Dec. 1909. Col. 7 Apr. 1911. Major-Genl. 21 June 1918. R. 26 June 1920. ———. Brother of T. H. Hendley, No. 1953, supra, 1869. K.H.S. 22 Sept. 1915. C.S.I. 1 Jan. 1920. Sudan, 1885, Suakin, medal with clasp, bronze star. Burma, 1886–88, operations, 1st Brigade, medal with two clasps.

*2184. Banatvala, Hormusjee Eduljee. b. 20 Oct. 1859. Bombay Univ. and Bart's. L.M.S. Bo. 1881. L.S.A. 1882. L.R.C.P. Lond. 1882. M.D. Brux, 1883. Surgeon, Bombay, 1 Apr. 1884, transferred to Bengal, 16 Dec. 1884. S.M. 1 Apr. 1896. Lt.-Col. 1 Apr. 1904. S. List, 1 Jan. 1910. Col. 2 Apr. 1914. R. 23 Apr. 1919. Employed in India after retirement, 27 Apr. 1920. ———. C.S.I. 14 June 1917. K.H.S. 22 Dec. 1917. Kt. 3 June 1920. Burma, 1886–87, operations, 1st Brigade, pursuit of Hla Oo, medal with clasp. N.-E. Frontier, Lushai, 1892.

* H. E. Banatvala was the first Indian member of the I.M.S. to rise to administrative rank.

2185. **Fink, George Herbert.** b. 27 July 1860. Univ. Coll. Lond. L.S.A. 1882. M.R.C.S. 1883. Surgeon, Madras, 1 Apr. 1884, transferred to Bengal, 16 Dec. 1884. S.M. 1 Apr. 1896. R. 13 July 1901, ―――. N.-W. Frontier, Tirah, 1897–98, medal with two clasps. Author of Methods of Operating for Cataract, 1894 ; Cancer and pre-cancerous changes, 1903 ; Fungi, Protophyta, and Protozoa, 1903 ; The Mosquito malarial theory and malarial prophylaxis, 1905.

2186. **Alpin, William George Patrick.** b. 15 Sept. 1859. St. Thomas'. M.R.C.S. 1881. L.R.C.P. Lond. 1882. M.D. Brux, 1884. Surgeon, Bombay, 1 Apr. 1884, transferred to Bengal, 16 Dec. 1884. S.M. 1 Apr. 1896. Lt.-Col. 1 Apr. 1904. R. 6 Jan. 1910. Afterwards in practice at Ealing. Rejoined for Service in war of 1914–18, 6 Apr. 1915 to 9 June 1919. ―――. O.B.E. 31 Jan. 1920. Sudan, 1885, Suakin, action of Tofrek, medal with two clasps, bronze star. N.-W. Frontier, Chitral, 1895, relief of Chitral, medal with clasp. War of 1914–18, Hosp. ship, 'Egypt,' and England, 1914–15, star, two medals, O.B.E.

2187. **Leslie, John Tasman Waddell.** b. 1 Dec. 1861. M.B. C.M. Ab. 1882, Surg. 1 Oct. 1884. S.M. 1 Oct. 1896. D.P.H. Oxon. 1900. Lt.-Col. 1 Oct. 1904. S. List, 2 Feb. 1910. d. at Marseilles, on passage to England, 27 Mar. 1911. Burma, 1885–86, medal with clasp.

2188. **Prain, David.** b. 11 July 1857. M.A. 1878, M.B. C.M. (Honours), 1883, Ab. L.R.C.S. Ed. 1883. Surg. 1 Oct. 1884. S.M. 1 Oct. 1896. Lt.-Col. 1 Oct. 1904. R. 31 July 1906. Director, Royal Botanic Gardens, Kew, Dec. 1905 to 28 Feb. 1922. Trustee, British Museum, Dec. 1924. ―――. LL.D. Ab. 1900. F.R.S. 1905. C.I.E. 29 June 1906. Polar Star (Sweden), 1910. LL.D. St. A. 1911. C.M.G. 1 Jan. 1912. Kt. 14 June 1912. Chevalier of Leopold II (Belgium), Mar. 1920. Albert Medal, Royal Society, 1925. Author of Report on Ganja, 1893 ; Bengal Plants, 1903 ; Flora of Sundribuns, 1903 ; Life of Francis Hamilton, once Buchanan (No. 438, supra, 1794), 1905 ; Life of Sir George King (No. 1876, supra, 1885), in vol. ii, 2nd Suppt. Dict. Nat. Biog. 1912.

2189. **Bown, Arthur Thomas.** b. 15 Dec. 1860. St. George's. M.R.C.S. 1882. L.R.C.P. Lond. 1883. Surg. 1 Oct. 1884. S.M. 1 Oct. 1896. Lt.-Col. 1 Oct. 1904. R. 17 Feb. 1905. ―――. N.-W. Frontier, Hazara, 1888 ; Hazara, 1891, medal with clasp ; Chitral, 1895, relief of Chitral, actions of Malakand Pass and at Khar, medal with clasp ; 1897–98, Fort Jamrud, clasp.

2190. **Mukerji, Upendro Nath.** b. 14 Sept. 1860. M.B. C.M. Ed. 1883. M.R.C.S. 1883. Surg. 1 Oct. 1884. S.M. 1 Oct. 1896. Lt.-Col. 1 Oct. 1904. R. 17 Feb. 1905. ―――. N.-W. Frontier, Zhob Valley, 1890. N.-E. Frontier, Manipur, 1891, medal with clasp. Author of Nutrition and Dysentery, 1905.

2191. **Price, William Locking.** b. 15 Mar. 1861. M.B. C.M. Ed. 1883. Surg. 1 Oct. 1884. S.M. 1 Oct. 1896. Lt.-Col. 1 Oct. 1904. R. 4 Dec. 1904. d. in Edinburgh, 17 May 1905. Burma, 1886–88, operations of 1st, 2nd, and 5th Brigades, Wuntho expedition, medal with clasp.

1885

2192. Campbell, Ernest Kenneth (d). *b.* 1 Sept. 1861. Ed. T.C.D. and Paris Univs., and Bart's. M.R.C.S. 1881. M.B. C.M. Ed. 1884. Surg. on probation, 1 Apr. 1885. Resigned from Netley, never joined in India. ————. F.R.C.S. 1886. Afterwards in practice in London, and Surgeon, Westminster Oph. Hosp. Author of Refraction of the Eye, and anomalies of ocular muscles, 1903.

2193. Drury, Francis James. *b.* 17 May 1860. B.A. 1881; M.B. B.Ch. 1883; T.C.D. Surg. 1 Apr. 1885. S.M. 1 Apr. 1897. Lt.-Col. 1 Apr. 1905. S. List, 1 Mar. 1910. Col. 1 Apr. 1912. *d.* at Ranchi, 30 Nov. 1915. Burma, 1886–88, operations of 4th Brigade, and Pouk column, medal with clasp.

2194. Dyson, Herbert Jekyl. *b.* 10 July 1860. St. Mary's. L.S.A. 1882. M.R.C.S. 1882. F.R.C.S. 1885. Surg. 1 Apr. 1885. S.M. 1 Apr. 1897. Lt.-Col. 1 Apr. 1905. *d.* in Presy. Genl. Hosp. Calcutta, 1 Sept. 1907. Burma, 1886–88, operations of 1st and 4th Brigades and in Pagyi, medal with clasp.

2195. Rogers, Frederick Arthur. *b.* 7 Sept. 1861. St. Mary's. M.R.C.S. 1883. L.R.C.P. Lond. 1883. Surg. 1 Apr. 1885. S.M. 1 Apr. 1897. D.P.H. Cantab. 1897. Lt.-Col. 1 Apr. 1905. R. 16 Dec. 1905. *d.* 2 Dec. 1912. Son of M. Rogers, M. No. 1030, 1839. D.S.O. 28 July 1890. Burma, 1885–87, and 1889, Desp. G.G.O. Nos. 434 of 1887 and 782 of 1889, medal with two clasps. N.-E. Frontier, Chin Lushai, 1889–90, Desp. G.G.O. No. 677 of 1890, clasp, D.S.O.

2196. Carroll, Edward Richard William Charles. *b.* 13 Apr. 1859. Westminster Hosp. M.R.C.S. 1884. L.R.C.P. Lond. 1884. Surg. 1 Apr. 1885. D.P.H. Cantab. 1893. S.M. 1 Apr. 1897. Lt.-Col. 1 Apr. 1905. S. List, 29 Mar. 1910. R. 25 Aug. 1912. ————. Burma. 1886–87, operations of 4th Brigade and Salin column, medal with clasp.

2197. Woolbert, Henry Robert. *b.* 21 Dec. 1858. Univ. Coll. Lond. M.B. (Honours), Lond. 1884. M.R.C.S. 1884. F.R.C.S. 1885. Surg. 1 Oct. 1885. S.M. 1 Oct. 1897. Lt.-Col. 1 Oct. 1905. S. List, 1 Apr. 1910. R. extra pension, 30 June 1913. Rejoined for service in war of 1914–18, 7 Nov. 1914 to Mar. 1919. ————. War of 1914–18, Hosp. ship, star, two medals. Author of Medico Topographical account of Deoli, Rajputana, with medical history of Deoli Irregular Force, 1899.

2198. Baker, George Henry. *b.* 11 May 1860. Charing Cross. L.S.A. 1884. M.R.C.S. 1885. Surg. 1 Oct. 1885. S.M. 1 Oct. 1897. Lt.-Col. 1 Oct. 1905. S. List, 1 Apr. 1910. R. 24 Dec. 1913. Rejoined for service in war of 1914–18, 27 Nov. 1914–1918. ————. Burma, 1886–87, operations, 6th Brigade, medal with clasp. N.-W. Frontier, Tirah, 1897–98, medal with clasp.

2199. Grainger, Thomas. *b.* 25 Dec. 1862. Q.C. Belfast. M.D. (Honours), M.Ch. B.A.O. R.U.I. 1884. Surg. 1 Oct. 1885. S.M. 1 Oct. 1897. S. Lt.-Col., specially promoted for Tirah, 20 May 1898. S. List, 1 June 1904. Col. 3 Dec. 1909. S.G. 25 May 1914. R. 29 Apr. 1918. ————. C.B. 19 June 1911. G.S.P. 2 Apr. 1914. K.H.S. 1 Apr. 1915. N.-E. Frontier, Sikkim, 1888, forcing of Jelapla Pass, medal with clasp. N.-W. Frontier, Hazara, 1891, clasp; Tirah, 1897–98, actions of Dargai and of Sampagha and Arhanga passes, operations in Bara Valley, Desp. G.G.O. No. 244 of 1898, promoted to Surg. Lt.-Col., medal with two clasps.

2200. Adie, Joseph Rosamond. b. 22 Mar. 1859. Univ. Coll. Lond. M.R.C.S. 1884. M.B. Lond. 1884. Surg. 1 Oct. 1885. S.M. 1 Oct. 1897. Lt.-Col. 1 Oct. 1905. D.T.M. Liverpool, 1906. S. List, 17 May 1910. R. extra pension, 22 Mar. 1914. d. at Ambala, 24 Jan. 1915. Burma, 1885-87, medal with clasp.

2201. Younan, Arthur Charles. b. 19 Dec. 1861. Calcutta and Ed. Univs. M.B. C.M. Ed. 1883, (Vans Dunlop Scholar, 1882). Surg. 1 Oct. 1885. S.M. 1 Oct. 1897. Lt.-Col. 1 Oct. 1905. S. List, 17 May 1910. R. extra pension, 1 Jan. 1915. ———. Burma, 1886-89, medal with two clasps. N.-W. Frontier, Hazara, 1891, clasp; Isazai, 1892; Chitral, 1895, relief of Chitral, medal with clasp; Tochi, 1897-98, clasp; Mekran, 1898; Mohmand, 1908, medal with clasp.

2202. Alcock, Alfred William. b. 23 June 1859. M.B. C.M. (Honours), Ab. 1885. Surg. 1 Oct. 1885. S.M. 1 Oct. 1897. Lt.-Col. 1 Oct. 1905. R. 29 Dec. 1907. Lecturer on Medl. Entomology, London School Trop. Med. 1913. Rejoined for service in war of 1914-18, 1 Feb. 1915 to June 1915. ———. LL.D. Ab. 1901. F.R.S. 6 June 1901. C.I.E. 1 Jan. 1903. Author of A Naturalist in Indian Seas, 1902; Entomology for Medical Officers, 1911; Article on Snakes and Snake Venom, in Daniels' Tropical Medicine, 1910; (with P. H. Manson Baker), Life and Works of Sir Patrick Manson, 1927.

2203. Edwards, Arthur Rea. b. 22 Apr. 1859. King's Coll. Lond. M.R.C.S. 1881. L.R.C.P. Lond. 1883. Surg. 1 Oct. 1885. Resigned, 16 Apr. 1890. Afterwards residing in Munich. d. at Munich, 4 Aug. 1921. Author of Human Nature, and the principles of Physiognomy.

2204. Cadell, John MacFarlane. b. 8 Mar. 1862. M.B. C.M. Ed. 1884. Surg. 1 Oct. 1885. S.M. 1 Oct. 1897. Lt.-Col. 1 Oct. 1905. S. List, 16 June 1910. R. 5 Mar. 1913. Rejoined for service in war of 1914-18, Major, R.A.M.C. (T.F.), 10th Royal Scots, 21 Oct. 1914 to Feb. 1922. ———. Burma, 1886-89, operations, 4th Brigade, Mogaung column, medal with two clasps. N.-W. Frontier, Hazara, 1891, clasp; Tirah, 1897-98, medal with two clasps. War of 1914-19, Egypt, 24 Nov. 1915 to 15 Mar. 1916, Egyptian Expedition Force, 19 Mar. 1916 to 9 Oct. 1916.

1886

2205. Thorold, William Grant. b. 4 Aug. 1863. Bristol and Univ. Coll. Lond. M.R.C.S. 1885. L.R.C.P. Lond. 1885. Surg. 1 Apr. 1886. S.M. 1 Apr. 1898. T.H.P. 15 Apr. 1901. R. 15 Apr. 1903. ———. Son of Asst. Surg. H. O. Thorold, Bo. No. 840.

2206. Hehir, Patrick. b. 17 May 1859. Calcutta and Ed. Univs. Hosp. App. S.M.D. Bengal, Oct. 1873. Asst. Apy. 31 Jan. 1882. Resigned, 8 Feb. 1884. L.S.A. 1883. M.D. and D.Ch. Brux, 1883. L.R.C.S. Ed. 1883. L.R.C.P. Ed. 1885. M.R.C.S. 1885. F.R.C.S. Ed. 1885. S.S.C. Cantab. 1886. Surg. 1 Apr. 1886. S.M. 1 Apr. 1898. D.T.M. Liverpool, 1904. M.R.C.P. Ed. 1905. Lt.-Col. 1 Apr. 1906. F.R.C.P. Ed, 1908. S. List, 12 July 1910. Col. 25 Mar. 1912. S.G. 13 Mar. 1918, afterwards gazetted Major-Genl. from same date. R. 9 Dec. 1919. ———. C.B. 29 Oct. 1915. C.M.G. 15 Feb. 1917. C.I.E. 4 June 1918. K.C.I.E. 1 Jan. 1920. Burma, 1886-87, medal with clasp. N.-W. Frontier, Tirah, 1897-98, medal with clasp. War of

1914–19, Mesopotamia, advance on Kut, battle of Ctesiphon, defence of Kut, as P.M.O. of Genl. Townsend's force, taken prisoner at Kut, Desp. L.G. 5 Apr., 13 July, and 19 Oct. 1916, and 18 May 1918. C.B. C.M.G. C.I.E. Afghanistan and N.-W. Frontier, 1919, K.C.I.E. Author of Sanitation for Indian Schools, 1890; Alcohol, its effects, 1890; Hygiene of water supplies, 1891; (with J. B. Gribble), Medical Jurisprudence for India, 2nd ed. 1891 (1st ed. 1885, by Gribble alone); Report of first Hyderabad chloroform commission, 1892; Hygiene and Sanitary Science, 1894; Prevention of Disease in Indian frontier warfare, 1911; The Medical Profession in India, 1923; Malaria in India, 1927.

2207. **Pisani, Lionel John.** *b.* 9 Aug. 1861, at Gibraltar. Charing Cross Hosp. M.R.C.S. 1886. L.S.A. 1886. Surg. 1 Apr. 1886. F.R.C.S. 1895. S.M. 1 Apr. 1898. Lt.-Col. 1 Apr. 1906. R. 10 June 1911. *d.* in London, 22 June 1926. N.-W. Frontier, Hazara, 1888, action at Kotkai, medal with clasp. Author of The Pathology of Relapsing Fever, 1897.

2208. **Basu, Basanta Kumar.** *b.* 28 Mar. 1859. Cal. and Ed. Univs. and Univ. Coll. Lond. M.B. C.M. 1882; M.D. 1884; Ed. Surg. 1 Apr. 1886. S.M. 1 Apr. 1898. R. 21 Aug. 1903. *d.* in Bengal, 16 Jan. 1913. China, 1900–01.

2209. **Sinha, Narendra Prosanna.** *b.* 30 Sept. 1858. Cal. Univ. and Univ. Coll. Lond. Civil Asst. Surg. Bengal, 1881–82. M.R.C.S. 1882. M.R.C.P. Lond. 1883. Surg. 1 Apr. 1886. S.M. 1 Apr. 1898. R. 1 June 1904. Afterwards in practice at Ealing. Rejoined for service in India in war of 1914–18, 30 Jan. 1915 to 10 Jan. 1922. Lt.-Col. 5 Feb. 1917. *d.* 14 Feb. 1930. Brother of Lord Sinha. Burma, 1885–89, medal with two clasps.

2210. **Edwards, William Rice.** *b.* 17 May 1862. London Hosp. M.R.C.S. 1884. M.B. (Honours), Dunelm, 1884. Surg. 1 Apr. 1886. S.M. 1 Apr. 1898. Lt.-Col. 1 Apr. 1906. S. List, 26 Oct. 1910. Col. 25 May 1914. S.G. 1 Apr. 1915, afterwards gazetted Major-Gen. from same date. D.G. 8 Jan. 1918. Hony. F.R.C.S. Ed. 1919. R. 8 July 1923. *d.* in London, 13 Oct. 1923. C.M.G. 29 Nov. 1900. C.B. 22 June 1914. G.S.P. 1 Apr. 1915. K.H.P. 18 Feb. 1917. K.C.I.E. 4 June 1921. K.C.B. 1 Jan. 1923. South Africa, 1899–1900, as personal Surgeon to Lord Roberts, Commr.-in-Chief, operations in Cape Colony, Orange River Colony, and Transvaal, actions at Johannesburg, Diamond Hill, and Belfast. Desp. L.G. 2 Apr. 1901, Queen's medal with five clasps, C.M.G.

2211. **MacTaggart, Charles.** *b.* 27 Mar. 1861. M.A. 1881, M.B. C.M. (Honours), 1885, Glas. Surg. 1 Apr. 1886. S.M. 1 Apr. 1898. Lt.-Col. 1 Apr. 1906. S. List, 27 Nov. 1910. Col. 29 Mar. 1915. R. 29 Mar. 1920. ———. C.I.E. 11 Dec. 1911. C.S.I. 3 June 1919.

2212. **Evans, John Fenton.** *b.* 25 July 1858. Bristol and Ed. Univs. M.B. C.M. Ed. 1880. Surg. 1 Apr. 1886. S.M. 1 Apr. 1898. *d.* in Calcutta, 13 Mar. 1899, of plague, contracted in the execution of his duties; the first European to die of plague in Calcutta. Burma, 1887–89, medal with clasp. N.-E. Frontier, Lushai, 1892. Desp. . . . Author (with Chuni Lal Bose) of The Necessity for an act restricting the free sale of poisons in Bengal, 1894.

2213. **Bell, George James Hamilton.** *b.* 28 Feb. 1861. M.B. C.M. Ed. 1882. Surg. 1 Apr. 1886. S.M. 1 Apr. 1898. Lt.-Col. 1 Apr. 1906. S. List, 6 Dec. 1910. Col. 16 June 1915. R. 20 Aug. 1920. *d.* at Edinburgh, 9 July 1930. C.I.E. 22 June 1914. Burma, 1887–89, medal with clasp. N.-E. Frontier, Lushai, 1889, clasp.

2214. **Daly, Joseph Thomas.** *b.* 3 Jan. 1862. Cath. Univ. Dublin. M:D. (Honours), M.Ch. R.U.I. 1884. Surg. 1 Apr. 1886. S.M. 1 Apr. 1898. Lt.-Col. 1 Apr. 1906. S. List, 1 Jan. 1911. Col. 1 Apr. 1915. R. 1 Apr. 1920. ———. N.-W. Frontier, Waziristan, 1894–95, medal with clasp. China, 1900, medal. N.-W. Frontier, Mohmand, 1908, operations in Zakha Khel and Mohmand country, medal with clasp. War of 1914–18.

2215. **Fooks, Henry.** *b.* 26 Jan. 1863. Charing Cross Hosp. L.S.A. 1884. L.R.C.P. Lond. 1884. M.R.C.S. 1885. Surg. 1 Apr. 1886. S.M. 1 Apr. 1898. Lt.-Col. 1 Apr. 1906. S. List, 28 Mar. 1911. Col. 12 July 1915. R. 19 Apr. 1920. ———. N.-E. Frontier, Lushai, 1889–90, medal with clasp; Manipur, 1891, clasp. N.-W. Frontier, Zhob Valley, 1890; Waziristan, 1894–95, clasp. China, 1900, medal.

2216. **Hudson, Ernest.** *b.* 9 Apr. 1859. Univ. Coll. Lond. M.R.C.S. 1882. L.S.A. 1882. F.R.C.S. 1886. Surg. 1 Apr. 1886. S.M. 1 Apr. 1898. Lt.-Col. 1 Apr. 1906. S. List, 7 Apr. 1911. *d.* at Allahabad, 14 Oct. 1916. N.-E. Frontier, Chin Lushai, 1889–90, Desp. G.G.O. No. 667 of 1890, medal with clasp; Chitral, 1895, Relief of Chitral, action of Malakand Pass, medal with clasp.

2217. **Deare, Arthur Cecil.** *b.* 30 Sept. 1860. Guy's. L.R.C.P. Lond. 1883. M.R.C.S. 1884. Surg. 1 Apr. 1886. Killed by a tiger, Damoh, C.P. 27 May 1892. Brother of B. H. Deare, No. 2308, infra, 1891. N.-W. Frontier, Hazara, 1888, medal.

2218. **Dawson, Arthur William.** *b.* 11 Feb. 1859. Liverpool and King's Coll. Lond. M.B. 1884; M.D. 1892; Dunelm. M.R.C.S. 1886. L.R.C.P. Lond. 1886. Surg. 1 Apr. 1886. S.M. 1 Apr. 1898. Lt.-Col. 1 Apr. 1906. S. List, 24 June 1911. R. 19 July 1917. *d.* at Grange Park, North London, 7 Mar. 1923. Second name given as Willan in Army Lists from 1894–1921, before and after these dates as William. N.-E. Frontier, Chin Lushai, 1889–90, medal with clasp. N.-W. Frontier, Hazara, 1891, clasp; Chitral, 1895, relief of Chitral, medal with clasp; Tirah, 1897–98, actions of Dargai and of the Sampagha and Arhanga Passes, operations at Dwatoi and in Bara Valley, two clasps. China, 1900, medal. Tibet, 1903–04, medal. N.-W. Frontier, Mohmand, 1908, medal. War of 1914–18, hospital ship.

2219. **Robinson, William Henry Banner.** *b.* 7 Dec. 1865. Carmichael School and Meath Hosp. Dublin. L.R.C.S.I. 1883. L.K.Q.C.P. 1884. Surg. 1 Apr. 1886. D.P.H., R.C.P. and S.I. 1893. S.M. 1 Apr. 1898. Lt.-Col. 1 Apr. 1906. S. List, 5 July 1911. Col. 1 Dec. 1915. S.G. 8 Jan. 1918, afterwards gazetted Major-Genl. from same date. *d.* in Calcutta, 7 Feb. 1922. K.-i-H. 2nd class, 1 Jan. 1901. Order of Philip the Magnanimous (Hesse), Knight's Cross, 1st class, 1904. C.B. 29 Oct. 1915. K.H.S. 22 Apr. 1919. Burma, 1885–89. Desp. G.G.O. No. 782 of 1889, medal with two clasps. N.-W. Frontier, Waziristan, 1894–95, clasp; Chitral, 1895, relief of Chitral, medal with clasp; Tirah, 1897–98, operations in Bara Valley, clasp. War of 1914–18. P.M.O. Indian Forces in Egypt, 1914–16, Desp. L.G. 21 June and 1 Dec. 1916, C.B.

2220. **Sheppard, Henry Anderson.** *b.* 7 Apr. 1859. Charing Cross Hosp. L.S.A. 1883. M.R.C.S. 1884. Surg. 1 Apr. 1886. Superseded for absence without leave, 28 Nov. 1886. Afterwards in practice at Southampton. Name omitted from Medl. Regr. 1924.

2221. **MacNamara, Robert Joseph.** *b.* 5 May 1861. M.D. (Honours), M.Ch. R.U.I. 1884. Surg. 30 Sept. 1886. Major, 30 Sept. 1898. Lt.-Col. 30 Sept. 1906. S. List, 5 Dec. 1911. Col. 14 Mar. 1916. R. 11 Nov. 1916. ———. Brother of J. W. U. MacNamara, No. 2130, supra, 1879. Burma, 1887–89, medal with clasp.

2222. **Pilgrim, Herbert Wilson.** *b.* 10 Oct. 1858, in Barbados. Ed. Univ. Bart's, and Univ. Coll. Lond. L.S.A. 1884. M.R.C.S. 1884. M.B. Lond. 1885. Surg. 30 Sept. 1886. Major, 30 Sept. 1898. F.R.C.S. 1902. Lt.-Col. 30 Sept. 1906. S. List, 25 Dec. 1911. R. extra pension, 11 May 1914. *d.* at Brighton, 1 Oct. 1914. N.-E. Frontier, Chin Lushai, 1889–90, medal.

2223. **French, George Brooke.** *b.* 14 Sept. 1858. Ed. Univ. M.R.C.S. 1885. L.R.C.P. Lond. 1886. Surg. 30 Sept. 1886. M.B. C.M. (Honours), Ed. 1894. Major, 30 Sept. 1898. *d.* at Tonbridge Wells, 20 Aug. 1904.

2224. **Thomson, Francis Wyville.** *b.* 7 Feb. 1860. M.A. 1880; M.B. C.M. 1886; Ed. Surg. 30 Sept. 1886. Major, 30 Sept. 1898. D.T.M. Liverpool, 1905. Lt.-Col. 30 Sept. 1906. R. 14 Mar. 1908. Rejoined for service in war of 1914–18, 1914–17. *d.* at Linlithgow, 27 May 1918. N.-W. Frontier, Waziristan, 1894–95, medal with clasp. China, 1900, relief of Pekin, medal with clasp. N.-W. Frontier, Waziristan, 1901–02, medal with clasp.

2225. **Brown, Edwin Harold.** *b.* 21 July 1861. Bombay Univ., Univ. Coll. Lond. and King's Coll. Lond. L.M.S. Bo. 18—. L.R.C.S. Ed. 1884. L.R.C.P. Lond. 1884. Surg. 30 Sept. 1886. M.D. (Honours), Brux, 1894. Major, 30 Sept. 1898. M.R.C.P. Lond. 1902. M.D. Dunelm, 1903. F.R.C.S. Ed. 1903. D.P.H., R.C.P. and S. Lond. 1903. Lt.-Col. 30 Sept. 1906. R. 10 Nov. 1909. Afterwards in practice in Calcutta. ———. N.-W. Frontier, Tirah, 1897–98, medal with two clasps.

2226. **Bensley, Charles Norman.** *b.* 20 Oct. 1863. M.B. C.M. Ed. 1885. Surg. 30 Sept. 1886. Major, 30 Sept. 1898. Lt.-Col. 30 Sept. 1906. R. 12 Nov. 1911. Rejoined for service in India during war of 1914–18. 19 Feb. 1915–17. ———. Son of C. E. W. Bensley, No. 1740, supra, 1856.

2227. **Henderson, Selby Herriot.** *b.* 28 Mar. 1861. M.B. C.M. Ed. 1882. Surg. 30 Sept. 1886. Major, 30 Sept. 1898. Lt.-Col. 30 Sept. 1906. S. List, 25 Mar. 1912. R. extra pension, 5 Apr. 1919. ———.

2228. **Scotland, David Wilson.** *b.* 16 Nov. 1861. M.B. C.M. 1886; M.D. 1899; Ed. Surg. 30 Sept. 1886. Major, 30 Sept. 1898. Lt.-Col. 30 Sept. 1906. R. 26 Mar. 1907. *d.* at Colinton, Midlothian, 19 Feb. 1925. K.-i-H. 2nd class, 23 May 1900.

2229. **Green, Charles Robert Mortimer.** *b.* 21 May 1863. London Hosp. L.S.A. 1884. M.R.C.S. 1885. L.R.C.P. Lond. 1885. Surg. 30 Sept. 1886. F.R.C.S. 1895. D.P.H. Cantab. 1895. Major, 30 Sept. 1898. Lt.-Col. 30 Sept. 1906. M.D. Dunelm, 1906. S. List, 1 Apr. 1912. Col. 11 Nov. 1916. R. 28 Mar. 1921. ———. K.H.S. 15 June 1920. N.-W. Frontier, Hazara, 1888, medal with clasp; Tirah, 1897–98, medal with clasp. War of 1914–19, Hosp. Ships 'Ellora' and 'Sicilia,' Feb.–Mar. 1917; Mahsud operations 27 Mar. to 10 Aug. 1917. Edited (with V. B. Green-Armytage), 5th ed. of Birch's Diseases of Children, 1913.

2230. **Sellick, James Henderson.** *b.* 17 Jan. 1863. Guy's. M.R.C.S. 1885. M.B. Lond. 1885. Surg. 30 Sept. 1886. Major, 30 Sept. 1898. *d.* at Mandalai, 29 Nov. 1900.

2231. **Hare, Edward Christian.** *b.* 4 Dec. 1863. Guy's M.R.C.S. 1886. L.R.C.P. Lond, 1886. Surg. 30 Sept. 1886. Major, 30 Sept. 1898. D.P.H. Cantab. 1902. Lt.-Col. 30 Sept. 1906. R. 3 Aug. 1917. ———. Son of E. C. Hare, No. 1314, supra, 1839. N.-W. Frontier, 1897–98, operations on Samana and in Kurram Valley, medal with two clasps. Author of Memoirs of Edward Hare, C.S.I. 1900.

2232. **Clarkson, Frank Cecil.** *b.* 27 May 1862. St. Thomas'. M.R.C.S. 1885. L.R.C.P. Lond. 1835. Surg. 30 Sept. 1886. Major, 30 Sept. 1898. Lt.-Col. 30 Sept. 1906. R. 1 Mar. 1912. Rejoined for service in war of 1914–18, 31 Mar. 1917 to Nov. 1918. ———. Brother of J. W. Clarkson, No. 1017, Bombay, 1875. N.-E. Frontier, Chin Lushai, 1889–90, medal with clasp; Manipur, 1891, clasp. Burma, 1891, Thetta column, clasp.

2233. **Jordan, John Gregory.** *b.* 6 Dec. 1859. M.B. C.M. Ed. 1883. M.R.C.S. 1884. Surg. 30 Sept. 1886. Major, 30 Sept. 1898. Lt.-Col. 30 Sept. 1906. R. 18 Apr. 1918. ———. N.-W. Frontier, second Miranzai, 1891, medal with clasp.

2234. **Swinburne, John Digby Marsh.** *b.* 9 Dec. 1861. St. George's. L.R.C.P. Ed. 1884. L.R.C.S. Ed. 1885. Surg. 30 Sept. 1886. *d.* in London, 14 Sept. 1890. N.-E. Frontier, Sikkim, 1888, medal with clasp.

2235. **Morris, Herbert MacKinlay.** *b.* 23 Jan. 1863. M.R.C.S. 1885. L.R.C.P. Lond. 1885. Surg. 30 Sept. 1886. Major, 30 Sept. 1898. Lt.-Col. 30 Sept. 1906. R. 14 May 1907. *d.* at Utakamand, 1 May 1914.

2236. **Russell, Allan Rupert Postance.** *b.* 5 Feb. 1865. M.B. C.M. Ed. 1886. Surg. 30 Sept. 1886. Major, 30 Sept. 1898. Lt.-Col. 30 Sept. 1906. R. 11 Oct. 1907. Rejoined for service in war of 1914–18, 18 Nov. 1914–1917. ———. Burma, 1887–89, medal with clasp.

2337. **Morwood, James.** *b.* 7 Sept. 1862. Q.C. Belfast and Univ. Coll. Lond. M.D. (Honours), M.Ch. 1884; M.A.O. 1897; R.U.I. Surg. 30 Sept. 1886. Major, 30 Sept. 1898. Lt.-Col. 30 Sept. 1906. R. 11 Nov. 1918. ———. N.-W. Frontier, Hazara, 1888, medal with clasp; Tirah, 1897–98, medal with two clasps. War of 1914–21.

2238. **Hall, Edmund Alexander William.** *b.* 29 Nov. 1864. M.B. C.M. Ed. 1886. Surg. 30 Sept. 1886. Major, 30 Sept. 1898. Lt.-Col. 30 Sept. 1906. S. List, 18 July 1912. R. 20 May 1920. ———.

1887

2239. **Elliot, William Henry Wilson.** *b.* 7 Oct. 1864. Guy's. M.R.C.S. 1886. L.S.A. 1886. Surg. 31 Mar. 1887. M.B. Lond. 1895. Major, 31 Mar. 1899. Lt.-Col. 31 Mar. 1907. R. 15 Nov. 1908. D.P.H. R.C.P. and S. Lond. 1911. Rejoined for service in war of 1914–18, 20 Nov. 1914–1918. Hony. Col. 1 Jan. 1919. Tempy. Lt.-Col. R.A.M.C. 15 Oct. 1919 to 15 Apr. 1922. ———. D.S.O. 26 June 1901. N.-W. Frontier, Hazara, 1888, medal with clasp; first Miranzai, 1891; Tochi, 1897–98, medal with clasp. South Africa, 1899–1901, operations in Natal, action at Lombard's Kop, defence of Ladysmith; operations in Transvaal, Desp. L.G. 8 Feb. 1901 and 10 Sept. 1901. Queen's medal with three clasps, D.S.O.

2240. **Murray, James.** *b.* 23 Apr. 1865. M.B. C.M. Ab. 1886. Surg. 31 Mar. 1887. *d.* at Simla, 8 Nov. 1897. N.-W. Frontier, Hazara, 1888, medal with clasp. Collaborated with Dr. Watt in Dictionary of Economic Products, 1889–96.

2241. **Clark, William Ronaldson.** *b.* 18 Sept. 1860. M.A. 1881; M.B. C.M. (Honours), 1884; D.P.H. 1897; Ab. Surg. 31 Mar. 1887. M.R.C.P. Lond. 1896. Major, 31 Mar. 1899. Lt.-Col. 31 Mar. 1907' R. 8 Dec. 1915. Rejoined for service in war of 1914–18, 12 Mar. 1916 to Nov. 1918. *d.* 4 Feb. 1919.

2242. **Braide, George Frederick William.** *b.* 5 Sept. 1862. Manchester. M.R.C.S. 1886. M.B. Vict. 1886. Surg. 31 Mar. 1887. Major, 31 Mar. 1899. Lt.-Col. 31 Mar. 1907. S. List, 28 Aug. 1912. *d.* at Lahore, 6 Jan. 1916.

2243. **Marks, Robert John.** *b.* 19 Oct. 1862. Bristol. M.R.C.S. 1886. L.S.A. 1886. Surg. 31 Mar. 1887. Major, 31 Mar. 1899. Lt.-Col. 31 Mar. 1907. S. List, 27 Dec. 1912. R. 26 Feb. 1918. ———. N.-E. Frontier, Lushai, 1891. N.-W. Frontier, Tochi, 1897–98, medal with clasp.

2244. **Sunder, Charles Edward.** *b.* 22 Nov. 1859. Univ. Coll. Lond. M.R.C.S. 1886. L.S.A. 1886. M.B. B.S. Lond. 1887. Surg. 31 Mar. 1887. Major, 31 Mar. 1899. Lt.-Col. 31 Mar. 1907. S. List, 5 Mar. 1913. R. 1 Apr. 1922. ———. N.-E. Frontier, Sikkim, 1888, medal with clasp. N.-W. Frontier, first Miranzai, 1891.

2245. **Ker, Malcolm Albert.** *b.* 26 Dec. 1862. M.B. C.M. Ed. 1884. Surg. 31 Mar. 1837. Major, 31 Mar. 1899. D.P.H., R.C.P. and S. Lond. 1904. Lt.-Col. 31 Mar. 1907. S. List, 30 June 1913. *d.* in London, 24 Feb. 1915. N.-W. Frontier, Hazara, 1888, medal with clasp; Hazara, 1891, clasp; Second Miranzai, 1891, clasp; Waziristan, 1894–95, clasp; Tirah, 1897–98, medal with two clasps; Waziristan, 1901–02, Desp. G.G.O. No. 611 of 1902, clasp.

2246. **Buchanan, Andrew.** *b.* 17 May 1861. Q.C. Belfast. B.A. (Honours), 1882; M.A. 1882; M.D. 1885; M.Ch. 1886; R.U.I. Surg. 31 Mar. 1887. Major, 31 Mar. 1899. Lt.-Col. 31 Mar. 1907. R. 20 Mar. 1921. ———. N.-E. Frontier, Chin Lushai, 1889–90, medal with clasp. Author of Diseases of the Gums in Indian Jails, 1899; Malarial fevers and Malarial parasites in India, 1901; Lathyrism in the Central Provinces, 1904; Plague prevention in Nagpur, Cats as plague preventers, 1909.

2247. **Hailey, Percy Oswald Ward.** *b.* 11 Apr. 1864. Guy's. M.R.C.S. 1885. L.R.C.P. Lond. 1885. Surg. 31 Mar. 1887. *d.* at Apazai, Zhob Valley, 2 May 1890. N.-W. Frontier, Zhob Valley, 1890.

2248. **Jolliffe, Albert Robert.** *b.* 9 Jan. 1862. Charing Cross Hosp. L.S.A. 1884. M.R.C.S. 1885. Surg. 31 Mar. 1887. *d.* at Kohat, 14 Aug. 1888.

2249. **Fischer, Lewis Gordon.** *b.* 2 Aug. 1862. M.B. C.M. Ed. 1885. Surg. 31 Mar. 1887. Major, 31 Mar. 1899. Lt.-Col. 31 Mar. 1907. R. 28 Oct. 1920. ———.

2250. **Vost, William.** *b.* 23 Nov. 1861. M.B. C.M. Glas. 1883. M.R.C.S. 1886. Surg. 31 Mar. 1887. Major, 31 Mar. 1899. Lt.-Col. 31 Mar. 1907. S. List, 24 Dec. 1913. R. extra pension, 24 Aug. 1919. ————. N.-W. Frontier, Hazara, 1888, medal with clasp; Second Miranzai, 1891, clasp, China, 1900, medal. Author of Jaunpur and Zafarabad Inscriptions, 1905.

2251. **Garvie, John.** *b.* 3 May 1863. M.B. C.M. Ed. 1885. Surg. 31 Mar. 1887. Major, 31 Mar. 1899. Lt.-Col. 31 Mar. 1907. S. List, 22 Mar. 1914. Col. 24 Mar. 1917. R. 25 Mar. 1922. ————. K.H.S. 20 June 1920. N.-W. Frontier, Zhob Valley, 1890.

2252. **Gilbert, Clarence Edward Lloyd.** *b.* 22 June 1862. St. Mary's. M.R.C.S. 1886. L.K.Q.C.P. 1886. Surg. 31 Mar. 1887. Major, 31 Mar. 1899. Lt.-Col. 31 Mar. 1907. R. 21 Sept. 1912. Rejoined for service in war of 1914-18, 7 Nov. 1914-1918. ————. N.-E. Frontier, Sikkim, 1883, medal with clasp; Manipur, 1891, clasp. N.-W. Frontier, Isazai, 1892; Waziristan, 1894-95, clasp; Chitral, 1895, relief of Chitral, medal with clasp; Tirah, 1897-98, operations in Bazar Valley, clasp. East Africa, Somaliland, 1902-04, medal with clasp. War of 1914-18, Hosp. ship.

2253. **MacLeod, Herbert William George.** *b.* 7 July 1860. Ed. Univ. and St. Mary's. M.B. C.M. 1886; M.D. 1895; B.Sc. 1904; Ed. Surg. 31 Mar. 1887. Resigned, 25 Apr. 1892. Afterwards in practice in London. D.P.H., R.C.P. and S. Lond. 1900. D.P.H. Cantab. 1900. M.R.C.P. Lond. 1907. *d.* 30 May 1930. N.-W. Frontier of India, 1888, Samana, medal and clasp. Author of Calculations in Hygiene and Vital Statistics, 1903; Hygiene for Nurses, 1911.

2254. **Manifold, Courtenay Clarke.** *b.* 3 Apr. 1864. Ed. Univ. and St. Mary's. M.B. C.M. Ed. 1886. Surg. 31 Mar. 1887. Major, 31 Mar. 1899. Lt.-Col. 29 Nov. 1900, specially promoted for services in China. S. List, 4 July 1907. Col. 29 Mar. 1910. S.G. 29 Dec. 1917, afterwards gazetted Major-Genl. from same date. R. 24 June 1923. ————. Son of Surg.-Genl. M. F. Manifold, A.M.D. (Johnston's Roll of R.A.M.C. No. 4855). MacGregor silver memorial medallist, 1903. C.B. 22 June 1914. C.M.G. 4 June 1917. Croix de Guerre, Belgium, 12 July 1918. K.H.P. 7 July 1918. K.C.B. 2 Jan. 1922. N.-W. Frontier, Tirah, 1897-98, operations in Waran Valley and in Bazar Valley, medal with clasp. China, 1900, relief of Pekin, actions at Peitsang and Yangtsun, Desp. L.G. 14 May 1901, medal with clasp, promoted Lt.-Col. War of 1914-18, Desp. LG. 4 Jan. and 1 June 1917. Operations in France and Belgium, Aug. 1914 to 26 May 1915, and Apr. 1916. Egypt, 3 June 1915 to 27 Mar. 1916; Belgian Croix de Guerre, C.M.G. K.C.B. G.S.P. 3 June 1930.

2255. **Irvine, Gerard Beatty.** *b.* 15 Aug. 1863. Carmichael School, Dublin. L.R.C.S.I. 1885. L.K.Q.C.P. 1885. Surg. 31 Mar. 1887. Major, 31 Mar. 1899. Lt.-Col. 31 Mar. 1907. S. List, 2 Apr. 1914. R. extra pension, 12 Oct. 1918. ————. N.-W. Frontier, Waziristan, 1894-95, medal with clasp; Tochi, 1897-98, medal with clasp. East Africa, Somaliland, 1903-04, medal with clasp. War of 1914-18, Desp. L.G. 5 Apr. 1916, 10 May 1916, 19 Oct. 1916, and 15 Aug. 1917, C.B.

2256. **Roberts, Alfred Ernest.** *b.* 3 Dec. 1859. Ab. Univ. and London Hosp. M.B. C.M. (Honours), Ab. 1884. M.R.C.S. 1887. Surg. 1 Oct. 1887. D.P.H. Cantab. 1898. Major, 1 Oct. 1899. Lt.-Col. 1 Oct. 1907. R. 21 Apr. 1908. *d.* in Guy's Hosp. London, 20 May 1920. N.-W. Frontier, Hazara, 1888, medal with clasp. Author of Sanitation in India, 1901; Enteric Fever in India, 1906.

INDIAN MEDICAL SERVICE [1887

2257. Davidson, David MacDonald. *b.* 23 Mar. 1865, at Antananarivo, Madagascar. M.B. C.M. (Honours and Murray Scholar), 1887; M.D. 1896; Ab. Surg. 1 Oct. 1887. D.P.H., F.P.S.G. 1897. Major, 1 Oct. 1899. Lt.-Col. 1 Oct. 1907. S. List, 11 May 1914. R. 24 Oct. 1923. *d.* at Lahore, 13 Mar. 1927. C.I.E. 1 Jan. 1921. Author of Article on Dysentery in Davidson's Hygiene and Diseases of warm climates, 1893.

2258. Maynard, Frederic Pinsent. *b.* 10 Mar. 1864. Durham Univ. and Bart's. M.B. (Honours), Dunelm, 1885. M.R.C.S. 1885. L.R.C.P. Lond. 1885. Surg. 1 Oct. 1887. Major, 1 Oct. 1899. F.R.C.S. 1900. Lt.-Col. 1 Oct. 1907. S. List, 25 May 1914. R. extra pension, 11 Mar. 1919. *d.* at Audlem, Cheshire, 30 Sept. 1921. N.-W. Frontier, Hazara, 1891, medal with clasp. Author (with D. Prain, No. 2188, supra, 1884), of Botany of Baluch-Afghan Boundary Commission, 1896; Manual of Ophthalmic Operations, 1908; 2nd ed., 1920; Manual of Ophthalmic Practice, 1920; edited Indian Medical Gazette, 1898.

2259. Lamont, John Charles. *b.* 1 July 1864. M.B. C.M. Ed. 1885. M.R.C.S. 1885. Surg. 1 Oct. 1887. Major, 1 Oct. 1899. Lt.-Col. 1 Oct. 1907. R. 10 Mar. 1908. Lecturer on Anatomy, St. A. Univ. (Dundee), 1909. Rejoined for service in India, during war of 1914-18, 10 Feb. 1915. to 13 Mar. 1919. ————. C.I.E. 1 Jan. 1919. N.-E. Frontier, Chin Lushai, 1889-90, medal with clasp; Manipur, 1891, clasp.

2260. Nott, Arthur Holbrook. *b.* 28 Nov. 1861. Durham Univ. and Birmingham. M.R.C.S. 1886. L.R.C.P. Lond. 1886. M.B. 1887; M.D. 1897; Dunelm. Surg. 1 Oct. 1887. Major, 1 Oct. 1899. Lt.-Col. 1 Oct. 1907. S. List, 1 Jan. 1915. R. extra pension, 21 Apr. 1919. *d.* at St. Moritz, Switzerland, 26 Aug. 1920. N.-W. Frontier, first and second Miranzai, 1891, medal with clasp; Zhob Valley, 1890. War of 1914-18, Desp. L.G. 19 Oct. 1916.

2261. Coleman, Albert. *b.* 20 Dec. 1862. M.B. C.M. Ed. 1887. Surg. 1 Oct. 1887. Major, 1 Oct. 1899. Lt.-Col. 1 Oct. 1907. S. List, 25 Feb. 1915. R. 21 Feb. 1921. ————. Burma, 1888-89, medal with clasp. N.-E. Frontier, Chin Lushai, 1889-90, clasp; Manipur, 1891, clasp.

2262. White, William Westropp. *b.* 10 June 1862. Q.C. Cork. M.D. M.Ch. M.A.O. R.U.I. 1887. Surg. 1 Oct. 1887. Major, 1 Oct. 1899. Lt.-Col. 1 Oct. 1907. D.T.M. dist. London School Trop. Med. 1907. S. List, 29 Mar. 1915. Bt.-Col. 23 June 1915. R. 2 Aug. 1921. *d.* at Bampton, Devon, 21 Mar. 1927. C.B. 1 Jan. 1916. C.M.G. 3 June 1919. N.-W. Frontier, Hazara, 1891, medal with clasp; Chitral, 1895, relief of Chitral, medal with clasp; Tirah, 1897-98, operations on Samana and in Kurram Valley, Buner, two clasps. China, 1900, relief of Pekin, Desp. L.G. 14 May 1901, medal with clasp. War of 1914-19, Desp. L.G. 22 June 1915, 19 Oct. 1916, 14 June 1918, and 5 June 1919. France, Mesopotamia and Palestine. Brevet of Colonel, C.B., C.M.G.

2263. Lane, Daniel Thomas. *b.* 1 Oct. 1862. Q.C. Cork. M.D. (Honours), 1885; M.Ch. M.A.O. 1886; R.U.I. Surg. 1 Oct. 1887. Major, 1 Oct. 1899. Lt.-Col. 1 Oct. 1907. S. List, 1 Apr. 1915. R. 20 Mar. 1918. ————. N.-W. Frontier, first and second Miranzai, 1891, medal with clasp; Hazara, 1891, clasp; Chitral 1895, relief of Chitral, medal with clasp.

2264. **MacWatt, Robert Charles.** b. 22 Jan. 1865. M.B. C.M. 1886; B.Sc. 1897; Ed. Surg. 1 Oct. 1887. Major, 1 Oct. 1899. Lt.-Col. 1 Oct. 1907. F.R.C.S. 1911. S. List, 1 Apr. 1915. Col. 8 Jan. 1918. Major-Genl. and Dir.-Genl. 23 Jan. 1923. R. 1 Oct. 1926. K.-i-H. 1st class, 1 Jan. 1908. C.I.E. 1 Jan. 1916. K.H.S. 28 Mar. 1921. Knight, 1 Jan. 1925. N.-W. Frontier, Hazara, 1888, medal with clasp. N.-E. Frontier, Lushai, 1889, clasp. N.-W. Frontier, Hazara, 1891, clasp; second Miranzai, 1891, clasp.

2265. **Woodwright, William Henry Edward.** b. 10 July 1865. L.R.C.S.I. 1886. L.K.Q.C.P. 1886. Surg. 1 Oct. 1887. F.R.C.S.I. 1891. Major, 1 Oct. 1899. Lt.-Col. 1 Oct. 1907. S. List, 21 June 1915. R. 10 July 1920. ———. N.-W. Frontier, Hazara, 1888, medal with clasp; first Miranzai, 1891.

2266. **Buchanan, Walter James.** b. 12 Nov. 1861. T.C.D. and Vienna Univs. B.A. M.B. B.Ch. 1887; Travelling Medical Prizeman, 1887; Dip. State Med. 1888; T.C.D. Surg. 1 Oct. 1887. Major, 1 Oct. 1899. Lt.-Col. 1 Oct. 1907. S. List, 12 July 1915. R. 7 June 1919. d. in Dublin, 23 Mar. 1924. ———. C.I.E. 1 Jan. 1913. K.C.I.E. 4 June 1918. N.-E. Frontier, Chin Lushai, 1889–90, medal with clasp. Author of The Darwinism of to-day, 1891; Jail Manual, 1898; Article on Inflammation of Liver in Quain's Dictionary of Medicine, 3rd ed. 1902; chapter on Indian Medical Jurisprudence in Taylor's Medical Jurisprudence, 5th ed. 1905; edited Indian Medical Gazette, 1899–1919.

2267. **Close, Joseph Kinnear** (christened **William Joseph Close,** birth cert.). b. 22 Dec. 1864. Q.C. Belfast. M.D. M.Ch. M.A.O. R.U.I. 1886. Surg. 1 Oct. 1887. Major 1 Oct. 1899. Lt.-Col. 1 Oct. 1907. S. List, 1 Dec. 1915. Col. 15 Aug. 1918. R. 9 Nov. 1922. ———. K.H.S. 29 Sept. 1926. N.-E. Frontier, Sikkim, 1888, forcing of Jelapla Pass, medal with clasp; Manipur, 1891, clasp.

2268. **MacNamara, John Maurice.** b. 25 Aug. 1860. Q.C. Cork and Galway. B.A. M.D. MCh. R.U.I. 1887. Surg. 1 Oct. 1887. d. at Jhansi, 21 Aug. 1889.

2269. **Brabazon, Henry Moore.** b. 28 Aug. 1861. B.A. M.B. B.Ch. 1885; M.D. M.Ch. 1888; T.C.D. L.K.Q.C.P. 1886. Surg. 1 Oct. 1887. F.R.C.S.I. 1888. d. in Calcutta, 1 Aug. 1891. N.-W. Frontier, Hazara, 1891, medal.

1888

2270. **Marshall, Daniel Grove.** b. 4 Sept. 1860. M.B. C.M. Ed. 1885. Surg. 31 Mar. 1888. Major, 31 Mar. 1900. T.H.P. 15 Sept. 1904. R. 24 June 1905. Lecturer in Tropical Diseases, Edin. Extramural Medical School, 1905; ditto, Ed. Univ. 1909. Tempy. Lt.-Col. R.A.M.C. Oct. 1918 to Nov. 1919. Lt.-Col. 15 Oct. 1919. d. in Edinburgh, 16 Dec. 1923. Burma, 1889–92, medal with clasp. N.-W. Frontier, Isazai, 1892; Tochi, 1897–98, medal with clasp. China, 1900, relief of Pekin, medal with clasp.

2271. **Moir, David MacBeth.** b. 30 June 1860. M.A. St. A. 1881. M.B. C.M. 1885; M.D. 1899; Ed. Surg. 31 Mar. 1888. Major, 31 Mar. 1900. d. in Calcutta, 5 June 1907. Son of R. Moir, No. 1622, supra, 1853. N.-E. Frontier, Chin Lushai, 1889–90, medal with clasp. Edited Indian Medical Gazette, 1897 and 1903–04.

INDIAN MEDICAL SERVICE [1888

2272. **Whitchurch, Harry Frederick.** *b.* 22 Sept. 1866. Bart's. M.R.C.S. 1887. L.R.C.P. Lond. 1887. Surg. 31 Mar. 1888. Major, 31 Mar. 1900. *d.* at Dharmsala, 16 Aug. 1907. V.C. 16 July 1895.* Gold Medal, British Medl. Assn. 1896. N.-E. Frontier, Lushai, 1890, relief of Changsil and Aijal, medal with clasp. N.-W. Frontier, Chitral, 1895, defence of Chitral, Desp. G.G.O. No. 531 of 1895, medal with clasp, V.C.; Malakand, 1897–98, defence of Malakand, relief of Chakdara, action at Landakai, operations in Bajaur and in Mohmand country, Desp. G.G.O. No. 1089 of 1897, two clasps. China, 1900, relief of Pekin, actions of Peitsang and Yangtsun, Desp. L.G. 4 May 1901, medal with clasp.

2273. **Roberts, James Reid.** *b.* 24 Jan. 1861. Middlesex Hosp. M.R.C.S. 1884. L.R.C.P. Lond. 1884. M.B. (Honours), M.S. L.S.Sc. Dunelm, 1885. F.R.C.S. 1887. Surg. 31 Mar. 1888. Major, 31 Mar. 1900. Lt.-Col. 31 Mar. 1908. S. List, 31 Dec. 1915. R. 9 July 1919. ——— C.I.E., 11 Dec. 1911. Kt. 3 June 1913. N.-E. Frontier, Chin Lushai, 1889–90, medal with clasp. N.-W. Frontier, Hunza Nagar, 1891, as P.M.O. capture of Nilt fort, Desp. G.G.O. No. 397 of 1892, clasp.

2274. **Gee, Frederick William.** *b.* 11 Mar. 1863. Univ. Coll. Lond. M.R.C.S. 1886. L.S.A. 1886. M.B. B.S. Lond. 1887. Surg. 31 Mar. 1888. Major, 31 Mar. 1900. Lt.-Col. 31 Mar. 1908. S. List, 1 Apr. 1916. R. 5 Aug. 1920. *d.* in London, 2 June 1930. C.I.E. 3 June 1915. G.S.P. 18 Aug. 1928. N.-W. Frontier, Chitral, 1895, relief of Chitral, medal with clasp; Tochi, 1897–98, clasp. China, 1900, medal. East Africa, Somaliland, 1903–04, Desp. L.G. 2 Sept. 1904, medal with clasp. War of 1914–18, Desp. L.G. 15 Aug. 1917, 12 Mar. 1918, 17 Aug. 1918, 21 Feb. 1919; C.I.E.

2275. **Prasad, Kanta.** *b.* 17 May 1860. L.R.C.P. and S. Ed. 1886. L.F.P.S.G. 1886. M.B. C.M. 1887; M.D. 1913; Ed. Surg. 31 Mar. 1888. Major, 31 Mar. 1900. Lt.-Col. 31 Mar. 1908. R. 3 June 1913. Rejoined for service in India in war of 1914–18, 29 Jan. 1915 to 9 Sept. 1921. *d.* at Benares, 16 Dec. 1921. K.-i-H. 1st class, 4 June 1917. N.-E. Frontier, Manipur, 1891, medal with clasp. N.-W. Frontier, Isazai, 1892; Tirah, 1897–98, Malakand, operations in Bajaur and Mohmand country, medal with two clasps. Author of Health and Mortality among educated Indians, 1913.

2276. **O'Gorman, Patrick Wilkins.** *b.* 1 Mar. 1860. Calcutta and Ed. Univs. and King's Coll. Lond. Hosp. App, S.M.D. Bengal, 15 Apr. 1875; Asst. Apy. 13 Feb. 1883; Resigned 30 Nov. 1885. L.R.C.P. and S. Ed. 1886. L.F.P.S.G. 1886. Surg. 31 Mar. 1888. D.P.H. Cantab. 1898. M.R.C.P. Ed. 1899. M.D. Brux, 1899. Major, 31 Mar. 1900. Lt.-Col. 31 Mar. 1908. R. 11 July 1919. ———. C.M.G. 3 June 1918. N.-W. Frontier, first and second Miranzai, 1891, medal with clasp. War of 1914–19, Desp. L.G. 7 Oct. 1918; C.M.G. Author of Alcohol in Health, 1900.

2277. **Gray, William Henry.** *b.* 18 Sept. 1863. M.B. C.M. Ab. 1886. Surg. 31 Mar. 1888. Major, 31 Mar. 1900. Lt.-Col. 31 Mar. 1908. R. 24 Oct. 1913. *d.* at Aberdeen, 14 Jan. 1915. N.-W. Frontier, Waziristan, 1894–95, medal with clasp; Buner, 1897–98, medal with clasp.

* The first and only V.C. gained by a member of the Bengal Medl. Service. The first gained by any member of the I.M.S. was that bestowed on J. Crinunin, Bombay, in 1889, in Burma. A third has since been gained by J. A. Sinton, of the Genl. List, in Mesopotamia, in 1916. Hosp. App. A. FitzGibbon, Bengal Sub-Medl. Dept., received a V.C. in 1861, for the second China war, in 1860.

2278. **Mould, George Thomas.** b. 25 Nov. 1864, at Auckland, New Zealand. M.R.C.S. 1888. L.R.C.P. Lond. 1888. Surg. 31 Mar. 1888. Major, 31 Mar. 1900. R. 28 July 1905. d. in London, 13 Sept. 1915. N.-E. Frontier, Manipur, 1891, medal with clasp. N.-W Frontier, Tochi, 1897–98, medal with clasp. China, 1900, relief of Pekin, actions at Peitsang and Yangtsun, medal.

2279. **Drake-Brockman, Herbert Edward.** b. 14 Feb. 1865. St. George's. M.R.C.S. 1887. L.R.C.P. London, 1887. Surg. 29 Sept. 1888. F.R.C.S. Ed. 1889. Major, 29 Sept. 1900. Lt.-Col. 29 Sept. 1908. S. List, 1 Apr. 1916. R. 1 Oct. 1919. ———. Brother of V. G. Drake-Brockman, No. 2333, infra, 1893. N.-W. Frontier, first Miranzai, 1891.

2280. **Lane, William Byam.** b. 8 Sept. 1866, in Antigua. Bart's. L.R.C.P. Lond. 1888. M.R.C.S. 1888. Surg. 29 Sept. 1888. Major, 29 Sept. 1900. Lt.-Col. 29 Sept. 1908. S. List, 1 Apr. 1916. R. 8 Feb. 1921. ———. C.I.E. 1 Jan. 1918. C.B.E. 1 Jan. 1919. N.-W. Frontier, Hazara, 1891, medal with clasp; Waziristan, 1894–95, clasp; Chitral, 1895, relief of Chitral, medal with clasp. War of 1914–21; Desp. L.G. 30 Apr. 1919; C.B.E.

2281. **Lumsden, Philip James.** b. 2 Feb. 1864. M.B. C.M. Ab. 1886. Surg. 29 Sept. 1888. Major, 29 Sept. 1900. Lt.-Col. 29 Sept. 1908. S. List, 1 Apr. 1916. Col. 15 Oct. 1918. R. 27 Nov. 1920. ———. Brother of J. S. S. Lumsden, No. 2313, infra, 1891. N.-W. Frontier, first Miranzai, 1891. War of 1914–19, Desp. L.G. 21 June 1916.

1889

2282. **Ozzard, Fairlie Russell.** b. 22 July 1865. London Hosp. M.R.C.S. 1888. L.R.C.P. Lond. 1888. Surg. 30 Mar. 1889. Major, 30 Mar. 1901. D.T.M. dist. London School Trop. Med. 1907. D.P.H., R.C.P. and S. Lond. 1908. Lt.-Col. 30 Mar. 1909. S. List, 23 June 1916. Col. 10 Jan. 1919. R. 20 May 1920. ———. N.-W Frontier, first and second Miranzai, 1891, medal with clasp; Tochi, 1897–98, medal with clasp. China, 1900, medal. War of 1914–18, operations in France and Belgium. Desp. L.G. 22 June 1915 and 18 May 1918.

2283. **Anderson, Adam Rivers Steele.** b. 3 Mar. 1863. Cambridge and St. Mary's. B.A. (Honours), 1882; M.B. 1886; D.P.H. 1889; Cantab. M.R.C.S. 1885. Surg. 30 Mar. 1889. Major, 30 Mar. 1901. Lt.-Col. 30 Mar. 1909. R. 11 Sept. 1918. d. at Bournemouth, 5 July 1924. War of 1914–18.

2284. **Calvert, John Telfer.** b. 4 Feb. 1864. St. Thomas'. M.R.C.S. 1887. L.R.C.P. Lond. 1887. M.B. Lond. 1887. D.P.H. Cantab. 1889. Surg. 30 Mar. 1889. Major, 30 Mar. 1901. M.R.C.P. Lond. 1906. Lt.-Col. 30 Mar. 1909. S. List, 21 Sept. 1916. F.R.C.P. Lond. 1917. R. 6 Oct. 1919. ———. C.I.E. 1 Jan. 1919. N.-E. Frontier, Manipur, 1891, medal with clasp. N.-W. Frontier, Tirah, 1897–98, medal with two clasps. Author of Notes on Intestinal Worms, 1902; edited 4th ed. of Ghosh's Materia Medica, 1910.

2285. **Jennings, Edgar.** b. 3 Aug. 1864. King's Coll. Lond. M.R.C.S. 1886. L.S.A. 1886. Surg. 30 Mar. 1889. Major, 30 Mar. 1901. D.P.H. Cantab. 1907. Lt.-Col. 30 Mar. 1909. S. List, 11 Nov. 1916. Bt.-Col. 1 Jan. 1916. R. 5 Feb. 1920. ———. Brother of W. E. Jennings, No. 1092, Bombay, 1887. War of 1914–19; Desp. L.G. 5 Apr. 1916, Brevet of Colonel.

2286. **Stiles, Theodore Mayo.** *b.* 10 Dec. 1863. Bristol. M.R.C.S. 1887. L.R.C.P. Lond. 1887. Surg. 30 Mar. 1889. *d.* at Nongba, Kachar, 28 Apr. 1891. N.-E. Frontier, Manipur, 1891.

2287. **Hendley, Arthur Gervase.** *b.* 26 June 1866. Bart's. M.R.C.S. 1887. L.R.C.P. Lond. 1887. Surg. 30 Mar. 1889. Major, 30 Mar. 1901. Lt.-Col. 30 Mar. 1909. R. 26 June 1909. Bursar and Medl. Offir. Glenalmond. ———. Rejoined for service in war of 1914–18, Capt. R.A.M.C. T.F. 11 Aug. 1915. Retired, with rank of Lt.-Col. R.A.M.C. T.F. 30 Sept. 1921. Son of Surg.-Genl. J. Hendley, C.B. A.M.D. (Johnston's Roll of R.A.M.C. No. 5053). N.-W. Frontier, 1897–98, medal with clasp.

2288. **Melville, Henry Bruce.** *b.* 4 Sept. 1863. M.B. C.M. Ed. 1885. Cert. Med. Psych. Assn. Surg. 30 Sept. 1889. Major, 30 Sept. 1901. Lt.-Col. 30 Sept. 1909. S. List, 1 Apr. 1917. R. 22 Jan. 1921. *d.* at Tain, 15 Apr. 1923. N.-E. Frontier, Lushai, 1890.

2289. **Vaughan, Joseph Charles Stoelke.** *b.* 29 June 1862. M.B. C.M. (Honours), Ed. 1885. Surg. 30 Sept. 1889. Major, 30 Sept. 1901. Lt.-Col. 30 Sept. 1909. S. List, 1 Apr. 1917. R. 24 Jan. 1821. K.-i-H. 1st class, 1 Jan. 1910. C.I.E. 1 Jan. 1925. N.-W. Frontier, first and second Miranzai, 1891, medal with clasp; Malakand, 1897–98, Buner, actions at Landakai and Tanga Pass, medal with clasp.

2290. **Duke, Alexander Leonard.** *b.* 12 Oct. 1866. M.B. C.M. Ab. 1888. Surg. 30 Sept. 1889. Major, 30 Sept. 1901. Lt.-Col. 30 Sept. 1909. S. List, 1 Apr. 1917. *d.* at Quetta, 27 Feb. 1918. Brother of Sir F. W. Duke, K.C.S.I. Lt.-Govr. Bengal, 1911. Izzat-i-Afghanistan, 1907.

2291. **White, Joshua Chaytor** (afterwards **Chaytor-White, Joshua**). *b.* 25 Oct. 1864. Ed. Bonn, and Heidelberg Univs. M.B. C.M. 1887; M.D. 1893; Ed. Surg. 30 Sept. 1889. Took name Chaytor-White in 1891. Major, 30 Sept. 1901. D.P.H. Cantab. 1901. Lt.-Col. 30 Sept. 1909. R. 22 Dec. 1912. Rejoined for service in war of 1914–18, 13 Nov. 1914 to Nov. 1918. *d.* at Cannes, 30 Jan. 1924. C.M.G. 4 June 1917. N.-W. Frontier, Chitral, 1895, relief of Chitral, medal with clasp. War of 1914–19, Desp. L.G. 27 July 1917, C.M.G.

2292. **Elphick, Henry William.** *b.* 10 July 1865. Univ. Coll. Lond. M.R.C.S. 1888. L.R.C.P. Lond. 1888. M.B. Lond. 1888. Surg. 30 Sept. 1889. Major, 30 Sept. 1901. T.H.P. 6 Mar. 1905. *d.* at Rugby, 20 May 1906. N.-E. Frontier, Manipur, 1891, medal with clasp.

2293. **Bedford, Charles Henry.** *b.* 19 June 1866. M.B. C.M. 1887; B.Sc. 1889; M.D. (Honours), 1892; D.Sc. 1892; Ed. M.R.C.S. 1888. Surg. 30 Sept. 1889. Major, 30 Sept. 1901. Lt.-Col. 30 Sept. 1909. R. 18 Dec. 1911. Rejoined for service in war of 1914–18, 1916–19. ———. Kt. 11 Dec. 1911. LL.D. St. A. 1913. LL.D. Ed. 1923. D.C.L. Oxon. 1924. Author of The Enteric Fever of India, 1893; George Heriot's Hospital, 1901; Synopsis of Practical Chemistry, 1901; Memoir of F. W. Bedford, D.C.L. LL.D. 1902; Handbook of Urine Analysis, 1902; Elementary Hygiene, 1903; Symptoms and Treatment of Poisoning, 1903; edited Indian Medical Gazette, 1898.

1890

2294. MacNab, Allan James. b. 17 Aug. 1864, at Digby, Nova Scotia. King's Coll. Lond. M.R.C.S. 1887. L.R.C.P. Lond. 1887. Surg. 31 Mar. 1890. F.R.C.S. 1896. Major, 31 Mar. 1902. Lt.-Col. 31 Mar. 1910. Bt.-Col. 14 Jan. 1916. Col. 2 Apr. 1919. R. 15 Aug. 1921. ―――――. C.B. 4 June 1918. C.M.G. 3 June 1919. N.-W. Frontier, Hazara, 1891, night attack on Ghazikot, medal with clasp; Chitral, 1895, relief of Chitral, medal with clasp; Malakand, 1897–98, defence and relief of Malakand, relief of Chakdara, action at Landakai, operations in the Mamund country, Utman Khel, Buner, two clasps. East Africa, Somaliland, 1903–04, medal with clasp. War of 1914–19, Hosp. ship 'Syria,' in command; operations in France and Belgium, July to Sept. 1916, and Nov. to Dec. 1917; Egyptian Expeditionary Force, Apr. to Oct. 1918; Desp. L.G. 1 Jan. 1916, 11 Dec. 1917, May 1918. Brevet of Col., C.B., C.M.G.

2295. Smith, Henry. b. 16 Aug. 1862. Q.C. Galway and Richmond Hosp. Dublin. B.A. M.D. M.Ch. M.A.O. R.U.I. 1888. Surg. 31 Mar. 1890. Major, 31 Mar. 1902. Lt.-Col. 31 Mar. 1910. R. 6 Jan. 1921. K.-i-H. 1st class, 1 Jan. 1911. C.I.E. 1 Jan. 1918. Author of Treatment of Cataract, 1910.

2296. Luard, Hugh Bixby. b. 13 Oct. 1862. Cambridge and St. Thomas'. B.A. (Honours), 1884; M.B. B.S. 1887; Cantab. M.R.C.S. 1887. L.R.C.P. Lond. 1887. Surg. 31 Mar. 1890. F.R.C.S. 1897. T.H.P. 15 Mar. 1901. R. 15 Mar. 1907. Rejoined for service in war of 1914–18, Major, 25 Aug. 1916. ―――――. N.-W. Frontier, second Miranzai, 1891, medal with clasp; Hunza-Nagar, 1891, Desp. G.G.O. No. 397 of 1892, clasp; Chitral, 1895, relief of Chitral, P.M.O. Gilgit Force, medal with clasp.

2297. Wimberley, Charles Neil Campbell. b. 23 Sept. 1867. M.B. C.M. (Honours), Ed. 1889. Surg. 31 Mar. 1890. Major, 31 Mar. 1902. Lt.-Col. 31 Mar. 1910. S. List, 22 Sept. 1917. Col. 15 May 1919. R. 10 Sept. 1920. ―――――. C.M.G. 4 June 1917. N.-W. Frontier, Chitral, 1895, relief of Chitral, medal with clasp; Tirah, 1897–98, operations on Samana and in Kurram Valley, actions of Chagru Kotal, Dargai, Sampagha and Arhanga Passes, reconnaissance of Saran Sar, operations in Waran Valley, three clasps. Tibet, 1903-04, action at Niani, operations at and round Gyantse, march to Lhasa, Desp. G. of I. No. 1065 of 1904, medal with clasp. War of 1914–19, operations in France and Belgium, 14 Oct. to 7 Dec. 1915; operations in Mesopotamia, 1 Jan. 1916 to 31 Oct. 1918, Desp. L.G. 15 Aug. 1917 and 27 Aug. 1918; C.M.G.

2298. Hore, Ernest Wickham. b. 13 Sept. 1865. Univ. Coll. Lond. M.R.C.S. 1889. L.R.C.P. Lond. 1889. M.B. Lond. 1889. D.P.H. Cantab. 1890. Surg. 31 Mar. 1890. Major, 31 Mar. 1902. Lt.-Col. 31 Mar. 1910. R. 7 Dec. 1911. Rejoined for service in war of 1914–18, Tempy. Major, R.A.M.C. 20 Oct. 1917 to June 1919. ―――――.

1891

*****2299. Crawford, James Muir.** b. 5 Aug. 1866. Ed. and Bonn Univs. and St. George's. L.R.C.P. and S. Ed. 1888. L.F.P.S.G. 1888. M.B. C.M. Ed. 1888. Surg. 31 Jan. 1891. Major, 31 Jan. 1903. Lt.-Col. 31 Jan. 1911. S. List, 30 Sept. 1917. R. 1 Feb. 1921. ―――――. Brother of D. G. Crawford, No. 2071, supra, 1881. O.B.E. 4 June 1918. N.-E. Frontier, Lushai, 1892–93. N.-W Frontier, Malakand, 1897–98, Buner, action of Tanga Pass, medal with clasp. China, 1900, medal. War of 1914–19, Desp. L.G. 26 Nov. 1918, O.B.E.

* From Jan. 1891 first commissions dated from day of leaving, instead of from day of joining, Netley.

2300. **Wolfe, John William.** b. 22 Jan. 1868. Q.C. Cork. M.B. (Honours) ; B.S. B.A.O. R.U.I. 1889. Lecturer on Anatomy, Q.C. Cork, 1889–90. Surg. 31 Jan. 1891. T.H.P. 20 May 1900. d. 17 Oct. 1903.

2301. **Singh, Bawa Jiwan.** b. 6 May 1863. Panjab Univ. and St. Thomas'. L.M.S. Panjab, 1885. M.R.C.S. 1889. L.R.C.P. Lond. 1889. Surg. 31 Jan. 1891. Major, 31 Jan. 1903. Lt.-Col. 31 Jan. 1911. S. List, 18 Oct. 1917. R. 1 May 1920. Dir.-Genl. Medl. Sany. and Jails Depts. Haidarabad, 1921. ————. C.I.E. 1 Jan. 1918.

2302. **Barber, Hugh Robert Campbell.** b. 12 Dec. 1863. Cambridge and Bart's. B.A. 1885 ; M.B. B.S. 1888 ; Cantab. Surg. 31 Jan. 1891. d. at Marri, 20 Aug. 1896.

2303. **James, Charles Henry.** b. 4 Aug. 1863. St. Thomas'. M.R.C.S. 1887. L.R.C.P. Lond. 1887. Surg. 31 Jan. 1891. Major, 31 Jan. 1903. F.R.C.S. 1909. Lt.-Col. 31 Jan. 1911. S. List, 19 Dec. 1917. R. 17 Oct. 1921. ————. K.-i-H. 1st class, 23 May 1900. C.I.E. 14 June 1912. Author of Report on plague in Jullundur and Hoshiarpur districts, 1899.

2304. **O'Kinealy, Frederick.** b. 19 Aug. 1865. Bart's. M.R.C.S. 1888. L.R.C.P. Lond. 1888. Surg. 31 Jan. 1891. Major, 31 Jan. 1903. Lt.-Col. 31 Jan. 1911. S. List, 8 Jan. 1918. R. 1 Oct. 1922. ————. C.I.E. 1 Jan. 1921. C.V.O. 16 Mar. 1922. N.-W. Frontier, Tirah, 1897–98, medal with two clasps.

2305. **Cassidy, Christopher Clemons.** b. 23 Sept. 1864. L.R.C.P. and S. Ed. 1885. L.F.P.S.G. 1885. Surg. 31 Jan. 1891. d. 22 June 1897, of wounds received on 10 June, at Datta Khel, Tochi Valley. N.-W. Frontier, Tochi, 1897–98, Desp.

2306. **Buist-Sparks, Arthur William Tremenheere** (afterwards **Buist, A. W. T.**). b. 7 Aug. 1866. Assumed name of Sparks, 23 July 1884, while at Ed. Univ. ; dropped it in 1898. M.B. C.M. 1888 ; M.D. 1919 ; Ed. Surg. 31 Jan. 1891. Major, 31 Jan. 1903. Lt.-Col. 31 Jan. 1911. S. List, 28 Feb. 1918. R. 5 July 1921. d. at New Milton, Hants, 17 Dec. 1925. N.-W. Frontier of India, Tochi, 1897–98, medal with clasp ; War of 1914–19, Desp. L.G. 4 July 1916.

2307. **Burton-Brown, Frederick Hewlett.** b. 28 June 1863. Oxford (Magdalen Coll.) and Jena Univs., and Guy's. B.A. 1886, M.A. M.B. B.Ch. 1891 ; M.D. 1892 ; Oxon. L.S.A. 1890. Surg. 28 July 1891. Resigned, 2 June 1897. Physician to British Embassy, Rome, 1902–05. Afterwards in practice in London, and later in Wales, and in Queensland. Name omitted from Medl. Regr. 1923. Son of T. E. B. Brown, No. 1788, supra, 1858, brother of A. T. Brown, Madras, No. 1525.

2308. **Deare, Benjamin Hobbs.** b. 29 July 1867. Middlesex Hosp. M.R.C.S. 1889. L.R.C.P. Lond. 1889. D.P.H. Cantab. 1891. Surg. 28 July 1891. Major, 28 July 1903. M.R.C.P. Lond. 1910. Lt.-Col. 28 July 1911. S. List, 5 Mar. 1918. Major-Genl. 8 Feb. 1922. R. 27 Aug. 1924. ————. Brother of A. C. Deare, No. 2217, supra, 1886. C.I.E. 4 June 1921. K.H.S. 8 Feb. 1922. N.-W. Frontier, Tirah, 1897–98, operations on Samana and in Kurram Valley, relief of Gulistan, actions of Changru Kotal, Dargai, Sampagha and Arhanga Passes, reconnaissance of Saran Sar, medal with three clasps. Edited 5th and 6th edns. of Ghosh's Materia Medica, 1913–15.

2309. Oldham, Benjamin Curwen. *b.* 23 Mar. 1865. Bart's. M.R.C.S. 1888. L.R.C.P. Lond. 1888. Surg. 28 July 1891. Major, 28 July 1903. Lt.-Col. 28 July 1911. *d.* at Osborne, Isle of Wight, 9 Jan. 1912. N.-W. Frontier, Mohmand, 1897-98, medal with clasp.

2310. Bird, Robert. *b.* 4 Dec. 1866. Bart's. M.R.C.S. 1888. L.R.C.P. Lond. 1888. M.B. B.S. 1888; M.D. 1889; M.S. 1891; Lond. F.R.C.S. 1891. D.P.H. Cantab. 1891. Surg. 28 July 1891. Major, 28 July 1903. Lt.-Col. 28 July 1911. *d.* at Wellington, Nilgiri Hills, 30 Mar. 1918. Deputed to Kabul, to attend the Amir of Afghanistan, Habibullah, in 1904. C.I.E. 2 Jan. 1905. Izzat-i-Afghanistan, 7 Mar. 1907. Harmat (Afghanistan), 7 Mar. 1907. M.V.O. 4 Jan. 1912.

2311. Smith, Sidney Browning. *b.* 12 Nov. 1866. Bart's. M.R.C.S. 1890. L.R.C.P. Lond. 1890. Surg. 28 July 1891. Major, 28 July 1903. D.P.H. R.C.P. and S. Lond. 1910. Lt.-Col. 28 July 1911. S. List, 24 June 1918. R. 12 Nov. 1921. *d.* at Otford, Kent, 13 July 1930. C.M.G. 4 June 1917. N.-W. Frontier, Chitral, 1895, relief of Chitral, Desp. No. 8C of 26 July 1895, medal with clasp; Waziristan, 1901-02, clasp. War of 1914-18, operations in France and Belgium, Dec. 1914 to Jan. 1916, operations in Egypt, 4 Jan. 1916 to 22 Feb. 1916, Desp. L. G. 27 July 1917, C.M.G.

2312. Henvey, William. *b.* 21 June 1867. St. Mary's. M.R.C.S. 1889. L.R.C.P. Lond. 1889. Surg. 28 July 1891. T.H.P. 24 Mar. 1902. *d.* at Ealing, 11 Jan. 1904. N.-W. Frontier, Isazai, 1892.

2313. Lumsden, John Stuart Shepherd. *b.* 12 Nov. 1866. M.B. C.M. Ed. 1889. Surg. 28 July 1891. F.R.C.S. Ed. 1901. Major, 28 July 1903. *d.* in London, 16 Feb. 1906. Brother of P. J. Lumsden, No. 2281, supra, 1888. N.-W. Frontier, Waziristan, 1894-95, medal with clasp.

2314. Frost, George Hewitt. *b.* 2 Apr. 1867. Cath. Univ. Dublin. B.A. 1887; M.B. B.S. B.A.O. 1890; R.U.I. Surg. 28 July 1891. Major, 28 July 1903. Lt.-Col. 28 July 1911. S. List, 15 Aug. 1918. R. 1 Jan. 1921. ———. South Africa, 1899-1901, operations in Natal, action at Lombard's Kop, operations in Natal, Transvaal, and Orange River Colony, Queen's medal with five clasps. War of 1914-19, operations in France and Belgium, 26 Sept. 1914 to 1 June 1915.

2315. Wilkinson, Edmund. *b.* 9 Jan. 1867. Univ. Coll. Lond. M.R.C.S. 1888. L.R.C.P. Lond. 1888. D.P.H. 1891; D.T.M. and H. 1906, Cantab. Surg. 28 July 1891. F.R.C.S. 1892. Major, 28 July 1903. Lt.-Col. 28 July 1911. R. 13 Nov. 1914. Medl. Offr. Local Govt. Board, London, 1 Apr. 1914 (after 1919, Ministry of Health). ———. N.-W. Frontier Waziristan, 1894-95, medal with clasp; Mohmand, 1897-98, Buner, action of Tanga Pass, medal with clasp. Author (with C. W. Daniels) of Tropical Medicine and Hygiene, 1910.

2316. Ewens, George Francis William. *b.* 14 Apr. 1864. King's Coll. Lond. L.S.A. 1885. M.R.C.S. 1886. L.R.C.P. Lond. 1886. M.B. 1886; M.D. 1888; R.U.I. D.P.H. Cantab. 1888. Surg. 28 July 1891. Major, 28 July 1903. Lt.-Col. 28 July 1911. *d.* at Lahore, 9 Sept. 1914. Author of Insanity in India, 1908.

2317. Duer, Charles. b. 10 Dec. 1864. Univ. Coll. Lond. M.R.C.S. 1888. L.R.C.P. Lond. 1888. M.B. Lond. 1889. F.R.C.S. 1891. Surg. 28 July 1901. Major, 28 July 1903. Lt.-Col. 28 July 1911. R. 29 Nov. 1913. ————. Rejoined for service in war of 1914–18, 19 Oct. 1914 to 13 May 1919. War of 1914–18.

2318. Wood, Henry Stotesbury. b. 31 Mar. 1865. M.B. C.M. Ed. 1888. Surg. 28 July 1891. Major, 28 July 1903. Lt.-Col. 28 July 1911, S. List, 3 Sept. 1918. R. 28 July 1922. ————.

1892

*2319. Seton, Bruce Gordon. b. 13 Oct. 1868. Bart's. M.R.C.S. 1891. L.R.C.P. Lond. 1891. S. Lt. 30 Jan. 1892. S. Capt. 30 Jan. 1895. Major, 30 Jan. 1904. Lt.-Col. 30 Jan. 1912. Bt.-Col. 30 June 1913. Succeeded his cousin as 9th Bart. 6 Mar. 1915. R. 27 May 1917. Claimed Barony of Gordon, 1928. ————. C.B. 4 June 1917. N.-W. Frontier, Waziristan, 1894–95, severely wounded, medal with clasp; Tochi, 1897–98, medal with clasp. War of 1914–19, Desp. L.G. 27 July 1917, C.B. Author of Cavalry Elementary Veterinary Manual, 1895; (with J. Gould, No. 2352, infra), The Indian Medical Service, 1911; (with Pipe-Major J. Grant), The Pipes of War, 1920; edited The Orderly Book of Lord Ogilvy's Regiment, in the Army of Prince Charles, Edward Stuart, 10 Oct. 1745 to 21 Apr. 1744, 1924; The Prisoners of the Forty-five, 1928.

2320. Haig, Patrick Balfour (christened **Patrick James Haig**). b. 25 Aug. 1866. Ed. Univ. and Paris. M.B. C.M. Ed. 1889. M.R.C.S. 1891. L.R.C.P. Lond. 1891. S. Lt. 27 July 1892. S. Capt. 27 July 1895. Major, 27 July 1904. Lt.-Col. 27 July 1912. S. List, 15 Oct. 1918. R. 16 Mar. 1921. ————. Son of W. J. Haig, No. 1775, supra, 1858. K.-i-H. 1st class, 3 June 1913. C.B. 1 Jan. 1917. N.-W. Frontier, Waziristan, 1894–95, medal with clasp; Malakand, 1897–98, Utman Khel, Buner, action of Tanga Pass, medal with clasp. Uganda, 1899, operations against Kabarega, Desp. L.G. 2 Jan. 1900, medal with clasp; 1900, operations against Nandi tribe, Desp. L.G. 10 Sept. 1901, medal with clasp. War of 1914–19, Desp. L.G. 13 Mar. 1919, C.B.

2321. Fullerton, Thomas William Archer. b. 31 Mar. 1867. M.B. B.Ch. R.U.I. 1890. S. Lt. 27 July 1892. S. Capt. 27 July 1895. Major, 27 July 1904. F.R.C.S. 1907. d. at Lucknow, 15 Aug. 1907. K.-i-H. 1st class, 26 June 1902. N.-W. Frontier, Waziristan, 1894–95, medal with clasp; Malakand, 1897–98, operations in Bajaur and in Mamund country, Utman Khel, Buner, medal with clasp.

2322. Maddox, Ralph Henry. b. 27 June 1864. M.B. C.M. (Honours), Ed. 1887. M.R.C.S. 1887. S. Lt. 27 July 1892. S. Capt. 27 July 1895. Major, 27 July 1904. Lt.-Col. 27 July 1912. S. List, 10 Jan. 1919. R. 27 July 1922. ————. K.-i-H. 2nd class, 26 June 1902. C.I.E. 3 June 1919. N.-W. Frontier, Waziristan, 1894–95, medal with clasp. Sudan, 1896, Dongola expedition, medal and Khedive's medal. N.-W. Frontier, Tirah, 1897–98, action of Sampagha Pass, medal with clasp. War of 1914–19, Desp. L.G. 15 Aug. 1917, 27 Aug. 1918, and 5 June 1919, C.I.E.

---

* Compound titles, including Surgeon-Lieutenant, introduced by Royal Warrant of 14 Dec. 1891.

2323. **Hugo, Edward Victor.** *b.* 5 Jan. 1865. Bart's. M.R.C.S. 1889. L.R.C.P. Lond. 1889. M.B. (Honours), B.S. 1890; M.D. (Honours), 1892; Lond. S. Lt. 27 July 1892. S. Capt. 27 July 1895. Major, 27 July 1904. F.R.C.S. 1906. Lt.-Col. 27 July 1912. S. List, 4 Feb. 1919. R. 8 Apr. 1922. ————. Brother of J. H. Hugo, No. 5, I.M.S. Genl. List, 1897. C.M.G. 4 June 1917. N.-W. Frontier, Waziristan, 1894–95, medal with clasp; Chitral, 1895, relief of Chitral, medal with clasp; 1897–98, defence and relief of Chakdara, Buner, Desp. G.G.O. No. 1317 of 1897, two clasps. War of 1914–19, Desp. L.G. 15 Aug. 1917, and 12 Jan. 1920, C.M.G.

2324. **Melville, Harry George.** *b.* 24 Mar. 1869. M.B. C.M. 1890; M.D. 1896, Ed. F.R.C.S. Ed. 1890. S. Lt. 27 July 1892. S. Capt. 27 July 1895. Major, 27 July 1904. Lt.-Col. 27 July 1912. *d.* at Bagdad, 7 Dec. 1918. C.I.E. 3 June 1918. N.-W. Frontier, Waziristan, 1894–95, action at Wana, medal with clasp; Tirah, 1897–98, operations in Mohmand country and in Bara Valley, medal with two clasps. War of 1914–18, Mesopotamia.

2325. **Hubbard, Arthur Oldham.** *b.* 19 Nov. 1865. Bart's. M.R.C.S. 1890. L.R.C.P. Lond. 1890. S. Lt. 27 July 1892. S. Capt. 27 July 1895. *d.* at Cairo, 8 Apr. 1899.

2326. **Robson-Scott, Charles George.** *b.* 16 Aug. 1865. Ed. and Berlin Univs., and Middlesex Hosp. M.B. C.M. Ed. 1889. M.R.C.S. 1890. L.R.C.P. Lond. 1890. D.P.H. Cantab. 1891. S. Lt. 27 July 1892. S. Capt. 27 July 1895. *d.* in Calcutta, 27 Nov. 1896.

2327. **Smith, Herbert Austen.** *b.* 3 May 1866. Cambridge (Trinity College) and Guy's. B.A. 1887; M.B. B.Ch. 1890; Cantab. M.R.C.S. 1890. L.R.C.P. Lond. 1890. S. Lt. 27 July 1892. S. Capt. 27 July 1895. Major, 27 July 1904. Lt.-Col. 27 July 1912. S. List, 2 Apr. 1919. Col. 19 Apr. 1920. R. 3 Nov. 1923. ————. C.I.E. 4 June 1918. K.H.S. 26 Mar. 1922. N.-E. Frontier, Lushai, 1892–93. Sudan, 1896, Dongola expedition, medal and Khedive's medal. N.-W. Frontier, Tochi, 1897–98, medal with clasp. War of 1914–18.

2328. **Green, Douglas Richard.** *b.* 20 June 1868. Univ. Coll. Lond. M.B. B.S. 1891; M.D. 1892; Lond. S. Lt. 27 July 1892. S. Capt. 27 July 1895. Major, 27 July 1904. Lt.-Col. 27 July 1912. R. 1 Aug. 1912. Rejoined for service in India in war of 1914–18, 19 July 1918 to 26 May 1920. ————. N.-W. Frontier, Tirah, 1897–98, actions of Chagru Kotal, Dargai, Sampagha and Arhanga Passes, operations at and round Dwatoi and in Bara Valley, medal with two clasps.

2329. **Smith, George MacIver Campbell.** *b.* 13 May 1869. M.A. 1888; M.B. C.M. 1891; Ab. S. Lt. 27 July 1892. S. Capt. 27 July 1895. Major, 27 July 1904. M.R.C.P. Lond. 1907. Lt.-Col. 27 July 1912. S. List, 15 May 1919. R. 17 Sept. 1921. ————. C.M.G. 3 June 1919. N.-W. Frontier, Chitral, 1895, medal with clasp; Tirah, 1897–98, operations in Mohmand country, actions of Chagru Kotal, Dargai, and Sampagha Pass, operations in Waran and Bara Valleys, two clasps; Waziristan, 1901–02, clasp. War of 1914–19, operations in Mesopotamia, 15 Nov. 1917 to 25 May 1918. Egyptian Expeditionary Force, 26 May to 31 Oct. 1918. Desp. L.G. 5 June 1919, C.M.G.

INDIAN MEDICAL SERVICE [1893

2330. **Earle, Hubert Malins.** *b.* 12 Nov. 1868. Middlesex Hosp. M.R.C.S. 1890. L.R.C.P. Lond. 1890. S. Lt. 27 July 1892. S. Capt. 27 July 1895. Major, 27 July 1904. Lt.-Col. 27 July 1912. R. 23 July 1912. Rejoined for service in war of 1914–18, 27 Nov. 1914–1918. ———. Sudan, 1896, medal. N.-W. Frontier, Mohmand, 1908, medal.

2331. **Hulbert, Joseph George.** *b.* 14 Sept. 1867. Cambridge and Bart's. B.A. 1888; M.A. M.B. B.S. 1892; Cantab. M.R.C.S. 1891. L.R.C.P. Lond. 1891. S. Lt. 27 July 1892. S. Capt. 27 July 1895. Major, 27 July 1904. Lt.-Col. 27 July 1912. R. 12 May 1914. Rejoined for service in war of 1914–18, 19 Oct. 1914 to 23 Mar. 1919. ———. N.-E. Frontier, Kachin Hills, 1892–93, medal with clasp. N.-W. Frontier, Tirah, 1897–98, operations in Mohmand country and in Bara Valley, medal with two clasps. War of 1914–18, Hosp. ship, two medals and star.

1893

2332. **Milne, Charles.** *b.* 4 Aug. 1869. M.B. C.M. Ab. 1891. S. Lt. 30 Jan. 1893. S. Capt. 30 Jan. 1896. Major, 30 Jan. 1905. Lt.-Col. 30 Jan. 1913. S. List, 3 Aug. 1919. Col. 19 May 1920. R. 1 July 1921. ———. O.B.E. 3 June 1919. N.-W. Frontier, Waziristan, 1894–95, medal with clasp. Sudan, 1896, Dongola expedition, medal, and Khedive's medal. War of 1914–19, Desp. L.G. 13 Mar. and 15 June 1919, O.B.E.

2333. **Drake-Brockman, Vivian Godfrey.** *b.* 9 July 1869. Middlesex Hosp. M.R.C.S. 1891. L.R.C.P. Lond. 1891. S. Lt. 30 Jan. 1893. S. Capt. 30 Jan. 1896. Major, 30 Jan. 1905. Lt.-Col. 30 Jan. 1913. R. 13 Feb. 1915. Rejoined for service in war of 1914–18, 7 Sept. 1915 to Nov. 1918. ———. Brother of H. E. Drake-Brockman, No. 2279 supra, 1888. N.-W. Frontier, Tochi, 1897–98, medal with clasp.

2334. **Young, William.** *b.* 6 May 1871. M.B. C.M. Glas. 1892. S. Lt. 30 Jan. 1893. S. Capt. 30 Jan. 1896. Major, 30 Jan. 1905. F.R.C.S. Ed. 1907. Lt.-Col. 30 Jan. 1913. S. List, 8 Sept. 1919. Col. 28 Mar. 1921. *d.* at Perth, 20 Sept. 1922.

2335. **Bourke, John Joseph** (signs **Bourke,** name spelt **Burke** in birth cert.). *b.* 1 Apr. 1865. B.A. 1885; M.A. 1886; M.B. B.Ch. B.A.O. 1887; R.U.I. S. Lt. 30 Jan. 1893. S. Capt. 30 Jan. 1896. Major, 30 Jan. 1905. Lt.-Col. 30 Jan. 1913. R. 1 Apr. 1920. ———. C.I.E. 3 June 1919. N.-W. Frontier, Waziristan, 1894–95, medal with clasp. China, 1900, medal.

2336. **Hunter, George Yeates Cobb.** *b.* 15 Feb. 1868. St. George's. M.R.C.S. 1890. L.R.C.P. Lond. 1890. S. Lt. 30 Jan. 1893. S. Capt. 30 Jan. 1896. T.H.P. 19 Apr. 1901 to 6 Feb. 1903. Major, 17 Nov. 1905. Lt.-Col. 17 Nov. 1913. R. 25 Oct. 1914. ———. Son of G. Y. Hunter, No. 924, Bombay, 1858; brother of Major-Genl. G. D. Hunter, R.A.M.C.; (Johnston's Roll of R.A.M.C. No. 6990).

2337. **Chatterton, Bernard Robert.** *b.* 14 Dec. 1868. B.A. 1890; M.B. B.Ch. B.A.O. 1891; M.D. 1895; M.S. 1896; T.C.D. S. Lt. 30 Jan. 1893. S. Capt. 30 Jan. 1896. Major, 30 Jan. 1905. Lt. Col. 30 Jan. 1913. S. List, 15 May 1919. R. 16 Feb. 1923. ———. N.-W. Frontier, 1897–98, Samana, medal with two clasps; Tirah, clasp. War of 1914–19, operations against Mohmands and Swatis, 1915, Desp. L.G. 4 July 1916.

INDIAN MEDICAL SERVICE

2338. Prall, Cedric Barkley. *b.* 8 Mar. 1870. St. Thomas'. M.R.C.S. 1892. L.R.C.P. Lond. 1892. S. Lt. 30 Jan. 1893. S. Capt. 30 Jan. 1896. Major, 30 Jan. 1905. Lt.-Col. 30 Jan. 1913. *d.* at Mhow, 5 Apr. 1916. N.-W. Frontier, Tirah, 1897–98, operations in Samana and in Kurram Valley, defence of Gulistan, Desp. G.G.O. No. 1417 of 1897, actions of Chagru Kotal and of Sampagha and Arhanga Passes, reconnaissance of Saran Sar, operations in Waran Valley, at and around Dwatoi, and in Bara Valley, medal with three clasps.

2339. Williams, Charles Edward. *b.* 1 Nov. 1865. Cambridge and Bart's. B.A. 1887; M.B. B.S. 1890; D.T.M. 1905; Cantab. S. Lt. 30 Jan. 1893. S. Capt. 30 Jan. 1896. Major, 30 Jan. 1905. Lt.-Col. 30 Jan. 1913. S. List, 27 June 1919. R. 29 July 1923. ———. N.-W. Frontier, 1897–98, operations on Samana, medal with two clasps.

2340. MacLeod, John Norman. *b.* 8 May 1865. M.A. 1886; M.B. C.M. 1890; Glas. S. Lt. 30 Jan. 1893. S. Capt. 30 Jan. 1896. Major, 30 Jan. 1905. Lt.-Col. 30 Jan. 1913. R. 23 Aug. 1916. ———. K.-i-H. 2nd class, 9 Nov. 1901. C.I.E. 1 Jan. 1908. C.M.G. 4 June 1917. N.-W. Frontier, Chitral, 1895, relief of Chitral, medal with clasp; Tochi, 1897–98, clasp. War of 1914–19, Desp. L.G. 27 July 1917, C.M.G.

2341. Ogilvie, Walter Holland. *b.* 2 Sept. 1869. M.B. C.M. 1891; B.Sc. 1893; D.Sc. 1898; Ed. S. Lt. 30 Jan. 1893. S. Capt. 30 Jan. 1896. Major, 30 Jan. 1905. Lt.-Col. 30 Jan. 1913. Bt.-Col. 3 June 1919. S. List, 23 Mar. 1920. Col. 20 May 1920. Major-Genl. 24 June 1923. D.M.S. India, 3 Jan. 1927. R. 2 Sept. 1929. ———. C.M.G. 25 Aug. 1917. Nile, 3rd class, 26 Nov. 1919. C.B. 2 June 1923. K.H.P. 12 June 1923. K.B.E. 4 June 1928. Sudan, 1896, Dongola expedition, medal, and Khedive's medal. China, 1900, relief of Pekin, medal with clasp. Tibet, 1903–04, march to Lhasa, medal. War of 1914–19, Desp. L.G. 15 Aug. 1917, 21 Jan. 1919, and 3 June 1919. Brevet of Colonel, Nile, 3rd class, C.M.G.

2342. Langston, Thomas Edward Ollivant. *b.* 1 Sept. 1868. Bart's. M.R.C.S. 1891. L.R.C.P. Lond. 1891. S. Lt. 30 Jan. 1893. S. Capt. 30 Jan. 1896. Major, 30 Jan. 1905. R. 12 Dec. 1910. Rejoined for service in war of 1914–18, 6 Nov. 1914–1918. Lt.-Col. 25 Dec. 1915. ———. N.-W. Frontier, Waziristan, 1894–95, medal with clasp; Malakand, 1897–98, defence of Malakand, relief of Chakdara, action at Landakai, Desp. G.G.O. No. 1089, of 1897, medal with two clasps.

2343. Heard, Richard. *b.* 10 Jan. 1870. T.C.D. B.A. 1891; M.B. B.Ch. B.A.O. 1892; R.U.I. S. Lt. 30 Jan. 1893. S. Capt. 30 Jan. 1896. Major, 30 Jan. 1905. Lt.-Col. 30 Jan. 1913. Bt.-Col. 29 Nov. 1915. Col. 21 June 1920. Major-Genl. 27 Feb. 1924. R. 27 Feb. 1927. ———. K.H.S. 12 June 1923. C.I.E. 3 June 1924. N.-W. Frontier, Waziristan, 1894–95, medal with clasp; Chitral, 1895, relief of Chitral, medal with clasp. War of 1914–19, Brevet Colonel. Author of Feeding in Infancy and Early Childhood, 1906.

2344. Parry, Edgar Rowe. *b.* 15 Nov. 1868. M.B. C.M. Ed. 1891. S. Lt. 30 Jan. 1893. S. Capt. 30 Jan. 1896. Major, 30 Jan. 1905. Lt.-Col. 30 Jan. 1913. R. 25 Apr. 1921. ———. N.-W. Frontier, Chitral, 1895, relief of Chitral, medal with clasp. East Africa, Somaliland, 1903–04, medal with clasp.

2345. **Orr, Walter Hood.** b. 11 Dec. 1867. Bart's. M.R.C.S. 1892. L.R.C.P. Lond. 1892. S. Lt. 30 Jan. 1893. S. Capt. 30 Jan. 1896. Major, 30 Jan. 1905. d. at Bahraich, 28 Jan. 1909. C.I.E. 1 Jan. 1909.

2346. **More, Paxton St. Clair.** b. 14 June 1867. M.B. C.M. Ed. 1891. S. Lt. 30 Jan. 1893. S. Capt. 30 Jan. 1896. Major, 30 Jan. 1905. Lt.-Col. 30 Jan. 1913. S. List, 29 Nov. 1919. R. 1 Nov. 1923. d. at Bournemouth, 8 Jan. 1928. O.B.E. 3 June 1919. N.-W. Frontier, Chitral, 1895, relief of Chitral, medal with clasp. War of 1914–19, Desp. L.G. 11 June 1920, O.B.E.

*2347. **Stevens, Cecil Robert.** b. 16 Mar. 1867. Bart's. and Zurich. M.R.C.S. 1890. L.R.C.P. Lond. 1890. M.B. (Honours), B.S. 1891; M.D. 1892; Lond. F.R.C.S. 1892. S. Lt. 29 July 1893. S. Capt. 29 July 1896. Major, 30 Jan. 1905. Lt.-Col. 30 Jan. 1913. d. at Paignton, Devon, 18 Nov. 1919. Son of Sir Charles Stevens, I.C.S. Lt.-Govr. of Bengal, 1897, brother of A. F. Stevens, No. 2375, infra, 1895. N.-W. Frontier, Chitral, 1895, relief of Chitral, medal with clasp; Tirah, 1897–98, two clasps. War of 1914–19.

2348. **Barry, Cecil Charles Stuart** (signs **Stuart**, name spelt **Stewart** in birth cert.). b. 10 Dec. 1867. St. George's. M.R.C.S. 1891. L.R.C.P. Lond. 1891. S. Lt. 29 July 1893. S. Capt. 29 July 1896. Major, 29 July 1905. Lt.-Col. 29 July 1913. R. 9 Feb. 1920. ———. C.I.E. 3 June 1915. N.-W. Frontier, Chitral, 1895, relief of Chitral, medal with clasp.

2349. **Rogers, Leonard.** b. 18 Jan. 1868. St. Mary's. M.R.C.S. 1891. L.R.C.P. Lond. 1891. M.B. (Honours), B.S. 1892; M.D. 1897; Lond. F.R.C.S. 1893. S. Lt. 29 July 1893. S. Capt. 29 July 1896. M.R.C.P. Lond. 1898. F.R.C.P. Lond. 1905. Major, 30 Jan. 1905. Lt.-Col. 30 Jan. 1913. R. 1 Mar. 1921. Member Medl. Board, India Office, 1922. President, 3 Nov. 1928. F.R.F.P.S.G. 1925. Tempy. Major-Genl. 3 Nov. 1928. ———. C.I.E. 11 Dec. 1911. Kt. 22 June 1914. F.R.S. 1916. Author of Report on Epidemic Malarial Fever of Assam (Kala Azar), 1897; Inoculation for Rinderpest, 1900; Report on Fevers in Dinajpur District, 1904; Fevers in the Tropics, 1908; (with Sir J. Fayrer and Sir L. Brunton), On poison of venomous Snakes, and prevention of death from their bite, 1909; Cholera and its treatment, 1911; Dysenteries, their differentiation and treatment, 1913; Revision of MacConnell's Catalogue of Pathological Museum of Medical College, Calcutta, 1916; Bowel Diseases in the Tropics; Cholera, Dysentery, Liver Abscess, and Sprue, 1921; (with E. Muir), Leprosy, Croonian Lectures for 1924, 1925; Recent Advances in Tropical Medicine, 1928.

2350. **Newman, Ernest Alan Robert.** b. 12 May 1867. Cambridge and Bart's. B.A. (Honours), 1887; M.B. B.S. 1891; Cantab. M.R.C.S. 1890. L.R.C.P. Lond. 1890. S. Lt. 29 July 1893. S. Capt. 29 July 1896. Major, 30 Jan. 1905. Lt.-Col. 30 Jan. 1913. S. List, 1 Mar. 1920. R. 29 July 1923. ———. C.I.E. 3 June 1918. N.-W. Frontier, Malakand, 1897–98, defence of Malakand, relief of Chakdara, action at Landakai, operations in Bajaur and in Mamund country, medal with two clasps; Tirah, 1897–98, operation in Bara Valley, clasp. Author of Manual of Aseptic Surgery, 1906; Irrigation in Cataract Extraction, 1923.

* First case of accelerated promotion to Major, granted under Mily. Dept. Not. No. 139 of 17 Feb. 1905.

2351. Birdwood, Gordon Travers. b. 24 Jan. 1867. Cambridge (Peterhouse College) and Guy's. B.A. 1888 ; M.B. B.S. 1892 ; M.A. M.D. 1895 ; Cantab. M.R.C.S. 1892. L.R.C.P. Lond. 1892. S. Lt. 29 July 1893. S. Capt. 29 July 1896. D.P.H., R.C.P. and S.I.. 1896. Major, 30 Jan. 1905. Lt.-Col. 30 Jan. 1913. R. 2 Nov. 1920. ―――――. N.-W. Frontier, Waziristan, 1894–95, medal with clasp ; 1897–98, operations on Samana and in Kurram Valley, medal with three clasps. Author of Clinical Methods for Indian Students, 1915 ; Guide for Students and General Practitioners in India in Diagnostic and Therapeutic Measures ; Practical Bazar Medicines, 1920 ; Clinical Methods for Students in Tropical Medicine, 1920.

2352. Gould, Jay (first name **Jabez** in birth cert., changed to **Jay** before entering I.M.S.). b. 20 Jan. 1867. Liverpool. M.B. B.Ch. Vict. 1890. S. Lt. 29 July 1893. S. Capt. 29 July 1896. Major, 29 July 1895. Lt.-Col. 29 July 1913. d. at Aden, 2 June 1919. C.B.E. 25 Aug. 1917. N.-W. Frontier, Waziristan, 1894–95, medal with clasp ; Chitral, 1895, relief of Chitral, medal with clasp ; Malakand, 1897–98, operations in Bajaur and in Mamund country, Utman Khel, Buner, action of Tanga Pass, clasp, China, 1900, medal. Tibet, 1903–04, medal. War of 1914–18. Author (with G. B. Seton, No. 2319, supra, 1892) of The Indian Medical Service, 1911.

2353. Turner, Reginald George. b. 5 Feb. 1870. St. George's. M.R.C.S. 1891. L.R.C.P. Lond. 1891. S. Lt. 29 July 1893. S. Capt. 29 July 1896. Major, 30 Jan. 1905. F.R.C.S. 1907. Lt.-Col. 30 Jan. 1913. S. List, 19 Apr. 1920. Col. 15 Aug. 1921. R. 17 Aug. 1923. Son of Staff-Surgeon A. F. Turner, A.M.D. 1853 (Johnston's Roll of R.A.M.C. No. 5158). ―――――. D.S.O. 1 Jan. 1917. C.M.G. 3 June 1918. N.-W. Frontier, Waziristan, 1894–95, medal with clasp. Uganda, 1897–98, attack of Kymbo, capture of Kadagambiz and of Sudanese Forts near Mruli, Desp., medal with two clasps. China, 1900, medal. War of 1914–18, Desp. L.G. 30 June 1916, D.S.O., C.M.G.

2354. Davidson, James. b. 27 Nov. 1865. M.B. C.M. Ed. 1891. S. Lt. 29 July 1893. S. Capt. 29 July 1896. Major, 30 Jan. 1905. D.T.M. Liverpool, 1908. Lt.-Col. 30 Jan. 1913. R. 27 Nov. 1920. ―――――. D.S.O. 23 Aug. 1912. N.-W. Frontier, Waziristan, 1894–95, medal with clasp ; Chitral, 1895, relief of Chitral, medal with clasp. Sudan, 1896, Dongola expedition, medal, and Khedive's medal. N.-W. Frontier, Tirah, 1897–98, two clasps. Tibet, 1903–04, action at Niani, operation at and around Gyantse, march to Lhasa, medal with clasp. N.-E. Frontier, Abor, 1911–12 ; Desp. G.G.O. No. 480 of 25 May 1912, medal with clasp, D.S.O.

2355. Mulvany, John. b. 9 Apr. 1870. London Hosp. M.R.C.S. 1891. L.R.C.P. Lond. 1891. S. Lt. 29 July 1893. S. Capt. 29 July 1896. Major, 29 July 1905. Lt.-Col. 29 July 1913. R. 29 July 1920. ―――――. Son of Asst.-Surg. John Mulvany, R.N. N.-W. Frontier, Chitral, 1895, relief of Chitral, medal with clasp ; Tochi, 1897–98, clasp. China, 1900, medal.

1894

2356. Lamb, George. b. 30 June 1869. M.B. (Honours and Brunton Prizeman), 1890 ; M.D. (Honours), 1892 ; Glas. S. Lt. 29 Jan. 1894. S. Capt. 29 Jan. 1897. Major, 29 July 1905. d. in Edinburgh, 11 Apr. 1911. N.-W. Frontier, Waziristan, 1894–95, medal with clasp. Author of Serum Sedimentation, 1900.

INDIAN MEDICAL SERVICE [1894

2357. Burden, Harry. *b.* 22 Apr. 1867. St. Thomas'. M.R.C.S. 1892. L.R.C.P. Lond. 1892. F.R.C.S. 1893. S. Lt. 29 Jan. 1894. S. Capt. 29 Jan. 1897. Major, 29 July 1905. Lt.-Col. 29 July 1913. R. 24 Mar. 1921, with Hony. rank of Col. ———. C.I.E. 11 Dec. 1911. N.-W. Frontier, Chitral, 1895, relief of Chitral, medal with clasp; Tirah, 1897–98, two clasps. War of 1914–18, Desp. L.G. 21 June 1916.

2358. Fisher, John. *b.* 8 Jan. 1867. Cambridge and St. Thomas'. B.A. M.B. B.S. Cantab. 1891. S. Lt. 29 Jan. 1894. S. Capt. 29 Jan. 1897. Major, 29 Jan. 1906. Lt.-Col. 29 Jan. 1914. R. 25 Mar. 1919. ———. D.S.O. 20 May 1898. N.-W. Frontier, 1897–98, Utman Khel, Buner, operations in Bajaur and in Mamund country, Desp. L.G. 11 Jan. and 18 Mar. 1898, medal with clasp, D.S.O.

2359. Peck, Edward Surman. *b.* 23 Mar. 1866. Cambridge and Bart's. B.A. M.B. B.S. 1891; D.P.H. 1894; Cantab. S. Lt. 29 Jan. 1894. S. Capt. 29 Jan. 1897. Major, 29 Jan. 1906. R. 6 Dec. 1913. ———. Air Pilot's Cert. 1914. Rejoined for service in war of 1914–18, 19 Oct. 1914–16. Lt.-Col. 11 Dec. 1916. Brother of F. S. Peck, No. 2156, supra, 1880. N.-W. Frontier, Chitral, 1895, relief of Chitral, medal with clasp.

2360. Evans, Charles Harford (afterwards **Bowle-Evans, C. H.**). *b.* 19 Oct. 1867. Cambridge and Bart's. B.A. 1889; M.B. B.S. 1894; D.T.M. 1909; D.P.H. 1910; Cantab. M.R.C.S. 1893. L.R.C.P. Lond. 1893. S. Lt. 29 Jan. 1894. S. Capt. 29 Jan. 1897. Took name of Bowle-Evans in 1902. Major, 29 July 1905. D.T.M. London School Trop. Med. 1909. Lt.-Col. 29 July 1913. S. List, 20 May 1920. Col. 10 Sept. 1920. Major-Genl. 6 Sept. 1923. Director, Medl. Services, India, 6 Sept. 1923. R. 19 Dec. 1923. ———. C.M.G. 3 June 1915. C.B.E. 3 June 1919. K.H.P. 9 July 1923. N.-W. Frontier, Waziristan, 1894–95, medal with clasp; Chitral, 1895, action of Malakand Pass, relief of Chitral, medal with clasp; Tochi, 1897–98, clasp. China, 1900, medal. War of 1914–18. Desp. L.G. 22 June 1915, and 3 Feb. 1920, C.M.G., C.B.E.

2361. Harriss, Stanley Arthur (name on birth cert. **Alfred Arthur Stanley Harriss**, changed name while at Ed. Univ.). *b.* 4 Jan. 1869. M.B. C.M. Ed. 1891. M.R.C.S. 1893. L.R.C.P. Lond. 1893. D.P.H. Cantab. 1894. S. Lt. 29 Jan. 1894. S. Capt. 29 Jan. 1897. Major, 29 Jan. 1906. D.T.M. dist. London School Trop. Med. 1906. D.T.M. Cantab. 1906. Lt.-Col. 29 Jan. 1914. S. List, 18 July 1920. R. 29 Jan. 1924. ———. China, 1900, medal with clasp.

2362. MacLeod, Ewan Cameron. *b.* 18 Aug. 1868. Westminster Hosp. M.R.C.S 1891. L.R.C.P. Lond. 1891. S. Lt. 29 Jan. 1894. S. Capt. 29 Jan. 1897. Major, 29 Jan. 1905. Lt.-Col. 29 July 1913. S. List, 21 June 1920. R. 9 Feb. 1923. ———.

2363. Thomson, Charles. *b.* 5 Apr. 1870. M.B. C.M. Ed. 1892. S. Lt. 29 Jan. 1894. S. Capt. 29 Jan. 1897. Major, 29 Jan. 1906. R. 30 Jan. 1911. Major, R.A.M.C. T.F. 4th London Howitzer Brigade, R.F.A. 1 Nov. 1913. Rejoined for service in war of 1914–18, 19 Dec. 1914–18. Lt.-Col. 18 Dec. 1917. ———. N.-W. Frontier, Zakka Khel, 1908, medal with clasp. War of 1914–18.

2364. **Ramsay, George.** b. 25 Oct. 1868. King's Coll. Lond. M.R.C.S. 1892. L.R.C.P. Lond. 1892. S. Lt. 28 July 1894. S. Capt. 28 July 1897. d. at Bagdad, 24 Mar. 1902. N.-W. Frontier, Chitral, 1895, medal with clasp.

2365. **Sutherland, David Waters.** b. 18 Dec. 1871, in Grenville County, Victoria. Melbourne and Ed. Univs. M.B. C.M. (Honours), 1893; M.D. 1902; Ed. S. Lt. 28 July 1894. S. Capt. 28 July 1897. M.R.C.P. Lond. 1902. Major, 29 Jan. 1896. Lt.-Col. 28 Jan. 1914. S. List, 19 Aug. 1920. F.R.C.P. Lond. 1923. R. 12 Dec. 1926. ———. C.I.E. 3 June 1917. N.-W. Frontier, Chitral, 1895, action of Malakand Pass, relief of Chitral, Desp. G.G.O. No. 998 of 1895, medal with clasp. Author of Differential Diagnosis of Fevers, 1909.

2366. **Selby, William.** b. 16 June 1869, at Dunedin, New Zealand. Bart's. M.R.C.S. 1892. L.R.C.P. Lond. 1892. S. Lt. 28 July 1894. S. Capt. 28 July 1897. F.R.C.S. 1905. Major, 29 Jan 1906. Lt.-Col. 29 Jan. 1914. d. at Lucknow, 8 Sept. 1916. D.S.O. 29 May 1898. N.-W. Frontier, Chitral, 1895, relief of Chitral, medal with clasp; Tirah, 1897–98, operations on Samana, relief of Gulistan, actions of Chagru Kotal, Dargai, Sampagha and Arhanga Passes, operations in Waran Valley, at and around Dwatoi, against Khanni Khel Chamkannis, and in Bara Valley, Desp. G.G.O. No. 244 of 1898, three clasps, D.S.O.

2367. **Granger, Thomas Arthur.** b. 12 Aug. 1871. M.B. C.M. Ed. 1892. S. Lt. 28 July 1894. S. Capt. 28 July 1897. Major, 27 July 1906. Bt. Lt.-Col. 1 Jan. 1914. Lt.-Col. 29 Jan. 1914. S. List, 10 Sept. 1920. Col. 24 Mar. 1922. R. 1 Aug. 1922. ———. C.M.G. 4 June 1918. Mekran, 1898. N.-W. Frontier, 1898–99, operations against Para Chamkannis. War of 1914–18, Desp. L.G. 11 Dec. 1917, and 25 May 1918, C.M.G.

2368. **Bamfield, Harold John Kinahan.** b. 18 Sept. 1870. St. Mary's. M.R.C.S. 1893. L.R.C.P. Lond. 1893. S. Lt. 28 July 1894. S. Capt. 28 July 1897. Major, 28 July 1906. Lt.-Col. 28 July 1914. S. List, 1 Nov. 1920. Col. 1 Aug. 1922. Major-Genl. 24 Sept. 1924. R. 24 Sept. 1928. ———. D.S.O. 4 June 1917. K.H.P. 24 June 1923. C.B. 1 Jan. 1925. N.-W. Frontier, Tirah, 1897–98, action of Ublan Pass, operations on Samana and in Kurram Valley, Desp. G.G.O. No. 1141 of 1897, medal with three clasps; Waziristan, 1902, operations against Darwesh Khel Waziris; Zakka Khel, 1908, medal with clasp. War of 1914–18, Desp. L.G. 22 June 1915 and 1 June 1917, D.S.O.

2369. **Grant, John Weymiss.** b. 5 Apr. 1869. M.B. C.M. 1892; D.P.H. 1893; Ab. Cert. Med. Psych. Ass. S. Lt. 23 July 1894. S. Capt. 23 July 1897. Major, 23 July 1906. Lt.-Col. 23 July 1914. S. List, 2 Nov. 1920. R. 5 Oct. 1924. ———. K.-i-H. 2nd class, 23 May 1900. Star of Nipal, 3rd class, Nov. 1920. N.-W. Frontier, Chitral, 1895, relief of Chitral, medal with clasp.

2370. **Moorhead, Arthur Henry.** b. 20 July 1872, at Port Louis, Mauritius. M.B. C.M. Ed. 1893. S. Lt. 28 July 1894. S. Capt. 23 July 1897. Major, 23 July 1906. D.T.M. London School Trop. Med. 1911. Lt.-Col. 23 July 1914. Bt.-Col. 18 Feb. 1915. d. at Kyrle, Batheaston, 1 Mar. 1916. Son of Asst.-Surg. G. A. Moorhead, A.M.D. 1858 (Johnston's Roll of R.A.M.C. No. 5749). N.-W. Frontier, Chitral, 1895, relief of Chitral, medal with clasp; Tochi, 1897–98, clasp. China, 1900, relief of Pekin, medal with clasp. War of 1914–18, France, Desp. Bt.-Col.

2371. **Hayward, William Davey.** *b.* 1 Apr. 1870. Liverpool. M.B. Ch.B. Vict. 1893. S. Lt. 28 July 1894. S. Capt. 28 July 1897. Major, 28 July 1906. D.T.M. Liverpool, 1909. Lt.-Col. 28 July 1914. R. 5 Aug. 1920. ———. N.-W. Frontier, Chitral, 1895, relief of Chitral, medal with clasp; 1897–98, operations in Bajaur and in Mamund country, clasp.

2372. **Russell, Archibald William Forbes.** *b.* 1 Oct. 1868. Cambridge and Bart's. B.A. M.B. B.S. 1893; M.A. 1894; Cantab. S. Lt. 28 July 1894. S. Capt. 28 July 1897. *d.* at Bareli, 22 June 1898.

2373. **Scott-Moncrieff, William Elmsley.** *b.* 4 Mar. 1871. M.B. C.M. 1893; M.D. 1905; Ed. S. Lt. 28 July 1894. S. Capt. 28 July 1897. Major, 25 July 1906. F.R.C.S. Ed. 1912. Lt.-Col. 28 July 1914. R. 29 July 1914. Rejoined for service in India in war of 1914–18, 12 Nov. 1914–17. Afterwards in practice at Victoria, Vancouver Island. ———. N.-W. Frontier, Chitral, 1895, relief of Chitral, medal with clasp; Tochi, 1897–98, clasp. China, 1900, medal.

1895

2374. **Milne, Charles John** (afterwards **Robertson-Milne, C. J.**). *b.* 8 Jan. 1872. M.B. C.M. 1893; M.D. (Honours), 1909; Ab. S. Lt. 29 Jan. 1895. S. Capt. 29 Jan. 1898. Took name of Robertson-Milne in 1900. Major, 29 Jan. 1907. *d.* at Barhampur, 22 May 1911. N.-W. Frontier, Tirah, 1897–98, actions of Sampagha and Arhanga Passes, reconnaissance of Saran Sar, operations against Khani Khel Chamkannis and in Bara Valley, medal with two clasps. Author of Report on Epidemic Cerebro-spinal Meningitis in India, 1906; Bengal Lunatic Asylums Manual, 1910; chapter on Insanity in Lyons' Medical Jurisprudence for India, 4th ed. 1909. Son of R. M. Milne, No. 1890, supra, 1865.

2375. **Stevens, Algernon Francis.** *b.* 30 Aug. 1869. Bart's. M.R.C.S. 1893. L.R.C.P. Lond. 1893. S. Lt. 29 Jan. 1895. S. Capt. 29 Jan. 1898. Major, 29 Jan. 1907. Lt.-Col. 29 Jan. 1915. S. List, 31 Jan. 1921. *d.* at Gaya, 20 Aug. 1922. Son of Sir Charles Stevens, K.C.S.I. Lt.-Govr. of Bengal, 1897. Brother of C. R. Stevens, No. 2347, supra, 1893. War of 1914–19, Hosp. ship ' Erinpura,' 21 June 1916 to 29 Dec. 1918.

2376. **Bensley, Clement Henry.** *b.* 27 Sept. 1870. St. Mary's. M.R.C.S. 1893. L.R.C.P. Lond. 1893. S. Lt. 29 Jan. 1895. S. Capt. 29 Jan. 1898. Major, 29 Jan. 1907. Lt.-Col. 29 Jan. 1915. S. List, 1 Feb. 1921. Col. 8 Jan. 1923. R. 15 Feb. 1927. ———. Son of E. C. Bensley, No. 1807, supra, 1859. C.I.E. 1 Jan. 1925. K.H.P. 13 Apr. 1924.

2377. **Watling, Francis Hammond.** *b.* 14 Sept. 1869. M.B. C.M. Ed. 1893. S. Lt. 29 Jan. 1895. S. Capt. 29 Jan. 1898. Major, 29 Jan. 1907. Lt.-Col. 29 Jan. 1915. R. 29 Feb. 1924. ———. N.-W. Frontier, Chitral, 1895, relief of Chitral, medal with clasp. China, 1900, medal. War of 1914–18, Desp. L.G. 15 Aug. 1917.

2378. **MacMillan, John Duncan.** *b.* 24 June 1869. M.B. C.M. Ed. 1893. S. Lt. 29 Jan. 1895. *d.* at Loralai, 5 Feb. 1897.

2379. **Gwyther, Arthur.** *b.* 16 June 1870. M.B. C.M. Ed. 1893. S. Lt. 29 Jan. 1895. S. Capt. 29 Jan. 1898. F.R.C.S. Ed. 1904. Major, 29 July 1906. Lt.-Col. 29 July 1914. R. 29 Jan. 1918. ———. K.-i-H. 1st class, 11 Dec. 1911. N.-W. Frontier, 1897–98, medal with clasp.

2380. Morgan, Edgar John. b. 29 July 1870. St. Mary's. M.R.C.S. 1893. L.R.C.P. Lond. 1893. M.B. Lond. 1894. S. Lt. 29 Jan. 1895. S. Capt. 29 Jan. 1898. Major, 29 Jan. 1907. Lt.-Col. 29 Jan. 1915. R. 1 Oct. 1915. ————. N.-W. Frontier, Tochi, 1897–98, medal with clasp.

2381. Ward, Alfred Edward Joseph. b. 30 Oct. 1872. Q.C. Cork. L.R.C.P. and S. Ed. 1894. L.F.P.S.G. 1894. S. Lt. 29 Jan. 1895. Resigned, 3 Apr. 1896. Afterwards in practice at Salisbury. ————.

2382. Carr, William. b. 4 Jan. 1870. M.B. C.M. Ed. 1893. S. Lt. 29 Jan. 1895. S. Capt. 29 Jan. 1898. Killed by an explosion, at Meerut, 6 May 1902. N.-W. Frontier, Malakand, 1897–98, Desp. medal with clasp. China, 1900, medal.

2383. Hamilton, John Archibald. b. 4 Nov. 1869. M.B. C.M. Ed. 1892. S. Lt. 29 Jan. 1895. S. Capt. 29 Jan. 1898. F.R.C.S. Ed. 1903. Major, 29 July 1906. D.T.M. London School Trop. Med. 1913. Lt.-Col. 29 July 1914. S. List, 1 Mar. 1921. R. 8 June 1922, with Hony. rank of Colonel. ————. C.M.G. 14 Jan. 1916. China, 1900, relief of Pekin, medal with clasp. War of 1914–19, Desp. L.G. 1 Jan. 1916, 5 Jan. 1919, 12 Feb. 1920, 21 May 1920, C.M.G.

2384. Stephenson, John. b. 6 Feb. 1871. Owen's Coll. Manchester. B.Sc. (Honours), 1890; M.B. Ch.B. (Honours), 1893; Vict. M.B. (Honours) Lond. 1894. S. Lt. 29 July 1895. S. Capt. 29 July 1898. F.R.C.S. 1905. Major, 29 Jan. 1907. Lt.-Col. 29 Jan. 1915. R. 6 Sept. 1921. ————. C.I.E. 3 June 1919. War of 1914–19, Egyptian Expeditionary Force, 26 June to 31 Oct. 1918.

2385. Windsor, Frank Needham. b. 2 May 1868. Cambridge (Emmanuel Coll.), and Owen's Coll. Manchester. B.Sc. Vict. 1887. B.A. 1890; M.B. B.S. 1892; Cantab. L.R.C.P. Lond. 1892. M.R.C.S. 1892. S. Lt. 29 July 1895. S. Capt. 29 July 1898. Major, 29 Jan. 1907. Lt.-Col. 29 Jan. 1915. R. 15 Aug. 1920. ————. N.-W. Frontier, Malakand, 1897–98, operations in Bajaur and in Mamund country, medal with clasp. Author of Indian Toxicology, 1906.

2386. Turnbull, Walter Barrie. b. 2 Aug. 1872. M.B. C.M. Ed. 1893. S. Lt. 29 July 1895. S. Capt. 29 July 1898. Major, 29 Jan. 1907. d. at Mainpuri, 17 Nov. 1907. N.-W. Frontier, Malakand, 1897–98, operations in Bajaur and in Mamund country, Buner, medal with clasp. China, 1900, medal with clasp. N.-W. Frontier, Waziristan, 1901–02, clasp.

2387. Waters, Ernest Edwin. b. 21 July 1872. M.B. C.M. 1893; M.D. 1903; Ed. S. Lt. 29 July 1895. S. Capt. 29 July 1898. Major, 29 Jan. 1907. M.R.C.P. Lond. 1911. Lt.-Col. 29 Jan. 1915. S. List, 1 Mar. 1921. R. 19 July 1927. ————. N.-W. Frontier, Tirah, 1897–98, Malakand, actions of Dargai, Sampagha and Arhanga Passes, operations in Bazar Valley, medal with two clasps. Author of Diabetes, its Causation and Treatment, with special reference to the Tropics, 1927.

2388. Leventon, Asher. b. 29 Apr. 1870. T.C.D. and Cath. Univ. Dublin. L.R.C.P.I. 1894. L.R.C.S.I. 1894. S. Lt. 29 July 1895. S. Capt. 29 July 1898. F.R.C.S.I. 1906. D.P.H., R.C.P. and S.I. 1907. Major, 29 Jan. 1907. Lt.-Col. 29 Jan. 1915. S. List, 16 Mar. 1921. R. 29 Apr. 1925. ————. C.I.E. 2 June 1923.

2389. Chapman, Philip Francis. b. 11 Feb. 1870. M.B. C.M. Ed. 1894. S. Lt. 29 July 1895. S. Capt. 29 July 1898. Major, 29 July 1907. Lt.-Col. 29 July 1915. S. List. 24 Mar. 1921. Col. 24 Sept. 1922. R. 27 Oct. 1923. ————. C.I.E. 1 Jan. 1919.

1896

2390. Cochrane, Arthur Williams Rea. b. 22 Nov. 1872. Bart's. M.R.C.S. 1894. L.R.C.P. Lond. 1894. M.B. Lond. 1895. S. Lt. 29 Jan. 1896. F.R.C.S. 1898. Capt. 29 Jan. 1899. Major, 29 July 1907. Lt.-Col. 28 July 1915. S. List, 28 Mar. 1921. Col. 9 Nov. 1922. R. 8 Feb. 1929. ————. N.-W. Frontier, Malakand, 1897–98, medal with clasp. Author (with C. A. Sprawson, I.M.S.), of A Guide to the use of Tuberculin, 1915.

2391. Clemesha, William Wesley. b. 19 Apr. 1871. Owen's Coll. Manchester. M.B. Ch.B. (Honours), 1894; M.D. 1904; Vict. M.R.C.S. 1895. L.R.C.P. Lond. 1895. S. Lt. 29 Jan. 1896. Capt. 29 Jan. 1899. Major, 29 July 1907. Lt.-Col. 29 July 1915. R. 21 Feb. 1921. ————. C.I.E. 1 Jan. 1919. War of 1914–18, East Africa, Desp. L.G. 6 Aug. 1918, C.I.E. Author of Plague from the Sanitarian's point of View, 1903; Bacteriology of Drinking water supplies in tropical climates, 1909; Sewage Disposal in the Tropics, 1910; Bacteriology of surface water in the Tropics, 1912.

2392. Black, James Alexander. b. 1 Mar. 1870. M.A. 1890; M.B. C.M. 1894; Ab. S. Lt. 29 Jan. 1896. Capt. 29 Jan. 1899. Major, 29 July 1907. Lt.-Col. 29 July 1915. S. List, 15 Aug. 1921. Col. 27 Oct. 1923. d. at Marseilles, on board P.O. S.S. ' Caledonia,' on passage to England, 27 Mar. 1925.

2393. Wilson, Roger Parker. b. 13 May 1870. Liverpool. M.R.C.S. 1893. L.R.C.P. Lond. 1893. S. Lt. 29 Jan. 1896. Capt. 29 Jan. 1899. D.P.H. Cantab. 1900. Major, 29 July 1907. F.R.C.S. 1912. Lt.-Col. 29 July 1915. S. List, 6 Sept. 1921. R. 17 Mar. 1926. ————. C.I.E. 3 June 1925.

2394. Lindsay, Victor Edward Hugh. b. 24 May 1869. Owen's Coll. Manchester, and St. Mary's. M.B. Ch.B. Vict. 1893. S. Lt. 29 Jan. 1896. Capt. 29 Jan. 1899. Major, 29 July 1907. Lt.-Col. 29 July 1915. S. List, 17 Sept. 1921. R. 24 May 1924. ————. Royal Humane Society's Bronze Medal, Hrinho, North China, 28 July 1903. China, 1900, medal.

2395. Robertson, James Currie. b. 26 Nov. 1870. M.A. 1890.; B.Sc. (Honours), 1893; M.B. C.M. (Honours), 1894; Glas. S. Lt. 29 Jan. 1896. Capt. 29 Jan. 1899. Major, 29 July 1907. Lt.-Col. 29 July 1915. S. List, 12 Nov. 1921. d. at Simla, 14 May 1923. C.I.E. 1 Jan. 1914. C.M.G. 8 Aug. 1917. C.B.E. 3 June 1919. Silver medal della Saluta publica (Italy), Nov. 1920. Officer, Crown of Italy, Sept. 1920. Sudan, 1896, Dongola expedition, medal, and Khedive's medal. South Africa, 1902, operations in Transvaal, medal with two clasps. War of 1914–19, operations in Italy, 26 Nov. 1917 to 4 Nov. 1918, Desp. L.G. 27 July 1917, 30 May 1918, and 5 June 1919, Italian Public Health Silver Medal, C.M.G.

2396. Rainier, Norman Robertson Jones. b. 16 Apr. 1871. Charing Cross Hosp. M.R.C.S. 1893. L.R.C.P. Lond. 1893. S. Lt. 29 Jan. 1896. Capt. 29 Jan. 1899. Major, 29 July 1907. Lt.-Col. 29 July 1915. R. 1 July 1923. ————.

2397. **Dawes, Christopher Dering.** *b.* 22 Mar. 1872. St. George's. M.R.C.S. 1895. L.R.C.P. Lond. 1895. S. Lt. 29 Jan. 1896. Capt. 29 Jan. 1899. D.T.M. dist. London School Trop. Med. 1906. Major, 29 Jan. 1908. Lt.-Col. 29 Jan. 1916. R. 26 Oct. 1921. ―――. N.-W. Frontier, Tirah, 1897–98, Mohmand, medal with two clasps. China, 1900, medal. N.-E. Frontier, Abor, 1911–12, medal with clasp. War of 1914–19, operations in France and Belgium, 15 Nov. 1914 to 21 Aug. 1915; Gallipoli, 8 Sept. 1915 to 9 Dec. 1915; Hosp. ship. 'Glenart Castle'; Mesopotamia, 1 May 1916 to 21 Jan. 1918; Hosp. ship, 'Varsova'; Desp. L.G. 5 June 1919.

2398. **Perry, Edmund Ludlow.** *b.* 28 June 1871. St. Thomas'. M.R.C.S. 1895. L.R.C.P. Lond. 1895. S. Lt. 29 Jan. 1896. Capt. 29 Jan. 1899. Major, 29 July 1907. Lt.-Col. 29 July 1915. S. List, 8 Feb. 1922. Col. 24 June 1923. R. 24 June 1927. ―――. Son of Asst.-Surg. George Perry, Scots Fusilier Guards (Johnston's Roll of R.A.M.C. No. 5440), D.S.O. 3 June 1917. K.H.S. 5 Mar. 1925. N.-W. Frontier, 1897–98, operations in Bajaur and in Mohmand country, Desp. G.G.O. No. 1317 of 1897, medal with clasp; Waziristan, 1901–02, clasp. War of 1914–18, Desp. L.G. 19 Oct. 1916 and 15 Aug. 1917, D.S.O.

2399. **Walton, Herbert James.** *b.* 19 Jan. 1869. Bart's. M.R.C.S. 1893. L.R.C.P. Lond. 1893. F.R.C.S. 1895. M.B. (Honours), Lond. 1895. S. Lt. 29 July 1896. Capt. 29 July 1899. Major, 29 Jan. 1908. D.T.M. dist. London School Trop. Med. 1909. M.D. Oxon. Trop. Med. 1910. D.P.H. Cantab. 1910. Lt.-Col. 29 Jan. 1916. R. 1 Sept. 1921. ―――. N.-W. Frontier, 1897–98, medal with clasp. China, 1900, relief of Pekin, actions of Peitsang and Yangtsun, medal with clasp. Tibet, 1903–04, operations at and around Gyantse, march to Lhasa, medal with clasp.

2400. **Ainsworth, Hugh.** *b.* 28 Sept. 1871. Owen's Coll. Manchester. M.R.C.S. 1893. L.R.C.P. Lond. 1893. M.B. Ch.B. (Honours), Vict. 1895. S. Lt. 29 July 1896. Capt. 29 July 1899. F.R.C.S. 1907. Major, 29 Jan. 1908. Lt.-Col. 29 Jan. 1916. S. List, 24 Mar. 1922. Col. 3 May 1923. R. 28 Sept. 1928. ―――. K.H.S. 27 Aug. 1924. N.-W. Frontier, Tirah, 1897–98, actions of Chagru Kotal, Dargai, Sampagha and Arhanga Passes, operations at and around Dwatoi and in Bara Valley, medal with two clasps.

2401. **Pinch, Albert Edward Hayward.** *b.* 28 Feb. 1868. Bristol and Bart's. M.R.C.S. 1894. L.R.C.P. Lond. 1894. F.R.C.S. 1896. S. Lt. 29 July 1896. Capt. 29 July 1899. T.H.P. 17 Dec. 1899. R. 17 Dec. 1901. Supt. Medl. Graduates College and Polyclinic, London, 1899–1909. Director, Radium Institute, London, 1909. D.M.R.E. Cantab. 1921. M.R.C.P. Lond. 1926. ―――. Author of Clinical Index of Radium Therapy, 1925; Superficial Radium Therapy, 1927.

2402. **Dickson, Henry Arthur David.** *b.* 15 Nov. 1870. St. Thomas'. M.R.C.S. 1893. L.R.C.P. Lond. 1893. F.R.C.S. 1895. S. Lt. 29 July 1896. *d.* at Sandgate, Kent, 27 Jan. 1898.

2403. **Stevenson, John Stuart.** *b.* 24 Aug. 1872. Bart's. M.R.C.S. 1895. L.R.C.P. Lond. 1895. S. Lt. 29 July 1896. Capt. 29 July 1899. *d.* at Lucknow, 20 July 1900. Son of Asst.-Surg. afterward Surg.-Genl. W. F. Stevenson, C.B., A.M.D., (Johnston's Roll of R.A.M.C. No. 6296). N.-W. Frontier, 1897–98, Malakand, operations in Mamund country, medal; Tirah, 1897–98, clasp.

APPENDIX I

BENGAL

Supplementary Names

APPENDIX I contains the names of about 120 men, whose names appear in various records, but who were not, or who cannot be identified to have been, regular members of the Service. The first fourteen names are taken, one from the marriage register, thirteen from the burial register, of St. Anne's Church, Calcutta ; the old church in Fort William, destroyed at the capture of the fort in 1756. It is probable that these men were in Government service. It is not likely that there would be many, if any, medical men in private practice in Calcutta, before the middle of the eighteenth century. There were always, of course, many ship surgeons of the Indiamen lying in the river. But in the entries in the register of the burial of ship surgeons, of which there are many, the name of the ship is given.

The other names, of which there are over one hundred, are mostly, but not quite all, taken from the Service Army Lists, Medical, Bengal, and fall chiefly under three heads : first, Sub. Asst.-Surgeons, mostly men holding posts usually held by commissioned medical officers ; second, names entered by mistake, by misreading or miscopying the real name, Christian or Surname ; e.g. Robert, John, and George Bainbridge for Thomas Bainbridge, John Berilay for John Barclay ; third, towards the end, after 1840, uncovenanted medical officers.

1. **Stuart, John.** Witnessed William Hamilton's will at Surajgarh, 27 Oct. 1717 ; (B. Cons. 9 Dec. 1717). Buried in Calcutta, 1 Dec. 1726.
2. **Frasier, Thomas.** Buried in Calcutta, 21 Oct. 1719.
3. **Tanner, Henry.** Buried in Calcutta, 16 July 1721.
4. **Beal, William.** Buried in Calcutta, 28 Aug. 1727.
5. **Davis, Joseph.** Buried in Calcutta, 18 Sept. 1727.
6. **West, Robert.** Buried in Calcutta, 20 July 1729.
7. **Dipping, Anthony.** Buried in Calcutta, 22 June 1734.
8. **Cauty, John** (b). Surg. 'Godolphin,' 1735 ; 'Harrington,' 1732. In Calcutta, 15 Feb. 1741–42 ; (B. Cons.). Buried in Calcutta, 17 June 1748.

INDIAN MEDICAL SERVICE

9. **Hook, Joseph.** Surg. Mate, Fort St. David, 23 Aug. 1742 ; M. No. 78, 1742. Buried in Calcutta, 17 May 1748.
10. **Napier, Alexander.** Buried in Calcutta, 2 Nov. 1742.
11. **Paul, Thomas.** Buried in Calcutta, 8 Sept. 1746.
12. **Singat, Lewis.** Buried in Calcutta, 25 July 1748.
13. **MacDonald, John.** Married in Calcutta, 14 Nov. 1749.
14. **Hemmins, John.** Buried in Calcutta, 13 Oct. 1752.
15. **Talcutt, Samuel.** Surg. ' Suffolk,' 1754 ; (St. H. Cons. 18 Mar. 1754, and 11 Apr. 1757). Buried in Calcutta, 9 July 1762.
16. **Quaderson, Edward.** Buried in Calcutta, 25 Sept. 1762.
17. **Cornes,** or **Cornee, William.** Appointed A.S. and posted to schooner ' Cuddalore,' sent in search of survivors of ' Earl Temple,' lost in China seas in 1763 ; (B. Cons. 24 Feb. 1767). The name, which is not easy to read, has been miscopied ; should be William Carnae, B. No. 76, 1760.
18. **Nicholas,** or **Nicola.** Dresser serving under Surgeon William Anderson, (B. No. 55, 1753), at Patna, in 1763. For services to the British officers, killed in the Patna massacre, services rendered at great risk to himself, was granted pay and allowances of Asst.-Surg. but not the rank. v. Hist. of I.M.S. i. 190, 490.
19. **Orton, Thomas.** Nominated by Court, Bengal List of Packet, dated, London, 30 Apr. 1765 ; (S.A.L.M.B.). This is Thomas Orton, M. No. 145, 1765.
20. **Connellan, Peter.** A.S. (no date) ; Surg. 20 Apr. 1767 ; resigned (no date) ; (S.A.L.M.B.).
    Connellan, Patrick. Resigns, L. from B. 4 Feb. 1778 ; (S.A.L.M.B.). Both these entries refer to John Peter Connellan, B. No. 115, 1765.
21. **Symmonds, Mr.** (b). Late Surg. of ' Falmouth.' Nominated by Govt. Supy. Surg. (L. from B. 28 Nov. 1766, paras. 82, 84, S.A.L.M.B.). This is James Simmons, B. No. 125, 1766, whose name is also given in S.A.L.M.B.
22. **Grove, Daniel.** Buried in Calcutta, 7 Sept. 1767 ; (St. John's Burial Regr.). Possibly same as Daniel Grant, B. No. 117, 1766.
23. **Frolick, John.** Surgeon's Asst. Buried in Calcutta, 17 Nov. 1769 ; (St. John's Burial Regr.). Probably a subordinate or servant.
24. **Anderson, James.** Surg.-Genl. to Army, appointed on recommendation of Genl. Smith, on ten shillings a day, from 8 Nov. ; (L. from B. 25 Jan. 1770, para. 57 ; S.A.L.M.B.). A mistake in Christian name, is Thomas Anderson, B. No. 88, 1763.
25. **Manton, Thomas.** A.S. (no date) ; Surg. 19 Dec. 1771 ; d. at Fort William, July 1778 ; (S.A.L.M.B.). This is Thomas Martin, B. No. 180, 1771.
26. **Durham, Hercules.** b. 1744. Oxford (Brazenose), 1769. Cadet, Bengal, 1772. Ensign, 30 Mar. 1773. Resigned, 20 Jan. 1775. Afterwards Company's Attorney, Calcutta ; appeared for Crown against Nanda Kumar. d. in Calcutta, 18 Oct. 1776. Served as Surgeon in Kuch Bihar war, 1772–73 ; (L. to C. from Warren Hastings, of 20 Apr. 1779 : B.P. and P. Oct.–Dec. 1925, p. 163).

INDIAN MEDICAL SERVICE

27. **Ambrose, William.** Shown in muster roll of Patna Division for 1772 as Surgeon-Major, 25th Batt. Sepoys, age 37, enlisted Nov. 1765. His rank is quite clearly written as Surgeon-Major, not as Sergeant-Major, which is what it should be. He is shown as Sergeant in the Long Roll of the Second Brigade for 1773, and in that of the First Brigade for 1774. No mention found of any medical officer called Ambrose. At this time there were three Surgeon-Majors on the strength of the Bengal Army, one to each Brigade. v. Hist. of I.M.S. i. 306.

28. **Carnegy, Charles.** A.S. (no date); permitted to resign for ill-health; (L. from B. 24 Mar. 1775, para. 47; S.A.L.M.B.). A mistake in Christian name, should be Alexander Carnegie, B. No. 190, 1772.

29. **Bromfield, Charles** (b). Signs a medl. cert. 3 Feb. 1776; (B. Cons. 5 Feb. 1776). Cert. Corp. Surg. 1778. Surg. 'Halsewell,' 1783–84. Probably Surg. Mate of a ship in Calcutta in 1776. Afterwards Surgeon, Canton, 1776–77. China, No. 4.

30. **Jackson, Rowland.** Name and some references in S.A.L.M.B. b. 1720. M.D. Rheims, 1746. L.R.C.P. Lond. 1776. Permitted to practice in Bengal, and to attend prisoners in jail; (Desp. from C. 17 July 1777, para. 31). Appointed Medl. attendant to Civil and Mily. servants of Govt. 13 May 1779; (B. Cons.). d. in Calcutta, 29 May 1784. His widow recommended for pension; (Genl. L. from B. 23 Aug. 1784. paras. 83–85, in which he is called Physician to the Settlement), Pension refused by Court; (Fort Wm. Secret. L. 23 Aug. 1786, para. 289). Author of De vera phlebotomiae theoria sanguinis circulationis. innixa tentamen, 1747; Physical Dissertation on Drowning, 1747, v. Hist. of I.M.S. ii. 93–95.

31. **Claveland, John.** Appointed A.S. L. from B. 4 Feb. 1778, paras. 16, 17; (S.A.L.M.B.). Same as John Clevelands, No. 216, 1778, which name is also given in S.A.L.M.B.

32. **Magrath, Michael.** A.S. 10 Apr. 1780; R. 21 Sept. 1803; (S.A.L.M.B.). Same as Michael MacGrath, No. 244, 1780; whose name is also given in S.A.L.M.B.

33. **Bainbridge, John.**
34. **Bainbridge, George.**
35. **Bainbridge, Robert.**

All these three names appear to be mistakes in Christian name for Thomas Bainbridge, No. 248, 1781. Name John Bainbridge is entered in S.A.L.M.B. with date of appointment as A.S. as 14 Apr. 1784. The name of George Bainbridge is also entered for the same year. Mily L. from B. of 25 Nov. 1791, para. 120, reports transmission of a memorial from Asst.-Surg. George Bainbridge about his rank. In muster roll of Third Brigade for 1782 is entered name of Robert Bainbridge, Asst.-Surg. Sepoys, age 25, joined in London in 1781, came out in 'Monmouth.' In Proc. C.M.B. of 8 July 1788, Asst.-Surg. John Bainbridge is entered as appointed on 10 Sept. 1782, which is the date on which Thomas Bainbridge joined.

36. **Darris, John.** A.S. no date, in S.A.L.M.B. A misreading of the name of John Davis, No. 297, 1782, whose name is not entered in S.A.L.M.B.

INDIAN MEDICAL SERVICE

37. **Rolland, John.** A.S. 4 Nov. 1783; *d.* at Jaunpur, 5 July 1789; (S.A.L.M.B.). This is John Rowland, No. 300, 1782, whose name is also separately given in S.A.L.M.B. as A.S. 6 Jan. 1783 (no more).

38. **Mowland, John.** A.S. 1784; (S.A.L.M.B.). No more. This also is a misreading of the name of John Rowland or Rolland, No. 300, 1782.

39. **Rolland, William.** A.S. (no date); Surg. 1783; *d.* at Calcutta, 2 Aug. 1784; (S.A.L.M.B.). This is also probably a misreading of John Rolland, No. 300, 1782, though the date of death differs.

40. **Powles, James.** A.S. (no date); dismissed by Court Martial, 31 May 1784; (S.A.L.M.B.). A mistake in Christian name of Thomas Powles, No. 319, 1783.

41. **Skarrow, Thomas.** Permitted to proceed to Europe on 'Worcester'; (L. from B. 6 Apr. 1783, para. 176; S.A.L.M.B.). This appears to be Thomas Skarrow, M. No. 240, 1781.

42. **Cooke, Thomas.** Name given in Genl. Stibbert's list of 12 Nov. 1783, between H. Stewart, No. 350, and G. Fraser, No. 354. Probably a mistake for Thomas Cooper, No. 353, whose name is not given in this list. The name of William Cooke, No. 318, is given in its proper place, between Thomas Clarke and Thomas Powles.

43. **Berilay, John.** A.S. (no date), in S.A.L.M.B.; no more. A miscopy of name of John Barclay, No. 356, 1783.

44. **MacGrath, John.** A.S. 1784; (S.A.L.M.B.). A mistake in Christian name for Michael MacGrath, No. 244, 1780, whose name is also given in S.A.L.M.B.

45. **Milne, Alexander.** A.S. 1784; (S.A.L.M.B.). Appears to be a mistake for George Milne, No. 264, 1781.

46. **Milson, Robert.** A.S. 1784; (S.A.L.M.B.). A miscopy of the name of Robert Wilson, No. 307, 1783.

47. **Tyffe, Charles.** A.S. 1784; (S.A.L.M.B.). A miscopy of the name of Charles Fyffe, No. 336, 1783.

48. **MacCra, John.** Granted leave on half-pay to Europe; (Genl. L. from B. 23 Mar. 1785; S.A.L.M.B.). This is John MacRae, No. 302, 1782, whose name is also given again in S.A.L.M.B. as John MacRae, A.S. 13 Apr. 1784.

49. **Keir, Archibald.** Services for 35 years in India, with application for appointment (as Civil Surg. Bhagalpur), set out in Genl. L. from B. 22 Feb. 1785, para. 45; (S.A.L.M.B.). This is Archibald Keir, M. No. 104, 1753. v. Hist. of I.M.S. i. 167–169.

50. **Clisdale, James.** A.S. 1790; *d.* at Tajpur, Aug. 1795; (S.A.L.M.B.). This is James Clydsdale, No. 402, 1791.

51. **Whitefield, Thomas.** A.S. 1791; *d.* at Chunar, 13 Nov. 1793; (S.A.L.M.B.). This is William Whitefield, No. 412, 1792, which name is also given separately in S.A.L.M.B.

INDIAN MEDICAL SERVICE

52. MacLean, Charles (b, e). Stated in Dict. Nat. Biog. to have had charge of a hosp. in Calcutta in 1792, no other author found for his having served Govt. as a medl. officer on land in India. Name not in S.A.L.M.B. Cert. Corp. Surg. 1787. Surg. 'William Pitt,' 1788–89; 'Northumberland,' 1791–92; 'Haughton,' 1793–95. Deserted from 'Haughton'; (Comml. L. from B. 7 Feb. 1795, para. 87, where name is spelt MacLane). Ordered to be deported, for writings in Press, 1798; (Law L. from B. 29 Sept. 1798, paras. 2–7). M.D. Mar. Coll. Ab. 1800. Appointed to Army Medl. Dept. in 1804, served at York Hosp. Chelsea, and at Chelmsford; deserted, advertised in Hue and Cry as a deserter; (D.N.B.). Name not entered in Johnston's Roll of R.A.M.C. In 1809 or 1810 appointed Lecturer to E.I. Co. on Diseases of Hot Climates. Travelled in East, 1815–17. Reappointed to same Lectureship in 1818. d. about 1824. Author of Dissertation on Sources of Epidemic Disease, Calcutta, 1796; An Excursion into France, 1804; Affairs of Asia considered in their effects on the Liberties of Britain, 1806; Analytical View of the Medical Department of the British Army, 1810; View of the Consequences of laying open trade to India, 1810; Illustrations of progress of medical advancement during the last thirty years, 1818; Evils of Quarantine Laws, 1820.

53. Campbell, Archibald. A.S. 1794, name given in Genl. Mily. Regr. for 1795. A mistake for Archibald Campbell Clunes, No. 442, 1794.

54. Clunes, Andrew Carmichael. A.S. 1794; (C.G. 2 Oct. 1794). A mistake for Archibald Campbell Clunes, No. 442, 1794.

55. Durrand, Samuel. A.S. 1794; (C.G. 2 Oct. 1794). A mistake for Samuel Durham, No. 447, 1794.

56. Buirette, Jean. A.S. Madras, 9 Jan. 1769, till pensioned in 1795, M. No. 171. In 1803 allowed to draw pension in Bengal, where he was appointed Police Surgeon, Calcutta. d. in Calcutta, 4 June 1811.

57. Crusco, F. Nominated A.S. by Govt. 29 July 1799; (S.A.L.M.B.). No more. This is Francis Cruso, Bo. No. 294, 1798.

58. Russell, W. Nominated by Court, G.O. 29 July 1799; (S.A.L.M.B.). No more. This is Sir William Russell, B. No. 459, 1797.

59. Forbes, Andrew. A.S. 1805; (S.A.L.M.B.). No more. A mistake for Andrew Forbes Ramsay, No. 564, 1805.

60. Dick, William. A.S. transferred to P.W.I. Establishment, 1807; (S.A.L.M.B.). William Dick, P.W.I. No. 1, retired in 1807.

61. Fraser, Alexander. A.S. 4 Aug. 1807; (S.A.L.M.B.). A mistake in Christian name for Archibald Fraser, No. 610, 1807.

62. De Souza, Francis. M.D. Police Surgeon, Calcutta; d. at Monghir, Oct. 1816; (C.G. 24 Oct. 1816).

63. Monthaan, —, Mr. Arrived in Calcutta on transport 'Soudannee' in charge of sick from Java; to afford medical aid to troops on vessel in which he returns to Java; (G.O. 14 Jan. 1813; C.G. 21 Jan. 1813).

64. Sampson, —. A.S. serving at Banka Island (occupation of Dutch Colonies); applies for appointment on Bengal Establishment; petition forwarded to Court in Mily. L. from B. 27 Sept. 1816, para. 158. No further information; was not appointed.

INDIAN MEDICAL SERVICE

65. **Fallowfield, James.** A.S. served with 1/29th N.I. in Dekkan war of 1817–18; (S.A.L.M.B.). A mistake in Christian name for Jonathan Fallowfield, No. 669, 1810, whose name is also given in S.A.L.M.B.

66. **Baker, —.** A.S. served with Gardner's Frontier Cavalry in Dekkan war of 1817–18; (S.A.L.M.B.). This is Thomas Eld. Baker, No. 734, 1814, whose name is also given in S.A.L.M.B.

67. **MacKinnon, Charles.** A.S. 14 Mar. 1819; Appointed to Prince of Wales' Island; resigned, 1 May 1829; (S.A.L.M.B.). This appears to be a mixture of entries respecting No. 836B, Charles MacKinnon, appointed 14 Mar. 1819, and resigned 1 May 1829; and of Charles MacKinnon, P.W.I. No. 2.

68. **Guthrie, William.** Medl. Offr. to Moorcroft's expedition to Kashmir, Kabul, and Bokhara, 1819–25. *d.* at Balkh, Aug. 1825. v. Hist. of I.M.S. ii. 141.

69. **MacRae, James.** Query John (?) Nominated officiating Asst.-Surg.; served with 4th Co. 4th Batt. Artillery in Burmese war, 1824–25; (S.A.L.M.B.). This is John MacRae, No. 1030, 1825.

70. **Stewart, —.** Relieved from medl. charge of H.M. 54th Foot, and permitted to return to Calcutta; (Madras G.O.C.C. 7 Jan. 1826; S.A.L.M.B.). This appears to be temporary A.S. William Stewart, No. 1001, 1825.

*71. **Anderson, David.** *b.* 7 May 1809; A.S. 13 July 1833; failed to pass in Physic; (List of cancelled appointments).

72. **Good, —.** S.A.S. 3 Sept. 1838; (S.A.L.M.B.). Not apparent why name is given.

*73. **Bligh, Richard.** A.S. 1 Dec. 1838; passed exam., resigned appointment; (List of cancelled appointments). v. Bo. 671.

74. **Bell, Charles William.** Granted Rs. 200 per month for medl. aid to British detachment in Persia, 1839; (S.A.L.M.B.). Physician to British Embassy in Persia, 1838–42. Ordered by Sir John MacNeill to accompany British detachment to Bagdad, 1840; (S.A.L.M.B.). M.D. Ed. 1843. Afterwards in practice at Manchester and Physician Manchester Royal Infirmary. Order of Lion and Sun.

75. **Healy, Michael.** Asst. Apy. Bengal, S.M.D. 4 July 1839; Steward, 30 Nov. 1842. M.R.C.S. 1843. Medl. Offr. Malwa Bhil Corps, 1845; (C.G. 21 June 1845); Kasauli, 22 May 1847; (C.G. 10 Sept. 1847); 1st Panjab Infy. 1849; (G.O. 29 Dec. 1849). Murdered by Afridis near Kohat, 16 Mar. 1850; (F.I. 11 Apr. 1850). Afghanistan, 1839–42, with Shah Shuja's troops.

76. **Bain, Robert Henry.** M.D. (?) M.R.C.S. 1832. Police Surg. Calcutta. *d.* in Calcutta, aged 33, 19 Aug. 1839; (F.I. 29 Aug. 1839).

77. **Maxton, John.** C.M. Glas. 1830. Surg. Calcutta Police, 16 Sept. 1839; (C.G.). Also medl. charge of Mint and Custom house; (C.G. 16 Mar. 1845). Gave over charge, 21 Feb. 1846; (C.G.; S.A.L.M.B.). Probably same as James Maxton, No. 100, infra.

---

* List of Cancelled Appointments, Cadets and Asst.-Surgeons; Miscell. Cadet Books, No. 13, p. 189. The following names of Asst.-Surgeons are given. Bengal, D. Anderson, E. O. Baines, R. Bligh, H. Harding; Madras, S. H. Batson, T. B. Sanders, J. Tyser, J. S. Williams; Bombay, R. Ballantyne, H. Trevor, M. Thompson, J. Gutteres, R. F. Stott, F. E. Barton, R. D. MacNab.

INDIAN MEDICAL SERVICE

78. **Hamlyn, R. J.** Appointed Uncovd. Medl. Offr. Ramri, Dec. 1839; Manipur, 1840. d. at Manipur, Mar. 1843; (S.A.L.M.B.).

79. **Harris, Joseph.** b. 7 Nov. 1823. Appointed Medl. Offr. Shekhawati Brigade, 10 Mar. 1840; Jaipur Agency, 10 Nov. 1843; (C.G. 21 Feb. 1844; S.A.L.M.B.). d. at Jaipur, 29 Sept. 1846; (F.I. 22 Oct. 1846).

80. **Parrock, J.** Appointed to Medl. charge of Nuggur Division, Maisur, on salary of Rs. 250 a month, 1841; (S.A.L.M.B.). Probably a medical subordinate in Madras, but not identified.

*81. **Harding, Henry.** M.B. A.S. 3 May 1841; Rejected at exam.; (List of cancelled appointments).

82. **MacPherson, —.** To give medl. aid to detachment, Bengal Volunteers on board 'Nusseerut Shaw'; (G.O. 7 July 1841; S.A.L.M.B.). Probably Duncan MacPherson, M. No. 981, 1836.

83. **Imlay, C. T.** S.A.S. Sandoway, 1841; Moulmein; (C.G. 21 July 1847); Dakka; (C.G. 25 Dec. 1847; S.A.L.M.B.).

84. **Hemming, R. G. W.** S.A.S. Delhi, 1841; Civil Medl. Offr. Kalpi, 1841; Hamirpur, 1846; Etah, 1849; 1st class. S.A.S. 1 Jan. 1854; (S.A.L.M.B.).

85. **Doyle, J. H.** Formerly a gunner in Artillery; S.A.S. Jodhpur, 18 Apr. 1842; Civil Medl. Offr. Tippera; (C.G. 14 Feb. 1846); d. at Murshidabad, 3 Sept. 1847; (S.A.L.M.B.).

86. **Tranter, George.** b. 22 Mar. 1817. St. George's. M.R.C.S. 1841. S.A.S. and Medl. Offr. Mehidpur Pol. Agency and United Melwa Contingent, 15 July 1843; Interpreter, 6 Mar. 1847; Gazetted A.S. Madras, 7 Nov. 1855. d. at Mehidpur, before receiving news of his appointment, 10 Dec. 1855. M. No. 1229, 1855. Name also given as G. Franter, infra; (S.A.L.M.B.).

87. **Franter, George.** S.A.S. Mehidpur, 1843; (S.A.L.M.B.). A misreading of the name of George Tranter, supra.

88. **Fletcher, Frederick.** A.S. (no date); (S.A.L.M.B.). This is Frederick Fletcher, M. No. 1104, 1843, erroneously entered in S.A.L.M.B.

89. **Sheridan, A. J.** Civil Medl. Offr. Kyukphyu, May 1843; Serampur; (C.G. 25 Feb. 1848); Birbhum 18—. Sonthal Insurrection, 1857; (G.O. 22 Apr. 1857; S.A.L.M.B.).

90. **De Cruze, Fanshaw.** S.A.S. Budaon; (C.G. 4 Nov. 1843); 2nd class S.A.S. 16 Nov. 1854; (S.A.L.M.B.).

91. **Rolland, Patrick, Dr.** L.R.C.P. Ed. 18—. Had served in Indian Navy. Uncovd. Medl. Offr. Kotah; (C.G. 29 May 1844; 5th P.C. G.O. 29 Dec. 1849). Jhang, 18—; (S.A.L.M.B.). d. at Jhang, early in 1858; (Indian Mail, 20 May 1858).

92. **De Souza, L—.** S.A.S. Shahjahaupur; (C.G. 19 Oct. 1844; S.A.L.M.B.).

93. **Linton, J. W.** S.A.S. Kotah Contingent; (C.G. 22 Feb. 1845); cancelled; (C.G. 29 Mar. 1845; S.A.L.M.B.).

94. **Salder, M—.** S.A.S. Jodhpur Agency; (C.G. 22 Feb. 1845); Karauli; (G.O. 30 July 1851; S.A.L.M.B.).

* *Vide* note on p. 240.

INDIAN MEDICAL SERVICE

95. **Thorburn, W. C., Dr.** Head Clerk, Mily. Medl. Board, Aug. 1845; Uncovd. Medl. Offr. Goalpara; (C.G. 13 May 1846); Kyukphyu; (C.G. 14 June 1848; S.A.L.M.B.).

96. **Wright, Thomas B—.** M.D. Ed. 1842. L.R.C.P. Ed. 1842. S.A.S. Shekhawati Brigade, 22 Sept. 1845; Jaipur; (G.O. 17 Dec. 1846). First Sikh or Sutlej war, 1845-46, battles of Sobraon and Aliwal, medal with two clasps; (S.A.L.M.B.). In practice at Gainsborough in 1871.

97. **Abbott, J—** (b). M.R.C.S. 1835. Late Surg. 'Essex,' 18—. Appointed Surg. to Danish Settlement at Serampur, after Dr. Voight, the last Danish Surgeon, went to Europe in 1842. Taken over by British Govt. when Serampur was ceded to Britain in 1845; (M.S. Records in Office of Commissioner, Bardwan Division). Resigned, 1 Mar. 1848, handing over to Sheridan, No. 89, supra; (C.G. 25 Feb. 1848; S.A.L.M.B.). Probably same man as Temporary A.S. Abbott, M. No. 1097, 1842. China, 1842.

98. **Long, William Johnston.** M.R.C.S. 1839. Uncovd. Medl. Offr. Assam, 1845. Civil Medl. Offr. Lakhimpur, and 1st Assam Light Infy. 1845; Sibsagar, 1848; Dibrugarh, 1851. M.D. Mar. Coll. Ab. 1854. Gazetted A.S. Madras, 2 Jan. 1856. *d.* in Calcutta, on his way to join, 27 Jan. 1856. M. No. 1231, 1856. Sonthal Insurrection, 1855.

99. **Barton, Francis Ezechiel.** *b.* 1 Oct. 1821. L.S.A. 1846. Appointed A.S. Jan. 1846, but rejected for having only one eye; (List of cancelled appointments).

100. **Maxton, James.** Surg. Calcutta Police; (C.G. 14 Feb. 1846); removed 1848; (S.A.L.M.B.). Probably same as Thomas Maxton, No. 77, supra.

101. **Moore, Ralph, Dr.** M.R.C.S. 1845. Civil Medl. Offr. Midnapur; (C.G. 28 Mar. 1846). Physician and Tutor to Maharaja of Kuch Bihar, 1851; (S.A.L.M.B.).

102. **Norway, Samuel.** M.R.C.S. 1830. L.S.A. 1830. Temporary Civil Medl. Offr. Murshidabad; (C.G. 8 Apr. 1846; S.A.L.M.B.). Afterwards in practice in London. F.R.C.S. 1855. *d.* in London, 4 June 1870.

103. **Lazarus, Edward John.** S.A.S. Dakka; Leave, C.G. 9 Dec. 1846; (S.A.L.M.B.). M.R.C.S. 1850.

104. **O'Sullivan, Matthew, Dr.** Civil Medl. Offr. Jalandhar, 18—; Shekhawati Brigade; (C.G. 22 Dec. 1846); Sandoway; (C.G. 18 Nov. 1848); Manbhum; (C.G. 1 Dec. 1849); Furlough S.C. to Cape; (G.O. 4 Apr. 1850; S.A.L.M.B.).

105. **Pilkington, —.** S.A.S. Jhansi; (G.O. 26 Nov. 1847; S.A.L.M.B.).

*106. **Bose, Bhola Nath.** One of the four medical students taken to England, in 1845, by H. H. Goodeve, to complete their education. M.R.C.S. 1846. Uncovd. Medl. Offr. Bengal, 1847. For many years Civil Medl. Offr. of Faridpur. *d.* at Faridpur, Nov. 1884. Founded by legacy Bhola Nath Bose dispensaries at Barrackpur, and at Mandalai, Hughli district. Second Sikh or Panjab war, 1848-49, medal with clasp; Sonthal Insurrection, 1855-56; (S.A.L.M.B.). v. Hist. of I.M.S. ii. 441, 442.

* The other three were S. C. G. Chuckerbutty, B. No. 1672, 1855; G. C. Seal, No. 107, infra; and Dwarka Nath Bose. The three last took the M.R.C.S. in 1846, Chuckerbutty took it in 1848, as soon as he came of age.

INDIAN MEDICAL SERVICE

107. Seal, Gopal Chandra. M.R.C.S. 1846. Uncovd. Medl. Offr. Panjab. 1847; Gujrat 1850. Second Sikh or Panjab war, 1848-49, medal with clasp; (S.A.L.M.B.).

108. Bose, Umesh Chandra. S.A.S. Posted temply. to 10th N.I. Gorakhpur; (G.O. 13 Nov. 1848; S.A.L.M.B.).

109. Davis, J—, Dr. Civil Medl. Offr. Tezpur, 1848; Sandoway; (C.G. 24 July 1849; S.A.L.M.B.).

110. Tatlock, —, Dr. Civil Medl. Offr. Goalpara; (C.G. 26 July 1848; S.A.L.M.B.).

111. Picachy, David. *b.* Jan. 1830. Calcutta, and King's Coll. Lond. L.M.S. Cal. 1848. S.A.S. Muzafarpur; (C.G. 5 Aug. 1848); Purnea, 1849. M.R.C.S. 1855. Resigned, 1858. Planter's Doctor, Purnea, 1859-65. Civil Medl. Offr. Purnea, Jan. 1865-90. R. Sept. 1890. *d.* at Purnea, 16 Jan. 1911. Indian Mutiny, 1857-58. Name in S.A.L.M.B.

112. Woodford, Charles Ormond. M.R.C.S. 1841. L.R.C.P. Lond. 1842. Surg. Calcutta Police, 1848, and ex-officio Prof. Medl. Jurisprudence, Calcutta Univ.; (C.G. 12 June 1850; (S.A.L.M.B.). F.R.C.S. 1861.

113. Ellis, W. James. S.A.S. Civil Medl. Offr. Pabna; (C.G. 30 June 1849; S.A.L.M.B.). M.R.C.S. 1857.

114. Barry, John B. M.R.C.S. 1844. Civil Medl. Offr. Tezpur; (C.G. 8 Aug. 1849; S.A.L.M.B.). Afterwards in practice in Calcutta.

115. Thomas, A. S.A.S. Civil Medl. Offr. Ramri; (C.G. 7 Nov. 1849; S.A.L.M.B.).

116. Kearney, Daniel. S.A.S. Civil Medl. Offr. Chaibasa, Sinhbhum; (C.G. 4 May 1850); Kyukhpyu; (G.O. 25 Mar. 1852; S.A.L.M.B.). Afterwards in Madras Medl. Service; M. No. 1301, 1860).

117. Thomas, Samuel John. Name entered in A.S. Certs. vol. xxxvii, 1851-52, as Asst.-Surg. Bengal. Bapt. in London, 4 Apr. 1813. Never joined. No further information.

118. Renton, David William. Uncovd. Medl. Offr. 1st Sikh Infy.; (G.O. 24 Feb. 1854); Hazara; (G.O. 3 Nov. 1856); Furlough; (G.O. 22 Jan. 1857; S.A.L.M.B.). *d.* at Bedford, 18 Aug. 1858, aged 29; (Lancet, 4 Sept. 1858).

119. Nowal, J. Civil Medl. Offr. Sylhet; (G.O. 7 June 1854; S.A.L.M.B.).

120. Gasper, M. M. S.A.S. Saharanpur; dismissed; (G.O. 13 Jan. 1855; S.A.L.M.B.).

121. Heude, W. W. M. D. 18—. Civil Surg. Nagpur, to attend 1st Infy. Nagpur Force; (G.O. 17 Aug. 1855; S.A.L.M.B.). This is William Wentworth Heude, M. No. 1110, 1844.

122. Irwin, R. P. Surg. of ship 'Cornwall,' 1855. Served in Sonthal Insurrection, 1855; (S.A.L.M.B.).

123. Minas, P. A. S.A.S. Civil Medl. Offr. Sirsa; (G.O. 9 July 1856; S.A.L.M.B.).

II. MADRAS

1630

1. **Clarke, John.** Appointed Surg. at Armagon; (Court Minutes, 12 Nov. 1630; Sainsbury, vol. v. No. 92, p. 78). No further information.

1645

2. **Whiting, Edward.** Surg. at Jambi, 1645; Madras 1649; Bengal, Feb. 1662/63. v. B. No. 1.

1648

3. **Lumley, Nathaniel.** Ordered to return home from Madras; (Court Minutes, 11 Feb. 1649/50). Died at Madras, 7 Oct. 1650; (L. from Fort St. G. 15 Jan. 1650/51).

1651

4. **Seymour, Arthur** (b). Went out in service of Courten's Assn. Afterwards Surg. of 'Endeavour.' Appointed Surg. at Masulipatam, 19 Feb. 1650/51; (Masul. Cons.; E.F. in I. 1651–54, p. 44). No further information. Name not in list of Company's Servants on Coast, 10 Jan. 1651/52.

1652

5. **Cooper, or Cowper, Robert.** Surg. Pegu factory, Jan. 1651/52, also employed as Factor in Pegu; (list of servants on Coast, 10 Jan. 1651/52). Transferred to Madras, and appointed Surg. there, when Pegu factory was abolished, in Feb. 1655/56. Still Surg. at Madras, 18 Jan. 1657/58; (List of inhabitants, where name is spelt Cowper). No further information. A Surgeon Robert Cooper was buried at Madras, on 21 July 1690, (Malden), but this can hardly be the same man, over thirty years later.

1662

6. **Westrey, John.** Serving as Surg. at Masulipatam in 1662; (M. Cons. 20 Oct. 1662). Name given as Westrow, in List of officers, 1662. No further information.

1665

7. **Bradford, Philip.** Came out as Surg. to Fort St. George, with recruits of 1665; (Love, vol. i. p. 214). d. at Madras in 1668.

1668

8. **Jardin, —.** Surg at Madras in 1668: (E.F. in I. 1668–69, p. 157). No further information.

1670

9. **Waldo, John.** Arrived at Madras as Surg. 14 June 1670; (List of officers, Jan. 1676–77). Went home, 27 Jan. 1677/78. Afterwards Surg. of an interloping ship at Hughli, the 'William and John,' in 1683; (Hedge's Diary, Notes, vol. i. p. 94).

1673

10. **Heathfield, John** (b, c). *b.* 6 Oct. 1623; (tombstone, Cotton). Surgeon of 'President,' 1668–73, captured by Dutch. Appointed Surg. at Masulipatam, 25 Sept. 1673. Surg. Madras, Jan. 1680/81. Factor, 21 May 1685. Reverted to Surgeon, 25 July 1687. *d.* at Madras, 2 Apr. 1688; (M. Cons.). v. Hist. of I.M.S. i. 82–84.

1675 (?)

11. **Morris, Thomas,** (or **Woodward, Thomas**). Physician at Masulipatam, 1675. *d.* there, 21 Dec. 1675; when dying, declared that his real name was Woodward, of Ripley in Worcestershire; (S. Master's Diary, vol. i. 289). One Thomas Morris was Surg. of the 'Ruby' in 1652, can hardly have been the same man.

1676

12. **Mallory,** or **Malory, Henry** (b, c). Surgeon's Mate of 'President.' Appointed Surgeon's Mate at Madras, 31 Jan. 1675/76. Surg., v. Sherman, D. 9 Sept. 1680; (M. Cons.). Transferred to Madapollam, Mar. 1680/81. *d.* at Masulipatam, 5 Aug. 1682. v. Hist. of I.M.S. i. 81–82.

13. **Sherman, Bezaleel.** Appointed Second Surg. Madras, by Desp. from C. 24 Dec. 1675. Arrived, 7 Aug. 1676. *d.* at Madras, 25 Aug. 1680; (M. Cons.). v. Hist. of I.M.S. i. 81.

14. **Grudgfield, James** (c). Serving as Surgeon's Asst. at Bombay, 1676–80; (Bo. Cons. 14 June 1676 and 12 Nov. 1680). Appointed Surg. at Vizagapatam, 12 July 1683; (M. Cons.). Transferred Kadalur, 9 May 1684. Still at Kadalur, 10 Apr. 1688. *d.* before end of 1688. The name of his widow is included in list of unmarried women residing at Madras, at end of M. Cons. for 1688. Bo. No. 44.

1682

15. **Dunn, Isaac.** Surg. at Masulipatam, 12 Oct. 1682. Still serving there, 17 Nov. 1687. No further information.

16. **Bulkley, Edward.** Surg. at Pettipoli in Dec. 1682. Went home from there, date unknown. On return appointed first Surg. Madras, 29 Dec. 1692; (M. Cons.). Resigned, 29 Jan. 1708–09; (M. Cons.). Appointed "Land Customer," and sixth Member of Council from same date. Resigned all appointments, on account of broken health, 20 Jan. 1712/13; (M. Cons.). *d.* at Madras, 10 Aug. 1714; (L. from M. 29 Sept. 1714, para. 119). v. Hist. of I.M.S. i. 88, 89.

1683

17. **Willmott, Samuel** (b, c). Surgeon's Mate of 'Resolution.' Appointed Surgeon's Mate, Madras, 1 Jan. 1682/83; (M. Cons.). Surg. 1686. *d.* 7 Sept. 1687; (Malden).

1684

18. **Watson, Henry.** Surg. Mate, Bengal, 1684. Surg. of 'Hopewell,' at Madras, end of 1688. Went home, 1705. v. B. No. 5.

19. **Plomer, or Plummer, John** (b. c.). Surg. Mate, Madras, 1684. Surgeon, Calcutta, 1695. Resigned, 1697. v. B. No. 6, and Hist. of I.M.S. i. 105.
20. **Warren, William.** Surg. Madras, 1684, Bengal, 1698. Resigned, 1706, and settled at Madras. *d.* 1716. v. B. No. 7, and Hist. of I.M.S. i. 106–108.
21. **Atkins, —.** Surg. at Masulipatam and Pettipoli. *d.* there Feb. 1685; (M.P.L. No. 176 of 6 Mar. 1684/85).

1685

22. **Perce, Francis** (b, c). Surgeon's Mate of 'Rochester,' appointed for either Madras or Priaman (Sumatra), 9 Feb. 1684/85; (M.P.L. No. 106, 9 Feb. 1684/85). No further information. Probably sent to Priaman.
23. **Poyntell, Edmund** (c). Appointed Surg. Masulipatam, 10 Dec. 1685; (M. Cons.). No further information.

1686

24. **Hart, Samuel** (c). Surg. in Bay, 1686; Madras, 1689; discharged, 1692. War in Bengal, 1686–87. v. B. No. 8.

1687

25. **Burley, James** (b, c). Surg. of 'Rose.' Appointed Surg. Madras, 5 Sept. 1687; (M. Cons.). No further information.
26. **Ozler, Bernard** (b, c). Surg. of 'Loyal Adventure,' wrecked, 7 Oct. 1687. Appointed Surg. Madras, 10 Oct. 1687; (M. Cons.). No further information.

1688

27. **Browne, Samuel** (b, c, e). Surg. of 'Dragon.' Appointed Surg. Madras, v. Heathfield, D. 7 May 1688; (M. Cons.). Accidentally poisoned Mr. Wheeler, Member of Council, 30 Aug. 1693; (M. Cons.); Discharged, 30 Nov. 1697, Bulkley having returned to Madras in 1692, and Court disallowing appointment of a second Surgeon; (M. Cons. 2 Jan. 1697/98). Offered appointment of Surgeon at Chutanuti, (Calcutta), 13 Jan. 1697/98, but declined it. Assay Master, Madras, 11 Aug. 1698. *d.* at Madras, 22 Sept. 1698. v. Hist. of I.M.S. i. 89–92.

1689

28. **Blackwall, Richard Benoni Ebenezer** (b, c). Surg. Mate of 'Resolution,' appointed Surg. at Conimir, 24 June 1689; (M. Cons.). Surg. Fort St. David, 1693. Accused of treason, offering to betray Fort St. David to Nawab of Karnatak; (M. Cons. 31 Jan. 1693–94). Under trial over a year. Council found that his sanity rather than his loyalty was at fault. Released early in 1695. Permitted to practice as Attorney, 1 Apr. 1695. Appointed Surg. to West Coast (Sumatra), 25 Feb. 1696/97; (M. Cons.). *d.* there, date not given; (M. Cons. 3 Mar. 1700/01). v. Hist. of I.M.S. i. 92–96. S. No. 1.
29. **Jones, Rowland.** Surg. Mate, Madras; *d.* there, 15 Apr. 1690; (Malden).
30. **Cooper, Robert.** Surg. at Madras; *d.* there, 21 July 1690; (Malden). Possibly same as Robert Cooper, No. 5, supra, 1756; but hardly probable.

1692

31. Faucet, Thomas (c). Surg. Madras, 23 Nov. 1692. Appointed to Fort St. David, v. Blackwall, 12 Mar. 1693/94. Leave to sea, six months, 8 June 1699. Accountant and second in Council at Masulipatam, 1701. Factor at Fort St. George, 1703. Resident at Masulipatam, 15 Aug. 1704; (M. Cons.). Resigned, date not ascertained. Reappointed as junior Merchant, 1 Sept. 1707. Third in Council at Vizagapatam, 1710. Senior Merchant, 1718. d. at Ingeram, as Resident there, 11 July 1723; (M. Cons. Dec. 1723). Name often spelt Faucett in Records; in M.P.L. No. 862 of 1694 is misprinted Famet. v. Hist. of I.M.S. i. 96–97.

1696

32. Royer, Joseph (c). Appointed Surg. Mate, Fort St. David, 18 May 1696; (Fort St. D. Cons. 6 July 1696). Surg. there, v. Faucet, Jan. 1699. Mentioned as dead in M.P.L. No. 1232 of 30 Aug. 1704. Name spelt Royall in M.P.L. No. 282 of 11 May 1696.

33. Cotter, John (b, c). Surg. of 'Dragon,' dismissed for "Mutiny," (really intended desertion); (M. Cons. 17 Jan. 1786/87). Surg. at Vizagapatam in 1696; (List of officers, M. Cons. Jan. 1696/97). Name still in list, Jan. 1697/98; out of list, Dec. 1698.

1698

34. Rawdon, Edward (c). Had been apprentice to Dr. Bulkley for six years, appointed Surg. Mate, Madras, 13 Jan. 1697/98; (M. Cons.). Assay Master, Madras, 29 Sept. 1699; (M. Cons. 19 Oct. 1699). Chief Mate, 6 Mar. 1704; (M. Cons.). No further information.

1699

35. Thompson, — (c). Sent as Surgeon's Asst. to Fort St. David, 23 Mar. 1698/99; (M. Cons.). No further information.

1701

36. Gray, Michael. Surgeon, Masulipatam, 1701; Fort St. David, 1702; Calcutta, 1705; resigned, 1706. v. B. No. 16, and Hist. of I.M.S. i. 109.

37. Ingram, Robert (c). Appointed Hosp. Asst. at Madras, from Apr. 1701; (M. Cons. 5 June 1701). Called Second Mate, and pay increased, M. Cons. 12 Nov. 1702. Discharged at own request, 30 Aug. 1703; (M. Cons.).

1702

38. Supply, Anthony. Surg. to New Company, Masulipatam, 1702. Surg. Fort St. David, v. Atkins, 1 Feb. 1705; (M. Cons.). Resigned, 30 Mar. 1709, and went home as Surg. of 'Kent'; (M. Cons. 30 Mar. 1709). Returned as Surg. to Capt. Edward Harrison, the Governor, who took over charge on 19 Jan. 1710/11. Appointed Second Surg. Madras, v. Chadsley, D. 30 May 1711; (M. Cons. 21 July 1711). Resigned on account of ill-health, 16 Jan. 1715/16; (M. Cons.).

1703

39. Atkins, Charles. Surg. at Gombroon, sent to Fort St. George, on account of misconduct, May 1703; (M. Cons. 27 May and 10 June 1703). Surg. at Fort St. David, v. Royer, D. 30 Aug. 1704; (Letter from Madras to Fort St. David, of that date, where name is spelt Aitkins). Dismissed, 1 Feb. 1704/05; (M. Cons.). Bo. No. 58. S. No. 7.

40. Hall, Joseph (b, c). Surg. Mate of 'Colchester.' Appointed Surg. Mate, Madras, v. Ingram, R. 30 Aug. 1703 ; (M. Cons.). Sent home as Surg. of 'Queen,' M. Cons. 8 Nov. 1705. d. on 'Queen' on passage home ; (M. Cons. 7 Aug. 1710).

1705

41. Morton, David (c). Surg. Mate, Madras, v. Hall, 8 Nov. 1705 ; (M. Cons). Surg. Fort St. David, v. Supply, R. 30 Mar. 1709 ; (M. Cons.). Resigned, 19 Mar. 1710/11 ; (M. Cons.).

1707

42. West, Robert. Surg. at Vizagapatam, 5 Aug. 1707 ; (List of inhabitants). d. at Vizagapatam, 14 May 1718 ; (M. Cons. 20 June 1718).

1709

43. Morgan, ——. Surg. Mate at Madras. Resigned, 26 Aug. 1709 ; (M. Cons.).

44. Robson, Thomas. b. 1683. Surg. of 'Montague.' Appointed Second Surg. Madras, 29 Jan. 1708/09 ; (M. Cons.). Here, and in M. Cons. of 7 Feb. 1708–09, his name is incorrectly given as Robinson. First Surg. v. Chadsley, D. 30 May 1711 ; (M. Cons. 7 June 1711). d. at Madras, 6 May 1720, aged 37 ; (Malden, and tombstone, [Cotton]).

45. Westoby, John (c). Appointed Surg. Mate, Madras, v. Morgan, R. 26 Aug. 1709 ; (M. Cons.). No further information.

46. Douglas, William (c). Surg. Mate, Madras, 26 Sept. 1709 ; (M. Cons.). Appointed Factor and Surg. to West Coast (Sumatra), 2 Jan. 1709/10 ; (M. Cons.). Appointed fifth in Council and Storekeeper at Fort York, 4 Aug. 1710 ; (S. Cons.). d. at Fort York, 21 Sept. 1711 ; (S. Cons.). S. No. 11.

1710

47. Chadsley, Richard. Appointed Chief Surg. at Madras, by Desp. from Court, 13 Jan. 1709/10. Arrived, 14 July 1710 ; (M. Cons.). d. at Madras, 30 May 1711 ; (M. Cons. 7 June 1711).

48. Carasco, Nicholas. Appointed Surg. Mate at Kadalur, 2 Aug. 1710 ; (Fort St. D. Cons.). Had served in both Dutch and Danish service. No further information.

1711

49. Jolly, Francis (or **Henry,** or **John**) (c). Appointed Surg. at Fort St. David, v. Morton, R. 19 Mar. 1710/11 ; (M. Cons.). Called John Jolly, in list of officers, Dec. 1711. Called Francis Jolly, Chirurgien Major, in Fort St. D. Cons. of 4 Dec. 1711, where he gives evidence about an autopsy. Discharged at own request, 17 June 1711 ; (M. Cons. where he is called Henry Jolly).

50. Stevens, John George (c). Appointed Second Surg. Mate, Madras, 10 Sept. 1711 ; (M. Cons.). Sent to West Coast (Sumatra), 22 Jan. 1713/14 ; (M. Cons.). Posted Bantall, 29 Mar. 1714 ; (S. Cons. ; where his name is given as Stevenson). S. No. 14.

1712

51. **Pichier, Andrew** (c). Appointed Second Surg. Madras, v. Supply, R. in Jan. 1716, from Aug. 1716; (M. Cons. 17 Sept. 1716, which state that he had served for four years, since 1712, on West Coast, Sumatra). d. at Madras, 6 Sept. 1729; (Malden). S. No. 15.

1713

52. **Munro, Duncan.** Appointed Surg. Mate, Madras, 23 June 1713; (M. Cons.). Granted discharge and leave to England, 15 Sept. 1718; (M. Cons.). Sailed, 21 Sept. in ' Success,' wrecked next day at Trivambore; (M. Cons. 6 Oct. 1718). Appointed Surg. v. Robson, D. 24 May 1720, and Chief Surgeon, by order of Court, 4 Aug. 1720; (M. Cons.). Resigned, 14 Jan. 1725/26; (M. Cons.).

53. **Machan, Saxbee.** Appointed Surg. Mate, Madras, 22 July, 1713; (M. Cons.). No further information.

1717

54. **Holmes, Thomas** (b, c). Surg. of ' Katharine.' Appointed Surg. at Fort St. David, v. Jolly, R. 17 June 1717; (M. Cons.). d. there, 8 Sept. 1719, or earlier; (M. Cons. 14 Sept. 1719).

1718

55. **Wyche, Matthew** (c). Appointed Surg. Masulipatam, 14 Mar. 1717/18; (M. Cons.). Surg. Fort St. David, v. Holmes, D. 14 Sept. 1719; (M. Cons.). d. at Fort St. David, 17 June 1724; (Fort St. D. Cons.).

56. **Raworth, Samuel.** Came out as a private soldier by last ships, appointed Second Surg. Mate, Madras, 15 Sept. 1718; (M. Cons.). Paid 44 pagodas for discharge from military service, 9 Feb. 1720/21; (M. Cons.). No further information.

1719

57. **Strachan, John.** Surg. Fort York, 29 Aug. 1714; (S. Cons. 29 Sept. 1714). Given commission as Ensign, 31 Jan. 1716/17 (S. Cons.). Appointed Surg. and Ensign at Vizagapatam, 13 July 1719; (M. Cons.). Reported as ill past hope of recovery at Vizagapatam in M. Cons. of 16 Jan. 1719/20. S. No. 18.

1721

58. **Rider, William** (b, c). Surg. of ' Bridgwater,' Appointed Surg. at Vizagapatam, 26 Jan. 1720/21; (M. Cons.). Resigned, 27 July 1721; (M. Cons.).

59. **Ringer, C.** (c). Appointed Surg. at Vizagapatam, v. Rider, R. 27 July 1721; (M. Cons.). No further information.

60. **Farquharson, William** (b, c). Surg. Mate of ' Monmouth.' Appointed Surg. Mate, Madras, 5 Nov. 1721; (M. Cons. 29 Jan. 1721/22). Surg. Fort St. David, v. Wyche, D. 10 Nov. 1724; (Fort St. D. Cons.). d. at Fort St. David, 21 Nov. 1725; (Fort St. D. Cons. 25 Nov. 1725). His will is given in full: he came from Aberdeenshire, was unmarried, and left his property to his sisters.

1724

61. Armitage, John. Surg. Mate at Fort St. David in 1724, reports on murder of Ensign Key; (M. Cons. 3 Oct. 1724). Dismissed, 4 Nov. 1728; (Fort St. D. Cons.).

62. Munro, Andrew. Surg. Mate at Madras in 1724; (M.P.L. No. 945 of 1724). Surg. Fort St. David, v. Gray, R. 1733; (List of officers, M. Cons. 31 Dec. 1733). Surg. Madras, v. R. Douglas, R. 9 Feb. 1741/42; (M. Cons.). Mayor of Madras, 1754. Retired from active work, and appointed Consulting Physician, 28 Dec. 1756; (M. Cons.). *d.* at Madras, 25 Oct. 1757; (Malden). War in Karnatak against France, 1745–50. Siege of Madras, and capture by French, 10 Sept. 1746.

1725

63. Ramsay, George. Appointed by Court as Surg. Madras, 2 Feb. 1723/24; (Desp. from Court, 2 Feb. 1723/24, M.P.L.). Joined, June 1725, and appointed Surg. Mate, there being no vacancy as Surgeon; (M. Cons. 22 June 1725). Surg. v. Duncan Munro, R. 14 Jan. 1725/26; (M. Cons.). *d.* at Madras, 1 July 1726; (Malden).

1726

64. Thriepland, George (c). Surg. Fort St. David, 10 Jan. 1725/26; (Fort St. D. Cons.). *d.* at Fort St. David, 14 Jan. 1731/32; (Fort St. D. Cons.).

65. Douglas, Robert (c). Surg. West Coast, (Sumatra), 13 June 1726; (M. Cons.). Surg. Madras, v. Lindsay, D. 22 Aug. 1730; (M. Cons.). Resigned, 30 Jan. 1741/42; (M. Cons.). Went home in 'Wager,' sailed, 6 Feb. 1741/42. S. No. 32.

66. Lindsay, Matthew (b, c). Surg. of 'Lyell,' 1725–26. Surg. Mate, Madras, 18 June 1726. Surg. v. Ramsay, D. 4 July 1726; (M. Cons.). *d.* at Madras, 21 Aug. 1730; (Malden).

1728

67. Gordon, Thomas (c). Surg. Mate, Madras, 20 Jan. 1727/28, having paid four pagodas for discharge from military; (Genl. L. from M. 20 Jan. 1727/28, para. 38). At Arcot in 1740; (M.P.L. No. 122 of 1740). Physician to Mahfuz Khan, imprisoned at Kadalur in 1748; (M.P.L. No. 1998 and 2014 of 1748). No further information.

68. Barlow, Nathaniel. Surg. Mate, Calcutta, 1728. Surg. Madras, 1729, served up to 1749. v. B. No. 31, and Hist. of I.M.S. i. 135.

1729

69. Turing, Robert (c). *b.* Sept. 1711, fourth son of Sir Robert Turing, Bart. of Foveran, Aberdeenshire. Appointed Surg. Mate, Fort St. David, 27 Aug. 1729; (M.P.L. No. 1142 of 1729). Transferred to Madras as Surg. Mate, 31 Jan. 1735/36; (Fort St. D. Cons.). Surg. Vizagapatam, v. Gibson, D. 18 May 1741; (M. Cons.). Second Surg. Fort St. David, 22 Feb. 1748/49; (L. to C. 22 Feb. 1748/49, para. 40). Shown as Second Surg. Fort St. George, in list of 1749. Called Head Surgeon in M. Cons. of 22 Jan. 1760, also Medl. Storekeeper. *d.* at Madras, 26 Dec. 1764. Name wrongly spelt Turning in S.A.L.M.M. Karnatak war, 1745–50; siege of Madras and capture by French, 10 Sept. 1746. v. Hist. of I.M.S. i. 138, 139.

1732

70. **Gray, George** (c). Surgeon, Fort St. David, 1732; Kasimbazar, 1733; Calcutta, 1738; Resigned, 1760. *d.* 1781. Capture of Calcutta, 1756. v. B. No. 35, and Hist. of I.M.S. i. 142.

71. **Stringer, —.** Surg. Vizagapatam, date of appointment not recorded; succeeded by Gibson, in 1736; (M.P.L. No. 627 of 29 Jan. 1736/37).

1734

72. **Douglas, William.** Surg. Mate at Madras, allowed to go home sick, Jan. 1734/35; (Genl. L. from M. 13 Jan. 1734/35). Reappointed Surg. Mate, on return, 10 Aug. 1738; (M. Cons.). Dead in 1744, account of estate in L. from B. 11 Dec. 1744.

1735

73. **Gibson, William** (b, c). Surg. of 'Britannia,' 1733; of 'Beaufort,' 1735. Surg. at Vizagapatam, 1735; (M. Cons. 14 Feb. 1735/36). *d.* at Vizagapatam in 1739; (Genl. L. from M. 15 Jan. 1739/40).

1736

74. **Cooper, Samuel.** Surg. Mate at Fort St. David, *d.* there 9 July 1737; (Fort St. D. Cons.).

1737

75. **MacKnight, James,** (or **William**) (c). Appointed Surg. Mate, Madras, 19 July 1737; (M. Cons. where name is given as James Mackneight). Had come out as a free merchant; (Genl. L. from M. 5 Oct. 1737). Transferred Fort St. David, 19 Aug. 1737; (Fort St D. Cons.). Discharged, 7 Sept. 1741; (Fort St. D. Cons.). Reappointed Surg. Mate, Madras, 23 Aug. 1742; (M. Cons. where name is given as William MacKnight). *d.* at Madras, 11 Oct. 1743; (Malden).

1739

76. **Belsches, William** (b, c). Surg. " Winchelsea,' lost leg at Canton. Surg. Mate, Calcutta, 1740. Surg. Fort St. David, 1742. Resigned, 1750. v. B. No. 39, and Hist. of I.M.S. i. 139.

1740

77. **Welsh, J.** (d). Appointed by Court, Surg. Mate, Madras 2 Apr. 1740; (Desp. from C. that date, M.P.L.). No further information. Apparently never joined.

1742

78. **Hooke, (or Cooke), Joseph** (c). Appointed Surg. Mate, Fort St. David, v. MacKnight, 23 Aug. 1742; (M. Cons. where name is given as Cooke). Joined, 31 Aug. 1742; (Fort St. D. Cons. where name is given as Hooke. *d.* in Calcutta, 17 May 1748; (St. Anne's Burial Regr., where name is spelt Hook).

1743

79. **Scott, John.** (d). Appointed by Court as Surg. Madras, 11 Jan. 1742/43; Desp. from C, that date, M.P.L.). Appointment again made in Desp. from C. 7 May 1746, para. 43. No further information. Apparently never joined. In S.A.L.M.M. name is given as Scott, — (no Christian name).

80. **Lyon, William** (c). Appointed First Surg. Mate, Madras, from 10 Sept. 1743 ; (M. Cons. 22 Sept. 1743). *d.* at Madras, 11 Nov. 1745 ; (Malden).
81. **Sheafe, John** (b, c). Surg. of ' Scarborough,' Jan. 1741/42 ; (B. Cons. 27 Jan. 1741/42). Appointed Second Surg. Mate, Madras, 22 Sept. 1743 ; (M. Cons.). *d.* at Madras, 9 May 1745 ; (Malden).

1745

82. **Lightfoot, Stephen** (b, c). Surg. Mate of ' Benjamin,' 1744–45 ; (M. Cons. 4 Feb. 1744/45). Appointed Second Surg. Mate, Madras, 12 Oct. 1745 ; (M. Cons.). *d.* at Dakka, Sept. 1749. B. No. 42.

1747

83. **Munro, James.** Appointed Surg. Mate, Madras, 10 Feb. 1746/47 ; (Desp. from C. 6 Mar. 1750/51, para. 86). Surg. Vizagapatam, 22 Feb. 1748/49 ; (Fort St. D. Cons.). *d.* at Vizagapatam, 31 July 1751 ; (L. from Fort St. D. 30 Sept. 1751, paras. 22, 23, and S.A.L.M.M.).

1748

84. **Hinchley, Joseph.** Surg. Mate, Madras, 1748. Transferred Fort St. David, 21 Mar. 1750/51 ; (L. from M. to Fort St. D. that date, M.P.L. No. 1185 of 1751). Surg. to Forces at Arcot, 13 Feb. 1752 ; (M.P.L. No. 2308 of 13 Feb. 1752). Surg. 9 Jan. 1758 ; (M. Cons.). Declined appointment as Surg. Madras ; (M. Mily. Cons. 13 Nov. 1771). R. 9 Oct. 1775 ; (M. Cons. ; had served 28 years). Karnatak war, 1745–50 ; battle of Kaveripak, 29 Feb. 1752 ; (Orme, Various, vol. 287, p. 343).

1749

85. **Wilson, James** (b). Surg. of ' Princess Amelia,' 1743–44 ; of ' Kent,' 1745–46. Appointed Surg. Mate, Madras, 27 Jan. 1748/49, by Desp. from C. that date, para 41. Surg. Mate, Devecotta, 2 Oct. 1749 ; (M. Cons.). Surg. Fort St. David, v. Belsches, R. 8 Jan. 1749/50 ; (Fort St. D. Cons.). Surg. Mate, Madras, appointed to read prayers, and conduct Church duties there, 24 Dec. 1750 ; (M. Cons.). Called up from Trichinopoly, to be Second Surgeon, Madras, on resignation of Andrew Munro, 28 Dec. 1756 ; (M. Cons.). Resigned, 1 Oct. 1763 : (M. Cons. 4 Oct. 1763). Sailed on ' Plassey,' 12 Nov. 1763. Karnatak war, 1750–53, siege of Trichinopoly, 1753. Wrote an account of siege of Trichinopoly, which may be found in Orme MSS. Various, vol. xv, pp. 1–51 ; and Orme, India, vol. v. p. 1.
86. **Page, John** (b). Surg. Mate at Fort St. David in 1749 ; (List of 1749, where his name is also given under Bengal). Left Madras before 1756, noted as " come home," in above list, in a note of later date. Surg. of ' Portfield ' in 1756 ; (Bo. Cons. 15 Oct. 1756). Appointed Surg. Bombay, 25 Apr. 1759 ; (Desp. from C. to Bo. 25 Apr. 1759, para. 114). First Surg. v. Heriot, R. 25 Mar. 1760 ; (Bo. Cons.). Appointment cancelled, " choosing a mercantile way of life " ; (Bo. Cons. 28 Mar. 1760, and Genl. L. from Bo. 4 Apr. 1760, para. 29). Surg. Surat, 1763; (L. from Bo. 24 May 1763, para. 184). Surg. Bombay, Mar. 1764; (L. from Bo. 25 Mar. 1764, para. 121). Resigned, 14 Dec. 1764 ; (L. from Bo. that date, para. 118). Bo. No. 114.
87. **Hancock, Tyso Saul.** Surg. Mate, Fort St. David, 1748. Surg. Madras, 1758 ; Kasimbazar, 1759 ; Calcutta, 1760. Resigned, 1761. Reappointed, 1770. *d.* 1775. v. B. No. 46, and Hist. of I.M.S. i. 169–171.

88. **Taylor, John.** Surg. Mate, Madras, 1749; Bengal, 1754; Calcutta, 1760. Head Surgeon. Resigned, 1771. Siege and capture of Calcutta. v. B. No. 48.

89. **Bingley,** (or **Bangley,** or **Bengley**), **Thomas** (b). Surg. of 'York,' 1744, name spelt Bingley. Surg. Mate at Fort St. David in 1749, where name is given as Bangley. In pay lists of 1750 and 1751, name is spelt Bengley; in list of 1754, Bingley. No further information.

90. **Hamilton, Samuel.** Surg. Mate at Fort St. David in lists of 1749 and 1754. No further information.

91. **Harmston, Samuel.** Surg. Fort St. David, d. there in 1749; Will entered in Fort St. D. Cons. of 4 Dec. 1749, Robert Turing is one of the witnesses.

92. **Key, John.** Surg. Mate at Fort St. David in pay lists of July and Dec. 1751, and of Dec. 1752. No further information.

93. **Massey, Francis William.** Surg. Mate, Fort St. David, in pay list of 31 Jan. 1749/50. Granted sick leave, 16 Jan. 1756; (M. Cons.). d. at Madras, 23 Oct. 1758; (Malden).

1750

94. **Grindal, Richard** (d). Appointed Asst. Surg. Madras, in Desp. from C. 22 Mar. 1749/50, para. 20. "Does not go"; (Desp. from C. 28 Nov. 1752, para. 32). Never joined.

95. **De Wendler, Peter** (d). Appointed A.S. for Coromandel Coast in Desp. from C. 29 Nov. 1750, para. 33. Apparently never joined.

96. **Burrows, John.** Shown as Surg. Mate at Fort St. David in pay lists of 1750, 1751, and 1752. No further information.

1751

97. **Jennins, Moses.** Shown as Surg. Mate, Fort St. David, in pay list of 30 Sept. 1751. Name omitted in pay list of 12 Feb. 1751/52. No further information.

98. **Gregorio, Daniel.** Shown as Surg. Mate, Fort St. David, in pay list of Dec. 1751. No further information.

*99. **Wilson, James.** Nominated Surg. Mate, Madras, in Desp. from C. 19 Dec. 1755, para. 79; (S.A.L.M.M. where name is spelt Willson). But was serving at Arcot in 1751; (v. infra). Surg. Vizagapatam, 1755–57. Third Surg. Madras, 12 June 1759, v. Hancock, transferred to Bengal; (M. Cons.). d. at Madras, 7 Dec. 1761; (Malden). War in Karnatak, 1751–57; siege of Arcot, 1751; capture of Vizagapatam by French in 1757, taken prisoner. Author of A Diary of the Siege of Arcot, contained in Orme MSS. India, vol. ii. pp. 292–297; and Various, vol. xiv.

1752

100. **Swinton, Archibald.** b. 1731. A.S. 20 July 1752; (M. Cons.). Surgeon, 1758. Ensign, Bengal Infy. 1 Aug. 1759. Resigned his rank as Surgeon, 4 Jan. 1761; (B. Cons. 16 Jan. 1761). Lieut. 10 Feb. 1761.

---

* The two James Wilsons were both serving together as Surgeons of Madras in 1759–61. The account of the siege of Arcot in the Orme MSS., Various, is there stated to be by Dr. Wilson, "not the old." It appears, therefore, that the two Wilsons were both serving with the Army in 1751, J. W. senior at Trichinopoly, and J. W. junior at Arcot, and that the latter was serving in India when nominated by Court in 1755. The handwriting of the diaries of the two sieges, Trichinopoly and Arcot, is quite different.

Capt. 18 Oct. 1763. Resigned, 23 Jan. 1766. *d.* at Bath, 6 Mar. 1804. Raised the original 10th B.I. at Midnapur in 1763; it was called Sultin-Ki-Paltan, and mutinied at Phillour in 1857. Karnatak war, 1752–57, wounded at Vellore; (M. Cons. 30 Apr. 1753). Circars, 1758–59. Biderra, 25 Nov. 1759. Bihar war of 1763, battle of Undhwa Nala, capture of Monghir, wounded, and capture of Patna, wounded, lost right arm. Author of Narrative of the Disputes between the Dutch and the English in Bengal in 1759. v. Hist. of I.M.S. i. 240, 241.

101. **Boswell, Alexander.** Surg. Mate, Fort St. David, in pay list of Dept. 1752. At Trivedi, 2 Apr. 1753; (M. Cons.). Transferred from Arcot to charge of hosp. at Trichinopoly, 7 Feb. 1757; (M. Cons.). Appointed Surg. at Madras, v. J. Wilson, junior, D. 10 Dec. 1761; (M. Cons.). He never took up this appointment, but remained on military duty till he was appointed Surgeon to Nawab Muhammad Ali, of the Karnatak, in whose service he remained till his retirement on 12 Feb. 1776. Name spelt Boiswell in S.A.L.M.M. War in Karnatak, 1753–60.

102. **Cudmore, John.** Shown as Surg. Mate, Fort St. David, in pay list of Dec. 1752; omitted in that of Dec. 1753. No further information.

1753

103. **Maule, Charles** (b, c). Surg. of ' Bombay Castle,' 1748–53. To remain in India as Surg. 21 Mar. 1753; (L. from M. that date, para. 20). Posted to Negrais Island. Surg. Vizagapatam, v. Wilson, 28 June 1759; (M. Cons.). Resigned, 6 Feb. 1771, and went home on ' Vansittart.'

104. **Keir, Archibald** (b, c). Surg. of ' Godolphin,' 1752–53. Appointed Surg. Army, Madras, 20 Apr. 1753; (M. Cons.). To rank next below Boswell; (M. Cons. 30 Jan. 1855). Accompanied force under Clive to Bengal in 1756. Lt. Bengal Infy. 1757, Capt. 1758. Resigned, 27 Aug. 1758; (B. Cons.). Went to England. Returned as a free merchant, and settled at Patna. Rejoined army as Captain at the time of the officers' mutiny in 1766. Resigned, 1 Sept. 1768. Applied to rejoin as Surg. in 1785, but not accepted; (Genl. L. from B. 22 Feb. 1785, paras. 45–46). War in Karnatak, 1753–56; Recapture of Calcutta, 2 Jan. 1757. Probably at Plassey. Author of Thoughts on the Affairs of Bengal, London, 1772. v. Hist. of I.M.S. i. 167–169.

105. **Wolsey, —.** Appointed Surg. Mate, Madras, 20 Aug. 1753, came out with Col. Scott; (M. Cons.). No further information. Name is printed Horseley in M.P.L. No. 4101 of Aug. 1753.

106. **Anderson, William** (b, c). Surg. Mate of ' Edgbaston.' Appointed Surg. Negrais Island, 30 Oct. 1753. (M. Cons.). Sick leave 1756. Bihar war, 1763; killed in Patna Massacre, 11 Oct. 1763. v. Hist. of I.M.S. i. 187. B. No. 55.

1754

107. **Stewart, William.** Serving as Surg. Mate, Madras, in 1754; (M. Cons. 6 May 1754). Name in list of 1754. At Devecotta and Madras in 1756; (M. Cons. 17 May 1756). Possibly the same as William Stewart, (B. No. 70), who was appointed by Desp. from C. 1 Apr. 1760, para. 115 posted to Bengal on arrival, and died at Kasimbazar, in May 1763. Karnatak war, 1754–56.

108. **Thornton, Richard.** Surg. Mate, Madras, 25 Nov. 1754; (M. Cons.). Transferred from Chingleput to Trichinopoly, 13 Jan. 1757; (M. Cons.). No further information. Karnatak war, 1756–57.

1755

109. Warke, Robert (b). Surg. Mate of ' Dragon,' 1750 ; (St. H. Cons. 11 June 1750). Serving as Surg. at Fort St. David, ordered to proceed to camp, 4 Mar. 1755 ; (M. Cons.). Still serving in camp, 26 Apr. 1756 ; (M. Cons.). d. in Bengal, 1758 ; (" lately," L. from M. 13 Mar. 1759, para. 59). Name spelt Wark in S.A.L.M.M. Karnatak war, 1755–56.

1756

110. Briggs, Stephen. Appointed Surg. Mate, Fort St. David, 16 Jan. 1756, formerly Asst. in King's Hospital, i.e. Surg. Mate in A.M.D. ; (M. Cons. 16 Jan. 1756). Surg. 3 July 1759 ; (M. Cons.). Granted title of Surg. Genl. as Senior Medl. Officer of troops in field, from Dec. 1759 ; (M. Cons. 1 Dec. 1760) ; the first officer of the I.M.S. to receive this title. Troops having returned to cantonments, title of Surg. Genl. abolished; (M. Mily. Cons. 15 Feb. 1763). Second Surg. Madras, v. James Wilson, senior, R. 30 Jan. 1764 ; (M. Pub. Cons.). R. 11 Feb. 1771 ; (M. Mily. Cons.), went home on ' Vansittart.' Karnatak war, 1756–60, siege of Madura, 1764. v. Hist. of I.M.S. i. 300–301.

111. Nelson, James. Serving as Surg. at Vizagapatam when that factory was captured by French in Sept. 1757, and taken prisoner. No further information. Possibly same as James Nelson. (B. No. 136), A.S. Bengal, 14 Sept. 1767. Not to be traced.

1757

112. La Forge, —, alias Bernard. A French Surg. Mate, applied for appointment as Medl. Officer in Madras Service at Fort St. David, in Apr. or May 1757, and at Trichinopoly in Dec. 1757 ; doubtful if he was ever actually so employed. Hanged for treason at Trichinopoly, 28 Dec. 1757 ; Orme MSS. India, vol. xiii. p. 3444–3447, and Various, vol. lxi. pp. 123–130). v. Hist. of I.M.S. ii. 222–228.

1758

113. Brown, Abraham (b, c). Surg. of ' Triton,' wrecked off Fort St. David, Apr. 1758. Served temply. as Surg. at Fort St. David, in siege, captured by French under Lally, June 1758, and afterwards at Madras, without pay. Granted gratuity of 500 pagodas (M. Cons. 3 July 1759).

114. Sprat, or **Spratt, John** (b). Surg. of ' Winchelsea,' 1748. Surg. Mate, Madras, 1758. Served during unsuccessful siege of Madras by Lally, Dec. 1758 to Feb. 1759. No further information for twenty years, except name in list of inhabitants of Madras in Dec. 1762. d. at Madras, 9 May 1780 ; (Malden).

115. Gordon, William (a, c). Appointed First Surg. Mate, Madras, July 1759 ; (list of 1787). Promoted Surg. and posted Palamcotta, v. Sinclair, sick, 30 June 1766 ; (M. Cons.). Appointed Surg. to Nawab Amir-ul-Amra, second son of Muhammad Ali, Nawab of Karnatak, 8 Apr. 1771 ; (M. Cons.). Reverted to regular line, Mar. 1778 ; (M. Mily. Cons. 4 Mar. 1778). Passed over for promotion to Head Surgeon, 1786. Furlough to Europe, 15 Apr. 1792 ; (M. Cons.). Cert. Corp Surg. 1792. On return promoted Head Surg. and posted Masulipatam, 4 June 1793 ; (M. Cons.). Sick leave to Madras, 24 Aug. 1793. d. at the Luz, Madras, 4 Sept. 1793. Was the first to suggest the foundation of a hospital for Indians at Madras, on 19 Nov. 1787 ; (M. Mily. Cons. Miscell. Book, 1787). War with France, 1759–60, siege of Pondicherri,

1760. First Maisur war, 1764–69, taken prisoner at Erode, 23 Dec. 1768, dangerously wounded in trying to escape near Palamcotta, (reported as killed, M.P.L. No. 6875 of 7 Apr. 1769), kept as prisoner at Seringapatam till peace made. Second Maisur war, 1780–82, as Senior Surgeon of Southern Army. A long memorial on his services, dated, Tanjore, 28 Feb. 1777, is contained in M. Mily. Cons. of 24 Mar. 1777. v. Hist. of I.M.S. i. 277 ; ii. 190, 414.

1759

116. Tetch, William Just (c). A Dane, formerly in Danish service. Appointed Surg. Mate, 4 Jan. 1759 ; (M.P.L. No. 5526 of 16 Nov. 1758, and No. 3795 of 4 Jan. 1759). No further information.

117. Gray, William. Surg. in camp, Wandiwash, 1759 ; (M. Cons. 25 Oct. 1759). Surg. of hospital at Arcot, 26 Sept. 1761 ; (M. Cons.). Surg. at Manilla, 1762. Sick leave to Madras, 2 Sept. 1763. In M. Cons. of 12 Jan. 1764 spoken of as junior full Surgeon in list, now at Manilla ; Lucas to rank next Gray. Returned to Europe for ill-health ; (L. from M. 5 Nov. 1767, para. 87). Capture of Manilla, 1762. Siege of Madura, 1764 ; (M. Cons. 24 July 1764). E.F. 25.

118. Matthews, — (b, c). Surg. of ' Pocock.' Appointed Surg. Mate, Madras, 27 May 1760 ; (M. Cons.). Name given as Mathers in S.A.L.M.M. No further information.

119. Brindley, James (b, c). Surg. of ' Worcester,' 1758, deserted ; (M. Cons. 11 Sept. 1758). Late Surg. at Croee (Sumatra), entertained at Madras, 15 July 1760 ; (M. Cons.). No further information. S. No. 58.

120. Meyer, John Hendrik (a). b. 1725. Surg. Mate at Karikal, serving under Boswell, Apr. 1760 ; (M. Mily. Cons. 21 Apr. 1760, where name is spelt Meyers). d. at Trichinopoly, 24 Mar. 1767, aged 41 ; (tombstone, Cotton). Karnatak war, 1760 ; capture of Karikal.

121. Hunter, Robert. Surg. Mate, Fort Marlbro, 1753–60. Taken prisoner when Sumatra was captured by French, Apr. 1760. Served at Kadalur in 1764. Surg. Calcutta, 1765. d. in 1777. v. B. No. 54. S. No. 55.

122. Reeford, Nathaniel. Surg. Mate. d. at Madras, 3 Sept. 1760 ; (Malden).

123. Norbury, William. Surg. Mate. d. at Madras, 3 Jan. 1761 ; (Malden).

1761

*124. Pasley, Gilbert (a, c). b. 1733. Came to India in 1754 as Surg. Mate of Adlercron's regiment, the 39th Foot, " Primus in Indis," now 1st Batt. Dorset regt. Name not in Johnston's Roll of R.A.M.C. Appointed Surg. Madras Army, 16 Feb. 1761 ; (M. Cons.). When James Wilson, junior, Second Surg. Madras, died in 1761, Boswell was appointed Second Surg. in his place from 10 Dec. 1761 ; (M. Cons.), and Pasley to officiate for him. As Boswell never joined the appointment, Pasley was confirmed in it. Senior Surgeon, Madras, v. Briggs, R. 11 Feb. 1771. Appointed Surg. Genl. 25 Mar. 1780 ; (M. Pub. Cons.). d. at Madras, 22 Sept. 1781 ; (Malden). His name is spelt Paisley in S.A.L.M.M. and often in records ; but Pasley is the correct spelling. War in Karnatak, 1754–60. v. Hist. of I.M.S. i. 301, 302.

* Gilbert Pasley and James Anderson were the two most prominent figures in the Madras Medical Service in the eighteenth century. Before I began to compile the Madras Medical List I had never heard of Gilbert Pasley. On working out his history, I found that he was my own great-great-grand uncle. Gilbert Pasley was the fourth son of James Pasley, of Craig, near Langholm, Dumfriesshire. James Pasley married Magdalene, daughter of Robert Elliot, of Middlemiln, Roxburgh, and died on 13 Apr. 1773, aged 78, when his eldest son, Robert,

1762

125. Anderson, James (b, c, e). *b.* 17 Jan. 1738. M.D. Ed. 17—. Surg. Mate, afterwards Surg. 'Drake,' 1759–61 ; Surg. of 'Essex,' 1762. Appointed Surg. Madras Army, in 1762, for service in Manilla expedition ; and while at Manilla held a commission, he states, in King's and Company's service at the same time ; (M. Mily. Cons. 26 Oct. 1786). Name not in Johnston's Roll of R.A.M.C. In a letter dated 8 Aug. 1782 ; (M. Mily. Cons. Miscell. Book, 1782), he states that he was Surg. to King's Artillery and M.D. before entering I.M.S. Second Surg. Madras, v. Scott, D. 27 Apr. 1772 ; (M. Cons.). Surg. Major, 27 Nov. 1780 ; (M. Mily. Cons.). Senior Surg. Madras, with title of Surg. Genl. v. Pasley, D. 17 Oct. 1781 ; (M. Mily. Cons.). First President Medl. Board, with title of Physician Genl. 14 Apr. 1786. *d.* at Madras, 15 Aug. 1809. Philippine expedition, 1762, capture of Manilla. Field Service in Northern Circars, 1766–67. Author of Letters on Cochineal, 1781 ; Letters on Cochineal, Coffee, and Silk, 1789–96 ; Minerals of Coromandel, 1797 ; a volume of his correspondence was published at Madras in 1800. v. Hist. of I.M.S. ii. 14–16.

126. Cushing, James. A.S. Madras, 17—. *d.* at Madras, 1 June 1762 ; (Malden).

127. Dormond, William. A.S. 17—. *d.* at Madras, 3 June 1762 ; (Malden).

128. Dickie, George. A.S. 17—. *d.* at Madras, 13 Aug. 1762 ; (Malden).

129. Clarke, William. A.S. at Vellore, sick leave to Madras, 15 Dec. 1762 ; (M. Cons.). *d.* at Madras, 15 Feb. 1763 ; (Malden).

1763

130. Threlkeld, Jonas. A.S. 17—. *d.* at Madras, 19 Dec. 1763 ; (Malden).

131. Sinclair, Arthur (a, c). Surg. 89th Foot, Appointed Surg. Madras Army, 6 June 1763 ; (M. Mily. Cons.). Surg. Major, 16 May 1783 ; (M. Mily. Cons.). Passed over for appointment to Medl. Board or to Head Surg. in Apr. 1786, on account of ill-health. *d.* at Masulipatam, June 1786. Name not in Johnston's Roll of R.A.M.C. Karnatak war, 1763–64 ; siege of Madura, 1763–64.

---

succeeded to the estate. Robert Pasley's daughter Magdalene, married my great-grandfather (mother's father's father), Lt.-General Alexander Dirom, of Mount Annan, Dumfriesshire. James Pasley's second son, James, and third son, John, died without offspring. Gilbert was the fourth son. On 6 Sept. 1778 he married, at Madras, Hannah Dashwood, but left no children. Eight months after his death his widow, Hannah Pasley, married Thomas Elliot Ogilvie, at Madras, on 27 May 1782. The fifth son, Thomas, entered the Navy, rose to the rank of Admiral, and was created a Baronet for his share in Lord Howe's great victory over the French fleet on 1 June 1794. One of Sir Thomas' daughters was also christened Magdalene. The sixth son, Charles, was a merchant in London. James Pasley left also four daughters. His third daughter, Margaret, married George Malcolm, of Burnfoot, near Langholm, and became the mother of ten sons, among whom were the four "Knights of Liddesdale." Her second son became Sir James Malcolm, K.C.B., Colonel of Marines ; the third was Admiral Sir Pulteney Malcolm, K.C.B. ; the fourth was General Sir John Malcolm, G.C.B., Governor of Bombay ; and the tenth was Admiral Sir Charles Malcolm, K.C.B. James Pasley's fourth daughter, Gilbert Pasley's youngest sister, also a Magdalene Pasley, married in 1772, after his retirement, Stephen Briggs, No. 110, supra.

An obituary notice in Hickey's Gazette, of 20–27 Oct. 1781, states that Gilbert Pasley entered the army as a Lieutenant-Fireworker, but soon exchanged the sponge and rammer for the gold-headed cane ; i.e. left the Gunners to join the Medical Department. No other reference has been found to his ever having held a combatant commission, and it appears that the notice in Hickey's Gazette is mistaken. His name does not appear in Kane's List of Officers of the Royal Artillery, 1715–1865. The Madras Military Consultations of 16 Feb. 1761, appointing him a Surgeon in the Madras Service, state that he came to India as a Surgeon's Assistant in Colonel Adlercron's regiment, was stationed at Pondicherri at the time, and was well qualified in his profession.—D.G.C.

132. **Bowen, William** (a). A.S. 1763, mentioned as serving in the field in M. Mily. Cons. of 31 Jan. 1764. Surg. 1767. A list of Surgeons in M. Mily. Cons. of 8 Apr. 1771, shows his name as a full Surgeon, next below Carere and above Scott. *d.* at Ganjam, 23 Nov. 1776; (M. Mily. Cons. 9 Dec. 1776). Karnatak war, 1763–66; siege of Madura, 1763–64.

133. **Walker, Benjamin** (a). A.S. 17—. Shown as serving at siege of Madura in M. Mily. Cons. of 24 July 1764. No further information.

134. **Fowke,** —. (a). A.S. 17—. Shown as serving at siege of Madura in M. Mily. Cons. of 24 July 1764. No further information.

135. **Davis, or Davies, Thomas** (a). Appointed by Court, in Desp. to M. 30 Dec. 1763, para. 112. Arrived at Madras, and posted to Kadalur, 13 Aug. 1764; (M. Mily. Cons.); apparently joined as full Surgeon. Appointed Surg. Major in the Field, v. Lucas, transferred to Madras on Pasley's death, 18 Dec. 1781; (M. Mily. Cons.). Head Surg. Madras, and third M.M.B. 14 Apr. 1786. *d.* at Madras, 24 Apr. 1788. Name is indiscriminately spelt Davis and Davies in the Records. First Maisur war, 1767–69. Karnatak war, 1778–80. Second Maisur war, 1780–82. v. Hist. of I.M.S. ii. 15–17.

1764

136. **Lucas, Colley Lyon** (c). *b.* 1730. Surg. A.M.D. in England, 12 June 1761. Chief Surgeon to the expedition to Manilla, under Sir William Draper, 1762. Half-pay, 1764, v. Johnston's Roll of R.A.M.C. No. 633. Appointed Surg. Madras Army, to rank next Gray, 9 Jan. 1764; (M. Cons.). [The wording of this order, "to rank next Gray," gave rise to a long dispute as to seniority between Anderson and Lucas, when both were appointed to the Medical Board in 1786. Apparently Anderson, who was absent at Manilla at the time, was simply forgotten, when Lucas was ranked next Gray. The question was finally settled in Anderson's favour.] Appointed Surg. Major in Field, 14 Jan. 1779; (M. Mily. Cons.). Chief Surgeon and second M.M.B. 14 Apr. 1786. *d.* at Madras, 25 Mar. 1797. D. and M. give his name, incorrectly, as L. Lucas Colley; the date of his first commission as 1765, and that of his promotion to Surgeon as 14 Apr. 1786, the date when he was appointed to the Medl. Board. Philippine expedition, 1762, capture of Manilla. Karnatak war, 1764–65; siege of Madura, 1764. Northern Circars, 1766–67. Capture of Mahé, 1779. Second Maisur war, 1780–84, siege of Vellore. Third Maisur war, 1790–91, as P.M.O. Madras Army, with title of Surg. Genl.; capture of Seringapatam. v. Hist. of I.M.S. i. 302–303; ii. 14–19.

137. **Suffrein-Tonnelle, Bartholomew** (a, c). A Frenchman. A.S. 9 Jan. 1764; (M. Mily. Cons. where name is spelt Soffrain). Not entitled to promotion; (M. Mily. Cons. 23 Oct. 1767. Here he is stated to have served eight years with the army, which would date his appointment in 1759). In list of 1771 shown as "assistant in hospital, not to rise." *d.* at Ellore, 5 May 1774; (M. Mily. Cons. 16 May 1774). Karnatak war, 1764–66.

138. **Buchanan, Duncan** (a, c). Had served in Navy; appointed Surg. 30 Jan. 1764; (M. Mily. Cons.). Surg. Trichinopoly Hosp. v. Hinchley, 18 Oct. 1775; (M. Mily. Cons.). Surg. Tanjore, 13 Jan. 1777; (M. Mily. Cons.). Resigned, 25 Dec. 1782; (M. Mily. Cons.). Karnatak war, 1764–66; siege of Madura, 1764, wounded, lost a leg; (Orme MSS. Various, vol. xxvii. p. 125). In L. from M. of 13 Aug. 1783, para. 514, reporting his retirement, he is called **William Buchanan**.

139. **Raine, William** (c). Surg. Mate, A.M.D. Mentioned as Asst. to Mr. Lucas in H.M.'s hospital in M. Cons. of 3 Jan. 1764. Appointed A.S. Madras Army, and posted to Vizagapatam, 26 Mar. 1764; (M. Mily. Cons.). Name not in Johnston's Roll of R.A.M.C. Surg. 1 Jan. 1765; (List of 18 Sept. 1787). In list of 8 Apr. 1771 is shown seventh on list of full Surgeons, between Gordon and Davis. Surg. Ellore, 25 Apr. 1771; (M. Mily Cons.). When Medl. Board was constituted, on 14 Apr. 1786, was passed over for promotion, both to Board and to Head Surg. at his own request, in order to retain his civil appointment. Head Surg. Madras, and Third M.M.B. v. Davis, D.; appointed by Court, after supersession at Madras, from 4 July 1790. Lost Seat at Board, and reduced to Head Surg. when Board was reduced to two members, 7 Jan. 1796. Second M.M.B. v. Lucas, D. 25 Mar. 1797. Furlough to Europe, 1800. d. on board 'Asia,' on passage to Europe, 7 July 1800. Karnatak war, 1776–78. Second Maisur war, 1780–84, wounded and taken prisoner in Col. Baillie's defeat at Perambakan, 9 Sept. 1780; (Proc. Med. Board, 29 Apr. 1794), prisoner at Bangalore till end of war. Third Maisur war, 1791–92; (M. Mily. Cons. 26 and 29 Apr. 1791). v. Hist. of I.M.S. ii. 16–19.

140. **Rockholt,** — (a). Mentioned as Surg. or A.S. at Trichinopoly, in M. Mily. Cons. 14 Mar. 1764. No further information.

141. **Charlton, John** (a, d). Nominated by Court, Desp. 1 June 1764, para. 27; (S.A.L.M.M.). Never joined.

142. **Duncanson, Neil** (a, d). Nominated by Court, Desp. 1 June 1764, para. 27; (S.A.L.M.M.). Never joined.

143. **Taylor, Cheek** (a, d). Nominated by Court, Desp. 1 June 1764, para. 27; (S.A.L.M.M.). Apparently never joined. He was in Calcutta towards end of 1764, a Cert. signed by him is quoted in B. Cons. of Dec. 1764; (C.P.L.).

144. **Carere, John** (really **Jean**) (a, c). A Swiss Protestant, in service of Muhammad Yusuf, Governor of Madura, in 1763. Deserted to English, 26 Feb. 1764. A.S. Madras Army, 13 Aug. 1764; (M. Mily. Cons.). Surg. 20 Apr. 1767. Was living on 15 Feb. 1780, when he addressed a letter to Madras Government; d. before 1 Apr. 1780; (M. Mily. Cons.). Karnatak war, 1764; siege of Madura.

1765

145. **Orton, Thomas** (a). C.C.S. 1760. M.D. Mar. Coll. Ab. 1765. Nominated by Court, List of Packet, 30 Apr. 1765; (S.A.L.M.M.). Appointed Surg. at Vellore, 15 July 1765; (M. Mily. Cons.). Resigned and went home in 'Vansittart,' Jan. 1771; (M. Mily. Cons. 11 Feb. 1771).

146. **Whyte, James** (a, c). A.S. June 1765. Surg. 8 Apr. 1771; (M. Mily. Cons.). Head Surg. 14 Apr. 1786. R. 15 Feb. 1788; (M. Mily. Cons.). First Maisur war, 1768–69. Second Maisur war, 1780–84; taken prisoner in Col. Braithwaite's defeat at Anagudi, 18 Feb. 1782, released Apr. 1784; (M. Mily. Cons. 22 Apr. 1784). v. Hist. of I.M.S. ii. 16, 17, 191.

147. **Walker, Thomas** (a, c). Had been educated as a medical man, enlisted in Company's Army, and went out as a private soldier in the 'Pitt.' Appointed A.S. 24 June 1765; (M. Mily. Cons.). Appointed Cadet, on recommendation of Genl. Caillaud, 30 Dec. 1766; (M. Mily. Cons.). Ensign, 1 Jan. 1767, Lieut. 9 May 1768; (M. Mily. Cons.). Shown

as dead in Madras M.S, Army list at end of Mily. Cons. of 1778. D. and M. do not give his name in their lists, either as combatant or medical officer.

1766

148. Simoens, Antonio (or **Anthony**) (c). A.S. June 1766. In a petition, dated 21 Jan. 1780 ; (M. Mily. Cons. Miscell. Book for 1781), says he has served 14 years. In list of 1771 shown among " assistants, not to rise." Promoted Surg. Supy. 20 July 1782 ; (M. Mily. Cons. where name is given as Simson). Invalided, 1788. d. at Kadalur, Feb. 1803. Name given as Simson in list of 1767, Simmons in list of 1771, Simons in M. Mily. Cons. of 31 May 1781, Simones in list of 1786 ; Simeon in M. Mily. Cons. 20 July 1782. First Maisur war, 1768–69, siege of Tanjore.

149. **Turing, Robert (a). A.S. appointed by Court, joined, 4 Aug. 1766 ; (M. Mily. Cons.). Surg. 8 Apr. 1771. Head Surg. 14 Apr. 1786, posted Masulipatam. R. 16 Feb. 1788 ; Second Maisur war, 1780–84, affair in Devalampetta Pass, 22 Oct. 1781 ; (M. Mily. Cons. 28 Dec. 1781). v. Hist. of I.M.S. i. 139.

150. Barry, John (a). Surg. appointed by Court, joined, 4 Aug. 1766 ; (M. Mily. Cons.). Resigned, 26 Jan. 1770 ; (M. Mily. Cons.).

151. Doak, — (a). Surg. Accidentally killed at Sikandramali, Dec. 1766. Poligar war, 1766. v. Hist. of I.M.S. ii. 189.

152. Laney, F. (a, c). A.S. 1766. In a petition, dated, 6 Apr. 1773, in M. Mily. Cons. of 24 Apr. 1773, says he has served seven years, and asks to be promoted to Surg. ; refused. In list of 1771 is shown among " assistants, not to rise." Transferred to Masulipatam, on account of ill-health, suffering from consumption, 2 Mar. 1778 ; (M. Mily. Cons.). Probably died soon after. His name is variously given in Records as Lamie, Lamee, and Laney, but the signature on the above petition (a copy), is F. Laney.

153. Knappe, Elias (a). Surg. d. at Madras, 4 June 1766 ; (Malden).

154. Saunders, David (a, c). A.S. Madras, end of 1766, complains of supersession by Peters, in M. Mily. Cons. 29 May 1769. d. at Madras, 21 Dec. 1769 ; (Malden).

155. Peters, James (a). Surg. 4th New York Independent Co, A.M.D. 17 Nov. 1760. Resigned, 6 Apr. 1763. v. Johnston's Roll of R.A.M.C. No. 604. Appointed by Court, Surg. Madras, 12 Dec. 1766, had served in A.M.D. since 1760 ; (L. of 27 May 1782, in M. Mily. Cons. Miscell. Book for 1782). Joined as full Surgeon. Spoken of as acting Surg. Major at Mahé, 7 June 1781 ; (M. Mily. Cons.). Superseded for promotion, and allowed to reside where he likes, on pay of 40 pagodas a month ; (M. Mily. Cons. 29 May 1782). This seems to be the last mention of him ; no further information as to date of death or retirement. Karnatak war, 1778–79, capture of Mahé. First Maratha war, 1780, with Madras detachment. Second Maisur war, 1780–82.

1767

156. Wilson, Richard (a). Appointed Surg. Bombay Marine, 4 Apr. 1767 ; (Desp. to Bo. 4 Apr. 1767, para. 27). Never joined at Bombay. A.S. Madras, 23 Oct. 1768 ; (M. Pub. Cons.). Serving at Pondicherri in Jan. 1779 ; (M. Mily. Cons. 11 Jan. 1779). No further information. Capture of Pondicherri, 1778.

* Turing appears to be Sir Robert Turing, sixth Baronet, who succeeded his brother Sir Inglis, fifth Baronet, in 1791, and died, leaving no male issue, on 21 Oct. 1831. Burke makes no mention of the sixth Baronet as having served in Madras, but says nothing about his life before his succession to the Baronetcy.

157. Nott, Joseph (a). Appointed Surg. Bombay Marine, 4 Apr. 1767 ; (Desp. to Bo. 4 Apr. 1767, para. 27). Never joined at Bombay. A.S. Madras Army, 18 Sept. 1767 ; (M. Mily. Cons.). Name in list of 1767, but not in that of 1771. No further information.

158. Duffin, William (a, c). A.S. 4 Aug. 1767 ; (M. Pub. Cons.). Surg. 8 Apr. 1771 ; (M. Mily. Cons.). Head Surg. 14 Apr. 1786. M.M.B. v. Davis, D. 30 Apr. 1788. Court ordered his removal and reversion to Head Surg. in favour of Raine (q.v.), from 4 July 1790, but as Lucas was absent on deputation, he retained his seat on the Board after Raine joined. On return of Lucas, retired and went home ; (Mily. L. from M. 15 Mar. 1792, para. 27). Permitted to return to India, in Mily. Desp. to M. 6 May 1795, para. 3. Did not rejoin. Given a gratuity of 1,000 pagodas, and considered to have relinquished the service, 30 June 1797 ; (Mily. Desp. to M. 30 June 1797, para. 8). Was Churchwarden of St. Mary's Church, Madras, 1790–91. v. Hist. of I.M.S. ii. 16–18.

159. Gahagan, or Geoghegan, Terence (c). b. 1750. A.S. 4 Aug. 1767 ; (M. Pub. Cons.). In list of 8 Apr. 1771, his name is entered as one of the six " assistants in hospital, not to rise." Cert. Corp. Surg. 1777. Surg. 12 June 1778, after taking diploma. Head Surg. 1 May 1788. M.D. K.C. Ab. 1798. Head Surg. Presidency, and Third M.M.B. 31 Dec. 1799. R. 29 Feb. 1812. d. in London, 21 Jan. 1814 ; (G.M. Mar. 1814). First Maisur war, 1767–69, action at Trinomali, siege of Tanjore. Karnatak war, 1778–80. Second Maisur war, 1780–84, Col. Baillie's defeat at Perambakam, 11 Sept. 1780, affair in Devalempetta Pass, 23 Oct. 1781. v. Hist. of I.M.S. i. 209 ; ii. 19–22.

160. Tenier, or Tennier, — (a. c). A Frenchman. A.S. 1767. Name in list of 1767, stationed at Chingleput. In list of 1771, shown as one of the six " assistants in hospital, not to rise." Superannuated, 18 Dec. 1781 ; (M. Mily. Cons. where name is spelt Ternay). d. 22 Jan. 1782, at Chingleput ; (Letter of that date from John Ruding, Surg. at Chingleput, in M. Mily. Cons. Miscell. Book, 1782).

161. Serpieter, — (a, c). A.S. 1767. Name in list of 1767, serving in 3rd Regt. Not in list of 1771. No further information.

162. Ash, — (a, c). A.S. 1767. Name in list of 1767, serving at Vellore. Not in list of 1771. No further information.

163. Swallow, — (a, c). A.S. 1767. Name in list of 1767, serving at Fort St. George. In list of 1771, shown as one of the six " assistants in hospital, not to rise." No further information.

164. Martin, Jean (a, c). Surg. 8 Dec. 1767. A Frenchman, who had been in the service of Haidar Ali, and deserted to English, bringing with him all Haidar's European cavalry, at Vaniambadi, on 8 Dec. 1767. Was appointed full Surg. at once, and posted to Corps of Foreigners. A letter, dated 29 Sept. 1767, from Fort St. George to Col. Joseph Smith, states that Martin had been in British service at Madura, before he joined Haidar Ali. In list of 1771 his name appears last on the list of full Surgeons, with the note " not considered as on the Establishment." In Aug. 1786 was arrested on a charge of murder, tried at Madras in July 1787, and acquitted. Restored to service in Oct. 1787, and reposted to Foreign Corps ; (M.P.L. No. 1652 of 9 Aug. 1786, and No. 1961 of 31 Oct. 1787). His history is given in a Memorial, dated 1 Jan. 1795, in M. Cons. of 20 Feb. 1795. No further information, as to death or retirement. He is usually called John Martin in the Records, but his real Christian name was Jean. v. Hist. of I.M.S. ii. 239–240.

1768

165. **Fabre, or Favré,** — (a, c). A.S. to Corps of Foreigners, 2 Jan. 1768; (M. Mily. Cons.). Unable to join on account of ill-health, ordered to be admitted to hospital, to receive pay until his recovery, and then to be discharged; (M. Mily. Cons. 11 Sept. 1769). Name spelt Fabre on first, Favré on second occasion. No further information.

166. **Scott, Samuel** (a). Surg. 29 Mar. 1768. Second Surg. Madras, v. Briggs, R. 11 Feb. 1771; (M. Mily. Cons.). d. at Madras, 20 Apr. 1772; (Malden).

167. **Beckett, James** (a). C.C.S. 1764. M.D. Mar. Coll. Ab. 1768. Nominated by Court, List of Packet, 27 Mar. 1768; (S.A.L.M.M.). Joined, 24 Aug. 1768, posted to Army; (M. Mily. Cons.). Surg. Vellore, v. Anderson, transferred, 18 May 1772; (M. Mily. Cons.). Senior Surg. to troops attacking Mahé, v. Lucas, 17 Feb. 1779; (M. Mily. Cons. where he is called Thomas Beckett). No further information. Name not in List of 1787. Possibly the same James Becket who served in Sumatra, 1762–66. S. No. 62. Capture of Mahé, Mar. 1779.

168. **Buchanan, John** (a, d). Nominated by Court, List of Packet, 29 Mar. 1768; (S.A.L.M.M.). Never joined.

169. **Crane, John** (a, d). Nominated by Court, List of Packet, 29 Mar. 1768; (S.A.L.M.M.). Never joined.

170. **Rank, Thomas** (a, d). Nominated by Court, List of Packet, 29 Mar. 1768; (S.A.L.M.M.). Never joined.

1769

171. **Buirette, Jean** (a, c). A.S. Madras army, 9 Jan. 1769; (M. Mily. Cons. where name is spelt Bouriett). In list of 1771, where name is spelt Buret, shown as one of the six "assistants in hospital, not to rise." After he was taken prisoner at Jinji, 19 Sept. 1781, said to have entered Haidar Ali's service, and to have served therein till he deserted back to English, in 1786; (M. Mily. Cons. 6 June 1787). Granted a pension of 20 pagodas per month, 1795; (Mily. L. from M. 4 Mar. 1795, para. 12) and posted to Corps of Pensioners. Pension increased to 40 pagodas per month, from 16 Oct. 1804, " was badly treated in 1787;" (Mily. Desp. to M. 30 July 1806, paras. 417, 418). Allowed to draw pension in Bengal, from 1803; (Mily. Desp. to M. 22 Aug. 1804, para. 264). Subsequently appointed Police Surgeon, Calcutta. d. in Calcutta, 4 June 1811; (C.G. 6 June 1811). Name spelt in many different ways in the Records; Buirette, most commonly; Buiretti in S.A.L.M.M.; Bourrett in M.P.L. 9 Jan. 1769. Second Maisur war, 1780–84, taken prisoner at Jinji, 19 Sept. 1781. v. Hist. of I.M.S. ii. 95, 191, 192.

172. **Goodsir, Walter** (a). Nominated by Court, List of Packet, 22 Mar. 1769; (S.A.L.M.M.). Asks for appointment as Surg. at Calcutta, 3 Apr. 1770; (C.P.L.). A.S. Madras, 19 Nov. 1770, posted Ingeram; (M.P.L. No. 1844 of 19 Nov. 1770). d. at Madras, 7 Mar. 1772; (Malden). Karnatak war, 1771, siege of Tanjore.

173. **Forbes, John** (a). Nominated by Court, List of Packet, 22 Mar. 1769; (S.A.L.M.M.). Went out in 'Plassey,' joined at Madras, June 1769, and died there before the end of June; (Hickey's Memoirs, vol. i. 185).

174. Court, Dennet (a, b). Surg. of 'Prince of Wales,' 1765–67. Nominated by Court, List of Packet, 22 Mar. 1769; (S.A.L.M.M.). Went out in 'Plassey,' joined June 1769, and resigned at once; (Hickey, vol. i. 212). Surg. of 'Earl of Ashburnham,' 1779; 'Speke,' 1771–72; 'Wessex,' 1773–74; 'Europa,' 1774–75; 'Nassau,' 1776–77; 'Osterley,' 1778. d. in Calcutta, 16 Sept. 1778; (St. Anne's Burial Regr.). Hickey calls him Denil Court (i, 133), and Dermit (iv. 487).

175. Balfour, Thomas (a, d)
176. Burnett, William (a, d)
177. Lee, William (a, d)
178. Mathewson, John (a, d)

All four nominated by Court, List of Packet, 22 Mar. 1769; (S.A.L.M.M.); but never joined. Burnett may be the same William Burnett, who joined as A.S. Bengal, 14 Aug. 1771, resigned 7 Jan. 1779; d. in 1784. B. No. 212.

1770

179. Wilson, Thomas (a, c). Came out as a recruit, had been bred a Surgeon, and had been acting as Asst. in hospital at Vellore; appointed A.S. in army, 26 Jan. 1770; (M. Mily. Cons.). Surg. 27 Apr. 1772; (M. Mily. Cons.). Second Maisur war, 1780; killed in action in Col. Baillie's defeat at Perambakam, 10 Sept. 1780.

180. Munro, Walter Ross. A.S. Madras, Apr. 1770, transferred Bengal, 27 July 1771. v. B. No. 157.

181. Pringle, Patrick (a, c). A.S. 13 July 1770; (M. Pub. Cons.). Surg. 27 Oct. 1773; (M. Mily. Cons.). d. at Arcot, Nov. 1787; (C.G. 29 Nov. 1787, and G.M. May 1788). Second Maisur war, 1779–81.

182. Binny, or Binney, George (a, c). Mily. Cadet 1770, had been bred a Surgeon, appointed A.S. 13 Aug. 1770; (M. Mily. Cons.). Surg. 27 Oct. 1773; (M. Mily. Cons.). Head Surg. Masulipatam, v. Turing, R. 15 Feb. 1788; (M. Mily. Cons.). d. at Masulipatam, 20 May 1793; (M. Mily. Cons. 28 May 1793). v. Hist. of I.M.S. i. 235, 236.

183. Carthy, Ambrose (a, b, d). Nominated by Court, Lists of Packets, 1770, and 26 Apr. 1771; (S.A.L.M.M.). Never joined. Surg. Mate, 'Royal George,' 1765; Surg. Sumatra, 1765–68, and 1771–73. Accompanied expedition to Borneo, 1773, and died at Passir, Borneo, 15 May. 1773. S. No. 64.

184. MacDowall, James (a, d). Nominated by Court, List of Packet, 1770; (S.A.L.M.M.). Never joined. Surg. 'Talbot,' 1768–69. Surg. Sumatra, 1770. S. No. 69.

185. Morris, George (a). Nominated by Court, List of Packet, 1770; (S.A.L.M.M.). d. at Madras, 30 May 1771; (Malden).

186. Rush, James (a, d). Nominated by Court, List of Packet, 1770; (S.A.L.M.M.). Never joined. Surg. Sumatra, 1770. d. at Fort Marlbro', 26 Feb. 1771; (S. Cons.). S. No. 70.

1771

187. Huggins, James (a, b, d). Surg. of 'Duke of Grafton,' 1768–69. Nominated by Court, List of Packet, 26 Apr. 1771; (S.A.L.M.M.). Apparently never joined. In S.A.L.M.Bo. occurs what is probably the same name, James Huygens, Surg. of 'Mercury,' dismissed at Madras for private trading.

188. Weston, Thomas (a, b). Surg. of 'Britannia.' Appointed by Court, Surg. for Balambangan, 1 June 1771; (list of 1787). Apparently never joined there. A.S. Madras, 1773. Surg. 12 May 1780 (Desp. from C. to M. 12 May 1780, para. 1. " Thomas Weston appointed youngest Surgeon, next below John Simpson "). Ranks above Ferguson ; (Letter of 23 June 1786, M. Mily. Cons. Miscell. Book, 1786). *d*. at Madras, 30 Sept. 1787 ; (Malden). Second Maisur war, 1780-82 ; captured on board ship by Spaniards, taken prisoner to Cadiz ; (M. Mily. Cons. 11 Feb. 1782). Capture of Trincomali, 1782.

189. **Mallet, William** (a, c). C.C.S. Formerly Surg. H.M.S. ' Stag,' appointed A.S. Madras, 18 Nov. 1771 ; (M. Mily. Cons.). Surg. 10 Mar. 1777 ; (M. Mily. Cons.). Dismissed by Court Martial, 30 Jan. 1787 ; (M. Mily. Cons. No particulars given).

1772

190. **Hutton, Thomas** (a, b, d). Surg. of ' Devonshire,' 1767-68 ; of ' Duke of Kingston,' 1769-71. Nominated by Court, List of Packet, Mar. 1772 ; (S.A.L.M.M.). Apparently never joined. Surgeon of ' Asia,' 1785-92. C.C.S. 1787. Probably same as Thomas Hutton, Surgeon, Canton, 1775-76. China, No. 3.

191. **Mein, Nicol** (c). *b*. 1754. Cadet of 1772, had been bred to Surgery, appointed A.S. 20 July 1772 ; (M. Mily. Cons.). Surg. 19 Jan. 1778 ; (M. Mily. Cons.). Head Surg. Trichinopoly, *v*. Whyte, R. 15 Feb. 1788 ; (M. Mily. Cons.). M.M.B. 20 May 1800. *d*. at Madras, 3 Apr. 1804. Second Maisur war, 1781-82, taken prison in ' Yarmouth,' by French frigate ' La Fine,' 15 June 1782 ; (Letter, 7 Sept. 1782, in M. Mily. Cons. Miscell. Book for 1782). *v*. Hist. of I.M.S. i. 235, 236.

192. **Simson**, or **Simpson, John** (a, b, c). Had made three voyages as Surgeon of an Indiaman ; (M. Mily. Cons. 19 Feb. 1776). A Cadet, appointed A.S. from 18 Aug. 1772 ; (Sep. L. from M. 15 Oct. 1772, para. 80). Surg. 19 Feb. 1776 ; (M. Mily. Cons.). Reported dead, 1 Apr. 1780 ; (M. Mily. Cons.).

1773

193. **Mitchell,** — (a, c). An Artilleryman, who had some knowledge of Surgery, appointed to act as A.S. to detachment under Col. Bonjour, from 7 Apr. 1773 ; (M. Mily. Cons. 24 Apr. 1773). No further information.

194. **Leslie, James** (a, b, c). Surg. of ' Anson,' 1769-73. A.S. 26 Apr. 1773 ; (M.P.L. No. 7316 of 26 Apr. 1773). *d*. at Palamcotta, 24 Jan. 1785 ; (tombstone ; Cotton).

195. **Ferguson** or **Fergusson, Finlay** (a, b, c). Surg. Mate, ' Queen,' 1768-69. Surg. Mate, R.N., in fleet under Admiral Harland, appointed A.S. Madras, 24 May 1773 ; (M. Mily. Cons). Surg. 28 May 1779. Surg. Major, Centre Army, 7 Sept. 1790 ; (M. Mily. Cons.). Furlough, S.C. 1792 ; (Mily. L. from M. 31 July 1792, para. 20). Did not rejoin. Struck off in 1795. Third Maisur war, 1790-91.

196. **Campbell, George** (a, b, c). Surg. Mate of ' Ponsborne,' appointed A.S. Madras, 26 July 1773 ; (M. Mily. Cons.). Surg. 1780. Second Maisur war, 1780, severely wounded and taken prisoner in Col. Baillie's defeat at Perambakam, 10 Sept. 1780, and died of wounds as a prisoner at Arni, 18 Sept. 1780.

197. **Ferrier, Alexander** (a, c). Cadet, 1770, Ensign, 1771, Madras Army, allowed to resign his commission, and appointed A.S. Madras, 27 Oct. 1773 ; (M. Mily. Cons.). Had served as Ensign and Surgeon at Achin in 1772. Surg. 28 May 1779. Furlough to Europe, 1788 ; (Mily. L. from M. 1 Mar. 1788, paras. 62, 64). Did not rejoin. Struck off, 1791.

198. **King, —** (a). A.S. Madras, 1773, services lent to Bombay; "Assistant Surgeon in hospital, came from Madras, reported to be of very little use in hospital, ordered to return to Madras"; (Bo. Cons. 24 Dec. 1773, S.A.L.M.Bo.). Taken prisoner by Haidar Ali, after shipwreck on Malabar Coast, 1783, imprisoned at Seringapatam; (Memoirs of War in Asia, 1780-84, pp. 173-179). Received a passage to the Bay in Sept. 1776; (M.P.L. No. 836 of 17 Sept. 1776. No further information. Bo. No. 184.

199. **Jenkins, —** (a). A.S. Madras 1773, services lent to Bombay; Assistant Surgeon in hospital, came from Madras, reported to be of very little use in hospital, ordered to return to Madras"; (Bo. Cons. 24 Dec. 1773, S.A.L.M.Bo.). No further information.

1775

200. **Eastbrook, Thomas Coryndon** (a, c). A.S. 24 July 1775; (M. Mily. Cons.). Sick leave to Bombay, 17 Feb. 1778; (M. Mily. Cons.). No further information.

201. **Croker, S. —** (a, c). C.C.S. Had been first Surg. Mate in a ship of the Line. A.S. from Sept. 1775; (M. Mily. Cons. 19 Feb. 1786, where name spelt Crocar). Surg. 1 Apr. 1780; (M. Mily. Cons. name spelt Crocker). *d.* at Aska, July 1782.

1776

202. **Simpson, David** (b). Surg. Mate, 'Grenville,' 1768-69; Surg. of 'Admiral Pocock,' 1770-71; of 'Earl of Lincoln,' 1771-73. A.S. 1776. At Ongole in May 1776; (M.P.L. No. 463 of 15 May 1776). Transferred from Madura to Trichinopoly, 1 Apr. 1780; (M. Mily. Cons.). Furlough to Europe, 5 July 1786; (M. Mily. Cons.). Did not rejoin. Struck off, 1790.

203. **Rollo, Robert** (a). A.S. 12 Mar. 1776, appointed by Court; (List of 18 Sept. 1787). Surg. 28 Nov. 1780. *d.* at Kadalur, 4 Mar. 1793; (M. Mily. Cons. 12 Mar. 1793).

204. **Howell, Thomas** (a). A.S. 8 Apr. 1776; (M. Mily. Cons.). Surg. 1 Apr. 1780. Leave to England, p.a. 6 July 1787; (M. Mily. Cons.). In S.A.L.M.M. said to have returned to duty in 1791, but no further reference to service in India found. Second Maisur war, 1781-84. Author of Journal of a Passage from India through Armenia and Asia Minor, 1787.

205. **Roxburgh, William** (b, e). *b.* 3 June 1751. Surg. Mate, 'Haughton,' 1773-74. A.S. 28 May 1776. Surg. 27 Nov. 1780. M.D. Mar. Coll Ab. 1790. F.R.C.P. Ed. 1790. Succeeded Colonel Kyd, founder and first Supt. of Calcutta Botanical Gardens, in 1793. Name was never transferred to Bengal list. Furlough, 1813. *d.* in Edinburgh, 18 Feb. 1815. A notice in Annual Biography for 1817 gives date of death as 10 Apr. 1815. Name given as Roxburgh or Roxborough in S.A.L.M.M. Author of a new species of Mahogany, 1793; Plants of Coromandel Coast, three vols, 1795, 1802, 1819; Hortus Bengaliensis, 1814; Flora Indica, two vols, 1820 and 1824, third ed. 1874. Memoirs of Roxburgh were published in Asiatic Journal, vol. i. 1816, p. 28; in Annual Biography, 1817; in Annals of Royal Botanical Gardens, by George King, 1895; and in Dict. Nat. Biography.

206. **Ramsay, Charles** (a, c). A.S. 27 May 1776; (M. Mily. Cons.). Surg. 28 Nov. 1780. No further information. Name not in list of 1786.

207. **Briggs, John** (c). b. 1758. C.C.S. 1776. A.S. 1 Oct. 1776. Surg. 30 Nov. 1780. M.D. K.C. Ab. 1793. Head Surg. 11 Mar. 1796. R. 8 Apr. 1801. d. in Herefordshire, 5 Sept. 1830. Capture of Colombo, 1796, as Head Surgeon.

208. **Adderton, Jeremiah** (a, c). A.S. 21 Oct. 1776; (M. Mily. Cons.). Surg. 1 Dec. 1780. Head Surg. Nizam's detachment, 21 July 1792; (M. Mily. Cons.). Do. Masulipatam, v. Gordon, D, 10 Sept. 1793; (M. Mily. Cons.). d. at Ellore, 29 Sept. 1796. Capture of Mahé, 1779. Second Maisur war, 1780–82. Third Maisur war, 1790–92.

209. **Ruddiman, William** (a, b, c). b. 1756. Surg. Mate of 'Godfrey,' deserted, Sept. 1775; (M. Mily. Cons. 2 Oct. 1775). A.S. 1776. Admitted youngest Surgeon, 30 Apr. 1784, had acted for many years as Surg. to Native Cavalry; (M. Mily. Cons.). M.D. Mar. Coll. Ab. 1791. Resigned, 22 Jan. 1793; (M. Mily. Cons.). d. in London, 20 Jan. 1826; (A.J. Feb. 1826, p. 314).

1777

210. **MacFie, James.** A.S. 5 May 1777. Transferred Bengal, 26 Jan. 1778. d. 11 Apr. 1790. v. B. No. 211.

211. **Richardson, James** (b, c). M.D. Ed. 1770. C.C.S. 1776, or earlier. Surg. of 'Marquis of Rockingham,' 1776–77. A.S. 7 June 1777; (M. Mily. Cons.). Surg. 6 July 1781; (M. Mily. Cons.). Head Surg. Masulipatam, v. Adderton, D, 14 Oct. 1794; (M. Mily. Cons.). M.M.B. 4 Apr. 1804. d. at Madras, 13 Feb. 1807. Second Maisur war, 1780–82, Defence of Ambur under Capt. Harting, 8 Dec. 1780 till surrender on 13 Jan. 1781; (M. Mily. Cons. Miscell. Book, 1781).

212. **Watson, Alexander** (c). M.D. K.C. Ab. 1775. A.S. 7 June 1777; (M. Mily. Cons.). Surg. 6 July 1781. Head Surg. 9 Feb. 1796, v. Mein, on furlough; (M. Mily. Cons.). M.M.B. 6 Aug. 1809. R. 2 Apr. 1821. Second Maisur war, 1780–82, affair in Devalampetta Pass, 23 Oct. 1781; (M. Mily. Cons. 28 Dec. 1781).

213. **Gillespie, Joshua** (c). A.S. 7 June 1777. Surg. 23 Oct. 1781; (M. Mily. Cons.). Head Surg. Nizam's detachment, 10 Sept. 1793; (M. Mily. Cons.). Do. Circars, 18 Apr. 1797; (M. Mily. Cons.). R. 14 May 1799. Second Maisur war, 1780–82. Third Maisur war, 1790–92.

214. **Ogilvy, George.** C.C.S. 1777. A.S. 11 Dec. 1777. Brevet Surg. 9 Feb. 1785. Surg. 30 Sept. 1787. Head Surg. 9 Oct. 1795. R. 11 Aug. 1802; granted an extra pension of £100 a year, on account of long imprisonment in Maisur; (Mily. L. from M. 17 Aug. 1803, para. 192). Second Maisur war, 1780–84, taken prisoner in Col. Baillie's defeat at Perambakam, 9 Sept. 1780, released 1784; (M. Mily. Cons. 12 June 1784).

215. **Anderson, Alexander.** C.C.S. 1777. A.S. 15 Dec. 1777. Brevet Surg. 9 Feb. 1785. Surg. Oct. 1787. Head Surg. in Field, 18 June 1793; (M. Mily. Cons.). Do. Seringapatam, 10 Aug. 1799; (S.A.L.M.M.). d. at Barshwapatam, near Chitaldrug, 28 Apr. 1805. Third Maisur war, 1790–92. Capture of Pondicherri, 1793, as Head Surgeon. Fourth Maisur war, 1799, as Head Surgeon, storm and capture of Seringapatam. Second Maratha war, 1803–04.

1778

*216. **Simpson, Robert** (a, b, c). Surg. of 'Triton,' 1669–70. A.S. 6 Apr. 1778, and granted leave to go to China in the 'Lord North'; (M. Mily. Cons.). *d.* at Tanjore, Sept. 1782; (M. Mily. Cons. 26 Sept. 1782).

217. **Blackader, Alexander** (a, b, c). Surg. Mate, 'Queen,' 1771–72. C.C.S. 1778. A.S. 22 June 1778; (M. Mily. Cons.). Surg. 26 June 1782; (M. Mily. Cons.). Sentenced by Court Martial, in 1791, to eight months' suspension, for neglect of wounded; (Mily. L. from M. 25 May 1792, paras. 31, 32). While under suspension, permitted to resign, not to be employed again; (M. Mily. Cons. 18 May 1792). Still in India, asks to be reinstated, his memorial sent to Court of Directors, in M. Mily. Cons. of 1 Mar. 1796, where name is given as Adam Blackader. Christian name given as Adam in Roll of Corp. Surgeons. Capture of Mahé, 1779; Second Maisur war, 1780–82; Third Maisur war, 1790–91.

218. **Mein, Alexander** (a, c). A.S. 22 June 1778; (M. Mily. Cons.). Surg. 6 Oct. 1785; (M. Mily. Cons. Miscell. Book). *d.* of hydrophobia at Wallajabad, Oct. 1787; (M. Mily. Cons. 19 Oct. 1787). In notice of death, in C.G. of 8 Oct. 1787, is called Mayne.

219. **Konig, or Koenig, John Gerhard.** M.D. 17—. Appointed Botanist and Natural Historian to Company, 17 July 1778; (M. Pub. Cons.). *d.* at Jaganathpatam, 26 June 1785; (C. Pub. Cons. 5 Oct. 1785, No. 10).

220. **Bird, Robert Smith** (a, b, c). Surg. of 'Grenville,' 1768–69; of 'Worcester,' 1770–71; of 'Greenwich,' 1771–73; of 'Salisbury,' 1775–76. Appointed Surg. Madras, to rank next Nicol Mein, No. 191, supra, at particular request of Admiral Sir Edward Vernon, 28 Sept, 1778; (M. Mily. Cons.). Granted leave to return to England, with the late Governor, Mr. Whitehill, on the 'Duke of Kingston,' with permission to return to India in his rank; (M. Mily. Cons. 4 Jan. 1781). Did not rejoin.

1779

221. **Rankin, George** (a). Came out as A.S. for Madras, appointed to do duty at Mahé, 3 Apr. 1779; (M. Mily. Cons. 22 Apr. 1779). In S.A.L.M.M. his name is given as George Rankin. Nominated by Court, Desp. 16 Mar. 1784, para. 22. No further information as to service in Madras. Capture of Mahé, 1779. Probably the same as George Rankin, A.S. Bengal, 17 Mar. 1783. q.v. B. No. 323.

222. **Anderson, George** (c). C.C.S. 1788. A.S. 13 Sept. 1779; (M. Mily. Cons.). In list of 1787, date of appointment is given as Aug. 1778. Brevet Surg. 31 Aug. 1785. Head Surg. 22 May 1810. *d.* at Bangalore, 4 Aug. 1810. D. and M. give dates as, A.S. 1788, Surg. 1 June 1796.

223. **Thompson, Maxwell.** A.S. 1 Dec. 1779. Surg. 1 Nov. 1787. *d.* at Vepery, Madras, 23 May 1807; (C.G. 18 June 1807). Ceylon, 1781–82, capture of Trincomali, 5 Jan. 1782; (M. Mily. Cons. Miscell. Book, 1782).

224. **Rennie, —** (a). Surg. Madras detachment. Killed in action in Genl. Goddard's action of 24 Apr. 1781, in first Maratha war; (India Gazette and Cal. Pub. Advertiser, 9 June 1781). No further information.

---

* There were three medical officers named Simpson serving in the Madras army in 1778–80; John Simpson, No. 192, supra, 1772; David Simpson, No. 202, supra, 1776; and Robert Simpson. In M. Mily. Cons. of 1 Apr. 1780, are mentioned the promotion of Howell to Surgeon, v. Simpson, D.; and the transfer of another Simpson from Madura to Trichinopoly. All three names are given in S.A.L.M.M.

1780

225. Cowill, — (a). A.S. Madras 1780 (?). Posted to detachment at Madura, 9 Apr. 1781; (M.P.L. No. 748 of 9 Apr. 1781). Second Maisur war, 1780–84, taken prisoner, probably at Bednur, 30 Apr. 1783. Name, spelt Cowin, in list of prisoners released by Tipu Sultan, in C.G. of 13 May 1784. No further information.

226. Davidson, — (a). A.S. 1780 (?). Transferred to Condapili, 5 Mar. 1780; (M.P.L. No. 497 of 5 Mar. 1780). Surg. 18 Feb. 1782, v. Whyte, taken prisoner at Anagudi; (M. Mily. Cons. 7 May 1782). d. at Condapili, Kistna District, May 1782; (M. Mily. Cons. 31 May 1782).

227. Ogilvie, Charles. C.C.S. 1779. A.S. 10 May 1780; (list of 1787). D. and M. give date of appointment as 17 Aug. 1781. Surg. 12 Jan. 1790. R. 30 July 1800. War with France, 1780; taken prisoner in the ' Mount Stuart ' by combined fleets of France and Spain, May 1780, was a prisoner some time, after release returned to England, sailed again for India in Mar. 1781, on arrival served some time in Malabar, in Second Maisur war, 1781–82, reached Madras, 17 May 1782; (Memorial, dated, 26 June 1788, in M. Mily. Cons. Miscell. Book, 1788).

228. Miller, Henry. C.C.S. 1780. A.S. 22 May 1780. Surg. 11 Feb. 1789. Head Surg. Jan. 1801. R. 16 Aug. 1808. d. in Scotland, 26 Oct. 1819. First Maratha war, 1781–82, with Madras detachment to Bombay. Ceylon, 1782. Third Maisur war, 1790–91, taken prisoner at surrender of Doraporam; (M. Mily. Cons. 17 Dec. 1790). Fourth Maisur war, 1799.

229. Lord, Thomas (a, c). C.C.S. 1780. A.S. 19 June 1780; (M. Mily. Cons.). Surg. 22 Jan. 1788; (M. Mily. Cons.). d. at Madras, 8 Nov. 1790.

230. Stewart, or **Stuart, Edward** (a). C.C.S. 1780. A.S. 6 July 1780, appointed by Court, List of Packet, 6 July 1780, where name is spelt Stewart. Surg. 16 Feb. 1788; (M. Mily. Cons.). d. at Trichinopoly, 15 Mar. 1795; (M. Mily. Cons. 17 Mar. 1795, where name is spelt Stuart). In S.A.L.M.M. name gven as Stewart or Stuart. Date of appointment given as 18 May 1780 in list of 1787. Name spelt Stuart in Roll of Corp. Surg.

231. Bulman, Job (a, b). Surg. Mate, ' Earl of Elgin,' 1767–68. Surg. of ' Huntingdon,' 1770–74. Appointed Surg. Madras, 2 Dec. 1780; (M. Mily. Cons. 27 Nov. 1780). List of 1787 states that he joined as full Surgeon on 28 Nov. 1780. Furlough, S.C. 5 Jan. 1790; (M. Mily. Cons.). Did not rejoin. Christian name given as Job or John in S.A.L.M.M.; signature is Job; (M. Mily. Cons. 21 Dec. 1780).

1781

232. Trotter, Robert (a). C.C.S. 1780. A.S. 8 Jan. 1781; (List of 18 Sept. 1787). Nominated by Court, Desp. 2 Feb. 1781, para. 18. Surg. 1789. d. at Tanjore, 10 Nov. 1793. In M.P.L. No. 1856 of 25 May 1782, in an order posting him to Chingleput, his name is misprinted Fratter. First Maratha war, 1781–82, with Madras detachment; (B. Pub. Cons. 27 Mar. 1782). Second Maisur war, 1782–84; (M. Mily. Cons. 30 Apr. 1784). Third Maisur war, 1791–92; (M. Mily. Cons. 20 Apr. 1791).

233. **Dempster, William** (a, d).
234. **Foot, John** (a, d).
235. **Hay, John Silvester** (a, d).
236. **Mair, Patrick** (a, d).

Nominated by Court, Desp. 2 Feb. 1781, para. 18. Apparently none of these four ever joined. J. S. Hay was Surg. of ' Harcourt,' 1765–66 ; ' Tilbury,' 1768–69 ; ' Harcourt,' 1770–71 ; ' Gatton,' 1772–73 ; ' Houghton,' 1777–78 ; ' Nassau,' 1782–85 ; (Hardy).

237. **Stuart, George** (a, d). A.S. 2 Feb. 1781. Nominated by Court, Desp. 2 Feb. 1781, para. 18. Apparently never joined. Appears to have been an officer of the A.M.D. who may have been nominated to, but never joined, the I.M.S. Mentioned as King's Surgeon at Tanjore in M.P.L. No. 837 of 18 Mar. 1785. In M.P.L. No. 1631 of Aug. 1786 it is stated that George Stuart, late Surg. Mate, 78th Regt. goes home on the ' London.' Name not in Johnston's Roll of R.A.M.C.

238. **Morton, Joseph** (a). A.S. appointed by Court, 21 Mar. 1781. Arrived at Fort Marlborough on a private ship, en route for Madras, posted to Fort Marlborough (Sumatra) ; (M. Mily. Cons . 31 May 1782). Admitted A.S. Bengal from 13 Jan. 1784 ; (B. Mily. Cons.) ; but apparently never joined in Bengal. Joined at Madras July 1784, and ranked from 21 Mar. 1781 ; (M. Mily. Cons. 15 July 1784). Transferred to Fort Marlborough again as full Surgeon ; (M. Mily. Cons. 3 Aug. 1785). d. at Fort Marlbro', 10 Jan. 1787 ; (S. Cons.). B. No. 249. S. No. 79.

*239. **Ruding, John** (a). Nominated by Court, Desp. 2 Feb. 1781, para. 18. Admitted as " youngest Surgeon," and posted as Field Surgeon, to Army, 6 July 1781 ; (M. Mily. Cons.). Sick leave to England, 7 Feb. 1786 ; (M. Mily. Cons.). Did not rejoin. Second Maisur war, 1781–84.

240. **Skarrow, Thomas** (a, d). C.C.S. 1779. Nominated by Court, Desp. 2 Feb. 1781, para. 18. Never joined. Possibly the same Thomas Skarrow who joined as A.S. on 6 Apr. 1791. No. 347, infra, q.v.

241. **Bowie, Patrick** (b, c). Surg. Mate, ' Bute,' 1773–75 ; ' Granby,' 1776–77 ; Surg. ' Grosvenor,' 1778–81. A.S. 18 Sept. 1781 ; (M. Mily. Cons.). Surg. 13 May 1788. S.S. 1800. R. 13 June 1804. D. and M. give date of appointment as 1 Aug. 1781.

1782

242. **Wynne, John** (a, c). Cadet, Bo. Infy. 31 May 1781. Appointed by Sir Eyre Coote, acting A.S. Madras, from 15 Apr. 1782, having studied at School of Physic ; (M. Mily. Cons. 15 Sept. 1783, where he is also permitted to return to Bombay). Ensign, Bo. Infy. 21 Nov. 1782. Lt. 29 Mar. 1788. Capt. 6 Sept. 1797. d. at Bombay, 10 Sept. 1798. D. and M. give his name in their Bo. Army List. Second Maisur war, 1782–83.

243. **Scott, John** (a, c, d). Senior Surg. Mate, 73rd Regt. appointed A.S. Madras, 7 May 1782 ; (M. Mily. Cons.). No further information. Probably never joined. Name is not given in Johnston's Roll of R.A.M.C.

244. **De Villeneuve, Pierre Roger** (a, c). A French Surgeon, deserted to English, had been Surg. of ' Solomon ' fireship, and in French army, asks for appointment ; (M. Mily. Cons. 1 Aug. 1782). Asks pay for services as Surgeon at Pulicat ; (M. Mily. Cons. 26 Mar. 1785). No further information.

* John Ruding was the last officer who joined as a full Surgeon, without going through the rank of Asst. Surgeon, except Patrick Russell, No. 259, infra, 1785, who joined as a specialist, at an advanced age, and not for general service.

245. Kincaid, John (a, b, c). *b.* 1752. Surg. of 'Earl of Hertford,' 1781–82. A. S. 23 Nov. 1782; (M. Mily. Cons.). Surg. Feb. 1790. Sick leave to China and Europe, 1792. Applies for pension, in letter of 1 Dec. 1792, from Canton; (M. Mily. Cons. 22 Jan. 1793). *d.* at Raphoe, Ireland, 22 Aug. 1817; (G.M. Oct. 1817). Third Maisur war, 1790–92.

1783

246. Barter, James (c). Surg. Mate, 23rd Light Dragoons, appointed A.S. Madras, 14 Apr. 1783; (M. Mily. Cons.). Permission to join I.M.S. refused by his O.C. Col. Lloyd; (M. Mily. Cons. 11 Feb. 1784). Apparently did not join. Resigned, 26 Apr. 1785; (M. Mily. Cons.). Name not in Johnston's Roll of R.A.M.C. Reappointed, 23 Mar. 1790; (M. Mily. Cons.). Confirmed by Court; (M. Mily. Cons. 23 Sept. 1791). Surg. 20 June 1798. *d.* at Masulipatam, 22 Sept. 1807. D. and M. give 23 Mar. 1790 as date of appointment. Capture of Colombo, 1796; (P.R.). Poligar rising in Tinnevelli, 1801, severely wounded in attack on Fort Panjalam Kurchi; 31 Mar. 1801; (Wilson, Hist. Madras Army, vol. iii. 22).

247. Walker, John (a, c). A.S. 14 Apr. 1783; (M. Mily. Cons.). Appointed to act as Surg. of 36th Foot, 23 Aug. 1783; (M. Mily. Cons.). Came out to Madras as Supy. A.S. in 78th Foot; (L. of 17 Aug. 1787, M. Mily. Cons. Miscell. Book, 1787). Surg. 5 Mar. 1790. *d.* at Madura, 19 Feb. 1795; (G.M. Oct. 1795). Second Maisur war, 1781–82, dangerously wounded at Cannanore; (Cert. in L. of 17 Aug. 1787, supra).

248. Harris, Henry (c). *b.* 1759. M.D. Ed. 1780. A.S. 20 June 1783; (M. Mily. Cons.). Surg. 9 Jan. 1791. S.S. 22 Sept. 1801. M.M.B. 1 Mar. 1812. *d.* at Madras, 10 Aug. 1822. D. and M. give date of first commission as 4 July 1782. Expedition to Malacca, 1795. Third Maisur war, 1791–92. Capture of Bourbon, 1810, as S.S. Desp. L.G. 25 Oct. 1810.* Author of Dictionary, English and Hindoostanee, Madras, 1790. In the preface to Shakespeare's Dictionary, published in 1817, it it stated that that work is extensively founded on Dr. Harris' MSS. in India House.

249. Boswell, Alexander (a, c). A.S. 20 June 1783; (M. Mily. Cons.). Surg. 29 June 1793. S.S. 29 Apr. 1805. M.M.B. 10 July 1812. R. 17 Feb. 1819. The lists of 1787, 1788, 1789, and 1790, give the date of his first commission as 6 Mar. 1787, and spell his name Boiswell. There is no mention of his name in the Records from the date of his appointment on 20 June 1783, till he is again appointed A.S. in M. Mily. Cons. of 5 Mar. 1787. Third Maisur war, 1791–92; (M. Mily. Cons. 20 Apr. 1791). Capture of Ceylon, 1796. Expedition to Malay Isles, 1797.

250. Mort, Henry (a, b, c). Surg. of 'Yarmouth,' taken by French, 14 June 1782, released, 14 July 1783, and employed as A.S. from 14 July to 15 Sept. 1783; (M. Mily. Cons. 7 Oct. 1783). Went to England as Surg. Mate of 'Fortitude,' 13 Oct. 1783.

---

* This is the first occasion on which medical officers (Supy. Surg. H. Harris, Madras, and Surg. W. A. Davis, Bombay), were mentioned in despatches. The first occasion on which officers of the A.M.D. were thus mentioned is Wellington's despatch at the siege and storm of Badajoz, 8 Apr. 1812, L.G. 24 Apr. 1812. Henry Wise, No. 368, infra, 1792, had previously been mentioned in Bengal G.O. of 21 May 1806, for service in the Second Maratha war, but not in the London Gazette.

251. Bell, George (a, c). A.S. 22 Aug. 1783 ; (M. Mily. Cons. 20 Mar. 1784). *d.* at Nagore, 9 Nov. 1789 ; (M. Mily. Cons. 13 Nov. 1789). Name is in lists of 1787 and 1788.

1784

252. Sievewright, Alexander (a, c). A.S. 10 Jan. 1784 ; (M. Mily. Cons.). Surg. 10 Feb. 1791. Sick leave to sea, 5 Feb. 1793. *d.* at sea ; (M. Mily. Cons. 25 Mar. 1793).

253. Hopley, Hugh (a, c). A.S. 10 Jan. 1784 ; (M. Mily. Cons.). *d.* at Permacoil before end of Jan. ; (M. Mily. Cons. 3 Feb. 1784).

254. Laird, John (a, c). A.S. 16 Mar. 1784, posted Permacoil ; (M. Mily. Cons.). *d.* 4 Oct. 1789, at Masulipatam ; (M. Mily. Cons. 20 Oct. 1789).

255. Falconer, Alexander (a, c). Serving as Surg. to deputation to Tipu Sultan ; (M. Mily. Cons. 26 June 1784). Asked leave to Europe, Oct. 1784, told that he can only have it by resigning the Service ; (M. Mily. Cons. 31 Oct. 1784). Permitted to resign ; (Sel. Com. L. from M. 9 Feb. 1785, paras. 85, 86).

1785

256. Corbet, Michael (c). C.C.S. 1779. Late Surg. of H.M.S. ' Eurydice, Appointed A.S. 26 Apr. 1785 ; (M. Mily. Cons.). Surg. 15 Jan. 1793. *d.* at Prince of Wales Island, 9 May 1798. Date of appointment given as 26 Apr. 1785 in list of 1787, as 3 Nov. 1785 in list of 1788 and by D. and M. In these lists his name is spelt Corbet and Corbett, D. and M. spell it Corbitt. Name given as Cobby in Roll of Corp. of Surgeons.

257. Berry, Andrew (c). *b.* 1764. M.D. Ed. 1784. A.S. 4 Oct. 1785 ; (M. Mily. Cons.). Surg. 15 Apr. 1791. S.S. 30 Sept. 1801. M.M.B. 24 Feb. 1807. R. 10 Aug. 1814. *d.* at Newton House, Perthshire, 24 Aug. 1833 ; (G.M. Sept. 1833). First Secy. to Medl. Board, 28 Apr. 1786. D. and M. give date of appointment as 27 Sept. 1784 ; lists of 1787 and 1788 give it as 27 Sept. 1785. Third Maisur war, 1791. Author of Account of Columbo root, 1809.

258. Lepper, George, or James (a, c). C.C.S. 1784. A.S. 4 Oct. 1785 ; (M. Mily. Cons. where name is given as J. Leopard). Death reported in M. Mily. Cons. of 16 Jan. 1789, where name is given as George Lipper. In S.A.L.M.M. is called George Lepper, and date of appointment given as 27 Sept. 1785. George Lepper in Roll of Corp. Surg.

259. Russell, Patrick (a, e). *b.* 6 Feb. 1726/27. M.D. K.C. Ab. 1753. Physician to English Factory at Aleppo, 1753–71. Appointed Surg. Madras and Naturalist to Company, 4 Nov. 1785 ; (M. Pub. Cons.). Resigned, 26 Feb. 1789. *d.* in London, 2 July 1805. F.R.S. 1777. Author of Poisonous Snakes of Coromandel Coast, 1787 ; Treatise on Plague, 1791 ; Edited and Enlarged Natural History of Aleppo, two vols. 1794, (first edition by his brother, Alexander Russell, 1756) ; Indian Serpents, four vols. 1796–1809 ; Description of 200 Fishes collected at Vizagapatam, two vols. 1803.

1786

260. Bree, Thomas (a, b, c, d). Surg. of 'Ceres,' 1777–78. A.S. 20 May 1786; (M. Mily. Cons. and list of 1789). Granted leave to remain in Bengal, without pay, for the cold weather; (M. Mily. Cons. 6 Nov. 1786). Never joined. Struck off, 29 July 1788; (M. Mily. Cons. where name is spelt Brae). Possibly same as Thomas Bree, No. 2011, in Johnston's Roll of R.A.M.C.

261. Baird, George (c). Late Surg. Mate, 36th Foot, appointed A.S. 20 May 1786; (M. Mily. Cons. 26 May 1786, and list of 1789). Surg. 11 Dec. 1792. Invalided, 3 Jan. 1793. d. in Europe, 23 Feb. 1798. Name not in Johnston's Roll of R.A.M.C. Name spelt Beard in M. Mily. Cons. 26 May 1786; Baynard in S.A.L.M.M. D. and M. give 30 May 1786 as date of first commission.

262. Campbell, John (a, c). A.S. 20 May 1786; (M. Mily. Cons. 26 May 1786). Name is in lists of 18 Sept. 1787, and of 4 Mar. 1788, omitted in that of Dec. 1788. Appointed Ensign, 18 Aug. 1788; (List in M. Mily. Cons. of 6 Mar. 1789). Name not in D. and M.'s Army List. No further information.

263. MacMahon, Bernard (c). C.C.S. 1785. A.S. 13 June 1786; (M. Mily. Cons.). Surg. 16 Jan. 1793. d. at Motapilly in Ceylon, 4 June 1798, after escaping in boat from wreck of ship 'Crocodile.' Capture of Pondicherri, 1793.

264. Moore, Fowke (a, c). A.S. 13 June 1786; (M. Mily. Cons.). Passed over for promotion; (M. Mily. Cons. 15 Jan. 1793). d. at Wallajabad, 12 May 1793; (M. Mily. Cons. 21 May 1793).

265. Vaughan, Edward (a, b, c). Surg. of 'Worcester,' 1786. A.S. 26 July 1786; (M. Mily. Cons.). Resigned and gone to England; (M. Mily. Cons. 6 July 1787).

266. Ramsay, James (a, b, c). C.C.S. 1785. Surg. of 'Fort William,' 1785–86. A.S. 15 July 1786; (M. Mily. Cons.). d. at Madras, 28 Jan. 1795; (Urquhart).

267. Reid, James, or **Patrick** (a, c). A.S. 5 Sept. 1786; (M. Mily. Cons. where Christian name is given as Patrick). d. at Trichinopoly, 26 July 1790; (M. Mily. Cons. 3 Aug. 1790, where he is called James Reed). James Reid in list of 1787.

268. Ferguson, George (a, c). A.S. 30 Sept. 1786; (M. Mily. Cons.). d. at Bangalore, Jan. 1792; (M. Mily. Cons. 24 Jan. 1792). Third Maisur war, 1791.

269. Fleming, Charles (a, b, c). Surg. Mate of 'Ganges.' Appointed A.S. by Lord Cornwallis, 6 Nov. 1786; (M. Mily. Cons.). Surg. 5 Feb. 1793. Head Surg. 18 May 1804. R. 24 Jan. 1812. Operations in Ganjam, 1789–92. Fourth Maisur war, 1799.

270. Inglis, John. A.S. 1 Dec. 1786; (M. Mily. Cons. 5 Dec. 1786, and list of 1787). Surg. 12 Mar. 1793. Head Surg. 1802. d. Mar. 1809. Fourth Maisur war, 1799. Poligar war, 1801, wounded; (Welsh, Mily. Reminiscences, vol. i. 125).

*271. Gifford, Thomas (a, c). A.S. 20 Dec. 1786; (M. Mily. Cons.). Absent without leave, 1788; (M. Mily. Cons. 29 July 1788); under arrest; (M. Mily. Cons. 2 Sept. 1788). Out of list, 1792. No further information.

* Another Asst. Surg. Gifford, of the 100th Foot, who was taken prisoner in the surrender of Genl. Matthews at Bedmir on 30 Apr. 1783, and poisoned while a prisoner, by order of Tipu Sultan, is obviously a different man.

1787

272. **Bannantine, John** (a, c). A.S. 5 Mar. 1787; (M. Mily. Cons.). d. Dec. 1790; (M. Mily. Cons. 25 Dec. 1790).

273. **Cameron, James,** or **John** (a, b, c). Late Surg. of 'Tryal' and 'Intelligence' Packets. A.S. 6 June 1787; (M. Mily. Cons. where Christian name is given as John). d. 27 Oct. 1788; (M. Mily. Cons. 6 Mar. 1789, where Christian name is given as James, as it also is in list of 1787).

274. **Duncan, John** (c). M.D. Ed. 1785. A.S. 6 June 1787; (M. Mily. Cons.). Surg. 29 June 1793. M.D. Mar. Coll. Ab. 1805. L.R.C.P. Ed. 1806. Head Surg. 24 Mar. 1807. M.M.B. 22 Feb. 1819. d. at Madras, 10 Apr. 1819. D. and M. give date of first commission as 9 June 1787.

275. **Stuart, Robert** (a, c). b. 1766. C.C.S. 1787. A.S. 5 July 1787; (list of 6 Mar. 1789). Approved as A.S. 4 July 1788; (M. Mily. Cons.). Transferred to Bombay. A.S. Bo. 30 Sept. 1788. Surg. 19 Nov. 1795. S.S. 18—. M.M.B. 10 Aug. 1811. R. 22 May 1819. d. in London, 4 Nov. 1819. Date of appointment given as 5 July 1788 in list of Dec. 1788. Confirmed as A.S. by Mily. Desp. from C. 5 Mar. 1790, para. 16. D. and M. give name in Bombay list, where it is spelt Stewart, but not in Madras list. Name always spelt Stewart in Bombay records; spelt Steuart in Roll of Corp. Surgeons.

276. **Baillie, George** (c). b. 1763. A.S. 6 July 1787; (M. Mily. Cons.). Surg. 27 Jan. 1793; (S.A.L.M.M.). S.S. 17 Mar. 1809. M.M.B. 11 Aug. 1822. d. at Baitmunghuur, Madras, 20 Feb. 1826. Capture of Pondicherri, 1793.

277. **Copeland, Joseph** (a, b, c). Surg. Mate of 'Hillsborough,' deserted at Calcutta, 11 Nov. 1786; (C.G. 1 July 1790). A.S. 6 July 1787; (M. Mily. Cons.). Still serving in list of 1792. Out of list, 1793. No further information.

278. **FitzGerald, Maurice,** or **Morris** (c). A.S. 4 Dec. 1787; (M. Mily. Cons. where Christian name is given as Morris). Surg. 29 June 1793. Physician to Nawab Azam-al-danlat, 1802–08. Furlough, S.C. 18 Apr. 1808. R. 1 May 1811. d. 15 Mar. 1833. D. and M. give date of first commission as 5 Dec. 1785. Third Maisur war, 1791–92, as Secy. to S.G. capture of Seringapatam. Capture of Pondicherri, 1793.

1788

279. **Thompson,** or **Thomson, John** (a, c). A.S. 29 Jan. 1788; (M. Mily. Cons.); to rank next FitzGerald; (M. Mily. Cons. 25 Nov. 1788). d. Apr. 1791; (M. Mily. Cons. 26 Apr. 1791). In S.A.L.M.M. date of first commission is wrongly given as 27 Jan. 1787, and name spelt Thomson. In list of 1788 spelt Thompson, and date of appointment given as 6 Dec. 1787. Name spelt Thompson in first and second references above, Thomson in third.

280. **Spalding, Thomas** (b). C.C.S. 1781. Surgeon, 'Resolution,' 1777–78; 'Princess Royal,' 1779–81; 'Winterton,' 1783–84; 'Winchester,' 1785–86; 'Ranger,' 1786–87. A.S. 31 May 1788. Surg. 31 Dec. 1793. Invalided, 22 Dec. 1807. d. at Madras, 3 Nov. 1812.

*281. **Kennedy, Alexander.** C.C.S. 1787. A.S. 1 June 1788. Surg. 25 Mar. 1795. S.S. 1808; (1804 in S.A.L.M.M.). R. 1 Apr. 1812. *d.* in Edinburgh, 27 Mar. 1827; (A. J., May 1827, p. 763).

282. **Todd, William.** A.S. 2 June 1788. Surg. 1 June 1796. Invalided, 3 Nov. 1807. *d.* at St. Thomé, Madras, 12 Feb. 1808. Operations in Circars, 1795.

283. **Little, Robert** (a). C.C.S. 1790. A.S. 3 June 1788. *d.* at Masulipatam, Nov. 1792; (M. Mily. Cons. 20 Nov. 1792).

284. **Thackeray, Thomas.** A.S. 4 June 1788. C.C.S. 1790. Surg. 1 June 1796. R. 5 Oct. 1804.

285. **Barber, Samuel.** C.C.S. 1787. A.S. 5 June 1788. Surg. 4 Nov. 1795. *d.* at Chitaldrug, 17 Nov. 1802.

286. **Bingham, John** (a). C.C.S. 1787. A.S. 6 June 1788. Furlough, S.C. to Europe, 1792; (M. Mily. Cons. 21 Sept. 1792). Apparently did not rejoin. M.D. Glas. 1795. Third Maisur war, 1791–92, as apothecary on Staff.

287. **Wilson, George** (b). Surg. 'Britannia,' 1787–88. A.S. 7 June 1788. Surg. 3 Mar. 1795. R. 13 Nov. 1805. Expedition to Malacca, 1796–99.

288. **Morris, Henry** (a). C.C.S. 1787. A.S. 8 June 1788. Killed in action at Pongar, Maisur, 13 Sept. 1790; (C.G. 14 Oct. 1790, G.M. Apr. 1791, and S.A.L.M.M.). Third Maisur war, 1790.

289. **Norman, William.** C.C.S. 1788. A.S. 9 June 1788. Surg. 28 Jan. 1795. *d.* at Taunton, 17 July 1811. Date of first commission given as 9 Jan. 1788 in S.A.L.M.M.

290. **Hathaway, John Scudamore** (a). C.C.S. 1787. A.S. 10 June 1788. *d.* 9 May 1796; (S.A.L.M.M.); in England; (Desp. from C. 19 Apr. 1797, para. 2).

291. **Cooper, John** (a). *b.* 1762. A.S. 11 June 1788. Granted six months' leave to Bengal, 19 Aug. 1788; (M. Mily. Cons.). Struck off, having been transferred to Bengal; (M. Mily. Cons. 20 Jan. 1789). D. and M. give name in Bengal, but not in Madras list. v. B. No. 369.

292. **Pearson, William** (a, b, d). Surg. Mate, 'Bridgwater,' 1780–81; Surg. 'Vansittart,' 1786–87. A.S. 12 June 1788. Nominated in Desp. from C. 28 Mar. 1788, para. 4; (S.A.L.M.M.). C.C.S. 1790. Never joined.

293. **Duncan, Francis** (b). C.C.S. 1787. M.D. Ed. 1787. Surg. 'Tryal' Packet. A.S. 13 June 1788. Lent to A.M.D. from 1 Jan. 1792 to 10 Aug. 1796, and served as Surgeon, 36th Foot, in place of Surg. Alex. Home, taken prisoner and murdered at Seringapatam. v. Johnston's Roll of R.A.M.C. No. 1146. Surg. 1 June 1796. R. 26 Nov. 1800. *d.* 10 Oct. 1824. Third Maisur war, 1791–92.

294. **Spiers, Archibald.** C.C.S. 1788. A.S. 13 June 1788. Surg. 1 June 1796. *d.* at Cape of Good Hope, on passage to Europe, Apr. 1798; (G.M. Dec. 1800). Name spelt Spires in list of 1793. Capture of Colombo, 1796; (P.R.).

* The dates of appointment, from A. Kennedy, No. 281, to R. Galloway, No. 305, are taken from a list at end of M. Mily. Cons. of 1788, except A. Spiers, No. 294, whose name is omitted in that list.

295. MacKenzie, Alexander. C.C.S. 1787. A.S. 14 June 1788. Surg. 1 June 1796. M.D. St. A. 1803. S.S. 21 Apr. 1810. R. 2 May 1815. Capture of Pondicherri, 1793. Fourth Maisur war, 1799.

296. Phippard, Thomas. C.C.S. 1780. Surg. R.N. since 31 May 1779; (M. Mily. Cons. 29 May 1789). A.S. 15 June 1788. Surg. 1 June 1796. *d.* at Mogultur, Godaveri District, 26 Oct. 1797. Name spelt Phiphard in S.A.L.M.M.

297. Conolly, Valentine. C.C.S. 1787. A.S. 16 June 1788. Surg. 1 June 1796. R. 2 Feb. 1803. *d.* in London, 2 Dec. 1819. Founded Madras Lunatic Asylum, 1793. Fourth Maisur war, 1799, capture of Seringapatam. v. Hist. of I.M.S. ii. 415, 416.

298. Ainslie, Whitelaw (e). *b.* 1768. C.C.S. 1787. M.D. 17—. A.S. 17 June 1788. Surg. 17 Oct. 1794. S.S. 1810. R. 26 Feb. 1815. *d.* in London, 29 Apr. 1837. Knighted, 10 June 1835. Operations in Ganjam, 1789. Author of The use of Balsam of Peru, 1811; Edible Vegetables, 1811; Materia Medica of Hindustan, 1813, republished in enlarged form as Materia Indica, two vols. 1826; Clemanza, or the Tuscan Orphan, a drama, 1822; Observations on Cholera, 1825; Medical Observations (in Murray's British India), 1832; Historical Sketch of Introduction of Christianity into India, 1835.

299. Ponton, Andrew. *b.* 1766. M.D. Ed. 1787. C.C.S. 1787. A.S. 18 June 1788. Surg. 28 Jan. 1795. *d.* at Madras, 4 Nov. 1795. Third Maisur war, 1791–92.

300. Pollard, Thomas. A.S. 19 June 1788. C.C.S. 1789. Surg. 24 June 1796. Invalided, 22 Jan. 1800. *d.* at Pondicherri, 19 Mar. 1800. Third Maisur war, 1791–92. Capture of Amboyna, 1796.

301. Alexander, Alexander (a). C.C.S. 1788. A.S. 20 June 1788. *d.* 1791; death noted, without date, in M. Mily. Cons. 16 Jan. 1792.

302. Johnston, James. C.C.S. 1787. A.S. 21 June 1788. Surg. 1 June 1796. Furlough, S.C. 10 Aug. 1799. *d.* in England, 1800. Name spelt Johnstone in S.A.L.M.M.

303. Brady, James (a, b). Surg. 'Pigot,' 1786–87. C.C.S. 1787. A.S. 22 June 1788. *d.* May or June 1789; death noted, without date, in M. Mily. Cons. 16 June 1789.

304. Steele, James (a, c). C.C.S. 1785. M.D. Mar. Coll. Ab. 1790. Surg. Mate, 36th Foot, appointed A.S. Madras, 27 June 1788; (M. Mily. Cons.). Retransferred to King's service, as Surg. 52nd Foot, 16 Jan. 1792; (M. Mily. Cons.). Gazetted Surg. 52nd Foot from 26 May 1791. H.P. 25 Mar. 1798. *d.* 1819. v. Johnston's Roll of R.A.M.C. No. 1140. S.A.L.M.M. gives date of appointment as 28 June 1787.

305. Galloway, Robert (b, c). C.C.S. 1788. Surg. of 'Barwell,' deserted at Madras, 19 June 1788; (C.G. 1 July 1790). A.S. Madras, 30 June, 1788; (M. Mily. Cons. 27 June 1788, where name is spelt Galloway). Surg. 1 June 1796. *d.* at Masulipatam, 6 July 1803. D. and M. spell name Gallaway.

*306. King, John (b, c). Surg. 'General Coote,' 1782–88; left sick at Madras, 1788; (C.G. 1 July 1790). A.S. 21 Feb. 1789; (M. Mily. Cons.). Confirmed by Court, 21 Nov. 1789. Surg. 1 June 1796. Cashiered by Court Martial for insubordination, G.O. 10 May 1803. *d.* at Sea, 24 Oct. 1812. D. and M. give date of appointment as 21 Nov. 1789.

---

* M. Mily. Cons. of 23 Sept. 1791 note that Court have confirmed appointments of the following Asst. Surgeons, to rank from dates given: J. King, 21 Nov. 1789; John MacArthur, 22 Nov.; David Haliburton, 23 Nov.; J. Barter (No. 246, supra), 23 Mar. 1790; E. MacKay, 24 Mar. 1790; John Casterate (sic.), 2 June 1790.

307. **MacArthur, John** (b, c). Surg. 'Airly Castle,' left sick at Madras, 7 Feb. 1789; (C.G. 1 July 1790). A.S. 21 Feb. 1789. Confirmed by Court, 22 Nov. 1789. Surg. 10 Apr. 1797. *d.* at Madras, 18 May 1799. S.A.L.M.M. gives date of death as 18 May or 17 Sept. 1799. Capture of Ceylon, 1796.

308. **Haliburton, David** (b, c). Surg. Mate, 'Manship,' deserted at Madras, 7 Feb. 1789; (C.G. 1 July 1790). A.S. 21 Feb. 1789; (M. Mily. Cons.). *d.* at Monigall, 22 Nov. 1800. Capture of Pondicherri, 1793. Operations in Circars, 1795.

309. **Home, John** (a). A.S. 16 June 1789, appointed by Court; (M. Mily. Cons.). Death reported, without date, in Mily. L. from M. 15 Jan. 1790, para. 29.

310. **Booth, Charles Ferris** (a). A.S. 7 Aug. 1789, appointed by Court and arrived; (M. Mily. Cons.). *d.* at Madras 4 Oct. 1789; (Malden, and M. Mily. Cons. 6 Oct. 1789). Second name given as Ferrier in S.A.L.M.M.

311. **Voyle, John** (a, d) *b.* Oct. 1761. C.C.S. 1789. A.S. 2 Dec. 1789. Nominated by Mr. W. Bensley; (Desp. from C. 2 Dec. 1789, para. 5; S.A.L.M.M.). Resigned, 13 Jan. 1790; (S.A.L.M.M.). Shown as "not arrived" in lists of 4 Sept. 1790 and 18 Jan. 1792. Never joined. In Cadet Register, vol. 2a, noted as "resigned, 13 Jan. 1790, John Abernethie in his place." M.R.C.S. 1800. Afterwards in practice at Haverfordwest. *d.* at Haverfordwest, 21 July, 1819.

1790

312. **Tait William** (b). *b.* 1764. Surg. Mate, 'Woodcot,' 1787–88. C.C.S. 1788. A.S. 12 Jan. 1790. Surg. 24 Apr. 1797. S.S. 17 Aug. 1810. R. 16 Feb. 1813. *d.* in London, 7 May 1827. Name spelt Taitt in list of 1790, Tait or Taitt in S.A.L.M.M. Capture of Amboyna, 1796; (P.R.). Poligar war, 1801.

*313. **Goldie, John.** C.C.S. 1788. A.S. 12 Jan. 1790. Surg. 9 Jan. 1798. S.S. 10 July 1812. M.M.B. 15 May 1819. R. 31 Dec. 1823. *d.* in London, 11 June 1855. Fourth Maisur war, 1799, capture of Seringapatam, 4 May 1799, medal.

314. **Martin, William.** C.C.S. 1788. A.S. 14 Jan. 1790. Surg. 13 Nov. 1797. *d.* in camp near Jaulna, 9 Sept. 1804. Capture of Pondicherri, 1793.

315. **Hawkes, Henry.** C.C.S. 1788. A.S. 19 Jan. 1790. *d.* at Negapatam, 28 Nov. 1796; (M. Mily. Cons. 19 Dec. 1796). D. and M. say died in 1796 at Colombo. Third Maisur war, 1790–92. Capture of Colombo, 1796; (P.R.).

316. **Abernethie, John.** C.C.S. 1789. A.S. 20 Jan 1790; appointed in place of John Voyle; (Cadet Regr. vol. 2a). Surg. 16 May 1798. *d.* 21 Dec. 1804.

317. **Blake, Francis** (a). *b.* 1764. C.C.S. 1789. A.S. 29 Jan. 1790. *d.* at Palamcotta, 7 Mar. 1794. Name given as Black in list of 16 Jan. 1792.

— **Barter, James** (c). A.S. 23 Mar. 1790. v. No. 246, supra, 1783.

---

* Goldie. This appears to be the first mention, in the Medical Records, of a medal given for war service.

318. **MacKay, Edward** (c). A.S. 24 Mar. 1790. Surg. 3 Oct. 1798. Invalided, 4 Oct. 1803. *d.* at Negapatam, 21 Feb. 1810. Third Maisur war, 1790–92.

319. **Beckett, Thomas** (a). C.C.S. 1789. A.S. 11 May 1790, arrived at Madras; (M. Mily. Cons.). Nominated in Desp. from C. 2 Dec. 1789 para. 5. *d.* at Arni, 16 Jan. 1791; (C.G. 17 Feb. 1791).

320. **Benamor, Leopold** (a, d). C.C.S. 1788. A.S. 11 May 1790. Nominated in Desp. from C. 2 Dec. 1789, para. 5, next Beckett. Shown as " not arrived " in lists of 4 Sept. 1790 and 18 Jan. 1792. Never joined.

321. **Casterède, Jean.** A Frenchman, in service of Haidar Ali and Tipu Sultan, 19 years, escaped, 1789, asks for appointment; (M. Mily. Cons. 21 July 1789). A.S. 2 June 1790. *d.* at Kadalur, 1 Feb. 1798. In letter of 23 Sept. 1791 (M. Mily. Cons. 1791, Miscell. Book), notifying that Court have confirmed his appointment from 2 June 1790, his name is spelt John Casterate. D. and M. call him John Casterade, and his name is thus spelt in M. Mily Cons., but his signature is Jean Casterède. Second Maisur war, 1781–83. v. Hist. of I.M.S. ii. 11–14.

322. **Wood, David** (a, c). A.S. 18 June 1790; (M. Mily. Cons.). Transferred to Bengal, 3 Oct. 1790. v. B. No. 397.

323. **Morton, Ephraim** (a, c). An American. A.S. 1 Oct. 1790; (M. Mily. Cons.). Confirmed by Court from 6 July 1791. *d.* at sea, in 1793, on passage from Cape of Good Hope to Mauritius; (C.G. 13 Feb. 1794). Name struck off in M. Mily. Cons. of 7 Jan. 1794, as absent since Jan. 1793.

324. **Todd, Richard Jackson** (a, c). A.S. 5 Oct. 1790; (M. Mily. Cons.). Sick leave to sea, 15 Oct. 1793; (M. Mily. Cons.). *d.* at sea in Nov. 1793; (M. Mily. Cons. 7 Jan. 1794). Third Maisur war, 1790–92.

*325. **O'Donoghue, Michael** (c). A.S. 8 Oct. 1790; (M. Mily. Cons.). Surg. 19 Aug. 1800. *d.* at Chatarpur, 21 June 1806. D. and M. give date of appointment as 8 July 1791.

326. **Jones, John** (a, c). Surg. Mate H.M.S. ' Phœnix,' accidentally left behind at Madras, appointed tempy. A.S. Madras, 12 Oct. 1790; (M. Mily. Cons.). Dismissed, for abducting a Sergeant's wife, to be sent to England; (M. Mily. Cons. 1 Oct. 1791). Third Maisur war, 1790–91.

327. **Betty, William** (b, c). Surg. ' Rodney,' 1787–88; ' King George,' 1789–90; ' Swallow,' 1790. A.S. 23 Oct. 1790; (M. Mily. Cons.). C.C.S. 1796. Surg. 19 Oct. 1800. Cashiered, 6 Oct. 1803, for killing Lt.-Col. Sir Robert Hamilton in a duel at Amboyna. Restored to service, 7 Mar. 1805. *d.* at Vizagapatam, 6 May 1810. D. and M. give date of appointment as 9 July 1791. v. Hist. of I.M.S. ii. 234.

328. **O'Neil, Charles William** (c). A.S. 2 Nov. 1790; (M. Mily. Cons.). Confirmed by Court from 10 July 1791. *d.* at Nagore, 3 Nov. 1797. Name spelt O'Neile in S.A.L.M.M.

329. **Ritchie, William** (a, d). A.S. Madras, 1790 or 1791. " Did not proceed, John Steddy appointed in his place; " (Cadet Regr. vol. 2a). Never joined.

* In M. Mily. Cons. of 10 Feb. 1795 it is stated that, of four Asst. Surgeons who submitted a memorial about their rank, only two, M. O'Donoghue and W. Betty, are now alive. The other two, whose names are not given, were probably E. Morton and R. J. Todd.

1791

330. Freer, William (a, d). A.S. Madras, 1791. "Died, Robert Brydon appointed in his place"; (Cadet Regr. vol. 2a). Never joined.

331. Nash, Thomas (a). C.C.S. 1790. A.S. 5 Jan. 1791, appointed by Court; (Mily. Desp. to M. 5 Jan. 1791, para. 7). Arrived Madras, 3 June 1791; (M. Mily. Cons.). Furlough, S.C. 1792; (Mily. L. from M. 5 Oct. 1792, para. 78). Apparently did not rejoin. Third Maisur war, 1791–92.

332. Bond, Hodson, or **Harman** (a). C.C.S. 1789. A.S. appointed by Court, arrived, 18 Jan. 1791; (M. Mily. Cons., where he is called Hodson Bond). *d.* May 1792; (M. Mily. Cons. 29 May 1792, where he is called Harman Bond). Name given as Hodson Bond in S.A.L.M.M.

333. Lettsom, William Coakley (a). C.C.S. 1789. A.S. appointed by Court, arrived, 18 Jan. 1791; (M. Mily. Cons.). *d.* at Dindigul, 2 June 1794; (M. Mily. Cons. 24 June 1794). Third Maisur war, 1791–92.

334. Le Mesurier, William (a). C.C.S. appointed by Court, arrived, 18 Jan. 1791; (M. Mily. Cons.). *d.* at Salem, Sept. 1793; (M. Mily. Cons. 7 Oct. 1793).

335. Gilmour, James. *b.* 1767. C.C.S. 1790. A.S. 21 Jan. 1791. Surg. 3 Oct. 1798. S.S. 1806–07, and 1813. R. 22 Apr. 1818. *d.* at Herne Bay, Kent, 6 May 1828. Third Maisur war, 1791–92.

336. Nicol, Patrick (b). C.C.S. 1788. Surg. Mate, 'Rose,' 1789–90. A.S. 22 Jan. 1791. Surg. 16 Jan. 1799. *d.* at Peterhead, 21 Aug. 1804. Name spelt Nicol by D. and M.; Nicolls in M. Mily. Cons. 21 June 1791; Nicoll in M. Mily. Cons. 30 Aug. 1791; Nicholl in S.A.L.M.M.; Peter Nicoll in Roll of Corp. Surg. Author of a work on Seringapatam fever.

337. Wright, James (a). C.C.S. 1790. A.S. 23 Jan. 1791. *d.* at Attore, 8 Apr. 1794; (M. Mily. Cons. 28 Apr. 1794).

338. Stuart, or **Stewart, William.** C.C.S. 1791. A.S. 24 Jan. 1791. *d.* at Madras, 18 May 1799. Name spelt Stewart in S.A.L.M.M. and in M. Mily. Cons. 23 Oct. 1791; Stuart by D. and M. Third Maisur war, 1791–92.

339. MacMorris, Samuel (b). *b.* 1763. Surg. Mate, 'Dublin,' 1788–89. C.C.S. 1791. A.S. 25 Jan. 1791. Surg. 25 Sept. 1799. R. 24 July 1805; (Mily. Desp. to M. 31 July 1805, para. 8; S.A.L.M.M. and E.I. Regr.). D. and M. give 13 Feb. 1805 as date of retirement. *d.* in London, 29 Apr. 1850.

340. Peyton, Wynne. C.C.S. 1789. A.S. 26 Jan. 1791. Surg. 26 Nov. 1799. S.S. 16 Mar. 1813. M.M.B. 1 Jan. 1824. R. 16 June 1826. *d.* 10 Oct. 1848. Third Maratha or Pindari war, 1817–18; (P.R.).

341. Dunbar, George. M.D. Ed. 1789. C.C.S. 1790. A.S. 28 Jan. 1791. Surg. 26 Nov. 1799. *d.* at Ganjam, 26 Aug. 1805. Expedition to Malacca, 1795. Fourth Maisur war, 1799, as Field Apothecary.

342. Ord, William (b). Surg. 'Kent,' 1788–91. C.C.S. 1791. A.S. 29 Jan. 1791. Surg. 26 Nov. 1799. S.S. 9 Dec. 1814. R. 17 Mar. 1815. *d.* in London, 23 May 1818. Name spelt Orde in Roll of Corp. Surg.

343. La Rivé, Thomas (a, c). C.C.S. 1790. A.S. 30 Jan. 1791. *d.* at Condapili, 19 May 1795; (C.G. 11 June 1795).

344. **Mitchell, Adam** (b, c). A.S. 2 Feb. 1791 ; (M. Mily. Cons.). Struck off, transferred to Bengal, 4 June 1792 ; (M. Mily. Cons.). v. B. No. 400.

345. **Samuel, Emanuel** (a). C.C.S. 1790. A.S. 16 Feb. 1791, appointed by Court. Arrived, 20 June 1791 ; (M. Mily. Cons.). Resigned, and ordered to return to Europe, 25 Sept. 1792 ; (M. Mily. Cons.). Remained in Madras, as Advocate, Proctor, and Attorney, Recorder's Court ; (M. Pub. Cons. 18 Jan. 1799). One of the proprietors of Madras Courier in 1793, Joint Manager of Madras Gazette, 1795 ; (Lovey, vol. iii. 519). Name is in list of European inhabitants of Madras, in E.I. Regr. up to 1804, omitted 1805.

346. **Bell, William** (a, d). Asst. to John Hunter, the famous Surgeon, 1775–89 ; (B.M.J. 14 Dec. 1923). C.C.S. 1788. A.S. 6 Apr. 1791, nominated in Desp. from C. 6 Apr. 1791, para. 8. In S.A.L.M.M. is noted " arrived in India, 1790," but apparently never joined Madras. Shown in list of 16 Jan. 1792 as " not arrived." A.S. Sumatra, 1792 ; (S. Cons. 9 May 1792). d. at Fort Marlborough, 3 July 1792 ; (S. Cons.). S. No. 94.

347. **Skarrow, Thomas** (a, b). Surg. ' Mount Stuart,' 1780 ; ' Worcester,' 1783. A.S. 6 Apr. 1791 ; (C.G. 6 Sept. 1792). d. at Madras, 17 Oct. 1792 ; (Malden, who gives name as James Scarrow. Possibly same as Thomas Skarrow, nominated, 2 Feb. 1781, No. 240, supra. Third Maisur war, 1791–92.

348. **MacIntosh, Robert** (a). C.C.S. 1790. A.S. 7 Apr. 1791. d. at Tellicherri, May 1792 ; (M. Mily. Cons. 4 June 1792).

349. **Munro, James** (a). C.C.S. 1790. A.S. 8 Apr. 1791. Sick leave to Europe, 8 Apr. 1793 ; (M. Mily. Cons.). In S.A.L.M.M. noted as dead, without date. Third Maisur war, 1791–92.

350. **Price, John** (a, c). A.S. 20 Apr. 1791. Dismissed for insubordination, 4 Oct. 1791 ; (M. Mily. Cons.). Third Maisur war, 1791.

351. **Scott, Donald** (a). C.C.S. 1790. A.S. 6 May 1791, appointed by Court. Arrived, 10 Oct. 1791 ; (M. Mily. Cons.). d. at Vellore, Oct. 1792 ; (M. Mily. Cons. 19 Oct. 1792).

352. **Brydon, Robert** (a). C.C.S. 1790. A.S. 6 May 1791, nominated by Court, Desp. 6 May 1791, para. 58. Took place of W. Freer, No. 330, supra. Arrived, 10 Oct. 1791 ; (M. Mily. Cons.). d. at Bellamcondah, 15 Nov. 1793 ; (C.G. 19 Dec. 1793, where name is spelt Bredon).

353. **Crilley, or Crilly, John.** C.C.S. 1790. A.S. 25 June 1791. Arrived, 10 Oct. 1791 ; (M. Mily. Cons. where name is spelt Crilly). d. on board Cruiser ' Ternate,' in Straits of Malacca, 30 Sept. 1800 ; (C.G. 25 Dec. 1800). D. and M. give same date of death, and spell name Crilley. S.A.L.M.M. gives date of death as 8 Dec. 1800, and spell name Crilly ; also spelt Crilly in Roll of Corp. Surg. Expedition to Malay Isles, 1797.

354. **White, John Douglas.** C.C.S. 1791. A.S. 26 June 1791. Surg. 26 Nov. 1799. S.S. 9 Dec. 1814. M.M.B. 2 Apr. 1821. d. at Madras, 27 May 1824.

355. **Dalton, James.** C.C.S. 1790. A.S. 1 July 1791. Surg. 14 May 1800. S.S. 1815. d. in England, 16 Sept. 1823. His wife, Catharine Augusta Ritso, who died at Madras in 1813, was said to have been a daughter of George III, by Hannah Lightfoot. v. Hist. of I.M.S. ii. 416, 417. Third Maisur war, 1791–92.

56. **Oram, Charles** (b). Surg. Mate, ' Ceres,' 1790–91. C.C.S. 1791. A.S. 2 July 1791. d. at Madras, 11 Aug. 1798.

357. **Steddy, John.** b. 1769. C.C.S. 1790. A.S. 5 July 1791. Took place of W. Ritchie, No. 329, supra. Surg. 14 May 1800. S.S. 6 Feb. 1817. d. at Waltair, 14 Nov. 1817. Name spelt Steady in Roll of Corp. Surg. Capture of Pondicherri, 1793.

358. **Huckersley, Thomas** (a, b). C.C.S. 1788. Surg. ' General Goddard,' 1789–90. A.S., appointed by Court, and arrived, 23 Aug. 1791; (M. Mily. Cons. where name is spelt Huckersley). d. at Ranipet, North Arcot, 30 Sept. 1793; (tombstone, Cotton; where name is spelt Huckerby). S.A.L.M.M. spell name Huckersby.

359. **Burton, John** (a). A.S. 1791 (?). Shown as A.S. 9 Nov. in India Regr. of 1792; (S.A.L.M.M.). M.R.C.S. 1804. No further information.

1792

360. **Deeks, John.** A.S. Bengal, 22 Feb. 1792. Transferred to Madras, in exchange with Robert Riddick; (Madras G.O. 11 Dec. 1792). A.S. Madras 22 Aug. 1792, date of Riddick's commission. d. at sea, on passage to Malacca, Aug. 1796; (M. Mily. Cons. 15 Nov. 1796). v. B. No. 413.

361. **Mein, Pulteney** (a, b, c). b. 10 Jan. 1769. Ed. Univ. Regtl. Mate, 74th Foot, 25 Dec. 1790. Resigned, 17—. Surg. Mate of ' Asia,' 1791–92, left sick at Madras. Tempy. A.S. 1 May 1792; (M. Mily. Cons.). Discharged and ordered to return to England, 6 July 1792; (M. Mily. Cons.). A.S. 74th Foot, 25 Dec. 1796. Surg. 73rd Foot, 3 May 1800. R. on half-pay, 25 Aug. 1811. d. at Airth Castle, Scotland, 20 Sept. 1853. v. Johnston's Roll of R.A.M.C. No. 1577. Nephew of Nicol Mein, No. 191, supra.

362. **MacGibbon, Duncan** (b). C.C.S. 1791. Surg. Mate, ' Earl Cornwallis,' 1791–92. A.S. 22 May 1792. Surg. 18 July 1802. d. at Baribati, Cuttack, 16 Dec. 1804; (A.A. Regr. 1805, Chronicle, p. 154).

363. **Riddick, or Reddick, Robert.** C.C.S. 1789. Nominated by Court, List of packet, 17 May 1792; (S.A.L.M.M. where name is spelt Riddick). A.S. 6 Aug. 1792, arrived Madras; (M. Mily. Cons. where name is spelt Riddick). Transferred to Bengal, in exchange with John Deeks; (G.O. 11 Dec. 1792). Ranked in Bengal from 22 Feb. 1792, Late of Deeks' commission. d. at Port Cornwallis, Jan. 1796. v. B. No. 414.

364. **Fancourt, Jacob Casivelaunus.** C.C.S. 1791. A.S. 12 Aug. 1792. d. at Rayacotta, Salem district, 5 Apr. 1800.

365. **Babington, Anthony.** C.C.S. 1791. A.S. 13 Aug. 1792. Surg. 19 Aug. 1800. d. at Malacca, 1 Aug. 1808. Expedition to Malay Isles, 1797.

*366. **MacLean, John Field** (a). C.C.S. 1791. A.S. 14 Aug. 1792. d. at St. Thomas' Mount, 15 Aug. 1794; (M. Mily. Cons. 19 Aug. 1794).

367. **MacMillan, Archibald** (a). C.C.S. 1791. A.S. 15 Aug. 1792; (M. Mily. Cons. 25 Sept. 1792). d. 29 Dec. 1793; (M. Mily. Cons. 14 Jan. 1794). Capture of Pondicherri, 1793.

368. **Wise, Henry** (b, c). C.C.S. 1792. Surg. Mate, ' Ocean,' 1792. A.S. 16 Aug. 1792. Surg. 2 Dec. 1800. d. at Palamcotta, 25 Sept. 1809. Capture of Colombo, 1796; (P.R.). Second Maratha war, 1804–05, wounded in attack on camp of Mr. Jenkins, Resident with Scindia, 25 Jan. 1805, Desp. G.O. 21 May 1806; (Wilson, History of Madras Army, vol. iii. 135).

* J. F. MacLean and W. Colquhoun were wrecked on Madagascar, in the ' Winterton,' on passage to India, on 20 Aug. 1792, and did not reach Madras till Jan. 1794; (M. Mily. Cons. 22 Apr. and 25 May 1794).

369. **Street, Joseph.** b. 1768. C.C.S. 1791. A.S. 17 Aug. 1792. Surg. 11 Dec. 1800. d. at Masulipatam, 10 June 1809.
370. **Addison, Robert.** C.C.S. 1791. A.S. 18 Aug. 1792. Surg. 31 Mar. 1801. d. at Banda, 5 Nov. 1801. Capture of Colombo, 1796. Expedition to Malay Isles, 1797.
*371. **Colquhoun, William,** afterwards **Colquhoun-Stirling, W.** C.C.S. 1792. A.S. 19 Aug. 1792. Surg. 14 Apr. 1801. S.S. 15 Nov. 1817. Took name of Colquhoun-Stirling in 1818; (G.O. 10 Mar. 1818). M.M.B. 21 Feb. 1826. R. 21 Feb. 1831. d. 20 Jan. 1842. D. and M. spell name Colhoun. Surgeon to Sir John Malcolm's mission to Persia, 1810. Fourth Maisur war, 1799, capture of Seringapatam, 4 May 1799, medal.
372. **Mudie, David.** C.C.S. 1791. A.S. 20 Aug. 1792. Surg. 10 June 1801. d. at Pondicherri, 21 Jan. 1807. Fourth Maisur war, 1799. War with France, prisoner at Mauritius, 1801–03; (S.A.L.M.M.).
373. **Stone, Richard.** C.C.S. 1791. A.S. 21 Aug. 1792. Surg. 16 Aug. 1801. d. at Manantodi, 23 Sept. 1806. Capture of Colombo, 1796; (P.R.).
374. **Lockhart, Samuel.** C.C.S. 1791. A.S. 22 Aug. 1792. d. at Madras, 23 Apr. 1807.
375. **Prichard,** or **Pritchard, William.** C.C.S. 1791. A.S. 24 Aug. 1792. Surg. 13 Jan. 1802. S.S. 1 May 1818. M.M.B. 28 May 1824. R. 1 July 1828. d. 30 Nov. 1847. D. and M. spell name Prichard. In M. Mily. Cons. of 15 Jan. 1793, reporting his arrival, it is spelt Pritchard, also in Roll of Corp. Surg. In S.A.L.M.M. it is given as Prichard or Pritchard. Father of W. G. Prichard, No. 996, infra, 1837.
376. **Carnie, John.** C.C.S. 1792. A.S. 25 Aug. 1792. Surg. 2 Mar. 1802. R. 15 Mar. 1805.

1793

377. **Heyne, Benjamin** (c). A Dane, "a gentleman from Tranquebar"; (S.A.L.M.M.). Appointed Supt. of Pepper and Cinnamon plantations, Madras, Sept. 1793; (M.P.L. No. 3799 of 30 Sept. 1793). Locally appointed A.S. 30 Apr. 1799, confirmed by Court from that date; (Desp. from C. 10 June 1801, para. 35). Surg. 2 Jan. 1807. d. at Vepery, Madras, 6 Feb. 1819. Author of Tracts, Historical and Statistical, on India, 1814.

1794

378. **Little, Archibald** (b, c). Surg. Mate, 'Fox,' 1780–87. C.C.S. 1788. Surg. 'Princess Royal,' 1787–93, taken by French privateer, 29 Sept. 1793, five months prisoner in Isle of France, had served Company 15 years, appointed tempy. A.S. 8 July 1794; (M. Mily. Cons.). Confirmed by Court from that date; (Mily. Desp. to M. 10 June 1795, para. 27). Invalided, Aug. 1802. d. at Madras, 26 Aug. 1804. Expedition to Malacca, 1795.

1795

379. **MacCoy, James** (a, d). C.C.S. 1794. A.S. 6 May 1795, appointed by Court; (Mily. Desp. from C. 6 May 1795, para. 9). Never joined. Struck off, having been appointed Surg. Mate, 98th Regt.; (Mily. Desp. from C. 10 June 1795, para. 36, and M. Mily. Cons. 17 Nov. 1795). Name not in Johnston's Roll of R.A.M.C.

* *Vide* note to Maclean, No. 366, p. 280.

380. **Bischoff, Frederick** (a, d). C.C.S. 1794. A.S. 10 June 1795 appointed by Court; (Mily. Desp. from C. 10 June 1795, para. 35). Name struck off, not having joined; (G.O. 26 July 1803). Was in Calcutta in 1795. The Proc. C.M.B. 7 Nov. 1795 note that Asst. Surg. Bischoff, Madras Establishment, is ordered to do duty at the Genl. Hosp. Fort William, pending further orders, by Bengal G.O.C.C. 10 Nov. 1795.

381. **Yates, William.** M.D. Ed. 1792. C.C.S. 1794. A.S. 26 Dec. 1795. Surg. 3 Feb. 1803. R. 31 Aug. 1808. *d.* in England, July 1809. Author of Hindustani-English Dictionary.

382. **James, John.** C.C.S. 1795. A.S. 27 Dec. 1795. Surg. 28 Apr. 1803. R. 29 July 1814. *d.* 16 Oct. 1825.

383. **Underwood, John** (b). Surg. 'Hawke,' 1787–88; Surg. Mate, 'Warley,' 1789–90. C.C.S. 1790. Surg. 'Raymond,' 1791–92; 'Hawke,' 1793–94. A.S. 28 Dec. 1795. Surg. 1 July 1803. R. 22 Feb. 1814. *d.* in Europe, 30 Nov. 1839. Founded the first hospital for Indians in Madras, 1797. v. Hist. of I.M.S. ii. 414.

384. **Peat, James.** C.C.S. 1794. A.S. 29 Dec. 1795. *d.* at Rajamandri, 18 Apr. 1802; (C.G. 27 May 1802). D. and M. say *d.* at Palaveram, Apr. 1802. Capture of Colombo, 1796; (P.R.).

385. **Bullman, William Robert.** C.C.S. 1794. A.S. 30 Dec. 1795. Surg. 2 Aug. 1803. R. 27. Nov. 1804.

386. **Heward, Simon.** C.C.S. 1793. A.S. 31 Dec. 1795. Surg. 5 Oct. 1803. S.S. 23 May 1819. M.M.B. 17 June 1826. R. 17 June 1831. F.R.C.S. original list, 1843. *d.* at Carlisle, 14 Apr. 1846. Knighted, 5 June 1837. D. and M. (wrongly) call him a Baronet. Fourth Maisur war, 1799, capture of Seringapatam, 4 May 1799, medal. Burma, 1824–25, as S.S. medal.

1796

387. **Stephenson, John** (b). Surg. 'Royal Charlotte,' 1792–94. C.C.S. 1794. A.S. 1 Jan. 1796. *d.* on board 'Matilda,' on passage to Europe, 20 Jan. 1804. In S.A.L.M.M. date of first appointment is given as 1 Jan. 1795, and name spelt Stevenson, also so spelt in Roll Corp. Surg. Second Maratha war, 1802–04, as Field Apothecary; (Mily. L. from M. 22 Feb. 1803, para. 95).

388. **Shuttleworth, John Robert Sutton** (b). C.C.S. 1793. Surg. 'Swallow,' had previously served to Eastward, appointed to act as A.S. 2 Jan. 1796; (Malacca G.O. 2 Jan. 1796, M. Mily. Cons. 2 Feb. 1796). Confirmed from 9 Jan. 1798, by Mily. Desp. from C. 7 May 1800, para. 148. *d.* at Madras, 11 July 1803. Expedition to Malacca, 1795–96.

389. **Owen, Thomas.** *b.* 1773. C.C.S. 1795. A.S. 3 Jan. 1796. Surg. 21 Jan. 1804. S.S. 11 Apr. 1819. M.M.B. 1 July 1828. *d.* at Madras, 14 Jan. 1833. Father of W. G. Owen, No. 810, infra, 1825; and of J. S. Owen, No. 845, infra, 1827. Capture of Colombo, 1796; (P.R.).

390. **Connell, Arthur** (b). C.C.S. 1794. Surg. 'Busbridge,' 1794–95. A.S. 4 Jan. 1796. Surg. 1 May 1804. *d.* at Sikandarabad, 27 Oct. 1819. Fourth Maisur war, 1799. Third Maratha or Pindari war, 1817–18; (P.R.).

391. **Fallowfield, William** (b). Surg. Mate, 'Francis,' 1790–91; 'Ganges,' 1791–92; Surg. 'Kent,' 1793–95. A.S. 5 Jan. 1796. Surg. 10 Sept. 1804. *d.* at Madras, 3 Aug. 1819.

392. **Inverarity, Alexander,** or **John.** C.C.S. 1795. A.S. 6 Jan. 1796. Surg. 10 Sept. 1804. *d.* at Trichinopoly, 22 Sept. 1808. D. and M. give John as first name. In S.A.L.M.M. it is given as John or Alexander E.I. Regr. and tombstone (Cotton), give Alexander.

393. **Humpage, Benjamin.** A.S. 7 Jan. 1796. Surg. 21 Sept. 1804. *d.* at Seringapatam, 27 Aug. 1806. Fourth Maisur war, 1799.

394. **Vernon, Joseph.** C.C.S. 1795. A.S. 3 Jan. 1796. *d.* at Haidarabad, 31 May 1800.

*395. **Daniel, Joseph.** Surg. ' Barwell,' 1788–89. C.C.S. 1794. A.S. 9 Jan. 1796. *d.* at Pondicherri, 6 May 1797 ; (M. Mily. Cons. 15 May 1797).

396. **Brydie, Charles.** C.C.S. 1794. A.S. 10 Jan. 1796. *d.* at Arni, 24 June 1797 ; (M. Mily. Cons. 27 June 1797).

*397. **Rogers, Colin.** C.C.S. 1795. A.S. 11 Jan. 1796. Surg. 21 Sept. 1804. S.S. 27 Oct. 1820. R. 22. May 1825. *d.* in London, 25 Nov. 1855. Capture of Colombo, 1796 ; (P.R.). Author of De Beriberia Ceylonica, 1808.

398. **Holloway, Henry.** C.C.S. 1795. A.S. 12 Jan. 1796. Murdered at Kandi, Ceylon, 23 June 1803 ; (S.A.L.M.M.).

399. **Davies,** or **Davis, Thomas Hart.** C.C.S. 1795. A.S. 13 Jan. 1796. Surg. 21 Sept. 1804. S.S. 3 Apr. 1821. M.M.B. 18 June 1831. R. 22 Feb. 1836. *d.* in Guernsey, 18 Feb. 1845. D. and M. spell name Davis. E.I. Regr. S.A.L.M.M. and Roll Corp. Surg. spell it Davies.

400. **Brown, Alexander Noble.** C.C.S. 1794. A.S. 14 Jan. 1796. *d.* at Pondicherri, 22 June 1798 ; (M. Mily. Cons. 3 July 1798). Capture of Colombo, 1796 ; (P.R.).

401. **Gordon, John.** C.C.S. 1795. A.S. 15 Jan. 1796. *d.* 7 Feb. 1802. D. and M. give no place of death, Urquhart gives Madras, S.A.L.M.M. gives Calcutta. The C.G. of 11 May 1802 gives the same date, but no place, of death. Expedition to Malay Isles, 1796–97.

402. **MacKintosh, William** (b). C.C.S. 1794. Surg. ' Ocean,' 1794–95. A.S. 16 Jan. 1796. Surg. 21 Sept. 1804. R. 15 Feb. 1815. *d.* 19 Jan. 1847. Father of A. Mackintosh, No. 890, infra, 1830 ; and of J. Mackintosh, No. 1056, infra, 1840.

403. **Robertson, John** (a, d). C.C.S. 1795. A.S. 17 Jan. 1796. Never joined. " Not arrived " in Madras Army List of 1803.

1797

†404. **Hay, John.** C.C.S. 1797. A.S. 1 Jan. 1797. Surg. 6 Nov. 1804. S.S. 21 Feb. 1826. M.M.B. 22 Feb. 1831. R. 25 Feb. 1836. *d.* at Ramsgate, 29 Dec. 1842. Father of J. M. Hay, B. No. 1437, 1843.

* The dates of first commission of Daniel and Rogers are taken from D. and M.'s list. They were actually in Madras somewhat earlier. M. Mily. Cons. of 20 Dec. 1795 notes the arrival of Asst. Surgeons J. Peat, J. Daniel, W. R. Bulman, A. N. Brown, and C. Rogers.

† There is some confusion as to the dates of appointments of the Asst. Surgeon of 1797 and 1798. D. and M. give the date of 1 Jan. 1797 for Hay, Ingledew, Trotter, Scott, Harrison, A. Jones, Tozer, Thomas, Briggs, Grant, Cordiner, and Scarman ; 1797 for Adamson ; 1 Jan. 1798 for Gilchrist, Horsman, Loftie, Taylor, J. Jones, Evans, Gordon, Jameson, and Foljambe ; 1799 for Alves ; 26 Aug. 1799 for Maxton ; Bowden is not entered at all ; Mardon is given as 30 July 1798, in Bombay list. S.A.L.M.M. give the same dates, except that 1798 is given as date of first commission of Adamson and Bowden. Mily. Desp. from C. 23 May 1798, para. 47, notifies appointment of Mardon, A. Jones, Trotter, Harrison, Adamson, Ingledew, Thomas, Tozer, Cordiner, and Scarman ; and in para. 48 of G. Briggs, now in India, if found qualified on exam.—Mily. Desp. from C. 29 May 1799, para. 4, notifies appointment of Maxton, Palmer, Horsman, J. Jones, Gilchrist, Loftie, Evans, and Foljambe. Mily. Desp. from C. 5 Mar. 1800, para. 5, notifies appointment of Jameson, Andrew, Taylor, Greaves, and Annesley. Adamson reported his arrival at Madras in Sept. 1798 ; (M. Mily. Cons. 25 Sept. 1798) ; Ingledew, Cordiner, (spelt Gardiner), Tozer, Trotter, Hay, Scott and Grant in Oct. 1798 ; (M. Mily. Cons. 9 Oct, 1798).

405. Ingledew, William. A.S. 1 Jan. 1797. C.C.S. 1798. Surg. 28 Nov. 1804. R. 10 Jan. 1821. In M. Mily. Cons. of 9 Oct. 1798, noting his arrival, name is wrongly spelt Engledew. In Roll Corp. Surg. it given as Ingledon. Fourth Maisur war, 1799. Author of Treatise on Vaccination, 1808 ; Treatise on Venereal Disease, 1809.

406. Trotter, Gaven. C.C.S. 1797. A.S. 1 Jan. 1797. Surg. 17 Dec. 1804. *d.* at Madras, 17 Apr. 1807.

407. Scott, David. C.C.S. 1797. A.S. 1 Jan. 1797. Surg. 31 Dec. 1804. *d.* at Madras, 4 June 1816. Capture of Mauritius, Dec. 1810 ; (P.R.).

408. Harrison, Charles Elliott. C.C.S. 1797. A.S. 1 Jan. 1797. *d.* at Fort Marlborough, 2 Jan. 1799.

409. Tozer, Aaron (b). Surg. Mate, ' General Elliott,' 1794–95. C.C.S. 1795. Surg. ' Bridgwater,' 1796–97. A.S. 1 Jan. 1797. Surg. 29 Mar. 1805. *d.* at Coimbatore, 12 Mar. 1814.

410. Jones, Alfred. C.C.S. 1797. A.S. 1 Jan. 1797. Surg. 29 Mar. 1805. Sent to England in charge of French prisoners in ' Matilda ' cartel, 1803 ; (Mily. L. from M. 20 Oct. 1803, para. 6). Did not rejoin. Struck off, 18 July 1809, absent from India over five years.

411. Thomas, William. C.C.S. 1797. A.S. 1 Jan. 1797. Resigned, 6 June 1804. War with France, came to England on furlough as a prisoner on parole, exchanged ; (Mily. Desp. from C. 17 Jan. 1810, para. 25).

412. Briggs, Gilbert. C.C.S. 1795. Cadet, Madras Infantry, 1795. Second Lt. 21 Mar. 1796. A.S. 1 Jan. 1797. Lieut. 29 Nov. 1797. Confirmed as A.S. by Mily. Desp. from C. 23 May. 1798, para. 48. Struck off Infantry List from 17 Dec. 1799, remaining in Medl. Dept. Surg. 29 Mar. 1805. *d.* at Madras, 4 Nov. 1820. D. and M. give name in both Madras Infantry and Madras Medl. List. Served on staff of Sir John Malcolm on his first mission to Persia, 1799–1807.

413. Grant, John. C.C.S. 1797. A.S. 1 Jan. 1797. Surg. 29 Mar. 1805. *d.* at Nellore, 24 Jan. 1814. In S.A.L.M.M. his name is given as Sir John Grant. Fourth Maisur war, 1799.

414. Cordiner, MacDuff. C.C.S. 1797. A.S. 1 Jan. 1797. Surg. 29 Mar. 1805. Invalided, 19 Dec. 1819. *d.* at Nellore, 13 Apr. 1821. In M. Mily. Cons. of 9 Oct. 1798, his name is wrongly given as MacDuff Gardiner. Fourth Maisur war, 1799.

415. Scarman, Jeremiah. *b.* 1779. C.C.S. 1797. A.S. 1 Jan. 1797. Surg. 29 Mar. 1805. S.S. 16 Jan. 1823. *d.* at Bangalore, 12 Apr. 1830. Fourth Maisur war, 1799. Third Maratha or Pindari war, 1817–18 ; (P.R.).

416. Peters, —. Formerly in Dutch service. Appointed tempy. A.S. to attend sick at Ostenburgh ; (M.P.L. No. 2260 (141) and No. 2329 of 24 Oct. 1797). No further information.

1798

417. Adamson, Robert. C.C.S. 1797. A.S. 1 Jan. 1798. *d.* at Hullial, 1 Dec. 1799. D. and M. give date of first commission as 1797, S.A.L.M.M. as 1798, no month or day being given by either.

418. Gilchrist, Donald. A.S. 1 Jan. 1798. *d.* at Gurumkonda, 10 Mar. 1801.

*419. **Horsman**, or **Horseman, William.** *b.* 21 Nov. 1758. Regtl. Mate 71st, afterwards 73rd Foot, 21 Jan. 1777. Surg. 3 Jan. 1782. R. on half-pay, 20 Oct. 1798. v. Johnston's Roll of R.A.M.C. No. 1000. On 3 Feb. 1786, along with James Anderson and Colly Lyon Lucas, the two Senior Members of the Madras Service, Horsman was appointed a Member of a Committee to administer the Medl. Services in Madras. Two months later, the Madras Medl. Board was instituted. As it was not concerned with King's troops, Horsman was not appointed to the Medl. Board, the third place being taken by Thomas Davis. A.S. Madras, 1 Jan. 1798. Surg. 29 Mar. 1805. S.S. 2 Feb. 1823. Furlough P.A. by G.O. 18 Oct. 1825. R. 21 June 1828. *d.* 22 Mar. 1845. His name is repeatedly spelt both Horsman and Horseman in records. Johnston spells it Horsman, but gives both spellings in index. D. and M. and S.A.L.M.M. spell it Horseman. Mily. Desp. from C. of 29 May 1799, para. 4, notifying his appointment, spells name Horsman. Surg. to Commander-in-Chief, 1800–01. Personal Physician to Nawab of Carnatic, 20 Feb. 1802; (M. Mily. Cons.), to 1813. Medl. Storekeeper, 1813–20. Second Maisur war, 1780–84. v. Hist. I.M.S. ii. 14.

420. **Loftie, Billington.** A.S. 1 Jan. 1798. Surg. 29 Mar. 1805. Head Surgeon, P.W.I. 8 Dec. 1808 to 29 Mar. 1811, with rank of S.S. from 26 Apr. 1810; (P.W.I. Cons.). *d.* at Samarang, Java, 12 Mar. 1812. Capture of Java, 1811; (P.R.).

421. **Taylor, Anthony.** C.C.S. 1797. A.S. 1 Jan. 1798. Surg. 29 Mar. 1805. *d.* 22 Mar. 1808. Egypt, 1801; (P.R.).

422. **Maxton**, or **Maxtone, Patrick** (b). Surg. ' Glatton,' 1796–97. A.S. 1 Jan. 1798. *d.* 11 July 1803, on board ' United Kingdom,' on passage to England. D. and M. spell name Maxtone. Mily. Desp. to M. 29 May 1799, para. 4, notifying his appointment, spells it Maxton. S.A.L.M.M. spell it Maxton, and give date of appointment as 26 Aug. 1799.

423. **Jones, John.** C.C.S. 1797. A.S. 1 Jan. 1798. Surg. 29 Mar. 1805. S.S. 22 Feb. 1823. *d.* at Masulipatam, 30 June 1825. Second Maratha war, 1803–04. Suppression of mutiny at Vellone, 10 July 1806; (Wilson, Hist. Madras Army, iii. 179).

424. **Evans, Thomas** (b). Surg. ' Lord Hawkesbury,' 1796–97. A.S. 1 Jan. 1798. Surg. 29 Mar. 1805. S.S. 1 Jan. 1824. R. 19 Feb. 1829. *d.* 11 Feb. 1845.

425. **Bowden, Charles** (a, b, d). Surg. ' Lord Macartney,' 1797–98. C.C.S. 1798. A.S. 1 Jan. 1798. Never joined. " Declined proceeding ; " (Mily. Desp. from C. 26 Feb. 1802, para. 4). Hans Gordon took his place.

426. **Gordon, Hans** (b). A.S. 1 Jan. 1798; appointment notified, vice Charles Bowden, with effect from 1 Jan. 1798, in Mily. Desp. from C. 26 Feb. 1802, para. 2. Surg. ' Walthamstow,' 1800–01. Surg. 24 Sept. 1805. *d.* at Tanjore, 19 June 1820.

---

* That the William Horsman, who entered the Madras Medl. Service as Asst. Surgeon on 1 Jan. 1798, was the same man as William Horsman, Surg. 73rd Foot, is shown by a discussion in the M. Mily. Cons. of 29 Aug. 1807, where his claim to the appointment of Medl. Storekeeper is urged, on account of his services, described at length, in the Second Maisur war. This war was over nearly fourteen years before he entered the Madras Service; but he certainly served in it as Surgeon of the 73rd Foot.

427. Jameson, John. A.S. 1 Jan. 1798. Surg. 24 Sept. 1805. *d.* 17 Feb. 1812.

428. Foljambe, James. C.C.S. 1798. A.S. 1 Jan. 1798. Surg. 24 Sept. 1805. Invalided, 31 Mar. 1819. R. 27 Feb. 1822. *d.* 25 June 1830.

429. Alves, John. A.S. 1 Jan. 1798. Appointed in Mily. Desp. from C. 7 May 1800, para. 36, as " of season 1798." *d.* at Bednur, May 1802. D. and M. and S.A.L.M.M. both give 1799 as date of first commission.

430. Mardon, Thomas Tod (a, d). *b.* 1776. C.C.S. 1797. A.S. 30 July 1798. Appointed A.S. Madras in Mily. Desp. from C. 21 May 1798, para. 47. Never joined Madras, struck off in G.O. of 22 July 1800, having been appointed to Bombay. D. and M. give name in Bombay, but not in Madras list. v. Bo. No. 288.

1799

431. Sherwood, Richard Crozier. C.C.S. 1799. A.S. 29 Apr. 1799. Surg. 24 Sept. 1805. R. 5 Jan. 1822. War with France, was on board East Indiaman ' Kent ' when she was taken by French privateer ' La Confiance ' off Sandheads on 7 Oct. 1800, dangerously wounded. v. Hist. of I.M.S. ii. 202.

432. White, John. A.S. 29 Apr. 1799. Surg. 24 Sept. 1805. Furlough, S.C. G.O. 16 Mar. 1803. Did not rejoin. Struck off 12 Dec. 1807, having exceeded furlough ; (G.O. 12 Dec. 1807).

433. Greaves, William Dodd. A.S. 29 Apr. 1799. M.R.C.S. 1801. Surg. 24 Sept. 1805. *d.* at Seringapatam, 23 Mar. 1816.

434. Andrew, John Alexander. *b.* 1778. A.S. 29 Apr. 1799. Surg. 24 Sept. 1805. *d.* at Nellore, 15 Apr. 1817. Father of P. A. Andrew, No. 950, infra, 1833. War with France, was on ' Kent,' when she was taken by ' La Confiance,' (v. Sherwood, No. 431, supra) ; dangerously wounded, left for dead. Name in list of killed in G.M. of Mar. 1801.

435. Annesley, James (b, c). *b.* 1780. Surg. ' Deptford,' 1795–96. C.C.S. 1797. Surg. ' Sulivan,' 1797–98. A.S. 29 Apr. 1799. Surg. 24 Sept. 1805. S.S. 20 Feb. 1829. M.M.B. 18 June 1831, appointment cancelled and again, 15 Jan. 1833. R. 18 Jan. 1838. *d.* at Florence, 14 Dec. 1847. F.R.S. 1840. F.R.C.S. original list, 1844. Knighted, 13 May 1844. Poligar wars, in Wynaad, Malabar, and Travancore, 1801–05. Capture of Java, 1811, capture of Weltevreden and Fort Cornelius, Desp. G.O.C.C. 13 May 1815. Third Maratha or Pindari war, 1817–18, battles of Mehidpur and Talnair, Desp. G.O.C.C. 22 Dec. 1817 and 17 Mar. 1818. Author of Sketches of most prevalent diseases of India, comprising a treatise on cholera, two vols., 1825, third edn. 1841 ; Treatment of prevalent diseases of India, 1828 ; Digest of Madras Medical Reports, 1788–1829.

436. Stewart, Alexander. A.S. 29 Apr. 1799. M.D. Mar. Coll. Ab. 1802. Surg. 24 Sept. 1805. *d.* at Madras, 11 Feb. 1820. Capture of Java, 1811 ; (P.R.). Author of Medical Discipline, rules for preservation of health on board H.E.I. Co.'s ships, 1796.

437. Best, John. A.S. 29 Apr. 1799. Surg. 2 Jan. 1807. *d.* at Bombay, 30 Sept. 1808.

438. MacKenzie, Gregory. M.D. Ed. 1799. A.S. 29 Apr. 1799. Lost on the voyage to India, in the ' Queen,' burned at San Salvadore on 9 July 1800.

439. Mealine, William Lewis (a, d). A.S. 29 Apr. 1799. Never joined.

440. MacCabe, Charles (b). C.C.S. 1796. Surg. ' Earl Spencer,' 1797-98. A.S. 29 Apr. 1799. Surg. 2 Jan. 1807. S.S. 8 May 1824. R. 15 Jan. 1830.

441. Patterson, James. A.S. 29 Apr. 1799. Surg. 2 Jan. 1807. Struck off, 18 June 1821, having been sentenced to transportation to New South Wales for forgery; (G.O. 6 Nov. 1821). d. in New South Wales in 1821; (S.A.L.M.M.).

442. Palmer, Henry (b). C.C.S. 1796. Surg. ' King George,' 1797-98. A.S. 26 Aug. 1799. d. at Tinnevelli, 10 Mar. 1801.

1800

443. Dove, Hugh (b). Surg. Mate, ' Hindostan,' 1793-94; Surg. ' Lord Walsingham,' 1795-96; ' Hindostan,' 1797-1800. A.S. 1 Jan. 1800. Surg. 2 Jan. 1807. d. at Vizagapatam, 3 June 1814. Second Maratha war, 1803-04; (C.G. 7 July 1814).

444. Campbell, John. M.D. Ed. 1800. A.S. 1 Jan. 1800. Surg. 2 Jan. 1807. d. at Sikandarabad, 2 Mar. 1816.

445. Cormick, John. M.R.C.S. 1800. A.S. 1 Jan. 1800. Surg. 2 Jan. 1807. Served on staff of Sir John Malcolm on his second mission to Persia, 1810. d. in Khorassan, 28 Sept. 1833. Lion and Sun, 2nd Class, 1825.

446. Boodle, John. M.R.C.S. 1800. A.S. 1 Jan. 1800. Surg. 2 Jan. 1807. d. at Madura, 31 Dec. 1809.

447. Smith, Adam Lockhart. A.S. 1 Jan. 1800. Surg. 2 Jan. 1807. d. at Vellore, 12 Feb. 1814. Author (with W. Ainslie, No. 298, and M. Christy, No. 509), of Medical report on epidemic at Coimbatore.

448. Alexander, George. M.D. K.C. Ab. 1798. A.S. 1 Jan. 1800. M.R.C.S. 1801. Surg. 2 Jan. 1801. Serving at Prince of Wales Island from 10 Oct. 1811; (P.W.I. Cons.), and transferred to P.W.I. Establishment, 9 Aug. 1818. M.D. Mar. Coll. Ab. 1818. S.S. 1823. R. 11 Apr. 1830. d. in London, 7 Aug. 1846. Capture of islands of Banda and Neira, 9 Aug. 1810; (P.R.). Capture of Java, 1811. P.W.I. No. 3.

449. Stuart, John. C.C.S. 1800. A.S. 1 Jan. 1800. d. at Nellore, 9 Feb. 1803; (D. and M. and S.A.L.M.M.). E.I. Regr. gives 9 Jan. 1803 as date of death.

450. Stephen, Thomas. A.S. 1 Jan. 1800. d. at Trichinopoly, 29 Oct. 1803.

451. Wyse, James. b. Aug. 1776. C.C.S. 1799. A.S. 1 Jan. 1800. Surg. 18 Apr. 1807. S.S. 26 Oct. 1824. d. at Tanjore, 7 Oct. 1828.

452. Trotter, Thomas. A.S. 1 Jan. 1800. M.R.C.S. 1801. Surg. 24 May 1807. S.S. 31 Jan. 1826. d. at Masulipatam, 26 Sept. 1826.

453. Tennant, Alexander. A.S. 1 Jan. 1800. d. at Bellary, 23 Oct. 1803.

454. Edwards, Robert (b). Surg. ' Belvidere,' 1790–91. A.S. 1 Jan. 1800. *d.* at Tindewanum, en route to Madras, 20 Sept. 1802.

455. Jones, James Howell. A.S. 1 Jan. 1800. M.R.C.S. 1806. Surg. 20 Sept. 1807. *d.* at Seringapatam, 24 Nov. 1818. Capture of Isle of France, Dec. 1810; (P.R.). Third Maratha or Pindari war, 1817–18; (P.R.).

456. Williamson, Henry. A.S. 1 Jan. 1800. M.R.C.S. 1801. Surg. 12 Dec. 1807. *d.* at Sikandarabad, 10 Aug. 1808.

457. Ainslie, Daniel. M.D. Ed. 1800. A.S. 1 Jan. 1800. Surg. 12 Dec. 1807. Appointed to accompany commercial mission from Java to Japan; (Java Mily. Cons. 3 Apr. 1813). *d.* at Weltevreden, Java, 21 July 1816. Capture of Java, 1811.

458. Harley, John (b). Surg. ' Earl St. Vincent,' 1800. A.S. 1 Jan. 1800. M.R.C.S. 1801. *d.* at Negapatam, 7 June 1803.

459. Jeffreys, John. A.S. 1 Jan. 1800. M.R.C.S. 1801. Surg. 23 Dec. 1807. R. 30 Sept. 1828. D. and M. spell name Jefferys.

1801*

460. Painter, Henry (b). Surg. Mate, ' Cirencester,' 1800–01. M.R.C.S. 1801. A.S. 1 Jan. 1801. *d.* in camp near Cuttack, 21 Nov. 1803. D. and M. give 1800 as date of first commission. His appointment is noted as " of season 1801," in Mily. Desp. from C. 26 Feb. 1802, para. 3, along with H. Fowle, S. Dyer, R. MacAulay, and W. Willyams, all of whose first commissions are dated 1 Jan. 1801.

461. Willyams, William (b). C.C.S. 1798. Surg. ' Marquis of Lansdown,' 1799–1800; ' Hawke,' 1800. A.S. 1 Jan. 1801. *d.* 29 Nov. 1805, in camp of Subsidiary Force in Dekkan.

462. Dickson, Thomas. A.S. 1 Jan. 1801. Surg. 23 Mar. 1808. *d.* at Bombay, 19 Jan. 1814.

463. Fowle, Henry. A.S. 1 Jan. 1801. Surg. 1808. *d.* in camp near Jaulna, 7 Mar. 1810, from a fall from his horse.

464. Riviére, Samuel James. A.S. 1 Jan. 1801. Surg. 20 Jan. 1811. Invalided, 8 Aug. 1816. *d.* at Pondicherri, 24 Oct. 1816.

465. Dyer, Samuel. A.S. 1 Jan. 1801. M.R.C.S. 1808. Surg. 12 Feb. 1811. M.D. St. A. 1822. S.S. 17 June 1826. R. 15 Dec. 1828. *d.* in London, 13 Jan. 1846.

466. Currie, William (b). Surg. ' Earl Spencer,' 1800. A.S. 1 Jan. 1801. Surg. 22 Feb. 1811. R. 5 Dec. 1821. Third Maratha or Pindari war, 1817–18.

467. Whitfield, or **Witfield, John.** A.S. 1 Jan. 1801. *d.* on board the ' Baring,' on passage to England, 31 May 1803. Name is spelt Whitfield in Mily. Desps. from C. 28 Apr. 1802, notifying his appointment, and 15 Feb. 1804, announcing his death, also in E.I. Regr. and in G.M. Suppt. 1803. D. and M. and S.A.L.M.M. spell it Witfield.

---

* The appointments of Asst. Surgeons of 1801–02 are notified in the following Desps. from Court, 28 Apr. 1802, para. 185, T. Dickson, S. Riviére, W. Currie, J. Whitfield, M. S. Moore, W. Scot, W. S. Mitchell. 5 Jan. 1803, para. 6, J. Stock, J. Leyden (of season 1801); para. 9, J. Gordon, B. P. Longdill. 14 Jan. 1803, para. 6, D. Brodie (of season 1801), J. Upton, A. High, (both of season 1802). 4 Feb. 1803, para. 6, S. Cotton (of season 1802). 27 Apr. 1803, para. 5, G. Rose. 1 June 1803, para. 6, R. Davies, A. Napier, C. MacDonald. 6 July 1803, para. 7, T. Wyllie (of season 1802). Most of them did not join at Madras till about a year after their appointment.

468. **Mitchell, William Somervell.** M.D. Ed. 1800. A.S. 1 Jan. 1801. Surg. 3 June 1811. *d.* at Madras, 24 Nov. 1819.

469. **MacAulay, Kenneth.** *b.* 1779. A.S. 1 Jan. 1801. Surg. 29 July 1811. S.S. 5 Oct. 1827. M.M.B. 23 Feb. 1836. *d.* at Kilpak, Madras, 2 Feb. 1841. Cousin of Lord MacAulay. Third Maratha or Pindari war, 1817–18; (P.R.).

470. **Moore, Matthew Scott.** A.S. 1 Jan. 1801. Surg. 10 Aug. 1811. S.S. 1 July 1828. R. 31 Dec. 1832; (E.I. Regr. and S.A.L.M.M.). D. and M. give 31 Dec. 1833 as date of retirement. *d.* in London, 26 Apr. 1852.

1802

471. **Scot, William.** A.S. 1 Jan. 1802. Surg. 13 Mar. 1814. S.S. 5 Oct. 1827. R. 1 Jan. 1835; (D. and M.). S.A.L.M.M. gives 30 May 1834 as date of retirement. *d.* 21 Oct. 1863. Capture of Mauritius, Dec. 1810. Author of Report on epidemic cholera in Madras, 1824, 2nd edn. 1849; On abuse of spirituous liquor by European troops in India, 1834.

472. **Leyden, John** (e). *b.* 8 Sept. 1775. Licensed as Preacher in Church of Scotland at St. Andrews in May 1797. M.D. St. A. 1802. L.R.C.S. Ed. 1802. A.S. 1 Jan. 1802. Appointed of season 1801, in Mily. Desp. from C. 5 Jan. 1803, para. 3. Joined, 18 Aug. 1803. Surg. to Maisur Survey, 1804. Professor of Hindustani, College of Fort William, 1807. Third Commissioner of Court of Requests, Calcutta, 4 Nov. 1808. Asst. Master, Calcutta Mint, 29 Sept. 1810. *d.* at Fort Cornelis, Java, 27 Aug. 1811. D. and M. give only 1802 as date of commission. Capture of Java, 1811. Author of Sketch of Discoveries and Settlements of Europeans in North and West Africa, 1799; 3rd edn. 1818; Indo-Persian, Indo-Chinese, and Dekkan Languages, 1807; Language and Literature of Indo-Chinese nations, 1810; Malay Grammar, 18—; Prakrit Grammar, 18—; Translation of Malay Annals, published 1821; and of Memoirs of Babar, published 1826. Edited The Complaynt of Scotland, 1801; and Scottish Descriptive Poems, 1802; helped Sir Walter Scott with first two volumes of Border Minstrelsy, 1802; Edited Scots Magazine, 1802. Memoir by Sir Walter Scott in Edinburgh Annual Register for 1811, vol. iv.; Poems republished, with memoir by Rev. J. Morton, 1819; again as Scenes of Infancy, with memoir, 1844; as Poems and Ballads, with Scott's memoir, 1858; as Scenes of Infancy, a centenary volume, with memoir by Rev. W. W. Tulloch, 1875.

473. **Stock, James.** A.S. 1 Jan. 1802. *d.* at Palamcotta, 24 Apr. 1809. D. and M. give only 1802 as date of commission.

474. **Gordon, James** (a). M.R.C.S. 1802. A.S. 1 Jan. 1802. Surg. 1 Jan. 1815. *d.* at Tokah, near Bombay, 9 Nov. 1824. Third Maratha or Pindari war, 1817–18, battle of Sitabaldi.

475. **Brodie, Duncan** (b). Surg. Mate, 'Deptford,' 1793–94. Surg. 'Northumberland,' 1795–97. A.S. 1 Jan. 1802. Joined, 1 Aug. 1803. *d.* 20 May 1811. D. and M. give no date for first commission; S.A.L.M.M. give only 1803.

476. Davies, Robert (a, d). C.C.S. 1800. A.S. 1 Jan. 1802. M.R.C.S. 1803. Never joined. T. Kennedy appointed in his place; (G.O. 7 Sept. 1804).

477. Kennedy, Thomas (a, d). A.S. 1 Jan. 1802, in place of R. Davies. Never joined. No further information.

478. Stewart, Archibald Douglas. A.S. 6 Sept. 1802. Furlough, S.C. 12 Feb. 1806. Did not rejoin. Struck off, 16 Mar. 1810, absent beyond prescribed period.

479. Longdill, Benjamin Proud (b). M.R.C.S. 1801. Surg. 'Monarch,' 1801–02. A.S. 6 Sept. 1802. Surg. 1 Jan. 1815. R. 22 Jan. 1828. *d.* at Exeter, 13 June 1829. Third Maratha or Pindari war, 1817–18; (P.R.).

480. Anderson, George. M.R.C.S. 1802. Surg. 6 Sept. 1802; (S.A.L.M.M.; D. and M. give no date of first commission). Surg. 1 Jan. 1815. *d.* at Madras, 24 Aug. 1819. Capture of Java, 1811; (P.R.).

481. Upton, John. M.R.C.S. 1802. A.S. 6 Sept. 1802. *d.* 25 Apr. 1805. D. and M. give no date of first commission. S.A.L.M.M. gives only 1803.

482. Pender, James Baillie. A.S. 6 Sept. 1802; (S.A.L.M.M.; D. and M. give only 1802). Surg. 1 Jan. 1815. *d.* at Madras, 20 Aug. 1817.

483. Balmain, John. M.R.C.S. 1802. A.S. 6 Sept. 1802. *d.* at Tripasore, 7 Sept. 1811. D. and M. give no date of first commission; S.A.L.M.M. gives only 1803, and gives 19 Sept. 1811 as date of death.

484. High, Andrew. M.D. St. A. 1788. Surg. 24th Dragoons, 20 Mar. 1794. Half-pay, regiment reduced, 25 Sept. 1802. M.R.C.S. 1802. A.S. Madras, 6 Sept. 1802. Resigned, 29 Oct. 1805, on appointment as Inspector of Hosps. in Ceylon. Full pay, A.M.D. on Staff, 3 Sept. 1805. Dy. Inspector of Hosps. 21 Dec. 1813. R. on half-pay, 1817. *d.* at Camberwell, 7 Mar. 1818 (Johnston's Roll of R.A.M.C. No. 1240). D. and M. give no date of first commission; S.A.L.M.M. gives Sept. 1803, the date when he joined.

485. Rose, George Robinson. A.S. 6 Sept. 1802. *d.* 18 Dec. 1807; (D. and M. and S.A.L.M.M.). E.I. Regr. of 1809 gives 13 Feb. 1807 as date of death. D. and M. give no date of first commission; S.A.L.M.M. gives 1803.

486. Wyllie, Thomas. A.S. 6 Sept. 1802. Surg. 15 Feb. 1815. *d.* at Badullah, Ceylon, 5 Nov. 1818.

487. Napier, Andrew. M.D. Glas. 1802. A.S. 6 Sept. 1802. Lost on passage to England, 28 Oct. 1808, in Indiaman 'Glory,' which parted company from fleet in South Indian Ocean on that day, and was never heard of again.

488. MacDonald, Charles. M.R.C.S. 1802. A.S. 6 Sept. 1802. Cashiered, 17 June 1812. D. and M. give no date of first commission; S.A.L.M.M. gives only 1802.

489. Dean, John. M.R.C.S. 1802. A.S. 6 Sept. 1802. Surg. 1 Mar. 1815. R. 14 May 1827. *d.* 15 Feb. 1866. Third Maratha or Pindari war, 1817–18; (P.R.). Burma, 1824–25; (P.R.).

490. **Strachan, James** (b). Surg. 'Lord Nelson,' 1800–02. A.S. 6 Sept. 1802. *d.* at Madras, 9 May 1810. D. and M. and S.A.L.M.M. both give only 1802 as date of first commission.

1803

491. **Johnston, James** (b). Surg. 'Carnatic,' 1798–1802. M.A. Mar. Coll. Ab. 1801. A.S. 1803. *d.* at Tellicherri, 10 Dec. 1804. D. and M. give no date of first commission. S.A.L.M.M. gives only 1803.

492. **MacKenzie, William.** *b.* 1785. A.S. 22 May 1803. Surg. 17 Mar. 1815. R. 1 Apr. 1830. *d.* in Edinburgh, 28 Mar. 1866. Capture of Java, 1811 ; (P.R.).

493. **Underwood, John.** A.S. 22 May 1803. Surg. 17 Mar. 1815. S.S. 8 Oct. 1828. M.M.B. 20 Feb. 1836. R. 26 Feb. 1839. *d.* 30 Nov. 1839 ; (Times, 3 Dec. 1839 ; S.A.L.M.M.).

494. **Cuddy, James.** M.R.C.S. 1803. A.S. 22 May 1803. Surg. 22 Mar. 1815. S.S. 16 Dec. 1828. M.M.B. 18 Jan. 1838. *d.* at Madras, 17 Dec. 1841.

495. **MacCaskill, Alexander.** A.S. 22 May 1803. Surg. 2 May 1815. *d.* at Hawalghi, near Bellary, 8 Sept. 1815.

496. **Hendry, Thomas.** *b.* 1775. Formerly in Royal Navy. A.S. 22 May 1803. Surg. 2 May 1815. R. 7 Apr. 1819. *d.* at Hull, 10 May 1836.

497. **Stephenson, Samuel Martin.** M.A. Glas. 1799. A.S. 22 May 1803. Surg. 29 Mar. 1816. S.S. 20 Feb. 1829. *d.* on the 'Alfred,' on passage to England, 13 Aug. 1833. Capture of Bourbon and of Mauritius, 1810 ; (P.R.). Capture of Java, 1811 ; (P.R.). Third Maratha or Pindari war, 1817–18, battle of Mehidpur, Desp. G.O.C.C. 23 Jan. 1818.

498. **Cotton, Samuel.** M.R.C.S. 1803. A.S. Bengal, 26 May 1803. Transferred Madras, 1803. Pensioned, 19 June 1810. *d.* 12 Aug. 1811. D. and M. give name in both Bengal and Madras lists. B. No. 538.

1804

499. **MacDowall, William.** A.S. 23 July 1804. Surg. 4 June 1816. R. 5 May 1827. Third Maratha or Pindari war, 1817–18 ; (P.R.).

500. **Ford, Lacy Gray.** A.S. 23 July 1804. M.R.C.S. 1805. Surg. 21 July 1816. S.S. 31 Jan. 1831. M.M.B. 26 Feb. 1839. Phys. Genl. 18 Dec. 1841. R. 31 Dec. 1843. *d.* at Southampton, 24 May 1844. Father of C. G. E. Ford, No. 999, infra, 1837.

501. **Jones, William** (b). M.R.C.S. 1803. Surg. 'Tottenham,' 1804. A.S. 23 July 1804. *d.* at Tinnevelli, 16 Dec. 1812. D. and M. give no date of first commission, S.A.L.M.M. gives 15 July 1805. Capture of Mauritius, Dec. 1810 ; (P.R.).

502. **MacDonald, James.** A.S. 23 July 1804. M.D. St. A. 1805. *d.* at Prince of Wales Island, 27 Nov. 1806.

503. Burton, John. M.R.C.S. 1804. A.S. 23 July 1804. Surg. 7 Aug. 1816. R. 1 Jan. 1831; (G.O. 4 Jan. 1831). D. and M. give date of retirement as 18 Apr. 1830. *d.* at Cheltenham, 18 Apr. 1852. Capture of Cape of Good Hope, 1806; (Mily. L. from M. 10 Mar. 1815, para. 77).

504. Haines, William. A.S. 23 July 1804. Surg. 15 Apr. 1817. S.S. 1 Mar. 1831. *d.* at Bangalore, 19 Mar. 1838. Capture of Cape of Good Hope, 1806; (S.A.L.M.M.). Capture of Java, 1811; (P.R.).

505. Rich, John (b). Surg. 'Ann,' 1803–04. A.S. 23 July 1804. Surg. 27 Aug. 1817. M.R.C.S. 1818. *d.* at Vellore, 23 July 1820; (D. and M. and S.A.L.M.M.). A.J. of Feb. 1821 states that he died at Vellore on 23 June 1820.

506. Gibbon, Richard. A.S. 23 July 1804. Surg. 15 Nov. 1817. M.R.C.S. 1820. S.S. 1 Feb. 1832. R. 1 Feb. 1835. *d.* at Cheltenham, July 1835; ('lately,' G.M. Aug. 1835). Capture of Cape of Good Hope, 1806; (P.R.).

*507. Johnstone, Alexander (b, c). Surg. 'Earl St. Vincent,' 1802–03; 'Princess Charlotte,' 1804. A.S. 23 July 1804. Surg. 22 Apr. 1818. R. 1 Sept. 1830. *d.* in Edinburgh, 31 Jan. 1831.

*508. Hume, George (b, c). Surg. 'Admiral Aplin,' 1803–04. A.S. 23 July 1804. Murdered at Alleppey, Travancore, 29 Dec. 1808; (Wilson, Hist. Madras Army, iii. 218). D. and M. give no date of first commission, S.A.L.M.M. gives Feb. 1805.

509. Christy, Matthew. M.D. Ed. 1799. A.S. 74 Foot, 20 Feb. 1802. Resigned, 13 July 1809; (Johnston's Roll of R.A.M.C. No. 2146). A.S. Madras, 23 July 1804. *d.* at Cuddapah, 12 Apr. 1818. Third Maratha or Pindari war, 1817–18; Desp. G.O.C.C. 23 Jan. 1818. Author, with W. Ainslie, No. 298, supra, and A. L. Smith, No. 477, supra, of Medical Reports on Epidemic at Coimbatore.

510. Jullion, John. A.S. Oct. 1804. *d.* at Arni, 10 May 1805. D. and M. give no date of first commission, S.A.L.M.M. gives "1804, arrived in India, Oct. 1804."

1805

511. Rumsey, Henry William (b). Surg. Mate, 'Earl Camden,' 1802–03. M.D. St. A. 1805. A.S. 30 Jan. 1805. *d.* at Prince of Wales Island, 1 Nov. 1806. D. and M. give no date of first commission. S.A.L.M.M. gives 1805, reported 30 Jan. 1805, arrived, 28 Aug. 1805.

512. Cook, or **Cooke, John.** *b.* Sept. 1765. C.C.S. 1805. A.S. 15 July 1805. Surg. 1 May 1818. *d.* at Mallagaum, 17 May 1821. Name spelt Cooke by D. and M. S.A.L.M.M. and E.I. Regr.; Cook in Mily. L. from C. of 14 Aug. 1805, para. 5, announcing his appointment.

513. Timon, Fabricius (a). A.S. 15 July 1805. Resigned, 18 Feb. 1807. A.S. 22nd Dragoons, 1 Nov. 1806. *d.* in Java towards end of 1812; (Johnston's Roll of R.A.M.C. No. 2691, where name is spelt Tymon). Capture of Java, 1811.

* Mily. L. from M. 18 Mar. 1805, paras. 305, 306, reports that A. Johnstone, Surg. of 'Princess Charlotte,' and G. Hume, Surg. of 'Admiral Aplin,' have been locally appointed Asst. Surgeons.

514. Goldie, Robert. b. 17 Jan. 1763. A.S. 15 July 1805. d. at Madras, 19 May 1811.

515. Jones, William. M.R.C.S. 1805. A.S. 15 July 1805. Surg. 10 Aug. 1818. R. 23 Jan. 1826. Capture of Java, 1811 ; (P.R.).

516. Hunter, Robert. b. 24 June 1783. M.R.C.S. 1804. A.S. 15 July 1805. Surg. 1 Sept. 1818. d. on passage to England on board the ' Bencoolen,' 3 June 1820.

517. Adams, George. b. Jan. 1784. A.S. 15 July 1805. Surg. 1 Sept. 1818. S.S. 3 Feb. 1832. I.G. Hosps. 2 Feb. 1841. S.G. 18 Dec. 1841. Phys. Genl. 31 Dec. 1843. R. 31 Jan. 1846. d. in London, 11 July 1852. Third Maratha or Pindari war, 1817–18 ; (P.R.).

518. Agnew, George (b). Surg. Mate, ' Lady Jane Dundas,' 1801–02. Surg. ' True Briton,' 1804–05. A.S. 15 July 1805. Cashiered, 19 Dec. 1811. Drowned, 2 Mar. 1812, on passage to England, on board the ' Streatham.'

519. Bruce, George. b. 26 July 1779. M.D. Ed. 1800. A.S. 15 July 1805. Surg. 1 Sept. 1818. R. 12 Feb. 1827. d. in London, 11 Sept. 1830.

520. Rule, John (b). b. 24 Mar. 1783. Surg. Mate, ' Asia,' 1802–04. M.R.C.S. 1805. A.S. 15 July 1805. d. in camp near Barhampur. Ganjam, 2 Mar. 1817.

521. Peppin, Arthur Bedford. b. Jan. 1784. M.R.C.S. 1806. A.S. 15 July 1805. Surg. 25 Nov. 1818. R. 12 July 1830.

522. Serjeant, Thomas. b. 29 Dec. 1775. A.S. 15 July 1805. Surg. 7 Feb. 1819. R. 18 Oct. 1826.

523. Richardson, Robert (b). M.R.C.S. 1802. Surg. Mate, ' Ceres,' 1802–03. Surg. ' Canton,' 1804–05. A.S. 15 July 1805. Surg. 18 Feb. 1819, d. at Madras, 31 May 1824. S.A.L.M.M. gives date of first commission as 15 July 1807. Capture of Bourbon, 1810.

524. Milne, John (b). Surg. ' Carnatic,' 1794–98. Surg. Mate, ' Lord Walsingham,' 1800–01 ; ' Lady Burges,' 1802–03. Surg. ' Worcester,' 1804–05. C.C.S. 1804. A.S. 15 July 1805. d. on board transport ' Darriah Beggy,' in Straits of Sunda, 4 Nov. 1811. Capture of Java, 1811 ; (P.R.). Author of Diseases which prevailed on two voyages to the East Indies, 1803.

525. Cother, Thomas. b. Nov. 1784. A.S. 15 July 1805. Surg. 1 Apr. 1819. d. in camp at Bochatti, 25 June 1820 ; (C.G. 8 Mar. 1821).

526. Towell, James. b. Mar. 1782. B.A. 1805 ; M.A. 1831 ; T.C.D. A.S. 15 July 1805. Surg. 8 Apr. 1819. S.S. 18 June 1831. R. 27 Mar. 1832. d. in England, 7 Jan. 1833.

527. Piper, Samuel Ayrault (a). b. 13 Mar. 1785. A.S. 15 July 1805. M.R.C.S. 1806. A.S. 30th Foot, 27 Dec. 1806. Discharged, having entered H.M.'s 30th Regt. without leave of Govt. ; (G.O. 18 Feb. 1807). Surg. 88th Foot, 21 Feb. 1823 ; 19th Foot, 19 Nov. 1830 ; Provn. Batt. 5 Dec. 1834. M.D. Glas. 1830. F.R.C.S. original list, 1844. R. on half-pay, 22 Dec. 1846. Employed while on retired list, at Mily. Prison, Fort Clarence, 25 June 1852. d. at Richmond, 19 Jan. 1867 ; (Johnston's Roll of R.A.M.C. No. 2704). S.A.L.M.M. spell name Samuel Agrault Pepper. His signature, in A.S. Certs. vol. ii, 1806, is Samuel Ayrault Piper. Third Maratha or Pindari war, 1817–18 ; (P.R.).

528. Sladen, Ramsay. *b.* May 1782. M.R.C.S. 1805. A.S. 15 July 1805. Surg. 11 Apr. 1819. S.S. 3 Feb. 1832. I.G. Hosps. 18 Dec. 1841. S.G. 31 Dec. 1843. Phys. Genl. 31 Jan. 1846. R. 18 Dec. 1846. *d.* at Madras, 5 Apr. 1861. Father of Col. Sir Edward Sladen. Commissioner in Burma. Capture of Kittur, Dec. 1824 ; (P.R.).

529. MacLeod, John. *b.* 14 Feb. 1784. M.D. Ed. 1805. A.S. 15 July 1805. Surg. 3 July 1819. S.S. 28 Mar. 1832. I.G. Hosps. 1 Jan. 1844. S.G. 31 Jan. 1846. *d.* at Champ-de-Mars, Mauritius, 19 Aug. 1846. Father of A. C. MacLeod, No. 1066, infra, 1841.

530. MacAndrew, Donald. *b.* Apr. 1786. A.S. 15 July 1805. Surg. 4 Aug. 1819. *d.* at Madras, 28 Nov. 1821.

531. Newlyn, William Fleet. *b.* 26 July 1783. M.R.C.S. 1805. A.S. 15 July 1805. Surg. 25 Aug. 1819. S.S. 15 Jan. 1833. *d.* at Madras, 14 Aug. 1833.

532. Croker, Robert Nettles. *b.* 17 Jan. 1782. M.D. Ed. 1804. M.R.C.S. 1805. A.S. 15 July 1805. Resigned, 20 May 1814. *d.* in London, 18 June 1856. Travancore Rebellion, 1810-11.

533. Kellie, James. A.S. 15 July 1805. Surg. 28 Oct. 1819. M.D. Ed. 1820. *d.* at Punamali, 21 May 1824. Third Maratha or Pindari war, 1817-18 ; (P.R.).

534. Stewart, Charles. *b.* 12 May 1784. M.R.C.S. 1805. A.S. 15 July 1805. *d.* in camp at Hindiah, 15 Dec. 1817. Third Maratha or Pindari war, 1817-18 ; (P.R.).

535. Norris, John. *b.* 2 Apr. 1782. A.S. 15 July 1805. M.R.C.S. 1806. Surg. 25 Nov. 1819. S.S. 18 Mar. 1833. R. 10 Dec. 1833. Third Maratha or Pindari war, 1817-18 ; (P.R.).

536. Jones, John. *b.* 1782. A.S. 15 July 1805. *d.* in England, 15 Oct. 1812.

537. Spiers, Archibald (b). M.R.C.S. 1803. Surg. Mate, ' Charlton,' 1802-03. Surg. ' Sir Stephen Lushington,' 1804 ; ' Earl Howe,' 1805. A.S. 15 July 1805. Surg. 20 Dec. 1819. *d.* at Rangoon, 22 July 1824. Burma, 1824, capture of Ava ; (P.R.).

538. Sutton, Thomas. *b.* 5 Oct. 1783. M.R.C.S. 1805. A.S. 15 July 1805. Surg. 12 Feb. 1820. *d.* near Benares, 8 July 1821 ; (tombstone in old Benares cemetery, " near this place "). D. and M. say died at Calcutta, 8 July 1821.

539. Anderson, William Stewart. *b.* June 1786. M.A. 1805 ; M.D. 1806 ; Glas. M.R.C.S. 1805. A.S. 15 July 1805. Surg. 4 June 1820. R. 1 Feb. 1833. *d.* 1 Jan. 1847. Third Maratha or Pindari war, 1817-18 ; (P.R.). Burma, 1824-25, capture of Ava ; (P.R.).

540. Tolmé, William. *b.* 29 May 1784. A.S. 15 July 1805. *d.* on board ship, near Goa, 13 Sept. 1809 ; (S.A.L.M.M.). D. and M. give 30 Sept. 1809 as date of death.

541. Williams, John (a, d). Appointed 1805. Name erased " ineligible for age." Never joined.

542. Harmer, Carrington (a, b, d). Bapt. 10 Oct. 1779. Surg. ' Maria,' 1803-04. Nominated A.S. 1805 ; (S.A.L.M.M., and A.S. Certs. vol. i, 1804-05). Never joined.

543. **Thomson, Andrew** (a, b, d). Surg. Mate, ' Royal Charlotte,' 1802–03. C.C.S. 1804. Surg. ' David Scott,' 1804–05. Nominated A.S. 1805 ; (S.A.L.M.M. and A.S. Certs. vol. i, 1804–05). Never joined. Name also in S.A.L.M. Bo.

1806

544. **Beattie, George** (a, d). Nominated A.S. Madras, Jan. 1806, in place of A. Thomson. Declined appointment ; (A.S. Certs. vol. ii. 1806). Never joined. Name also in S.A.L.M. Bo.

545. **Parrock, Stephen** (b). *b.* 18 May 1782. Middlx. Hosp. M.R.C.S. 1804. Surg. ' Metcalfe,' 1805–06. A.S. 11 Apr. 1806. Surg. 19 June 1820. R. 28 June 1820. *d.* at Hayes Park, Middlesex, 6 Apr. 1862. Capture of Mauritius, Dec. 1810 ; (P.R.). Capture of Java, 1811 ; (P.R.).

546. **Brown, Thomas** (b). Surg. Mate, ' Boddam,' 1799–1800. Surg. ' Boddam,' 1801–02 ; ' Henry Addington,' 1802–04 ; ' Royal George,' 1805–06. M.D. Ed. 1803. A.S. 11 Apr. 1806. *d.* at Tanjore, 21 Aug. 1818.

547. **Davidson, James** (b). *b.* Dec. 1785. Surg. Mate, ' Lady Burges,' 1805–06, lost on island of Bonavista, 20 Apr. 1806. A.S. 11 Apr. 1806. *d.* in India, 2 Jan. 1812. Travancore Rebellion, 1809, action at Quilon, wounded ; (Wilson, Hist. Madras Army, iii, 215).

548. **Morgan, Charles** (b). *b.* 26 May 1779. C.C.S. 1797. Surg. ' Princess Mary,' 1799–1805. A.S. 11 Apr. 1806. *d.* at Gazalhati, Maisur, 17 Dec. 1808.

549. **Currie, Claud.** *b.* 22 Dec. 1785. A.S. 11 Apr. 1806. Surg. 26 June 1820. S.S. 14 Aug. 1835. I.G. Hosps. 31 Jan. 1846. S.G. 19 Aug. 1846. Phys. Genl. 18 Dec. 1846. R. 31 Jan. 1851. *d.* in London, 8 Aug. 1854. Father of C. D. Currie, No. 1031, infra, 1840 ; W. F. Currie, No. 1091, infra, 1842 ; A. O. Currie, No. 1122, infra, 1845 ; and of G. V. Currie, B. No. 1624, 1854.

550. **Houghton, Michael Morley** (b). Surg. ' Britannia,' 1802–05. M.R.C.S. 1806. A.S. 11 Apr. 1806. *d.* at Manantodi, 17 Aug. 1816.

551. **Mather, George.** *b.* 1780. A.S. 11 Apr. 1806. Surg. 24 July 1820. *d.* in England, 25 Aug. 1823.

552. **Simpson, Charles.** *b.* Oct. 1784. M.R.C.S. 1806. A.S. 11 Apr. 1806. Surg. 1 Aug. 1820. *d.* near Jaulna, 27 Oct. 1824.

553. **Bordman, or Boardman, Thomas.** *b.* 20 Sept. 1775. A.S. 11 Apr. 1806. Pensioned, 11 Mar. 1814. *d.* at Arcot, 4 Sept. 1817 ; (D. and M. and S.A.L.M.M.). E.I. Regr. and Madras Army List of 1818 give 4 Dec. 1817 as date of death.

554. **Gillespie, Thomas.** *b.* 11 Dec. 1785. A.S. 11 Apr. 1806. M.R.C.S. 1807. Pensioned on Lord Clive's Fund, 12 May 1815.

555. **Hastie, John.** *b.* 1774. M.D. Ed. 1806. A.S. 11 Apr. 1806. Surg. 5 Nov. 1820. *d.* at Balpili, 8 Aug. 1822.

556. Irving, John. *b.* 7 Feb. 1787. A.S. 11 Apr. 1806. Surg. 5 Nov. 1820. R. 1 Feb. 1833. *d.* at Cheltenham, 21 Dec. 1873. S.A.L.M.M. gives date of first commission as 11 Apr. 1808, and of retirement as 28 Sept. 1831.

557. Conwell, William Eugéne Edward. *b.* Sept. 1785. M.R.C.S. 1806. A.S. 11 Apr. 1806. Surg. 11 Jan. 1821. S.S. 11 Dec. 1833. Reverted to Surg. G.O. 31 Jan. 1834. S.S. 17 Jan. 1836. *d.* at Bangalore, 18 May 1836. Author of Observations on Pulmonary Disease in India, 1829; Medical Regulations for Presidency of Prince of Wales Island, 1828; Treatise on the Liver, 1835.

558. Coombs, William (a, d). *b.* 3 Dec. 1776. A.S. 1806; (S.A.L.M.M.). Apparently never joined. No further information.

559. Ramsay, James (a). A.S. 1806; arrived, 22 Dec. 1806; (S.A.L.M.M.). Allowed to remain at Prince of Wales Island; (Mily. L. from M. 6 Apr. 1809, para. 61). No further information. Name not in P.W.I. List.

1807

560. Butler, John (a). A.S. 11 May 1807. *d.* 3 Jan. 1808; (S.A.L.M.M.).

561. Henderson, David (b). *b.* Apr. 1785. M.D. Paris. Surg. ' Sovereign,' 1804–05; ' Bengal,' 1806–07. A.S. 5 July 1807. Surg. 3 Apr. 1821. R. 12 Jan. 1831. *d.* in Edinburgh, 3 Jan. 1832.

562. Provan, David (b). *b.* 10 Oct. 1777. M.R.C.S. 1801. Surg. ' Belvidere,' 1801–02; ' Lord Melville,' 1803–05; ' Europe,' 1805–07. A.S. 5 July 1807. Surg. 18 May 1821. R. 13 Aug. 1829.

563. Atkinson, Henry. *b.* 17 May 1784. C.C.S. 1807. A.S. 5 July 1807. Surg. 9 July 1821. R. 8 Feb. 1834. *d.* at Bideford, Devon, 13 Oct. 1845. Father of J. J. Atkinson, No. 657, Bombay, 1837; and of A. R. Atkinson, No. 1501, Bengal, 1846.

564. Chalmers, James (b). *b.* 1780. C.C.S. 1797. Surg. ' Woodford,' 1799–1800. A.S. 5 July 1807. *d.* at Palamcotta, 3 Jan. 1821. Capture of Bourbon, 1810.

565. Wyllie, John. *b.* 17 July 1787. A.S. 5 July 1807. Surg. 29 Nov. 1821. R. 12 Oct. 1831. F.R.C.S. original list, 1843. *d.* 1848. Third Maratha or Pindari war, 1817–18; (P.R.).

566. Hunter, Matthew. *b.* 8 July 1787. A.S. 5 July 1807. *d.* at Palchitti Choultri, Java, 5 June 1813. Capture of Java, 1811.

567. Shadforth, James. *b.* July 1786. M.R.C.S. 1807. A.S. 5 July 1807. *d.* at Madras, 6 Oct. 1819.

568. Campbell, Archibald. *b.* 21 Dec. 1786. M.D. Ed. 1806. A.S. 5 July 1807. M.R.C.S. 1808. Surg. 6 Dec. 1821. *d.* at Moulmein, 1 Dec. 1833. Burma, 1824–25; (P.R.).

569. Meikle, George (b). *b.* 22 June 1788. L.R.C.S. Ed. 1807. Went out as Surg. of packet ' Georgiana.' A.S. 5 July 1807. Surg. 6 Jan. 1822. S.S. 23 Feb. 1836. *d.* at Sikandarabad, 16 May 1838. Date of first commission given as 22 June 1808 in S.A.L.M.M. Third Maratha or Pindari war, 1817–18, battle of Mehidpur; (P.R.).

570. Jones, Charles. *b.* 3 July 1785. A.S. 5 July 1807. M.R.C.S. 1808. Sentenced by Court Martial to be reduced to rank from 28 July 1811, next below Asst. Surg. Peter Crawfurd; (G.O. 13 Mar. 1820). Surg, 11 Oct. 1824. Pensioned, 25 Apr. 1829. *d.* in London, 7 May 1859. Author of Narrative of a Voyage from India in the Free Trader ' Arab,' 1823.

571. Conran, John Trebeck. *b.* 11 Dec. 1783. M.R.C.S. 1804. A.S. 5 July 1807. Surg. 9 Aug. 1822. S.S. 26 Feb. 1836. F.R.C.S. original list, 1844. *d.* at the Cape of Good Hope, 19 Apr. 1846.

572. Nixon, John. *b.* 14 Mar. 1786. M.R.C.S. 1807. A.S. 5 July 1807. *d.* at Masulipatam, 10 May 1811.

1808

573. Veitch, John (a, c). A.S. 12 Jan. 1808. Nominated by Govt. G.O. 12 Jan. 1808; confirmed by Desp. from C. 29 Apr. 1814, para. 67; (S.A.L.M.M.). No further information.

574. Donaldson, David. A.S. 28 June 1808. M.R.C.S. 1809. Surg. 11 Aug. 1822. *d.* at Jaulna, 27 Sept. 1833.

575. Monteath, John. *b.* 15 June 1787. M.A. 1804; M.D. 1808; Glas. M.R.C.S. 1808. A.S. 28 June 1808. *d.* at Aurangabad, 1 July 1815.

576. Harwood, John. *b.* Nov. 1785. C.C.S. 1808. A.S. 28 June 1808. M.R.C.S. 1813. Surg. 23 Jan. 1823. *d.* at Madras, 10 Oct. 1824. Capture of Java, 1811. Third Maratha or Pindari war, 1817-18; (P.R.).

577. Smart, James. *b.* Dec. 1787. A.S. 28 June 1808. Surg. 16 Aug. 1823. *d.* at Negapatam, 20 Aug. 1825. Capture of Java, 1811; (P.R.). Third Maratha or Pindari war, 1817-18; (P.R.). Burma, 1824-25, capture of Mergui.

1809

578. Napier, Adam (a). *b.* 24 May 1780. Originally posted to Madras, arrived there, 12 Feb. 1809. Transferred to Bengal, 26 May 1809; (G.O. 26 May 1809). *d.* at Cape of Good Hope, 16 Apr. 1825. v. B. No. 647.

579. White, John. *b.* 6 Sept. 1789. A.S. 16 July 1809. Surg. 17 May 1823. S.S. 15 May 1836. R. 29 Feb. 1844. *d.* in London, 12 Nov. 1873. Third Maratha or Pindari war, 1817-18; (P.R.).

580. Sevestre, Thomas (b). *b.* 1784. Surg. Mate, ' Thames,' 1803-04. M.R.C.S. 1805. Served in Royal Navy, 1806-09. A.S. 16 July 1809. Surg. 1 Jan. 1824. S.S. 3 Sept. 1837. R. 5 Dec. 1837. *d.* at Florence, 15 Feb. 1842. Knight of Tower and Sword, (Portugal), 1816. Capture of Cayenne, 14 Jan. 1809, as Surg. of H.M.S. ' Confiance.' Capture of Java, 1811.

1810

581. Rae, Alexander. *b.* 26 Mar. 1790. A.S. 22 Aug. 1810. *d.* at Bellary, 5 June 1816.

582. **Braid, Norman.** *b.* 2 Feb. 1789. A.S. 22 Aug. 1810. Arrived in India with H.M.'s 69th Foot, Oct. 1810; (S.A.L.M.M.). *d.* at sea, 22 July 1811. D. and M. give only 1810 as date of first commission; S.A.L.M.M. gives 1808.

583. **Milne, Alexander** (b). *b.* 10 Feb. 1790. Surg. Mate, 'Lord Melville,' 1808–09. A.S. 22 Aug. 1810. *d.* at Banda, Dutch Indies, 24 Jan. 1813. Capture of Java, 1811.

584. **Prince, Richard.** *b.* 20 Mar. 1788. A.S. 22 Aug. 1810. Surg. 1 May 1824. *d.* at Chittur, 12 Mar. 1829. Third Maratha or Pindari war, 1817–18; (P.R.).

585. **Stuart, Robert Hunter.** *b.* 5 June 1788. A.S. 22 Aug. 1810. *d.* at Madras, 5 Oct. 1820.

586. **Aitken, James** (b). *b.* 15 Jan. 1790. C.C.S. 1808. Surg. 'Ocean,' 1808–10. A.S. 22 Aug. 1810. M.D. K.C. Ab. 1820. Surg. 1 May 1824. R. 1 Apr. 1833. *d.* in London, 13 Oct. 1880.

587. **Smith, William.** *b.* 13 Sept. 1788. M.R.C.S. 1810. A.S. 22 Aug. 1810. *d.* at Masulipatam, 17 June 1819. Third Maratha or Pindari war, 1817–18; (P.R.).

588. **Gilder, Jonathan.** *b.* Aug. 1779. A.S. 22 Aug. 1810. *d.* at Riahcharuwa, 22 July 1817.

589. **Woolcott, John** (b). *b.* 16 Jan. 1783. Surg. 'Lord Keith,' 1804–10. M.R.C.S. 1810. A.S. 22 Aug. 1810. *d.* on board 'Marquess of Wellington,' on passage to India, 12 May 1823. Third Maratha or Pindari war, 1817–18; (P.R.).

590. **Wilson, William.** *b.* 22 Aug. 1787. M.D. Ed. 1809. A.S. 22 Aug. 1810. Surg. 1 May 1824. *d.* near Benares, 25 Mar. 1837. Third Maratha or Pindari war, 1817–18; (P.R.).

591. **Mann, James.** *b.* 26 Oct. 1788. A.S. 22 Aug. 1810. C.C.S. 1811. *d.* at Arcot, 17 June 1812.

592. **Taylor, William Hammond.** *b.* 26 Feb. 1784. M.R.C.S. 1810. A.S. 22 Aug. 1810. *d.* near Seringapatam, 17 Apr. 1813.

593. **Neilson, Robert.** *b.* 10 July 1787. M.D. Glas. 1808. A.S. 22. Aug. 1810. M.R.C.S. 1812. Surg. 1 May 1824. *d.* at Sholapur, 1 Oct. 1828. Third Maratha or Pindari war, 1817–18; (P.R.).

594. **Cruickshank, John Morris.** *b.* 1783. A.S. 22 Aug. 1810. M.R.C.S. 1811. M.A. Mar. Coll. Ab. 1823. Surg. 22 May 1824. R. 1 Feb. 1835.

595. **Duncan, James Johnston.** *b.* 23 Aug. 1791. A.S. 22 Aug. 1810; gazetted to Bengal in C.G. of 14 Nov. 1811, but never joined there, struck off Bengal list in C.G. of 7 May 1812. M.A. Mar. Coll. Ab. 1812. *d.* at Cannanore, 11 Nov. 1821. D. and M. give name in Madras, but not in Bengal list. B. No. 670.

596. **Tomkinson, Thomas.** *b.* Feb. 1789. A.S. 22 Aug. 1810. M.R.C.S. 1811. Surg. 28 May 1824. R. 21 Nov. 1826.

597. **Monach, Andrew** (a, b). Surg. 'Earl Camden,' 1807–10, burned at Bombay, 23 July 1810. A.S. 1810; (S.A.L.M.M., which gives no date of commission, but states that he served at reduction of Isle of France, in Dec. 1810, P.R.). Probably temply. employed after loss of his ship.

Lightning Source UK Ltd.
Milton Keynes UK
UKOW05f1104201215

265024UK00002B/4/P

9 781847 345622